Abortion Law in Transnational Perspective

PENNSYLVANIA STUDIES IN HUMAN RIGHTS

Bert B. Lockwood, Jr., Series Editor

A complete list of books in the series is available from the publisher.

Abortion Law in Transnational Perspective

Cases and Controversies

Edited by

Rebecca J. Cook, Joanna N. Erdman,
and Bernard M. Dickens

PENN

UNIVERSITY OF PENNSYLVANIA PRESS

PHILADELPHIA

Published by
University of Pennsylvania Press
Philadelphia, Pennsylvania 19104-4112
www.upenn.edu/pennpress

Printed in the United States of America on acid-free paper
10 9 8 7 6 5 4 3 2 1

Library of Congress Cataloging-in-Publication Data
Abortion law in transnational perspective : cases and controversies / edited by Rebecca J. Cook, Joanna N. Erdman, and Bernard M. Dickens. —1st ed.
    p. cm. — (Pennsylvania studies in human rights)
    Includes bibliographical references and index.
    ISBN 978-0-8122-4627-8 (hardcover : alk. paper)
    1. Abortion—Law and legislation—Case studies. 2. Abortion—Law and legislation—Cross-cultural studies. 3. Reproductive rights—Law and legislation—Case studies. 4. Reproductive rights—Law and legislation—Cross-cultural studies. I. Cook, Rebecca J. II. Erdman, Joanna N. III. Dickens, Bernard M. IV. Series: Pennsylvania studies in human rights.
    HQ767.A1853 2014
    342.08'4—dc23

                                                    2014003052

Contents

Introduction

Rebecca J. Cook, Joanna N. Erdman, and Bernard M. Dickens

The field of abortion law has survived several revolutions. Perhaps the greatest is the shift in focus to human rights. Although today it is exceedingly difficult to encounter any legal treatment of abortion without some comment on the rights involved, this was not always the case. Abortion law evolved "from placement within criminal or penal codes, to placement within health or public health legislation, and eventually to submergence within laws serving goals of human rights."[1] Reflecting on historical revolutions led us to think of new transitions in hand and in prospect. With this collection, we are looking for new ideas in abortion law. We seek to take stock of the field, but in a dynamic way, to ask which ideas are changing the way we advocate, regulate, and adjudicate on abortion.

The collection builds on significant transnational legal developments in abortion law. Innovation in case strategies and an abundance of decisions from constitutional and human rights courts have produced a rich jurisprudence, which remains largely unexamined and undertheorized by legal scholars. Technological change, such as new medical methods of early abortion, has given rise to new legal controversies and rendered former legal frameworks outdated. While the United States and Western Europe may have been the vanguard in abortion law reform in the latter half of the twentieth century, Central and South America are proving the laboratories of thought and innovation in the twenty-first century, as are particular countries in Africa and Asia. Too often though, barriers of language and legal form impede the transnational flow of these developments and the thinking behind them. Country-specific case studies are published as stand-alone reviews that fail to reflect on larger global trends. Yet often, revelations about why a law has developed in the way that it has, and how strikingly different it is from what came before or what can be, are visible only in comparison and contrast.

In this collection, we seek to build primarily on this century's legal developments—judicial decisions, constitutional amendments, and regulatory reforms—to ask about change of a larger order. We seek change in the frameworks of ideas that influence, underlie, and give meaning to these legal developments. These are the frameworks that define the relevant questions, the persuasive arguments, and the foreseeable answers in the field. By bringing together legal scholars engaged with different legal controversies, in different legal fields and national contexts, we seek to create a collaborative space for rethinking abortion and the law. The chapters are organized around four themes: constitutional values and regulatory regimes, procedural justice and liberal access, framing and claiming rights, and narratives and social meaning, recognizing that some chapters explore multiple themes.

Constitutional Values and Regulatory Regimes

The chapters in the first part of this volume focus on the evolution of constitutional values associated with women and prenatal life in various constitutional court decisions on abortion, and how these values are expressed and protected in different legal regimes. The term "legal regimes" is used to communicate the variety of legislative and policy instruments employed by legislatures and reviewed by courts in the regulation of abortion. These include criminal abortion laws, but increasingly laws that allow women to access abortion on request, albeit subject to counseling to ensure women's free and informed decisions, and even more notably, policies to facilitate family formation, such as child care and child welfare benefits. These alternative non-punitive regimes are being recognized for their unique property of protecting prenatal life, while supporting women in their reproductive decision making.

The first chapter in this part examines the decline of the conflict-of-rights paradigm in abortion law. To think of abortion as a conflict between the rights of women and the rights of the unborn seems truly of a past era. In her study on the constitutionalization of abortion, Reva Siegel tracks how, over time and across jurisdictions, courts have rejected the view of abortion as a "zero-sum game" in which more accommodation of one set of rights means proportionately less for another. Siegel explores the origin and evolution of constitutional abortion law, and the influences of social movement that led courts increasingly to acknowledge, accommodate, and even respect women's agency in abortion—most strikingly on the constitutional ground that this provides a more expansive way to protect the right to life of the unborn. She reveals how today regulatory regimes are no longer exclusively tied to the priority of one or the other constitutional value, but vindicate competing values to the advantage of each.

Ruth Rubio-Marín and Adriana Lamačková explore this evolution with country-specific case studies. Rubio-Marín reads the 2010 decision of the Portuguese Constitutional Court validating a mandatory, open-ended abortion counseling regime as an instance of this emerging doctrine. The Court recognizes the regime as protective of unborn human life but also respectful of women's dignity and autonomy as constitutional values worthy of protection. Rubio-Marín identifies a shifting vision, underlying this evolution, of the pregnant woman, now viewed as a responsible actor who makes her own legitimate decisions informed by available means and support, suggesting an alternative, positive course of action for the state. Lamačková explores the 2007 decision of the Slovak Constitutional Court, again validating a counseling regime as consistent with the right to life of the unborn. This decision is especially noteworthy in the region because it does not consider protection of unborn life to be the sole or even primary right in constitutional abortion law. A woman's right to reproductive self-determination enjoys full and equal standing in the constitutional order. Lamačková attributes this jurisprudential shift to the Court's use of balancing as an analytical framework, according to which multiple constitutional rights and values are vindicated, none completely overruling any other, and favoring compromised rather than absolute regulation.

Verónica Undurraga expressly takes up judicial methodology in constitutional abortion law, focusing on proportionality as a reasoned analytical framework that allows courts to move beyond the abstract, intuitive decision making that characterized abortion judgments of the past. Proportionality, Undurraga explains, brings into consideration substantive issues too often neglected in abortion law adjudication and forces judges to assess not merely the rationale, but also the impact of criminalization; that is, whether the protection it affords unborn life is worth the sacrifice it demands of women.

Rachel Rebouché maintains a methodological focus but departs from constitutional law as the primary field of engagement. Her chapter questions the costs of continuing to prioritize the relationship between constitutional values and regulatory regimes, rather than that between law and practice. She makes a compelling case that the practice of abortion is not determined by legislative form or constitutional norm, but by a complex relationship among formal, informal, and background rules, and thus she sets out an alternative functionalist methodology to capture this web of rules, and to study its impact on access to services.

Procedural Justice and Liberal Access

The chapters in the second part of the book develop the relationship between abortion law and practice introduced by Rebouché. These chapters focus on a preoccupation in abortion law with the prospects of procedural justice to secure women's access to lawful services. The claim is that legality of services is a necessary precondition to service accessibility. However, unless women are aware of their legal rights and have the means to exercise them, services to which they are lawfully entitled remain beyond their reach. The historical proposition of the Common law that substantive legal rights emerged within the interstices of procedure is relevant today. Women's access to safe, lawful abortion depends on women and service providers actually knowing the legal grounds and the conditions under which abortion services may lawfully be rendered and legal procedures of timely review and appeal in the event of disagreement on whether the grounds are met in an individual case. The authors explore the promises and uncertainties of procedural justice in abortion law from three different geographic vantage points.

Joanna Erdman explores the procedural turn at the European Court of Human Rights, asking whether and how procedural abortion rights can serve the substantive end that advocates claim for them: access to services. She begins with a complicating factor of discretion in abortion law, through which women may be denied services to which they are entitled, or granted services to which they are not. When discretion is challenged in the latter case, procedural claims for standards, review, and oversight threaten to restrict rather than enlarge access and thereby to confound the liberalizing promise of the procedural turn. Erdman looks to redeem this ambivalence by shifting focus, asking about the procedural turn from the perspective not of the advocate, but of an international court seeking to engender change on an issue of deep democratic conflict. Procedural rights may serve as a means for the European Court to respect the plurality of rights-based norms on abortion in Europe by working through rather than against the state, enlisting its democratic forces and its institutions in the effective protection of abortion rights. In a final shift of perspective, Erdman tests this theory in practice, asking about the impact of procedural rights on access to services as mediated through the ambitions and actions of legislatures, doctors, and women themselves, using Ireland as her case study.

Paola Bergallo explores the procedural turn in Argentina through a contest between formal law and informal norms in access to abortion. She recounts how legal grounds for access to services are continually undermined through the use of informal norms by conservative opposition, leading to de facto prohibition. Bergallo explains how government ministries, through procedural guidelines and judicial rulings on implementation, struggle to ensure formal law governs practice. She explores how the struggle to implement the legal indications for abortion may help to promote a gradual change in conceptions of the rule of law, revealing a fertile terrain for moving toward decriminalization. The chapter shows that guidelines have not solved the unworkability of regulating abortion through legal grounds and concludes that the procedural turn in Argentina may ultimately show its greatest potential in reinforcing the normative claims for decriminalization.

Charles Ngwena draws principally on decisions of United Nations treaty bodies but also references decisions of the European Court of Human Rights and national tribunals to illustrate the potential of the procedural turn for facilitating access to lawful abortion in Africa. He sets out a case for how rendering states accountable for lack of effective implementation of existing legal grounds can be an important juridical tool to secure access to safe abortion. He finds that states no longer satisfy individuals' human rights by simply legislating the difference between lawful and unlawful resort to abortion, but must actively create identifiable means by which women can access, and providers deliver, lawful services. He explores whether the promulgation of abortion guidelines by ministries of health in certain African countries meets the procedural standards. He also explains that their legitimacy would be more substantial if they had the support of ministries of justice and offices of attorneys general, and their assurances that there will be no prosecutions where abortions are done safely with due regard to the rights and dignity of women.

Framing and Claiming Rights

The chapters in the third section of the book address how arguments are framed and how claims are made, investigated, challenged, and may be resolved within these frames. A frame shares common reference points and parameters that determine how knowledge is constructed and debated. The authors investigate frames of argumentation, whether in public debate or judicial proceedings. They examine the origins of frames of argumentation, why they have come into use and by whom, forums in which they are used, and most notably, the plurality of competing claims within them.

This set of chapters opens with Sally Sheldon and Bernard Dickens examining frames of reasoning in public debates, and how they may accommodate an increasing cast of social actors with different policy agendas. Sheldon uses early medical (i.e., nonsurgical) abortion, a routine procedure in many countries, as a focus for exploring the strengths and weaknesses of the highly medicalized framework for the provision of abortion services in Britain. While this frame, entrenched in statute and broadly accepted, has contributed to significant depoliticization and liberalization of access to abortion, it has also obstructed other ways of conceptualizing what is at stake in the debate on abortion, notably, women's reproductive rights. Sheldon explores the resilience of this medicalized control despite a court challenge to repeal the clinically unsupported restrictions on the use of nonsurgical abortion, and evidence from other countries regarding the safety of its home use.

Dickens explores variants of the human right to freedom of conscience in abortion debates, focusing on the claim that the human right to act lawfully according to one's individual conscience is not a monopoly of abortion opponents. Equally conscientious may be providers' commitment to delivery of abortion care, according to which they are entitled by conscience to participate in such lawful procedures, to advise patients about the option, and to refer patients to where appropriate services are available. Moreover, much in the same way that secular health facilities must accommodate providers' rights of conscientious objection, religiously inspired health facilities must accommodate providers' rights of conscientious commitment to undertake or make provision for services, and women's conscientious rights to receive them.

Julieta Lemaitre and Luís Roberto Barroso focus on specific frames of legal argumentation. Lemaitre explores the emergence of Catholic constitutionalism in abortion law; that is, the advancement of Catholic theological reasoning through the secular discourse of human rights. Believing that engagement with these arguments, on their own merits, is crucial for the pro-choice community, she elaborates core Catholic constitutional arguments about the legal regulation of abortion and explores the productive effects of this engagement in exposing the moral order implicit in liberal convictions and its shortcomings, and in building bridges with Catholic concerns for social justice.

Barroso recounts his advocacy before the Brazilian Supreme Court in successful arguments that the termination of an anencephalic pregnancy, a fetal condition of brain tissue deficiency incompatible with survival outside the womb, does not constitute abortion. He compares and contrasts the decision of the Brazilian Supreme Court with court decisions of other countries and with those of human rights treaty bodies. He explains how this extreme case offered a chance to bypass the most crucial moral claim against abortion—the fetus' potentiality for life. Barroso explores how the advocacy helped to overcome the taboos around abortion in Brazil and how it benefitted the broader advocacy effort to assert women's right to abortion.

Similarly reflecting the interaction of reasoning in public debates and advocacy before courts, Melissa Upreti addresses the shifting frames of reference through which a constitutional court analyzes abortion. She examines the decision of the Supreme Court of Nepal in the *Lakshmi Dhikta* case, which addressed the rights of a poor woman from rural western Nepal to have the cost of her abortion covered by the government. The Court's decision reinforced the transition from the country's earlier punitive repression of abortion, based on Hindu religious precepts of patriarchy and the high value that they place on women's fertility, to guarantee economic access to safe and legal abortion services for poor women. Upreti explains how the Court, guided by a frame of transformative equality, required the government to ensure that women marginalized by poverty and geographical remoteness have timely access to free services.

Narratives and Social Meaning

The chapters in the fourth part of the book identify the recurring narratives that arise from legal debates on abortion. They explore the significance of narratives that are produced by laws, litigation, and language about abortion, and how these narratives convey social meaning. The authors encourage readers to consider the consequences of stories told through the legal contests about abortion and the social meanings they convey about women, their sexuality, and their pregnancies and what these consequences may portend for legal strategy. Understanding the broader narratives within which legal argument resides opens opportunities to rethink strategies of old, and to reimagine new approaches of engagement.

Lisa Kelly studies narratives of adolescence and sexuality in contemporary transnational abortion rights litigation from Latin America. She identifies in these cases a recurring narrative that invokes sexual innocence, violation, and parental beneficence in the pursuit of a lawful abortion, which when denied, identifies the state as the shameful antagonist. She warns, however, that with these legal and discursive openings, reproductive rights advocates face a "knife-edge dilemma." By narrating sympathetic cases of violated young girls, advocates risk reinforcing ideas of deservedness in abortion law. By mobilizing the cultural and legal power of the family, advocates may vest greater legal rights in parents to act against their minor daughters' wishes and interests. By deploying tropes of youthful suffering and vulnerability, advocates may reinforce protectionist discourses to restrict adolescents' access to lawful services they favor.

Alejandro Madrazo examines the significance of the legal debates in Mexico and beyond about prenatal personhood for women's exercise of their reproductive rights. His concerns lie not in the narrow legal issues of interpretation, but rather their role in shaping the public debates over abortion. Leaving the fundamental question of prenatal personhood unattended can have catastrophic consequences for women's rights in general, and their sexual and reproductive rights in particular, in part by facilitating resort to criminal rather than constitutional law as the modality of reasoning. Moreover, the protection of prenatal personhood is usually not taken self-critically by its proponents but is rather an argument for justifying restrictions on women's sexual and reproductive rights and, more specifically, for trumping women's right to choose. Claims of prenatal personhood enable oversimplified narratives centered on the act of abortion rather than on the circumstances of women that give rise to unwanted pregnancies.

Rebecca Cook concludes the collection with a study on the stigmatizing effects of criminal law on abortion, asking whether the negative social implications of stigma that affect women considering or resorting to abortion, and that similarly affect providers of abortion services, outweigh the reasons for regulating abortion though criminal law. The answer requires acknowledging that stigmatization is a dehumanizing process by which power is exerted to spoil individuals' status, dignity, and self-image, justifying their degrading treatment. Cook explains that, as a decentralized mode of social control, stigmatization has unending rippling effects. Its consequences extend well beyond the formal criminal law, which often allows abortion only as a narrow exception from criminal guilt, to facilitate the development of informal rules that misapply the formal law and ignore the background rules on patients' rights and professional duties with impunity. As a result of the stigmatizing effects of criminally constructing women, Cook concludes that addressing abortion primarily through criminal law cannot be justified.

This book's contributors are differently located in the world and differently situated vis-à-vis the abortion field. Some are steeped in abortion scholarship and activism. Others have written relatively little in the field and have come to the study of abortion as an incident of some other project. Fragmentation is critical to our concept for the book, which subscribes to the view that "[a]lthough to a substantial extent it is what scholars share that makes discourse possible, it is what they do not share that makes it valuable."[2] Too much cohesion or too much connection can be stagnating, even corrosive, for a field of study. It is the wandering of different but related ideas that generates novelty and innovation.[3]

It is increasingly implausible to speak of a purely domestic abortion law, if one ever existed. The chapters of this collection illustrate various dimensions of the transnational enterprise. Lemaitre and Upreti explain the influence of Catholic and Hindu religious teachings respectively on framing of abortion law and legal debates. Siegel describes the influence of transnational social movements on the constitutionalization of abortion, while Ngwena describes colonial influence on African abortion laws. Sheldon points to how women's safe use of nonsurgical abortion in their homes in some countries inspired efforts to allow the same in Britain, and why these efforts proved unsuccessful given the British medical framework. Rubio-Marín and Lamačková address a form of cross-regime borrowing and grafting, where constitutional frameworks from afar are reimagined in new jurisdictions in a new era. Dickens explores how the debates on providers' right of conscience to refuse to provide services have been monopolized across jurisdictions by those opposed to abortion, without regard to the equal right of conscience to provide and use services.

Undurraga examines how constitutional courts have used and could use the principle of proportionality, a common legal doctrine in many countries, to discipline and resolve the reasoning about whether abortion regimes comply with constitutional and human rights. Recognizing the transnational phenomenon of the turn to procedural or adjective law to ensure access to lawful services, Erdman explores its promises and perils in the hands of an international court of human rights that seeks to engender change by drawing on the strength of democratic forces within, and acting in concert with, institutions of the state; that is, by integrating legal systems of rights protection. Bergallo explains how abortion guidelines of other countries and technical guidance from the World Health Organization inspired similar guidelines in Argentina to ensure women's access in practice to lawful abortions. Barroso compares and contrasts the decision of the Supreme Court of Brazil with court decisions of other countries on the same issue. Rebouché and Kelly describe the workings of a transnational reproductive advocacy network on domestic litigation. Madrazo and Cook document social meanings of law traveling across the boundaries of legal jurisdictions, suggestive of cultural values transcending geopolitical boundaries.

This book does not represent all geographic regions equally, and we recognize that some regions are underrepresented. The intention of the book is in part to encourage more transnational engagement and to invite identification and sharing of innovative lawyering and theorizing. We hope that this book will stimulate readers to imagine alternative ways to engage with abortion in law.

PART I

Constitutional Values and Regulatory Regimes

Chapter 1

The Constitutionalization of Abortion

Reva B. Siegel

Comparative constitutional study of abortion has generally focused on the decisions of a few influential jurisdictions, particularly Germany and the United States, where constitutional frameworks begin from dramatically divergent premises—protecting, respectively, unborn life and decisional autonomy.[1] Some comparative studies are dynamic, observing that constitutional doctrine in Germany and the United States has evolved to allow forms of abortion regulation that have more in common than the divergent constitutional frameworks authorizing them would suggest.[2]

This chapter analyzes constitutional decisions concerning abortion in the United States and Germany, their evolution over time, and their influence across jurisdictions. But rather than assume the existence of constitutional law on abortion—as so much of the literature does—the chapter asks how abortion was constitutionalized.[3] Examining the conflicts, within and across borders, that led to the first judicial decisions addressing the constitutionality of abortion laws in the 1970s sheds light on questions that prompted the birth of this body of law, and continue to shape its growth. The first constitutional decisions on abortion grew out of debates over women's citizenship, engendering doctrine that to this day is haunted by "the woman question" and conflicted about whether government may or must control women's decisions about motherhood. Attention to this question in turn sheds light on the relationship of constitutional politics and constitutional law: it demonstrates how political conflict shapes constitutional law and constitutional law endeavors to shape political conflict.[4]

Constitutional decisions on abortion began in an era when a transnational women's movement was beginning to contest the terms of women's citizenship, eliciting diverse forms of reaction, both supportive and resisting. As I show, the woman question haunts the abortion decisions, where it is initially addressed by indirection, and over time comes to occupy a more visible role, whether as an express concern of doctrine, *or* as a problematic nested inside of the growing body of law articulating a constitutional obligation to protect unborn life.

The body of constitutional law on abortion that has grown up since the 1970s is concerned with the propriety, necessity, and feasibility of controlling women's agency in decisions concerning motherhood. Some courts have insisted that government should respect women's decisions about motherhood, while many others have insisted that protecting unborn life requires government to control women's decisions about motherhood. Over the decades a growing number of courts have allowed government to protect life by persuading (rather than coercing) women to assume the role of motherhood. Across Europe, a growing number of jurisdictions are now giving women the final word in decisions about abortion—on the constitutional ground that it is the best way to protect unborn life. These remarkable developments suggest deep conflict about whether law should and can control women's agency in decisions about motherhood. Reading the cases with attention to this conflict identifies questions that courts are grappling with in the latest generation of abortion decisions, illuminating ambiguities in the normative basis of constitutional frameworks and in their practical architecture.

At the same time, this approach to the abortion cases offers a fascinating vantage point on constitutional decision making in the face of persistent social conflict. On one familiar view, constitutional adjudication raises the stakes of the abortion debate because it requires courts to choose between competing principles, and so inhibits compromise and incites polarization. But this chapter offers a more complicated story in which escalating political conflict precipitates constitutional adjudication, and, over time, constitutional adjudication endeavors to mediate political conflict. Recent judicial decisions on abortion seem to appreciate the tenacity of the abortion conflict, and in varying ways have come to internalize its implications for constitutional adjudication. Judgments frequently integrate opposing normative perspectives into one constitutional framework, in order to channel conflict that courts lack power to settle. Rather than endeavoring to impose values, courts often employ techniques that inform politics with constitutional value, just as

recent abortion legislation aspires to shape judicial reasoning about constitutional matters. These judicial and legislative frameworks endeavor to vindicate contested constitutional values by means that preserve social cohesion.

This chapter's interest in the conflicts that engendered the constitutionalization of abortion shapes its focus. The chapter does not systematically compare abortion legislation worldwide or investigate social practices concerning
its enforcement.[5] The chapter considers legislation for the purpose of exploring the roots and dynamic logic of constitutional law. These same interests
shape its coverage of constitutional doctrine. The chapter's focus is on the
development in national constitutions of broad normative frameworks concerning abortion.

The chapter proceeds in three sections. The first part briefly considers
developments in the 1960s and 1970s, a time when reformers of many kinds
persuaded legislatures around the world to liberalize access to abortion; when
a mobilizing feminist movement first claimed that repeal of abortion restrictions was required as a matter of justice for women; when those who sought
to preserve abortion's criminalization began to mobilize against change in the
name of a "right to life"; and when courts in five nations first issued judgments explaining what forms of abortion regulation their respective constitutions required or allowed.

The second part of the chapter examines key constitutional decisions in
the United States and Germany which together illustrate differences and sim-
ilarities in the logic of constitutionalization. In the 1970s, courts in both jurisdictions struck down abortion laws and provided guidelines for future
legislation, reasoning from very different constitutional norms. In 1973, the
Supreme Court of the United States interpreted the U.S. Constitution to require legislatures to respect the decision of a woman and her physician
whether to terminate a pregnancy, as long as the fetus was not viable;[6] in
1975, the West German Federal Constitutional Court interpreted its Basic
Law to require legislatures to protect unborn life, by prohibiting abortion in
all cases except those that would impose extraordinary burdens on the pregnant woman.[7] In the 1990s, commentators observe, in the midst of domestic
political conflict, each court significantly modified its judgment, to allow access to abortion after abortion-dissuasive counseling. Less remarked on is the
way that the reasoning of the courts in the 1990s was shaped by constitutional
struggles of the preceding decades. I consider in particular how the view of
women as citizens expressed in the U.S. and German abortion opinions of the
1970s and 1990s evolved.

The final section looks to the logic of constitutional law today, considering how several dominant frameworks address the woman question. Some jurisdictions now require constitutional protections for women's dignity and welfare in government regulation of abortion of a kind unheard of before the modern women's movement. Many jurisdictions require constitutional protection for unborn life, providing for these purposes detailed judgments about what legislatures may or must do in regulating women's conduct. Perhaps the most remarkable aspect of this story is how understanding of this recently articulated duty to protect unborn life has evolved: over time and across jurisdictions, the constitutional duty to protect unborn life has been articulated in terms that increasingly acknowledge, accommodate, and even respect women citizens as autonomous agents—even in matters concerning motherhood. A growing number of jurisdictions now invoke the constitutional duty to protect unborn life as reason for giving women the final word in decisions concerning abortion.

From Constitutional Politics to Constitutional Law

In the mid-twentieth century, abortion laws around the world varied greatly. Some countries allowed abortion on request; others criminalized abortion except to save the life of the pregnant woman. Between these extremes, countries permitted abortion on various "indications" (therapeutic, eugenic, juridical [e.g., in cases of rape], and socioeconomic), subject to different procedures and requirements.[8] From 1967 to 1977, at least forty-two jurisdictions changed their abortion laws, with the vast majority expanding the legal indications for abortion.[9] It was during this same period that courts in the United States, Canada, and Europe began to review laws regulating abortion for conformity with their constitutions.[10]

Comparativists who have addressed the constitutionalization of the abortion debate as a historically specific development have tended to equate constitutionalization with adjudication or judicialization.[11] Some commentary in this vein views judicialization of abortion as accelerating polarization or backlash.[12] But at least one constitutional comparativist has located the dynamics of polarization and constitutionalization of the abortion debate in politics[13]—an approach that my own work on the history of abortion conflict in the United States inclines me to adopt.[14] Although the matter plainly deserves further investigation, the record suggests that shifts in the form of political debate about abortion prompted and shaped subsequent constitutional litigation over the practice.

In the 1960s, abortion was not generally understood as presenting constitutional questions. Arguments for liberalizing access to abortion were couched in practical and policy-based terms. In Western Europe and North America, where abortion was criminally banned but available when authorized by doctors for particular indications, poor women often relied on illegal and unsafe providers; critics argued that criminalization imposed health harms on women that were unequally distributed by class.[15] A different kind of public health concern arose in the 1960s as pregnant women who sought to become mothers discovered that they had been exposed to drugs or illness known to cause developmental harms to the unborn (e.g., thalidomide, measles).[16] Doctors endeavoring to care for their women patients worried about erratically enforced criminal abortion laws and sought freedom in which to practice their profession.[17] In some jurisdictions, advocates for liberalization raised concerns about overpopulation—a concern that could take eugenic or environmental forms.[18]

These arguments for liberalizing abortion laws on public health, professional, and populationist grounds were not initially expressed or understood in constitutional terms. But youth movements challenging traditional sexual mores and a newly mobilizing women's movement advanced very different kinds of arguments for liberalizing access to abortion.[19]

By 1971, feminists on both sides of the Atlantic were calling for complete repeal of laws criminalizing abortion. They used "speak-out" strategies to publicize their claims, conducting "self-incrimination" campaigns in which women "outed" themselves as having had abortions, and so exposed themselves to criminal prosecution—asserting, through these acts of civil disobedience, a claim to dignity, in defiance of custom and criminal law. In France, 343 women drew international attention by declaring in a public manifesto that appeared in *Le Nouvel Observateur* in April 1971 that they had had abortions.[20] The text of the manifesto, written by Simone de Beauvoir and signed by many prominent French women, called for an end to secrecy and silence and demanded access to free birth control and to abortion services.[21] Two months after the release of the French manifesto, Aktion 218, a women's organization in West Germany named after the Penal Code Section criminalizing abortion, followed the French example, publishing abortion stories and the names of 374 German women in *Der Stern* in a statement asserting that the law criminalizing abortion subjected women to "degrading and life-threatening circumstances," coerced women, and "branded them as criminals."[22] Within months, women in Italy undertook their own self-incrimination campaign, releasing on August 4, 1971, a statement that women signed, acknowledging that they had had an abortion, and calling for abolition of the crime, on the ground that abortion should be "available for each class" and that motherhood should be a "free, conscious choice."[23] Women in the United States also joined in, with a petition, on the model of the French campaign, published in the spring 1972 edition of *Ms. Magazine*.[24]

Feminists changed the shape of the debate about abortion. Public health advocates and others who sought to liberalize access to abortion in the 1960s argued for incremental reform on the indications model, which they defended by appeal to shared values (health, class equity). By contrast, feminists sought categorical change—repeal of laws criminalizing abortion—which they justified on symbolic as well as practical grounds.

Feminists protested the criminalization of abortion as a symptom of a social order that devalued and disempowered women and asserted that repeal of laws criminalizing abortion was a necessary first step in women's emancipation. In 1969, Betty Friedan, president of the National Organization for Women, mobilized these arguments in a call for the repeal of laws criminalizing abortion:[25]

> Women are denigrated in this country, because women are not deciding the conditions of their own society and their own lives. Women are not taken seriously as people. Women are not seen seriously as people. So this is the new name of the game on the question of abortion: that women's voices are heard.
>
> . . . Women are the ones who therefore must decide, and what we are in the process of doing, it seems to me, is realizing that there are certain rights that have never been defined as rights, that are essential to equality for women, and they were not defined in the Constitution of this, or any country, when that Constitution was written only by men. The right of woman to control her reproductive process must be established as a basic and valuable human civil right not to be denied or abridged by the state.[26]

Friedan insisted: "there is no freedom, no equality, no full human dignity and personhood possible for women until we assert and demand the control over our own bodies, over our own reproductive process. . . . The real sexual revolution is the emergence of women from passivity, from *thingness*, to full self-determination, to full dignity."[27] Long shrouded in silence, the practice of abortion was now the object of political struggle, and increasingly a site of fundamental rights claims premised on the understanding that the regulation of abortion defined the standing of citizens and the nature and values of the polity. French feminists challenging the criminalization of abortion appealed to the ideals and traditions of the French revolutionary founding.[28] A leaflet spread in Vienna, Austria, announced: "The fight against the law prohibiting abortions is part of the fight for the women's right of self-determination, for their equal rights, in the law, in the public, at the places of work and within the families!"[29]

Growing calls for liberalization of abortion law provoked countermobilization in defense of the status quo. Opponents of abortion reform, often led by lay and clerical leaders of the Catholic Church who mobilized before feminists even entered the debate,[30] tended also to employ a categorical and symbolic style of politics. In the United States, for example, the Catholic Church created a national organization in 1967 designed to block any relaxation of criminal restrictions on abortion;[31] that same year, Church leaders mobilized parishioners against passage of an indications law in New York by invoking a God-given "right of innocent human beings to life" and equating incremental reform of the law criminalizing abortion with murder and genocide.[32]

In West Germany, conservative Catholic opponents of abortion reform invoked Nazism.[33] As in the United States, conservative Catholics argued that incremental reform of abortion law would put in jeopardy the moral fabric of the nation. In 1970, the Central Committee of German Catholics, an association of Catholic lay persons, objected that "the respect of human life is not subject to compromise" and warned that "a state that denies to becoming life the protection of law puts life in general in danger. It thereby puts its own inner legitimacy at stake."[34] Catholic opponents of decriminalization, like feminist proponents, tied abortion to fundamental questions of human dignity.[35] The Central Committee of German Catholics argued that decriminalizing abortion would violate West German constitutional guarantees of dignity: "If becoming life is not protected, including with the means of the criminal law, unconditional fundamental principles of a society founded on human dignity are not assured for long."[36] As the West German Parliament considered liberalizing access, the conference of German Catholic Bishops called for a suit challenging the constitutionality of the abortion reform legislation if enacted,[37] and Robert Spaemann, a Catholic philosopher and public intellectual, observed in 1974 that the proposed abortion liberalization "would, in the eyes of many citizens of our country, violate the legitimacy of the State at its very foundations for the first time since 1949. . . . With the periodic model our State would, to them, cease to be a Rechtsstaat."[38]

During the 1970s, these national and transnational debates led to the enactment of legislation in a number of countries that liberalized access to abortion, either on the indications model (doctors given authority to perform abortion upon verification of conditions satisfying a therapeutic, juridical, or social indication) or periodic model (women allowed to obtain abortion during a specified period, often in the first ten to twelve weeks of pregnancy). But conflict over the new laws spilled out of the legislative arena, and those frustrated in politics increasingly brought their claims to court,[39] where conflict was readily intelligible as a *constitutional* conflict because it had *already* been expressed as an argument about justice and the fundamental character of the polity.

In the 1970s, courts in the United States, France, the Federal Republic of Germany, Austria, and Italy reviewed for the first time the constitutionality of abortion laws.[40] As Machteld Nijsten has observed, "The European courts had no discretionary power in deciding the issue: In Germany, France and Austria, the courts were seized under the power of abstract review, and as such they served as a political instrument for the defeated opposition in Parliament."[41] In the United States and Italy, courts struck down laws criminalizing abortion; in France and Austria courts upheld laws liberalizing access to abortion; while in the Federal Republic of Germany, the Federal Constitutional Court declared unconstitutional legislation allowing abortion in the early weeks of pregnancy.

Foundational Frameworks and Their Evolution: United States and Germany

Much attention has been devoted to the 1970s decisions of the U.S. and West German courts because there is such a dramatic difference in their normative frameworks: the U.S. case struck down legislation criminalizing abortion in order to protect decisional autonomy, while the West German case struck down legislation legalizing access to abortion in order to protect unborn life.[42] Each judgment provided a framework to ensure that future abortion legislation would respect constitutional values. Decisions in the 1990s reaffirmed these constitutional frameworks, in the course of moderating them.

Commentators have attributed the difference in constitutional concern animating the1970s judgments to differences in constitutional or political culture.[43] For example, Gerald Neuman contrasts the U.S. and German legal systems in their willingness to recognize a constitutional duty of protection and to impose affirmative obligations on the state.[44] Donald Kommers points to differences in political culture, asserting that U.S. constitutional law expresses a "vision of personhood [that] is partial to the city perceived as private realm in which the individual is alone, isolated, and in competition with his fellows, while the [German] vision is partial to the city perceived as a public realm where individual and community are bound together in reciprocity." Given these differences in political culture, Kommers reasons, the "authority of the community, as represented by the state, to define the liberty interest of mothers and unborn life finds a more congenial abode in the German than in American constitutional law."[45]

Practices of comparison may exaggerate intergroup differences and occlude intragroup conflicts. Differences in political culture could well have made the West German judgment more acceptable in West Germany than it would have been in the United States; but polls showed widespread disagreement with the West German Court's decision to strike down the new abortion legislation.[46] Comparative constitutional inquiry can consider how judicial decisions respond to political conflict, and not simply to political culture.[47] In the United States and the Federal Republic of Germany, courts issued constitutional judgments on abortion after protracted debate over whether to liberalize access to abortion—a debate joined in the years immediately preceding the judgments by a mobilizing feminist movement calling for repeal of the criminal law.[48] Close comparative analysis of how this conflict shaped the judgments, or how the judgments aspired to shape this conflict, is beyond the scope of this chapter. But a few observations about the relation of the judgments and the conflict suggest that further comparative inquiry of this kind would be fruitful.

In what follows, I show that in the first round of decisions constitutionalizing abortion, each court responded to feminist claims. And the response of each court changed over time. By the 1990s, the autonomy claims of women came to play a more significant role in the abortion cases of *each* nation. The inquiry illustrates how constitutional judgments about the agency of women citizens are nested within constitutional protections for life, and how these judgments evolved in the late twentieth century.

The 1970s

In 1973, the U.S. Supreme Court struck down a nineteenth-century criminal law that banned abortion except to save a woman's life, as well as a twentieth-century law that permitted abortion on the basis of more expansive indications. *Roe v. Wade*[49] held that the constitutional right to privacy (a liberty right protected by the Fourteenth Amendment) encompassed a woman's decision in consultation with her physician whether to terminate a pregnancy. At the same time, the Court recognized that the privacy right "is not absolute; . . . at some point the state interests as to protection of health, medical standards, and prenatal life, become dominant."[50] To coordinate the right and its regulation, the Court set forth a "trimester framework" that allowed increasing regulation of women's abortion decision over the course of a pregnancy, permitting restrictions on abortion to protect unborn life only at the point of viability (when a fetus is deemed capable of surviving outside a woman's womb).[51]

Roe responded both to public health and feminist claims. The decision offered an account, unprecedented in constitutional law, of the physical and emotional harms to women that criminal abortion laws inflict and declared that the law's imposition of these harms on women was a matter of constitutional concern: "The detriment that the State would impose upon the pregnant woman by denying this choice altogether is apparent."[52] The Court declared these harms constitutionally significant after years of public health reporting and feminist testimony, on the street and in court, about the ways that criminalization of abortion harms women.[53]

Even so, the Court's opinion in *Roe* seems mainly responsive to public health arguments, and at best only indirectly responsive to feminist claims. While the appellant's brief in *Roe* argued that the Texas law banning abortion "severely impinges [a woman's] dignity, her life plan and often her marital relationship,"[54] the *Roe* decision focused much more clearly on the *doctor's* autonomy than on his patients," repeating statements of this kind: "The decision vindicates the right of the physician to administer medical treatment according to his professional judgment up to the points where important state interests provide compelling justifications for intervention. Up to those points, the abortion decision in all its aspects is inherently, and primarily, a medical decision, and basic responsibility for it must rest with the physician."[55] As importantly, the Court's account of the harms to women that criminal abortion laws inflict focused on the physical and psychological difficulties of pregnancy that "a woman and her responsible physician necessarily will consider in consultation."[56] The Court's account of harms did not speak in the register of citizenship or status about the injury to a woman's dignity in being coerced by government to bear a child and to become a mother.[57] The opinion's discussion of the state's interest in restricting abortion to protect potential life makes no mention of these concerns.[58]

By contrast, the 1975 decision of the German Federal Constitutional Court was much more explicit in its engagement with feminist claims. The West German Court held that a 1974 law, which decriminalized abortion during the first twelve weeks of pregnancy for women who received abortion-dissuasive counseling, violated the Basic Law: "The life which is developing in the womb of the mother is an independent legal value which enjoys the protection of the Constitution."[59] The Court reasoned that the duty of the state to protect unborn life was derived from the Basic Law's protection for life and for dignity: "Where human life exists, human dignity is present to it."[60]

The Federal Constitutional Court warned the legislature not to "acquiesce" in popular beliefs about abortion that might have developed in response to "passionate discussion of the abortion problematic."[61] The Court expressly and rather brusquely dismissed the Parliament's efforts to devise a framework that respected the dignity of women *and* of the unborn: "The opinion expressed in the Federal Parliament during the third deliberation on the Statute to Reform the Penal Law, the effect of which is to propose the precedence for a particular time 'of the right to self-determination of the woman which flows from human dignity vis-à-vis all others, including the child's right to life' . . . is not reconcilable with the value ordering of the Basic Law."[62] Given the overriding importance of the dignity of human life, the Court concluded, "the legal order may not make the woman's right to self-determination the sole guideline of its rulemaking. The state must proceed, as a matter of principle, from a duty to carry the pregnancy to term."[63]

Thus, the Federal Constitutional Court engaged with feminist dignity and autonomy arguments for decriminalizing abortion by striking down legislation enacted in response to them as unconstitutional in principle, and, further, by recognizing a constitutional duty to protect life that requires law to enforce the maternal role and responsibilities of women.

Judgments about the maternal role and responsibilities of women are nested throughout the opinion's account of the constitutional duty to protect life. The duty to protect life was "entrusted by nature in the first place to the protection of the mother. To reawaken and, if required to strengthen the maternal duty to protect, where it is lost, should be the principal goal of the endeavors of the state by the protection of life"; the duty to protect life obliged government to "strengthen the readiness of the expectant mother to accept the pregnancy as her own responsibility"[64] Having established that government had a duty to protect life enforceable against pregnant women, the Court distinguished between the "normal" burdens of motherhood, which the duty to protect life obliged government to exact by law, and extraordinary burdens of motherhood, such as those posing a threat to a woman's life or health, which are nonexactable by law.[65] The Court reasoned that when a pregnant woman faced difficulties other than the "normal" burdens of motherhood, her "decision for an interruption of pregnancy can attain the rank of a decision of conscience worthy of consideration," and in these circumstances it would be inappropriate to use criminal law or "external compulsion where respect for the sphere of personality of the human being demands fuller inner freedom of decision."[66] By contrast, women who "decline pregnancy because they are not willing to take on the renunciation and the natural motherly duties bound up with it" may decide "upon an interruption of pregnancy without having a reason which is worthy of esteem within the value order of the constitution."[67] The Court recognized a woman's concern about continuing a pregnancy that posed a threat to her life or grave risk to her health as respectworthy, hence warranting an exemption from legal compulsion. The Court authorized the legislature to permit abortion on the basis of other analogously nonexactable indications.[68] "Even in these cases the state may not be content merely to examine, and if the occasion arises, to certify that the statutory prerequisites for an abortion free of punishment are present. Rather, the state will also be expected to offer counseling and assistance with the goal of reminding pregnant women of the fundamental duty to respect the right to life of the unborn, to encourage her to continue the pregnancy."[69]

The 1990s

In the 1990s, acting under different forms of political pressure, the U.S. and German courts each revisited their judgments of the 1970s, reaffirming and modifying them.[70] Each court continued to reason from its original premises, yet did so in ways that gave far greater recognition to women's autonomy in making decisions about motherhood.

The Supreme Court's 1992 decision in *Planned Parenthood of Southeastern Pennsylvania v. Casey*[71] analyzed the constitutionality of a Pennsylvania statute that imposed a twenty-four-hour waiting period before abortions could be performed; required a woman seeking an abortion to receive certain information designed to persuade her to choose childbirth over abortion, required a minor to obtain parental consent; and required a woman seeking an abortion to provide notice to her spouse.[72] The Court reaffirmed what it termed the central principle of *Roe*: "the woman's right to terminate her pregnancy before viability."[73] But the *Casey* Court rejected *Roe*'s trimester framework and announced that it would allow government regulation for the purpose of protecting potential life *throughout* the term of a pregnancy, *as long as* the law did not impose an "undue burden" on the pregnant woman's decision whether to bear a child. To determine whether regulation imposed an undue burden the Court announced it would ask whether the statute has "the purpose or effect of placing a substantial obstacle in the path of a woman seeking an abortion of a nonviable fetus."[74]

Even as the Court revised the *Roe* trimester framework to allow restrictions on abortion throughout pregnancy, it restated the constitutional basis of the abortion right in terms that gave far more recognition to women's decisional autonomy. *Casey*'s "undue burden" framework allowed government to deter abortion, but only by means that inform, rather than block, a woman's choice about whether to end a pregnancy: "What is at stake is the woman's right to make the ultimate decision."[75]

At the same time, *Casey* emphasized, in ways *Roe* did not, that constitutional protections for decisions about abortion vindicate women's dignity, their liberty, and their equality as citizens.[76] The portion of the plurality opinion attributed to Justice Kennedy invoked dignity to explain why the Constitution protects decisions regarding family life: "These matters, involving the most intimate and personal choices a person may make in a lifetime, choices central to personal dignity and autonomy, are central to the liberty protected by the Fourteenth Amendment."[77] Protecting women's authority to make their own decisions about motherhood simultaneously vindicates constitutional values of equality as well as liberty. Reaffirming the abortion right, *Casey* locates its constitutional basis in evolving views of women's citizenship that give to women, rather than the state, primary authority in making decisions about their roles: "Her suffering is too intimate and personal for the State to insist, without more, upon its own vision of the woman's role, however dominant that vision has been in the course of our history and our culture. The destiny of the woman must be shaped to a large extent on her own conception of her spiritual imperatives and her place in society."[78] In *Casey*, the Court applied the undue burden standard and upheld all of Pennsylvania's regulations, except for the provision requiring a woman to inform her spouse before she could end a pregnancy—which the Court characterized as inconsistent with modern understandings of women as equal citizens.[79]

In striking down the spousal notice provision, the Court again invoked liberty and equality values, explaining how women's standing as citizens had evolved with changing understandings of women's roles: "Only one generation has passed since this Court observed that "woman is still regarded as the center of home and family life," with attendant "special responsibilities" that precluded full and independent legal status under the Constitution. These views, of course, are no longer consistent with our understanding of the family, the individual, or the Constitution. . . . A State may not give to a man the kind of dominion over his wife that parents exercise over their children."[80] *Casey* protected women's dignity in making the very decisions about motherhood that the Federal Constitutional Court held were governed by natural duty—as, for example when the German Court reasoned that women who "decline pregnancy because they are not willing to take on the renunciation and the natural motherly duties bound up with it" may decide "upon an interruption of pregnancy without having a reason which is worthy of esteem within the value order of the constitution."[81]

In 1990s, the Federal Constitutional Court would reaffirm this understanding, but in a framework that indirectly afforded far greater recognition to women's autonomy in making decisions about motherhood. The reunification of Germany required reconciling the law of East Germany, which allowed women to make their own decisions about abortion in early pregnancy, with the law of West Germany, which did not.[82] The German Parliament enacted legislation that allowed women to make their own decisions about abortion in the first twelve weeks of pregnancy after participating in a counseling process designed to persuade them to carry the pregnancy to term—a form of regulation presented as more effective in deterring abortion than a criminal ban and respecting both "the high value of unborn life and the self-determination of the woman."[83] The Federal Constitutional Court invalidated the legislation but shifted ground as it did so.

The Court reaffirmed that protection for the unborn vis-à-vis its mother is only possible if the legislature forbids a woman to terminate her pregnancy.[84] The legislature was obliged to use the criminal law to demarcate obligations exactable of the woman, in order clearly to communicate the scope of the duty to protect—an obligation bearing not only on the pregnant woman herself, but also on others in a position to support her in carrying the pregnancy to term.[85] But the legislature was not obliged to protect unborn life through the threat of criminal sanction itself. The legislature could devise a scheme of counseling to persuade pregnant women to carry to term and, as long as the counseling was effective to that end, could even decide to dispense with the threat of criminal punishment "in view of the openness necessary for counseling to be effective."[86] The legislature could base its protection concept "on the assumption—at least in the early phase of pregnancy—that effective protection of unborn human life is only possible *with* the support of the mother. . . . The secrecy pertaining to the unborn, its helplessness and dependence and its unique link to its mother would appear to justify the view that the state's chances of protecting it are better if it works together with the mother."[87]

The Court presented this new account of the state's duty of protection as in "conformity with the respect owed to a woman and future mother,"[88] observing that the counseling concept endeavors to exact what the pregnant woman owes "without degrading her to a mere object of protection" and "respects her as an autonomous person by trying to win her over as an ally in the protection of the unborn."[89] While the Court presented the decision as requiring legislative adherence to its 1975 judgment, the Court's willingness to accept the substitution of counseling for threat of criminal prosecution augured a new view of the citizen-subject that abortion regulation addresses, and a transformed understanding of the constitutional duty to protect unborn life. In this emergent view, women citizens are persons who exercise autonomy even as to the ways they inhabit family roles; that exercise of autonomy is sufficiently respect-worthy that women would be degraded were abortion law to treat them as a mere object or instrument for protecting unborn life.

In the wake of the 1993 decision, abortion remains criminally prohibited except under restricted indications, but a woman who completes counseling can receive a certificate granting her immunity from prosecution for an abortion during the first twelve weeks of pregnancy.[90] In this new framework, Catholic lay groups are involved in counseling, and where necessary, issuing abortion certificates and providing the sex education required by law, although this has been the subject of much and extended controversy.[91]

Contemporary Constitutional Frameworks

As we have seen, courts in the United States and Germany imposed different frameworks on the regulation of abortion designed to vindicate competing constitutional values; but within two decades, courts in each nation had reaffirmed and modified those frameworks to give greater recognition to women's agency in the abortion decision, while simultaneously emphasizing the importance of protecting unborn life. The 1990s cases reject the view that constitutionalization of abortion is a "zero-sum game" and present frameworks that vindicate competing constitutional values, endeavoring to mediate conflicts among them.

Today, we can see constitutionalization of abortion taking several forms. Some jurisdictions require government to respect women's dignity in making decisions about abortion and consequently require legislators to provide women control, for all or some period of pregnancy, over the decision whether to become a mother. Many jurisdictions require constitutional protection for unborn life, criminalizing abortion while permitting exceptions on an indications basis to protect women's physical or emotional welfare, but not their autonomy. Yet other jurisdictions protect unborn life through counseling regimes that are result-open; these jurisdictions begin by recognizing women's autonomy for the putatively instrumental reason that it is the best method of managing the modern female citizen, and then come to embrace protecting women's dignity as a concurrent constitutional aim of depenalizing abortion.

In what follows, I explore these three forms of constitutionalization, in order of their historical emergence, and briefly illustrate with contemporary examples. The forms are distinguishable along several dimensions. As will become apparent, the frameworks of review that jurisdictions have adopted vary in the *constitutional values* that courts expect abortion legislation to vindicate (e.g., respecting women's dignity, protecting unborn life, protecting women's welfare), and the *legislative regimes* associated historically and symbolically with the vindication of these constitutional values (e.g., "periodic" regimes which allow abortion at a woman's request for a period of pregnancy; "indications" regimes which prohibit abortion except on indications determined by a third party; and "result-open" dissuasive counseling regimes which allow a woman to make the ultimate decision after she is counseled against abortion). Historical and symbolic ties between constitutional values and particular legislative abortion regimes have endowed those regimes with powerful social meaning, even as enforcement of abortion legislation may provide women access in striking variance. Finally, there is variance within these forms in the *judicial constraints* courts impose on representative government (do courts allow, require, or prohibit legislation vindicating particular constitutional values?). In some cases, these differences in judicial constraint seem connected to the values the case law vindicates; but in others they suggest an interesting story about the interaction of courts and representative government in the articulation of constitutional law.

There are other expressions of this evolving relationship between courts and legislatures. Over the decades, constitutions have been amended to address abortion more or less directly, and statutes have been enacted that include constitutionalized preambles, either in response to antecedent constitutional law or in an effort to call into being new bodies of constitutional law. With the growth of legislative constitutionalism in abortion regulation, the boundaries between constitutional law and politics grow ever blurrier.

Respecting Women's Dignity: Periodic Legislation

This approach, originating in the United States, constitutionalizes the regulation of abortion with attention to women's autonomy and welfare. It is associated with periodic legislation, which coordinates values of decisional autonomy and protecting life by giving women control over the abortion decision, often for an initial period of the pregnancy, thereafter allowing restrictions on abortion except on limited indications (e.g., for life or health).

This approach begins in court decisions but now also finds expression in constitutionalized preambles. In South Africa, for example, the preamble to a statute allowing abortion on request in the first twelve weeks of pregnancy announces that it vindicates "the values of human dignity, the achievement of equality, security of the person, non-racialism and non-sexism, and the advancement of human rights and freedoms which underlie a democratic South Africa."[92] The High Court upheld the legislation's constitutionality in a 2004 decision: "the Constitution not only permits the Choice on Termination of Pregnancy Act to make a pregnant woman's informed consent the cornerstone of its regulation of the termination of her pregnancy, but indeed requires the Choice Act to do so."[93]

Legislation recently enacted in Mexico City providing for abortion on request during the first twelve weeks of pregnancy appeals to a constitutional provision that guarantees Mexican citizens the freedom to decide the number and spacing of children;[94] the preamble to the Mexico City statute provides: "Sexual and reproductive health care is a priority. Services provided in this matter *constitute a means for the exercise of the right of all persons to decide freely, responsibly and in an informed manner on the number and spacing of children*."[95] The Supreme Court of Mexico recently confirmed the constitutionality of the legislation.[96] The state was constitutionally permitted to decriminalize abortion.

Protecting Life/Protecting Women: Indications Legislation

Other jurisdictions follow the German tradition in constitutionalizing a duty to protect life; these jurisdictions require action in furtherance of the duty to protect and typically require or authorize legislatures to criminalize abortion with certain exceptions or indications determined by a committee of doctors or some decision maker other than the pregnant woman. As we have seen, constitutional judgments about women are inevitably nested within the constitutional duty to protect life and emerge in any effort to specify the terms on which abortion is to be banned (and thus also permitted). Constitutionalization in this form has tended to incorporate gender-conventional, role-based views of women's citizenship—for example that the burdens of pregnancy are naturally assumed by women, or by women who have consented to sex, except when such burdens exceed what is normally to be expected of women, at which point women may be exempt from penal sanction for aborting a pregnancy.[97]

Constitutionalization in this form is paternalist, in its conception of women as well as the unborn, reasoning about women as dependants who may deserve protection, and protecting them against injuries to their physical and emotional welfare, rather than to their autonomy. (Jurisdictions that protect unborn life by banning abortion except on third-party indication typically excuse women from the duty to bear a child to protect women's physical survival and to protect women's physical and emotional welfare; only recently have some considered protecting women's dignity.) Courts reasoning in this tradition typically permit but do not require abortion legislation to protect the welfare and autonomy of women citizens who are pregnant; courts may, however, hold that a constitution requires the state to allow abortion to save a woman's life.

The Republic of Ireland, which first amended its Constitution to address abortion, expressly relates the protections it accords the life of the unborn and the life of the mother: "The State acknowledges the right to life of the unborn and, *with due regard to the equal right to life of the mother*, guarantees in its laws to respect, and, as far as practicable, by its laws to defend and vindicate that right."[98] Ireland seems to construe a woman's "equal right to life" as including protection for a woman's physical survival but not her dignity. When an adolescent woman who was pregnant by rape was enjoined from traveling abroad for an abortion, the Irish Supreme Court overturned the injunction, reasoning that the young woman's risk of suicide satisfied the standard of a "real and substantial risk" to the pregnant woman's life.[99] In other words, in order to fit the case within the right to life that Ireland guarantees equally to women and the unborn, the Court had to efface the young women's agency—her refusal to have sex with her rapist and the consequent risk she might harm herself if compelled to bear her rapist's child; instead the Court approached the young woman's case as if it concerned a physiological risk from pregnancy. The Court explained that its Constitution's abortion clause should be interpreted in terms informed by the virtue of charity: "not the charity which consists of giving to the deserving, for that is justice, but the charity which is also called mercy."[100]

In 1985 the Spanish Constitutional Court declared that its Constitution protected the life of the unborn, in the tradition of the first West German judgment, yet declared that it was constitutional for the legislature to allow abortion on several indications, including rape. In discussing the justification for the indication for rape, the Spanish Court emphasized that in such a case "gestation was caused by an act . . . harming to a maximum degree her [a woman's] personal dignity and the free development of her personality," emphasizing that "the woman's dignity requires that she cannot be considered as a mere instrument."[101] Even so, the Court reasoned that the exceptions to Spain's abortion law were constitutionally *permitted*, not required, and emphasized that the legislation was enacted for the purpose of protecting unborn life.[102]

A more recent decision of the Colombian Supreme Court interpreting a constitution understood to protect unborn life offers a striking contrast. The Colombian Court held that a statute banning abortion was constitutionally *required* to contain exceptions for certain indications in light of "the constitutional importance of the bearer of the rights . . . the pregnant woman."[103] "When the legislature enacts criminal laws, it cannot ignore that a woman is a human being entitled to dignity and that she must be treated as such, as opposed to being treated as a reproductive instrument for the human race."[104] "A criminal law that prohibits abortion in all circumstances *extinguishes the woman's fundamental rights*, and thereby *violates her dignity* by reducing her to a mere receptacle for the fetus, *without rights or interests of constitutional relevance worthy of protection*."[105]

Thus, the Colombian Court held that the legislature was constitutionally obliged, and not merely permitted, to include indications in its abortion law. The Court explained that failure to allow for abortion in cases of rape would be in "complete disregard for human dignity and the right to the free development of the pregnant woman *whose pregnancy is not the result of a free and conscious decision*, but the result of arbitrary, criminal acts against her in violation of her autonomy."[106] "A woman's right to dignity prohibits her treatment as a mere instrument for reproduction, and her consent is therefore essential to the fundamental, life-changing decision to give birth to another person."[107] By this same reasoning, however, the legislature *was* allowed to criminalize abortion in cases of consensual sex, as long as the legislature provided exceptions for women's life, health, and cases of fetal anomaly.[108] This approach presumes that, for women, consent to sex *is* consent to procreation.

Protecting Life/Respecting Women: Result-Open Counseling

Yet other jurisdictions begin from a constitutional duty to protect life, and, like Germany, have begun to explore approaches for vindicating the duty to protect life that do not involve the threat of criminal prosecution. These jurisdictions constitutionally justify depenalization of abortion, coupled with abortion-dissuasive, result-open counseling, as more effective in protecting the unborn than the threat of criminal punishment. The justifications for life-protective counseling, as well as its form, are evolving over time, in ways that progressively incorporate values of women's autonomy. At a minimum, these jurisdictions recognize women as the type of modern citizens who possess autonomy of a kind that law must take into consideration if it hopes to affect their conduct; some go further and are beginning to embrace protecting women's dignity as a concurrent constitutional aim.[109]

Constitutional review of counseling regimes originates in the German cases. In 1975, the German Court endorsed abortion-dissuasive counseling as a mode of protecting life in cases where the legislature deemed abortion nonexactable;[110] in 1993, the German Court expanded that approach, reasoning that a legislature might find counseling coupled with depenalization of abortion generally more effective than the threat of criminal punishment in meeting its duty to protect life, observing that depenalization was *also* consistent with women's autonomy.[111]

The Hungarian Court has amplified the woman-respecting aspects of this approach. In 1998, the Hungarian Court held that it was unconstitutional for the state to make verification of a "situation of serious crisis" indication depend *solely* on a woman's signature: "Such provisions themselves cannot secure for the foetus the level of minimum protection required by the [Constitution] . . . and in fact, they do not secure any protection, as the regulation is concerned with the mother's right to self-determination, only."[112] The Court explicitly rejected this legislative scheme as a concealed version of periodic regulation,[113] while holding that the state could remedy the legislation through directed counseling measures or third party verification. The Court then discussed abortion-dissuasive counseling as a method of protecting unborn life that was *also* respectful of women's rights. "In principle, such a consulting service would not . . . violate her freedom of conscience."[114] While "the state may not compel anyone to accept a situation which sows discord within, or is irreconcilable with the fundamental convictions which mould that person's identity" obligatory participation in counseling violates neither principle "having particular regard to the fact that she [the pregnant woman] is only obligated to participate without any [further] obligation. . . . [A]s far as *its outcome is concerned, the consultation*—while clearly focusing on the protection of the fetus—*must be open.*"[115]

Portugal has taken further steps in this direction.[116] In upholding legislation that allowed abortion during the first ten weeks of pregnancy after a waiting period and result-open counseling, the Portuguese Constitutional Court emphasized that the new law was an effective means of protecting life. However, a counseling regime the Court upheld was not expressly dissuasive.[117] Strikingly, the recent Portuguese decision employed the reasoning of the 1993 German decision to dispense with the need for expressly dissuasive counseling of the kind mandated by the 1993 German decision. As it did so, the Portuguese decision invoked women's dignity as a justification for result-open counseling.[118] The Portuguese case thus features emergent elements of women's rights, both as to justification and as to legislative form. But the constitutional framework yet remains at some distance from the women's dignity–periodic access cases of jurisdictions such as the United States and South Africa. The Portuguese Court ruled that a result-open counseling framework in the early period of pregnancy is constitutionally *permitted*, not required, as it would be in a traditional woman's rights framework.

The abortion legislation Spain enacted in 2010 presses result-open counseling in ways that even more robustly associate it with protecting women's rights. The legislation allows abortion on request in the first fourteen weeks, subject to counseling. Its preamble reasons in constitutionalized terms about the values the legislation is designed to vindicate, including both "the rights and interests of women and prenatal life." The preamble asserts that "protecting prenatal life is more effective through active policies to support pregnant women and maternity," and therefore that "protection of the legal right at the very beginning of pregnancy is articulated through the will of the woman, and not against it," and directing public officials to "establish the conditions for adopting a free and responsible decision."[119]

In the decades since the German Court's 1993 decision, this hybrid framework has spread, legitimating result-open counseling early in pregnancy as a method of protecting unborn life,[120] while increasingly acknowledging, accommodating, and sometimes even explicitly respecting women's autonomy in making decisions about motherhood.[121] Whether or not the fetal-protective justification for results-open counseling is accompanied by a women's dignity-respecting justification, women are accorded the final word in decisions about whether they become mothers. Drawing elements from two disparate forms of constitutionalization, this hybrid form has transformative potential: one day it might combine community obligation to support those who nurture life with community obligation to respect their judgments. Realization of this potential depends on both expressive and practical aspects of implementation.

The emergence in the last two decades of fetal-protective justifications for providing women control over decisions concerning abortion is especially striking in light of the concurrent spread of woman-protective justifications for denying women access to abortion (e.g., banning or restricting abortion for the asserted purpose of protecting women from harm or coercion).[122] In both cases, a particular legislative regime is justified by appeal to constitutional values historically associated with an opposing form of abortion regulation: legislation that allows abortion is associated with the constitutional protection of unborn life, and legislation that restricts abortion is associated with the constitutional protection of women. Rhetorical inversions of this kind may be produced through social movement struggle, or they may emerge as movements employ the discourse of a reigning constitutional order in order to challenge it.[123]

After decades of conflict, a constitutional framework is emerging in Europe that allows legislators to vindicate the duty to protect unborn life by providing women dissuasive counseling and the ability to make their own decisions about abortion. Constitutionalization in this form values women as mothers first, yet addresses women as the kinds of citizens who are autonomous in making decisions about motherhood, and may even warrant respect as such. The spread of constitutionalization in this form attests to passionate conflict over abortion and women's family roles; it also suggests increasing acceptance of claims the women's movement has advanced in the last forty years, however controverted they remain. Jurisdictions that permit result-open counseling in satisfaction of the duty to protect unborn life express evolving understandings of women as citizens, in terms that reflect community ambivalence and assuage community division, while continuing to engender change.

Chapter 2

Abortion in Portugal:
New Trends in European Constitutionalism

Ruth Rubio-Marín

Despite persistent variation, abortion legislation in Europe has experienced a common and gradual liberalizing trend. Most European countries exempt from punishment abortions performed to protect a woman's health and life, in cases of serious fetal malformations, and where pregnancy results from rape (the commonly known therapeutic, eugenic, and ethical indications). This progressive trend has continued with most European countries adopting ever more liberal interpretations of the indications, or adding a social indication to the regime. Many countries even allow women themselves rather than third parties to verify the existence of a social indication, for example, to declare themselves in a situation of distress.

Still further liberalization can be seen in an increasing number of countries embracing a periodic model, where women can freely decide whether to carry their pregnancies to term before an upper gestation limit ranging from twelve to eighteen weeks. Coupled with this periodic model are regulations that often require counseling and reflection periods, though countries differ in the rationale for these requirements. Some counseling regulations seek only to ensure women's informed decision making. Others intend counseling to dissuade women from having an abortion.

Of note, this progression toward liberalization in Europe has tended not to rely on constitutional law. Neither women nor those defending women's reproductive rights have relied primarily on constitutions or constitutional courts to advance their position. European constitutional texts, for the most part, are silent on abortion or matters of reproduction generally, and it has not been women or rebellious doctors but conservative political forces that have seized the courts, seeking to resist legislative liberalization. In some countries such as France[1] and Austria,[2] such attempts were unsuccessful from the start, with the courts allowing legislators to proceed unimpeded. In others such as Germany,[3] Hungary,[4] and Poland[5] the courts did step in to curb progressive legislation.

Perhaps the most influential of these decisions was that of the German Federal Constitutional Court, which in 1975 struck down a periodic legislative reform. This case proved paradigmatic in the region and beyond, by framing abortion constitutionalism primarily in terms of the protection of unborn human life, linked to the normalization of women's duty of motherhood. In time, even the German constitutional doctrine would come to validate the periodic model of abortion regulation, now widespread across the region. But this was first accomplished merely on strategic grounds, namely on the view that dissuasive counseling and social assistance might prove the only effective way to deter abortions.

More important in the history of European liberalization of abortion constitutionalism is the fact that, in more recent times, we have come to see a shift in rationale. The emergence of a constitutional doctrine of abortion that respects the German legacy and grants constitutional protection to unborn human life but also accepts periodic legislation in respect of women's constitutional dignity and autonomy rights. In other words, although the state's obligation to show respect to unborn life is maintained, the normalization of pregnant women's duty of motherhood is challenged. An articulate expression of this doctrine was provided by the Portuguese Constitutional Court in a 2010 decision[6] validating the 2007 periodic legislation that allows women to decide whether to have an abortion within the first ten weeks of pregnancy.[7] Women are required to undergo counseling, but the counseling is explicitly nondirective.

Portugal has a rich history of abortion constitutionalism, its Constitutional Court having delivered five abortion decisions since the mid-1980s, in every case validating yet ever more progressive reform. In the first set of decisions, dating from 1984[8] and 1985,[9] the Constitutional Court backed an indication-based reform against an otherwise complete criminal prohibition. In the second set of decisions, in 1998[10] and 2006,[11] the Court again upheld the constitutionality of progressive reform through national referenda on the legislative introduction of a periodic regime. In its most recent 2010 decision, the Court pushed the development of European constitutional abortion law by validating a periodic regime with nondissuasive counseling, relying on a reading of the Portuguese Constitution that requires state protection of both intrauterine life and women's reproductive autonomy.[12]

The chapter seeks to unravel this evolution in Portugal's abortion constitutional jurisprudence, and to isolate the legal and political developments in the formation of the new constitutional doctrine now governing abortion law in the country. The next two parts focus on the early history of abortion constitutionalism in Portugal. They explain how the first cases of the 1980s, and then the referenda decisions of later decades, both conformed to and departed from the German doctrine. These sections describe the main features of the German doctrine against which the Portuguese case law was shaped, while also emphasizing the main points of departure that eventually allowed the Portuguese Court to hold a periodic model of abortion legislation constitutional. The fourth part of the chapter focuses on Portugal's most recent constitutional abortion case, the 2010 decision upholding the constitutionality of the periodic law. Particular attention is paid to why, in contrast to developments under German law, the lack of dissuasive counseling was not considered an insurmountable flaw by the Portuguese Constitutional Court. The chapter concludes by assessing changing conceptions of the pregnant women within abortion law and the ultimate meaning behind the protection of unborn human life under this new doctrine.

The Dawn of Abortion Constitutionalism in Europe and Portugal

Modern constitutionalism, born at the end of the eighteenth century with the French and American Revolutions, produced a vision of political equality among propertied, free, and white men. Women, who at the time did not enjoy civil or political equality, were unable to seize the historical opportunity to articulate their views on the enlightened ideals of liberty and equality or on which expressions of human autonomy should be deemed so fundamental as to be constitutionally enshrined.[13] It should not come as a surprise that, in this context, the freedom to decide whether or not to beget children was not considered *constitutional* in substance, despite the arguably fundamental way in which this decision impacts women's bodies and lives. In the 1960s, a transnational women's movement, coinciding with second wave feminism, started to challenge the terms of women's citizenship.[14] Feminist ideas about women's citizenship converged with broader health concerns about the high morbidity and mortality of illegal abortions, to spur on legislative liberalization efforts.[15] Church leaders in turn resisted these reforms by invoking the sanctity and dignity of life.

This was the context of abortion's constitutionalization in the West. In 1973, relying on the right to privacy the U.S. Supreme Court decided the landmark case of *Roe v. Wade*,[16] by reading women's reproductive freedom into a silent constitutional text to strike down a restrictive criminal statute. The Court endorsed a trimester scheme that banned state interference in the first trimester; it permitted regulation to protect the woman's health in the second trimester; and it permitted prohibition after viability to protect a state interest in unborn life.[17] The Court would later abandon this trimester scheme, allowing state interference short of an undue burden throughout pregnancy.[18]

In the European imagery *Roe* became the American paradigm, marked by a constitutional framing of abortion that begins with recognition of women's reproductive freedom. This paradigm has always represented an extreme against which European courts have sought more moderate positions. This is perhaps a consequence of the way in which European courts were brought into constitutional struggles over abortion. Between 1974 and 1975, in four European countries (Austria, France, Germany, and Italy) constitutional decisions on abortion were issued, but in every case with the exception of Italy,[19] it was groups resisting liberalization rather than those fighting for it, that resorted to the courts. This is how European abortion constitutionalism started off and has remained to this day *reactive* in nature.

The primary question asked in these cases was whether liberal reform violated the constitutional right to life of the unborn. As such protection was not explicit in constitutional texts, European courts—like the U.S. Supreme Court—were asked to "read in" constitutional protection, albeit for the life of the unborn rather than for women's reproductive freedom. In 1975, in the case that would be become a clear point of reference in Europe, the German Constitutional Court struck down a legislative attempt to decriminalize abortion in the first twelve weeks of pregnancy.[20] The law was held to provide insufficient protection of the right to life and dignity. Although few other European courts would reproduce the German doctrine in its entirety, the 1975 German decision has had an outsized influence on European abortion constitutionalism, primarily in its framing of the constitutional question in terms of state protection of unborn or intra-uterine life, and a naturalized duty of women as mothers.

The Portuguese Constitutional Court was no exception in this regard. The German paradigm is plainly evident in the early abortion decisions of the Court. Abortion in Portugal was banned under the Criminal Code until 1984, when the legislature introduced an indications model declaring abortion nonpunishable where necessary to protect the life or health of the woman, in cases of severe fetal abnormality, or when pregnancy resulted from rape.[21] Following the continental trend, this legislative reform triggered reactive litigation, which ultimately proved unsuccessful. The Court first defended the legislation in 1984 in an a priori challenge by the president of the republic, and then again in 1985[22] against a challenge by the ombudsman, after the legislation was enacted.

Framing the case within the German paradigm, the Portuguese Court interpreted the constitutional right to life (Art. 24[1]) and personal integrity (Art. 25), in harmony with the principle of human dignity, to require state protection of "intra-uterine life."[23] The 1975 German decision had also read such protection into the Constitution by reasoning that as an "unborn *human being*," the fetus enjoyed the full protection of the rights to life and human dignity.[24] This ruled out different degrees of protection based on different stages of fetal development. The fetus at all stages of development was a human being, and as such, entitled to full protection. Moreover, connecting life and dignity, the German Court elevated human life to a supreme value in the German constitutional order.[25] Thus, although the Court admitted in passing that a woman's right to self-determination was implicated by the criminalization of abortion, the life of the fetus was granted priority as a matter of principle for the entire duration of pregnancy.[26] Proportionality was simply out of the question. Women, whom the decision referred to as *mothers,* had a prima facie constitutional duty to carry their pregnancies to term.[27] This duty could be superseded only in extraordinary circumstances, namely the typical therapeutic, eugenic, ethical, and social indications.[28]

The legislative reform challenged in the first Portuguese cases was an indications-based law and thus could have passed constitutional scrutiny under the German doctrine, fully and faithfully applied. The Portuguese Court, however, departed from its German counterpart in two important respects.

First, the Court specified that state protection was owed to intra-uterine life as an *objective value* worthy of constitutional promotion. Reasoning that only persons could hold fundamental rights, the Court departed from German doctrine by explicitly refusing to recognize the unborn or individual fetus as a rights holder.[29] This allowed the Portuguese Court to also depart from the absoluteness of state protection that followed in reasoning. Rather than declare the superiority of unborn life, the Court stated that the objective value of intra-uterine life may need to be sacrificed when in conflict with the fundamental rights of pregnant women, not only to life and health, but also reputation, dignity and conscientious motherhood.[30]

Second, recognizing the full humanity of prenatal life had two implications for legislative form. Although the German Court acknowledged that the form of protection of unborn life was a matter of legislative discretion, the chosen means had to be shown as effective in deterrence as criminal punishment.[31] Also, the legal order was *always* required to condemn abortion as wrong, even when it decided to tolerate it and exempt women from punishment.[32] As a consequence, before having an abortion, women were expected to go through explicitly dissuasive counseling and to be reminded of their fundamental duty to respect the life of the unborn.[33]

Notwithstanding dissenting voices, a majority of the Portuguese Court refused to recognize any constitutional obligation for punitive protection of intra-uterine life. Nor did it require, as had the German Court, that other protective mechanisms be shown to be as effective as criminalization. From its first constitutional cases, the Portuguese Court respected legislative discretion to adopt alternative means of protection, if criminalization was deemed unnecessary, inadequate or disproportionate.[34] The Court was not willing to depart from the general principle that in a rule-of-law-based system, the criminal law was to remain an *ultima ratio*, a last resource.

Thus while the Portuguese Court cited the 1975 German decision and reproduced the primary features of it, it introduced fundamental differences that would show their critical significance in the constitutional review of periodic reform. Like the Austrian, French, and Italian courts of the 1970s, the Portuguese Constitutional Court would support the legislator in moving toward more liberal abortion legislation.

A Shift in Strategy: The Referenda Decisions

In 1997 and 1998, there were several legislative initiatives to introduce a periodic law that would allow women to freely choose abortion in the early stages of pregnancy. A claimed motivation for reform was the ineffectiveness of criminalization in preventing illegal abortions or in stopping women with the necessary means from traveling abroad for legal abortion. The growing European convergence toward a periodic solution was also in the air. None of the reforms, however, could find success through the ordinary political process.

In view of the legislative stalemate, following a proposal from the center-left Socialist and the center-right Social Democratic parties, a binding referendum was called in 1998 to let the Portuguese people directly pronounce itself on the matter.[35] The draft referendum asked about agreement on: the *decriminalization of abortion when performed during the first ten weeks, at an officially recognized health service and by a doctor or under his direction, and with the pregnant woman's consent.*

As required by the Constitution, the president of the republic submitted the draft referendum to the Constitutional Court to assess its constitutionality. The Court was to decide whether the question presented voters with an outcome that would *necessarily* lead to legislation incompatible with the Constitution. In other words, the Court was asked whether a periodic model in principle was compatible with the Constitution.

In April 1998, the Portuguese Constitutional Court handed down an affirmative decision and the referendum went ahead in June 1998. For a binding result, the referendum required that half of all registered electors participate.[36] The quorum was not achieved: 68.1 percent of the registered electors did not take part. Moreover despite public opinion polls that consistently showed broad societal support for liberalization, a slim majority of those who voted—50.9 percent to be exact—rejected the proposal.

Several factors explained the "no" victory. First, civil society groups, including conservative law professors,[37] and, more significantly, the Catholic Church[38] had waged a strong and evidently successful fight against liberalization. The church proved to be the most engaged actor—bishops and priests seized both the pulpits of rural areas and national mass media to aggressively combat liberalization, including by drawing comparisons between abortion and the Nazi holocaust.[39] As for political parties, whereas conservative parties including the Christian Democrats and the Social Democrats consistently backed the "no" position, left-wing parties, including the Socialist Party and the Communists failed to create a common front for liberalization. The Socialist Party was internally divided on the question, and maintained a lukewarm position in the referendum campaign, allowing for votes of conscience not along party lines. The Socialist Party's leader and prime minister António Guterres (himself a Catholic), took an open position against changing the law. In turn, the Communists failed to get actively involved, with the matter not considered a priority, probably because of the party's moral conservatism.[40]

The referendum was not for nothing though. While the law remained unchanged, the constitutional abortion landscape was transformed. In its 1998 decision, the Constitutional Court explicitly endorsed periodic reform, in principle, as constitutionally valid. The decision relied and continued to build on the Court's creative work within the German paradigm, but in departure from its doctrine.

While the 1998 decision started with protection due to the unborn, it reaffirmed unborn life as an objective constitutional value. Building on its 1984 and 1985 precedents, the Court further insisted on the need to balance the protection owed to this constitutional value against the protection owed to a pregnant woman, in light not only of her constitutional rights to life, health, and dignity, but also her constitutional right to responsible motherhood and to the free devolvement of her personality (Art 26[1]).[41] Expanding its prior doctrine, the Court applied the interpretive principle of harmonization ("princípio da concordância práctica"), which required it "to coordinate and combine conflicting legal values to avoid (entirely) sacrificing one for the sake of the other."[42]

The Court reasoned that in this exercise of harmonizing countervailing values and rights, the legislator could opt for a method of gradual protection that allowed women to request abortion in the first ten weeks and the state to limit abortion subsequently through indications or even generally prohibit abortion in the last stage of pregnancy.[43] Moreover, the Court stressed that the protection of the unborn, and thus the constitutionality of the law, cannot be assessed by isolating and focusing only on the first ten weeks. Rather constitutional protection must be considered in light of the pregnancy as a whole. This law granted greater protection to woman's autonomy in the early stages of the pregnancy, while making the protection of the unborn more dominant in the later stages of pregnancy.[44] The Court insisted that none of this was tantamount to endorsing "the American paradigm." The apparent underwriting of the trimester framework was not an endorsement of *Roe*. Any affirmation of abortion as a constitutional right under the Portuguese Constitution was explicitly rejected.[45]

Instead, the Court situated the Portuguese law squarely within a European context,[46] concluding that, with the exception of Ireland, abortion was not punished when performed within a certain period of time for therapeutic, eugenic, or ethical indications in most European countries. Moreover, in an overwhelming majority of Europe, abortion was allowed during the early stages of pregnancy when carried out at an officially recognized health service center and following an informed decision by the pregnant woman.

In the decision, the Court also reaffirmed the *discretion* of the legislator to favor more effective means than criminalization to deter abortions in early pregnancy.[47] There was simply no constitutional obligation of criminal protection for intra-uterine life, a claim the Court tried to support empirically. Not only was there a lack of social consensus on the criminalization of abortion, there was also the widespread knowledge that in a border-free Europe, women with means could subvert the law by traveling to other parts of Europe, including Spain, with lax enforcement.[48]

Even if periodic legislation were passed, the Court emphasized, there were other more effective, nonpunitive means to protect unborn life, such as those embraced by other European countries. These included sexual education measures to avoid unwanted pregnancies, and employment and social benefits to assist women in childbirth and care. The Court specifically noted that most European countries mandated counseling procedures, which provided a woman with "the necessary information about her social rights and the assistance measures that she could rely on if she decided to continue her pregnancy," as well as a mandatory reflection period between counseling and the procedure,[49] to ensure that she "took her decision freely, informed and non-rushed, thereby ruling out the interruption of pregnancy out of rushed despair."[50]

Granted, none of these requirements was included in the referendum question (which the legislator might have wanted to keep reasonably short) but the Court noted in its judgment that nothing prevented the legislator from introducing them in the reform.[51] In other words, in 1998 the Portuguese Court was already sending hints to the legislator to consider mandatory counseling as an alternative and sufficient protection of unborn life were it to embrace periodic legislation. Nothing however was said about the need for counseling to be explicitly dissuasive, as required by the German Court in its decisions.

The judgment of the Court, while building on past precedent, was hardly unanimous. Strongly opposing the majority position, the dissenting justices divided into two groups. Some justices did not reject the possibility of balancing per se, but did not agree with the specific type of balancing that the Court had accepted, mostly because of what they thought was an insufficient protection of unborn life in the first ten weeks.[52] Others went further and, reproducing the tenor of the 1975 German decision, rejected the possibility of legislative balancing altogether on the basis of what they argued was the absolute protection owed to the right to life, including the life of the unborn.[53]

This debate was resurrected almost a decade later, when once more a public referendum was called on exactly the same terms as the previous one. It asked the Portuguese people to endorse periodic legislation allowing a woman to choose abortion within the first ten weeks of pregnancy. The second referendum was supported by similar claims about the continuing practice of clandestine abortion, the ineffectiveness of criminalization, its underenforcement, and the growing perception that Portugal was simply lagging behind its European neighbors.[54]

This time around the referendum campaign was different. Only the Christian Democratic Party campaigned for a vote against the referendum. And whereas the conservative Social Democrats allowed individual members to vote on conscience, the Socialist Party was actively committed to a campaign in support of approval, with the personal support of Socialist prime minister José Sócrates. Several pro-choice and pro-life movements had been formed and took part in the campaign. Pro-choice supporters included physicians (such as "doctors for choice"), as well as actors, singers, and other prominent public figures.

In 2006, the Constitutional Court again approved the terms of the referendum,[55] later held on February 11, 2007. Only 43.57 percent of registered electors voted rendering the vote nonbinding, but unlike in 1998, of those who did vote, 59.25 percent backed the proposed legislative change. This time around, the government announced that regardless of the turnout, it would legislate according to the views of the majority.[56] And it did. That the legislative reform was preceded by the referendum significantly shaped its form as it provided the Court with the opportunity to shape the law.

The 2006 decision of the Court essentially reproduced the doctrinal lines of its 1998 precedent. The Court once again confirmed that there was no constitutional obligation to protect unborn life through criminal law, and that forms of protection could vary to reflect the different stages of pregnancy.[57]

Against the claim that a periodic law was tantamount to a complete lack of protection for the first ten weeks of pregnancy, the Court reiterated that constitutional protection must be assessed comprehensively, and not by reference to one specific moment of pregnancy.

The 2006 judgment, however, pushed nonpunitive measures beyond simply being a permissible alternative. For the first time, the Court stressed the *importance*, if not yet the *obligation*, of nonpunitive measures to reduce unintended pregnancy, such as sexual education and family planning, and measures to encourage women to opt for motherhood, such as employment-related protections and social support for student-parents.[58] The Court reasoned that these measures should be preferred, given that "during pregnancy, [women] normally establish a strong emotional connection, of proximity and love towards the being in gestation, and not simply a 'relationship of respect' towards an alien good."[59] In other words, if the state creates the social conditions to allow women to become mothers, they will.

Most importantly, in 2006, the Court directly acknowledged that any debate on the constitutionality of abortion could not be limited to the protection of intra-uterine life. Such protection must always be balanced against the woman's freedom to choose her life project. Intra-uterine life had no constitutional or ontological priority. Using this analytical framework, the Court then affirmed that the legislator's decision to allocate primary protection to women's autonomy during the first phase of pregnancy constituted a valid constitutional balance.[60] In doing so, the Court again referenced mandatory counseling and waiting periods to accompany a periodic law, in what may clearly be interpreted as an attempt to guide the legislative reform.[61] This judgment, however, like the last was hardly unanimous, with six dissenting opinions replicating the two strands of disagreement expressed in 1998. Some of the justices rejected the notion that proper balancing had taken place.[62] Others considered balancing altogether prohibited.[63] It is also important to note that while the majority of the Court affirmed a periodic law as constitutionally permissible, it said nothing of any constitutional requirement. That is, whether women's constitutional right of autonomy required the law to provide some period for freedom of choice was simply not the question at hand.

A Shift in Doctrine: The 2010 Decision

In April 2007, legislation was finally passed amending Portugal's Criminal Code. Women could now access abortions on request during the first ten weeks of pregnancy after mandatory counseling and a reflection period. The purpose of the counseling was to provide a woman with information to support her "free, conscious and responsible" decision making.[64] Explicit dissuasion was not intended. Rather the new regulation mandated that at the counseling session the pregnant woman be informed about the circumstances under which abortion could be performed and its possible health effects, about the assistance provided by the state both for the termination of pregnancy and for motherhood, and, finally, of the option for women to avail themselves of both state-funded psychological support and assistance by a specialized social worker during the mandatory reflection period of three days.[65]

The new law on abortion also included a conscientious objection clause allowing doctors and other health professionals to refuse to participate in any abortion-related act, but conscientious objectors could not take part in the counseling session.[66] The only consent required for termination was the written consent of a competent pregnant woman, at least sixteen years of age. The publicly funded health care system was to cover the full costs of the abortion, similar to any other pregnancy-related medical procedure. In the end then, the chosen legislative model represented a compromise between the options defended during the referendum campaign by different political parties, a compromise arguably inspired by the Constitutional Court's implicit endorsement of mandatory (but not explicitly dissuasive) counseling as an alternative to criminalization.

In 2007, thirty-three conservative members of Parliament asked the Constitutional Court to strike down the new abortion law on two main grounds. First, they argued that the law violated the constitutional precept that "human life shall be inviolable"[67] since it left human life unprotected in the first ten weeks of pregnancy when abortion is available on the request of the pregnant woman. Second, the plaintiffs argued that mandatory counseling could not adequately compensate for this lack of protection, since the counseling was not dissuasive in nature. It included no measures to encourage the protection of the unborn, such as the mandatory exposure to ultrasound images, nor did the legislation require a referral to institutions that support pregnancy and motherhood or to the child adoption system.[68]

In February 2010, the Constitutional Court rejected both arguments and upheld the constitutionality of the legislation.[69] This outcome was perhaps predictable given the 1998 and 2006 referenda decisions that had already validated a periodic law in abstract. Rather than simply rely on precedent, however, the Court used the challenge as yet another opportunity to push the margins of the German paradigm even further.

In the judgment, the Court begins at its fixed starting point: the constitutional obligation to protect unborn life. Following precedent, unborn life is protected as an objective value, and as such, a value to be balanced against the constitutional rights of women.[70] One might therefore say that the starting point of the Court is actually one of balance, on which the legislator enjoys a wide margin of discretion. This discretion, however, is not absolute. The legislator can grant neither too much protection to the unborn, since this would unduly limit women's constitutional rights, nor give insufficient protection to the objective value of human life. The Court thus affirmed once again that at no point during pregnancy, including its earliest stages, can the legislator give absolute priority to women's rights, sacrificing entirely the value of life.[71] This would amount to an unconditional recognition of a woman's right to have an abortion, a right that the Court claimed the American, but not the Portuguese legal order, recognized.[72]

Within the two extremes, there is much room for maneuvering since positive duties (i.e., duties to actively promote and protect rights or values) are much more undetermined in nature[73] than negative duties (i.e., duties not to infringe constitutional rights or values).[74] The Court makes two important points about the positive duties of the legislator. First, it is the whole scheme of positive measures that must provide an adequate degree of protection of intra-uterine life.[75] Second, the legislator may take into account the gestational stage of fetal development in deciding how to properly harmonize the duty to protect intra-uterine life and women's fundamental rights. The Portuguese Court here refers to a relationship between the pregnant woman and the unborn as a "duality within unity," a phrase originally used by the German Constitutional Court in 1993.[76] This peculiar relationship, the Portuguese Court elaborates, "does not remain static throughout the pregnancy, but instead 'during the first weeks the woman and the *nascituro* . . . fully appear as unity, whereas with the growth of the embryo the 'duality' becomes more apparent.'"[77] In other words, the Court recognized that the legislator is allowed to take into account the relevance of the passage of time, reflecting the fact that as the pregnancy progresses so does the existential reality of the fetus.

Applying this carefully calibrated balancing framework, the crucial question becomes: has the legislator fulfilled its obligation of minimum protection, even when women are permitted a free, conscious, and responsible choice during the first ten weeks of pregnancy, ensured by a counseling system that is not explicitly dissuasive? The plaintiffs focused heavily on the counseling requirement under the 2007 Act and argued that it was not sufficiently dissuasive and hence protective of unborn life. The counseling procedure, they claimed, was primarily informative. Ensuring that an abortion decision is fully informed hardly protects unborn life. The plaintiffs thus hoped that the Portuguese Court would follow German doctrine, making the counseling requirement explicitly dissuasive.

In a 1993 decision, the German Constitutional Court revisited the abortion question in a challenge to periodic legislation permitting abortion on request early in pregnancy.[78] The German Court accepted in principle the constitutionality of periodic legislation strictly on strategic grounds but subjected this acceptance to two preconditions. First, the legislator had to ensure that the responsibility of motherhood did not fall entirely on women but that it was a shared one since raising children was a service for the benefit of society. This meant that measures to ensure a child-friendly society had to be put in place, including, for example, legislation to prohibit termination of tenancy because of the birth of a child, and ensuring equality between men and women in employment.[79] Second, and critically, before deciding on abortion, women were required to undergo counseling duly reflective of the constitutional value system. This meant that the counseling must not only seek to enhance the autonomy of a woman (ensuring a free and informed decision, or even a responsible and conscientious decision), but to persuade a woman to continue the pregnancy by reminding her of her duty of motherhood.[80]

In its 2010 decision, the Portuguese Court declined to follow German precedent and, in this respect, made an important statement in European abortion constitutionalism. In validating the counseling requirement of the 2007 Act as sufficiently protective of unborn life, the Court first relied on comparative law to show both an increasing prevalence of periodic legislation in Europe, but also the wide variation in mandatory counseling under these laws.[81] In its comparative review, the Court found that explicit dissuasive counseling, as required by the German Court, was the exception rather than the norm. The Court attributed this anomalous standing to the German law having recognized the unborn as a rights holder, which demanded more definitive protection. Without this recognition in Portuguese constitutional law, the Court reasoned, similar protective measures such as dissuasive counseling were simply not justified.[82] In a vociferous dissent, Chief Justice Rui Manuel Moura Ramos challenged this distinction between rights holder and objective value, arguing that each individual instance of unborn life requires protection of its existential reality.[83]

The majority of the Portuguese Court also responded to the claim that because counseling was not explicitly dissuasive, it was merely informative and not protective. The Chief Justice, for example, claimed that nondissuasive counseling failed to intervene directly in the mental decision-making process of the woman and to discourage her from having an abortion. The majority of Court countered that the very existence of any mandatory counseling could only have the "objective effect of [helping the pregnant woman] gain awareness about the value of the life she carries inside her" and hence, of the seriousness of her decision.[84] The objective of counseling was "to explain, in a climate of tranquility and utter respect for the decisional autonomy of the pregnant woman, the existence of assistance measures which may lead, from her own initiative, to consider an alternative solution to that of the interruption of the pregnancy."[85] In other words, if alternatives to abortion were provided and women were made aware of them, one could expect that some women would choose to take advantage of them.

The new law, then, could not be interpreted as the state giving up on its duty to protect unborn life. For the Court, a sort of "soft law" approach—more promotional than repressive in nature—was justified as more conducive to altering a woman's motives and making her reconsider her decision in the few cases in which a woman has not made up her mind, that is, in the only cases where the unborn have a chance to be spared.[86] The legislator, the Court reasoned, could have endorsed verbal formulae more expressive of the importance of the value of life, but while this might produce symbolic meaning, it would not necessarily offer any greater degree of protection to the unborn. There is no empirical evidence that the German dissuasive counseling requirement is particularly effective. On the contrary, the Court continued, it is reasonable for the legislator to assume that, at an early stage, protection of the unborn is most effectively realized *through* the protection of the woman (i.e., relying on her sense of responsibility and trusting her judgment), making sure only that the decision is both informed and deliberate.[87]

More fundamentally, leaving aside strategic considerations of effectiveness and focusing on the constitutionally protected dignity of women, the Court maintained that an understanding of women as "responsible and sensitive to the reasons that speak against abortion" was not compatible with an infantilizing and paternalistic counseling system. In other words, a model that assumes the responsible choice of the pregnant woman and her inclination to cooperate with the state's duty to protect life cannot easily be reconciled with one that pressures her and interferes in her decisional process by appealing to her emotions and psychological vulnerability.[88] Such an approach is likely to provoke the opposite of the desired result and therefore prove ineffective, but more so such an approach denies women respect as full constitutional subjects, as rights holders. Interestingly, for the first time in its jurisprudence, the Portuguese Court in the 2010 decision held that the value of *dignity* did not express itself only through the intra-uterine life, but also through the woman who is, after all, a rights holder. The dignity of women, the Court reasoned, must also shape the counseling requirement.

The Court thus rejected a vision of pregnant women contemplating abortion as acting out of hedonistic and selfish reasons and backed its claim with sociological data.[89] The decision to have an abortion is taken, despite the anxiety it generates, out of a genuine conviction that this is the right course of action, after pondering responsibly the value of unborn life as well as the existence of other types of harms to be avoided.[90] These included, the Court was ready to acknowledge, the positive obligation of taking care of a person for many years at the expense of burdening her own entire existence. It is motherhood, and not just pregnancy, the Court seemed to recognize, that is normally at stake.

In recognizing that it is motherhood that is ultimately at stake in the abortion debates, the Court asserted that rather than regulating the behavior of women through abortion criminalization, the protection of unborn life fundamentally "falls on the state [which has] to fight against 'risk factors' . . . through education and to adopt social policies favoring responsible conception as well as willingness to continue pregnancy."[91] Providing sexual education and family planning services, as well as ensuring decent living and working conditions, through social policies in favor of motherhood and family life, are all necessary to protect unborn life. It is ultimately these measures through which the Portuguese state shows that it is not indifferent to abortion.[92]

In the end, the language of protection proved discursively valuable on all sides. The plaintiffs agreed that women need protection, not only for the burdens of motherhood, but against the harms of abortion itself. Much like with the debates over tobacco legislation, the plaintiffs argued that women's freedom should be limited for the sake of their own protection. Although the plaintiffs cited no empirical evidence to support their claim, the Court did accept that "harmful consequences, including those of a non-transitory nature could ensue especially for women's psychological well-being, given frequent feelings of loss and guilt following abortions."[93] But the Court contended that the legislator had been sensitive to this when mandating the need to inform women, through counseling, of the possible health-related consequences of abortion, and by the requirement that abortion be performed by a doctor in a recognized health establishment.[94] Beyond that, it was a mistake to think that the prohibitions of abortion would protect women. Rather the likely consequences would be to drive women to unsafe abortions, much more threatening to women's health.[95] Indeed, if the concern was truly with women's health, the focus, according to the Court, should be on social policies rendering the option of responsible motherhood more available since, as the Court noticed, the "best protection of pre-natal life is the protection of existing life."[96]

The Evolving Vision of Women in Constitutional Abortion Law

The 1975 German precedent looms large in European abortion constitutionalism. As a result, constitutional abortion architecture has often been constructed around the protection of the unborn. In some countries, this has impeded the liberalization of abortion, particularly, the adoption of periodic legislation. Although the 1993 German decision lent constitutional support to abortion on request within early pregnancy, it mandated, if not endorsed, explicit dissuasive counseling to meet minimum constitutional standards.

The turn of the present century brought a doctrinal shift. Even those constitutional systems inspired by the German paradigm have started to abandon punitive measures and are endorsing preventive and promotional measures at the early stages of pregnancy. These changes are not merely strategic concessions (i.e., a most effective alternative), but a principled turn that challenges the core of the German doctrine.

The 2010 Portuguese decision represents the most sophisticated expression of a doctrine that provides principled support for periodic abortion legislation affirming constitutional protection for both women's reproductive interests and the unborn. While this doctrine still starts with the constitutional obligation to protect unborn life, and, in this sense, remains within the

German paradigm, the unborn is not considered a rights holder. Human life is rather characterized as an evolving process with qualitatively relevant milestones, which allows different degrees of protection throughout the process. Crucially, women's constitutional rights and interests are recognized to matter, including free development of their personalities and self-determination in reproduction. Accordingly, the state obligation to protect unborn life cannot automatically, and as a matter of principle, lead to the normalization of women's duty of motherhood. The state is required to find a way to harmonize both the interests of women and the protection owed to unborn human life.

Underlying this jurisprudential evolution is a shifting vision of the pregnant woman. The relationship between the woman and the fetus inside her is no longer seen as antagonistic; so the need to protect the fetus from the selfish or whimsical motives of the woman, by forcing her to accept her destiny as a mother, is replaced by a vision of the *pregnant woman* as a single entity (a duality within unity) and a responsible decision maker. This woman is constructed not as somebody inclined to take the decision whether to proceed with or discontinue her pregnancy lightly, or out of selfish or hedonistic reasons. Rather, she is said to be influenced by the existence of means and support (or lack thereof), or the conviction that she must avoid harm to others and to herself.

Periodic abortion legislation is thus supported on both effectiveness and principled grounds, in the conviction that punitive measures are not adequate means to fight against abortion and that, during stages of pregnancy, the unborn can be best protected through the pregnant woman. This requires both trust in her judgment and making sure that her decision is free and informed. This vision of women recognizes that it is the life-long task of motherhood that is at stake in the abortion decision, not just the biological process of pregnancy and delivery.

This principled basis of the Court's constitutional validation, that is, due regard for the autonomy and dignity of pregnant women, is reflected in the nature and characteristics of the counseling procedure accompanying the law. Plainly distancing itself from German precedent, the 2010 Portuguese Court recognized that explicitly dissuasive counseling to pressure women into motherhood was not a necessary, or even permissible constitutional requirement. An understanding of women as responsible and sensitive to the reasons that speak against abortion could not be reconciled with an infantilizing and paternalistic counseling system. Much the same could be said about women-protective rationales, which, in the name of women's health, seek to protect women from themselves instead of facilitating access to the information and means to make free and informed reproductive decisions.

Reconciling the respect due to human unborn life and women's reproductive autonomy in this way (i.e., respecting women as responsible decision makers, even when what they decide to do is discontinue their pregnancies) requires accepting that the protection of unborn human life may not be as much about maximizing the actual number of fetuses that make it into full human beings, as about placing human reproduction at the center stage. Doing so requires both that the reproductive process not be trivialized, and that the burdens of human reproduction be equitably and socially shared. The state must adopt education policies that seek deliberate and responsible conception and ensure a reproduction-friendly society. It cannot expect women to act as mere reproductive vessels but must create the conditions to ensure that their disposition to pregnancy and mothering is truly free. Only under this logic can we understand how recognizing women's reproductive freedom and ensuring a reproduction-friendly society can be seen as part of a legal system that respects the dignitary value of unborn life.

Conclusion

In the end, a combination of both constitutional provisions that explicitly recognize women's reproductive rights and the state obligation to facilitate a reproduction-friendly and equitable society for the sake of all would likely provide much stronger constitutional foundations for the protection of women and human life than do silent constitutional texts, subject to the whims of changing interpretations by overwhelmingly male benches and parliaments. The great weakness of the Portuguese doctrine is that it still frames abortion as a matter of legislative discretion. The legislator *may* adopt a periodic law and do so without explicit dissuasive, invasive, and patronizing counseling. But without a more explicit recognition of both women's constitutional standing and the state's positive obligations to create a reproduction-friendly society, backlash can be hard to prevent.

One may fool oneself into believing that backlash is unlikely, but recent events in Spain prove the opposite. In 2010, under the socialist Zapatero government, legislation was passed in Spain that departed from an indications model, with lax enforcement. Women were entitled to decide freely on abortion within the first fourteen weeks of pregnancy, after mandatory but not explicitly dissuasive counselling.[97] As stated in its preamble, the law was intended to provide protection for women's sexual and reproductive rights as aspects of gender equality and as part of a broader public policy on sexual and reproductive health. This legislation, however, is now being challenged at the Spanish Constitutional Court. Even if the 2010 law is upheld, the newly elected right-wing Rajoy government has stated its intention to at least revert to the indications model in force before the legislative reform.

Given the very lively and contentious nature of abortion constitutionalism in many Latin American countries, many of which have powerful Catholic movements and have inherited through Spain the seeds of the German doctrine, much hinges on whether the constitutional path opened by the Portuguese Court is consolidated in Spain and noticed overseas. The 2010 Portuguese decision offers a framework to support abortion on request in a balance between women's dignity and reproductive autonomy, and the dignity and respect due to unborn human life, as long as the state lives up to its task of ensuring that sufficient preventive and enabling policies are adopted to properly convey the constitutional imperative of not trivializing human reproduction.

Chapter 3

Women's Rights in the Abortion Decision of the Slovak Constitutional Court

Adriana Lamačková

In 2007, the Constitutional Court of the Slovak Republic held that abortion on a woman's request is consistent with the constitutional obligation to protect unborn human life.[1] The question of compatibility between a liberal abortion law and the right to life is not a new question in European constitutional law. After the end of state socialism, constitutional courts across Central Europe, including Germany, Hungary, and Poland, asked and answered this question.[2] The Slovak Court, however, is the only Court in the region to validate abortion on request by reference to state obligations *both* to protect unborn human life and to respect the right of women to reproductive self-determination. Abortion on request was held not merely consistent with the rights of women, but required by them. These rights imposed obligations and related limitations on the state in its regulation of abortion, constitutionally requiring rather than merely permitting abortion on request.

The decision of the Slovak Constitutional Court is noteworthy in the region for this reason. It does not consider the protection of unborn human life to be the sole nor even the primary value of constitutional abortion law. A woman's right to reproductive self-determination enjoys full and equal standing in the constitutional order. This chapter seeks to show how the decision of the Slovak Court, by giving full recognition and effect to the rights of women, reflects a fundamental shift in European constitutional abortion law. This shift is captured in the Court's use of *balancing* as an analytical framework, according to which multiple constitutional rights and values are vindicated, none completely overruling any other.

The chapter proceeds in three sections. In the first section, I outline the development of abortion regulation in Slovakia, with attention to an evolving discourse around women's reproductive decision making. Next I focus on the 2007 Slovak Court decision upholding abortion on request. This section highlights the uniqueness of the Court's reasoning, specifically its robust analysis of women's rights in reproductive self-determination, against constitutional abortion decisions of other courts in Central European countries. The final section briefly describes the legislative developments after the decision and the related change in anti-abortion discourse and argument in Slovakia.

The Woman in Abortion Decision Making and Regulation: 1918–2001

The significance of the 2007 decision can best be appreciated against the history of abortion regulation in Slovakia from 1918 until 2001, the year the constitutional challenge was filed. This history cannot be told without attention to larger political and social change in the country, namely the creation of Czechoslovakia in 1918, the period of state socialism from 1948 to 1989, and the dissolution of the federal state of Czechoslovakia in 1992, leading to the successor sovereign states of the Slovak Republic (Slovakia) and the Czech Republic. This section is divided into two parts, marked by the critical transition from state socialism in 1989.

From 1918 to 1989

Until 1950, abortion was criminally prohibited in Czechoslovakia under all circumstances.[3] During this prohibition, hundreds of women were punished for having illegal abortions, and each year thousands of women were reported to have died from unsafe abortions, with countless more women suffering severe health effects.[4] The impact of illegal abortions on the health of women and the well-being of their families, especially those of lower income, led to several unsuccessful legislative initiatives to decriminalize abortion in the interwar period.[5] Support for these proposals was largely based on protecting women's health and well-being, but some members of parliament, formerly active in the women's movement, supported the proposals on the basis of a woman's right to decide the fate of her pregnancy.[6] The proposals ultimately failed, until 1950, when a new Criminal Code introduced life and health exceptions to the prohibition under certain conditions.[7]

Spurred by Soviet developments in abortion regulation and the efforts of several individuals in Czechoslovakia who advocated for liberalization of abortion before and after WWII,[8] further liberalization occurred in 1957 when the first abortion-specific law[9] was adopted in Czechoslovakia. The new law cancelled the regulation of abortion in the Criminal Code and permitted abortion until the twelfth week of pregnancy on health grounds and for "other reasons of special importance," to be later specified in ministerial and governmental decrees.[10] After twelve weeks, a pregnancy could be legally terminated only in the case of a severe genetic disease of one of the parents, or when the life of the pregnant woman was in danger.[11] The law also expressly exempted women from criminal liability for illegal abortions.

Support for the law was again not framed in women's rights. Rather, arguments about "healthier motherhood" and the protection of women's health and "healthy population" dominated the debates.[12] These arguments were reflected in the purpose of the law, which was to "expand care for the healthy development of famil[ies] threatened by damage to the health and lives of women caused by [illegal abortions]."[13]

The liberalization of 1957 did not enable women to decide on abortion of their own accord. Each request for abortion was to be reviewed by a so-called abortion commission, whose purpose was to control and limit the number of abortions by assisting women to overcome their concerns about childbirth and raising their children.[14] This procedure was seen as necessary to protect against women's abuse of the new law, and to protect women from the potential health risks that even legal abortions presented.[15] According to sociologist Radka Dudová, many women requesting abortion criticized these commissions as an invasion of privacy. As one woman explained in a popular magazine, it was appalling "to have to explain and confide such sensitive problems to complete strangers."[16]

In the 1970s, social and political changes in Czechoslovakia led to a restrictive turn in abortion regulation. The restrictions were motivated not by religious or moral concerns, which were nearly absent from abortion discourse at the time. Rather the restrictive reforms stemmed in large measure from the pro-natalist policies of political elites concerned with the country's declining birth rate. As Dudová notes, "legal abortion was not interpreted [anymore] as a way of protecting women's health (from the consequences of illegal abortions), but, on the contrary, as a threat to women's health and . . . to *population development*."[17] A ministerial decree instructed abortion commissions to assess requests carefully, especially in the case of childless married women or married women with only one child seeking abortion on social grounds, and to allow abortions only exceptionally.[18] The decree proved to have little effect in practice, however, with commissions still approving more than 95 percent of all requests.[19] The perceived futility of the abortion commissions no doubt led to their abolition in the next liberalization.

The reform in 1986 not only brought an end to abortion commissions but also entitled women to receive abortion services upon request until the twelfth week of pregnancy, without requiring any additional therapeutic or social reason.[20] This liberalization was attributed primarily to two factors. First, an early vacuum aspiration method called "mini-abortion" or "menstruation regulation" was developed, which experts and legislatures agreed had a lower risk of health complications and was less demanding on health system infrastructure and less costly. Since the "mini-abortion" could be performed only in the early weeks of pregnancy, the delays of the commission authorization process rendered this new method inaccessible.[21] Second, a psychological study conducted in Prague in the 1970s showed the negative impact of unwanted pregnancies on the well-being of children born to women denied abortions by commissions.[22] These two factors dominated the call to abolish the commission system and expand access.

Although the reform was primarily and publicly defended on expert medical and psychological arguments, the explanatory report to the new abortion bill and related parliamentary debate cited women's reproductive rights.[23] The law was understood and claimed to be "establishing a new principle of a woman's will, whether to end her pregnancy by birth or by induced abortion . . . giv[ing] a woman the right to terminate [her] pregnancy."[24] A woman's free decision making in pregnancy and motherhood were highlighted as a principle of law in the debate itself.[25]

This 1986 law, with a few changes adopted recently, remains valid in Slovakia today. Since the fall of state socialism in 1989, however, the law has been the target of repeated criticism and attempted restriction. One such attempt was the constitutional challenge to the law in 2001, ultimately leading to the constitutional decision of 2007, the focus of this chapter.

From 1989 to 2001

In 1989, the political and social landscape in Central and Eastern Europe changed dramatically with the fall of state socialism. Since then, in Czechoslovakia and later in Slovakia, as well as in other countries in the region,[26] reproductive politics became an important tactical space for social groups and political parties to advance a conservative agenda in the newly democratic state. In Slovakia, where the majority of the population identifies as Catholic, the Catholic Church hierarchy has also come to play an increasingly influential role in state politics. Opposition to the liberal abortion law was no longer dominated by health protectionist or pro-natalist arguments. Rather, abortion was publicly condemned as "killing an unborn child," leading to calls for state protection of "unborn human life" in the form of legal restrictions on abortion.

Protecting the "right to life" from the moment of conception proved to be one of the most contested subjects in 1991, when the Federal Assembly of the Czech and Slovak Federal Republic debated the draft of a new constitutional document—the Charter of Fundamental Rights and Freedoms. Arguing that Communist and materialist ideologies had corrupted social morals and undermined respect for life, a few parliamentarians proposed the reformulation of the right-to-life provision to include protection of human life from conception.[27] This reformulation was intended to render unconstitutional the 1986 abortion law. One parliamentarian explicitly stated that a woman could not have a right to terminate her pregnancy, she being "only a vessel" for new life.[28] Opponents of the proposal emphasized the absence of any national consensus on when human life begins and referred to Czechoslovakia's international human rights obligations to respect women's right to decide on the number and spacing of children, and to the extreme effects of the anti-abortion pro-natalist policy in Romania under the Ceaușescu regime, which led to illegal abortions and high maternal mortality rates.[29] Czechoslovakia, they argued, should resist following the same course.

After a protracted debate, the Federal Assembly adopted a compromise provision, which read: "Everyone has the right to life. Human life is worthy of protection even prior to birth."[30] After Czechoslovakia split into two republics and the Slovak Republic was formed in 1993, the text of the Charter including this provision became a part of the Constitution of the Slovak Republic.[31] Since then, parliamentarians opposed to abortion on request—with support from the Catholic Church hierarchy and anti-abortion organizations—have sought to restrict the law on abortion using this constitutional provision.

In 2001, a group of conservative parliamentarians proposed an amendment to the provision itself, as part of a broader constitutional reform. A proposal was introduced and debated in the Slovak Parliament to replace the
second clause of the provision, "Human life is worthy of protection even prior
to birth," with the following more explicit prescription: "Intentional termination of unborn human life is disallowed. The right of a mother to a treatment
aimed at saving her life is guaranteed."[32] The intention was to eliminate any
difference in the protection of human life prior to and after birth, as was in
the existing Constitution, but more importantly, to directly incorporate a
prohibition on abortion (except to save the life of the pregnant woman) into
the Constitution. The liberal abortion law was said to have been "brutally
imposed" by the old Communist regime and, if unrepealed, threatened "the
existence and survival of the state and the nation."[33] Other parliamentarians,
backed by women's and human rights groups, criticized the proposed constitutional amendment and argued in favour of the 1986 abortion law. Their
resistance was firmly rooted in a women's rights discourse. They argued that
the proposed amendment infringed on the fundamental right of a woman to
make decisions about her pregnancy. Referencing the situation in Poland
after restrictive reforms were introduced in 1993,[34] they also pointed to negative public health consequences of "underground" abortions and to "abortion
tourism."[35]

The proposed constitutional amendment ultimately failed, leading to a
change in strategy. Parliamentarians turned to the Constitutional Court in an
effort to repeal the law. At the time of this challenge, the law permitted abortion on request without restriction as to reason during the first twelve weeks
of pregnancy. Thereafter, abortion could be performed on genetic grounds up
to twenty-four weeks, or without a time limit in the case of severe fetal impairment or when a woman's life was in danger.[36] The next section addresses
this constitutional challenge, and the decision of the Slovak Constitutional
Court in upholding abortion on request. Highlighted is the Court's explicit
recognition and robust analysis of women's rights, which renders the decision
unique within post-1989 constitutional abortion jurisprudence in the Central European region.

The Slovak Abortion Decision

In 2001, thirty-one members of the Slovak Parliament belonging primarily to conservative and nationalist political parties challenged the 1986 abortion law before the Constitutional Court under the so-called abstract judicial review.[37] Under this procedure available to state bodies, the Constitutional Court may be asked to review a law or parts thereof for compliance with the Constitution and international treaties ratified by Slovakia.[38] The petitioners claimed that the law permitting abortion on request within the first twelve weeks of pregnancy violated Article 15(1) of the Slovak Constitution, which reads: "Everyone has the right to life. Human life is worthy of protection even prior to birth."[39]

By requiring no justification other than the request of the woman, the petitioners argued, the abortion law gave no recognition and thus no protection whatsoever to unborn human life within the first twelve weeks of pregnancy. In support of this claim, the petitioners cited Article 15(4) of the Constitution, under which "it is not a violation of rights . . . , if someone is deprived of life as a result of an action that is not deemed criminal under the law." This provision was interpreted to constitutionally allow the legislator to decriminalize abortion only in exceptional situations, justified by reference to another and competing constitutional right. This was claimed not to be the case with abortion on request, which the petitioners supported by reference to German and Polish case law, in which regulation more restrictive than the Slovak law was declared unconstitutional for failing to afford due protection to unborn life. In 2007, almost seven years after the petition was filed, the Slovak Court issued its decision, holding that abortion on request, as regulated in the abortion law, was constitutional.[40] After noting the diversity of constitutional decisions and regulatory laws on abortion from countries in Europe and beyond, the Court reached an outcome that was also consistent with prevailing public opinion in Slovakia, which favored the challenged abortion law and even its further liberalization.[41]

This chapter, however, focuses not so much on the outcome of the decision, but on the Court's departure from the constitutional jurisprudence on abortion in the Central Europe region, particularly the German and Polish decisions placed before it. To fully appreciate the degree of this departure, it is perhaps best to begin with the balancing framework that the Slovak Court adopted for the constitutional adjudication of abortion according to which multiple constitutional rights and values are validated, none completely overruling any other.

A Balancing Framework

To understand the significance of adopting a balancing framework in European constitutional abortion law, it is important to note the outright rejection or weakening of this framework by other courts in the Central Europe region, most notably the Federal Constitutional Court of Germany in its highly influential 1993 decision invalidating an on-request regime. In refusing to balance competing legal values, the German Court explained that "what is being weighed up on the side of the unborn life is not just a matter of a greater or fewer number of rights nor the acceptance of disadvantages or restrictions, but life itself. A balance which guarantees both the protection of the unborn's life and, at the same time, grants the pregnant woman a right to terminate is not possible because the termination of a pregnancy is always the killing of an unborn life."[42] Rather than balancing, the Court established a fetal protective framework that, as a matter of principle, required pregnancy termination to be fundamentally prohibited by law, and that subjected women to a fundamental duty to carry a "child" to term. This duty could never be suspended but in certain exceptional circumstances, when pregnancy poses extraordinary burdens for the woman, it is constitutionally permissible for this duty not to be applied.[43] While other courts in the region proved more amenable to a balancing framework to structure their analysis, they effectively undermined the framework in application.

The Constitutional Court of Hungary, for example, applied balancing as an analytical framework for abortion adjudication but recognized quite limited rights for women within this framework, thereby fixing the balance to be struck. In its 1998 decision, the Court reviewed a law that permitted abortion in a "situation of serious crisis" without requiring the indication to be verified by a third party.[44] The Court explained that "it consider[ed] a proportional mutual restriction of the mother's constitutional rights and the State's constitutional duty to protect the life of the foetus the criterion of judging constitutionality."[45] While acknowledging a women's right to self-determination, it limited the application of the right to "exceptional cases . . . [of the right] being seriously endangered."[46] Women are entitled to exercise their right to self-determination, in other words, only in exceptional circumstances. This of course precludes abortion on request as a constitutional arrangement. The right to access abortion must be circumscribed by the exceptional circumstances of an indications-based law.[47]

In the decision of 1997, the Polish Constitutional Tribunal also chose balancing as an analytical framework when assessing whether a law permitting abortion on social grounds—that is, the difficult living conditions or difficult personal situation of a pregnant woman—with a mandatory waiting period and counseling, was constitutional.[48] The balancing performed by the Tribunal, however, did not give due regard to women's rights invoked by the social indications and instead focused solely on the protection of the fetus.[49] The Tribunal found that a balance was impossible to achieve because the constitutional values related to the social situations cannot take precedence over the constitutional value of human life, even at the prenatal stage.[50] Like the Hungarian Court, the Tribunal held that the protection of human life may be limited or even waived only in certain exceptional circumstances, but deemed that the above listed social situations did not fall within this category.

The Slovak Court—unlike its counterparts—did not shy away from framework in application. It explicitly identified its task as assessing whether the legislator had struck an appropriate balance between the duty to protect the value of unborn human life and the duty to protect women's rights to privacy, dignity and the principle of freedom in permitting abortion on request.

Grounding its decision on the constitutional principle under which Slovakia is described as "a sovereign, democratic state governed by the rule of law [and] not bound to any ideology or religion," the Court explained that its role in this case was to determine "the constitutional boundaries that the Constitution sets to the legislator in relation to the legal regulation of artificial interruption of pregnancy [abortion]."[51] Determining the *constitutional boundaries* suggests that the Court was not only looking to the minimum limits that the Constitution establishes with regard to protection of the value of unborn human life, but also to the maximum limits on this protection set by the rights of women. In other words, the Court recognized that there are limits from both sides that must be balanced in the regulation of abortion. Balance suggests acceptable rather than absolute regulation.

The crucial question is this: How did the Slovak Court arrive at *balancing* as an appropriate constitutional framework for the adjudication of abortion regulation? The Court's interpretation of several key constitutional provisions, including the rights to life and to privacy, proved crucial to this outcome.

The Objective Value of Unborn Human Life

The legal status of unborn human life has been an important determinant in abortion adjudication in Central Europe, and, in particular, in the application of the balancing framework. The German Court refused to adopt balancing in the context of abortion on request, primarily because unborn life was recognized as an *independent human life* with its own elementary and inalienable right to life stemming from the dignity of the person.[52] The Hungarian Court, meanwhile, which applied a balancing framework, refused to find that the fetus was a rights holder and instead recognized the state's "objective duty" to protect unborn human life. As a logical consequence, "the focus of the constitutional review of the provisions on abortion . . . has shifted from the field of the 'competing' rights to life and to human dignity to the examination of the relationship and the balance between the pregnant woman's right to self-determination and the State's (not absolute) objective duty . . . to protect life."[53]

Like these courts, the Slovak Court began with an interpretation of the state's constitutional duty to protect unborn human life, recognizing that it must determine the legal status of a fetus in order to identify the constitutional framework in which to adjudicate the claim. Like the Hungarian Court, the Slovak Court found that "unborn human life" is a constitutional "value" that warrants protection from the state but noted that this protection is of a lower intensity than the protection awarded to a "right." The Court adopted several modes of reasoning to reach this conclusion.

First, the Court reasoned textually. Article 15(1) of the Constitution states that: "Everyone has the right to life. Human life is worthy of protection even prior to birth." The petitioners argued that the second clause should be read conjunctively with the first, thus guaranteeing a right to life to unborn life. The Court disagreed and read the clauses disjunctively. It emphasized that the first clause protects a subjective right to life for every born person. The second clause protects human life prior to birth as an objective value. The Court buttressed its textual analysis by noting that rights guaranteed in the Constitution are accorded at birth and not prenatally.[54]

Second, the Court reasoned by comparison, noting that a "majority of European and North American states do not consider *nasciturus* [the unborn] a subject of law that disposes of an absolute subjective right to life."[55] The Court also referenced international law, specifically the International Covenant on Civil and Political Rights, which recognizes the right to life only at birth. Referring to the jurisprudence under the European Convention on Human Rights, the Court noted that the Convention also does not recognize the unborn (*nasciturus*) as a person entitled to the "right to life" under Article 2(1)—and most significantly—"that granting a fetus the same rights as persons would place unreasonable limitations on the Article 2 rights of women, as persons already born."[56]

This led the Court into its third mode of analysis, reasoning by consequence, to consider the implication for women's access to abortion if the Court was to recognize a fetal right to life. If the second clause of Article 15(1) were interpreted to provide for an absolute right to life prior to birth, abortion for any reason other than to protect the life of the pregnant woman would effectively be prohibited, for under a strict measure of proportionality the right to life of the unborn would always prevail over any other right except the woman's right to life. Such an approach would therefore require a prohibition of abortion on all grounds other than risk to life—a position, as the Court noted, that not even the petitioners advanced.[57]

In the Court's view, granting the fetus an absolute right to life, and at the same time allowing for abortions other than on the ground of protection of the woman's life, would also have resulted in "a dangerous emptying of the very concept of the fundamental right to life." This, the Court explained, was an untenable position because the constitutional right to life "has the same weight regardless of its holder (subject)"; thus "creating various categories of right to life out of which not all would have the same weight, or even creating new subjects of law by means of jurisprudence (next to the classical dichotomy of natural persons v. legal persons) would be in conflict with the constitutional postulate on equality of people in rights." Awarding the unborn a *sui generis* right, then, would have dramatic consequences for equality in rights, affecting "the general structure of fundamental rights according to the Constitution."[58]

For these reasons, the Court decided to interpret the provision on unborn human life as expressing an objective value and not a right. The Slovak Constitution, it explained, is a values-oriented document that protects not only rights and freedoms but also values and principles, objective in the sense that they express a general "good" accepted by a society, and which the state cannot create but can only recognize, and respect.

The objective values, when explicitly guaranteed in the Constitution, become constitutional values and subject to constitutional protection.[59] They include freedom, equality, human dignity, marriage, parenthood and family, health, environment, and morality, as well as the value of unborn human life. These values admit to different forms and intensity of protection. Values of freedom, equality, and human dignity, for example, are considered to be universal constitutional principles imposing an obligation of state protection of the highest degree. The objective value of unborn human life also imposes an obligation of state protection, but the Court reasoned "the [Constitutional] text clearly shows, compared with other . . . objective values, both a lower degree of concreteness of this obligation ('is worthy of protection') and a different degree of intensity of its constitutional protection."[60] In other words, constitutional values, unlike constitutional rights, allow for greater discretion in the protection afforded to them, thus moving away from thinking in terms of absolute regulation toward acceptable legal regulation.[61]

To summarize, the Slovak Court's interpretation of unborn human life as a constitutional value that mandates a lower degree of intensity of state protection enabled the Court to adopt a balancing framework as a criterion of judging the constitutionality of abortion on request.

Women's Self-Determination as a Constitutional Right

By interpreting unborn human life as an objective value with protection that is less absolute than that afforded an individual right, the Slovak Court softened the minimum standards for abortion regulation. More critically, the Court recognized what may be termed maximum standards for abortion regulation, or constitutional limitations on state regulation that are derived from the fundamental rights of women to privacy informed by the right to dignity, and the constitutional principle of freedom. The Slovak Court, it may be said, turned from an analysis of action by the state required to protect unborn human life, to an analysis of the limitations on the state action required to protect the rights of women.

This was untrue of other Central European courts mentioned above. In its decision of 1997, the Polish Constitutional Tribunal, for example, declared a law permitting abortion on social grounds unconstitutional in part because according to the Tribunal a right to decide whether to have a child was not an individual right of a woman, but a "joint right of a child's mother and father." Moreover, this right, if understood as a right to decide not to have a child, was reduced only to the entitlement to "refus[e] to conceive a child."[62] The Hungarian Court specifically required that a social or serious crisis indication be maintained in the law, so that "the State, at least in principle and on constitutional grounds, does not give a free way to abortion, an act acknowledged by the law only in exceptional cases."[63] The Slovak Court, in contrast, incorporated a strong analysis of women's right to privacy informed by the right to dignity and the principle of freedom, to find that abortion on request is constitutionally justified.

The recourse to privacy in constitutional abortion law might seem unspectacular from a North American perspective, the most famous abortion-as-privacy case being the U.S. Supreme Court decision *Roe v. Wade*. What is remarkable, however, is that a court working within the fetal-protective framework of the European constitutional jurisprudence should reference the U.S. case law on abortion, as did the Slovak Court.[64]

The Court identified two relevant constitutional provisions regulating privacy. The first, Article 16(1), reads: "The inviolability of a person and her privacy shall be guaranteed. It may be restricted only in cases specifically provided by a law." In reaffirming its previous case law, the Court elaborated this provision as protecting a person's physical integrity and his or her right "within certain spheres of social relations to live according to his or her own conception—free from undue restrictions, commands or prohibitions laid by bodies of public authority."[65]

The second provision regulating privacy, Article 19(2), states that "everyone has the right to protection against unjustified interference in his or her private and family life." This provision, according to the Court, is based on "the right of an individual to decide according to his or her own deliberation on whether and to what extent facts from his or her private life should be made available to others."[66]

Constitutional protection for privacy is therefore multilayered, covering various aspects of individual integrity and social interaction. The Court explained that the respect for private life, which also involves the right to form and develop personal relationships, is central to the liberal notion of personal autonomy and self-determination, emphasizing the close connection between the rights to privacy and the principle of freedom. According to the Court, the constitutional principle of freedom is "one of the fundamental values of a democratic state governed by the rule of law" and mandates the state "to respect and protect the sphere of personal autonomy of an individual."[67] Under this principle "everyone may do what is not forbidden by a law and no one may be forced to do what the law does not enjoin."[68] Interpreting these rights and principles together, the Court explained that they: "guarantee a certain "internal sphere," in which the individual can live according to his or her own conception. . . . The right to privacy and to protection of private life in connection with the principle of freedom in its most basic specification, relying also upon the fundamental right to human dignity, . . . guarantees a possibility of autonomous self-determination to the individual."[69]

In this explanation, the Court identified the central pillars of the privacy doctrine as applied to women's reproductive decision making. This realm of privacy includes "the woman's decision making about her own mental and physical integrity and its layers [including] whether she will conceive a child and [about] the course of her pregnancy." The woman's decisional autonomy lies at the center of the right to self-determination, and the Court made plain that "by becoming pregnant . . . a woman does not waive [this] right."[70] Even though the Court did not provide in-depth analysis of dignity, it adopted the right-to-dignity language to support its reading of women's privacy rights. The Court also referenced the Convention on the Elimination of All Forms of Discrimination against Women (CEDAW) in elaborating the women's right to reproductive self-determination, emphasizing the principle of equality and the right to freely decide on the number and spacing of children, as guaranteed by the CEDAW.[71] The reference to CEDAW and other United Nations international human rights treaties in support of women's rights is a distinctive aspect of the Slovak decision, which none of the decisions of other courts in Central Europe mentioned above can claim.

To summarize, the Slovak Court's reasoning on women's right to privacy, interpreted in light of the constitutional principle of freedom and the right to dignity and supported by the principle of equality, delivers a strong foundation for the protection of women's reproductive autonomy, and an understanding of the abortion decision as an act of decisional autonomy. Without doubt, this interpretive work played a decisive role in assessing the abortion law within a balancing framework. Proceeding from the observation that pregnancy is a condition for a woman that may "significantly limit [her] possibilities to freely fulfill her personality," the Court concluded that "any restriction upon a woman's decision making whether she means to bear such obstacles in her autonomous self-realization, and hence whether she means to remain pregnant until its natural completion, constitutes an interference with the woman's constitutional right to privacy."[72]

Yet the right to privacy is not absolute but can be protected only against *unjustified* interference.[73] Balance or proportionality is an anticipated feature of the scheme. As the Court explained, "examination of proportionality of the interference with the right to privacy . . . is a question of balancing this fundamental right with other fundamental rights and freedoms as well as with the constitutional principles and the constitutional values that find themselves in mutual tension with it."[74] This balancing is governed by the principle of practical concordance (*praktische Konkordanz*), developed in German constitutional theory and jurisprudence. In essence, this principle "requires a holistic view of the constitution"[75] and demands achieving "harmonization of the relevant constitutional values and maintenance of their creative tension."[76] As the Court noted, all rights and freedoms anchored in the Constitution are prima facie of the same value. Their relative weight or priority "does not depend upon some doctrinal predetermination, but it is a function of the specific context and circumstances under which the concerned rights, principles and values find themselves in mutual tension."[77] Applying this to the present case, the Court affirmed that the value of unborn human life as expressed in the Constitution cannot stand *a priori* higher than other constitutional rights, principles, and values relevant to the abortion issue, in particular the right to privacy. A holistic view must be taken, where: "on the one hand the legislator must not ignore . . . the obligation to provide protection to unborn human life. On the other hand, the legislator must respect the fact that everyone, including a pregnant woman, has the right to decide on her or his private life and to protect the implementation of her or his own conception of [the private life] against unlawful interference."[78]

In seeking a balance through justified limitation, "respect must be given to the essence and meaning of [fundamental] rights and freedoms."[79] This is a guiding principle through which the Court worked. As applied to the case at hand, the Court set the following standard: that "the constitutional value of unborn human life can . . . be protected only to such extent, that this protection did not cause an interference with the essence of a woman's freedom and her right to privacy."[80] The focus on encroachment upon the *essence* of a woman's freedom and her right to privacy is the core of the Slovak decision, and the ultimate basis on which the Court finds the legal regulation of abortion on request constitutional. While the Court gives little guidance on what exactly it means by the essence of personal freedom and the right to privacy, a general idea can be derived from the following statement: "if a woman, during a certain phase of her pregnancy, could not decide of her own accord whether to carry the fetus to term or have her pregnancy interrupted, then it would mean an obligation to carry the fetus to term, an obligation which has no support in the Constitution and at the same time it would infringe upon the essence of her right to privacy as well as her personal freedom."[81]

The Court makes clear that a woman is entitled to some opportunity to decide on whether she wishes to carry a pregnancy to term. The time period and the procedures by which the woman may exercise her right to "abortion on request" remain within the legislature's discretion, but the entitlement remains to "a real decision by the woman on the artificial interruption of her pregnancy."[82] This constitutes the fundamental difference between the Slovak decision and those of other Central European courts: abortion is not merely an exception from the protection of unborn life, it is a woman's constitutional entitlement, at least for a certain period of pregnancy.

A Balance Within: Procedural Requirements and Gestational Limits

Having established *balance* between the protection of unborn human life and the rights of women as the standard for constitutional review, where does the Court find this balance in a law that allows abortion on a woman's request in the first twelve weeks of pregnancy?

First, the Court made an important observation that constitutional protection for unborn human life must be viewed from the perspective of the whole legal order and not limited to the regulation of abortion alone. The Court thus identified measures that the state is taking to fulfill its duty, and divided them into two groups: (1) measures protecting unborn human life "through" the protection awarded to a pregnant woman; and (2) measures protecting unborn human life "against" a pregnant woman.[83]

The measures protecting unborn human life *through* a pregnant woman include, according to the Court, protection of pregnant women in labor relations, and Criminal Code provisions on illegal abortion, and the protection of life and health that also apply to pregnant women. It also mentioned the civil law protection of the *nasciturus* (unborn), while noting nevertheless the application of the born alive rule. These measures, the Court reasoned, provide some protection of unborn human life in the first twelve weeks of pregnancy.

Measures protecting unborn human life *against* the pregnant woman are expressed through the abortion law. Referring to the statement of the European Court of Human Rights that "the 'life' of the foetus is intimately connected with, and it cannot be regarded in isolation from, the life of the pregnant woman,"[84] the Court affirmed that the legislator is constitutionally permitted to regulate a "social relationship" between the pregnant woman and her fetus in a specific way. This specific relationship is expressed through the abortion law, where the legislator tries to find a balance between the constitutional imperative to protect the value of unborn human life and "the fundamental right of a pregnant woman to decide about herself."[85]

Taking this into account, the Court finds this balance in two elements of the law: in procedural requirements, and in the gestational limit of twelve weeks.

The Court found that protection for unborn human life was secured in the abortion law through certain procedural requirements: (1) filing a written request for an abortion, (2) undergoing a medical examination, (3) consulting a physician who must inform the woman of potential health consequences of abortion, and (4) paying an abortion fee if the woman still insists on pregnancy termination after counseling. These requirements, stated mainly in Section 7 of the abortion law, are alleged to protect the interests of unborn human life by ensuring against a "woman's ill-considered and premature decision on artificial interruption of pregnancy."[86]

Of these statutory prerequisites, the Court elaborated, albeit quite poorly, only the counseling requirement. The choice to focus on this requirement was not unusual. Counseling has been the critical feature in the European case law to date that has rendered liberal abortion laws constitutional in the fetal protective framework. For example, even though the German Court invalidated the particular law permitting abortion on request, it accepted that directive mandatory counseling oriented toward the protection of unborn life in the early stages of pregnancy could provide sufficient protection of unborn life,[87] and termination of pregnancy would thus be constitutional. However the counseling requirement in the Slovak law, as read by the Court, differs in important respects from the one articulated by the German Court.

With regard to the statutory obligation to inform a woman "of the potential health consequences of [abortion]," the Court explained that the "instruction is undoubtedly provided with the aim of acting upon the pregnant woman so that she considers backing out of her intent to perform the intervention, by which not only the protection of the woman's health is ensured, but . . . also the protection of the unborn human life."[88] In this explanation, the Court seemed to imply a form of directive counseling, like that of German law, intended to dissuade a woman from her decision.

Rather than informing women of their fundamental duty to carry a pregnancy to term as stressed by the German Court, in the Slovak decision, to the extent that the counseling requirement offered protection for unborn life, it was through the empowerment of physicians. Referring to the ethical disapproval of abortion in the Hippocratic Oath, the Court submitted that the doctor would protect unborn human life through counseling. There thus seemed an expectation that the doctor would counsel in accordance with this ethical directive.

Moreover, the Court identified the objective of counseling as providing the woman with relevant medical information,[89] and of the potential health consequences of abortion. It is unclear how such counseling, if scientifically accurate information on the relative safety of abortion is provided in a non-manipulative manner, would have a necessarily discouraging effect on a woman's decision. The Court did not address whether a woman must or may also be informed of the comparative health risks of continuation of pregnancy.

Of crucial distinction from previous jurisprudence, the Slovak Court interpreted the counseling requirement as nondirective albeit, as mentioned above, implying some dissuasive aspects, which suggests incoherence in the Court's approach to counseling.

The Court also found the law constitutional in limiting abortion on request to the first twelve weeks of pregnancy. In subsequent weeks, abortion was accessible only on strict indications. The petitioners, however, considered the twelve-week limit arbitrary, arguing that a difference in legal protection of unborn life prior to and after twelve weeks was constitutionally unsupportable.[90]

In refusing the claim, the Court referred to jurisprudence of the European Court of Human Rights as well as the U.S. Supreme Court, which recognized a gradual protection of unborn human life throughout pregnancy.[91] This gradual protection was based on the understanding that "the course of pregnancy and the relation between the fetus and the mother can be defined best as a *unity in duality*, where the unity of the mother and the fetus prevails in the first phase of pregnancy, while in the subsequent phases the duality of the mother and the fetus is emphasized more."[92] Borrowed from the dissenting opinion of the 1993 German abortion decision,[93] this concept of "unity in duality" was key to the Slovak Court's balancing framework, because it enables the legislator to allow different forms and intensity of protection throughout pregnancy.

In deciding that the twelve-week limitation was constitutional, the Slovak Court held that the legislator struck an acceptable balance: neither allowing abortion on request for too short or too long a period, nor offering too little protection to the value of unborn human life, or the rights of women. Referring to the prevailing legislative practice on time limits in other European countries, the Court reasoned that the twelve-week period is not arbitrary, but importantly, given a "real possibility of ascertaining the very existence of pregnancy, [it] provides the mother with a sensible chance to consider the option of pregnancy interruption and its possible performance." Shorter gestational limitations may run counter to the purpose of the law, "which is to enable the woman to decide on her motherhood."[94] Even in reference to gestational limitations, the Court maintained its commitment to the full recognition of the rights of women.

After the Decision

The petitioners and their supporters criticized the decision, arguing that the abortion law did not balance the competing values and rights adequately. As a result, a few petitioners introduced an amendment to the abortion law in an attempt to restrict access to abortion by adding additional procedural barriers. The amendment extended the parental consent requirement to include all minors and mandated a seventy-two-hour waiting period for abortion on request and new counseling requirements, requiring a doctor to inform the woman about the alternatives to abortion, about "physical and mental risks associated with the induced abortion," about "the current developmental stage of an unborn child, . . . and on her entitlement to obtain a recording from an ultrasound examination."[95] Even though this proposal was not adopted, just one year later, in 2009, Parliament was persuaded and adopted a similar proposal.[96] Besides introducing a forty-eight-hour mandatory waiting period and the above-mentioned counseling and parental consent requirements, the enacted legislation imposes a duty on health professionals to send a report on the provision of the mandated information about abortion and its alternatives to a state institution. The report must be submitted before an abortion is performed and contains the personal data of women whose pregnancy shall be terminated including those who filed a request for an abortion, creating a space for potential abuse of women's right to privacy, which includes "the right of an individual to decide . . . whether and to what extent facts from his or her private life should be made available to others,"[97] as articulated by the Court in its 2007 decision.

Proponents of both amendments argued that the proposed measures would enable a woman to make a "more qualified and freer" decision about her pregnancy, because she would be provided with a "qualified instruction" about the procedure and its alternatives by her doctor.[98] In order to support this claim the proponents of the adopted proposal referred to the 2007 decision arguing that their claim had a basis in the Court's reasoning on the instruction (counseling) requirement. In particular, they cited the Court's discussion of the counseling objective, namely to encourage a woman to change her mind, and the confidence it placed in the doctor as the protector of unborn human life.[99] Although the Court found the existing procedural measures sufficient for the protection of unborn human life, noting that they ensured that a woman decides "only after a due consideration based also on relevant medical information provided in an accessible form,"[100] the proponents used the Court's reasoning to strengthen their claim that a woman had to be provided with "qualified" information and subjected to the mandatory waiting period necessary for absorbing that information. These new measures, they explained, were supposed to enable a woman to decide in favor of the protection of unborn life.[101]

These proposals demonstrate a change in argumentation against abortion after the Court recognized the women's autonomous decision making in the early phase of their pregnancy. In addition to focusing on the protection of the life of an "unborn child," those against abortion added arguments claiming to protect women and their decision making. Because women are allowed by the law to decide on their pregnancy in the first trimester without restriction as to reason, their decisions must be supplemented through additional measures that aim at influencing women to carry the pregnancy to term and thus at helping women make "more rational, qualified" decisions. Similar measures, known also as "woman-protective" anti-abortion measures, have been found in other contexts to undermine women's agency.[102]

Conclusion

The Slovak decision is progressive in its robust analysis of the right to privacy, recognizing that this right includes a woman's right to reproductive self-determination, and affirming that in order for a woman to effectively exercise this right, she must be able to decide on abortion of her own accord in a certain phase of her pregnancy. This distinguishes the Slovak decision from the decisions of other constitutional courts in Central Europe, which understood abortion as an exception from the protection of unborn life rather than the woman's constitutional entitlement, at least for a certain period of pregnancy. From the point of view of women who experienced the end of state socialism in 1989 and in whose countries courts reviewed the constitutionality of abortion law—that is, East German, Hungarian, Polish, and Slovak women—the Slovak Court was the only one that upheld a liberal abortion law permitting abortion on request without the need to specify a reason.

Strong support for women's autonomous decision making means that the right to terminate a pregnancy cannot be taken away from women in Slovakia so easily. Paradoxically, and perhaps logically, this also resulted in a shift in the anti-abortion rhetoric and consequently led to the adoption of restrictive measures that focus on women's capacity to make rational and competent decisions. Through these "woman-protective" anti-abortion measures, those against abortion try to undermine women's access to abortion on request. One can only hope that, were the "woman-protective" anti-abortion measures to be challenged at the Court one day, the Court would find them in conflict with the essence of the women's right to privacy and their personal freedom.

Chapter 4

Proportionality in the Constitutional Review of Abortion Law

Verónica Undurraga

Constitutional abortion judgments are often characterized by two primary traits. Courts tend to be categorical in their approach, grounding decisions in abstract moral and legal principles that are difficult to relate to women's experiences. Courts are also prone to rely on rarely justified intuitive premises, especially the assumed effectiveness of criminalization in protecting unborn life and gender stereotypes that minimize the perceived effects of criminalization on women's lives. Courts are increasingly becoming more sensitive, however, to the need for a less categorical approach, one that recognizes competing interests, and seeks to resolve constitutional conflicts through a reasoned balance. As the shape of constitutional abortion judgments shift, courts are searching for and experimenting with different frameworks through which to articulate their reasoning. In this chapter, I explore proportionality as a methodology that when applied by courts has resulted in a more balanced treatment of abortion in constitutional law, curbing the tendency of judgments to be one-sided and insufficiently justified.

Proportionality as a methodology requires judges to order the questions they must address in consecutive stages and encourages them to reflect on certain substantive issues too often neglected in abortion adjudication. Judges are required, for example, not merely to assert the protection of unborn life as a constitutional duty or a constitutional legitimate interest, but to assess the effectiveness of law in this protection. With assessment of effectiveness, empirical data on the causes of abortion, best practices to lower abortion rates, and the effect of criminalization on the lives of women become relevant considerations. Assessments of effectiveness, in other words, require judges to account for the harms of criminalization against its alleged benefits, and to thus consider alternative measures of protection that are equally effective, but less infringing on competing interests. Proportionality explicitly asks about the gains and costs of protecting unborn life, and about the allocations of those costs, which up to the present have been disproportionately borne by women, thus limiting their constitutional rights. Once these considerations are incorporated into judicial analysis and given due consideration, the usual result is support for approaches to abortion regulation other than through criminal law.[1]

The chapter is divided into three parts. In the first part, I describe a core premise of proportionality doctrine, namely the interpretation of rights as *principles* rather than *rules*. I use the 1975 German constitutional abortion decision—regarded as a paradigm-setting judgment in the field—to demonstrate early and unrefined applications of the doctrine based on this core premise, and to set a baseline against which to explore the development of proportionality in contemporary case law.

In the second part, I describe how proportionality works as an analytical tool to shape, or perhaps discipline, constitutional review. I explain the three standards of the doctrine—suitability, necessity, and strict proportionality—and highlight the substantive issues they raise. By reference to contemporary comparative jurisprudence, I show how constitutional courts have progressively refined the standards and application of the doctrine to defend ever more liberal legislative reforms.

In the third part, I tackle a particularly challenging aspect of proportionality analysis in constitutional abortion law: how courts have reconciled positive duties to protect unborn life with negative duties to abstain from interfering with women's rights.

The Principle and Doctrine of Proportionality

Proportionality refers to an analytical framework of constitutional review. It assumes that the legal system is a consistent value system, and that the judicial task is to reach an interpretation in which competing values accord ("practical concordance"). These values include rights but may also encompass other objective interests that are constitutionally protected.

In constitutional law, rights may be structured as either rules or principles, a distinction that has a particular consequence for whether and how they may be balanced, in other words, whether and how they may be analyzed within a proportionality framework. "Rights as rules" are categorical in structure: they are always either fulfilled or not. The right of a detainee to be presented before a judge within forty-eight hours of arrest, for example, is a right as rule. Two contradictory rules therefore cannot be applied at the same time to the same situation. A conflict between two rules can be resolved only by reading an exception into a rule or by declaring one of the rules invalid or of no effect.[2] Judicial interpretations that conceive constitutional rights as categorical and absolute claims (every right is absolute within a specifically delimitated space) assign rights a rule-like structure. As such, they are incompatible with the idea of balancing that is at the heart of proportionality. The Supreme Court of Costa Rica, for example, declared a statute permitting in vitro fertilization unconstitutional on the reasoning that the loss of embryos in the procedure violated the absolute right to life of human beings from the moment of conception.[3] The Court's categorical conception of the right to life precluded a proportionality approach. Most constitutional rights, however, are better understood if structured as principles rather than rules.

Robert Alexy defines *principles* as "norms which require that something be realized to the greatest extent possible given the legal and factual possibilities"[4] Rights as principles cannot, by definition, be absolute—they are "optimization requirements characterized by the fact that they can be satisfied to varying degrees."[5] Competing principles may therefore not only coexist in a legal system but may be applied simultaneously to resolve a given situation. There is no abstract or absolute hierarchy between principles. Rather they are balanced in the context of a case, whereby a *conditional* precedence of one principle over the other is established in the light of the particular circumstances of a case.[6] Rights as principles are thus well suited to a proportionality analysis, which seeks to maximize all rights to the greatest extent possible. The application of proportionality makes possible a clear decision on a case and resolves the competition between principles *for that specific case.* This particular decision is categorical and thus can be expressed in the form of a rule. The characterization of rights as rules or principles is helpful to understand constitutional abortion law. In the landmark 1975 decision of the German Federal Court, the Court was asked to decide whether a statute that legalized abortion in the first twelve weeks of pregnancy violated the right to life of the unborn. According to the Court, the duty to protect unborn life resulted from the recognition of its dignity, which must be read into the sentence "human dignity shall be inviolable," contained in Article 1, paragraph 1 of the Basic Law. The decision identified as the competing interest the right of the pregnant woman to the free development of her personality, which it said is also connected to human dignity.[7]

The German decision is often read as categorical in nature—that is, that it reads the right to life as a rule to deny any recognition to women's right of self-determination. This reading tends to be based on the Court's statement that the state must regulate abortion from "a duty to carry the pregnancy to term. . . . The condemnation of abortion must be clearly expressed in the legal order."[8]

I read the German Court, however, as having adopted a rudimentary proportionality analysis even in this early decision. The Court, in fact, expressly commits itself to "a principle of the balance which preserves most of the competing constitutionally protected positions"[9] and describes its task as finding that "required balance" under which "both constitutional values [life and self-determination] are to be viewed in their relationship to human dignity, the center of the value system of the constitution."[10]

The Court's statement privileging unborn life may thus be read as a statement on the "required balance" of competing values rather than as a rule. The Court's reasoning supports this reading of the case. The Court explains that as applied to *normal pregnancy*—circumstances of pregnancy that do not seriously burden the woman, but represent the normal burdens with which every pregnant woman must cope—the balance tilts decisively in favor of the protection of unborn life. A compromise to guarantee the value of life of the unborn and the right of women's self-determination (i.e., freedom of abortion), the Court explains, is simply "not possible since the interruption of pregnancy always means the destruction of the unborn life . . . [while the woman may nonetheless enjoy] many opportunities for development of [her] personality."[11] The Court thus concludes that the "decision . . . must come down in favor of the precedence of the protection of life for the child *en ventre sa mère* over the right of the women to self-determination."[12]

In cases of "extraordinary burden," which lead to a burdening of the woman that goes beyond that normally associated with pregnancy, such as a risk to life or health,[13] the balance turns out differently. In such circumstances, the Court finds, a woman's continuation of pregnancy cannot be demanded or enforced by the state. Motherhood, in the words of the Court, is "non-exactable."[14] The same holds true for other situations, such as severe fetal malformation or where pregnancy results from rape, or where the woman confronts extreme economic or social hardship, that impose "extraordinary burdens for the pregnant woman, which, from the point of view of *non-exact-ability*, are *as weighty as*" the danger to her life or health.[15] In all these cases, the Court explains, "another interest equally worthy of protection . . . asserts its validity with such urgency that the state . . . cannot require that the pregnant woman must, under all circumstances, concede precedence to the right of the unborn."[16]

On this reading of the case, the German Court treated both the value of life of the unborn, and the rights of women—to life and health but also to self-determination—as principles. They are rights and values that coexist, that admit to degrees of protection, and that are interpreted in balance with one another and in a manner to maximize the protection of all. That in a particular case, the balance may decisively come out in favor of one value over the other does not strip the exercise of its "balancing" character. For this reason, the proportionality methodology—however rudimentary in form—can be considered to have been a feature of abortion jurisprudence from the earliest of decisions.

Proportionality as an Analytical Tool in Constitutional Review

Even courts that treat *rights as principles* nevertheless often find it difficult not to give absolute priority to life when in conflict with other rights. That life unlike other rights does not allow for gradation is a persuasive claim, leaving judges to reason that there is little accommodation if any that can be permitted in abortion regulation. This can be seen in the 1975 German judgment: the life of the unborn is extinguished in abortion, whereas pregnancy does not deny all opportunity for women's self-determination, thus a criminal ban on abortion is favored.

Proportionality as an analytical framework, however, rejects this form of crude balancing. For even if life is considered the utmost right to be protected in a constitutional order, it still seems reasonable, if not necessary, to ask whether and if so, to what extent criminalization protects unborn life and whether the same purpose can be achieved in a more or equally effective way, less infringing of the rights of women.

Proportionality works as an analytical tool to shape, or perhaps discipline, judicial review by setting three consecutive standards of assessment, through which a court must proceed in assessing the constitutionality of a statute. These are the tests of *suitability, necessity,* and *strict proportionality* (also called *proportionality in the narrow sense).* The doctrine requires that a court assess a statute against each test, and that the law pass each test in order to be declared constitutional. If one fails, there is no need to continue with the others and the law must be deemed unconstitutional.

The suitability test requires that a statute that infringes a constitutional right or value be rationally connected to a constitutionally legitimate aim. A court must thus assess both the legitimacy of the objective and the appropriateness of the means chosen to pursue it. In abortion law, the typical suitability question asks whether criminalization is a suitable legislative measure to protect unborn life.

The necessity test requires that a statute that infringes a constitutional right be necessary to achieve its legitimate constitutional aim, that is, that there is no less intrusive but equally effective measure to achieve the objective of the law. In abortion law, the necessity test usually asks whether criminalization is the least restrictive means available to pursue the protection of unborn life.

The strict proportionality test offers a version of crude balancing: it asks that the benefits of a statute that encroaches on a constitutional right clearly outweigh its burdens. In abortion law, this requires the Court to ask whether even if criminalization is found suitable to the protection of unborn life, and the least infringing of all alternatives, the sacrifice it demands of women is justified.

By reference to contemporary comparative jurisprudence, I seek to show how constitutional courts continue to refine the tests of the proportionality analysis and how their application has resulted in the support of abortion regulations based on prevention rather than criminal repression.

The Suitability Test

The first question a court must ask itself in review of a criminal abortion statute is whether the law is based on a constitutionally legitimate objective. This question is often omitted because the legitimacy of protecting unborn life is taken for granted as both a legitimate objective, and as the objective of the law. Increasingly however courts are taking a more deliberate approach and scrutinizing both the objective of the law and its legitimacy.

Recent judgments overturning criminal bans on the termination of anencephalic pregnancies, for example, have reassessed the legitimate objective of the law based on an interrogation of the definition of the life to be protected.[17] The common argument that unborn life is worthy of protection as part of the process of human development, and that protection of that life is to make possible its future enjoyment of rights, does not hold with nonviable fetuses. The legitimate objective of criminalization is thus questioned in such cases.

In other cases, the wording of statutes may be interrogated to reveal that criminalization does not have as its sole or main objective the protection of unborn life. Often a primary objective is to affirm a certain religious or moral order, seeking to protect the virtue of women or providers involved in abortion. In Chile, the law excludes criminal punishment only in cases where the requirements of the Catholic doctrine of double-effect are met, that is, for example, where pregnancy termination is not the intended effect of life-saving treatment for the pregnant woman (e.g., chemotherapy), but may be an inadvertent effect.[18] When the conception of the "good" pursued by a law is confined to a particular religion, but the state according to the constitution should be denominationally neutral in religious matters, the legitimacy of such an objective may be questioned.

Abortion laws that reinforce traditional gender roles may also be challenged on this basis. Laws that punish women more severely than third parties (including male partners) for their role in illegal abortion, for example, suggest greater wrongdoing. Yet viewed from the protection of unborn life, the harsher treatment of women does not advance any objective. Such laws thus suggest that criminalization is perhaps also intended to reinforce the traditional maternal role of women by penalizing those women who deviate from what is seen as their natural and special duty to protect fetuses. Another ground for the defense of criminalization is the paternalistic idea that criminal deterrence is justified in order to prevent the woman from suffering the consequences of a wrong decision. Such consequences include the so-called post-abortion syndrome, despite the fact that the evidence supporting its alleged psychological harms has been widely criticized.[19] Neither of these laws pursues legitimate aims because they are based on harmful stereotypes incompatible with the recognition of the dignity and equality of women as subjects of law.

Rarely, however, do criminal abortion laws fail constitutional review for lack of a legitimate aim. Most courts recognize laws that seek to protect human life and create a culture of respect for human dignity, rightly, as serving legitimate aims. The suitability test thus carries the greatest bite in assessment of criminalization as a means to achieve these ends. Suitability increasingly calls for empirical assessment of the law's effectiveness, namely evidence of whether criminalization is associated with lower or reduced abortion.

Courts have ventured down this path and stated that criminalization of abortion "is only legitimate when efficiency can be attributed to it, as a minimum requirement."[20] The claim is now well substantiated that highly restrictive abortion laws are not associated with lower abortion rates.[21] For example, the abortion rate is twenty-nine per one thousand women of childbearing age in Africa and thirty-two per one thousand in Latin America, which correlates with the fact that abortion is illegal under most circumstances in most of the countries of these two regions. In contrast, Western Europe has an abortion rate of twelve per one thousand, where abortion is generally permitted on broad grounds. The proportion of women living under liberal abortion laws is inversely associated with the abortion rate in the subregions of the world, which might be explained by the fact that the unmet need for modern contraception is lower in subregions dominated by liberal abortion laws than in those dominated by restrictive laws.[22]

The deterrent effect of criminal law cannot be assumed. Criminal law may be effective in deterring some crime, but its effectiveness depends in large measure on the kind of conduct sanctioned. Most criminal laws require people *to abstain* from harming someone else engaging in conduct that most of us would not engage in even if they were legal. In the case of criminal abortion laws, women are required to perform highly demanding *positive* duties related to pregnancy and child rearing, and when they abort they usually do not see themselves as harming others but acting upon their own persons. This point is key to understanding why the criminal law has proved so ineffective in deterring pregnancy termination throughout time. Courts must also confront legislatures with the insurmountable practical limitations in using criminal law to protect unborn life. To make these laws effective, it would be necessary for the state to know the existence of pregnancies at risk of being aborted, to take measures to prevent abortion in such cases, and, to prosecute and punish those who averted detection and prevention. None of these three conditions can be met in our societies. If abortion is criminalized, women simply hide their pregnancies and resort to clandestine services, which are very difficult to prosecute because they are done in secrecy and with the complicity of all concerned. Current abortion methods, such as medication abortion, have further privatized the act. Unless totalitarian policies are adopted, such as those in Romania under Ceauşescu in the 1980s, where all fertile women were required to undergo monthly gynecological examinations to identify and monitor pregnancies and ensure they were brought to term,[23] criminalization is an ill-suited means to prevent abortion.

In the past, courts tended to simply accept and to assess criminalization on its face, paying little if any attention to its effectiveness as a means of protection. This can be seen in the 1975 German decision, favoring a criminal approach in principle, even against the evidence provided by the legislature that a preventive regime could be more effective in saving lives. The Court argued that the obligation owed is that of "individual protection to each single concrete life,"[24] and that a less categorical approach than criminal prohibition that would sacrifice the life of any one fetus would thus be an unacceptable trade-off. The underlying assumption of the Court, of course, was that criminalization does not itself "sacrifice" lives. But this is a mistaken assumption because of the ineffectiveness of criminalization in practice. As the dissent pointed out, "the sacrifice" argument of the Court works both ways: criminalization sacrifices the lives of those fetuses that die in clandestine abortions and that could have been saved through the alternative means proposed by the legislature. That abortion under one regime happens with the sanction of the law, and in another with its condemnation, should not matter in assessment of "lives lost." Rather it is the overall efficacy of the state's protective measures that matter in a constitutional review premised on the protection of unborn life. Courts almost everywhere have shown a similar unwillingness to assess the effectiveness of criminalization. Proportionality, however, requires consideration of the suitability of law to its task.

It was only with a turn to asking about the relative effectiveness of different legal measures that courts began to endorse more liberal abortion regimes, for example, those that substitute counseling for punishment. The German Court was among the first to do so, in 1993, when it revisited and accepted the constitutionality of law that allowed women to elect abortion early in pregnancy following dissuasive counseling and a waiting period, reasoning that "at least in the early phase of pregnancy . . . effective protection of unborn human life is only possible with the support of the mother."[25] The Court held that "the secrecy pertaining to the unborn, its helplessness and dependence and its unique link to its mother would appear to justify the view that the state's chances of protecting it are better if it works together with the mother."[26] The Court in other words acknowledged that criminalization had failed to protect unborn life and that the legislature was entitled to enact an alternative and more effective mode of regulation.

In 2010, the Portuguese Court followed suit, citing the ineffectiveness of criminal law in affirming the constitutionality of a statute decriminalizing abortion in the first ten weeks of pregnancy. The Court stated: "We are confronted not with the limits of criminal law, but with the limits of law."[27] In the judgment, the Court reviewed the suitability of criminalization not only in failing to lower abortion rates, but also in failing to create "an atmosphere that would favor a decision to maintain a pregnancy."[28] Even if we ignore the rarity of convictions, the Court argued, "when exceptionally [a conviction] happens, the social reaction is more of uneasiness than of applause."[29] As the Court's reasoning suggests, a justification of criminalization exclusively based on the idea that criminalization is the symbolic way in which society expresses the wrongness of abortion, is not a sufficient reason. According to the Court, effectiveness requires a showing of lower abortion rates.

The suitability test requires that any limitations imposed on the rights of women are not imposed without purpose. That is, suitability requires that an abortion statute that encroaches on a constitutional right at least achieve some legitimate aim to justify its burdens. A law that fails this requirement, that imposes burden without benefit, is disproportionate, and should be declared unconstitutional.

The Necessity Test

If there is evidence that criminalization is effective in achieving some aim—lowering abortion rates or creating a culture of respect for human life—the next question that must be asked is whether criminalization is a necessary means to achieve these ends. Phrased differently, under proportionality doctrine, courts must ask whether there are less intrusive but more or equally effective alternative means to achieve the objectives of the law. If so, criminalization fails the necessity test and must be declared unconstitutional. The law is once again disproportionate, this time imposing burdens on the lives of women and interfering with their fundamental rights unnecessarily.

In criminal law theory, the necessity test is expressed in the well-known *ultima ratio* principle: the threat of criminal punishment must be the last resort of the legislator. The idea behind this principle is that there is a continuum of protective measures: ranging from the least to the most invasive. The legislator should opt for measures that maximize conflicting interests, that is, measures that are least infringing, but sufficiently effective.

In its 1975 decision, the German Court acknowledged the *ultima ratio* principle but, having assumed the effectiveness of criminalization, created a high burden on the legislator to prove that a liberal law was as effective as criminal punishment in protecting the life of the unborn. The Court reasoned from assertion that "the worth and importance of the legal value to be protected demand[ed]" the protection of criminal law.[30] A dissenting opinion in a 2008 Mexico Supreme Court abortion case reasoned in a similar vein. "It is not up to the discretion of the ordinary legislature to punish or not punish conduct that threaten[s] the minimum essential values of society. . . . When the legal interest protected is essential it must be protected by criminal law."[31]

This reasoning is flawed on several grounds. First, as argued by the dissent in the 1975 German case, by imposing a burden on the legislator to prove that alternative protective measures were as effective as criminalization, the majority flipped the *ultima ratio* principle. Criminalization must be demonstrated rather than assumed necessary under the principle.[32] Second, there is not necessarily a relationship between the invasiveness of a measure and the degree of protection it affords, that is, its effectiveness. It is probably the case, for example, that paid maternity leave and public childcare may be much more effective in preventing abortion than criminal sanction.

Following this reasoning, the Colombian Constitutional Court applied the *ultima ratio* principle very differently in its landmark 2006 decision, which liberalized a near complete criminal prohibition on abortion.[33] In an earlier judgment unrelated to abortion, the Court has explained that the principle of proportionality requires criminalization to be avoided when the state has less restrictive means to achieve its objectives: "It is disproportionate that the legislature chooses the means that most impinges on personal liberty, criminal law, when it has other tools that are less harmful to those constitutional rights to secure the same values."[34] The same principle applies in the abortion context. The Court concluded that the legislator may resort to criminal law only where there is an "insufficiency of other means to guarantee the effective protection of the life of the unborn."[35]

In 2008, the Mexico Supreme Court declared constitutional the decriminalization of abortion in the first twelve weeks of pregnancy.[36] This decision adds an interesting component to the application of the *ultima ratio* principle. The reform had been challenged as violation of the right to life of the unborn. A majority of the Court, however, held that unless the Constitution or an international human rights treaty mandates the legislature to criminal-ize abortion, it is free to decide on the most appropriate measure to protect unborn life.[37] The Court also declared that if the legislature decides to crimi-nalize abortion, it must respect the limits on the use of criminal law set by the constitutional rights of women. The Mexican decision is particularly impor-tant in contemporary constitutional abortion law because it definitely disso-ciates the status of unborn life from any necessary means of protection. This break rejects the common notion that if the fetus is recognized as a holder of a constitutional right, there is necessarily a constitutional duty to criminalize abortion. This move away from an absolutist, rule-like conception of the right to life allows proportionality to play a more prominent role in the analysis.

It is a jurisprudential break increasingly common in constitutional abor-tion law. In 2010, the Portuguese Court also deferred to legislative choice of protective measures, rejecting any assumed necessity of criminalization. It expressly declared that any assumed legitimacy of criminal law was mistaken: "criminal punishment is the most intrusive instrument . . . [and] cannot es-cape a positive examination; . . . the efficiency of criminal law cannot be auto-matically deduced from the inefficiency of other means."[38]

A proportionality analysis thus requires a relative assessment of different legal measures of protection, forswearing any assumption that the most inva-sive is the most effective. Rather it calls for studies and better understanding of the causes of abortion, and best practices of prevention. The experience of those countries that have achieved the lowest rates of abortion having the least restrictive criminal laws on abortion should guide the courts in the ap-plication of the necessity test. Against such evidence criminal laws cannot be reasonably defended as necessary if the objective of the law is to reduce abor-tion rates. Rather, advocates and courts should make use of growing research that demonstrates the key interventions to reduce abortion rates are effective and sustainable programs, including education and access to family planning, to reduce unwanted pregnancy, as well as those ensuring social and economic support for women who wish to continue their pregnancies and become mothers.[39]

Like effectiveness, the necessity of criminalization cannot be taken for granted. Under proportionality, the use of penal measures is justified only as a last resort, where alternative measures are proven insufficient to the protec-tion of unborn life.

The Strict Proportionality Test

Given the ineffectiveness of criminal law and the availability of less intrusive measures, most laws criminalizing abortion during the first stage of pregnancy probably would not pass the suitability and necessity tests and hence would not need to be scrutinized under the strict proportionality test. Should a court find criminalization suitable and necessary to protect unborn life, an assessment of proportionality *strict sensu* is required under the doctrine. This test asks whether the benefits of a statute that encroaches on a constitutional right clearly outweigh its burdens. It is a crude form of balancing, asking whether the sacrifices demanded by the law are justified by the legitimate aims it pursues. It favors one set of values over the other: the rights of women over the life of the unborn.

Three considerations can be described under this test: (a) the "abstract weight" or constitutional importance of the interests independent of the specific circumstances of the case; (b) the intensity of the negative and positive impacts on these interests; and (c) the certainty that these impacts will materialize in the specific circumstances of the case.[40]

An Abstract Weighting: Women and Unborn Life

Interests (rights and values) are assigned different significance in different constitutional orders. In the United States, for example, free speech is given much more weight than in most other constitutional systems. In Germany, the value of dignity is the supreme value of the state, reflected in the express prohibition against any reform of the constitutional provision that guarantees its protection. Alexy refers to this conferred status of different constitutional rights and interests as their "abstract weight."

The abstract weight of the right to life of the unborn is often regarded as a determinative factor in constitutional abortion law. Whether unborn life is given the status of a constitutional right, an objective value protected by a constitution, or simply a legitimate interest the state *may* pursue, but is *under no obligation* to pursue, the abstract weight assigned to unborn life influences, but does not necessarily determine, the balancing exercise under proportionality doctrine.

By treating the fetus as a rights holder, for example, the proportionality test is cast between values of a similar kind: subjective individual fundamental rights (of the fetus and the woman, respectively). In Ireland, the fetus enjoys a constitutional right to life, and the law permits abortion only to save the life of the pregnant woman.[41] In the United States, in contrast, which constitutionally guarantees abortion on request (albeit not unimpeded), the Supreme Court expressly denied the fetus the status of rights holder, recognizing the protection of unborn life only as a legitimate state interest that *may* be pursued.[42]

German, Spanish, Portuguese, and Slovak among other European constitutional courts, have taken more intermediate positions, declaring unborn life a constitutional (objective) value that states *must* protect. The same is true of the Colombian Court in Latin America. Where the protection of prenatal life is a constitutional objective value and not a right, the interests in conflict differ in kind. This distinction does not have significant consequences in the rudimentary proportionality analysis made by the German Court, but it does in the decisions of the Colombian, Portuguese, and Slovak courts, which have emphasized the *prima facie* priority of rights over objective values. In the language of proportionality, this means that rights have more abstract weight than interests that are not rights. Constitutional courts have thus reasoned that as a constitutional value, unborn life is not entitled to the same degree of protection of life as a subjective constitutional right, to which born people are entitled.[43] The Colombian Court, for example, explained that "while it is true that the legal system gives protection to the fetus, it does not do so to the same degree or with the same intensity that it gives to the human person."[44] Expressed differently, rights are considered by these courts to have more weight vis-à-vis constitutional interests that are not rights because their status is different and superior in the constitutional system. The Portuguese Court added another consequence of considering unborn life a value and not a right. "As a value worthy of protection that is independent from the personal interest of someone, human life is not bound to an 'all or nothing' protective logic that would reject gradations of 'more or less.'"[45] Life as a value allows for a gradualist approach to protection. The abstract weight of the life of a recently fertilized ovum is less than the weight of the life of a six-month-old fetus.

Abstract weight, however, attaches not only to the designation of right or value, but also to the nature of the specific interest invoked. Even though privacy, autonomy, liberty, and equality may be prized as abstract ideals, their weight is often lessened when invoked in the context of women's lives. In a decision by the Chilean Constitutional Court declaring public distribution of emergency contraception a violation of the right to life, the Court does not consider women's rights involved in the case and alludes to them indirectly, only *after* it has given its holding, stating that "this court is aware of the evident impact [the judgment] . . . will produce in a matter that also has very strong emotional implications for people, which are, no doubt, fully respectable."[46] The rights of women, in other words, were reduced to "strong emotional implications."

The discounted "abstract weighting" of the rights of women requires advocates and courts to expressly ask the "woman question."[47] That is, to assess the relative weight of rights from the lives and perspective of women, and to thereby, in some way, challenge the claimed 'abstractness'—and assumed gender neutrality—of the exercise. How can we understand the decision to keep or terminate a pregnancy as an exercise of the right to privacy or autonomy? Although feminist scholars have incorporated the term "reproductive rights" into legal vocabulary to designate and make visible the cluster of human rights connected to the reproductive lives of women and men, courts sometimes regard reproductive rights as "new rights"—and thus of less established status than traditional rights of liberty or equality. When considered newcomers, reproductive rights are often accorded less weight than traditional rights, influencing any balance among competing values. It is for this reason perhaps necessary for legal argument to explicitly make the connection between reproductive rights and traditional rights, to show how reproductive rights reflect an exercise in application, an effort to make rights meaningful in the reproductive lives of women (and men).

One such traditional right is human dignity, regarded as foundational of all human rights and accorded significant abstract weight in most constitutional orders. Dignity, however, is a contested concept with different and often conflicting uses in abortion contests.[48] Advocates of criminalization claim the intrinsic dignity of unborn life and its inherent worth. Yet in comparative constitutional law, dignity is increasingly invoked as an argument to limit state control over the reproductive lives of women, in a claim that women cannot be considered an instrument for procreation and that forced motherhood denies respect for women's dignity as full and equal citizens.[49] This argument not only rescues dignity as a constitutional value exclusively aligned with prenatal life but also expressly associates dignity with autonomy, which is its primary meaning in the broader realm of law. As expressed by the Portuguese Court: "the axiological [that is the valued] weight of the principle of human dignity does not fall on the side of intrauterine life, exclusively. It also falls on the constitutional legal position of the woman."[50] When courts begin to speak of abortion law in terms of the dignity of women, women become visible as full subjects of the law.

The Relative Positive and Negative Impacts of Criminalization

Strict proportionality further requires a crude balancing of concrete impact: the positive impact of criminalization on protection of unborn life against its negative impact on the rights and lives of women. Even if important rights are at stake, it does make a difference in the balancing if the intensity of the restrictions affecting these rights is high or low.

Many decisions that constitutionally require criminalization speak to the absolute negative effect of abortion: the destruction or complete loss of individual fetal life. The benefit of criminalization—to the extent it effectively deters abortion—thus entails a complete realization of the constitutional value, protection of unborn life. In contrast, the rights of women—autonomy, privacy, equality, health, and other rights—may be limited, but not fully extinguished by criminalization. The restriction on women's rights is sometimes framed in terms of limited duration, namely that of the nine months of pregnancy.

Such reasoning, however, again suffers from a failing to assess the impact of criminalization from the perspective of women. Although there is not a perfect correlation between the legal status of abortion and its risks, it is well documented that morbidity and mortality resulting from abortion tend to be high in countries and regions characterized by restrictive abortion laws, but very low where abortion laws are liberal.[51] Courts that justify the legalization of abortion for the reason of preserving the woman's health, in cases of severe fetal malformation, and when pregnancy results from rape or will result in extreme social hardship tend to assess the impact of criminalization beyond the physical endurance of pregnancy. The intensity of the impact on a woman might may be such that, as the German Court said "[this right] asserts its validity with such urgency that the state's legal order cannot require that the pregnant woman must, under all circumstances, concede precedence to the right of the unborn."[52] Further, in the experiences of real women, the more intense impacts of unwanted pregnancy do not always coincide with circumstances recognized as legal indications for abortion. This evidence has led legislatures—supported by courts—to increasingly forgo regimes based on indications for abortion in favor of time-frame regimes, recognizing women as the moral agents entitled to determine the balance. Instrumentalization of a woman's body, as when the law requires the continuation of a pregnancy when it implies risk to the woman's life or integrity, is now recognized as a form of inhuman and degrading treatment.[53]

There is disagreement on whether and in what situations it is against a woman's dignity to prohibit her access to legal abortion. The 1975 German decision is grounded on the belief that the woman's responsibility for the fetus is accorded by nature: "developing life itself is entrusted by nature in the first place to the protection of the mother. To reawaken and, if required, to strengthen the maternal duty to protect, where it is lost, should be the principal goal of the endeavors of the state for the protection of life."[54] According to this decision, the negative impacts of pregnancy on women are not attributable to law, but to nature itself, and as such they may not be considered encroachment on dignity. Criminalization of normal pregnancies does not "seriously burden [women] . . . since they [i.e., the limitations on autonomy] represent the normal situation with which everyone must cope."[55] The reasoning of the German Court may be contrasted with that of courts that do not read the burdens of pregnancy through traditional gender stereotypes. In *Planned Parenthood v. Casey*, for example, the U.S. Supreme Court recognizes that although women have always carried the burdens of pregnancy, this cannot justify the state in insisting "upon its own vision of the woman's role, however dominant that vision has been in the course of our history and our culture. The destiny of the woman must be shaped to a large extent on her own conception of her spiritual imperatives and her place in society."[56] The Constitutional Court of Colombia further developed the implication of dignity regarding abortion. The Court held that the criminalization of abortion is unconstitutional when the pregnancy is the result of rape, incest, or the application of a reproductive technique without the woman's consent, because it infringes upon the dignity of the pregnant woman. The law cannot demand perfectionist standards of conduct or heroic behavior.[57] A woman cannot be forced to make unusual sacrifices or to renounce her right to personal integrity to protect fetal life. Forcing a woman to bear a pregnancy and deliver a nonviable fetus is also an excessive burden, which amounts to cruel, inhuman, and degrading treatment, and which impinges on her spiritual welfare and her right to dignity.[58] In the language of the German doctrine of nonexactability: this is simply too much to ask.

Considerations of dignity were decisive in the 2006 Colombian decision. Dignity as a foundational principle of the constitutional order was defined to include autonomy to pursue one's life plan, which thus prohibited the assigning of women stigmatizing gender roles or the deliberate infliction of mental suffering.[59] According to the Court, a complete prohibition on abortion does not respect the dignity of women but reduces them to mere instruments for reproduction, depriving them of full recognition as constitutional subjects.

In defining the harms of criminalization in terms of dignity, the Court gave full recognition to the reproductive rights of women, understanding them as basic to the constitutional order. The pregnant woman is treated as an autonomous rights bearer, and "her consent . . . [is deemed] essential to the fundamental, life-changing decision to give birth to another person."[60]

Lawful abortion in Colombia is restricted to three indications. Merely looking at the form of the law, is it obvious that access to legal abortion is more limited than in Germany. However, looking beyond mere form, one is able to see the different logics behind the idea of nonexactability as applied by both courts. Nonexactability in German law is anchored in the logic of exceptionality: "that a pregnancy termination can be legal only in those exceptional circumstances where carrying a child to term would place a burden on the woman which is so severe and exceptional . . . that it would exceed the limits of exactable self-sacrifice."[61] The reasoning of the Colombian Court in constitutionally requiring indications is different, avoiding the language of exceptionality and grounded in a more—although still not fully—consistent application of the proportionality principle. The Court claimed that criminal law must not be used to enforce pregnancies if there are less restrictive suitable means to achieve unborn life protection, and it assessed the proportionality of the sacrifices imposed on the pregnant woman's rights. The Colombian Court limited its holding to three specific situations in which criminalization would represent disproportionate burdens because the harm to women outweighs any benefit in the protection of unborn life. However, consistent with its approach based on proportionality, the Court admitted that there might be other situations where the prohibition of abortion is disproportionate and left the door open for the legislature to further decriminalization.[62]

A Question of Certainty: A Realistic Assessment of the Negative and Positive Impacts of Criminalization

The strict proportionality test also requires an assessment of the certainty that is to be accorded to the empirical assumptions that sustain the claims about the benefits and harms of criminalization. This calls courts to review, for example, the reliability of the scientific knowledge used by the legislature and to be cautious when criminalization is based on questionable evidence. Although uncertainty about the effects of a law in the future cannot exclude the power of the legislature to pass the law, uncertainty cannot immunize such law from constitutional review either. Sometimes the harms of criminalization are countered by suggesting that given medical progress rarely is termination ever required to save the life or health of the pregnant woman, making the claim for life or health indications under the law more fiction than fact. Criminal laws, in other words, are said to rarely deny women access to therapeutic care. Alternatively, proponents of criminalization sometimes use its very ineffectiveness to argue that the law rarely threatens women's life or health: doctors routinely flout the law and perform therapeutic abortions regardless of legal sanction. Both claims disregard relevant evidence. In many countries, the *chilling effect* of criminalization overextends its reach, whereby women lawfully entitled to services are routinely denied access.[63] Moreover many women cannot access state-of-the-art medical care such that while it may be scientifically possible to survive a dangerous pregnancy, the reality for a woman without access to health care will be death. The same skepticism of criminalization is rarely shown with respect to its positive impacts, to question whether criminal law successfully deters women from seeking or accessing abortion, or that it breeds a culture respectful of human life and dignity.

The proportionality principle brings into consideration substantive issues too often neglected and forces judges to assess the actual impact of criminalization. In the final stage of the analysis, courts must assess the law on balance: asking whether the protection it affords unborn life is worth the sacrifice it demands of women.

Reconciling Negative and Positive Duties

Perhaps one of the most challenging aspects of applying proportionality in the constitutional review of abortion laws is the reconciling of positive and negative duties. Some courts, such as the Colombian Constitutional Court in 2006, have been called on to decide whether criminalization violates women's rights. The constitutional duty that is said to be violated in the case is negative: the state is obligated to refrain from encroaching on the rights of women to life, health, self-determination, and so on. Abstention is the action required of the state in fulfillment of its constitutional duty.

The case is different where courts are called on to decide if decriminalization violates the life of the unborn. The constitutional obligation allegedly infringed in this case is positive, and the violation results from a deficiency of state action. The challenge is that the obligation may be fulfilled through any number of different means, provided the means chosen are sufficient to the task.

This difference is relevant in the application of the proportionality principle. It is much easier for courts to declare when a negative obligation has been violated than to determine whether a threshold of protection has been reached. Thus we have tended to see—especially in contemporary case law—a greater degree of deference being shown to the legislature. In the 1993 German decision, for example, the Court explained that the Constitution identifies protection of unborn life as a goal, but does not define the form it should take. It is the legislature's task to determine the form of protection and only in "the prohibition on too little protection [is it] . . . subject to constitutional control."[64] Recent decisions of the Slovak and Portuguese courts similarly emphasized legislative discretion to decide the means and intensity of protection of unborn life, providing a threshold minimum level is satisfied.

The challenge of applying a proportionality analysis in these cases, however, is that the legislature finds itself constrained by both minimum and maximum standards. State action must be sufficient to protect the life of the unborn, but cannot impose too excessive a burden on the rights of women. The state must both intervene and abstain. The Slovak Court in a 2007 decision, for example, cautioned that "the constitutional value of unborn life can be therefore protected only to such extent that this protection does not cause an interference with the essence of woman's freedom and her right to privacy."[65] In its 2010 decision, the Portuguese Court weighted the two duties differently, reasoning that "the protective function [of rights or values] . . . [is a] substantially weaker function than rights as prohibitions against intervention . . . [such that] the observance of this protective function does not justify the unconditional invasion of the protected sphere of rights of other subjects."[66]

Of course it is worthwhile to recall that there is no necessary relationship between the invasiveness of a measure and the degree of protection it affords. The Portuguese Court thus decided the case largely on the view that the decriminalization of abortion does not necessarily entail a weaker degree of protection. On the contrary, the state may fully comply with its positive duty to protect unborn life by taking measures to prevent unwanted pregnancy, such as through the public provision of sexual education and contraceptives, as well as affirmative policies that support motherhood.[67]

Conclusion

In this chapter I have sought to demonstrate the opportunity provided by proportionality analysis in judicial review to usher in a new era of progressive abortion law reform. Proportionality as a methodology requires judges to reflect on substantive issues too often neglected, or considered only in an abstract and intuitive way. Proportionality asks about the true effects of the law. Tracing the origins of the doctrine to the 1975 German constitutional decision, my intention was to show its deep roots in the field and the significant advances made by European and Latin American courts in the understanding and application of proportionality in constitutional decisions on abortion. The most relevant change is the transition from an indication-based model sustained in the idea that only exceptional situations would justify the retreat from criminal law, to a periodic model based on the idea that criminal law can be used only if it proves suitable, necessary, and strictly proportional to achieve the aim of protecting unborn life.

Chapter 5

A Functionalist Approach to Comparative Abortion Law

Rachel Rebouché

This chapter critiques the present comparative methodology in abortion law and explores the possibilities of a new comparative approach. The current method relies on high-profile but dated constitutional abortion decisions from the United States and Germany. Courts continue to rely on these cases to justify their decisions as consistent with a modern, global convergence around women's rights and to minimize national resistance to contested law reform. These comparisons, however, oversimplify legal developments of the past forty years by focusing on constitutional norms and legislative regimes, rather than on the relationship between abortion law and practice.

Courts in countries as diverse as Portugal, South Africa, Mexico, and Colombia consistently refer to an emerging consensus on the liberalization, if not decriminalization, of abortion law. Each court has relied on comparative law to balance the rights of women with potential life and to position their decisions along a spectrum of legislative regimes on abortion. At one end of the spectrum, courts invoke the 1973 U.S. decision *Roe v. Wade*[1] as the high-water mark of liberalization and abortion-on-request. At the other end, courts rely on the then West German Federal Constitutional Court 1975 decision[2] to support protections for "unborn life."[3]

Based on a right of privacy, the U.S. Supreme Court in *Roe v. Wade* declared that women, in consultation with their physicians, are constitutionally entitled to elect abortion for any reason in the first trimester.[4] Thereafter the state is permitted, though not constitutionally required, to regulate abortion to protect maternal health in the second trimester, and to protect potential life in the third.[5] Although based on a judicial interpretation of domestic constitutional rights, *Roe* became a global symbol of abortion rights that encouraged legislative liberalization around the world.[6] This was true even after the Supreme Court replaced its trimester framework with the more restrictive undue burden standard of *Planned Parenthood of Southeastern Pennsylvania v. Casey.*[7] *Roe* "both informed and was informed by a larger global movement to recognize reproductive health and self-determination as integral components of women's equality."[8]

This is precisely the vein in which the South African Supreme Court of Appeal cited *Roe* to reject a constitutional challenge to the Choice on Termination of Pregnancy Act (CTOPA). Passed in 1996, the act substantially liberalized South Africa's abortion law, allowing abortion on request within the first twelve weeks of pregnancy.[9] In defense of the act, the Court quoted from *Roe* at length as a symbol of progressive reform inspired by women's autonomy and equality: "the same considerations as applied in the [United States] would compel one to conclude that our Constitution protects a woman's right to choose."[10] Referring to *Casey* as having "affirmed the essential findings of *Roe*,"[11] the Court used U.S. case law to defend a shared legislative framework—abortion on request—as the hallmark of progressive law.

The South African Court described German law, in contrast, as an exception to the international consensus.[12] In its 1975 decision, the Federal Constitutional Court held that the German Basic Law imposes positive obligations on the state to protect the "unborn" or "developing life."[13] In the regulation of abortion, the German Court affirmed, "precedence must be given to the protection of the life of the child about to be born."[14] On this basis, the Court declared a dissuasive counseling regime unconstitutional,[15] and it affirmed that abortion could be made lawful only in exceptional circumstances (severe birth defect, a threat to maternal life or health, rape or incest, or a "general social situation" when continuation of the pregnancy would impose extraordinary burdens).[16] While the German Court reinforced the constitutional protection of potential life in its 1993 decision, it allowed a dissuasive or pro-childbirth counseling regime but required that abortion performed under it remain unlawful though unpunished.[17] These legislative permissions for abortion in the German case law—whether in indications or counseling—accord some respect to the rights of women, albeit always subordinated to the protection of unborn life.

U.S. and German case law now correspond to two ends of a spectrum of reform options that tied constitutional rights to legislative form. Often when courts cite the 1975 and 1993 German decisions, they do so for the constitutional protection of fetal life. In 2010, the Constitutional Court of Portugal upheld a law permitting early abortion with nondirective counseling and a three-day waiting period. Although the Court referred to women's rights in its holding,[18] it aligned with the German Constitutional Court and against the U.S. Supreme Court to make its decision palatable to anti-choice Portuguese residents. The Court was quick to contrast Portugal's law with what it perceived to be the U.S. standard, in which women make "spontaneous decisions."[19] Citing *Roe*, the Court argued that U.S. women make their abortion decisions alone, while Portuguese women have the support of the state in considering whether to choose abortion or childbirth.[20] In distancing the new law from that of the United States, the Court cited the 1993 German decision as an example of a legislative counseling regime that relies on social services and preventative, rather than punitive, measures to deter women from abortion.[21] The Portuguese and German legislative regimes, it argued, accomplish the same goals, among them, the protection of unborn life.

Increasingly, however, courts are finding the middle ground between U.S. and German case law to be a means to defend moderate reforms. "Meeting in the middle" was arguably the comparative approach taken in a 2006 Colombian case. The Constitutional Court of Colombia cited comparative abortion law to introduce limited exceptions to the country's criminal abortion prohibition, allowing for pregnancy termination in cases of risk to maternal health or life, serious fetal malformation, and pregnancy resulting from rape, incest, unwanted artificial insemination or implantation.[22] The Court cited the German Constitutional Court 1975 decision in affirming constitutional protection for unborn life,[23] but it noted that this protection did not require women to bring a pregnancy to term in instances of "extraordinary and oppressive burden," such as fetal anomaly, criminal act, or risk to life or health.[24] The trimester framework of *Roe*, the Court then explained, could be used to justify an indications-based legislative regime as a balance between the rights of unborn life and of women.[25] As pregnancy progresses, the Court reasoned, the constitutional protection of unborn life becomes stronger, permitting greater limitations on the right to abortion, except in instances in which a woman's life or health is at risk.[26]

A common pattern of comparative engagement emerges. U.S. and German case law is used—now in almost any combination—to legitimatize abortion law reform. The comparative methodology may almost be thought of as one of anointment: a process employed ritualistically, to consecrate a law by the token reference to these historical authorities. Whether comparative law is cited to align a country's law with the United States in its affirmation of the rights of women, or with Germany in its affirmation of the protection of unborn life, or to suggest a compromise between the two, these comparisons provide a consistent and readily identifiable framework for adjudicating on abortion law reform.

The weakness of the methodology is that abortion law reform is evaluated, as well as legitimatized, against a highly stylized, abstract set of rights demarcated by what the U.S. and German decisions have come to represent. What abortion law reform achieves in practice—be it access, prohibition, or compromise—is not assessed, comparatively or otherwise. Constitutional litigation simply does not serve this purpose. The case law sets up an abstracted relationship of legislative form to constitutional rights: we must have limitations to or grounds for abortion in order to protect unborn life; we must have freedoms to respect the rights of women. What either means for access to abortion services—whether services are more available, more affordable, or more convenient to access—is not within assessment. There appears to be faith in liberal laws promising liberal access, and in restrictive laws restricting access. But empirical studies, often in the field of public health, show this faith to be unfounded. Neither legislative form nor constitutional norm wholly determines the practice of abortion. Formal legal rules are not necessarily the rules of access.

The objective of this chapter is to offer an alternative comparative methodology that privileges an assessment of abortion laws in their functional capacity, that is, a methodology that studies how law functions in practice to facilitate or to impede women's access to safe abortion. I ground this *functionalist approach* in public health law, a discipline suited to understanding the gaps between law and practice.

The chapter is set out in three parts. The first part takes up the challenge first posed by Günter Frankenberg to show "what is left out, marginalized, or taken for granted by the official discourse" of comparative constitutional abortion law.[27] This part describes the inadequacies of the current favored methodology, focusing on how courts misconstrue the state of abortion law in the United States and Germany and thereby perpetuate a myth about the relationship between legislative form and abortion practice. Permissive laws, in other words, do not always result in permissive access, and the same holds true for restrictive laws and practice. This section concludes by considering why courts nonetheless remain committed to this formalist comparative method.

The second part proposes an alternative comparative method, described as functionalist in that it focuses on how legal norms influence the practice of abortion. This section describes the value of a functionalist approach, namely in the way in which it can develop an expanded understanding of different types of legal rules—formal, informal, and background—and their relationship to one another and to the delivery of abortion services.

The third part locates this alternative functionalist approach within the emerging field of public health law research and its methodologies. Public health law research proves instrumental in the study of abortion law because it starts from the premise that rules outside of formal abortion law shape practice. It thereby seeks to discover and to describe these local influences. This section explores the promise of two research methods in particular: implementation studies and field-based assessments.

The chapter concludes by suggesting that advocates can begin to change courts' comparative engagement on abortion law reform by introducing functionalist considerations into their briefs, that is, by combining legal argument with the lived practice of abortion.

The Limitations of the Current Comparators

Current comparative references to U.S. and German abortion law may be unrecognizable to those living under the law in the United States or Germany. Take the 2010 decision of the Constitutional Court of Portugal as an example. The Constitutional Court of Portugal described U.S. abortion law as the height of liberalization—abortion is treated in law as an entirely private decision, to be made by the woman alone at any time and for any reason. Legislative developments after *Roe* make this a questionable assertion. Counseling requirements and waiting periods are widespread across the United States and, moreover, have been declared constitutional by the U.S. Supreme Court time and time again.[28] Contrary to the Portuguese Court's description, women are hardly "alone" in their decisions but encounter a dense network of laws that make abortion anything but a "spontaneous" undertaking.

Courts citing comparative law are not necessarily concerned with the practice of abortion under the laws they cite. Interestingly, the suggestion that the

United States and Germany are at the opposite ends of a spectrum marked by liberalization and criminalization may be flipped. Abortion services are less available in certain regions of the United States, where women have a constitutional right to abortion on any ground before viability, than they are in Germany, where abortion remains an unlawful, though not a punishable, act.[29]

German women, for example, appear to have several choices of counseling centers, some of which offer minimal counseling that sounds in tones of women's rights rather than protection of fetal life. In a report issued by the European Women's Health Network, a counseling center, Pro Familia, stated its position as letting women decide whether to continue pregnancies on their own, "as a consequence of the human right to family planning."[30] For women who are "undecided," Pro Familia's advice "consider[s] different world-views, . . . a secular concept of human being, [women's] individuality, equality of rights and . . . autonomy."[31] Groups like Pro Familia maintain that this style of counseling complies with German law because it is consistent with "science and the respect for the final decision and responsibility of the woman (openness of result)."[32] In the United States, in contrast, it is common for states to statutorily require that information about possible physical or psychological consequences of abortion and about the development of the fetus be given to the deciding woman.[33] Several states mandate that women receive counseling information detailing only negative risks, including suicidal tendencies,[34] infertility,[35] depression, anxiety, and eating disorders.[36] A handful of laws inaccurately link abortion to breast cancer or include information about fetal pain.[37]

The cost and affordability of abortion might also cause one to question assumptions about the nature and operation of U.S. and German abortion law. In Germany, over 80 percent of the country's abortions are state funded through the state welfare program. This includes abortions with counseling, which remain formally unlawful but unprosecuted, when women demonstrate financial need. In contrast, almost 60 percent of U.S. women pay out of pocket for abortion services,[38] and only 13 percent of women receiving abortions in the United States rely on some form of state funding.[39] Enacted in response to the *Roe* decision, the Hyde Amendment bars the use of certain federal funds, including Medicaid, the health insurance program for low income Americans, to pay for abortions with the exception of threat to the pregnant woman's life and in cases of incest or rape.[40] As Mary Anne Case summarized, in the United States abortion is "famously protected, but unsubsidized," but in Germany it is "at once condemned and subsidized."[41]

Given these realities of access under the U.S.-German constitutional regimes, why do the almost forty-year-old comparisons persist? This question is even more striking considering that courts citing comparative law seem unconcerned with fidelity to the letter of the law. For example, although the Portuguese Court in its 2010 decision aligned itself with German precedent, it upheld nondirective counseling that resembles the counseling proposed in German legislation, which the German Constitutional Court struck down in 1993 for being too neutral in respect to the value of potential life. The South African Supreme Court of Appeal similarly quoted from *Casey* to support a holding that minors can seek abortion without parental permission. Yet in *Casey*, the U.S. Supreme Court upheld a Pennsylvania law that required parental permission.

Courts' willingness to oversimplify the authorities they cite may be an effort to fix the law to the facts. In other words, courts confer legal authority to new legislative or constitutional interpretations in order to open access to abortion, and citation to foreign comparators is one means to justify that exercise of power. But the question remains, why do courts need comparative legal authority, especially when the standards cited no longer seem to have the influence attributed to them? Why do courts so assiduously resort to comparative legal authority, even when they undermine their own credibility in its misstatement?

First, comparative constitutionalism has gained traction as the global recognition of rights became increasingly important to social justice movements. Over the last several decades, international and national organizations, with the mission of advocating for reproductive rights and bringing about abortion law reform, have made significant gains in marrying human rights and women's reproductive health before national courts.[42] Reva Siegel recently mapped how feminists successfully challenged criminal abortion laws in the 1960s and 1970s by arguing for women's rights to control their reproductive lives and against state imposition of traditional sexual mores.[43] U.S. and German abortion jurisprudence reflects this activism, responding to and incorporating feminist claims.[44] The U.S. and German case law represent, in the abstract, judicial assertion of constitutional rights to strike down abortion legislation, which has been conceived as the lynchpin of legal and social reform.

Since the 1990s, women's rights groups have played a crucial role in urging courts to liberalize abortion laws, relying on the comparative experiences of other countries and human rights principles. Comparative examples travel, in part, because they are used as evidence that countries are moving toward a consensus on expanded rights to abortion. For example, in liberalizing the Colombian law, the Constitutional Court stated that "sexual and reproductive rights . . . have finally been recognized as human rights, and as such, belong to constitutional law, a fundamental basis for every democratic state."[45] These rights recognize and promote "gender equality in particular and the emancipation of women and girls [as] essential to society."[46] Comparative law and international human rights law are described in the same section of the Colombian decision and support the same objective—to align the court with international trends that earmark progress and modernity.[47] The same can be seen in Portugal, where the Constitutional Court defended a liberal abortion law as following a model "widely prevalent" in Europe,[48] in compliance with human rights standards.[49] A circular issued by Portugal's Ministry of Health likewise announced that "the government's recent decriminalization of abortion represents a move toward joining the most modern, developed and open European societies."[50]

Second, the comparative examples of U.S. and German law travel because they serve formalist ends, in that they stand for an easy typology of reform. Grounds or time limits are often used as the metric for whether laws are restrictive or progressive. The purpose is to describe what the law allows formally per statute, code, or constitution. Fernanda Nicola has described this comparative methodology broadly as "comparison by columns," or "comparing the language of legal norms understood as positive law in specific legal regimes."[51] Comparative law by columns is a snapshot in time of what countries either permit as reasons for abortion or consider justifiable exceptions to criminal prohibitions that have been codified into law. A formalist approach succeeds at fitting all law reform into prescribed boxes of what formal law allows.

Consider a map of the world's abortion laws, published by the Center for Reproductive Rights.[52] Countries are shaded a different color depending on whether the country: prohibits abortion altogether; permits abortion only to save the woman's life; permits abortion to preserve physical health, to preserve mental health, or on socioeconomic grounds; or permits abortion without restriction as to reason. The map helpfully provides a snapshot of countries' laws on the books and the level of global support for different types of abortion law. Because of its format and function, however, the map cannot represent the nuance of how law is implemented, interpreted, or ignored. The map does not depict how the law functions in practice.

In comparative law theory, the critique of comparativism being overly formalist is longstanding. Comparative inquiries of the late 1800s and early 1900s were "dubious and non-scientific typologies of the world's legal systems based on a crude evolutionary model of social and legal development."[53] Said another way, the comparative project for most of its history has been concerned with categorizing laws and distinguishing between legal systems.[54] Yet a defining debate in comparative law is whether comparison should merely seek to categorize the formal laws of countries, or whether comparative examples should expose the deep differences between laws that appear similar.[55] Does comparison reveal shared doctrines, which can apply across borders, or are laws on abortion too divergent, too local, too embedded in culture to harmonize? Can laws on reproduction be meaningfully compared?

These questions challenge the practice of comparing formal laws for the purpose of showing a trend toward liberalization, without regard to the local and regional practices that shape how law is interpreted and implemented.[56] Darren Rosenblum, writing about comparative approaches to women's rights, envisions a comparative approach as a means "to acknowledge vast differences in national legal cultures" and "to expose important weaknesses in the neorealist understandings of human rights."[57] If the purpose of comparison is "emphasizing difference over universality," comparative examples can help uncover "the dynamic interaction between law, culture, and context."[58]

Comparative inquiry in abortion law, at present, makes little room for considering how law intersects with culture and context.[59] One reason for this deficiency is that the constitutional rights and legislative forms compared in U.S. and German case law represent only a narrow slice of the legal rules and norms that affect abortion practices. A critical comparativist, however, might look to foreign examples to yield insights into implementation and effectiveness of legal reform.[60] Instead of starting from the formal law on abortion (permitted grounds or timing for legal abortion), a comparative inquiry might ask: how do women seek abortion inside and outside of law? That is, what forms of regulation facilitate or impede abortion access in a country? Comparison of constitutional rights, and of abortion statutes, is important, but a singular focus on these forms of law may not account for the other legal rules that shape abortion access on the ground.

Legal Rules and the Functionalist Approach

The dominant comparative approach may allow courts to justify abortion law reform, but it does so in formalist terms that channel that reform into predetermined regimes, marked by permission for certain legal grounds or time limits. Abortion in practice tests the meaningfulness of these formal categorizations. A country with a functioning but submerged market for abortion may be coded as restrictive, but women may gain access to abortions for which the formal law does not account. Conversely, the law on the books may grant broad legal permission for abortion services, but practical impediments and other legal rules may make it difficult for women to gain access. To understand how abortion services are provided under the law, a new comparative method is needed—one that may be described as functionalist insofar as it focuses on how legal norms influence the practice of abortion. This requires an expanded appreciation of formal, informal, and background rules and their relationship to one another and to abortion services.

Formal Rules

The study of abortion law is often limited to the formal rules of constitutional rights and largely penal statutory provisions. There are, however, other kinds of formal rules that directly shape abortion practice. These include guidelines on health service delivery. Health care guidelines are rules of particular importance to a functionalist approach because, as the recent World Health Organization (WHO) *Safe Abortion: Technical and Policy Guidance for Health Systems* signals, guidelines seek to provide technical assistance and to create tools to help health providers and women negotiate health systems.[61] Guidelines are issued, in other words, because the constitutional or statutory law that structures the health system does not itself provide sufficient direction to guide practice. For this reason, some countries use administrative processes to clarify the terms of access to lawful abortion, especially after constitutional or statutory reform.

For example, in 2010, Kenya adopted a new Constitution states that, "Abortion is not permitted unless, in the opinion of a trained health professional, there is need for emergency treatment, or the life or health of the mother is in danger, or if permitted by any other written law."[62] Evidence suggested, however, that the terms of permission were not widely understood or being fully implemented. Sections of the Kenyan penal code had not been revised to reflect the language of the new Constitution, and thus the law formally reflected a contradiction in permission.[63]

Despite a "liberalized" law and concerted efforts to promote contraception, sex education, and post-abortion care, the numbers of unsafe abortion and related maternal deaths in East Africa remained among the highest in the world. The Kenyan Ministry of Medical Services responded in 2012 by issuing service delivery guidelines for abortion care, the purpose of which was to improve the quality of care in health facilities across the country.[64] The guidelines clarified the constitutional permissibility of abortion; provided detailed standards for who may perform an abortion, with what training, and in what facilities; and recommended well-being and options counseling to prevent unsafe abortion if permission was denied. The guidelines emphasized the importance of appropriate clinical assessment of patients terminating pregnancies and the importance of preventing infection and disease, as well as protecting the patient's dignity, privacy, and comfort.

The Kenyan Ministry of Medical Services intends frontline health workers to use these guidelines when treating women seeking reproductive services and designed the guidelines to aid in decision making about patient care. The guidelines, in other words, are expressly intended to change the practice of abortion, and the success of the guidelines is measured against resulting improvements in women's health. It is this orientation of the guidelines that mark them as an important formal rule to study in a functionalist approach. A functionalist method starts by "identifying the purpose of a rule" and then "provid[ing] a standard by which the merits of the rule can be evaluated: how well do [rules] serve their purposes."[65] That is, if the purpose of a guideline is to reduce unsafe abortion and related mortality by increasing access to lawful abortion and averting unsafe abortion practices, then the abortion law may be assessed against both these ends.[66] The enactment and content of guidelines—what they target—reveals and describes the current dysfunctions of the law they seek to redress.

Like a rights-based approach, however, guidelines are dependent on state implementation for their success. In Colombia, lawyers returned to court following the 2006 judicial liberalization to ask for government-issued guidelines on the legal duties of health professionals and state officials.[67] The Colombian Ministry of Social Protection in response issued guidelines to define the limits of providers' lawful exercise of conscientious objection, to instruct providers on what constitutes "good medical attention," and to require basic insurance coverage for abortion.[68] The guidelines themselves, however, ultimately proved ineffective. Like the constitutional and statutory law they were intended to implement, the guidelines too remained vague and unenforced.[69] Guidelines, as other formal rules, may be difficult to implement when the enforcement powers of the state are weak, suggesting that both the source of and remedy for the problem lie elsewhere. This is an insight gained by examining the effect of formal rules and seeking to identify why they succeed or fail in practice. If there are severe limitations on state enforcement—on which constitutional law, statutory regimes, and guidelines depend—then the promulgation of additional formal rules is likely to do little to solve enforcement or implementation problems.

The underenforcement of formal administrative measures, like guidelines, proves only half the problem. New standards for providers and facilities can open up access, but these rules can also impose bureaucracy or create processes that deter women from seeking legal abortions.[70] In 2007, the Legislative Assembly of Mexico City redefined the crime of abortion as the interruption of pregnancy after the twelfth week of gestation and established that, prior to that point, termination of a pregnancy for any reason was a free health service available in public hospitals, regardless of the patient's financial need.[71] However, a recent study revealed that, even though abortion care is free in public facilities, many women still seek informal or private services due in part to privacy concerns and bureaucratic hassles.[72] In 2012, Colombian advocates brought a case on behalf of a minor who had complied with all the requirements for a legal abortion, but was forced to continue her pregnancy after ten weeks of administrative delays.[73] One question a functionalist approach might ask is how revision of formal laws influences previously complicit, indifferent, or somewhat supportive providers to oppose abortion. In Colombia, women knew where to obtain abortions before liberalization and their choices were "socially tolerated" by health professionals; after the Constitutional Court judgment, physicians expressed skepticism and hesitation about deciding whether a termination fit within the legal grounds.[74] These are again findings learned only from watching the practice under the rule, rather than assuming that a practice necessarily follows the rule. A comparative functionalist method uses a legal rule to investigate the variable practices around and within it.

This orientation avoids, for example, a simple dichotomy of defining abortion practice as either legal or not legal. Rather the approach asks how practice itself shapes the formal rules, sometimes effectively changing the meaning of the rule. Informal practices can fold into formal rules that straddle legality and illegality, such as in the case of "menstrual regulation."[75] Joanna Erdman discusses the prevalence of practices that skirt or reinterpret the law, using "menstrual regulation," a practice relied on by women in various jurisdictions, as an example.[76] Women approach health care providers, including midwives, after they miss a menstrual cycle.[77] The provider performs an early medical or surgical abortion to "start menstruation." Because a woman never confirms her pregnancy by taking a pregnancy test, the provider and patient do not consider it a termination.[78] Formal legal rules have most profound effect on abortion practice in the shadow of the law.

Informal Rules

Courts and advocates typically conflate illegal abortion with the risks of unsafe abortion as the problem that formal law cures. In Portugal, the Constitutional Court's decision reflects women's rights advocates' argument that if the law did not allow time-limited abortion, women would inevitably seek dangerous, illegal terminations.[79] According to the Court, this was "the empirical reality of social life" and "incontrovertible data gathered from past experience."[80]

For many women in many countries, however, this is not the reality. In countries like South Africa and Colombia, a well-known informal sector for abortion provision persisted well after legal reform.[81] In South Africa, the illegal abortion rate remains high despite the CTOPA, which guarantees abortion on request through twelve weeks of pregnancy.[82] Studies in Colombia demonstrate that self-induced abortion via over-the-counter drugs persists even for women who could have obtained legal abortions.[83] Given that formal rules may not govern practice as expected or as designed, recognizing and understanding the complex informal norms and rules that govern abortion makes the practice of abortion law intelligible. We might consider, for example, countries with state tolerance of widespread quasi- or extralegal abortion practice.[84]

The increasing availability of safer self-use methods, such as misoprostol, is challenging the common pairing of illegal and unsafe abortion. Multicountry surveys conclude that "misoprostol is widely available" and that "there is an informal network of medical providers and pharmacists" who dispense the drug for pregnancy termination.[85] This "network" is often expanded to include "partners, family and friends, and lay or traditional healers," who offer advice about where to find the drug and how to use it.[86] The nonprofit

organization Women on Waves, for example, maintains country-specific ho-
tlines that explain to callers how to order misoprostol, how to use it, what to
do if complications arise and provide other information relevant to self-
administered abortion. Generally, the drug's appeal is its low cost and the
option to administer at home and the ability it allows for the woman to think
about the termination in whatever terms suit her personal beliefs.[87] Where
state power is diffuse and state resources are limited, reformers might concentrate on building the capacity of these informal networks. State authorities
may even allow efforts to strengthen informal avenues if such measures alleviate the burdens or costs of unsafe abortion and avoid the public controversy
of law reform.[88]

It is a mistake, however, to pretend informal practices are not without
their own dysfunctions or controversies. When administered according to
clinical instruction, the majority of women who use misoprostol complete
their abortions without any complications.[89] But without information, instructions, and supplies, women can face serious consequences from unsupervised or incorrectly supervised use.[90] Given inevitable variations among
localities' informal networks, as well as in information and drug availability,
self-induced termination will not be an acceptable or viable option for certain
populations of women.

Nevertheless the fact that some women in some jurisdictions self-use
misoprostol, after formal liberalization, is a valuable insight into the relationship between abortion law and practice. Informal norms or rules can help
advocates assess what statutory or regulatory interventions will be more or
less useful in protecting women's reproductive health.[91] This requires, however, a more pragmatic comparative method, one that analyzes how law reform intersects with the culture of abortion practice. Close engagement with
existing attitudes as well as family and community structures through which
informal networks operate—considerations largely absent from current litigation strategies—might help reproductive rights advocates and others see
new opportunities and costs of law reform.[92] Strategies that cater to tailored,
local solutions, with the backdrop of state resources, require learning from
local and informal practice.

Background Rules

To learn from practice, however, requires attention not only to the practice itself, but also to the environment of that practice. In the field of public

health law research, Scott Burris gives the example of how land-use laws are pivotal to understanding the efficacy of health care policies: laws governing land use determine options for physical activity, levels of environmental threat, and access to geographically bound services.[93] Understanding how these factors interact with and influence health depends on participatory research that "enlists community members as full partners [and] promises to ground research in local knowledge while at the same time unleashing community capacity."[94]

Background rules include statutes, regulations, and policies that govern health services, families, and individual or group conduct, but do not specifically regulate abortion. These laws nonetheless play an important role in influencing abortion practice. For example, spousal support and child care policies influence many women's choices about pregnancy by shaping their relationships to and responsibilities for partners, parents, or existing children. In many ways, this is already explicit in abortion counseling requirements that include description of the social resources available to mothers and pregnant women. One can think of these counseling scripts as providing a list of the background rules that shape women's roles as caretakers. Broader regulations on health resources within a country's primary care system are background rules that affect abortion practice. The World Health Organization, in its *Safe Abortion: Technical and Policy Guidance for Health Systems*, takes up this issue. It notes that abortion service delivery depends on employment policies to recruit diverse health care professionals, such as nurses, midwives, and health care assistants, and that these policies should standardize how professionals are licensed and what tasks they may perform.[95] Reproductive health campaigns also increasingly recognize that tackling problems in the primary health care system are critical strategies for improving abortion access.[96]

As with informal rules, it is exceptionally difficult to identify background rules from a formalist methodology alone because their influence depends on context and law in practice. An appreciation of how background rules operate fits with a broader trend in comparative law that embraces legal realism and expresses an appreciation for ethnographical research—"the concrete study of norms in their regulatory context."[97] The next section of the chapter turns to research methods by which a comparative functional approach can be undertaken.

Functionalist Research Methods

A functionalist comparative methodology can be found in the emerging field of public health law research (PHLR). This discipline has received increasing attention in recent years because it offers a methodology to improve "investment in and implementation of [health] policy" by collecting data.[98] PHLR studies health outcomes and externalities and seeks to understand these outcomes by using monitoring and evaluation tools. This depends on not only knowing the law but also understanding the social determinants of health, which, as Scott Burris recently noted in the context of the U.S. health care system, means studying family income, social and class status, and other individual and aggregate characteristics.[99]

Public health law research can impart invaluable lessons about how abortion is practiced under law. Among the most important, PHLR starts from the premise, which it more often than not confirms, that the influence of rules other than formal law shape abortion practice. That is, constitutional provisions and criminal prohibitions do not exclusively define "law." Moreover, it is on-the-ground implementation that matters: "It is not just the formal rules, but how these rules are enacted every day in offices by case workers—and clients—who have their own understandings of what the law is, how it relates to other set of rules, and how it can advance or hinder their own goals."[100]

Indeed, a premise of PHLR is that law cannot be taken for granted as a determinative factor in why certain health outcomes occur.[101] PHLR asks, is law having an effect and what sort of effect does law have? Researchers look outside of law to other strategies that can help explain law's effects. To that end, PHLR describes a legal rule and how it operates—does law deter or shame or incentivize or educate?[102] Strategies for reform are then tailored to and around law's influence and function. In reviewing laws that criminalized the unprotected sex of HIV positive individuals, researchers studied the role of self-reporting behavior and whether deterrence, norms of procedural justice, or stigma caused people to comply, ignore, or disobey the law. Researchers concluded that easing access to condoms, altering the physical layout of sex venues, and improving employment among at risk populations helped reduce HIV transmission.[103] The policy prescription was not to strengthen criminal prohibition or rewrite poorly drafted statutes.

In this vein, what might prove important to the study of abortion law is how formal law works in unintended ways, often frustrated by competing background and informal rules. This is what marks PHLR as distinguishable from other kinds of public health research. It evaluates not only the effectiveness of public health intervention in abortion practice, but also the effectiveness of *law* as the tool used to implement or facilitate the intervention.[104] It can provide meaningful comparison by asking what a law achieves and *why* within a given context.

Methodology tools range from quantitative studies of rates and percentages of the number of abortions performed, and by what method and under what circumstances, to qualitative research interviews of women seeking (and providers delivering) services. A key research tool in the field is an implementation study. The method is broadly defined as "the process of putting a law into practice . . . [focusing on the] mediating factors, including the attitudes, management methods, capacities and resources of implementing agencies and their agents; the methods and extent of enforcement; the relationship between the legal rules and broader community norms; and the attitudes and other relevant characteristics of the population whose behavior is targeted for influence."[105]

An implementation study, for example, would examine why women continue to resort to clandestine abortion methods even after law reform. Why in South Africa, even after Parliament amended the law to allow nurses to perform early-term abortions and to increase the number and distribution of approved facilities, do women continue to resort to informal practices?[106]

Rachel Jewkes and her colleagues examined that question. They first reviewed the methods by which women procured abortions, such as through traditional healers, providers working outside of law, or self-induction using medicines.[107] Researchers conducted interviews with women who had resorted to illegal abortion, despite living in a metropolitan community where legal services were available. Researchers spent a total of three weeks with 151 women presenting at hospitals with incomplete abortions and gathered information through questionnaires as well as one-on-one conversations.[108] The study found that most women did not know the CTOPA existed, and, when they had knowledge of the CTOPA, many women did not know the circumstances or the facilities in which an abortion could be performed.[109] For other women who knew what the law provided, they preferred self-induced abortion because they distrusted the health care system, faced long delays in obtaining legal services, or feared the negative attitudes of physicians and health care staff.[110] Thus, the Jewkes study suggests a need for policies and programs that meet those concerns—services, attitudes, education—rather than revision of statutory text or *more* law.

The WHO's *Safe Abortion: Technical and Policy Guidance for Health Systems* offers another public health law methodology—"field-based assessment," which assesses the needs of the community and the capacity of the current system to meet those needs. WHO guidelines recommend that small-scale changes should be undertaken first to determine the feasibility of legal intervention before proposing sweeping law reform. The WHO advises that "it is important that actions to strengthen policies and services are based on a thorough understanding of the service-delivery system, the needs of providers, the needs of women, and the existing social, cultural, legal, political and economic context."[111] This context assessment could include many background rules of influence: laws on sexuality and contraception, policies setting the curricula of medical and other relevant professional schools; rules governing private and public health insurance or other measures that reduce out-of-pocket expenditure.

The purpose of these research methods, including the implementation of pilot programs, is to determine the effect of new rules. Moving from assessment to pilot programs to broader reform, the WHO calls for systematic approaches to "scaling-up," that is, expanding or citing successful legal interventions to recognize "real-world" complexity, with multiple (and often competing) participants and interests. The WHO guidelines acknowledge that "attention to technical concerns is essential, but equally important are the political, managerial and ownership issues that come into play, since interventions to improve access and quality of care often call for changes in values as well as practices."[112] "Scaling-up" is inherently a comparative project that takes as its goal improvement in abortion practice. It models an alternative way of seeing routes to reform, outside of litigation and outside of a closed set of formal rules.

Returning to the example of South Africa, a report on provider attitudes toward the country's abortion services[113] relied on in-depth interviews and discussion groups in eight public hospitals, four nongovernmental organizations, and two clinics linked to educational facilities. Researchers interviewed abortion providers, physicians who did not provide abortion, nurses, and counselors. The study is an example of "scaling-up." Researchers found that health care providers were an impediment to abortion access for reasons of "circumstance and personal interest," which included religious or moral refusal, but also misunderstandings of what law required, lack of facility resources (too many patients, not enough space or beds, for example), and fears of being ostracized given the still prevalent stigma surrounding abortion.[114]

Thus, the report focused first on steps that might address microlevel and community needs, such as increasing providers' compensation. After addressing these measured interventions, the report turned to broader recommendations on the background conditions of health care, including counseling and support for providers and rewards for quality health care services. The study, of note, did not focus on maneuvering judicial or legislative processes.[115]

The approach this chapter describes embraces a certain amount of divergence and disagreement about how to reduce mortality and morbidity for women. How law influences health outcomes; the external and internal pressures on state and community resources; and the bureaucracy of health agencies and administration will change from region to region, place to place. Comparative questions provide a shared starting point: what are the structural and operational determinants for implementing new policies? What individual and system characteristics allow health systems to develop legal initiatives that promote better health care?[116] It is a framework in part defined by what it is not. That is, this approach suspends the assumption that law has a direct or immediate or even a necessarily casual relationship with health outcomes.

Conclusion

A concluding question for this chapter might concern how functionalist comparisons should travel. Advocates bring cases and shape litigation, and often their strategies transfer from case to case. Reproductive rights advocates support the use of comparative and international law in their legal advocacy, but along conventional lines of formalist analysis. In the South African litigation, for example, a brief filed on behalf of the Reproductive Rights Alliance, a nonprofit organization, outlined the comparative arguments that surfaced in the Supreme Court of Appeal's opinion.[117] The brief referred to "three basic human rights norms that protect reproductive rights: freedom, human dignity, and equality;"[118] it then proceeded to rely on U.S. law and legal literature.

This suggests that advocates are important in defining the terms of comparison, as they are often the experts providing courts with information about abortion law at home and abroad. Advocates' briefs could use this influence to introduce a new form of comparative legal argument premised on a functionalist approach. Taking the South African litigation as an example, imagine a strategy in which the purpose of jurisprudential borrowing would be to elucidate implementation problems that may or can follow newly articulated rights. Such a comparative methodology would be concerned with what is compared and with the reasons for comparison: not to authorize a legal reform, but to ask what makes it a legal reform worth adopting, what are its benefits, and what are its risks.[119] Thus, instead of mining foreign texts for support for rights, the Reproductive Rights Alliance might have considered why women continue to consult traditional healers first before seeking care in health institutions,[120] or contemplated the need for information campaigns in rural areas, or explored the option of supporting self-induced medication abortion.[121] This suggestion is not intended to minimize the resources and time that infusing practical considerations, grounded women's experiences, takes. The advantage of a comparative project is that it is one in which models are shared and evolve across countries and time, and is also one in which lessons about gathering useful data and using it effectively travel. Legal advocates' writings could be a means to share this information among national reform projects—not only the solutions for reform, but also the ways of asking questions about reform. Such a methodology may better approach law and interpret rights and rules, vis-à-vis practice.

PART II

Procedural Justice and Liberal Access

Chapter 6

The Procedural Turn:
Abortion at the European
Court of Human Rights

Joanna N. Erdman

A change can be seen in the international world of abortion advocacy, a movement from the reform of laws to their implementation, from legal rights to legal services. This is perhaps a consequence of success, an unmistakable global trend toward decriminalization. More likely, it is a consequence of that success being widely undermined, of abortion services allowed by law but too often denied in practice.[1] Abortion rights advocates have encountered what reform movements have long known: the extraordinary discretion that characterizes criminal justice.[2] Abortion laws themselves do not determine what is or is not allowed. More often the law empowers others—doctors and public prosecutors—to make this determination.

In much of the world, abortion is partially decriminalized, that is, it is regulated by criminal law, but not strictly prohibited. Abortion is allowed in certain prescribed circumstances, commonly where pregnancy endangers a woman's life or health, or results from a criminal act, and where the fetus suffers serious impairment. These circumstances are referred to as the legal grounds for abortion. Common too is third-party authorization, a requirement that doctors or a public prosecutor certify that a legal ground is met in an individual case. In authorization, the problem of discretion arises.

Discretion sometimes manifests in disagreement. Where legal grounds are written in vague terms, interpretive conflicts may arise between doctors and women, or among doctors themselves, on whether a ground is met in the circumstances of an individual case. Doctors may also deny authorization because of their own legitimate fears in the face of an uncertain law. In both cases, the source of the problem ultimately resides in the law. The legal position of a woman cannot be known with any confidence, and rare are the opportunities for review or appeal. This breeds not merely inconsistent but arbitrary practice. Authorizations denied in bad faith, for improper purpose, or in light of irrelevant considerations. In fact the problem of discretion may eventually manifest in arbitrariness writ large. The criminalization of abortion affords doctors coverage to impose their views on women, to deliberately obstruct women's exercise of their legal rights, and to thereby frustrate the intentions of the law.

A transnational litigation strategy has thus emerged, premised on the duties of the state to implement abortion laws through clear standards and procedural safeguards, and to thereby curb the arbitrary exercises of discretion that deny women access to lawful services.[3] Cases can be found in the U.N. system,[4] as well as domestically, in Argentina[5] and Northern Ireland.[6] The strategy explicitly trades on a relationship between substance and procedure: that no law on abortion—however liberal in its substantive rights—can guarantee access to services without procedures of implementation.

This chapter focuses on the turn to procedural abortion rights under the European Convention for the Protection of Human Rights and Fundamental Freedoms.[7] It explores whether and how procedural abortion rights can serve the substantive end that liberalization advocates claim for them: access to services. Through this inquiry, the chapter encounters a well-traveled complexity in the relationship between procedural and substantive rights, how procedure is always related to some substantive end, but often in indirect and complex ways, and sometimes in defiance of intention and expectation.

To capture this complexity, the chapter reads the procedural turn at the European Court of Human Rights from intersecting interpretive worlds. The first part of the chapter traces the turn in the recent abortion case law of the Court and seeks to identify wherein its appeal and danger lie for liberalization advocates. Highlighted is a stumble of arbitrariness: women may be denied services to which they are entitled, or granted services to which they are not. In the latter case, procedural claims for strict standards, review, and oversight are likely to threaten from the other side, with red tape to tighten restrictions on access. This is an especially threatening prospect in countries like Poland and Ireland, the respondent states of the Court's procedural cases, where the law on abortion is primarily framed as protecting the right to life of the unborn. On the logic of the procedural turn, once the state recognizes a substantive right, it is obligated to ensure its effective protection. That procedural rights may be used to both open and restrict access speaks to an ambivalent, if not conservative bent in the turn.

The second part of the chapter takes up this concern, but in a shift of perspective from the advocate to the Court and in light of the political realities of human rights protection in Europe. In Poland and Ireland, abortion carries a symbolic import, bound to conflicts over the very identity of the nation-state. This is the political reality against which a turn to procedure must be read. That is, how can an international human rights court engender change on an issue of deep democratic conflict? The theory offered is that of a pluralistic ethic. By requiring the state under procedural rights of the Convention to make effective the substantive rights of its national law, the Court can accommodate a plurality of rights-based norms, and thereby keep the state engaged rather than alienated from the European human rights project. Even more so, a problem that resides in everyday acts of discretion demands a systemic remedy. Procedural rights enable the Court to work through rather than against the state, to enlist its democratic forces and its legal and political institutions in the effective protection of human rights.

The third part of the chapter shifts perspective again to test the theory of procedural rights in practice. In a final variation, the procedural turn is approached from the pragmatics of reform. The chapter asks about the impact of procedural rights on access to services mediated through the ambitions and actions of legislatures, doctors, and women themselves. Proposed legislation to implement a European Court judgment against Ireland contextualizes the study. With the legislation not yet in effect, the chapter explores feared consequences of the law as voiced in public debate. These mirror the appeal and danger of procedural rights identified in the first part of this chapter. Liberalization advocates fear the state will interpret and use procedural rights to restrict rather than open access. Conservative critics fear procedural rights will liberalize access beyond what the substantive law allows. The chapter tracks the mechanisms by which each consequence is likely to come about.

The Promise of Procedure: The Claim Turns

Tysiąc v. Poland marks the first case under the European Convention in which a woman claimed a right of access to *lawful* abortion.[8] Though abortion is a criminal offense in Poland, statutory law admits to three exceptions, including where pregnancy endangers the woman's life or health.[9] Medical certification of therapeutic need is required for the exception. In *Tysiąc*, certification was refused. The case centered on a disagreement between a pregnant woman fearful of losing her eyesight after a third delivery, and doctors who did not consider that pregnancy or delivery constituted any threat to life or health. The case, however, was not decided by resolution of this conflict. The European Court would not question the doctors' clinical judgment, nor would it decide whether the applicant was entitled to an abortion under Polish law. In fact, the Court would decide no substantive claim at all, especially "whether the Convention [itself] guarantees a right to have an abortion."[10]

The Court turned away from any substantive claim for a right to abortion, and rather resolved *Tysiąc* on the applicant's claim to a "comprehensive legal framework to guarantee [this] right by . . . procedural means."[11] Since Polish law already guaranteed a right to therapeutic abortion, the Court reasoned the case was better decided from the perspective of positive obligations alone, what is required of the state to "secure the physical integrity of mothers-to-be."[12] This is a claim of procedural rights, a claim that would find success at the European Court again and again.

The Court in *Tysiąc* focused on *disagreement*, namely disagreement over whether the therapeutic ground for abortion had been met in a given case, disagreement between the pregnant woman and her doctors, and among doctors themselves.[13] The question was with whom decision-making authority should reside. Polish law granted doctors significant discretion to interpret and apply the law and provided women with no opportunity to challenge refused certification through review or appeal. Not only were doctors free in this manner to act arbitrarily, but they too were vulnerable under law, with no certainty and little security in their actions. In these circumstances, doctors were understandably cautious in their assessments, referred to as the "chilling effect" of the law.[14] Viewed as a whole, the legal system in Poland worked to deny rather than to protect a woman's access to abortion as entitled by law.

The Polish state had failed to provide the applicant with any effective mechanism to determine whether the conditions for a lawful abortion were met in her case, and in this failure breached its positive obligations under the

Convention.[15] The Court explained that "once the legislature decides to allow abortion, it must not structure its legal framework in a way which would limit real possibilities to obtain it."[16] To avoid situations of conflict and to alleviate the chilling effect of the law, "the applicable legal provisions must, first and foremost, ensure clarity of the pregnant woman's legal position."[17]

A clear and certain abortion law was the primary focus of *A, B, and C v. Ireland*,[18] which the Court decided a few years after *Tysiąc*. Once again the case was structured on a division between substantive and procedural abortion rights, which proved consequential in judgment. Applicants A and B argued but lost a substantive challenge to the Irish law, seeking to legalize abortion in cases of risk to health. Applicant C won a procedural right to life-saving abortion, the only legal ground for abortion in Ireland. Unlike in Poland, there are no statutory exceptions to an otherwise strictly worded criminal prohibition in Ireland.[19] In fact, fearing that a court might read liberal exceptions into the prohibition, the Constitution of Ireland was preemptively amended by referendum. By Article 40.3.3, the Constitution now reads, "the State acknowledges the right to life of the unborn and, *with due regard to the equal right to life of the mother*, guarantees in its laws to respect, and, as far as practicable, by its laws to defend and vindicate that right."[20] Interpreted by the Irish Supreme Court, this constitutional provision allows for abortion if "there is a real and substantial risk to life, as distinct from the health of the mother, which can only be avoided by the termination of her pregnancy."[21]

Applicant C suffered from a rare form of cancer and was advised that her pregnancy might affect her prognosis and treatment. She argued that because of the chilling effect of the law, she could not receive accurate information about the risks of pregnancy. Given this uncertainty, and believing she could not therefore establish her entitlement to an abortion in Ireland, she terminated her pregnancy in England.[22] Her claim against the state mirrors that of *Tysiąc*, that authorization for lawful abortion cannot be treated like any other medical matter. This legal responsibility cannot be vested in doctors alone "given the lack of clarity as to what constitutes a 'real and substantial risk' to life . . . [and] the chilling effect of severe criminal sanctions for doctors whose assessment could be considered *ex post facto* to fall outside that qualifying risk."[23]

The European Court agreed. To leave authorization to the ordinary process of a woman consulting her doctor was inappropriate, but so too was the alternative the government offered, constitutional or other judicial proceedings.[24] For the Court in *A, B, and C*, the primary deficiency of the legal framework was not conflicts of interpretation per se, with whom interpretive authority should lie, but that the law on abortion needed to be interpreted over and over again. "That the ground upon which a woman can seek a lawful abortion in Ireland is expressed in broad terms . . . [and] [w]hile a constitutional provision of this scope is not unusual, no criteria or procedures have been subsequently laid down in Irish law, whether in legislation, case law or otherwise, by which . . . risk is to be measured or determined, leading to uncertainty as to its precise application."[25]

After *A, B, and C*, the European Court decided two more cases in the procedural paradigm: both successful and both against Poland. These cases build the jurisprudence of procedural rights incrementally, but subtle shifts are perceptible in the reiteration of the claim. In *R.R. v. Poland*, the applicant developed the information-deficiency claim of *A, B, and C*,[26] that she was denied full and reliable information about the risks of pregnancy, a prerequisite to establish her right to a lawful abortion. Rather than a risk to the woman's life or health, the case concerned a risk of severe or irreversible impairment, a second legal ground under Polish law. The Court found that the applicant's persistent efforts to access prenatal tests were marred by procrastination, confusion, and deliberate obstruction by doctors and administrators.[27] This delayed the diagnosis of fetal impairment and so disqualified the applicant from a lawful abortion within the statutory time limit.[28] Though recognizing the delay and denial of services came at the hands of reticent doctors, the Court again followed the applicant's lead in attributing the rights violation to the state, specifically its regulatory failure to protect women against the obstructive actions of doctors. "If the domestic law allows for abortion in cases of foetal malformation, there must be an adequate legal and procedural framework to guarantee that relevant, full and reliable information on the foetus' health is available to pregnant women."[29]

R.R. differed from *Tysiąc* and *A, B, and C* in that the central controversy of the case was not uncertainty or conflict about whether the applicant qualified for a lawful abortion. Rather it seemed precisely because of the belief that she would qualify, that her efforts to access prenatal testing were frustrated. The regulatory framework was deficient not in its failure to clarify the legal grounds for abortion, nor to resolve conflict about them, but in its failure to constrain the arbitrary actions of doctors–the discretion the law afforded them to impose their views on women, and to thus frustrate the intentions of the law.

This deficiency of Polish law surfaced plainly in the last of the cases, *P. and*

S. v. Poland.[30] The applicants, a mother and daughter, received certification that the daughter's pregnancy had resulted from a criminal act, the last of the Polish statutory grounds. Her formal right to a lawful abortion was uncontested, but she encountered strong resistance in what the Court termed the "procedural and practical modalities" of exercising this right.[31] She was subjected to unwarranted requirements for medical certification, notarized consent, waiting periods, and counseling; was refused an abortion on an administrator's conscientious objection; and eventually received abortion services in a hospital more than five hundred kilometers from her home. The maze-like character of the case, with new frustrations at every turn, led the Court to conclude, "the staff involved . . . did not consider themselves obliged to carry out the abortion . . . on the strength of the certificate issued by the prosecutor."[32] Once again, the state could not rely on its doctors to implement the law on abortion. This was the crux of the applicants' claim and the Court's holding. There was a systemic failure of the state to enforce its own laws and to regulate the arbitrary actions of doctors; that is, actions deliberately intended to frustrate the intentions of the law.

On this reading of the case law, the European Court turned to procedural rights in vindication of claims brought by advocates with the unequivocal goal of liberalization. For this reason, critics have labeled the case law "an attempt to promulgate a full-fledged 'Right to Abortion'—not openly, but through the backdoor."[33] Despite its assertions otherwise, the European Court is accused of vindicating a substantive right to abortion under the guise of procedure.

That a relationship between procedural and substantive rights exists is indisputable, but the nature of that relationship is less certain. The stumble comes in the reality that arbitrariness—where the procedural turn lands in *R.R.* and *P. and S.*—can result in both under- and overinclusion.[34] With vague and broadly written legal grounds, women may be denied services to which they are formally entitled, or granted services to which they are not. Overinclusion may even be endemic to the system as a whole. In these contexts, arbitrariness is the source, not the constraint of liberal access. This being so, procedural claims for strict standards, review, and oversight may come from the other side, as "red tape" to tighten restrictions on access and to ensure that women receive nothing less but also nothing more than the law allows. A contemporary case from New Zealand proves the point.

Right to Life New Zealand filed a claim against the country's Abortion Supervisory Committee for having neglected its statutory duty to oversee the interpretation and application of legal grounds for abortion.[35] A High Court judge found "reason to doubt the lawfulness of many abortions authorized by certifying consultants [doctors] . . . who are apparently employing the mental health ground in much more liberal fashion than the legislature intended."[36] When the case reached the Supreme Court, the committee was reminded not merely of its power, but also of its obligation to "do what is reasonable and practical to ensure the consistent administration of the abortion law through-out New Zealand."[37] While review of individual authorizations was beyond its remit, the Committee could make inquiries of doctors about their general practices, and if the inquiry revealed views inconsistent with the tenor of the abortion law, the committee could report its concerns to disciplinary authorities.[38] Thus lifted from the facts of the European cases and the specific contexts of Poland and Ireland, the procedural turn may not have a liberalizing effect in countries like New Zealand where access relies on the free exercise of discretion.

One may argue that because the procedural turn at the European Court is premised on making effective a legal right, it cannot threaten to deprive access in this way. That is, procedural rights do not require the state to implement restrictions, but only rights. Yet this argument neglects that in many European countries abortion restrictions are treated as a state obligation deriving from the right to life of the unborn. This of course is the case in Ireland, its Constitution not merely acknowledging the right to life of the unborn, but expressly obligating the state to respect, defend, and vindicate it. In Poland, the first provision of the abortion statute on which the applicants relied guaranteed that "every human being shall have an inherent right to life from the moment of conception."[39] The government even argued in *R.R.* that the "Polish law protected the human foetus in the same manner as the mother's life and it therefore allowed for termination of pregnancy only in the circumstances prescribed."[40] In fact, the Polish statute is known as the Anti-Abortion Act, and its legal grounds were drafted to restrict the broad access to abortion formerly allowed under the Communist-era law.

What is more—in a controversial line of cases—abortion law is accepted under the Convention as a measure to protect the right to life of the unborn. In an early set of cases, putative fathers challenged legal grounds for abortion as a violation of the right to life.[41] Rather than decide whether the right to life extends to the unborn, the cases were resolved on the reasoning that even if it did, legal grounds meet "a fair balance between, . . . the need to ensure protection of the fetus and, on the other [hand], the woman's interests."[42] Though unsuccessful, these cases set a foundation for abortion regulation as a measure to safeguard the right to life of the unborn. In *Open Door Counselling and Dublin Well Woman v. Ireland*, the European Court expressly validated restrictive regulation, an injunction on information about legal abortion services abroad, as serving a legitimate aim in the protection of morals, of which in Ireland, the right to life of the unborn is one aspect.[43] This jurisprudential thread culminated in *Vo v. France*, a case about pregnancy termination not by intention, but by medical negligence.[44] The Court again demurred on whether the right to life extends to the unborn but reasoned that even if so, the final question is whether the law satisfies the procedural requirements inherent in the right.[45] With *Vo*, this line of cases merges with the procedural abortion rights cases, compelled by the same logic. A state that extends rights protection to the unborn incurs a positive obligation to ensure that protection is effective, in other words, a positive obligation to enact procedural safeguards.

For some, the ambidexterity of procedural rights—that they are available to both open and restrict abortion access—is not a buried fault, but deliberate in design. It allows an equivocation in the Court's jurisprudence, a feature more maligned than admired in commentary. Many reproductive rights supporters read the procedural cases with disappointment, a Court in retreat from the substantive issues of abortion rights, namely the "critical importance of reproductive control to women's lives."[46] In its abortion jurisprudence generally, the Court is described as unwilling to "come off the fence" and advance the law in this area.[47]

It is difficult, however, to infer the intention or to predict the effect of the procedural turn from doctrine alone. To read the European Court's case law apart from the political context in which it was delivered and in which it seeks to have effect is to miss or rather to misinterpret critical features of it. Human rights practice is located between the technical art of legal reasoning and the realities of political conflict.[48] The chapter's next section offers an account of the procedural turn from this perspective.

The Politics of Procedure: The Court Turns

In his dissent in *Tysiąc*, Judge Borrego Borrego did not criticize the European Court for its timidity. On the contrary, he claimed that the Court's judgment "in its approach and in its conclusions . . . goes too far."[49] Through positive obligations and procedural requirements, the Court was acting as a national parliament, in effect insisting that Poland join the rest of Europe and adopt liberal legislation. In direct provocation, he asked: "Is this the law that the Court is laying down to Poland?"[50]

These comments bring attention to a particular feature of the European Court's procedural cases. They all name Poland or Ireland as the respondent state. This is not a trivial detail. Democratic conflict over abortion runs deep in these countries, profoundly bound to the very definition of the nation-state. The collapse of communism in Europe and the rise of a new Catholic conservatism marked renewed debates on abortion in the former Eastern Bloc. Abortion in Poland became a symbolic issue of political transformation, the fight for the Catholic church's role in public life, and the Christian character of the Polish state.[51] The restrictive abortion law marks this character. "Separation of Church and State does not really exist in Poland today. The explicit language of public laws—especially of those controlling abortion—leaves no doubt about the . . . [Church's] authority."[52] Abortion carries a similar national burden in contemporary Ireland. The campaign for the constitutional amendment on the right to life of the unborn traded on Ireland's inherited religious-cultural traditions—traditions historically used to mark its sovereignty from England.[53] Abortion rights reform continues to be "perceived not only as hostile to religious-cultural beliefs and practices, but also to the very ties that bind the nation state."[54]

The national import of abortion in Poland and Ireland presses a structural principle of the European human rights system: subsidiarity.[55] In one of its formative cases, the European Court affirmed that it will not "assume the role of the competent national authorities . . . [lest it] lose sight of the subsidiary nature of the international machinery of . . . the Convention."[56] Within the system, states are to retain the primary responsibility for rights protection. This principle is defended on the unique character of international human rights law, concerned with matters within the internal order of the state, and which often elude consensus in a pluralistic Europe.

In the abortion case law, the principle of subsidiarity tends to find expression in the margin of appreciation,[57] a doctrine by which the European Court gives state authorities wide discretion to decide the substantive content of their abortion laws. In *A, B, and C*, the Court granted Ireland a wide margin in the substantive challenge to its law. It offered in justification that abortion is a moral issue on which no European consensus can be found, but more so, it is an issue that has engendered a "lengthy, complex and sensitive debate in

Ireland."[58] The Court reviewed the many political processes and consultations on abortion in Ireland, defending the margin of appreciation on the quality of democratic deliberation. By reason of their direct and continuous contact with these vital democratic forces, state authorities are claimed better situated than an international judge to balance the competing rights and restrictions of an abortion law.[59] Yet the margin of appreciation has many detractors, especially among reproductive rights supporters. In *A, B, and C*, the doctrine ultimately defeated the substantive challenge, raising ire in commentary on the case.[60] The central thrust of the doctrine's ill repute is its "caustic, uneven, and largely unpredictable nature," leading to its impression as a gesture of deference pure and simple, a form of rights minimalism.[61] The question is whether the procedural turn in abortion rights is destined to the same fate.

In *Vo*, the Court premised its "even assuming" formula of procedural protection on a margin of appreciation claim, that there was no European consensus on when life begins, but more so, that within France, there was significant debate about what legal protection should be afforded to prenatal life.[62] Commentary, however, reads the move as a pragmatic effort by the Court to avoid interfering with states' laws on abortion.[63] In the procedural abortion rights cases, the Court expressly nods to the modesty of its intervention. Procedural rights ask no more of the state than to make effective rights already accorded in national law. In *A, B, and C*, the Court thus reassured that no democratic injury would be caused. The obligations on the state "could not be considered to involve significant detriment to the Irish public since it would amount to rendering effective a right already accorded, after referendum, by . . . the Constitution."[64] These assurances have triggered criticism of the procedural turn as "deferential, avoidant and normatively neutral"—a Court turned in supplication.[65]

On the case law though, it is exceedingly difficult to maintain that the European Court's turn to procedure does not reach national law. Rather, in each procedural case, the Court finds a breach of the Convention in a structural defect of law, such that the remedy of the violation lies in the law's reform. Yet the Court reaches this conclusion cautiously, through the reasoning rather than the operative parts of its judgments. In these cases, the Court remains tethered, however tenuously, to a mandate of individual justice. The relief it offers is particular and retrospective, granting applicants damages to compensate for the violation of their human rights. The Court has long adhered to this modest conception of its powers in abortion cases, refusing to assess the general validity of laws against the Convention. The earliest abortion cases in the European system, men challenging newly enacted liberal laws for their effect on the "future of the nation," were declared inadmissible on this basis.[66] Even in its procedural cases, the Court has rejected claims on the reasoning that "its task is not to review . . . domestic law and practice in *abstracto*."[67]

Yet between the formal rules lies the practice. What the Court will and has reviewed are claims that attribute the discretionary acts of doctors to a structural defect of law. Where delay or denial in access to lawful abortion results from an interaction required by law, and so threatens to repeat over and over again, more than an ad hoc response is required. A positive obligation is thus claimed and, by judgment of the Court, imposed on the state to effectively prevent these interferences from arising.[68] By explaining how the state currently fails in this obligation, the Court implicitly guides the state on reform of its laws. In the procedural cases, while professing it is not for the Court to say how the state should comply with its positive obligations, the Court nevertheless draws attention to the legislative choices of other European states[69]— notably states with liberal laws on abortion.

More important, most states interpret the European Court's judgments of structural violation in this way: as a directive to change their laws, and follow in reform. In this respect, the European Court is said to perform a constitutional function; that is, its "most important rulings place national policymakers 'in the shadow' of future litigation, provoking a politics of adaptation akin to . . . [what] one finds in national systems of constitutional justice."[70]

The dilemma of the procedural turn is how the European Court may function in this constitutional way, setting standards and expectations for the legal regulation of abortion, while staying meaningfully committed to regime subsidiarity. The Court finds reconciliation in a pluralistic ethos.[71] By requiring the state under procedural rights of the Convention to make effective the substantive rights of its national law, the Court accommodates a coexistence of rights-based norms. Respect for subsidiarity comes first from the substantive rights to abortion being derived from national law, which makes their variation not merely acceptable, but crucial to a human rights system that seeks to build rather than impose consensus.

That the Court seeks to make these rights *effective*, however, is what saves the turn from the downfall of deference.[72] In the procedural cases, the Court reiterated—almost in mantra—that the "*Convention* is intended to guarantee not rights that are theoretical or illusory but rights that are practical and effective."[73] By turning to positive obligations and to procedural rights—by enlisting the state and its laws in making rights *effective*—the European Court seeks to work *through* rather than *against* the national legal order. Moving aside intractable conflicts of substance—the "right to abortion" question— judgments of procedure seek to reengage rather than alienate the state, asking it to return, to reconsider, and to deliberate the relationship between abortion law and practice in light of the Convention. Procedural rights allow the Court to perform a constitutional function, setting standards and expectations, by keeping the state a central actor in the system. Subsidiarity in pluralism thus derives not from deference, but from the recognition that rights protection demands integration. The aim is to have Convention rights *embedded* within the political and legal system of the state.[74]

This impulse is evident in the European Court taking sides, as it were, with national institutions favorable to rights protection.[75] In *A, B, and C*, the European Court is deliberate in tracking expressions of regret in the Irish Supreme Court that "Article 40.3.3 had not been implemented by legislation . . . that, when enacting that Amendment, the people were entitled to believe that legislation would be introduced so as to regulate the manner in which the right to life of the unborn and the right to life of the mother could be reconciled."[76] The Court throughout shares its authority with national legal institutions, blending their calls with its own for legislative clarity and procedure to make effective the constitutional right to abortion.[77] This aspect of the judgment shows continuity in the Court's abortion judgments against Ireland, a continuing effort to engender change from the inside. A few years before *A, B, and C*, the Court declared inadmissible a substantive challenge to the Irish law, for its lack of a legal ground on fetal impairment.[78] The Court refused the case, *D v. Ireland*, on the failure to exhaust domestic remedies; in other words, the applicant had not explored all domestic avenues of redress. That Court reasoned "that in a legal system providing constitutional protection for fundamental rights, it is incumbent on the aggrieved individual to test the extent of that protection and . . . to allow the domestic courts to develop those rights by way of interpretation."[79]

On one account then, the turn to procedure is essential to making human rights *effective*. If the European Court is to address not merely grave violations, but the everyday observance of human rights—to remedy the small acts of discretion that affect women's lives in fundamental ways—it must depend on and build up domestic institutions of rights protection. This is the theory of how substantive obligations and procedural rights work in the European system, and tempting as it may be to take this theory at face value, this chapter does not. The next section asks how procedural rights have or might work outside the Court, on the ground and in practice, focusing on the impact of *A, B, and C* in Ireland as mediated through the actions of legislatures, doctors, and women themselves.

The Pragmatism of Procedure: The Practice Turns

Following *A, B, and C*, the Irish government appointed a group of medical and legal experts to study the judgment and to recommend options for its implementation. Their report was long overdue when tragic circumstances intervened. Savita Halappanavar died in an Irish hospital after being refused an abortion following miscarriage. The fetus, while unviable, still had a beating heart, and so the doctors argued that their "hands were tied." An investigation into her death found "an apparent over-emphasis on the need not to intervene until the fetal heart stopped together with an under-emphasis on . . . managing the risk of infection and sepsis in the mother."[80] The lack of clear clinical guidance on lawful abortion was named a "material contributory factor" in the doctors' decision-making.[81]

The death led to nationwide protests calling for law reform. The abortion regime in Ireland could no longer be claimed a mere technical breach of abstract Convention rights, having shown its injustice in death. Public outrage eclipsed the European Court's judgment and quieted criticism accusing the Court of usurping the constitutional rights of the Irish people. The ruling was now seen as guiding rather than imposing change demanded by the Irish people themselves. Human rights were no longer taken under, but riding atop democratic forces. Within weeks of the death, the government published its expert report.[82] The Irish Human Rights Commission entered the fray, announcing its own review of the expert recommendations, and inviting comment from civil society.[83] Soon thereafter, draft legislation, the Protection of Life During Pregnancy Bill 2013, appeared.[84] At the time of this chapter's writing, the Irish Parliament is debating the bill, with intended enactment before summer recess. Ireland is a state reengaged, but to what end?

The debate on the proposed legislation reveals much about the theory and impact of the European Court's procedural turn. Liberalization advocates fear the Irish government will use procedural rights to restrict rather than open access. Conservative critics fear that procedural rights will crack the right-to-life exception wide open, with access well beyond what the substantive law allows. Both claims warrant further study, for the mechanisms by which their feared consequences are likely to emerge are indirect and complex, and sometimes in defiance of intention and expectation.

Liberalization advocates complained that the bill did not reflect access to lawful abortion as a constitutional right.[85] Rather than entitlement, the bill speaks in the language of permission: what shall be lawful, what shall not constitute an offense. Procedures are then set out to administer these permissions. Primary among them is certification, the very authorization procedure that proved so problematic in the Polish cases. An obstetrician and a relevant specialist, having examined the pregnant woman, must jointly agree that there is a "real and substantial risk" to her life, which can be averted only by termination of pregnancy. In the case of suicide, rather than risk from physical illness, the agreement of three specialists is required. If permission is denied, a woman may apply in the "prescribed form and manner" for a review of the decision. The review committee will examine the woman again, and may request any document or other record from a medical practitioner to assist in its determination. The woman is *entitled* to be heard by the committee, marking the only use of the word in the bill.

Liberalization advocates argue that these procedures *in practice* will prove overly complex and burdensome, that they will delay and deter rather than facilitate access.[86] Ironically the Irish government itself argued this point in *A, B, and C*, disputing that the situation would be improved by adopting a certification process like that of Poland and stressing the simplicity of the Irish system, where a woman who did not agree with the opinion of her doctor was free to seek another.[87] Nonetheless the bill reads like a checklist of the European Court's procedural criteria, and even if it did not, the state enjoys a margin of appreciation in its design. What positive obligations require is not clear-cut, and so the Court predicted or rather ordained that, "having regard to the diversity of the practices followed and the situations obtaining [in states] . . . requirements will vary considerably from case to case."[88] National authorities have the task of interpreting the European Court's judgment, the form and content of the procedures chosen, and the manner of their enactment. In the empirical reality of pluralism, European human rights law may show only as the sum of its implementation in national variation.[89]

The significance of this reality is the lasting relevance, even reassertion, of the national normative order in procedural reform. The restrictive character of the Irish bill is hardly disputed. What for some are access barriers are for others legal safeguards. This is the doublespeak of the bill, evident in its very title, which refers generically to "the protection of life during pregnancy," and so leaves open the intended beneficiary of protection. As described by the government, the objective of the bill is "to provide legal clarity, by way of legislation and regulations, of the circumstances where a medical termination is permissible."[90] It seeks only to regulate a narrow provision of constitutional law, guided by the Irish Supreme Court's narrow interpretation of the provision. It is not for economy alone that the otherwise strict prohibition on abortion is restated in the bill. The proposed law reaffirms and through procedure seeks to safeguard the protection of unborn life. Its adjudicatory and enforcement machinery is almost indistinguishable from procedures designed and used in countries worldwide to curb and control access. The bill follows a common knowledge, that "the greatest inhibitory effects can be expected from narrowly-formulated indications whose application is strictly controlled."[91]

That the European Court's judgment could be plausibly interpreted in this way is foreseeable in the cases themselves. In *Tysiąc*, Judge Bonello concurred with the Court but only insofar as its judgment concerned no substantive "right to abortion, . . . [no] fundamental human right to abortion lying low somewhere in the penumbral fringes of the *Convention*."[92] Dissenting in *R.R.* and *P. and S.*, Judge De Gaetano agreed. These were not "abortion rights" cases per se. They were cases about "regulatory frameworks and procedural mechanisms . . . to enforce a 'right' granted by domestic law in the face of opposition, direct or oblique from public authorities."[93] The content of the right was entirely irrelevant. For this reason, he argued, the claims should have been examined, if at all, under Article 6 of the Convention, which guarantees fair procedure in the determination of civil rights and obligations.[94] The Court, however, decided the cases under Article 8, which made things more difficult, and distorted the true meaning of the provision. On a reading of the case law, his claim speaks some truth.

Article 8 guarantees a *right to respect for private life*, and since the late 1980s, the Court has read implicit positive obligations and procedural protections into the right.[95] As the Court explained in the abortion cases, "while Article 8 contains no explicit procedural requirements, it is important for the effective enjoyment of the rights guaranteed [by this provision] that the relevant decision-making process is fair and such as to afford due respect to the interests safeguarded by it."[96] The problem is that the Court is less than clear about the content of these interests in the abortion cases.[97] It seems to work backward, declaring what procedures are required to protect the right, but hedging on the content of the right itself.

The Court is unequivocal that abortion law falls within the sphere of private life but describes private life as a broad concept, encompassing rights to personal autonomy and development, and to physical and psychological integrity, among others.[98] In *Brüggemann and Scheuten v. Federal Republic of Germany*, the first abortion case decided on the merits in the European system, abortion laws appeared to interfere with autonomy in sexual life.[99] By *Tysiąc*, the focus shifted to physical integrity in therapeutic abortion.[100] In *A, B, and C*, the Court troubled this interpretation by refusing to decide the procedural claim on life-saving abortion under positive obligations of the right to life, which would have been the logical extension of *Tysiąc*, reverting back to unspecified interests under the right to respect for private life.[101] In *P. and S.*, the Court returned to an interest in autonomy, specifically "decisions to become and not to become a parent," despite having earlier—in the very same judgment—confined the right to therapeutic abortion.[102] The case law leaves the most attentive reader confused, with the right to private life seeming to encompass everything, and nothing.

What the Court remained clear and firm about is the essential object of Article 8, "to protect the individual against *arbitrary interference* by public authorities."[103] Whatever interests Article 8 protects, it protects these interests against interference on bad faith, for an improper purpose, or in light of irrelevant considerations. The form of that protection is the rule of law, but of a formalist kind.[104] Arbitrariness is constrained by the rights and restrictions of the national abortion law being set out in clear terms, and strictly applied. Yet by saying nothing on what the content of these rights and restrictions must be—by recognizing no substantive abortion right under the Convention—the law by which the Court constrains arbitrariness is simply the abortion law of the state. The Court says as much, characterizing the violation of Article 8 in the striking *discordance* between the right to lawful abortion, as guaranteed in domestic law, and its practical implementation.[105] In other words, by tying procedural rights to the substantive value of lawfulness, the Court's judgments can be read to support the will of the majority through the rule of law, and to thus stand decidedly on the side of the state.[106] The threatened deference of the procedural turn emerges. This is how the Irish government can claim to implement *A, B, and C*, while reasserting restrictive norms in new legislative form. In *R.R.*, Judge De Gaetano spoke more freely than the Irish government ever would. The "law allows a woman to seek an abortion in the narrowly defined circumstances . . . . One may agree or disagree with that provision of law, but there is nothing this Court can do about it . . . and indeed this Court has not been called upon to do anything about it."[107]

For liberalization advocates, this reading of the case law breeds dangers beyond procedure as a means to tighten access. Other substantive ends threaten. If procedural rights impose no substantive limit on the content of criminal abortion laws, they can be easily evaded. The clearer and more effective a legal ground becomes, the greater the incentive to simply repeal the right of access altogether. This is described as a structural feature of counter-majoritarian procedural rights. The court defines them, but the state can undermine them in substantive reform.[108] Procedural rights, in other words, may drive a state to test its margin of appreciation in enacting a more restrictive law. In 2011, the Polish Parliament narrowly defeated a bill to introduce an absolute ban on abortion.[109] Recriminalization as a political response to procedural rights is especially threatening in Poland because of an underground abortion industry, staffed largely by the certified gynecologists who provide in their private offices what they deny in public hospitals.[110] With the legal prohibition on abortion as underenforced as the legal grounds allowing it, procedural rights may be resisted through substantive reform not on moral opposition, but on financial incentive.

Rather than resist procedural rights, the state may also find them useful in frustrating substantive reform efforts toward decriminalization. Procedural rights make the regulation of abortion through criminal prohibition and legal grounds seem more reasonable, and thus less objectionable. As protection against arbitrariness, they are premised on a belief that legal grounds can be made transparent and accessible, carrying an accepted meaning among those who implement them, and applicable to concrete situations without convolution or excessive difficulty.[111] Yet whether legal grounds are at all amenable to this task is never considered in the case law. Procedural rights only make sense if the underlying substantive law is not itself arbitrary. This is hardly true.[112]

The European Court proceeds on the assumption that legal grounds correspond to objective facts about the world. In *A, B, and C*, however, the applicant argued that a "legal distinction, without more, between a woman's life and her health was an unworkable distinction in practice."[113] This is because the distinction is based in normative, not empirical fact. As exemptions from criminal sanction, legal grounds reflect moral judgment. In *R.R.*, the Court explained that the applicant's entitlement to a lawful abortion could not be determined because there was "no consensus in Poland as to whether Turner syndrome . . . [was] a serious enough malformation within the meaning of the 1993 Act [statute] to justify a legal abortion."[114] Once again, the required seriousness for criminal exemption stems not from a medical but a moral determination.

Yet the promise of precise legal grounds suggests they do have an empirical validity. Legal grounds are treated as some kind of natural classification system, with designations like "therapeutic" a real property of the abortion, rather than a label assigned to it. By turning normative judgments into objective standards, the procedural turn serves a legitimating function. It creates an air of objectivity in authorization. That the criminal law looks more rational and so less threatening leads to its greater acceptance and so frustrates efforts to impugn the criminal regulation of abortion as arbitrary all the way down, to the very constituent parts of the law itself.

The doublespeak of the Irish bill and the chronic vacuity of legal grounds— that they are malleable, even manipulable in moral judgment—cut both ways. The second major claim about the Irish bill in public debate is that it is a gateway to liberalization beyond what the constitution and criminal law allow. Conservative critics claim the language of the bill is too vague, that through patient-doctor collusion and routine circumvention, it will facilitate ever-expanding access to abortion.[115] Its narrow permissions will stretch, and its onerous procedures will soften. Critics speak of the bill as a "legislative and political 'Trojan Horse'," which not tomorrow or the next day, but over time will lead to ever more permissive attitudes and practice.[116] The critics are not without precedent in their fear. Doctors who work the gaps and ambiguities of abortion law mark the history of informal decriminalization, that is, of regulatory schemes, toppling into ever more liberal variants.[117] New Zealand is not alone in this regard.

Given that legal grounds reflect contested norms of justification, the state cannot itself define the limits of its laws. For the state is not the only, not even the primary, source of norms within the system. Though authorization is a legal task, when performed by nonlegal actors in nonlegal settings, a variety of influences inform it. Doctors interpret the law in a way that coincides with what they otherwise think is the correct outcome, particularly where concepts like risk and illness carry an accepted meaning for them outside of law.[118] They come to their decision first and then sanctify it with law. Where doctors are secure in their determinations under law, without fear of prosecution or discipline—as proposed by the Irish bill—the law's interpreters become the lawmakers. That is, the problem of discretion in the procedural cases now threatens from the other side.

The most likely mechanism of an informal drift toward liberal access is marked in the Irish bill itself. It is the only procedure written as an entitlement of women, and one the European Court expressly named in its judgments. "What has to be determined is whether, having regard to the particular circumstances of the case and notably the nature of the decisions to be taken, an individual has been involved in the decision-making process."[119] To this end, abortion regulation must "guarantee to a pregnant woman at least a possibility to be heard in person and to have her views considered."[120]

In naming the right to be heard, the Court thickened its conception of the rule of law. Protection against arbitrariness is not confined to women being treated in accordance with the national law on abortion. The right to be heard introduces substantive norms into the regulation of abortion, sufficient to change its tenor. The potential and controversy of the right can be seen in the *Tysiąc* dissent, which rebuked the Court for having treated the applicant's fears as relevant to authorization, especially against medical expertise and the authority of law.[121] Yet this is precisely the point. In naming the right to be heard, the Court challenged, however obliquely, a basic premise of restrictive abortion laws: that women are things to be acted on, rather than respected as persons who act. The right to be heard is a procedural right classically tied to norms of respect, worth, and dignity.[122] That a woman is to be heard before authorization may be denied is the minimum required of the state to respect her worth as a person.

To involve a woman in the determination is to signal that her view on the subject matters. A woman's fear of blindness, or her risk of unemployment while raising three children alone, is relevant to the determination of her legal right. A woman's fear of caring daily for a severely ill child and of the toll it will take on her family are relevant to any decision taken. Within a right to be heard sits a respect for personal autonomy and development, substantive interests associated with the most liberal of abortion regimes. To the extent legal grounds are concealed judgments of moral worth, of which the Court now seems aware, the views of women are entirely relevant—and may even come to be the interpretive influence that will crack the legal grounds open, the mechanism of liberal access.

Yet access premised on voice raises concerns from social inequality. Which women can or will be heard? Misaligned incentives threaten to frustrate the liberalizing potential of this right. Women with means will exit rather than fight the system, accessing abortion clandestinely or abroad. The poor, the less able, and the less educated are resigned to access abortion within the system, but they are also the most burdened and threatened by it.

For a woman who does not know the words to say, the claims to convince, the right to be heard may seem a cruel gesture. Rather than being powerless in prohibition, a woman is enlisted—made a part—of the very process of her denial, an author of her own misfortune. The right to be heard becomes a procedure of placation, that having been heard, she might better accept the inevitable and quietly go home.[123] Procedural rights again threaten to legitimate what is ultimately an unjust law.

Conclusion

Even as they implement criminal abortion laws against women, procedural rights affirm that women must be treated with respect, worth, and dignity. Procedural rights may thus advance substantive ends distinct from, even at odds with, the substantive law they enforce. In this respect—as the chapters of this collection suggest—the European Court has adopted a primary modality of contemporary abortion law. In the constitutional review of liberal abortion laws, European courts have come to vindicate the autonomy rights of women within state protection of unborn life.[124] Procedures like counseling and authorization are repurposed to serve substantive ends that yesterday they frustrated.

Constitutional law appears to share the normative ambiguity of the procedural turn in international law. An ambiguity that lies not in fault, but in seeking to embrace a pluralistic ethos in the adjudication of abortion, to make room for the coexistence of contested norms. As Reva Siegel describes, "rather than endeavoring to impose values, courts often employ techniques that inform politics with constitutional value."[125] The European Court offers procedural rights as one such technique. By turning to positive obligations and to procedural rights, the European Court seeks to work *through* rather than *against* the state. It seeks to engender change by drawing on the strength of democratic forces within and by acting with rights-protecting institutions of the state, to keep the state at the center of the system, even while seeking to transform it.

Yet the passive virtue of procedural rights invites a large measure of indeterminacy in the substantive change engendered, sometimes even perverse outcomes. For this reason the chapter does not study the procedural turn of the European Court in doctrine alone, fearful of missing the complex and subtle ways in which the turn is likely to have its most profound effects.

Looking to how rights and obligations of procedure in abortion law are claimed, interpreted, and implemented over time, the chapter focuses on law as multivalent. The significance of the procedural turn in abortion law will not be heard in a solitary voice—of the advocate, the court, the state, a doctor, or a woman—but in their blended discord.

Chapter 7

The Struggle Against Informal Rules on Abortion in Argentina

Paola Bergallo

Since 1921, Argentina's National Criminal Code (NCC) has allowed abortion for specified indications. The text of NCC's Article 86 reads:

> Abortion performed by a licensed medical practitioner with the consent of the pregnant woman is not punishable:
>
> 1. If done in order to prevent danger to the life or health of the mother and if this danger cannot be avoided by other means.
>
> 2. If the pregnancy is a result of a rape or indecent assault on an idiot or insane woman. In this case, the consent of her legal representative shall be required for the abortion.[1]

Where abortions are not provided for these indications, Article 85 establishes penalties of up to ten years for providers and up to four years for women undergoing abortions. This original 1921 wording of Article 86 underwent modifications during the dictatorships, but in 1984, President Alfonsín rolled back the dictatorial reforms to the criminal code,[2] and the text recovered its 1921 wording. However, since 1984, abortions to save a woman's life or health and in cases of rape were rarely available in the different sectors of the Argentine health system. This lack of legal abortion services for the Article 86 indications could be described as the result of an "informal rule" banning the practice.

This chapter tells the story of the recurring confrontations between proponents of the "informal rule" establishing a de facto prohibition of legal abortion services, and those seeking to foster compliance with the "formal rule" allowing women's access to abortions authorized by Article 86. As scholars of informal institutions have argued, informal rules and procedures are key to structuring the "rules of the game" as they shape how democratic institutions work and can reinforce, subvert, or even overturn formal rules, procedures, and organizations.[3] Moreover, in weak democratic contexts, informal rules can operate in what is called the "brown areas" of the state. These areas are characterized by "low-intensity citizenship," where citizens are not engaged in the institutions of government, and the "(un)rule of law where there is the uneven and arbitrary application of the law by public officials, reinforcing inequalities."[4]

This chapter shows that since the late 1980s, conservative actors deployed an array of legal arguments and strategies that inhibited the provision of legal abortion authorized by Article 86. Such efforts succeeded in subverting formal rule and establishing a competing informal rule. But starting in 2005, progressive actors began to deploy new strategies to enforce the duty to provide legal abortions. These legal fights in provincial, national, and international settings signaled a shift toward the proceduralization of abortion regulation as a means to dismantle the informal rule. This procedural turn developed out of court orders following the litigation of individual cases to access legal abortions, the recommendation of international human rights committees, and the approval of legal abortion protocols by provincial ministries of health. Proceduralization involved establishing new precedents and rules regulating the provision of legal abortion services by public and private health providers. These precedents specified the legal criteria for assessing the danger to the life or health of the women, clarified the scope of the rape exception, and enforced the existing legal duties of medical professionals and institutions. What has been the trajectory of this procedural turn? Who were the actors involved in the confrontation between formal and informal rules? What are the changes and continuities brought about by the procedural turn? This chapter seeks to answer these questions and find lessons for further legal reform.

With that goal in mind, the first part of the chapter illustrates the power of informal rules to subvert formal law by examining the development of the de facto total ban on abortion services. It shows how, in the first two decades of democratic transition beginning in 1983, conservative groups succeeded in fostering a restrictive interpretation of Article 86 abortion indications. The second part of the chapter offers an account of the enduring struggle to overturn that informal rule and to reinstate the formal rule that mandated the provision of legal abortions. Since 2005, momentum to replace the informal rules has gained force through a procedural turn and a renewed interpretation of the NCC in light of the Constitution and human rights treaties. The final part of the chapter explores how the procedural turn accelerated its impact when the Supreme Court redefined the legal debates around Article 86 in its *F., A.L.* decision.[5] The chapter concludes with a brief discussion on the limits and possibilities of proceduralization.

The Consolidation of an Informal Rule Banning Abortion

For most of the twentieth century the Article 86 exceptions to the criminalization of abortion did not translate into the availability of legal abortion services. Indeed, throughout the first ninety years of its operation, the indications model worked as a set of exceptions only on paper. Evidence as to the availability of abortion services during this period is scarce since no official records were kept. However, there is no evidence of the services being available to the public or even evidence of the health care infrastructure necessary to provide lawful abortions.

Research into health providers' views on abortion in the late 1990s, suggests that a majority of actors within the health system understood that abortion was or should have been prohibited, irrespective of the text of Article 86.[6] The subversion of the formal law of Article 86 by an informal rule effectively banning abortion services could be explained by several factors. Scholars of informal institutions in Latin America have pointed to at least four reasons why informal institutions emerge.[7] They explain that informal institutions may result from the "incompleteness" of formal rules that cannot cover all possible contingencies. In such cases, actors exploit ambiguities in their favor. Second, informal rules might arise where there is weak enforcement capacity resulting from institutional deficiencies. Third, actors may push for the creation of informal rules when they lack power to foster formal rule change or think that it would be too costly. Finally, actors might use informal rules to set up publicly unacceptable goals—ranging from the unpopular to the illegal.

A combination of these four factors may explain why legal abortion services were not available from 1921 until very recently. Article 86's incompleteness and its lack of implementation for several decades led to uncertainty that could partially account for the failure of the health community to offer legal abortion services. It was not clear what type or magnitude of danger would justify a legal abortion. Similarly, the scope of the rape exception was not clearly defined—did the exception apply to all women who became pregnant as a result of rape or only to women with mental disabilities? Further, the persistent legal disputes among prestigious liberal and Catholic criminal law scholars may also have contributed to the misunderstanding in the health community about the validity of Article 86. On the other hand, the more fundamentalist conservative groups knew that they lacked the power to foster the reform of the Criminal Code to totally ban abortion as they learned during the 1994 constitutional convention, where they failed to establish a total prohibition of abortion. Moreover, a total ban on abortion would have also been politically unacceptable and unconstitutional given the women's rights incorporated into the 1994 constitutional amendments.

But how did conservatives move to establish the informal rule banning the provision of legal abortions? After the democratic reforms of the 1980s, some actors began to request an indications model to regulate abortion, and some rape victims reached out to the courts demanding legal abortions. As these demands were emerging in the late 1980s, conservative actors were already organized around the defense of the absolute right to life of the unborn, allegedly protected by Article 33 of the Constitution as an implicit right and by Article 4.1 of the American Convention on Human Rights protecting the right to life "in general" from the moment of conception.[8] In the course of the following decade, conservative groups succeeded in frustrating access to legal abortions by exploiting the uncertainties in the indications model and profiting from weak institutional enforcement mechanisms, thereby consolidating an informal rule subverting Article 86.

As a result of this conservative mobilization, the return of democratic rule did not mean much in terms of abortion liberalization for Argentine women. Unlike in Spain, where the transition to democracy resulted in the adoption of new divorce and abortion regimens, in the first decade of Argentina's democratic transition the approval of a new divorce law was not accompanied by the adoption of abortion reforms.[9] In fact, after the 1980s, actors in the health system and in the political and the judicial realms opposed the Article 86 exceptions, stating that the Constitution and human rights law required the prohibition of abortion. Neither enforcement institutions nor progressive actors were able to succeed in interpreting Article 86 as requiring the actual provision of legal abortion services. Conservative claims operated in establishing what has been called "a moral veto."[10]

Actually, in the mid-1990s some conservative groups organized to fight for the formalization of the total prohibition of abortion. During the 1994 Constitutional Convention, representatives of the right wing of the Menem government with strong ties to Opus Dei pushed for the adoption of a clause protecting life from conception in the reformed text of the Constitution. However, former president Raúl Alfonsín (leading the convention), some liberal members of the Constitutional Assembly, and an initiative put forward by several women's organizations that became known as MADEL succeeded in keeping the subject off the floor of the convention.[11]

In the following years, despite their failure to enshrine a formal constitutional clause recognizing the right to life from conception, conservative groups succeeded in further consolidating the informal prohibition of abortion services, through a series of legal debates that took place in legislatures and courts across the country until the 2002 crisis. Once conservatives failed to achieve formal legislative change of Article 86, they worked to inhibit access to Article 86 abortions. After the 1994 constitutional reform, conservatives argued that the granting of constitutional status to the Inter-American Convention on Human Rights and the U.N. Convention on the Rights of the Child implied that Article 86 of the NCC had become "prospectively unconstitutional." Conservatives continue to use these arguments in judicial cases opposing legal abortions of anencephalic fetuses[12] and in cases opposing emergency contraception.[13] They also appealed to this argument in the Senate to oppose the adoption of a national reproductive health statute that in 1996 was passed by the House of Representatives but lost parliamentary status two years later because of strong pressures from conservative groups and leaders of the Catholic Church.[14]

A turning point came with the final congressional passage in 2002 of the National Reproductive Health Law, creating a program to promote reproductive health counseling and access to contraception.[15] Although the new law excluded abortion services, the debate about abortion that followed its approval signaled the beginning of a new era in the overturn of the informal rule establishing the ban. In 2004, the Consejo Federal de Salud (COFESA), a gathering of the ministries of health of the twenty-four provinces and the National Ministry of Health, committed to reduce maternal mortality rates, a third of which were caused by unsafe abortions.[16] In 2005, the National Ministry of Health ended its historic inaction on the subject and established a post-abortion care program. Thanks to the Campaña Nacional para el Aborto Legal, Seguro y Gratuito (the National Campaign for the Right to Legal, Safe and Free Abortion) (hereinafter la Campaña), created that same year by the country's women's movement, a bill to decriminalize abortion was filed for the first time in Congress in 2006. Meanwhile, la Campaña began to claim the adoption of procedural regulations under Article 86, a short-term strategy, while pursuing the longer-term goal of decriminalization.

After some of these policies began to be implemented, debates on abortion involving high-profile figures focused the attention of the media.[17] Also, at the same time, a number of women requesting Article 86 abortions began to reach the public health systems of different provinces. When confronted with the demand for services they had not offered before, health care providers began to request court authorization to perform abortions they understood were prohibited. As explained below, these cases marked the intensification of the fight to destabilize the informal rule banning abortion, and to replace it by a practice where legal abortions gradually became available.

Overturning the Informal Rule Through Procedural Shifts

Formal-informal rule relationships are dynamic. During the first two decades of democratic rule, the informal rule on abortion had displaced the provisions of the NCC, producing a "crowding out" effect, that is, inhibiting the development of an effective formal rule by dampening demands for legal abortion services.[18] However, as this sections shows, informal rules can be subverted through recurring legal confrontations aimed at reinstating the valid formal rule. In the case of the fight for legal abortion, the strategy for enforcing Article 86 included a turn toward procedure that went through several rounds in provincial and national courts, legislatures, and ministries of health, and in international forums.

The Confrontation in Provincial Courts

Provincial courts became a setting for the enforcement of Article 86 of the NCC from 2005 to 2012. A systematic observation of the three main legal periodicals of the country (*La Ley, El Derecho,* and *Jurisprudencia Argentina*) and media coverage in national newspapers (*La Nación, Clarín,* and *Página*

12) and in the provincial newspapers (*El Día* and *La Voz del Interior*) between 2005 and 2012 shows different types of cases reaching courts in search of abortion services.

A first group of cases emerged when women facing acute illnesses or representatives of mentally disabled rape victims, often the victims' mothers, sought legal abortion services in public hospitals in the provinces of Buenos Aires, Mendoza, Entre Ríos, and Santa Fe. In such cases, courts were usually called on to authorize or deny Article 86 abortions, and in the case in Santa Fe, they were invited to investigate the physicians who had denied a legal abortion for a terminally ill woman. The cases received wide media coverage and inspired heated national debates. In all of these decisions, the courts insisted that women did not need to seek judicial permission for abortions when they found themselves in the circumstances specified under Article 86.[19] In the context of important interpretative disagreements within the health and legal communities, some of these decisions helped to clarify the constitutionality of the indications for lawful abortion.

In one of these lawsuits argued before the courts of the Province of Buenos Aires, *C.P. de P.A.K.*,[20] a mother was requesting the authorization of an abortion given the danger posed by the pregnancy to her health since she suffered from a chronic heart disease.[21] Although no rule required prior judicial authorization, the physicians of a provincial public hospital demanded it in order to proceed with a legal abortion. After the court of first instance and the Court of Appeals denied the authorization, the provincial Supreme Court finally granted it.

In a new conflict in the same province, the mother of *L.M.R.*,[22] a minor with a mental disability who had been raped, found herself in litigation, initiated by the prosecutor investigating the rape, after the mother had complied with the rape reporting requirement as a precondition to accessing abortion. The Supreme Court of the Province of Buenos Aires ultimately authorized the abortion, but the delays and difficulties in finding a doctor to perform the procedure revictimized *L.M.R.* and her family.

These two cases received extensive coverage from the media,[23] and, as a result, other women across the country began to apply to courts seeking access to Article 86 abortions. This was the case of Ana María Acevedo,[24] a pregnant mother of two children who had been diagnosed with terminal cancer and whose experience was particularly poignant as she died after being denied pain killers and was forced to continue the pregnancy in order to protect the fetus. Unlike other cases resulting in judicial refusals of necessary medical services, this case resulted in a criminal investigation of the doctors and the hospital director who had denied Ana María Acevedo the abortion.[25]

The emergence of these cases marked a turning point that provoked the approval of a first round of procedural guidelines. However, even after some guidelines were put in place the demand for courts' authorization as a precondition for the abortion services did not stop. Until early 2012, cases continued reaching the courts of Buenos Aires, Chubut, Entre Ríos, Mendoza, Misiones, Río Negro, Santiago del Estero, and Salta, when rape victims or severely ill women demanded termination of their pregnancies. In all of these cases, opposition to or mere restrictions of the actual availability of legal abortion services was often exercised without much substantive legal debate. Those defending restrictive interpretations of the legal indications for abortion basically advanced two main arguments. A first set of arguments questioned the constitutionality of the legal indications for abortion. Conservatives argued that Article 86 violated a constitutional duty to ban abortion that emerged out of the implicit protection of the right to life (Article 33 of Argentina's Constitution), and in Congress's ability to pass laws for the special protection of infancy from the moment of pregnancy (Article 75[23] of the Constitution). Furthermore, they appealed to Article 4.1 of the American Convention on Human Rights protecting life "in general, from the moment of conception." In the same manner, they cited Argentina's declaratory interpretations upon ratifying the Convention on the Rights of the Child.[26]

The second type of case accepted the constitutional status of Article 86 but questioned aspects of its design including (a) the scope of the exceptions, and (b) the legal status of the indications, either as a justification or an absolving excuse (in Spanish, *causal de justificación* or *excusa absolutoria*). Even among conservatives, there was no consensus about the scope of the exceptions or even the legal status of the indications. More moderate conservatives are open to interpreting the indications for abortion under Article 86 as legal. They accept that women could, under exceptional circumstances, obtain abortions under Article 86, but they vary in the extent to which they read the indications for cases of rape and of danger to women's health. Some defend a restrictive interpretation by demanding that the risks to women's health be severe and pertain only to physical health and narrowly interpret the rape exception to apply only to "idiot or demented" women.

The Fight for Legislative and Administrative
Procedural Guidelines

In some of the lawsuits mentioned above, women's activists and lawyers collaborated in the search for access to legal abortion services while contributing to bolster public discussions on the need for further reforms. Indeed, since the emergence of the first cases mentioned above, women's organizations, especially those gathered around la Campaña, also advocated for the adoption of new medical guidelines that could help avoid the judicialization of abortion demands, just as the judges in the aforementioned cases had called for. A number of different actors worked hard to establish procedural guidelines in order to destabilize the informal rules, which thrived on uncertainty. Ultimately the procedural guidelines were approved in a number of provinces and displaced the de facto ban on all abortion services.

This struggle for proceduralization began with a first stage characterized by the adoption of simple procedural rules followed by minor or nonexistent implementation policies. After a few experiences, the fight transitioned to a second phase, when the guidelines became justified in rights terms and accompanied by increasing degrees of compliance. A third stage of the procedural turn finally arrived when the Supreme Court decided *F., A.L.* in early 2012. All these changes coexisted, however, with extensive areas of the country still subject to the informal rule.

The First Stage: The Adoption of Simple Rules

The litigation of the cases discussed above prompted a number of regulatory initiatives seeking to destabilize the informal rule totally banning abortion. The first institutional reply to the demands for procedural guidelines that women's organizations had posed since La Campaña was created came from the Instituto Nacional contra la Discriminación, la Xenofobia y el Racismo (National Institute Against Discrimination, Xenophobia and Racism) (INADI), directed by a feminist advocate, María José Lubertino. The INADI issued a recommendation concerning the justification and regulation of "nonpunishable abortions." The recommendation, which followed a procedural rule model, framed the debate as an antidiscrimination issue.[27] Subsequently, a group of regulatory guidelines was adopted defining procedures for Article 86 abortions in the health systems of the cities of Buenos Aires and Rosario and the provinces of Buenos Aires and Neuquén.[28] Nine decades after the enactment of the NCC, more than half of Argentina's women were suddenly living in jurisdictions whose "books" regulated the provision of legal abortions. Even though the new procedural guidelines represented only a formal message in the path toward overcoming the prevalent informal rule, they revealed an unprecedented will in provincial public health authorities to redefine their role in interpreting the NCC and regulating the conditions for the provision of legal abortion services.

The guidelines of this first generation were brief explanations of procedures. They clarified the impropriety of requiring judicial authorization and reminded doctors of their duty to educate themselves on the procedures for legal abortion. They regulated the functioning of expert committees, the requirement for informed consent, and the formalities for the representation of minors and women with disabilities.

In 2007, the National Ministry of Health, then headed by Ginéz González García, took another important step in the struggle to replace the informal rule inhibiting the supply of legal abortions and asked the National Program on Reproductive Health and Responsible Parenthood (hereinafter the NPRHRP) to develop a national protocol following the World Health Organization's abortion guidance[29] and those approved in Brazil[30] and Colombia.[31] Late that year, the NPRHRP announced that the Guía para la Atención Integral de los Abortos No Punibles[32] (hereinafter, the Guide) was ready. However, the Guide was not approved and González García left his position in the Ministry of Health when Cristina Fernández de Kirchner became president in late 2007. Graciela Ocaña, the newly appointed minister of health took the position that abortion was a matter of criminal law and policy and remained silent about the Guide until she left office in mid-2009.

The frustration of the National Ministry of Health's project to adopt procedural guidelines was not an isolated case. The failure of two provincial initiatives in Mendoza and La Pampa reflected the determination of conservative groups to oppose the adoption of new rules and their temporary political success in the context of the change of presidential mandate. Moreover, the new ministers of health appointed for the city of Buenos Aires and the province of Buenos Aires at the time also stopped the implementation of the first procedural guidelines that had been approved during 2007.

A year later, only the province of Neuquén, well known for its more integrated and better functioning public health system, had moved forward to tenuously implement the first regulations and to guarantee legal abortions in some cases.[33] The development of policy initiatives to foster the implementation of the regulations in the province and the city of Buenos Aires was paralyzed, and the adoption of new guidelines or national standards in other provinces seemed out of the question. Moreover, an example of the lack of implementation policies of the guide approved in the province of Buenos Aires is addressed by the case of *S.G.N.*,[34] which reached the courts of the city of Bahía Blanca when the mother of a mentally disabled rape victim requested an abortion. The facts of the case were similar to those in *L.M.R.*,[35] but they took place in the province of Buenos Aires where guidelines had clarified the procedures to provide abortions for rape victims. The *S.G.N.* case showed that access to abortion for mentally disabled victims of rape was not available, in spite of the resolution requiring its provision.

The Second Stage: Guidelines Are Justified in Rights Terms

In spite of this bleak panorama, the struggle to overturn the informal rule continued as progressive actors put forward new strategies to fight in the open interstices. Feminists and other progressive players mounted a series of legal encounters to push for more ambitious procedural rules. The new regulatory proposals could be interpreted as part of a second phase in the procedural turn. In this second stage, new instances of congressional deliberation were organized and helped to inspire a more specific set of guidelines following the innovations proposed in the first version of the 2007 Guide developed at the request of the National Ministry of Health.[36]

At the national level, the initiatives that had a key antecedent in the Guide moved to Congress in 2008, where committee deliberations about a bill to amend Article 86 of the NCC took place. Two years later, once again, such initiatives returned to the Ministry of Health, where a second version of the Guide was commissioned.[37] Neither of these strategies was successful, however. Congressional deliberations to reform Article 86 were seen as untimely, given the more ambitious hope for the adoption of a repeal law promoted particularly by progressive actors and la Campaña.

Despite the blockages experienced at the national level, some provinces began to offer new opportunities to propose and debate procedural rules. A new stage in the turn to procedure took place when the city of Buenos Aires and the provinces of Santa Fe and Chubut considered, and in the last two, approved, procedures for the legal termination of pregnancy.[38]

This second phase of the procedural turn can be traced back to the initiative of four legislators of the city of Buenos Aires from different political parties, including a representative of the Frente para la Victoria, the president's party. These legislators kicked off the new stage in the procedural turn in 2008 when they filed draft bills to regulate the provision of abortion services through a statute.[39] The project generated a series of legislative committee meetings and open public hearings in which experts and civil society representatives argued for and against the bills. Although they were not passed, the bills provided for significant public deliberation on aspects of the procedural turn not discussed in the first stage of the procedural turn.

Moreover, other provincial regulatory initiatives continued to foster tenuous changes to overturn the informal abortion ban. In 2009, the socialist government of the province of Santa Fe was the first to adopt, through a ministerial resolution,[40] the 2007 Guide commissioned by the National Ministry of Health, but never implemented at the federal level.[41] However, the total prohibition of abortion was still the rule in most of the country, even in most of the provinces with procedural guidelines.

But the fight against the informal rule continued, and new judicial decisions from Río Negro and Chubut authorized the performance of abortions requested by victims of rape who were not mentally ill.[42] Building on these precedents, the cases of *F., A.L.*[43] and *M.*,[44] decided in 2010 by the Supreme Court of Chubut, represented milestones in the emergence of a new judicial perspective on the state's duty to ensure legal abortion services. In its *F., A.L.* decision, the Supreme Court of Chubut established an historic precedent by authorizing an abortion in the case of an adolescent victim of rape and urged other state bodies to regulate the procedures for the provision of legal abortions. The decision suggested that judges had begun to consider the institutional dimension of a right that required the regulation of access to services in order to subvert enduring informal obstructive practices. Two months later, Chubut's legislature unanimously approved a law establishing the procedures for Article 86 abortions.[45] Conservative groups were not able to veto the move, and once the law was approved, the provincial Ministry of Health began to work in its implementation.

These decisions and regulatory guidelines required that the NCC be interpreted according to the Constitution and human rights treaties. They referenced various women's rights and gender equality, and they reframed abortion demands in a language sensitive to women as rights holders. This expansion also reflected new norms and a constitutional duty to promote gender equality, which gave Article 86 a constitutional basis that was not envisioned by the congressmen who passed the NCC in 1921. Taken together, these developments reflected minor improvements toward the dismantling of the informal rule when compared to the first stage of the procedural turn.

With regard to the health indication, the guidelines clarified that health should be defined holistically according to the World Health Organization. And with regard to the rape indication, they clarified that the exception pertains to any rape victim, not just rape victims who were developmentally disabled. In doing so, the guidelines demanded a substantive interpretation of law, with a focus on human rights. Also, they exhibited a transformation in the understanding of regulatory guidelines as a tool to promote better interpretations of the indications, a function that even progressive legal scholars had opposed in earlier debates.

The new regulations further detailed procedures for the application of the indications, taking a clear position on controversial issues that had arisen in the earlier protocols. Thus, the new norms defined that health grounds will be confirmed only by a professional in the relevant area of medicine or mental health, while also waiving the requirement to report the rape, which had been a de facto precondition to have a request for abortion services considered. The new regulations also mandated that complete and accurate information be provided to women seeking abortions; prohibited treatment delays; warned about the possibility of administrative or criminal sanctions; and addressed the duties around confidentiality and conscientious objection.

The new phase in the procedural turn was also accompanied by a number of important changes at a political level that affected the legitimacy of the law reform processes. To begin with, the regulations were followed by the growing development of some *implementation tasks* by health care providers at the provincial level. In Buenos Aires, Chubut, Neuquén, and Santa Fe, ministerial provincial authorities led the implementation. Furthermore, in Santa Fe for example, the implementation advanced the regulation of other issues, such as requiring that the providers' rights of conscience are exercised without obstructing or denying women's access to services.

The expansion of channels for participation and public debate beyond the already committed feminist groups in la Campaña was also important. Deliberations involved (a) the presence of professionals from diverse disciplines in the legislative debates of the city of Buenos Aires, (b) the participation of national and international organizations through amicus curiae briefs presented in cases, such as the case before the Chubut Supreme Court, (c) the issuing of public statements by diverse actors to accompany public discussion of court cases, and (d) the emergence of new scholarly writings and professional opinions regarding the indications model of lawful abortion. The public debate was bolstered by important advocacy initiatives such as those mounted by the

Lesbianas y Feministas por la Liberalización del Aborto, who have tirelessly promoted access to information on medical abortion through the establishment of a hotline. The public debate also inspired wider awareness about the need to move toward decriminalization of abortion.

The struggle to overturn the informal ban on abortion services was also accompanied by a strategy of transnational legal mobilization that took place through the shadow reports submitted by nongovernmental organizations to international human rights bodies[46] that inspired their Concluding Observations concerning Argentina's lack of implementation of Article 86.[47] Transnational mobilization also took place around the *L.M.R.* case,[48] a case of a developmentally disabled adolescent rape victim who was denied abortion services in public hospitals. Having exhausted effective domestic remedies in national courts, her mother successfully pursued remedial justice for L.M.R. through the U.N. Human Rights Committee.[49] While the demand for a right to abortion had figured in these forums for several years, the new shadow reports to the committees called for the implementation of procedures for legal abortion, including the application of the Guide, and the implementation of existing provincial regulations and the development of provincial regulations where they did not exist.

A note of caution should be sounded here. Despite the significant material and symbolic effects that followed the advancements made in certain provinces in the fight for a rights-based procedural turn and the increase in support for the larger campaign for decriminalization experienced in recent years, by early 2012 legal abortion services were still not available in large areas of the country. The reconstruction of this second stage of the procedural turn, where guidelines become justified in rights-terms, could be read as a linear process toward increased access to legal abortion services. Such a simplified reading would be misleading, however. When fostering the different initiatives identified above, proponents of the procedural turn faced instances of challenge and resistance that explain, in practice, the "sticky" nature of the informal rule restricting the supply of legal abortion services. Conservative forces with strong political ties managed to frustrate the spread and the effects of many of the initiatives described so far. Also, in places where the procedural turn was reaching increasing degrees of compliance, fear of regression was always present, and the initiatives were therefore maintained without much publicity, limiting their actual potential for substantive change.

Deficits of the Procedural Turn

Despite the improvements in subverting the informal rule banning abortion, interpretive and implementation deficits limiting the effectiveness of the procedural turn persisted until the Supreme Court issued its decision in *F., A.L.*

Interpretive deficits. A review of the media coverage of cases where women were requesting access to legal abortions in the provinces with procedural guidelines and the interviews conducted in two hospitals of the city of Buenos Aires during 2009–2010 point to at least three types of interpretation problems around the guidelines that limited access to abortion: (a) legal uncertainty, (b) misguided application, and (c) underspecification.

Legal uncertainty. In certain provinces, existing guidelines did not clarify the scope of the indications, and hence rape victims without a mental disability were often denied abortions or asked for prior court authorizations.[50] This lack of clarity on the scope of the rape indication generated disparities in the application of Article 86 across provinces with guidelines like Neuquén and Chubut.

The same problem was also present with respect to the standards and prerequisites for the performance of the abortion. While some provinces required the judicial report of the rape, others had already replaced that requirement by an affidavit. Other inconsistencies or abuses in the application of the guidelines included the imposition of requirements not formally provided by the guidelines. These requirements delayed access to abortions that had often been sought at early stages of the pregnancy. Unforeseen formalities of that sort could include demanding the initiation of procedural investigations or a judicial report where the pregnancy was caused by rape. Similarly, women might be required to provide proof of judicial declarations of insanity or minors might be required to obtain the consent of both parents. Women were also denied service based on gestational periods not provided for by the regulations.

Misguided application. In a number of cases, the procedural guidelines have been applied in breach of patients' rights such as the right to confidentiality and the right to provide informed consent. The right to privacy was often breached when excessive information was released in the attempt to verify an indication. Minors were also denied the right to a hearing and the right to protection against potential conflicts of interest with parents or guardians. Women's right to enjoy the benefits of scientific knowledge and progress was also breached, for instance by restrictions on the use of pharmaceutical methods, like misoprostol, for performing abortions. Finally, the right to conscience was abused by doctors, for example by the failure to refer women to willing providers, with the tolerance of hospital and provincial authorities. This tolerance often resulted from the underregulation of the practice, and the total lack of accountability for its abusers.

Underspecification. The lack of clear and explicit rules often hampered the application of the procedural guidelines. For example, women's options were limited by the lack of legal recognition of the full menu of medical techniques for abortions including the authorization of misoprostol. This problem was exacerbated by the lack of training and dissemination of information to administrators and medical personnel. Apart from medical issues, women also faced financial barriers because there were no clear rules governing the duties of contributory health care providers and insurers. Conscientious objection remained a sticking point because there were no regulations or policies to guide its application. Nor were there adequate rules that required referral to other health care providers when conscientious objection was exercised. Finally there was a lack of coordination of services, like legal aid for vulnerable women who did not clearly fall within the Article 86 exceptions, victims of violence, women with disabilities, indigenous women, migrant women, and women in prison, required to obtain judicial authorization. More generally, the lack of infrastructure and rules for the health system resulted in a failure to protect women or their relatives from interference or harassment by third parties that sought to deter their abortions.

Implementation deficits. In the six jurisdictions where the procedural turn resulted in the adoption of new rules, interpretative and implementation restrictions persisted, not merely as a result of the explicit interpretative confrontations mounted by conservative actors but also as a consequence of weak institutional arrangements and low enforcement commitments. The actual application of the procedural rules varied from case to case, each exhibiting different degrees of compliance with the procedural standards. In that continuum, one could locate, for instance, cases such as the city of Buenos Aires where evidence suggests that the application of the rules in a few hospitals was contingent on the will of directors and individual physicians. At the other extreme are jurisdictions like Neuquén, where since 2007 the health care system has increasingly implemented the provincial guidelines. However, implementation of legal abortion services was never fully in place in either of these two jurisdictions. In Neuquén, despite significant progress toward availability of legal abortions, the provincial health system did not widely advertise the facilities and doctors delivering legal abortion services.

As a result, women could not obtain information about the location of services, their scheduling, or the names of professionals who did not conscientiously object to perform Article 86 abortions. Against this backdrop, the actual implementation of the procedural turn presented serious doubts about its potential to provide legal abortions to all the women who might have needed them.

Until early 2012, procedural guidelines had been adopted in only six provincial or city jurisdictions of the country, which implies an important fragmentation between the formal rights of women living in those locations and women inhabiting the rest of the country. In addition, within the provinces with guidelines, their uneven application seems to have been the rule, generating further intrajurisdictional inequalities. The absence of a procedural framework and standards for the supply of legal abortion services at the national level and the withdrawal of the national government's support from initiatives such as the Guide[51] have also contributed to delegitimize the development of further procedural rules and the implementation of the existing ones as a national constitutional requirement.

Moreover, the enforcement of the formal procedural rules on abortion has confronted new legal and illegal strategies put forward by conservative groups to defend the informal rule restricting the supply of abortion services. To begin with, obstructive strategies in litigation included the unbearable pressures imposed both by court officers and outsiders, who harassed the mothers of young rape victims, often eleven or twelve years old, so that they would withdraw their requests for abortion services.[52] In other cases, women running severe life or health risks were forced to sustain a pregnancy in inhuman conditions. This was evident in the plight of *E.A.*,[53] concerning a girl from Entre Ríos suffering from severely deteriorating health, who was forced to take the pregnancy to term alone in a hospital in another province, where for several months she lost almost total contact with her family. A few days after she gave birth, she suffered a mental stroke. On another level, resistance to the procedural turn was maintained by health care providers who continued to require prior judicial authorization before performing Article 86 abortions, even in the provinces where procedural guidelines clarified that such authorizations were unnecessary.

Other more organized legal challenges were brought to courts by conservative organizations to question old and new procedural guidelines like in the *Profamilia* case.[54] Political tactics were also mounted to defend the informal rule banning abortion. They were advanced, for instance, in the context of the change in provincial and national authorities that took place in late 2007. That same year, the appointed governors of the city of Buenos Aires and the province of Buenos Aires, as well as the new authorities at the National Ministry of Health, blatantly stopped the implementation of the first-generation guidelines and of the national Guide.[55] The lack of implementation of the procedural guidelines of the city and the province of Buenos Aires was sustained for most of the four following years.

Within the national government, conservative gestures of resistance also emerged from the president, who repeatedly opposed abortion legalization without distinguishing her opposition to full legalization from enforcement of the existing indications model during the debate over the adoption of a repeal law (a frequent strategy to avoid discussing the need to implement legal abortion services through medical guidelines that could be issued by the Ministry of Health). This was also the typical behavior of a majority of provincial governors, who stopped initiatives to adopt procedural guidelines under informal pressure from representatives of the Catholic hierarchy.

At the national level, resistance to the procedural shift has also characterized intradepartmental relationships. In 2010, the then director of the NPRHRP, Paula Ferro, commissioned a revision of the Guide, and a second version of the document was elaborated. However, before the announcement of its adoption by a ministerial order, Minister Juan Luis Manzur did not approve the guidelines and rejected any regulatory rules for Article 86 abortions.[56]

The Procedural Turn After the Supreme Court *F., A.L.* Decision

A new stage in the formal-informal rule relationship began in March 2012, when the National Supreme Court issued its opinion in *F., A.L.*, its first substantive judgment in an abortion case.[57] The Court was inaugurating a new stage in the turn toward procedure that clearly signaled the success of the constitutional and principled arguments put forward for years by the defenders of the formal rule. In the competition between the informal and the formal rules, the latter was finally beginning to impose itself over the former. In *F., A.L.*, the Court affirmed the decision of the Superior Court of Chubut that had authorized the abortion requested by an adolescent raped by her mother's partner.[58] In the majority opinion signed by five justices, the Court offered its key contribution to destabilize the arguments and the practices supporting the lack of legal abortion services.

To begin with, the opinion of the five justices outlined the different reasons why interpreting the Constitution as requiring a total ban on abortion was wrong. After rejecting each of the restrictive arguments used by conservative groups to justify the informal rule, the Court proceeded to detail the different provisions of the Constitution and human rights law supporting the constitutionality of Article 86, and its interpretation as grounding a right to abortion in the case of rape for all victims, irrespective of their mental health. The Court based this interpretation on the provisions of the Constitution protecting autonomy (Article 19) and equality before the law (Article 16).

The Court relied on human rights treaties, such as the Convention on the Elimination of All Forms of Discrimination against Women, especially those provisions obligating the state to condemn discrimination in all its forms, ensure women's full development, eliminate prejudices against women, and eliminate all forms of discrimination in private and family life (Articles 2, 3, 5 and 16), and the Inter-American Convention on the Prevention, Punishment and Eradication of Violence against Women (Convention Belém do Pará), which recognized women's right to equal protection before and of the law, the right of women to be free from all forms of discrimination, and the obligation of the state to condemn all forms of violence against women and prevent, punish, and eradicate such violence by appropriate means (Articles 4.f., 6.a, and 7). The Court drew on international jurisprudence like the U.N. Human Rights Committee's decision in *L.M.R.* to clarify that restrictive interpretation of the rape indication would violate a woman's entitlement to abortion under Article 86. The Court underscored the importance of dignity, the requirement not to impose heroic demands on persons, and the mandates of the legality principle, including the obligation not to alter the law retrospectively through discretionary interpretation.

The opinion in *F., A.L.* signaled a new stage in the turn toward procedure and the enforcement of the formal law because of the Court's recognition of both the negative and positive duties at stake as a result of a woman's right to an Article 86 abortion. The second part of the majority's opinion, in particular, showed a Court aware of the practical and institutional obstacles hindering access to Article 86 abortions. The Court reacted with a clearly nonessentialist approach toward rights, showing its understanding of the interlocking relationship between rights and remedies, as just two sides of the same coin. The Court identified some of the barriers resulting from an informal practice banning abortion for rape and exercised its power to clarify and issue instructions to overcome them at the level of structures and actors.

The National Supreme Court explained the duty of the state to remove all medical and judicial bureaucratic obstacles endangering the life or health of women, and to prevent the "implicit prohibition—and therefore a *contra legem* practice—of the abortions authorized by the criminal law legislators."[59] The Court required the state to make "available all the medical and sanitary requirements necessary to carry out the abortions in a rapid, accessible and safe fashion," without disproportionately burdening women.[60] Given its concern with effective access to legal abortions, the Court clarified several contested implementation issues reminding the governmental and other providers of:

(a) the duty to provide health care services for legal abortions,
(b) the prohibition of demanding prior judicial authorization,
(c) the need for a simple affidavit of the rape victim with respect to the rape,
(d) the duty not to impose any additional requirements by committees with the capacity to generate delays or diminish the safety of the abortion,
(e) the need to develop procedural safeguards for the appeal of decisions denying the abortion as a result of disagreements between health professionals and women, and
(f) the need to regulate health professionals' exercise their right of conscience to ensure that women's health care is not compromised.

The Court reminded legal and health professionals of their legal liability if they obstructed women's access to legal abortion services. Moreover, the Court urged the government to issue medical and hospital guidelines to ensure the provision of legal abortion services, including for victims of sexual violence, and to develop public information campaigns with special focus on vulnerable women. Although *F., A.L.* addressed the rape indication, the way the justices discussed the standards for implementation ensures that the decision applies to all Article 86 abortions.

The decision fostered broad social debate regarding abortion. Its efficacy in delegitimizing the resilient informal rule restricting legal abortions is still difficult to assess. Conservative resistance to the Court's demand for adoption of regulatory guidelines, including concrete standards, began immediately and generated an array of legal disputes a description of which exceeds the scope of this chapter. Within hours of the announcement of the decision, the National Ministry of Justice reported that the government had no plans to discuss abortion reform, signaling the lack of political will to comply with the Court's mandate. Moreover, President Fernández de Kirchner remained silent about the Supreme Court's decision. Had the president mandated compliance with the Supreme Court's order, all the government officials would have followed her order.

Similarly, the National Ministry of Health for Argentina has not advanced any significant initiative to promote the implementation of the Court orders in *F, A.L.*, and the minister addressed the need to comply with the Supreme Court decision only after a series of legal fights took place in the city of Buenos Aires.[61] In fact, disagreement within the same Ministry of Health about the duties regarding the enforcement of the Court decision led to the resignation of the director of the NPRHRP a few months after the judgment.

Most of the legal activity and debates sparked by *F, A.L.* have taken place below the federal level. After the decision, nine new provinces embraced the procedural turn, and only ten remain without specific regulations. Moreover, among the five subnational jurisdictions that had adopted procedural guidelines before, three of them (the city of Buenos Aires and the provinces of Buenos Aires and Santa Fe) issued new protocols replacing the old ones, while the provinces of Neuquén and Chubut applied the rules they had passed previously.

The move toward proceduralization has generated new legal contentions resisting the enforcement of the formal rule demanding the supply of abortion services. Among the provincial territories that have adopted some form of regulation, a first type of resistance resides in the content of the new guidelines. A recent survey reported that only the guidelines of Chaco, Chubut, Santa Fe, Jujuy, and Tierra del Fuego satisfy the standards delineated by the Court in *F, A.L.*[62] In the remaining ten provinces procedural requirements are more demanding than those defined by the Court or are incomplete, leaving room for uncertainties and the development of new obstacles to restrict access to abortions. Moreover, where new regulations have been adopted, there is still resistance through underimplementation or the failure to provide information and training to ensure effective service delivery.

Conservative opposition in the era after *F, A.L.* has reached courts through the filing of strategic cases in which right-wing organizations have either questioned the newly adopted rules or have attempted to obstruct women's access to abortions. In the city of Buenos Aires, in Córdoba, and in Santa Fe, organizations such as Profamilia, Portal de Belén, and others have requested injunctions to forbid the application of the guidelines and challenged their constitutionality. In all these cases, the litigants obtained restrictive preliminary injunctions that were either overturned or are still subject to revision by the courts of appeal,[63] helping to maintain uncertainty and misinformation about the status of the new regulations.

The new obstructions of women's access to legal abortion services are illustrated by an episode that took place in the city of Buenos Aires in late 2012, when a victim of trafficking who had escaped her captors reached a public hospital in the city. At the time, the governor announced the application of the new abortion guidelines to the case.[64] With this information published in the media, a conservative organization first approached a judge in a local court of the city, requesting an injunction to stop the abortion. When the local judge denied the petition, the conservative group informally contacted a national civil judge and obtained an injunction, which two days later was overturned by a decision of the Supreme Court.[65] While this episode was in the media, the governor vetoed a law approved some weeks before by all of the members of the opposition in the legislature of the city establishing more progressive procedural guidelines.

As these anecdotes illustrate, conservative tactics to resist the procedural turn and to defend the informal rule banning abortion continue to be deployed within and outside the law. These tactics have been transformed but not dismantled as a result of the Supreme Court's judgment. However, progressive actors mobilized to strengthen the procedural turn have multiplied and increased their arsenal of strategies to defend women's access to legal abortions. Women activists and several organizations have been involved in the fight for the adoption of progressive procedural guidelines within provincial ministries of health and legislatures. Other groups have been working in the training of professionals and assisting in the concrete implementation of newly approved guidelines. Others worked to defend guidelines challenged in the litigation conservatives took to courts in Córdoba, Santa Fe, or Buenos Aires. Similarly, others such as the members of Salta's Mujeres por la Igualdad de Oportunidades have developed more aggressive judicial strategies, going to court to challenge the restrictive procedural guidelines adopted by Resolution 1170/12. Despite all these efforts, by the end of 2012 the actual provision of Article 86 abortion services is far from a reality across the country.

Concluding Remarks on the Limits and Possibilities of the Procedural Turn

The exploration of the different stages of the journey to subvert the informal rule banning abortion and to replace it by a rights-based regulation to accessible abortion services exposes the limits of procedural turn's ability to guarantee women's access to their rights. This might be the most important lesson of the struggle for proceduralization. On the one hand, the fight to overturn the informal ban on abortion services in Argentina teaches us that while procedural rules may be needed to guarantee access to legal abortion rights and services, their power is constrained given their inherent legal uncertainty and the interpretative and implementation deficits to which they are subject. This has been clearly illustrated in the first and the second parts of the chapter by the struggles between proponents of the de facto ban on abortion services and those seeking the enforcement of Article 86 throughout the different branches of government against the backdrop of weak institutional commitments to the rule of law.

On the other hand, the very same flaws and inherent limits of the procedural approach offer a valuable argument to advance the legal reform of abortion law, as it provides new grounds to replace the indications model with the regulation of abortion on request. Actually, the failure of the procedural shift provides the basis for a claim of the violation of women's rights as a result of the health care and the legal systems' proven incapacity to guarantee access to fair procedures as established by formal rules regarding Article 86 abortions. Particularly after the Supreme Court's decision in *F., A.L.*, the deficiencies of proceduralization, as recognized by the Canadian Supreme Court in the *Morgentaler* decision,[66] reinforces the normative claims for decriminalization. The evolution of the struggle for proceduralization may help to promote a gradual change in conceptions of the rule of law, revealing a fertile terrain for moving toward decriminalization. The chapter shows that proceduralization has not solved the unworkability of the indications model. Indeed, the struggle for proceduralization may make sense only for its potential to show that there is no better option to respect women's rights than a regime allowing abortion on request.

Chapter 8

Reforming African Abortion Laws and Practice: The Place of Transparency

Charles G. Ngwena

Unsafe abortion that is linked to criminalization of abortion remains a major public health and human rights challenge in the African region. Reform of abortion law and practice in the African region can advance women's reproductive rights partly by appropriating and domesticating persuasive jurisprudence on the requirement of transparency in abortion laws. With the global trend toward the liberalization of abortion, of which the African region has been part,[1] efforts to reform abortion law and practice in order to promote women's access to safe, legal abortion need to also focus on ensuring that existing laws are effectively implemented. This does not imply abandoning the goal of ultimately securing the decriminalization of abortion,[2] or overlooking the indispensability of rendering abortion services accessible. Rather, it is to highlight that, while criminalization remains, rendering the state accountable for lack of effective implementation of existing abortion laws can be an important juridical tool for creating a legal framework for enabling access to safe abortion.

Partly on account of the recognition that highly restrictive abortion laws are linked to the African region's high levels of maternal mortality and morbidity,[3] the region has been liberalizing laws in the past three decades or so. A milestone development in this regard is the unprecedented recognition of abortion as a discrete and substantive human right under the regional human rights system established by the African Charter on Human and Peoples'

Rights.[4] Article 14(2)(c) of the Protocol to the African Charter on Human and Peoples' Rights on the Rights of Women in Africa[5] requires States Parties to permit abortion in cases of "sexual assault, rape, incest, and where continued pregnancy endangers the mental and physical health of the mother or the life of the mother or the foetus." The Women's Protocol, which was adopted in 2003, came into force in 2005 and has been ratified by two-thirds of the fifty-four states that make up the African Union.[6] If implemented effectively, the Women's Protocol can transform the regulation of abortion from a crime-and-punishment model to a reproductive health model.[7]

The persistence of high levels of unsafe abortion, notwithstanding the trend toward liberalization of abortion laws in the African region, suggests that it is no longer highly restrictive abortion grounds alone which necessarily constitute the major barrier to accessing safe abortion. Leaving aside abortion services that are unavailable or inaccessible, the lack of effective implementation of exceptions to the criminalization of abortion that are permitted under domestic law is also a major barrier. As part of addressing this shortcoming, this chapter submits that the African region can avail itself of new jurisprudence for rendering states accountable for failure to implement domestic abortion laws that is emerging from U.N. treaty-monitoring bodies.[8] The jurisprudence can be treated as persuasive authority as it constitutes quasi-judicial interpretation of treaties that have been ratified by nearly all the member states of the African Union.[9] In communications brought under Optional Protocols, both the Human Rights Committee and the Committee on the Elimination of Discrimination against Women (CEDAW Committee) have expressed views on the nature of state obligations as they apply to implementation of abortion laws.

The emerging jurisprudence shows that domestic regulation of abortion is no longer the sole prerogative of national authorities, as was the historical position before the age of human rights. State obligations emanating from human rights treaties can be applied to render states accountable for regulating abortion in a manner that violates human rights. The jurisprudence requires domestic laws to meet certain minimum human rights imperatives, including ensuring that any permitted exceptions to the criminalization of abortion are in practice accessible to women seeking safe abortion, so as to yield tangible legal rights. The human rights importance of requiring the state to ensure the effective implementation of abortion laws can be understood as emanating from the obligation of the state to guarantee "transparency" in the implementation of its domestic laws, including abortion laws.[10] This chapter seeks to highlight the place and rationale of transparency in abortion laws as a juridical tool and adjunct strategy for reforming African abortion laws and practice in ways that promote access to safe abortion.

When mainly drawing from the jurisprudence of U.N. treaty-monitoring bodies, the chapter also takes into account the complementary developments emanating from the European Court of Human Rights, the World Health Organization, and the African region. In recent years, the European Court of Human Rights has also been developing jurisprudence that highlights the state's duty to provide women seeking lawful abortion a clear and effective procedural framework.[11] The World Health Organization has provided governments with guidelines on implementing abortion laws in ways that respect, protect, and fulfill women's rights, including instituting administrative frameworks, which are aimed at ensuring that abortion services that are permitted under domestic laws are in fact "accessible in practice."[12] At the African regional level, the African Union has policies that require states to implement domestic abortion laws effectively. The main policy is the Maputo Plan of Action for the Operationalization of the Continental Policy Framework for Sexual and Reproductive Health.[13] The Maputo Plan of Action, which was adopted in 2006, requires African states to adopt administrative and legal frameworks aimed at reducing unsafe abortions, including providing comprehensive safe abortion services "to the fullest extent of the law," and "educating communities on available safe abortion services as allowed by national laws." At the domestic level, a number of African states have begun to develop and implement guidelines on the provision of safe abortion services, partly through clarifying domestic abortions laws.

The following section of this chapter provides an overview of the historical development of African abortion laws, highlighting, in the end, a general lack of implementation. The third section discusses the views of U.N. treaty bodies on transparency, while the fourth section attempts to explain the normative values underpinning transparency as a human rights imperative. The fifth section applies transparency to the African region, highlighting its transformative potential as well as its limits. The sixth and final section highlights that, in the final analysis, it is not so much transparency that is the solution for women seeking safe abortion in the African region, but decriminalization of abortion coupled with political commitment by African governments to provide requisite health services and to recognize women as equal citizens.

Historical Development of African Abortion
Laws and Its Link with Unsafe Abortion

Estimates of the global and regional incidence of maternal mortality due to unsafe abortion published by WHO underscore that, for women in the Global South, unsafe abortion remains a persistent danger.[14] On the one hand, the estimates show a welcome decline in the number of deaths from unsafe abortions globally, from sixty-nine thousand in 1990 and fifty-six thousand in 2003 to forty-seven thousand in 2008. On the other hand, as a proportion of global maternal mortality, unsafe-abortion-related deaths have hardly declined, remaining close to 13 percent. The African region accounts for 28 percent of the global incidence of unsafe abortions, and close to 62 percent of unsafe abortion-related mortality (twenty-nine thousand women). Such a high burden of unsafe abortion partly explains why the sub-Saharan region is least positioned to meet the Millennium Development Goal (MDG) number 5A to reduce maternal mortality by three-quarters by 2015.[15]

Addressing unsafe abortion ultimately requires a holistic approach to sexual and reproductive health that goes beyond discretely addressing abortion. At the same time, creating an enabling legal environment for the availability and accessibility of safe abortion services is absolutely critical. The critical role that abortion law plays is underscored by evidence showing, in the African region itself, that the historical criminalization of abortion has served as a major incentive for unsafe, illegal abortions. Tunisia[16] and South Africa,[17] following radical reforms, demonstrate that when abortion law is liberalized and accompanied by availability of accessible abortion services, unsafe, illegal abortions are drastically curtailed.

One of the major flaws with African abortion laws is that, though abortion is not absolutely prohibited and, furthermore, though there has been a discernible regional trend toward substantive liberalization of the grounds for abortion, in the overwhelming majority of countries, abortion laws have not been effectively implemented. The pervading public understanding in several African countries, including those that have liberalized abortion, is that abortion law is most prohibitive and abortion is something that is rarely, if ever, lawful.[18]

The Architecture of African Domestic Abortion Laws

The origins of Africa's abortion laws are colonial. Whether the laws originated from the codified laws of Belgium, France, Italy, Spain, or Portugal or from the common law or statutory law of England, a common feature of colonial abortion laws is that they all criminalized abortion.[19] Historically, African abortion laws have been singularly highly restrictive, being replicas of the laws of the colonizing countries. Saving the life of the pregnant woman was expressly or implicitly the only recognized exception. This exception, which became known as the therapeutic exception, was initially understood very restrictively to amount to what is required to satisfy the defense of necessity to save human life when faced with a criminal charge.

On the eve of independence, abortion law stood as it was during the colonial era, with no official guidance on how to apply the therapeutic exception save to a limited extent in Anglophone Africa[20] following a ruling in 1938 by an English court in the *Bourne* case.[21] *Bourne* equated threat to the life of the pregnant women with a serious threat to her physical or mental health. In this way, *Bourne* judicially broadened the compass of the therapeutic exception beyond an immediate threat to the pregnant woman's life to also cover a threat to her physical or mental health. However, the guiding effect of *Bourne* was limited. It could constitute a persuasive ruling only in jurisdictions that were aligned with the British common law tradition, which effectively meant only British or former British colonies. In any event, the efficacy of the *Bourne* ruling was undermined by the fact that, even in the jurisdictions in which it was formally received by colonial courts, such as in West Africa[22] and East Africa,[23] colonial states did not take more practical steps to implement the ruling. This omission left women seeking abortion largely ignorant of the circumstances in which abortion is lawful. It also served to deter health care professionals with competence to render abortion services for fear of attracting prosecution.

Several African states have retained abortion laws contained in colonially inherited penal codes. Countries that fall into this category are: Angola, Central African Republic, Congo (Brazzaville), Côte d'Ivoire, Democratic Republic of Congo, Egypt, Gabon, Guinea-Bissau, Madagascar, Malawi, Mali, Mauritania, Mauritius, Sao-Tome and Principe, Senegal, Somalia, Sudan, South Sudan, Tanzania, and Uganda. At the same time, an increasing number of African countries have liberalized abortion grounds beyond saving the life of the pregnant woman. The most liberal reforms have been those of Cape

Verde,[24] South Africa,[25] Tunisia,[26] and Zambia.[27] The laws of Cape Verde, South Africa, and Tunisia permit abortion on mere request in the first trimester, while all four countries explicitly permit abortion for socioeconomic reasons. Ethiopian reforms of 2004,[28] while not as extensive as those of Cape Verde, South Africa, Tunisia, and Zambia, constitute substantial liberalization partly because they permit abortion for social reasons, albeit only in respect of women who are minors and women who suffer from mental disabilities.

Leaving aside domestic law reforms that explicitly permit abortion on request or for social reasons, close to half of the African Union's fifty-four member states now permit abortion on the ground of the woman's health.[29] Rape, incest, and danger to fetal health or life are also increasingly recognized as grounds for abortion. But notwithstanding a discernible trend toward liberalization, domestic law reforms in the African region have, on the whole, not translated into tangible access to safe abortion services. This is not only because, for the majority of women, abortion services are frequently unavailable or inaccessible because of factors such as distance, cost of services, or ignorance about location of facilities. It is also because of the persistence of laws that have remained largely unknown and administratively inaccessible.

While liberalizing abortion, African states have failed to implement the grounds in ways that are sufficiently transparent or effective as to allow women seeking abortion to become aware of their legal rights, and to know how to realize them, including having recourse to administrative procedures in the event of being denied abortion. Equally, in most African jurisdictions, health care professionals have remained largely ignorant of what is permitted by the law. Zimbabwe serves as an example.

Zimbabwean abortion law illustrates legislative reforms that are lacking in transparency. Until 1977, Zimbabwean abortion law was a colonial bequest from the English Offences Against the Person Act of 1861 and the derivative Common law that made it an offence to "unlawfully" procure an abortion. In 1977, Zimbabwe (then Rhodesia) passed the Termination of Pregnancy Act, which was retained at independence in 1980. The Zimbabwean Termination of Pregnancy Act was passed ostensibly to clarify the law on abortion and render it more certain for women seeking abortion as well as health care professionals with the competence to provide abortion services.[30] Section 4 of the Zimbabwean Act permits abortion on the grounds that: "the pregnancy so endangers the life of the woman concerned or so constitutes a serious threat of permanent impairment of her physical health that the termination of pregnancy is necessary to ensure her life or physical health"; or "there is a serious risk that the child to be born will suffer from a physical or mental defect of such a nature that the child will permanently be seriously handicapped"; or "there is a reasonable possibility that the foetus is conceived as a result of unlawful intercourse."

But far from serving to clarify the circumstances in which abortion is lawful, the Zimbabwean Termination of Pregnancy Act has, instead, served as a deterrent both to women seeking abortion and to health care professionals with the competence to provide abortion services. The Zimbabwean Act is not supplemented by official guidelines or protocols that explain to women seeking abortion or providers of abortion services how the permitted grounds are to be applied in practice. The prohibitive language in which the abortion grounds are couched, such as the requirement of a "serious threat of permanent impairment of physical health," together with the implicit exclusion of mental health as a ground for abortion, and the burdensome certification requirements have also been factors in deterring provision of safe, legal abortion. Health care professionals have been reluctant to perform abortion even for women they believe meet the legal requirements for fear of prosecution.[31] The high incidence of unsafe abortions outside the health sector is not unconnected with inaccessibility of domestic law. In 2008, unsafe abortions accounted for 35 percent of maternal mortality.[32]

Regional Human Rights System Dimension

The Women's Protocol is the first international treaty to expressly recognize a right to abortion. Article 14(2)(c), which is part of a broader provision that guarantees a right to sexual and reproductive health, recognizes not just a threat to the life of the pregnant woman as a ground for abortion, which has been the historically recognized ground among African states. More significantly, it also recognizes threat to the health of the pregnant woman. Threat to the life of the fetus, rape, incest, and sexual assault are also alternative grounds. While falling short of recognizing socioeconomic grounds or mere request as grounds for abortion, it has transformative potential. By according abortion the status of an enumerated fundamental right at the regional level, the Protocol advances global consensus on combating unsafe abortion through an enabling legal environment; it promotes the legitimacy of liberalizing domestic abortion laws by providing abortion grounds that serve as a minimum threshold.[33]

As a supplement to the African Charter, the Women's Protocol seeks to augment the protection of women's rights.[34] However, while the protocol has a capacity to promote a paradigm shift in the regulation of abortion by supplanting the historical crime-and-punishment model with a reproductive health model, its abortion provisions have remained largely unoperationalized, even in ratifying countries. So far, among states whose abortion laws were incompatible with the Women's Protocol at the time of ratification, Rwanda is the only state that has reformed its domestic law to specifically align with the Protocol.[35]

The main protective and adjudicatory organs of the African Charter system, namely, the African Commission on Human and Peoples' Rights[36] and the African Court on Human and Peoples' Rights,[37] have, thus far, not played a significant role in applying the protocol's abortion provisions. There has been only one occasion where, in concluding observations, the African Commission has alluded to state obligations to prevent deaths and illness from unsafe abortion. In its concluding observations on the report of Nigeria,[38] the African Commission expressed concern that in its report, Nigeria had not indicated the steps it had taken to comply with state obligation under the Women's Protocol, which Nigeria has ratified.[39] But while recommending that Nigeria should take steps to prevent unsafe abortion-related mortality,[40] it did not specifically refer to obligations under article 14(2)(c) of the Protocol. It made no reference to the importance of clearly aligning with the protocol its abortion laws, which are a colonial legacy. Partly on account of lack of tangible implementation, the laws, which are contained in penal codes and expressly permit abortion on the ground of saving the woman's life, are generally understood restrictively as not recognizing threat to the woman's health as within the permitted exception. This is despite *Bourne*, which judicially broadened the woman's life ground, having been received into the Nigerian legal system in the *Edgal* case.[41]

Jurisprudence from United Nations
Treaty-Monitoring Bodies

In three cases, *K.L. v. Peru*,[42] *L.C. v. Peru*[43] and *L.M.R. v. Argentina*,[44] United Nations treaty-monitoring bodies have held that states are accountable for failure to implement abortion laws. The *K.L.* and *L.M.R.* cases were decided by the Human Rights Committee, while the *L.C.* case was decided by the

CEDAW Committee in the context of communications (that is, legal actions) alleging state violations of human rights under respective Optional Protocols. The Human Rights Committee and the CEDAW Committee are the treaty-monitoring bodies of the International Covenant on Civil and Political Rights (ICCPR) and the Convention on the Elimination of All Forms of Discrimination against Women (CEDAW), respectively, which, as alluded to in the introduction, have been so widely ratified by African states as to justify taking cognizance of these decisions as standard setting.

In *K.L.*, the Human Rights Committee found Peru in violation of its obligations under the ICCPR, when hospital authorities denied abortion to a seventeen-year-old girl who was pregnant with a fetus that was affected with anencephaly. The complainant was denied abortion regardless of medical and social evidence confirming that continuing with the pregnancy would seriously harm K.L.'s health, and of Article 119 of the Peruvian Criminal Code, which permitted abortion if it was the only way of saving the life of the pregnant woman or avoiding serious and permanent damage to her health. As a result, the complainant was compelled to carry the pregnancy to term. She gave birth to a baby with anencephaly that survived for only four days, during which she was obliged to breastfeed. She was severely traumatized by the experience. The committee found the conduct of Peru to constitute violations of Article 2 (right to an effective remedy), Article 7 (right to be free from inhuman and degrading treatment), Article 17 (right to privacy), and Article 24 (right to special protection as a minor) under the ICCPR. An important finding underpinning the committee's decision is that, though Peruvian law permitted abortion in given exceptions, there was no domestic administrative structure, short of constitutional litigation, to allow the complainant to challenge the decision to deny her abortion.

In the *L.C.* case, the CEDAW Committee found Peru to be in breach of its state obligations under CEDAW, partly because the state had failed to provide the complainant with effective access to exercise her right under domestic abortion law. The complainant was a thirteen-year-old girl who became pregnant following repeated sexual abuse by a thirty-four-year-old man. On discovering that she was pregnant, she became severely depressed and attempted suicide by jumping from a building. She suffered severe injuries, including paralysis of her lower and upper limbs. Although she required emergency surgery, hospital authorities did not render treatment because they took the view that treatment would harm the fetus. When she requested abortion through her mother, she was refused. This was notwithstanding that Article

119 of the Peruvian Criminal Code, as mentioned above, permits abortion to save the life of the pregnant woman or to prevent serious and permanent damage to her health. It took forty-two days for the hospital authorities to respond to her request, and decline it. The complainant lodged an appeal, but while awaiting a response from the hospital authorities, she miscarried spontaneously. It was only then that she was rendered treatment for the injuries she had sustained. Even then, the hospital authorities indicated that they would have declined the appeal as their initial decision was final and not appealable. Although the complainant was operated on, her health had, by then, deteriorated. She was unable to derive the benefit she would have derived had the treatment she required been rendered timely.

Among the reasons the CEDAW Committee gave in *L.C.* for finding several violations under CEDAW, including violation of Article 12, which guarantees women equal and nondiscriminatory access to health care, is that, although the Peruvian Criminal Code permitted therapeutic abortion, the complainant had been left without access to an effective procedure to establish her entitlement. The Committee noted that, because of the absence of laws and regulations for implementing the permitted exceptions under the Criminal Code, access to abortion was determined arbitrarily, with each hospital authority determining its own legal grounds, procedure, and time frame.[45] It highlighted that Article 12 of CEDAW imposes an obligation on states to "respect, protect and fulfil" women's right to health care. This duty includes ensuring that legislation, executive action, and policy all respect the three-fold obligations.[46] As part of addressing implementation, the Committee recommended that Peru establish a procedure to enable women seeking abortion to realize their entitlements timely under Peruvian law, including conducting education and training in the health care sector to sensitize health care professionals to respond positively to the reproductive health needs of women, and adopting guidelines or protocols to ensure the availability and accessibility of health care services, including abortion services.[47]

The *L.M.R.* case concerns a complainant who was nineteen years of age but had a mental age of about ten years. She had become pregnant following a suspected rape. She requested abortion through her mother but was refused. This was so regardless of Article 86(2) of the Argentinian Criminal Code, which permits abortion on the ground of danger to the life or health of the pregnant woman, or if the pregnancy results from rape or indecent assault. Despite evidently falling within the exceptions, especially the latter exception, the complainant was required to first obtain judicial authorization for abortion. A juvenile court refused the authorization, and its decision was confirmed by a higher court. On appeal to the Supreme Court, the complainant was successful. The Supreme Court ruled that judicial authorization was not necessary once a permitted ground was met. Notwithstanding, the complainant was unable to find a public facility willing to perform an abortion, mainly on account of public pressure opposed to abortion that was being brought on health facilities. In any event, the public hospital authorities said the pregnancy, whose gestation was at this stage around twenty weeks, was now too advanced for a safe termination. In the end, with the support of women's organizations, the complainant was, through her mother, able to arrange for a clandestine abortion.

In *L.M.R.*, the Human Rights Committee found violation of the Article 2(3) (right to an effective remedy) taken together with Articles 3 (right to equal enjoyment of rights), 7 (right to be free from inhuman and degrading treatment), and 17 (right to privacy) of the ICCPR. In reaching its conclusion on Article 2(3) especially, the Committee noted that despite meeting the criteria for legal abortion, the complainant had to appear before three courts, which had the effect of prolonging by several weeks the gestation period, which became the reason why the hospital ultimately declined to perform the abortion and the complainant had to resort to a clandestine procedure.[48] These facts, according to the Committee, highlighted that Argentina did not have an administrative framework for providing women seeking abortion under domestic law with an effective remedy.

As indicated earlier, there is also a parallel jurisprudence on transparency from the European Court of Human Rights. The essence of the European Court's new jurisprudence as apparent from its decisions in *Tysiąc v. Poland*, *A, B, and C v. Ireland*, *R.R. v. Poland* and *P. and S. v. Poland*[49] is that, where national authorities rely on criminal regulation of abortion but permit certain exceptions, the regulatory measures must meet two main procedural requirements. First, the state must take positive steps to ensure that the circumstances in which abortion is permitted are articulated in a way that is reasonably clear not just to women seeking abortion services, but also to health care professionals who provide or at least have the competence and responsibility to provide abortion services. Second, national authorities must take positive steps to establish an accessible and timely administrative procedure for allowing women who are aggrieved by a decision refusing them abortion to contest the decision. The administrative procedure must comply with the requirements of fairness and administrative justice, not least by affording the woman an opportunity to be heard, and providing her with written reasons. Significantly, the European Court has said that it does not consider litigation, including constitutional litigation, as a primary or regular route to follow for women seeking to challenge decisions denying them abortion. This is because such litigation is fraught with complexity and delay, which clearly militate against prompt outcomes, time being of the essence for women seeking to terminate pregnancies.

A Normative Framework for Understanding Transparency

In attempting to explicate the normative values underpinning transparency, it serves well to highlight that "transparency" is not, itself, a juridical term of art. It is not a term that has been specifically claimed by U.N. treaty-monitoring bodies or the European Court in the cases that were discussed or mentioned earlier. It is used in this chapter as convenient terminology for capturing the essence of jurisprudence that recognizes that, where abortion is permitted by domestic law, regardless of whether the law is highly restrictive, the state has a duty to take positive steps to render any attendant legal rights amenable to effective realization by women seeking access to legal abortion.

The jurisprudence on transparency can be understood as serving multiple normative purposes. Some purposes appeal to procedural or administrative justice, but others implicate more substantive principles of justice as to gesture toward substantive equality. Some purposes are more general and are aimed at securing the equal and effective exercise of rights in a liberal democracy in the age of human rights or constitutionalism and remedies in the event of breach. Some justifications implicate transparency as a principle that serves public health. It highlights that, even where there are permitted exceptions, criminalization of abortion is, itself, a barrier that endangers public health through illegal abortions that in many settings are frequently unsafe. The state must, therefore, make conscious efforts to implement any exceptions and thus facilitate access to safe abortions.

At a general level, the insistence by U.N. treaty-monitoring bodies in their decisions in *K.L. v. Peru*, *L.C. v. Peru* and *L.M.R. v. Argentina*, which is also echoed in the jurisprudence of the European Court, that once a legislature decides to allow abortion it must not structure its legal framework in a way that effectively undermines the real possibilities of exercising the rights permitted under the law, can be understood as serving the objective of securing equality under the law. The duty of the state to raise awareness about the legality of abortion among women and health care providers espoused most elaborately in *L.C. v. Peru*, and the duty to take *positive* steps to ensure that women seeking abortion have access to administrative procedures that facilitate timely review of any decisions, which runs through all the transparency cases, can be understood as both aligning transparency with administrative justice as a modality for securing equality under the law and ensuring that legal rights are not illusory for all rights holders, and not necessarily women seeking abortion alone.

Thus the use of transparency to require operationalization of abortion laws is a form of administrative or procedural justice that need not be limited to rights pertinent to abortion as it obtains for all rights in general. Philosophically, such procedural justice can be explicated as serving to fulfill the notion of "overlapping consensus" that is tethered to equality in a liberal or constitutional democracy that was espoused by John Rawls.[50] Rawls advanced the idea of an overlapping consensus as a political conception of justice and a principle for the organization of political and social institutions. It is possible to argue that the positive duty of the state to institute procedural structures that allow women to effectively realize rights conferred on them by domestic abortion laws emanating from the decisions of U.N. treaty monitoring bodies and the European Court is, in fact, a tangible expression of the state's duty to fulfill an overlapping consensus through guaranteeing equality under the law.

Justice as fairness among "free and equal" citizens is the impulse behind Rawls's idea of an overlapping consensus.[51] The overlapping consensus serves pluralism. It ensures that, even if we share different views about the moral rightness or wrongness of abortion, once our democratic institutions have recognized certain rights, such as when abortion is permitted, a reasonable conception of justice should seek to require the state to fulfill the rights and discharge its duties so that citizens who rely on the rights are treated equally. Equality is the fundamental intuitive value and idea from which to construct a reasonable political conception of justice, as indeed Rawls sought to do in his larger work, *Theory of Justice*.[52] In a plural democracy, at the very least, it should be possible to agree that equality under the law is a shared consensus, and that effective and accessible administrative justice is an adjunct to securing equality.

Against this philosophical backdrop, transparency is, therefore, a concrete juridical expression of a wider reasonable political conception of justice that intuitively appeals to the imperative of a fair system of social cooperation between citizens who enjoy equal protection under the law. Its rationale is enhanced in respect of rights that are morally contested, as abortion rights. In abortion, there is an established history of denial of rights guaranteed by the law. Even in the aftermath of reform, there might be uncertainty about the permitted legal parameters, or arbitrariness or illicit opposition on the part of health care providers who decide whether a woman seeking abortion is eligible as is borne out by the cases decided by the U.N. treaty-monitoring bodies and the European Court. In such a context, requiring the state to clarify abortion law and institute administrative justice guarantees is a means of specifically and concretely defining the content of a fair system of social cooperation among equal citizens. Further, requiring the state to take account of the needs of women seeking an abortion, including the vital importance of accessing services in a timely manner, and providing them with a right to administrative appeal, serves to enhance democratic participation in health care decision making. It ensures that transparency is not the unilateral gesture of paternalistic national authorities. Rather, it promotes the active participation of women.

The rationale for transparency is anchored in much more than the imperatives of administrative justice and procedural equality. Transparency also serves as an adjunct to antidiscrimination approaches. Taking equality seriously means taking steps to protect the equality rights of a vulnerable social group by countering discriminatory and obstructive barriers that are unconstitutional or superfluous and have the effect of delaying or ultimately thwarting the exercise of legal rights, and thus perpetuating the status quo. The historical criminalization of abortion and its moral stigmatization render women seeking abortion not just a marginalized political minority but also a vulnerable one. Women seeking abortion are vulnerable to being denied access to lawful services even after domestic liberalization of the law.[53] This is easily the case where influential political or religious majorities and their adherents among health care providers opposed to abortion are determined to frustrate the legitimate exercise of abortion rights regardless of the law as is implicit in the cases emanating from both Latin America and Europe.

The cases decided by U.N. treaty-monitoring bodies and the European Court demonstrate how religious opposition to abortion can be used by health care providers as well as domestic courts under different guises to discriminate against women seeking abortion by undermining abortion rights already conceded by the legislature. For example, conscientious objection may be abused to thwart the exercise of abortion rights. Where there is such abuse, transparency serves to counter unfair discrimination by clarifying reciprocal rights and duties and, ultimately, to highlight the relative rather than absolute nature of the right to conscientious objection.[54] Other unconstitutional anti-abortion stratagems might be to delay access to abortion until such time that the option of abortion is no longer safe for the woman. In *L.M.R. v. Argentina*, for example, the requirement of judicial authorization was an unnecessary and burdensome administrative requirement that was created by national authorities and health care providers antithetical to abortion. It was a Trojan horse that served to discriminate against women seeking abortion by overburdening them with an unnecessary certification requirement in order to frustrate timely access to safe abortion. In this case, the duty of transparency served to counter unconstitutional religiously inspired barriers in Argentinian legal and health systems and to provide a remedy.

As an antidiscrimination modality, transparency gestures toward substantive equality. In the abortion context, the achievement of equality should be measured not only by ascertaining whether the letter of the law recognizes reproductive agency, but also whether the rights it acknowledges are realizable in practice by women of all backgrounds and means, especially those that are most vulnerable and marginalized.[55] Requiring legislatures and health care systems to specifically provide women seeking abortion with sufficiently clear information about the legality of abortion and timely access to administrative procedures for vindicating their rights is a form of conferring "status recognition."[56] It is a mechanism that goes beyond merely requiring accountability and openness and ensuring equality under the law in order to also recognize women seeking abortion as moral agents. Ultimately, it requires responsiveness to the needs of women who seek access to abortion services, but are impeded by ignorance or are frustrated by unnecessary or deliberate unconstitutional barriers created, through an act or omission, by national authorities.

In a substantive equality sense, the requirement of transparency constitutes affirmation of a class of persons and a health service need that have been historically marginalized and stigmatized. By taking into account the peculiar information and procedural needs of women who wish to realize their abortion rights, the substantive equality of a social group advances through empowering women or giving them "capabilities" to overcome some of the socioeconomic disadvantages that serve as barriers to accessing safe, legal abortion.[57] In *L.C. v. Peru*, especially, one of the objectives of the CEDAW Committee's approach to transparency was giving women seeking abortion capabilities though the provision of requisite legal, administrative, and health information.

Finally, there is also a public health rationale to transparency. This is particularly the case in environments that have a high incidence of unsafe abortion, as does the African region. Where national authorities concede that abortion is lawful, especially when they liberalize the grounds for abortion but refrain from clarifying the circumstances in which abortion is permitted so as to allay uncertainties among women seeking abortion or providers of abortions services, they may be assisting in providing incentives for unsafe abortion. Equally, refraining from establishing administrative gateways to lawful abortion services is also an incentive for unsafe abortion for poor women especially. The next section will, in part, expand on the public health rationale because of its immediate relevance to the African region.

Application of Transparency Requirements to African Abortion Laws

The call for transparency in this chapter rests on a number of premises about its applicability and efficacy in the African region. As a juridical principle for vindicating procedural equality, administrative justice, and to a point substantive equality, transparency is predicated on an assumption that commitment to constitutionalism by all relevant organs of state, including the judiciary and the executive, will be forthcoming. Ultimately, political will is required among organs of state that are closely involved in its administrative implementation, especially ministries of health and ministries of justice. For the public health rationale to be realized and deter recourse to unsafe abortions, African abortion laws must ultimately translate into services that are accessible to all women, especially poor women and those who live in rural areas. Crucially, there must be a critical mass of willing health care professionals with recognized competence to provide abortion services. Furthermore, the call assumes willingness and capacity on the part of civil society to litigate, if necessary, to hold the state accountable for failure to effectively implement abortion laws and thus vindicate abortion rights. Each of these premises needs to be weighed carefully and factored in as part of contextualizing transparency in the African region.

There are reasons for being sanguine about the appropriateness and efficacy of transparency in the African region. Despite having a checkered history in constitutionalism, African states have been transitioning toward commitment to democratic governance since the 1990s, especially, as one of the outcomes of the end of the Cold War.[58] This transition has been accompanied by domestic constitutional reforms and the adoption of modern Bills of Rights that seek to respect, protect, and fulfill human rights, including rights to equality and administrative justice among other fundamental rights. The transition of the African region from the Organization of African Unity to the establishment of the African Union in 2000 signaled the African region's commitment to democracy and the promotion of "democratic principles and institutions" that are founded, inter alia, on the promotion and protection of human rights.[59] The establishment, in recent years, of an African Court on Human and Peoples' Rights with contentious and advisory jurisdictions to augment the protective role of the African Commission under the African Charter system is another sign of the region's renewed commitment to human rights. Appropriating, therefore, transparency to the African region as supplementary juridical value and principle in fulfilling equality under the law and a right to administrative justice in the provision of abortion services is not something that would require legal reform. Rather, it is tantamount to enforcing existing state duties through affirmation.

There is also emerging evidence of political goodwill for embracing transparency by executive organs at both the domestic and regional levels. Some of the African states that have liberalized abortion but have not implemented the law have found purchase mainly in the public health rationale for transparency. As an executive response, they have begun to develop guidelines and protocols to guide health care providers and professionals in the provision of lawful abortion services but also to educate communities on lawful abortion services. Ghana is one of the countries that has led the region in this connection.

Ghana liberalized its abortion law in 1985.[60] A risk of injury to the physical or mental health of the pregnant woman, without more, is a ground for abortion over and above risk to the life of the pregnant woman, rape, "defilement," incest, or fetal health. But despite liberalized abortion grounds, the reforms of 1985 have thus far not substantially broadened actual access to safe abortion. Services in the public sector have rarely been available, partly on account of ignorance of the law and the pervading assumption on the part of health care providers as well as the public that abortion is illegal.[61] To promote knowledge about the circumstances in which abortion is permitted, in 2006, the Ghanaian Ministry of Health adopted guidelines to clarify abortion law and guide health care providers on the provision of safe, legal abortion services as well as educate communities on the availability of abortion services.[62]

The Ghanaian guidelines underline that the law should be implemented in order to ensure women's access to comprehensive abortion care to which they are entitled under the law. They address common misconceptions about the illegality of abortion under domestic law. Furthermore, they attend to other pertinent rights and obligations associated with the provision of abortion. For example, they address conscientious objection and underline that only those "directly" involved in the performance of abortion procedures can exercise the right to conscientious objection, but subject to a legal duty to refer the woman to an "accessible" provider of abortion services. The guidelines, which have been shaped by the guidelines on safe abortion developed by WHO,[63] have been emulated by ministries of health in Ethiopia,[64] Zambia,[65] and Kenya.[66] The World Health Organization's guidelines, which emphasize the importance of implementing what is permitted under domestic abortions laws in ways that are ultimately consonant with fulfilling the human rights of women seeking abortion, are being used as important guidelines by African states.

At the regional level, the Maputo Plan of Action has also appealed to a public health rationale for transparency.[67] As a strategic plan for reducing the levels of unsafe abortions in the region, it has called on African governments to take steps to implement abortion laws maximally by, among other strategies, raising awareness among health care providers and communities about circumstances in which abortion is lawful. Embracing the emerging jurisprudence, therefore, should not be seen as deference to foreign values of little import to the African region. Instead, it should be seen as an opportune appropriation of important juridical adjuncts to the achievement of sexual and reproductive objectives that the region, itself, has set, including optimally using abortion laws to promote and protect the reproductive health of African women.

But much as there are hopeful signs particularly for the public health rationale for transparency to become an important catalyst in broadening access to safe abortion services in the African region, important caveats are warranted. It is important to ask whether domestic and regional efforts such as the domestic adoption of guidelines by Ghana and other jurisdictions clarifying the circumstances in which abortion is lawful and the adoption of the Maputo Plan of Action are making a difference in practice in terms of encouraging providers to provide safe abortion services and women to take up safe abortion services. Another question to ask is whether Ghana and the other African states that have followed suit have done what is sufficient to meet transparency requirements.

The first question cannot be reliably answered in the absence of research that is specifically designed to test the transparency efforts thus far. But even taking this limitation into account, some tentative inferences can be drawn from research conducted on unsafe abortion generally. A study conducted in Ghana in 2010 on unsafe abortion found that though abortion remains highly stigmatized, knowledge about circumstances in which abortion is permitted under domestic law, though not widespread, has substantially increased among health care professionals especially.[68] The numbers of women who are undergoing safe abortion is increasing, also suggesting raised awareness among women about lawful abortions. The study found that 57 percent of women sought a doctor to perform an abortion in contrast to 12 percent who did so in a 1997–1998 survey.[69] Though the study did not set out to measure the impact of the guidelines of 2006, it was cognizant of them. It specifically called for the intensification of public education efforts to raise awareness about domestic abortion law as a modality for increasing the proportion of safe abortions. The study seems to support the inference that efforts by the Ghanaian Ministry of Health to educate health care providers as well as the public about what is permitted under domestic law are impacting positively.

But even if the adoption of guidelines is having some effect in increasing access to safe abortion, a question remains whether guidelines on their own are sufficient to achieve transparency. The guidelines adopted by Ghana, and the countries that have followed suit—Ethiopia, Kenya, and Zambia—appear to be the effort solely of ministries of health. There is no indication that other organs of state that are responsible for providing guidance on the implementation of laws, such as the ministries of justice or the offices of attorneys general, actively collaborate in establishing and implementing procedures and frameworks for giving concrete expression to transparency so as to enhance its legitimacy and efficacy. Given the chilling effects of criminalization of abortion, especially where abortion provisions remain situated in penal codes, using transparency to create an enabling legal environment should also involve organs of state that have the constitutional standing to reassure health care providers as well as women seeking abortion that they will not be prosecuted for providing or accessing a service that is lawful.

On its own, transparency cannot deter unsafe abortion. Implementing abortion laws in ways that are responsive to the information, procedural equality, and the administrative justice needs of women would be a pyrrhic victory if, in the end, abortion services are not available or accessible in ways that cater to the needs of women from all socioeconomic backgrounds. The public health rationale for transparency assumes accessibility of services in ways that are responsive to General Comment 14 developed under the International Covenant on Economic, Social and Cultural Rights.[70] In Cape Verde, South Africa, and Tunisia access to safe abortion has been broadened with commensurate declines in unsafe abortion-related mortality not merely by raising awareness about the legality of abortion or instituting administrative structures, but more crucially, through rendering services available especially to the majority of women who are poor and rely on the public sector for health services. Transparency will be to no avail if abortion services cannot be assured. Though technologies and procedures for performing abortion have become more affordable as to be within the reach of African health care systems, one of the major barriers to provision of services is that the majority of African states continue to assume that only doctors have the competence to perform abortion. The call for transparency in the African region needs to go, hand in hand, with measures to render abortion services accessible, through, for example, conceding that where doctors are highly scarce, appropriately trained midlevel providers can safely perform abortions, using procedures such as manual vacuum aspiration in the first trimester, as South Africa has demonstrated.[71]

As with all human rights, especially in contested areas such as abortion, civil society should play its role in championing neglected rights. It should hold the state accountable where there is failure to render abortion services transparent in ways that make a difference to women seeking safe abortion. Simply cherishing rights in the abstract does little to change the status quo. Women's struggles in the African region, in contradistinction to the Latin American region, have thus far avoided constitutionalizing abortion through litigation even in the face of the Woman's Protocol, which recognizes abortion as a fundamental right and has been widely ratified. This is not to suggest that litigation assures success as it might even engender a backlash from patriarchal authorities and constituencies. Rather, it is to highlight that when addressing the human rights of a political minority such as women and a stigmatized need such as abortion, part of sensitizing the African human rights system, including civil society, about the place of transparency in vindicating reproductive agency can come from litigation. Even where litigation is unsuccessful, nonetheless it can succeed in raising public consciousness about how national authorities deny human rights though failure to implement rights already guaranteed and, in the process, foreground or reinforce transformative political struggles.

Conclusion

The arguments for transparency in this chapter are a way of appropriating to the African region a pragmatic jurisprudential strategy for working within a largely constraining legal environment that has yet to concede radical reform of abortion law as Cape Verde, South Africa, and Tunisia have done. Transparency is by no means intended to replace the struggles for the ultimate decriminalization of abortion so that women's reproductive agency is respected. The call for transparency in this chapter has been a way of constructing a legal and administrative pathway for giving women capabilities within legal systems that largely continue to criminalize abortion long after colonial rule. It is a strategy for countering a double discourse of domestic laws that give with one hand but take away with the other even the small concessions made to women.

The overwhelming majority of African states have retained a crime-and-punishment approach to the regulation of abortion, which was bequeathed to them by the colonial state. The retention of criminalization of abortion in the African region is not a case of benign indifference. Rather, it is part of patriarchal and religious resistance to women's sexual and reproductive self-determination. The continued exclusion and marginalization of women in the sexual and reproductive sphere is part of a larger exclusion and marginalization of women from African social and political economies. It is an outcome of contradictory tendencies in African nationalism, which, on the moment of emancipating Africans from white colonial rule, also sought to redomesticate women and which thus serve to reconstitute and legitimize old patriarchies.[72] Ultimately, it is not lack of transparency as such that is the main problem with African abortion laws but criminalization of abortion.

Equally, transparency is not a substitute for reforming African health care systems in ways that assure access to abortion services on the basis of need. The public health rationale for transparency crucially depends on availability and accessibility of services that are woefully lacking in the African region partly because of failure to develop health care systems that also allow mid-level health care professionals to provide abortion services.

PART III

Framing and Claiming Rights

The Medical Framework and Early Medical Abortion in the U.K.: How Can a State Control Swallowing?

Sally Sheldon

In this chapter, I use early medical abortion (EMA), a routine procedure in many countries, as a focus for exploring the strengths and weaknesses of a highly medicalized framework for supporting access to good, safe, legal abortion services. I focus on the example of Britain, where EMA has been legally available under medical control for over two decades and where such a medical framework is preeminent. I begin by explaining what I mean by this last claim and setting out what is involved in EMA and why it provides a useful focus for my analysis.

A Highly Medicalized Conceptual Framework

I have argued elsewhere that the dominance of the medical framework in debates regarding abortion contributes to an apparent depoliticization, defusing conflict and controversy surrounding it.[1] This is not to claim that the medical frame necessarily implies a strong consensus regarding the ethical acceptability of abortion. What it rather provides is a shared conceptual framework within which knowledge claims are constructed, investigated, and tested, and shared reference points for determining who has the authority to intervene in debates and what forms successful interventions must take. Within the dominant medical framework, even where disagreement regarding abortion remains fundamentally ideologically driven, it becomes articulated through disagreement regarding empirical questions of clinical fact. For example, an activist's claim that the use of EMA is unnatural or sinful (for example, that it constitutes "chemical warfare on the unborn")[2] will not be as effective as a clinician's argument that it has a particular harmful side effect. This latter operates within a set of shared reference points for determining what kinds of considerations "count" and can be tested against a medical evidence base, and the authority with which a clinician speaks is grounded within his or her training, experience, and privileged claim to interpret this expansive knowledge base.

The British example stands out for the dominance of the medical framework, with one necessary consequence of this being the occlusion of other ways of conceptualizing what is at stake in discussion of abortion, including, notably, the human rights frame that is so significant in many of the other contexts considered in this collection. Rather than having individual freedoms protected through a codified list of rights, the British were said traditionally to have enjoyed an "undifferentiated mass of liberty," with individuals free to act in any way not prohibited by the law.[3] While a significant change occurred with the introduction of the Human Rights Act 1998, rendering the European Convention on Human Rights directly enforceable in U.K. courts, this legislation has been in force for little more than a decade. As such, it may be that the habit of framing issues as conflicting rights claims is less well developed in the U.K. context than in some other countries. Nonetheless, some bioethical disputes—such as the acceptability of assisted dying—have become framed squarely within a human rights paradigm,[4] whereas in the context of abortion, human rights challenges have been infrequent. This may be partly attributable to potential litigants' awareness of the wide margin of appreciation that the European Court of Human Rights has tended to accord in matters of abortion law (making challenges to legislation unlikely to succeed) and partly due to timing, with the British legislation at the forefront of a wave of liberalizing reform measures across Europe and beyond. By the time that British lawyers were more readily framing moral disputes in a vernacular of human rights, the dominance of the medical framework was already entrenched in abortion law.

The medical framework must be distinguished from a reproductive health framework, with the latter dovetailing more neatly with discussion of human rights. I take "medicine" to mean the practice of dealing with the maintenance of health and the prevention, alleviation, or cure of disease. The role of doctors is central, with a strong claim to authority that relies on experience, expertise, and privileged access to an extensive scientific knowledge base. While the concept of "health" is notoriously difficult to define, a somewhat different emphasis is nonetheless evident. Health is typically understood as "soundness of body; that condition in which its functions are duly and efficiently discharged,"[5] or "the condition of an organism with respect to the performance of its vital functions especially as evaluated subjectively or non-professionally (as in the phrase, 'how is your health these days?')."[6] The focus is on the patient's overall well-being (rather than the doctor's ability to deliver one aspect of it), and, on most views, "health" goes beyond mere absence of disease and reliance on what might be thought of as purely "objective" clinical indicators. This broader understanding is clear in the World Health Organization's famously expansive definitions of "health" and "reproductive health":

> Within the framework of WHO's definition of health as a state of complete physical, mental and social well-being, and not merely the absence of disease or infirmity, reproductive health addresses the reproductive processes, functions and system at all stages of life. Reproductive health, therefore, implies that people are able to have a responsible, satisfying and safe sex life and that they have the capability to reproduce and the freedom to decide if, when and how often to do so.[7]

"Reproductive health" thus foregrounds individual well-being (broadly understood) and emphasizes the individual's right to make reproductive choices, supported by access to information and services. This is a more explicitly political framework, expressed in the grammar of human rights, foregrounding patients' needs and capacities rather than scientific knowledge or medical authority. As the WHO continues: "Implicit in this are the right [*sic*] of men and women to be informed of and to have access to safe, effective, affordable and acceptable methods of fertility regulation of their choice, and the right of access to appropriate health care services that will enable women to go safely through pregnancy and childbirth and provide couples with the best chance of having a healthy infant."[8]

Along with rights comes the possibility of arguing for duties on the part of governments: for example, to reduce maternal mortality, to ensure access to post-abortion care, and to provide affordable reproductive health services.[9] In centering the patient's experience, autonomy, and rights, a "reproductive health" frame can also be seen as more woman centered, aligning with much feminist academic work and activist mobilization around abortion. While shared substantive concerns may occupy the two frameworks, "reproductive health" thus speaks a language of needs, capacities, rights, and duties, incommensurable with the medical frame's focus on knowledge, expertise, skill, and authority.

Early Medical Abortion

In an EMA, it is best practice for a woman to take mifepristone (RU486), an antiprogestin, which acts to block the production of progesterone and thus impairs her body's ability to hold onto a fertilized egg, followed one to two days later by misoprostol, a prostaglandin that acts to induce uterine contractions and expel the contents of the womb. If mifepristone is not available or is too expensive, misoprostol may be taken alone, offering a less—but still highly—effective method of termination.[10] In terms of efficacy and safety, EMA is broadly comparable to early surgical methods of termination as performed by a skilled operator in hygienic conditions.[11] Where such conditions exist, it is considered best practice to offer women a choice of medical or surgical abortion, with the relative risks and benefits explained.[12] Where legal abortion is highly restricted or unavailable, however, EMA can offer a significantly safer method of achieving an abortion clandestinely. Yet while clinicians discuss EMA as just one medical procedure among others, broader contestation surrounding it cannot be understood as involving straightforward disagreements regarding its medical merits. Rather, concerns that EMA offers the potential to ease access to, and disrupt legal and medical control of, abortion appear to offer the most convincing explanation for much of the opposition to it. After all, as one early commentator asked, "How [can] a state control swallowing?"[13]

EMA offers a series of important challenges to how we conceptualize abortion. First, it focuses attention on early pregnancy, blurring the line between contraception and abortion. Antiprogestins can be readily understood as part of a continuum of mechanisms that prevent the egg from being fertilized (condom, spermicides, diaphragm, female condom), those that may prevent fertilization or implantation (combined pill), those that may prevent implantation or may dislodge the implanted embryo (IUD), and those that cause the womb to shed its lining along with the implanted embryo (antiprogestins).[14] Indeed, this disruption of boundaries was actively encouraged by the scientist that developed mifepristone, who described it as an "unpregnancy pill" or "contragestive," in order "to diffuse the strength of the word 'abortion.'"[15] Complex issues are also raised regarding whether or not EMA falls within legal prohibitions on abortion in various countries.[16]

Second, that EMA is in pill form may also influence popular perceptions, with confusion with the "morning-after" pill relatively common in popular and political discourse[17] and early commentators noting that women described EMA as "bringing their periods back."[18] For some, this has raised concerns that if abortion becomes seen as a medically less serious procedure, this will inevitably slide into treating it as a morally less serious decision. Thus, critics have claimed that EMA trivializes abortion: "You take a tablet to get rid of a headache. You take a tablet to stop getting pregnant. And now you take a tablet to get rid of a child. . . . Terrifyingly, some people now talk of the death and destruction of the tiny unborn human life by a powerful chemical steroid as being more convenient."[19]

Finally, and significantly for current purposes, EMA offers the potential to demystify abortion as a specialized medical event, with the doctor's role necessarily decentered. In this sense it has been noted that EMA tends to collapse any neat distinction between safe and unsafe abortion,[20] and also, potentially and radically, to uncouple the demand for "safe" abortion from the demand for "legal" abortion.[21] In EMA, women can monitor their own miscarriages, administer pain relief, and take responsibility for reporting any side effects as necessary. Where abortions are performed clandestinely, this is a far safer means of "unsafe" abortion.[22] Where abortion is legal, EMA also increases the potential for abortions to occur off medical premises, including in the woman's own home. Locating much opposition to EMA in this potential to give women greater control, one veteran reproductive rights campaigner has noted that "the abortion pill potentially puts the control of abortion into women's hands, and a lot of conservative men and women aren't sure they like that."[23]

It is EMA's potential to challenge assumptions regarding abortion practice, potentially disrupting the boundaries of the medical framework that make it a useful focus for this study. With this in mind, I will now move on to consider the development of the British law over the last five decades.

The Medical Framework: The British Example

The 1960s: the Introduction of the Abortion Act (1967)

Abortion in the U.K. is subject to longstanding criminal prohibition under the Offences Against the Person Act, 1861. In response to widespread maternal mortality resulting from backstreet abortions, the Abortion Act 1967 was introduced in England, Wales, and Scotland, largely as a public health measure, to provide that abortions might be lawful where certain conditions were met.[24] These conditions include that an abortion must be performed by a doctor, on the basis of the good-faith opinion of two doctors that one of a number of broad contraindications to pregnancy is present. The first and most commonly used of these grounds provides for the legality of abortion where two doctors believe that "the pregnancy has not exceeded its twenty-fourth week and that the continuance of the pregnancy would involve risk, greater than if the pregnancy were terminated, or of injury to the physical or mental health of the pregnant woman or any existing children of her family."[25] The Act does not extend to Northern Ireland, where medical understandings failed to displace understandings of abortion based in religious values, and access to legal abortion remains extremely restricted.

Those encountering the Abortion Act for the first time might be surprised by what appears to be a disjuncture between the relatively liberal upper time limit within which abortions are available (up to twenty-four weeks, with provision for later abortions if the woman's life or health would be put at serious risk by continuing the pregnancy, or in the event of substantial risk of serious fetal handicap[26]) and what appears to be, at least in comparative Western European terms, a contrasting illiberal refusal to allow the woman a formal right to decide on termination without prior medical approval, even very early in pregnancy. Yet this apparent paradox dissolves if the Abortion Act is understood not as balancing female autonomy against a concern for fetal life but rather, within the medical framework, as recasting the social problem of unwanted pregnancy as a public health question. Within such an understanding, there is no basis for recognizing a woman's "right to choose" at any stage in pregnancy but, equally, the ground is laid for recognizing broad clinical discretion to act in the best interests of one's patients, even where this mandates access to abortion later in pregnancy.

Why was the medical framework so strongly accepted? I have argued in detail elsewhere that the British law is grounded, firstly, in the view that women are not capable of making their own reproductive decisions, and, secondly, in admiration for those highly skilled, dedicated, and responsible "medical men," who might be trusted to manage this problem sensitively and ethically.[27] The law thus aimed to ensure that women with unwanted pregnancies would be passed "into the hands of the medical profession",[28] with doctors offering support and, ultimately, deciding whether terminations were justified. In making these decisions, doctors were charged to take account of women's "actual and reasonably foreseeable environment".[29] A clear recognition that abortions are frequently sought for social reasons is thus combined with a belief that doctors remain the best judges even when the abortion decision involves not an understanding of medical factors so much as a close knowledge and scrutiny of the woman's broader environment and her ability to cope as a mother within it. Importantly, the role envisaged for doctors here is twofold: to provide a safe abortion service and to act as gatekeepers to it, scrutinizing individual cases in order to determine where a termination would be justified.

The medical framework was also grounded in a strong distinction between highly qualified professionals, operating openly and in good faith, and unqualified, financially motivated amateurs operating in the backstreets. Here the Abortion Act entrenched in statute a dichotomy that had already emerged repeatedly in the case law that preceded it. To take one significant example: the case of *Bourne* had formed the legal basis for such abortions as were performed lawfully prior to 1967 in Britain (and remains the legal basis for the very small number of lawful terminations performed in Northern Ireland). Here, a leading doctor was acquitted, despite having openly performed an abortion on a fourteen-year-old, pregnant as a result of a gang rape. His acquittal rested squarely on the fact that he was a qualified doctor, despite the fact that the Offences Against the Person Act, 1861 made no distinction regarding the professional status of the abortionist. In summing up, the judge contrasted the doctor's actions with those of another defendant, who had come before the court earlier in the month. In the first case,

> a woman without any medical skill or any medical qualifications did what is alleged against Mr. Bourne here. . . . She did it for money. £2 5s. was her fee, and she came from a distance to a place in London to do it. . . . The case here is very different. A man of the highest skill, openly, in one of our great hospitals, performs the operation . . . as an act of charity, without fee or reward, and unquestionably believing

that he was doing the right thing, and that he ought, in the performance of his duty as a member of a profession devoted to the alleviation of human suffering, to do it.[30]

The distinction between medical professionals and backstreet abortionists remained central following the introduction of the Abortion Act, with the Court of Appeal noting that: "the legality of an abortion depends on the opinion of the doctor. [The Abortion Act] has introduced the safeguard of two opinions: but, if they are formed in good faith by the time the operation is undertaken, the abortion is lawful. Thus a great social responsibility is firmly placed by the law on the shoulders of the medical profession."[31] Henceforth, abortions would be lawful provided that they were provided by doctors and in approved medical facilities; certification requirements meant that abortions must be performed openly and were subject to monitoring; and, combined with the need for a second signature and the good-faith requirement, this should ensure that abortions were performed for sound medical reason and not for the mere pecuniary advantage of the provider.[32] Taken together, these measures aimed to ensure that abortion would be lawful only under tight medical control, with amateurs remaining subject to onerous criminal sanction.

The entrenchment of the medical framework was not immediately accepted and has not been without challenge. Indeed, over twenty attempts had been made to reform the Abortion Act by the end of the 1980s, with anti-choice Members of Parliament (MPs) attempting to restrict access to abortion "salami fashion", slice by slice. Yet the Act has survived largely unchanged and has become subject to increasingly liberal interpretation by doctors, with charitable abortion providers playing a major role in opening up those areas where abortions had proved difficult to obtain because of the hostility of local doctors. Further, while access to National Health Service (NHS) funding (again, historically controlled by local doctors) was for a long time subject to striking regional variations, currently 96 percent of abortions are funded by the state.[33] The Abortion Act is thus currently serving as the basis for providing British women with high quality, readily available, free abortion services.

The 1990s: Minor Reform and the Arrival of EMA in Britain

Despite other attempts at reform over the years, successive governments have been reluctant to give parliamentary time to the issue of abortion, and the 1967 Act has been amended only once, when another piece of legislation—the Human Fertilisation and Embryology Act 1990—provided a vehicle for some minor amendments to it. The dominance of the medical framework is clearly visible in that process: MPs voted to allow abortion where there was a "substantial risk of serious handicap" until term (serving to free doctors to exercise their clinical discretion with regard to providing late terminations) yet refused to vote to limit medical control to the extent of allowing abortion in the first twelve weeks of pregnancy on the authority of just one, rather than two, doctors.[34] One further small change, also introduced in 1990, served to emphasize a broad acceptance that the legislation must move with the development of new medical technologies. With an eye to the imminent licensing of mifepristone, an amendment gave the Government the power to extend approval of premises for the provision of abortions to further "classes of places" for the use of specified abortifacient drugs.[35] The fears that this might loosen control over abortion were expressed at that time by the Conservative MP Anne Widdecombe, who warned that the amendment "gives the Secretary of State powers to enlarge the classes of premises that will be licensed. I believe that that is merely a paving measure—even if it is not intended as such—for self-administered home abortion."[36] The introduction of EMA in Britain followed soon after, with a product license for mifepristone granted in 1991, ten months after an application had been submitted.[37] This was not accompanied by the same level of controversy and political manipulation that has often dogged the drug's approval elsewhere,[38] and there may thus be an element of truth in the somewhat envious conclusion of one U.S. commentator that "in Great Britain equitable access to health care is more important than political pressures brought to bear by a vocal minority."[39] Subsequent parliamentary debate regarding the decision to license mifepristone clearly split down pro- and anti-choice lines. However, both sides chose to frame their arguments within an essentially medical framework,[40] with anti-choice MPs arguing that "women in their dilemma may be subjected to [EMA]"[41] with long-term dangers to their health, and long-term costs to the NHS.[42] The scientific objectivity of the research base demonstrating the safety and efficacy of EMA was also questioned, with it noted that tests had been financed by the manufacturer, Roussel Uclaf, or had involved at least one Roussel scientist.[43] Such claims were countered by those who asserted the ease, convenience, and clinical merits of EMA, the saving to the NHS, and the extra choice for women and doctors.[44]

EMA was licensed for use in Britain on the basis that it must be provided within the same legal framework as any other kind of abortion. Specifically, as noted above, the Abortion Act imposes practical limitations concerning who may authorize abortions, who may perform them, and where they may be provided. These two latter restrictions are of particular interest with regard to EMA, as they are less obviously grounded in the kinds of clinical considerations that may apply in the context of surgical procedures. First, for abortion to be lawful, pregnancy must be "terminated by a registered medical practitioner."[45] The issue of whether this required a doctor physically to hand over EMA drugs was preempted by a commonsense judicial interpretation of the relevant provision in a case regarding late medical terminations (where prostaglandins are used to expel the contents of the uterus in late pregnancy, in a process largely conducted by nursing staff). Here, the House of Lords found that, provided that a doctor remains in charge of the course of treatment, it is permissible for suitably qualified personnel acting under medical guidance to perform such actions which, in accordance with good medical practice, would normally be performed by such staff.[46] This somewhat circular line of reasoning reflected a hierarchical medical model, understanding the actions of the nurses as being essentially those of the doctors in the eyes of the law, with the relationship between the two professionals construed as one in which "the nurse is little more that the doctor's handmaiden."[47] However, it is also an interpretation that facilitated good and effective medical practice, accepting that doctors need be physically involved in performing terminations only where clinically necessary.

This judgment has had particular significance in clarifying that there is no legal requirement for a doctor to hand over mifepristone tablets, provided s/he remains in control. Further, it is an interpretation that offers significant flexibility with regard to a medical framework that is not static. While one might criticize the hierarchical relationship implicit in the *RCN* judgment, the decision nonetheless provides a continuing legal basis for protecting the health care team involved in providing abortion services, where each individual performs a role determined with reference to best medical practice.

The second restriction, that any treatment for the termination of pregnancy must be carried out in a place approved by the Government,[48] has proved more problematic. As was noted above, the Abortion Act was reformed in 1990 to accord the Health Secretary the power to authorize the use of specified abortifacient drugs in "classes of places" (including, potentially, GPs' surgeries, family planning clinics, or women's homes). Successive governments have shown no desire to make use of this power, and, as discussed below, the provision has been subject to recent challenge on the basis that it imposes a clinically unnecessary restriction. This illustrates a significant limitation of the current, highly medicalized, tight regulatory model in operation in Britain. Other countries, such as the United States, which might be thought in other respects to have far more restrictive abortion laws, are able to offer home use of EMA subject only to the constraints of clinical safety and best medical practice, because they lack the detailed regulatory framework laid down in the Abortion Act.

The 2000s: Challenges Within and Against the Medical Framework

When the Human Fertilisation and Embryology Act 1990 came back before Parliament for revision and reform in 2007–2008, there was again considerable activity among parliamentarians who saw a second opportunity to use it as a vehicle for abortion law reform. Again, the medical framework was accepted in this process. First, it was the House of Commons Science and Technology Committee (S&TC) that chose to launch a major review of the Abortion Act, aiming to provide a solid evidence base to inform MPs' voting.[49] Ethical and political issues do not fall within the S&TC's remit, and it trained its focus purely on the scientific evidence, resulting in a careful and authoritative report that operated entirely within an evidence-based, scientific—and predominantly medical—framework. The S&TC found no evidence in favor of lowering the upper time limit within which abortion is available, and no evidence for either the need for two doctors' signatures or the claim that only doctors can safely perform terminations. Finally, neither did the S&TC find any evidence to support the requirement that both courses of drugs involved in an EMA must be administered (as well as prescribed) on approved premises.[50]

While the two "pro-life" members of the S&TC, Nadine Dorries and Bob Spink, MPs, were critical of the liberalizing conclusions of the final report, they nonetheless accepted the medical frame of reference, grounding their dissent in criticism of the objectivity of the evidence received.[51] Yet having accepted the medical framework for debate, the two dissenters struggled to make their case against the weight of evidence, leaving themselves open to criticisms that their intervention was "a rollercoaster ride of pseudoscience and dubious data," which differed from the main report primarily in terms of "the quality of the science, the selectivity of the quoting, and the quality of the referencing."[52]

The focus on scientific evidence continued in the parliamentary debates regarding various amendments to the Abortion Act, which were then tabled during the passage of the Human Fertilisation and Embryology Act 2008. A first set of amendments, which attempted to restrict the upper time limit within which abortion is available, were defeated in large part because of research demonstrating that while the survival rates of neonates born at twenty-four weeks had improved since 1990, there had been no significant improvement for babies born at earlier gestational ages.[53] However, the fate of a second set of proposed amendments, including many that would have liberalized access to abortion and loosened medical control over it, is also noteworthy. These amendments, supported by the evidence base set out in the S&TC report, sought broadly to ensure that abortion services could be provided in line with good medical practice, safety, and patient welfare, in a way that was untrammeled by clinically unnecessary limitations. They envisaged the removal of the need for two doctors' signatures to authorize abortions performed before twenty-four weeks; the extension of the Abortion Act to Northern Ireland; permitting suitably trained nurses and other health care professionals to carry out abortions; the extension of the range of locations where abortions may take place to primary care level; and provision for home use of EMA. Rather than allowing these amendments to come to a vote, however, the Labour Government blocked debate of them, allegedly as a secret quid pro quo to secure political support for an entirely unconnected piece of legislation.[54]

The S&TC report and subsequent failure of these liberalizing reforms provide powerful illustrations of how actors may be ideologically driven, yet nonetheless conduct debates in a language of medical fact and scientific advance. Behind the scenes, the availability of abortion services may even become a bargaining chip in backroom deals regarding questions seen as "real" political issues. However, while the Labour Government's track record with regard to abortion services may thus appear poor, it by no means reflected the level of hostility that has become visible since the change of government in 2010.

Since 2010: Abortion Under the Coalition Government

In May 2010, the Labour Government lost power and a new coalition government, with a Conservative majority and Liberal Democrat minority, took office. The change in government was shortly followed by a legal challenge launched by the U.K.'s largest charitable abortion provider, the British Pregnancy Advisory Service, which uses the acronym bpas, regarding the home provision of EMA. Bpas argued that s.1(3) of the Abortion Act should be interpreted to include the situation whereby misoprostol was self-administered at home, citing the experience of a number of other countries to demonstrate that this would be safe, effective, and acceptable to women.[55] It contended that contemporary abortion best practice was radically different from that of the late 1960s, when Parliament's intention that the whole process must take place in licensed premises would have made sound clinical sense. Even in 1990, the protocol for an EMA was very different, with the second stage of the process then involving side effects that justified close medical monitoring.[56] The High Court was invited to interpret the Act as a "living statute," ensuring that it kept up to date with advances in medicine. Specifically, bpas suggested, the meaning of "treatment" should now be taken to include cases where only prescription and supply of a drug took place on approved premises, with administration taking place elsewhere.

The High Court, however, preferred the submission of the Government that the words "any treatment" must include not just the prescription but also the administration of an abortifacient drug and this must, therefore, also take place on approved premises. This interpretation was supported by the introduction of a new s.1(3A) in the Abortion Act in 1990, giving the power to the health secretary "to react to further changes in medical science" and "to approve a wider range of place, including potentially the home." The fact that this provision referred directly to the "use" of medication and reserved powers to the health secretary, gave powerful weight to the Government's reading of the statute.[57]

No human rights arguments were expressed in support of bpas's preferred interpretation of the Abortion Act. Rather, it articulated the rationale for its court challenge as a matter of responding to scientific progress and shifting standards in clinical best practice, explaining that it concerned "whether the 1967 Abortion Act could be interpreted in line with advances in medical science" and bringing "UK medical abortion practice, governed by laws dating back to the 1960s (when abortion pills would have seemed like futurist science fiction), into line with international standards of care."[58] The Department of Health's response is less easily understood in clinical terms, with just one relatively weak medical argument offered in favour of their position: that a new practice should not be introduced simply because it had been deemed safe elsewhere in the world without fully piloting and evaluating the system and ensuring appropriate protocols in Britain.[59] Yet, even if the rejection of direct relevance of international medical data is accepted, this claim would seem merely to justify the need for further research.

The BPAS court decision has been attacked as ignoring the "golden rule" of statutory interpretation: that legislation should be interpreted so as not to lead to an "absurd and irrational result."[60] And, indeed, the result of the case is indefensible when the medical framework is accepted as providing the exclusive compass. What is perhaps most interesting about the BPAS decision for current purposes, however, is the fact that the Government refused to conduct this dispute wholly or, indeed, primarily on this terrain. Rather, the emphasis in the Department of Health's skeleton argument was firmly on the need to maintain *political* control of a controversial and morally sensitive procedure. The Government reminded the Court of the basis for the introduction of s.1(3A), with Parliament having been reassured that EMA would be subject to both medical and political control, and advised that such drugs "would be administered only in closely regulated circumstances under the supervision of a medical practitioner." The Government argued that Parliament had specifically considered home use and "elected to retain political control" over the assessment of which premises might be approved. Later, it emphasized again that the "power is conferred on [the health secretary] and not on the medical profession" and further noted that what bpas proposed would "represent, in a highly controversial area, a very significant shift of responsibility from the democratically elected and accountable Secretary of State to the medical profession."[61]

More generally, relying on the House of Lords judgment in the *RCN* case discussed above, the Government asserted that the Abortion Act is underpinned by two broad purposes. The second of these ("to ensure that abortion is carried out with all proper skill and in hygienic conditions") was accepted in the bpas submission. However, the Government argued, the first purpose— "to broaden the grounds on which abortion may be lawfully obtained"—must also be given its full weight. In this sense, "particularly importantly given the controversial nature of the context," the Act "allocated responsibility— including as between the medical profession and the Secretary of State."[62]

The acceptance of this political case for tight regulatory control of abortion, even where particular restrictions find no basis in medical necessity, is reflected in Supperstone J's reference to abortion as a "controversial" issue, involving "deeply-held views."[63] The tight medical control of abortion (including restrictions on who can authorize and perform abortions, and where they can be performed) is thus justified not merely by clinical considerations but also by virtue of the morally sensitive, controversial nature of the proce-dure, which distinguishes it from other medical treatments. The Govern-ment's response to bpas might thus be read as clearly drawing the boundaries of medical control and reasserting the more general political control within which it operates. The same shifts may be seen in further developments since the BPAS decision all of which suggest a more hostile environment toward abortion and abortion providers and all of which present challenges to the medical framework.

First came unsuccessful proposals for two statutory amendments, intro-duced by the Conservative MP Nadine Dorries and tabled during the passage of recent, controversial NHS reforms.[64] The first sought to remove responsi-bility for drawing up clinical guidelines regarding best practice in abortion provision from the relevant professional body, the Royal College of Obstetri-cians and Gynaecologists (RCOG). The RCOG working group which had drawn up the current clinical guidelines regarding treatment of women seek-ing induced abortion was attacked as including eleven members who "are immediately and easily identifiable as abortionists who make their living wholly or partly through the abortion process." Suggesting that "it is time for self interest in the £60 million abortion industry to cease," Dorries argued that the amendment would "remove the incestuous behaviour of the RCOG and bring the care of vulnerable women back to a balanced, impartial, ac-countable and caring footing."[65] A second amendment sought to ensure that women would be offered counseling from an independent provider, with "in-dependent" defined as meaning that the provider should have no financial interest in provision of abortion services. This definition would have permit-ted Catholic "pro-life" charities to offer such counseling while simultaneously excluding charitable abortion providers, such as bpas, whose income is gen-erated primarily from providing abortions (albeit with any surplus then rein-vested into furthering the organization's charitable aims). While the amendment was defeated by 368 votes to 118, a subsequent Department of Health consultation was launched to explore nonstatutory means of achiev-ing a similar result. This was later quietly dropped.

Second, further controversy centered on a "sting" operation carried out by a British newspaper, whereby an actor approached a number of abortion providers, pretending to be seeking a termination on the grounds of fetal sex.[66] While most of the clinics refused her request, a small number of doctors were captured on film agreeing to authorize the requested termination. This led to significant public debate, with near universal condemnation of the doctors concerned. The then Health Secretary, Andrew Lansley, responded swiftly to promise criminal investigations. Noting that the limits of doctors' discretion are bounded by the parameters set by Parliament, Lansley stated: "I was appalled. Because if it happens, it is pretty much people engaging in a culture of both ignoring the law and trying to give themselves the right to say that although Parliament may have said this, we believe in abortion on demand."[67] Within the medical framework, providing abortion "on demand" suggests an abdication of the doctor's (legally entrenched) responsibility.

Third, Andrew Lansley ordered the Care Quality Commission (CQC) to undertake mass inspections of abortion clinics in order to check compliance with certification requirements. Media reports based on early leaked findings reported the "scandal" of around one-fifth of inspected clinics breaking the law, with doctors presigning authorization forms and patients receiving unsatisfactory levels of advice and counseling. Many clinics were reported to be in line to be stripped of the licenses that allow them to offer abortions.[68] However, the final report issued by the CQC cited presigning of forms at only fourteen of 249 inspected clinics, with none of the clinics concerned accused of providing poor care to their patients.[69] The Abortion Act provides only that doctors must form an opinion in "good faith," with regulations providing that any certificate of an opinion must be given before the termination takes place but remaining silent on the question of when forms should be signed.[70] While the legality of presigning per se is thus moot,[71] two points can be made about Andrew Lansley's actions in this instance. First, they appear to reflect a concern that medical control is not being rigorously exercised, with doctors accused of treating the authorization process as "rubber stamping" rather than exercising independent scrutiny and clinical judgment. In this sense, the accusation might be that doctors are abdicating the decision-making role foreseen for them in the 1967 Act. Second, however, the political dimension to the Health Secretary's actions is clear, with Lansley criticized for interference with the priorities of an independent regulatory body that is known to be struggling to meet existing commitments, and which was forced to cancel planned hospital inspections in order to target abortion providers.[72] Lansley was also attacked for announcing details of the inspections while they were still underway, allegedly in a bid to chase more positive headlines, following widespread, vocal criticism of his highly unpopular NHS reforms.[73] This led some to question whether "precious time and money was being wasted on an essentially political scheme to placate elements of the Conservative party."[74]

Fourth, hostility toward abortion services has not diminished following Lansley's removal as Health Secretary, with his successor creating headlines within two weeks of his appointment, by suggesting that he would like to see the upper time limit within which abortion is legally available halved from twenty-four to twelve weeks.[75] Jeremy Hunt initially reported that he had reached his conclusion after studying "the evidence" rather than for religious reasons but, in later interviews, he refused to be pushed on precisely what scientific facts he believed would support a twelve-week limit.[76] While the Prime Minister intervened to confirm that the Government has no plans to reform abortion law,[77] Hunt was supported by a number of other Conservative MPs, including the Minister for Women who expressed her own support for a reduction in the abortion time limit to twenty weeks. Like Hunt, Maria Miller claimed her view was grounded in "evidence," apparently relying on a misreading of the data regarding survival rates of extremely premature babies.[78]

Finally, one further recent and highly tragic case is also of relevance here. In September 2012, Sarah Catt was found guilty of unlawful procurement of miscarriage under the Offences Against the Person Act. She was initially sentenced to eight years of imprisonment (reflecting a one-third reduction of the maximum twelve-year term, in view of her guilty plea).[79] Catt had bought misoprostol over the Internet, and, on the basis of evidence obtained from scans performed at two abortion clinics (which had each advised Catt that she was too late for a lawful termination), the judge found that she must have taken the drug "as near to term as makes no difference." Catt claimed that her baby had been stillborn and that she had buried the body at a location that she refused to disclose. Despite some evidence of a chaotic lifestyle, including previous concealed pregnancies, Catt was found to have no mental disorder. Rather, Cooke J found that she had made a "cold calculated decision" taken for her "own convenience and in [her] own self interest alone," despite having the "intelligence, education and experience [to] know just how early on a child's characteristics and features are seen in the womb and the extent of a child's development at 38–40 weeks." Further, while "suffering emotional distress," she was found to have demonstrated no remorse for her actions.[80]

While Catt's guilty plea meant that the Court did not need to consider legal argument on whether all aspects of the crime charged had been met,[81] the harshness of the sentence in her case has been widely criticized as pointlessly punitive and reflecting the strong pro-life bias of a judge who was later revealed to be a leading member of the Lawyers' Christian Fellowship,[82] an organization committed, in its own words, to "applying God's justice on the ground."[83] Cooke J's general hostility toward abortion services is clearly visible in his highly unusual *obiter* attack on the exercise of medical discretion under the Abortion Act, which, he opined, is "wrongly, liberally construed in practice so as to make abortion available essentially on demand prior to 24 weeks with the approval of registered medical practitioners." Cooke J further describes Catt's offence as one that "all right thinking people would consider . . . more serious than manslaughter or any offence on the calendar other than murder," and certainly more serious than causing death by dangerous driving, given her "calculated intentionality."[84] As one commentator noted, such language would be "as at home in the pulpit as it was in the court," moving on to criticize the judicial articulation of the worrying principle that "the closer a defendant gets to giving birth, the closer she gets to being categorized as a murderer."[85] While the Court of Appeal later reduced the 'manifestly excessive' sentence imposed on Catt to three and a half years, it declined to comment on Cooke J's *obiter* remarks regarding the exercise of medical discretion under the Abortion Act or the assumptions made regarding the views of "right thinking people."[86]

While *Catt* raises many issues, two points are of specific relevance for current purposes: the appropriateness of current criminal sanctions in this context and the enforceability of existing law. First, the case serves to emphasize that while the Abortion Act may have led to the widespread availability of abortion in Britain, those terminations that take place outside the strict regime of medical control foreseen within it may be subject to extremely onerous criminal sanction. While the judge's sentencing comments suggest that it was the lateness of the termination that justified such a lengthy prison term, a woman who used drugs purchased online earlier in her pregnancy is still, on the face of the statute, potentially subject to the same onerous penalty. Second, however, the case also indicates the difficulties of enforcing this law in a world of widespread Internet availability of abortion medication. Catt's use of misoprostol was detected only because of the suspicions of clinic staff following her late scans. If Catt had not attended a clinic, her use would almost certainly have gone undetected, and the wide publicity given to this case will undoubtedly provide useful lessons in how to avoid discovery for other women considering the self-administration of abortion drugs.

The attacks on British abortion providers and abortion law described above were framed in two subtly different ways, operating both within and against the medical framework. *Within* the medical framework, concerns have been advanced that abortion service providers are motivated by financial incentives, that medical control has become a matter of "rubber stamping," or that doctors are wrongly construing the legislation too liberally, rather than offering the impartial, individualized, discriminating act of clinical scrutiny intended by Parliament. What is needed, say such critics, is not less but simply better (uncorrupted and more rigorous) medical control. Jeremy Hunt's criticism of the law was likewise claimed (albeit with no substantiation) to be grounded in medical fact, with Hunt repeatedly reassuring critics that he would be "guided by the science" in any decisions that he would make as Health Secretary. Other of these attacks rather operate *against* the medical framework, refuting its preeminence, and seeking to delineate more tightly the parameters within which it should be contained. Here, the argument is that the place for medical judgment must be strictly limited to a more tightly defined role, with the work of setting such parameters an inherently political task.

Conclusions

In this chapter, I have described how a shared conceptual framework can operate to establish common reference points and parameters for determining both *how* one may speak with legitimacy and *who* has authority to do so. I focused on Britain as a significant case study of where the preeminence of the medical framework has been entrenched in statute and broadly accepted. While this has contributed to significant depoliticization and liberalization of access to abortion, the limitations of the medical frame as a basis for defending and furthering women's reproductive rights should nonetheless be apparent. In Britain, the provision of abortion services remains restricted by clinically unnecessary requirements regarding where, and by whom, terminations can be performed and authorized. Notably, women have no formal legal right to demand a termination at any stage of pregnancy. Further, as was seen in the BPAS decision, clinically unsupported restrictions on abortion provision have been retained as part of a system of tight, medicalized control, whereas elsewhere, the absence of any specific rule regarding place of provision has allowed home use of EMA. The difficulties of enforcing this tight regulation in a context where mifepristone and misoprostol may be bought online is, nonetheless, clear.

I suggested that the dominance of the medical framework does not necessarily imply a deeper moral consensus regarding abortion, and, again, this was clear in the British example, where attitudes to abortion have remained divided in a way only explicable through ideological differences. The MPs who debated the decision to license mifepristone were, by and large, not trained scientists, reaching different, informed views on the clinical merits of EMA following their own extended study of the trial data. Rather, their perspectives were informed by existing views on the morality of abortion and, in some cases, a network of contacts outside Parliament that fed them information and arguments. To intervene in the parliamentary debates, however, these broader moral beliefs were typically translated into medical arguments regarding patient safety and the scientific objectivity of the available data. The same dynamic is equally apparent in subsequent debates including, notably, the S&TC report, where the minority's ideological opposition to abortion is expressed through disputing the scientific validity of the evidence in favor of liberalizing the law.

It was seen that the medical framework has been used partly to distinguish between ethically motivated doctors, who perform abortions openly, in sanitary conditions, and in the best interests of their patients, on the one hand; and unskilled, profiteering, backstreet abortionists who prey on vulnerable women, on the other. While such a clear-cut dichotomy never reflected reality, it signally fails to offer a useful framework for considering the actions of women who choose to purchase abortion drugs online in order to perform their own abortions. Further, its inability to offer either a descriptive or normative framework capable of understanding current abortion provision is starkly visible in the light of the abortion services offered in Britain by charitable providers, which operate closely within the law, relying on the work of doctors and evidence-based medicine, yet are explicitly motivated to empower women to make their own reproductive choices. I distinguished the "medical" framework from a "reproductive health" one. British charitable providers find themselves caught in the tension between offering reproductive choice and the best possible care for the women they treat, yet being constrained to abide by the highly medicalized model of control entrenched in statute (with this tension illustrated in the legal dispute regarding home use of EMA).

One further observation is also significant at this point: the medical framework is not static. The 1967 Act is grounded within a particular understanding of medicine that fossilized the broader assumptions of a time in which medical control was intended to achieve two specific and quite

separate ends: clinical safety and a significant gate-keeping role, filtering requests for access to abortion. Notwithstanding this second aim, abortion on
demand has been largely realized in Britain because the medical framework
in which the Act is grounded has evolved since 1967, with the ethos of the
medical relationship at its core gradually shifting away from a model of "doctor knows best" paternalism towards a model of partnership. The doctor's
role, within this reframed medical relationship, is to provide the information
and advice that a duly empowered, informed and autonomous patient needs
to make his or her own healthcare choices.

Early feminist commentators made extravagant claims regarding the future development of EMA drugs:

> An anti-progestin drug could develop in the future in such a way that
> sudden decisions could be put into effect, so that spontaneous con-
> tacts from which no consequences are desired would become increas-
> ingly devoid of risk of pregnancy. This would likely change the
> behaviour of women entirely around reproduction and their sexual
> behaviour. They would be in a position to act and react like men,
> meaning they would, in every single case, be able not to let the conse-
> quences of sexual intercourse take place.[87]

While twenty years on, such early hopes (and the corresponding fears provoked in others) have remained largely unrealized, the potential of EMA to
challenge received understandings of abortion and existing regulatory frameworks is nonetheless striking. The possibility to purchase EMA drugs online
brings safer abortion outside of medical control into the reach of many
women. In future years, in many parts of the world, legal disputes regarding
abortion may come to be focused on pharmaceutical licensing procedures,
the regulation of telemedicine, conflicts of laws, and customs restrictions.
And while abortion has long been a difficult crime to detect and prosecute,
the challenges involved in any attempt to regulate EMA—or to contain it
within tight medical control—will be very significantly greater.

Chapter 10

The Right to Conscience

Bernard M. Dickens

The aim of this chapter is to release "conscience" from capture by those who object to participation in induced abortion. It argues that, while opponents of induced abortion are properly entitled to invoke conscientious objections to participation, others are equally entitled conscientiously to participate in such lawful procedures, to advise patients about the option, and to refer patients to where appropriate services are available. This includes taking such actions in institutions that, for religious or other reasons, oppose such procedures on principle. The human right to act lawfully according to one's individual conscience is not a monopoly of abortion opponents. As a legally protected human right, however, the right to conscience may be considered an entitlement primarily of human individuals, and available to corporate or other institutions on only a limited basis. Individuals may accordingly invoke conscientious reasons to participate, or not to participate, in abortion procedures, and to offer advice and referral without suffering sanctions or discrimination on grounds of their religious or philosophical convictions.

The origins of conscientious objection in health care precede the legalization of abortion. In England, for instance, legislation of mandatory vaccination of children against smallpox in 1867 triggered violent objections to vaccination.[1] Among medical practitioners, historical conservative attitudes rooted in different religions, religious denominations, and laws influenced practitioners conscientiously to object to advise and assist artificial contraception, contraceptive sterilization, artificial insemination, and abortion.[2] The transition to legality of these procedures was traced in 1966 by two gynecologists regarding artificial insemination when they observed, "Any change in custom or practice in this emotionally charged area has always elicited a response from established custom and law of horrified negation at first; then negation without horror; then slow and gradual curiosity, study, evaluation, and finally a very slow but steady acceptance."[3] It was growing legalization of abortion, however, from the late 1960s in Europe and beyond, that made this procedure the prime center of health service providers' claims to object to participation in lawful medical care on grounds of conscience.

An important factor easing enactment of the U.K. Abortion Act, 1967,[4] for instance, was inclusion of section 4(1), which provides that "no person shall be under any duty, whether by contract or by any statutory or other legal requirement, to participate in any treatment authorised by this Act to which he has a conscientious objection." Section 4(2) provides the exception, however, of: "any duty to participate in treatment which is necessary to save the life or to prevent grave permanent injury to the physical or mental health of a pregnant woman."

The section is consistent with the Universal Declaration of Human Rights, of 1948, which provides in Article 18 that: "Everyone has the right to freedom of thought, conscience and religion; this right includes freedom . . . to manifest his religion or belief in teaching, practice, worship and observance." When legal effect was given to this right, however, in the International Covenant on Civil and Political Rights, it was made clear that the right is not absolute. Article 18(1) repeats that everyone "shall have the right to freedom of thought, conscience and religion," but 18(3) provides that: "Freedom to manifest one's religion or beliefs may be subject only to such limitations as are prescribed by law and are necessary to protect public safety, order, health, or morals or the fundamental rights and freedoms of others."

The protection under human rights of "conscience and religion" shows that conscience is separate from religion. Religious convictions may well shape individuals' conscience, but religion has no monopoly on conscience and is indeed subject to scrutiny and evaluation on grounds of conscience. Conscience may be shaped by social, philosophical, political, professional, and other convictions apart from those founded on religious faith. Religious institutions and hierarchies that, for instance, do not include women, and that expressly exclude women from positions of doctrinal authority, may be considered conscientiously flawed, and to lack relevance in their pronouncements, particularly on a matter such as abortion, in which women's health and interests are centrally involved.

Religious convictions may inspire individuals to enter the health care professions, for instance as doctors or nurses. This conforms to a long, honourable tradition of religious commitment to care for the sick and for disabled individuals. When health care practitioners would place their personal conscience above serving their dependent patients' health needs, however, they risk violation of their duties of conscientious professionalism, with legal implications, which this chapter addresses, and ethical implications.[5]

The four historic reputable professions, namely religious ministry, the profession of arms, medicine, and the law, are founded on a calling to self-sacrifice. In times of plague, for instance, ministers of religions tended to the sick and dying at the risk of contracting infections and sharing the fate of those they comforted. The status of mercenary soldiers is now discredited, but volunteers and conscripts who serve their nations have paid, and still pay, with their health and very lives. Doctors who treated infectious patients have faced risks of contracting their infection in past and present times. For instance, Dr. Carlo Urbani, who in 2003 discovered and named the severe acute respiratory syndrome (SARS), died of contracting that viral infection. Lawyers may be obliged to defend those accused, and guilty, of atrocious crimes, and to advance the purposes of clients, including governments, whose motivations they deplore, with professional detachment and disregard for their own interests. Against this background of self-sacrifice, health care professionals who will serve their own religious or other interests by sacrificing the interests of their dependent patients, by reliance on the claim of conscientious objection, are in a conflict of interest, with legal and ethical accountability, and risk committing a travesty of professionalism.

The challenge in law is to address how health care providers conscientiously opposed to abortion and comparable procedures that serve their patients' wishes and interests should conduct themselves. A related challenge is how health care institutions founded on religious traditions opposed to such procedures should accommodate health care providers who are conscientiously committed to delivering such services when, in their clinical judgment, the providers consider the procedures to best serve their patients' wishes and health interests.

The latter challenge bears attention, since in the abortion context the focus in the literature, legislation, and jurisprudence has been on conscientious objection, and accommodation of objectors' human rights of conscience. Respect for and accommodation of conscience should in justice be symmetrical, however. Institutions with no policy opposing particular medical procedures such as forms of reproductive health care, and end-of-life care, should accommodate practitioners who object to participation in them on grounds of conscience, without censure or discrimination, and institutions whose leadership is opposed should accommodate practitioners conscientiously committed to deliver care to patients for whom such procedures appear medically indicated, equally without censure or discrimination.[6]

States must protect practitioners' conscientious commitment to undertake abortion care, so that states are able to discharge their legal responsibilities to patients. The European Court of Human Rights has observed, regarding abortion services, that " States are obliged to organise the health services system in such a way as to ensure that an effective exercise of the freedom of conscience of health professionals in the professional context does not prevent patients from obtaining access to services to which they are entitled under the applicable legislation."[7]

Laws designed to restrict access to abortion services may violate human rights, of both women and service providers, and justify challenge. Deliberate defiance of laws, amounting to civil disobedience, has been advocated by opponents of abortion restriction who assert the superiority of human rights, and by religious advocates of abortion restriction who claim the superiority of divine law.[8] However, this chapter lacks space to address arguments for legal accommodation of noncompliance with states' abortion laws.

The Nature and Scope of Conscience

The foundation of rights to conscience in leading international human rights instruments, reflected in the constitutional laws and human rights codes and provisions of many countries, confirms the importance of these rights to human dignity and identity. Although rights to conscience are formally distinguishable from rights to religion in Article 18(1) of the International Covenant on Civil and Political Rights (CCPR), Article 18(3) addresses limits on the freedom "to manifest one's religion or beliefs," indicating that freedom of belief is allied with religious freedom. This is of particular significance in some sectors of the Roman Catholic tradition regarding induced abortion, where this is considered a mortal sin, constituting death of the soul and a risk of forfeiture of eternal life in heaven after the end of one's life on Earth. To those who have faith in this or a comparable belief system, the risk of committing this sin is too fearful to take. Their spiritual anguish can deny them their physical, mental, and/or social well-being; that is, what the World Health Organization considers their "health."[9]

Conscientious objection based on religious beliefs must accordingly be accommodated to the fullest extent consistent with, in the language of CCPR Article 18(3), "the fundamental rights and freedoms of others." No less worthy of profound respect than religiously guided conscience is conscience based on secular convictions, such as philosophical, social, political, professional, or other beliefs. If individuals are to be free to be true to themselves, the diversity of their rights to conscience must be accommodated as a key human right. In international human rights law, three "generations" of human rights have been identified, the first being civil and political rights, the second equality or socioeconomic rights, and the third collective or solidarity rights.[10]

Collective rights may be possessed by members of social or communal groups of individuals, and by private or public corporate bodies recognized by law to have artificial personality as an administrative or commercial convenience, including, for instance, rights of property ownership and to commercial speech. They can also bear responsibility for violation of individuals' rights, such as to nondiscrimination in recruitment for employment. Jurisprudence, for instance under Article 9 of the European Convention on Human Rights, recognizes rights of religious institutions such as churches and mosques to invoke human rights in their own name,[11] acting as representatives of their members, for instance to resist state intervention in their internal affairs and denial of their rights. However, a legal entity such as a hospital corporation, as a civic, nonecclesiastical institution, cannot claim a right to religious conscience.

In a 2008 judgment of international significance, for instance, the Constitutional Court of Colombia ruled that a hospital corporation could not claim a right of conscientious objection on its own behalf to justify denial of a medically indicated abortion procedure.[12] The Court held that the human right to respect for conscience is enjoyed only by natural human beings. By requiring and allowing its gynecologists' conscientious objections to limit its services, the hospital was unlawfully asserting a conscientious objection of its own. The hospital's legal duty is to have physicians available to conduct timely procedures for patients' care in which others may object to participate on grounds of conscience.

The Court recognized individuals' right to object to direct participation in abortion but ruled that hospital administrative officers responsible for such tasks as admitting patients and booking operating theaters, and, for instance, those conducting routine nursing procedures such as for postoperative care, do not attract the protection of conscientious objection. This ruling is consistent with a body of jurisprudence holding that, in the absence of specifically directed legislation, administrative personnel in health facilities where abortions are conducted, who are not directly clinically engaged in such procedures, cannot invoke conscientious objection to refuse to discharge their routine responsibilities. The Constitutional Court indicated that religious objections to complicity in sin have no legal substance when such objections would deny "the fundamental rights and freedoms of others" to receive medically indicated lawful treatment.

The Court required that patients for whose care abortion is indicated, and who request the procedure, have to be promptly referred by, or on behalf of, those who have conscientious objections to physicians who would conduct the procedure. This touches on an area of professional sensitivity, since it is known in many countries, but rarely reflected in their jurisprudence, that some gynecologists who invoke conscientious objection to participate in abortions in public hospitals perform the procedure for fee-paying patients in their private clinics. Physician self-referral, meaning referral by physicians of their public hospital patients to be treated in their private practices, usually as fee-paying clients, raises legal and ethical concerns regarding conflict of interest. Gynecologists may want to maintain a public appearance of opposing abortion, thereby avoiding stigma and risk of condemnation for being "abortionists," and to offer patients the greater confidentiality of private care, where pregnancy termination can be recorded by medical euphemisms unrelated to abortion.

That conscientious objection may be publicly invoked insincerely and unconscionably stands in contrast to the moral worthiness of practitioners whose objections are authentic, uniform, and sincere. Their discharge of a religious duty to tend to the sick and needy, but within a framework of serving their own spiritual salvation, explains why they are prepared to place their own spiritual interests above the interests their patients intend to pursue by obtaining indicated health care. In a sense, they may be using their dependent patients instrumentally, as a means to achieving their own spiritual ends, even though they may self-servingly rationalize their conduct as protecting the unborn or, more paternalistically, as protecting the patients themselves.[13] This would violate the Kantian ethic that people should treat others as ends in themselves, and not purely as means or objects through which to serve their own ends.

Conscientious objection to abortion raises concerns about medical education and training for medical students of gynecology, for medical schools, and for medical licensing authorities. It is common that medical students and qualified doctors do not make efforts to learn the types of skills that they do not intend to practice. For instance, intended pediatricians do not seek the skills of geriatricians, nor vice versa. However, those who intend careers in gynecology are expected to learn the skills of that specialty even if they intend not to induce abortions. They may be called on, for instance, to treat patients suffering threatened spontaneous miscarriage, and to remove a dead fetus from the uterus according to professional techniques and standards, even if those skills may be applied in other circumstances in termination of pregnancy. A student's refusal to learn these procedures, a medical school's acceptance not to teach them to prospective gynecologists, and a medical licensing authority's grant of an unrestricted licence to a specialist who is incompletely trained, all raise legal questions of holding out to the public that qualified gynecologists are fit to practice who may be unable to provide adequately trained care.

Gynecologists should disclose the limits of their training to the agencies interested to engage their services, and the areas of practice expected of gynecologists to which they object. Similarly, as will be addressed below, their patients and prospective patients should be informed of what services patients may reasonably expect from practitioners in their specialty that they are not able or willing to undertake.

The same applies to midlevel providers of gynecological services, such as nurse practitioners, who can be trained for competent discharge of selected services where fully qualified gynecologists are not available. Women should not be denied care because gynecologists trained and qualified to the highest levels are unavailable. If such personnel would decline to undertake services reasonably expected of them on grounds of conscientious objection, however, this should be appropriately disclosed to agencies liable to recruit them.

An approach to encourage medical and related students who conscientiously object to inducing abortion to learn to assist women with threatened loss of pregnancy may be through use of appropriate language. The use of language in the sensitive area of abortion is notoriously euphemistic, imprecise, or casual.[14] If "abortion" is taken to refer to deliberately induced abortion, however, while spontaneous loss of pregnancy, whether before or after fetal viability, is described as "miscarriage," gynecologists who object to participation in abortion procedures may be trained and willing to assist women who suffer spontaneous threatened or actual miscarriage. That is, the legitimate scope of their objection may be narrowed to its conscientious focus.

A less tractable definitional concern is the status of emergency contraception. The medical evidence is that the emergency contraceptive pill levonorgestrel is not abortifacient, since it will not affect an actual pregnancy, but may prevent pregnancy.[15] This reasoning is based on the definition of pregnancy applied by the International Federation of Gynecology and Obstetrics (FIGO), the only organization that brings together professional societies of gynecologists on a global basis, which is that "pregnancy . . . commences with the implantation of the conceptus in a woman, and ends with either the birth of an infant or an abortion."[16] Implantation is usually completed in the lining of the uterus. A conceptus is an ovum that has become fertilized by a sperm. The view that there cannot be abortion until pregnancy, and that before completion of implantation there is no pregnancy, has been endorsed at a governmental level, for instance in the U.K., where the Attorney-General explained that disposal of unimplanted embryos following in vitro fertilization (IVF) is not governed by the abortion law.[17]

Underlying this issue is contention about when protected human life commences. Scientific approaches vary,[18] as do religious traditions, and legal judgments. Many religious denominations accept the medical view that prevention of implantation constitutes contraception, and not abortion. Doctrine in the Roman Catholic denomination of Christianity has varied historically on when human life warrants protection, but in 1869 Pope Pius IX fixed this time as "conception." The words "fertilization" and "conception" were synonymous at that time, since the only evidence of fertilization of an ovum, and of conception by implantation of the fertilized ovum in the uterus, was that a woman had become pregnant. The development of IVF, however, showed fertilization to occur before conception and pregnancy, and even when there would be no conception or pregnancy. Roman Catholic doctrine, which condemns IVF, was then interpreted to equate deliberate wastage of unimplanted human embryos[19] with abortion.

Those who for religious reasons conscientiously object to abortion may therefore equally object to deliberate wastage of embryos, should they exist, in emergency contraception, since an embryo will be prevented from survival, which depends on completion of uterine implantation. Indeed, their approach may consider the distinction between abortion and routine or emergency contraception inconsequential, since they are as much opposed to any form of artificial contraception as to abortion. For instance, many pharmacists who object to filling prescriptions for emergency contraception also object to delivering prescribed contraceptive products.

The distinction between abortion and emergency contraception remains significant, however, in law, since what constitutes abortion is a legal as well as a religious matter. A rape victim treated in the emergency department of a Roman Catholic hospital in California once complained of violation of her constitutional and civil rights because she was not offered nor informed of her option of using emergency contraception, which she described as "the morning-after pill" and the court as "estrogen pregnancy prophylaxis."[20] The hospital invoked its statutory protection against any obligation to perform or to permit abortion. The California Court of Appeal ruled, however, that prevention of pregnancy by emergency contraception is different from abortion, and that the rape victim's rights had been violated. The Court accepted the victim's claim that her "right to control her treatment must prevail over [the hospital] respondent's moral and religious convictions,"[21] to the extent of being informed of her right to emergency contraception, and of means to acquire that treatment within seventy-two hours of the assault.

In requiring hospital emergency or gynecological staff to provide information of emergency contraception, and to supply it or refer the patient, in a timely manner, to where she could avail herself of it, notwithstanding their personal conscientious objections, the Court was not denigrating or dismissing the significance of religious convictions, but acting as a secular court does. When the English Court of Appeal (Administrative Court) in 2002 similarly ruled that the morning-after pill was not abortifacient, and that in using it, "hundreds of thousands, indeed millions, of ordinary men and women" in England and Wales were not causing (arguably illegal) abortions, Mr. Justice Munby (as he then was) observed, "I sit as a secular judge serving a multi-cultural community of many faiths in which all of us can now take pride, sworn to do justice 'to all manner of people.' Religion—whatever the particular believer's faith—is no doubt something to be encouraged but it is not the business of government or of the secular courts. So the starting point of the law is an essentially agnostic view of religious beliefs and a tolerant indulgence to religious and cultural diversity."[22]

In contrast, courts in several Latin American countries have applied legislation, including their national constitution, that provides that human life is afforded protection "from conception," to find emergency contraception unlawful.[23] In Peru in 2009, for instance, the Constitutional Court required the Ministry of Health not to distribute emergency contraception, which remained accessible in the private sector.[24] This prohibition followed a 2002 decision of the Supreme Court of Argentina,[25] which prohibited production, distribution, and sale of an emergency contraceptive product, and a similar decision of the Constitutional Court of Ecuador in 2006.[26] Some conscientious objectors, fearful of excommunication from the Catholic Church, suspected scientific assurances that abortion is not implicated in emergency contraception, and their doubts were echoed by courts that found the scientific evidence inconclusive. The Constitutional Courts of Chile[27] and Peru[28] resolved the uncertainty in favor of a potential for human life and upheld prohibition of emergency contraception.

The Latin American jurisprudence may be superseded, however, by the 2012 ruling of the Inter-American Court of Human Rights, that an embryo, prior to implantation, has no legal right to life. [29] The Court's ruling that any wastage of surplus embryos from in vitro fertilization does not justify prohibition of that reproductive means supports the legal conclusion that emergency contraception, preventing possible implantation, is not abortifacient.

For the same reason, menstrual extraction, for instance following a woman being late in her menstrual period, cannot be equated with abortion. This simple vacuum suction technique removes menstrual blood and other products from the uterus and restores the woman's menstrual cycle. Menstruation may be delayed for a variety of reasons, but the procedure is not preceded by a pregnancy test. In contrast is restoration of regular menstruation by manual vacuum aspiration, which is a clinic or hospital procedure that requires dilation of the cervix, may require use of a vacuum machine, and must be preceded by a positive pregnancy test. The latter procedure is clearly intended to terminate pregnancy, justifying conscientious objection.

Patients'/Women's Conscience

The preamble to the U.N. Convention on the Elimination of All Forms of Discrimination against Women (CEDAW) notes that the U.N. Charter "reaffirms faith in fundamental human rights, in the dignity and worth of the human person and in the equal rights of men and women." It further notes that the Universal Declaration of Human Rights promotes equality in dignity and rights of all human beings "without distinction . . . based on sex," and that states must "secure the equal rights of men and women to enjoy all economic, social, cultural, civil and political rights." Article 12 of CEDAW addresses equal access to health care services, including family planning.

Adopted in 1979 and in force since 1981, CEDAW remains unratified by, among others, the United States and the Holy See. Identifying U.N. declarations requiring the equality of women and men, the preamble expresses concerns that "despite these various instruments extensive discrimination against women continues to exist." These concerns remain pertinent today, particularly regarding women's unimpaired access to abortion services that they conscientiously consider in the best interests of their families and themselves. A continuing concern, for instance, is that "in situations of poverty women have the least access to food, health, education [and] training." These are interactive concerns regarding pregnancy, since malnutrition leading to anemia and related ill-health, as well as illiteracy, dependency on others for sustenance, and lack of means to cope with family and related responsibilities, can combine to make continuation of pregnancy medically contraindicated, and contraindicated on wider grounds of "health," described by the WHO as a state of "physical, mental and social well-being."[30]

Even the most culturally, socially, and economically advanced of countries have not shed the legacy of denying women's moral agency as conscientious decision makers, for their societies, families, and even their own bodies. Male-led institutions in which women are underrepresented, not included, or deliberately excluded, such as legislatures, government ministries, judicial benches, religious hierarchies, and medical professional associations, often consider themselves better capable of serving women's health care and other interests than are women themselves. Insensitive to or unaware of the particular circumstances of individual women, they stereotype women[31] through often crude characterizations, for instance as impetuously, or in panic, making hurried decisions to abort, uninformed of the implications of abortion procedures.

Both religious and secular intruders into pregnant women's choices are often more preoccupied with protection of unborn human life than with protection of women's health and the welfare of their families, including their dependent children.[32] Rejecting pre-natal baptism and so requiring live birth as the precondition to achieving a child's spiritual salvation, they fear that, without their intervention, the unborn child will lose not only its life, but its heavenly afterlife too. Opposing abortion through denial or obstruction of procedures is seen as merciful rescue, and a legitimate, necessary initiative, whether or not in conformity with human laws.

The woman who proposes to terminate her pregnancy is myopically viewed in relation only to her embryo or fetus. This is especially so in religious environments conditioned by celibate priesthoods whose members exist outside the lived experience of family life, with its trade-offs of interests, its difficult judgments on whose interests to privilege, postpone, or subordinate, and its assessments of how the interests of past and future generations should weigh in the balance. For instance, a woman aged thirty with two young children, a husband who requires her assistance in his small business that supports the family, elderly dependent parents and/or parents-in-law, and commitments to other family members, may conscientiously judge that these competing interests weigh against continuation of a pregnancy. The welfare of the parents for the foreseeable future, and the well-being of her young children and their rearing, depend on her availability, which she sees being jeopardized by birth and caring for a newborn, if she survives childbirth and maintains her health. Depending on the health care and other resources to which she has access, none of these outcomes may be assured.

It is arrogant and impertinent for strangers to this woman's circumstances, whether they have the power of legislators, the authority of judges, the piety of ministers of religion, or the learning and experience of doctors, to believe that their conscientious resolutions of this woman's competing family interests are superior to hers. Her health, meaning her physical, mental, and social well-being, is denied security by the claims of third parties, perhaps empowered by law, to impose their preferences in decision making over hers. This is the basis on which the Chief Justice of Canada, in a landmark ruling in 1988 declaring the restrictive national criminal law on abortion unconstitutional, observed: "Forcing a woman, by threat of criminal sanction, to carry a foetus to term unless she meets certain criteria unrelated to her own priorities and aspirations, is a profound interference with a woman's body and thus a violation of security of the person."[33]

The previous law made abortion dependent on decisions of committees no agency was legally required to establish, that many medical institutions were ineligible to establish, and that could ignore an applicant's "own priorities and aspirations." Their purpose was to ensure compliance with statutory criteria, although evidence showed that they often added their own arbitrary, idiosyncratic conditions.[34] In many countries, access to professional care for abortion has been made dependent on compliance with patronizing conditions that infantilize women applicants, and with others designed to dissuade or deter women from pursuing their intentions.

For instance "reflection delay" laws, initiated in France,[35] require women requesting abortion to reflect for a time, measured in hours or days, before their consent is legally effective. These laws presuppose that women request abortions without prior reflection. The stereotype this demonstrates of women as impulsive, and unreflective unless made to be so by legislatures, is profoundly disrespectful of the conscientious, sometimes agonizing but responsible thought that usually precedes an abortion request. Such a legal provision approaches pregnant women as immaturely incapable of personal, social, or moral reflection without legal compulsion. No other medical procedure, however invasive or long-lasting its effect, attracts this type of discriminatory statutory requirement. Doctors are required to ensure, as far as they reasonably can, that patients understand the information they are given for their consent to proposed treatment to be adequately informed, and will recommend counseling when desirable, but patients who are resolved in their choices may waive these opportunities and consent when they want to.

Similarly, laws such as introduced in Germany that make documented receipt of dissuasive counseling by governmentally approved non-physician counselors a precondition to lawful abortion subordinate the moral agency of women to perceived state duties to the unborn.[36] Laws of this nature further compromise women's access to care since eligible counselors may arbitrarily decline to meet with women.

Several U.S. state legislatures under control of anti-abortion politicians have abused informed consent laws to compel doctors to recite, and women to hear, "information" that the legislators have scripted. Some, such as Texas, go further, and require women to see ultrasound pictures of their fetuses, including real time images of their pulsating hearts.[37] In regular law, to obtain adequately informed consent to proposed treatment, doctors must offer to provide material information, and give it to patients who want to receive it, without statutory compulsion. There is no obligation on the part of patients, however, to receive it. The aim of these clinically unnecessary, often cynical laws is to deter women from having abortions, and to punish those who have them by implanting memories for guilt and remorse. The role of U.S. state legislatures in inducing abortion-based regret has attracted academic analysis (see below).[38]

Women's capacities for conscientious judgment on abortion may be denied concerning their own bodies, and also concerning their capacities and duties as mothers of their daughters. When young or adolescent girls are victims of sexual abuse and become pregnant, their mothers often initiate abortion requests on their behalf. This is liable to bring them into contact, and in some countries not uncommonly into conflict, with hospital adminis- trations, government health care agencies, criminal law enforcement agen- cies, hospital chaplains, and senior clerics.[39]

An incident that generated public reaction occurred in Recife, Brazil, in 2009 when a nine-year-old girl, whose stepfather reportedly admitted sexu- ally abusing her, was found to have a life-endangering twin pregnancy. In Brazil, abortion is lawful when pregnancy is due to rape. Local doctors ac- cepted the mother's abortion request, but Archbishop Sobrinho of Olinda and Recife condemned the mother and doctors, declaring their excommuni- cation from the Catholic Church. In an unusual reaction, another archbishop wrote to the Vatican's newspaper that this approach to the girl's plight "hurts the credibility of our teaching, which appears in the eyes of many as insensi- tive, incomprehensible and lacking mercy."[40] Perhaps embarrassed at public condemnation of Archbishop Sobrinho and support for the girl's mother and doctors,[41] the diocese later advanced a more compassionate explanation in accordance with Catholic teaching.

The incident reflects a disdain for mothers' conscientious judgments made in their daughters' best interests. In a 2012 case, the European Court of Human Rights held Poland in violation of the European Convention for the Protection of Human Rights and Fundamental Freedoms[42] when the mother of a fourteen-year-old pregnant rape victim seeking abortion was asked to sign a statement including that "this procedure could lead to my daughter's death," was told by a priest brought into the case in breach of confidentiality that she was a bad mother, and later was subjected to proceedings in the Lu- blin Family and Custody Court to terminate her parental rights regarding her daughter. The Family Court initially divested the mother of her legal status, but quashed that decision on a re-hearing of the case. The doctor at the hos- pital to which the girl was first taken offered to adopt the girl's baby, and the girl herself,[43] showing how women's status in relationship to their pregnant daughters can be minimized and denied when they conscientiously request abortion. The European Court found violations of the mother's and daugh- ter's rights to respect for their private lives by the doctors' and hospital's inter- vention between them, and by breach of medical confidentiality affecting them both.

Conscientious Objection

The right to act or to refrain in accordance with one's conscience, whether based on religious, philosophical, or other convictions, is a central human right protected by leading international and national legal instruments such as treaties and constitutions. As such, conscientious objection warrants maximum protection. Laws may require, as for instance in Poland, that objection be made in writing and included in the individual patient's medical record, with referral to another physician competent to perform the same service.[44] The burden of proof of conscientious objection usually falls on the person who claims the right. In Scotland, for instance, a statement made on oath or affirmation is sufficient proof,[45] with legal liability for speaking falsely.

Like other human rights, the right of conscientious objection is not absolute. It must yield, as CCPR Article 18(3) provides, to legal "limitations . . . necessary to protect public safety, order, health, or morals or the fundamental rights and freedoms of others." There is a nice point of interpretation regarding whether "public" qualifies only "safety," to contrast public with private safety, or whether it provides protection only for public order, comparable to the French *ordre public* which underpins operation of the state's legal system, public health and public morals.[46] If the disallowance of exercise of rights of conscience applies only for protection of public health but not of private or clinical health, then abortion to protect or promote individual health will need to be defended under the CCPR as a "fundamental" right and freedom.

Such right or freedom may be recognized for medically necessary procedures, but not elective procedures. For instance, the U.K. Abortion Act, 1967, section 4(2), excludes rights of conscientious objection only from "any duty to participate in treatment which is necessary to save the life or to prevent grave permanent injury to the physical or mental health of a pregnant woman."[47] This may appear to allow conscientious objection to participation in abortion procedures for lesser health risks. However, mental health may be permanently and gravely impaired if a woman is compelled to gestate and deliver an unwanted child, and to feel responsible for its welfare for the rest of her life. This is particularly so where, as section 1(1) (d) of the Act provides, "if the child were born it would suffer from such physical or mental abnormalities as to be seriously handicapped." Conscientious objection to abortion that would leave the applicant with grave permanent injury to her mental health, and perhaps, by psychosomatic causation, similar injury to her physical health, would fall within the scope of section 4(2), so that the immunity for conscientious objection provided by section 4(1) would be inapplicable.

Subject to section 4(2), conscientious objection is available to a person who would otherwise be "under any duty . . . to participate in any treatment authorised by this Act." This seems to preclude hospitals and comparable institutions as such from claims to conscientious objection, since, while as corporate bodies they may facilitate procedures, they do not participate in them. This is consistent with the 2008 decision of the Constitutional Court of Colombia.[48] However, corporate bodies such as hospitals must accommodate the objections of health care providers they engage, without censure or discrimination, while also ensuring patients' access to lawful treatment, including abortion as allowed by prevailing law.[49]

What extent of immunity or protection is afforded conscientious objectors varies among jurisdictions. In the U.S., for example, at least forty-five states have so-called conscience clauses in laws to allow objection to participation in health care procedures.[50] Some, such as California, permit objection to abortion, but not other services.[51] Others allow objection to sterilization, contraceptive, and, for instance, medically assisted fertility or reproduction services, and to forms of end-of-life care, and some define "participation" expansively to cover indirect services such as those of pharmacists, ambulance drivers, medical instructors, and students. Most if not all of these laws were enacted in the aftermath of the U.S. Supreme Court 1973 decision recognizing the legality of abortion in *Roe v. Wade*,[52] to accommodate an expanding anti-abortion backlash.

An instance of this type of law is the Mississippi Health Care Rights of Conscience Act,[53] which was initially directed only to abortion, but was expanded comprehensively to accommodate the full agenda of the right-to-life movement. This covers any broadly defined "health care service," including "patient referral, counseling, therapy, diagnosis or prognosis . . . prescribing, dispensing or administering any device, drug, or medication, surgery, or any other care or treatment rendered by health care providers or health care institutions."[54] Protection of conscience is available to a "health care provider," defined as "any individual who may be asked to participate in any way in a health care service, including . . . any professional, paraprofessional, or any other person who furnishes, or assists in the furnishing of, a health care procedure."[55]

The Act does not recognize patients' rights of conscience but grants such rights to a "health care institution," defined as "any public or private organization . . . that is involved in providing health care services, includ-ing . . . institutions or locations where health care procedures are provided to any person."[56] The Act similarly grants rights of conscientious objection to any entity or employer that pays for health care services. It addresses the right not to "participate" in health care services, meaning "to counsel, advise, provide, perform, assist in, refer for, admit for purposes of providing, or participate in providing, any health care service or any form of such service."[57]

A key provision is the underlying protection of "conscience," which is ex-plained as "the religious, moral or ethical principles held by a health care provider, the health care institution or health care payer." Conscience shall be determined by reference to "existing or proposed religious, moral or ethical guidelines, mission statement, constitution, bylaws, articles of incorporation, regulations, or other relevant documents."[58] However, institutions' accommo-dation of refusals of care does not allow refusal of care "because of the pa-tient's race, color, national origin, ethnicity, sex, religion, creed or sexual orientation."[59] Similarly, while "no health care provider shall be civilly, crimi-nally, or administratively liable for declining to participate in a health care service that violates his or her conscience," there is no such exemption when refusal is because of the patient's race or other characteristic identified in the Act.[60]

Health care providers, institutions, officials, and others are fully protected against suffering discrimination for invoking rights of conscience covered by the Act, which provides that it shall be unlawful "to discriminate against any health care provider in any manner based on his or her declining to partici-pate in a health care service that violates his or her conscience." Discrimina-tion includes termination, transfer, refusal of staff privileges, refusal of board certification, adverse administrative action, demotion, loss of career specialty, reassignment to a different shift, reduction of wages or benefits, refusal to award any grant, contract, or other program, refusal to provide residency training, or any other penalty, disciplinary, or retaliatory action.[61] Comparable protections are enacted for health care institutions and payers for services.

The Act is enforceable by a civil action for treble damages and/or injunc-tion, and no defense is allowed that violation of the Act "was necessary to prevent additional burden or expense on any other health care provider, health care institution, individual or patient."[62] This means that violations of the Act are not defensible on the ground that conformity would impose sig-nificant additional burdens or expenses on health care institutions, or patients.

It is not clear whether legislation of this nature entitles gynecologists or obstetricians to refuse to inform prospective patients that they will not participate in particular services that fall within the usual range of services that members of the public reasonably expect of practitioners in this medical specialty, such as prescribing contraceptive products, offering contraceptive sterilization, or abortion. The legislation protects refusals to render treatments, but disclosure of treatments that will and will not be rendered is not itself treatment. Before any treatment is begun, prospective patients legally should know of any deviations from services that patients reasonably expect to receive. These include any proposed treatment that is experimental or unproven, and any usual service within the specialty of obstetrics and gynecology that is not provided. This serves patients' legal option to forgo that service, or change to another practitioner. Some private health insurance policies cover treatments only through designated providers, which makes it important for prospective patients to know whether such providers will refuse to render services within their specialty on grounds of personal conscience.

In many circumstances, prospective patients do not enjoy a choice of practitioners but receive care from whichever practitioner is available to them from the hospital, clinic, or comparable facility to which they have access. It is important that facility administrators know what services potential providers are able and willing to offer, and in particular what services within their specialty they refuse to provide. For patient care, administrators must ensure that they can direct personnel to render necessary care, and can adequately cover those who object to provide care by recruiting others who do not object. They must therefore enquire if potential recruits object to provide any services within their medical or other specialty.

Potential recruits are usually protected against discriminatory hiring practices, but it is not discriminatory to decline to hire them if they do not meet the reasonable employment requirements of positions for which they apply. If a hospital where many gynecologists object to participate in abortion procedures wants to recruit one who does not object, willingness to participate is an explicit, essential bona fide condition of recruitment. Those not willing to participate make themselves ineligible for appointment. The requirement must be central to the proposed employment, however, and not be a cover for unlawful discrimination.

Refusals of health care services related to abortion have been reviewed in the United States in the National Health Law Program (NHeLP) 2010 report,[63] showing how appropriate health care for women has been denied, postponed, and undermined. An instance is recorded of a patient nineteen weeks pregnant when her membranes ruptured. The fetus was not viable, and the patient was septic. Her doctor considered termination of pregnancy necessary, but the hospital administration refused to allow this because a fetal heartbeat was recorded. The patient spent ten days in intensive care and nearly died. The fetus died in utero, the woman surviving but with substantial internal bleeding and pulmonary disease resulting in lifelong oxygen dependency.[64]

The report identifies how claims of conscientious objection and related administrative barriers to care that is required according to medical professional guidelines, such as provided by the American College of Obstetricians and Gynecologists,[65] jeopardize pregnant women's health. In addition to delayed care on premature rupture of membranes, treatment of preeclampsia and eclampsia by medically indicated delivery of the fetus may be postponed to increase the chance of fetal viability. Medically indicated care may be postponed or denied when a fetal heartbeat exists in cases of anencephaly, in which the fetus, lacking an upper brain, is not viable, and when comparable conditions exist that are dangerous to women's health. Some therapeutic drugs may be withheld from pregnant patients lest fetal health be compromised, and from women affected by health- and life-endangering cardiovascular conditions that make continuation of pregnancy contraindicated. Such health conditions affecting pregnant patients may be left inadequately treated for fear of religiously construed liability for causing abortion.

Of special note is delay in treating tubal or ectopic pregnancy, a life-threatening condition occurring when an embryo implants outside the uterus, most commonly in the fallopian tube. There are surgical and nonsurgical means to remove the embryo before it causes the fallopian tube to rupture, risking permanent damage to the woman's future fertility, morbidity, and even death. However, on grounds of conscientious objection to deliberately inducing what some Catholic theologians rule is abortion, practitioners may wait until the fallopian tube ruptures or is close to rupturing before undertaking an emergency, life-saving intervention. In all of the circumstances outlined above, the Ethical and Religious Directives for Catholic Health Care Services ("the Directives") applied in Roman Catholic associated health care facilities, and by Catholic health care providers engaged outside such facilities, give priority to survival of embryos and fetuses, and subordinate regard to preservation of women's health and fertility.[66]

Institutions and individual practitioners intending to apply priorities of this nature and effect, without regard to their patients' wishes, should provide potential and actual patients with timely information of that intention. Patients who have been induced to rely on their health care institutions and providers for medically indicated care, in accordance with professional standards, should not suddenly be confronted, perhaps in moments of crisis, with denial of indicated care based on personal claims to conscientious objection.

The inclusion in conscientious objection immunity laws, such as in Mississippi,[67] of protection of objecting health care providers who do not refer patients whom they refuse to treat to nonobjecting providers confirms that, in the absence of such laws, objecting doctors have a duty to refer their patients, in good faith, to providers of such care. As an English High Court judge ruled in 1999, "once a termination of pregnancy is recognised as an option, the doctor invoking the conscientious objection clause should refer the patient to a colleague at once."[68] Failure to refer violates professional standards of care, exposing a defaulting practitioner to professional discipline. Some jurisdictions in the Common law tradition consider the unequal doctor-patient relationship to be fiduciary, so that the doctor, with the power of professional knowledge, is under a fiduciary duty to assist the patient, who is dependent on the conscientious application of that knowledge to serve his or her interests.[69] Further, conformity to professional standards may be an implied term of a doctor-patient contract.

A distinction must be drawn between duties owed to patients and those owed to other people requesting to become patients. A doctor can decline to treat an applicant for care, on such grounds as inability to accept any additional patients, but not on discriminatory grounds such as race or religion. The doctor has no duty to refer the applicant for care to another provider. When a doctor-patient relationship exists, however, following from a past association or, for instance, because the doctor is appointed to care for the patient by the hospital the patient attends, the doctor owes duties to the person who has thereby become the doctor's patient, particularly duties of nonabandonment. The doctor cannot withdraw from care, such as on grounds of conscientious objection, without first ensuring the patient's continuous access to appropriate care.

The doctor cannot legally claim, unless supported by legislation as expansive as that in Mississippi, that there is an additional right of conscientious objection to referral. That claim is often founded on complicity, that is, that it is as wrong or sinful to be complicit in another's wrongdoing as it is directly to perpetrate the wrong oneself. This misconstrues the purpose of abortion referral, however, which is not simply for abortion but for consideration of a range of legitimate options, of which abortion is one. Not infrequently, referral does not lead to abortion.

Conscientious objection is accommodated so that the objector does not have to participate directly in abortion. However, referral for consideration of a treatment does not constitute participation in it. For instance, the referring doctor does not share any fee the doctor to whom referral is made may earn, is not party to any negligence the other doctor may commit, and does not share in any criminal liability that doctor may incur. The duty to refer may be discharged by referring the patient, in good faith, to another practitioner or agent known not to object. In New Zealand, for instance, the Health Practitioners Competence Assurance Act of 2003 provides that, when a health practitioner conscientiously objects to providing a reproductive health service, "the health practitioner must inform the person who requests the service that he or she can obtain the service from another health practitioner or from a family planning clinic."[70]

One author has built on this model to propose mediation between the practitioner who objects to referral and the patient requesting a service in which the practitioner refuses to participate.[71] She advances the concept that the medical profession itself, through specialist and/or local associations, can maintain lists of practitioners who are prepared to undertake procedures to which others conscientiously object. Objecting practitioners unwilling or unable to refer their patients to others who will undertake such procedures may then refer their patients to the associations. This would be a service both to maintain the objecting practitioner's sense of integrity, and to provide patients with the referral to which they are entitled.

Manifesting Conscience

While Article 18(1) of the International Covenant on Civil and Political Rights (CCPR) protects freedom "of thought, conscience and religion," limitations under Article 18(3) may reduce freedom "to manifest one's religion or beliefs" in order to protect "health . . . or the fundamental rights and freedoms of others." Individuals are free passively to reach judgments based on their ideas, conscience, and/or religion, perhaps as an aspect of their privacy protected under Article 17, and to express their convictions as protected under Article 19, but they may be subject to limitations on how they actively manifest their religious or other beliefs.

National courts have addressed whether limitations on the right to manifest one's religion can be imposed to protect one's own health, for instance whether to prohibit Jehovah's Witnesses from refusing blood transfusions. International tribunals have not elaborated on the application of Article 18 in a substantive way,[72] but its equivalent in the European human rights system has founded a sophisticated jurisprudence in the European Commission and the European Court of Human Rights,[73] and in domestic courts of states that are parties to the European Convention for the Protection of Human Rights and Fundamental Freedoms.

Article 9(1) of the European Convention echoes Article 18(1) of the CCPR on freedom of thought, conscience, and religion, and Article 9(2) similarly provides that: "Freedom to manifest one's religion or beliefs shall be subject only to such limitations as are prescribed by law and are necessary in a democratic society . . . for the protection of the rights and freedoms of others." The contrast between subsections (1) and (2) was crisply summarized in a Scottish court in the judicial observation that "Article 9 encapsulates a duality of rights, namely the freedom to hold a belief and freedom to 'manifest' it. The former is absolute. The latter is qualified."[74] While freedom of religious or other beliefs cannot be contained, limits may legally be set upon, or result from, how individuals may manifest such beliefs. For instance, the Constitutional Council in France has upheld legislation providing that departmental heads of public health facilities cannot refuse to allow conduct of lawful abortions on grounds of their personal conscience, although they may refuse direct participation in an individual procedure.[75]

The European Court of Human Rights addressed Article 9 in the *Pichon* case.[76] Two French pharmacists operating the only pharmacy in a remote area refused to sell contraceptives to women presenting valid prescriptions, on grounds of their religious beliefs. French courts upheld their criminal convictions for breach of the national Consumer Code by refusal to supply services without a legitimate reason. Health service providers are allowed nonparticipation in abortion-related services, but by law other religious or moral beliefs do not provide legitimate reasons for breach of the Consumer Code. The pharmacists appealed to the European Court of Human Rights alleging violation of their rights to conscientious objection, protected under Article 9(1). The Court found the claim inadmissible, however, on the ground that the appellants' freedom of religious belief had not been violated.

The finding was more procedural than substantive,[77] not expanding on the scope of Article 9(2),[78] but observed that "the applicants cannot give precedence to their religious beliefs and impose them on others . . . since they can manifest those beliefs in many ways outside the professional sphere." Alternative means to express beliefs may set a limit to undertaking employment with responsibilities from which the employee seeks legal exemption on grounds of conscientious objection. The European Commission of Human Rights ruled in 1981 that: "The freedom of religion, as guaranteed by Article 9 is not absolute, but subject to the limitations set out in Article 9(2). Moreover, it may, as regards the modality of a particular religious manifestation, be influenced by the situation of the person claiming that freedom."[79]

This ruling was cited by a Scottish judge in a 2012 decision concerning two midwives employed as labor ward coordinators in a hospital where abortions were performed.[80] They had accepted employment requiring them to supervise midwives, without themselves directly treating patients, but claimed rights of conscientious objection to supervising participants in abortion procedures. They petitioned for reversal of dismissal of their employment grievance actions, and for declarations that they were not required to delegate, supervise, and/or support staff in the conduct of induced abortions. They invoked rights of conscientious objection under section 4(1) of the U.K. Abortion Act, 1967, and Article 9 of the European Convention.

The trial judge rejected the claim brought under section 4(1) of the 1967 Act, which affords rights of conscientious objection regarding "any duty . . . to participate in any treatment" authorized by the Act, because the petitioners were not direct participants in such treatment. Regarding Article 9, the judge observed that "the European Court of Human Rights has been reluctant to impose obligations on employers to take positive steps to accommodate an employee's wishes to manifest his religious beliefs in a particular manner."[81] She also cited the highest U.K. court, now named the U.K. Supreme Court, in which it was observed that "Article 9 does not require that one should be allowed to manifest one's religion at any time and place of one's choosing."[82] However, citing the practical difficulty of knowing what part of "treatment" is direct participation and which is not, the appeal court reversed the trial decision. Its expansive ruling that rights of objection "should extend to any involvement in the process of treatment, the object of which is to terminate a pregnancy"[83] unfortunately creates serious doubts about patients' rights to indicated, dignified care, for instance from nursing and administrative staff, and ignores limits under Article 9(2) of the European Convention binding on the U.K. This wide ruling is being further appealed to the U.K. Supreme Court, whose decision may conceivably be yet further appealed to the European Court of Human Rights for application of the European Convention.

Conscientious Commitment

In contrast to practitioners whose personal conscience compels them to refuse participation in abortion procedures is the half-century and longer history of practitioners whose conscience commits or allows them to advise, offer and/or provide abortion.[84] Most conscientious commitment to undertake abortion is derived from secular and professional convictions. One is that, since doctors enjoy a state-granted monopoly over the practice of medicine, and therefore over lawful abortion procedures, they would abuse that monopoly were they to refuse to undertake such procedures, on patients' requests, so widely as to deny patients effective means of access. This is reinforced by experience of how women denied the lawful, safe procedures to which they are entitled may resort to unsafe interventions, including medically unsupervised, self-induced abortions, with high resulting rates of mortality and morbidity.

A related ground of conscientious commitment is that doctors publicly licensed to practice, particularly though not only in public hospitals and facilities, and whether or not educated at public expense, are public officers, who must accordingly serve the public neutrally, without favor or disfavor on religious or other personal grounds. This principle was supported by Chief Judge Posner, of the United States Court of Appeals for the Seventh Circuit, in 1998.[85] The case concerned a Chicago police officer assigned to protect an abortion clinic against protesters' violence and assaults. As a devout Roman Catholic, he considered this assignment to facilitate abortion, and to violate his freedom of conscience. Judge Posner observed, however, that as an agent serving a public function, the police officer was not free to choose which premises he would protect and which not, like a firefighter cannot choose which buildings to protect and which to let burn. By analogy, doctors should not deny lawful procedures that patients want when they are the only ones trained, qualified, and available to undertake them, on the basis of their personal beliefs.

As against this approach, however, committed doctors may claim the same rights of conscientious objection to discharge certain tasks that they find personally offensive as their colleagues enjoy. For instance, when required by legislation to make certain statements to women requesting abortion that they find medically incorrect, or liable to subvert women's responsible judgment of their own and/or their families' interests, they may object and refuse. They may invoke grounds of professional conscience, for instance to be truthful in dealings with patients, and to do no harm. Several states' abortion laws in the U.S. require that specified information be given only when it is medically accurate. This is unobjectionable but may compromise a doctor's clinical judgment about whether the disclosure is material to the patient, and whether she will afford it proportionate weight. When doctors consider mandated disclosures contrary to the best scientific information and understanding, however, they may conscientiously object to make such disclosures. Refusal to comply with mandatory disclosure ("compelled speech") laws may be defensible under protection of conscience laws such as in Mississippi, which protect conscientious objection against civil, criminal, and administrative sanctions.

An informative research article provides details of U.S. state laws on abortion disclosure requirements.[86] Many are being challenged in court.[87] For instance, the Texas counseling booklet requires doctors to inform prospective patients seeking abortion that complications "may make it difficult or impossible to become pregnant in the future or carry a pregnancy to term."[88] However, most abortions are conducted in the first trimester, most commonly by vacuum aspiration, which "poses virtually no long-term risk of infertility, ectopic pregnancy, spontaneous abortion or congenital malformation."[89] Many states' laws require emphasis on psychological or mental health hazards of abortion. Michigan's law requires disclosure "that as the result of an abortion, some women may experience depression, feelings of guilt, sleep disturbance, loss of interest in work or sex, or anger."[90] In West Virginia, material to be given to abortion patients states that "many women suffer from Post-Traumatic Stress Disorder Syndrome following abortion. PTSD is a psychological dysfunction resulting from a traumatic experience."[91] The material includes reference to associated symptoms of depression, drug abuse, eating disorders, chronic relationship problems, and, inter alia, suicidal thoughts or acts.

This material draws from an alleged condition not recorded in the reputable psychiatric literature, post-abortion syndrome,[92] against which anti-abortion advocates propose to protect women.[93] Scientific studies show that, while any medical experience is liable to have a psychological effect, that of abortion is no more significant than that of any other procedure. It is observed, for instance that: "The relative risk of mental health problems among adult women who have a single, legal, first-trimester abortion of an unwanted pregnancy for non-therapeutic reasons is no greater than the risk among women who deliver an unwanted pregnancy."[94]

Another study finds no increased resort to psychiatric services for mental disorder after induced abortion, but a slight increase after childbirth.[95] This scientific literature supports doctors who conscientiously object to having to provide their patients with false or misleading "information." Doctors may indeed be guarded against providing accurate information for fear of the so-called nocebo effect, the reverse of the better-known beneficial placebo effect. The nocebo effect arises when suggestible patients are induced to expect specific negative side-effects of interventions and, by psychosomatic causation, may experience them. Doctors, in their clinical judgment, are entitled to exercise a narrow "therapeutic privilege" not to disclose information they conscientiously believe will cause their patients harm.[96]

Some states claim concern that women having abortions may suffer psychological harm, but the explicit disclosures they require of alarming, unproven, or largely discredited risks, such as of breast cancer and early fetal pain, may aggravate women's distress. The states' main purpose may in fact be to deter women from pursuing abortion. Similarly, requirements that ultrasound examinations be conducted before women have abortions make a legal necessity of an invasive procedure, whether by abdominal or vaginal transduction, that is medically unnecessary, though possibly useful. Ultrasound examinations will be recommended by doctors who consider them desirable, without a legislative mandate. The explanations that legislators provide make it evident, however, that the requirement is primarily designed so to bond women to their fetuses in utero that they decide to continue their pregnancies, and punitively to burn an image into their memories if they do not.[97] Doctors who find their patients resolved on abortion may conscientiously object to enforce ultrasound examination and viewing, consistently with the historical medical ethic to do no harm.

Doctors who choose to comply with laws that mandate disclosures to patients considering abortion are entitled to place that "information" in context. State justifications of compelled speech do not justify prohibitions of speech. Doctors may therefore disclose what the legislature requires, but inform patients that such disclosure is scientifically suspect or false, for instance regarding first-trimester procedures. On physical risk, they may point out, for instance, that medical evidence in the United States shows that risk of death from routine childbirth is about fourteen times higher than from legal abortion, and that overall morbidity associated with childbirth exceeds that with abortion.[98] On mental health risk, they may add that post-abortion syndrome has little if any recognition in psychiatry, whereas postpartum depression has an established history in both psychiatry and law. A 2006 study mainly across Western countries showed postpartum depression to affect ten to fifteen percent of mothers.[99] In law, a woman who kills her child within twelve months of delivering it may be convicted not of murder but only manslaughter (infanticide) if "at the time . . . the balance of her mind was disturbed by reason of her not having fully recovered from the effect of giving birth to the child or . . . lactation consequent upon the birth."[100]

Doctors conscientiously committed not to abortions but to their patients being properly informed may therefore counter false mandated speech with scientifically established and professionally accepted facts. The right conscientiously to tell the truth is violated, however, when doctors are prohibited from truthful, relevant discussions with their patients. In the United States, for instance "some religiously affiliated hospitals forbid employees from providing information or counseling about abortion, [from] referring patients to other facilities for abortions, or [from] performing or assisting with abortion procedures at other medical facilities."[101]

Not all countries have religiously affiliated hospitals, or such public hospitals, but among countries that do, Roman Catholic hospitals are prominent. Such hospitals are increasingly delivering care, for instance, in the United States and Canada as Catholic and non-Catholic hospitals merge, often for economy, and the new entity functions as Catholic.[102] This poses questions of how patients, particularly women, access services barred by the Church, and of how health care providers, particularly doctors, discharge conscientious commitments they feel toward patients. In Kentucky, for instance, in December 2011, the Governor refused to approve a merger between a Roman Catholic and a non-Catholic hospital, on the ground that the prospective withdrawal of services, particularly from women, would not be in the public interest.[103]

In the same way as the right to conscience properly protects conscientious objection to participation in lawful medical care, it should equally protect the conscientious commitment to deliver such care. Doctors engaged in hospitals whose administrations condemn abortion, contraception, and, for instance, contraceptive sterilization, should remain free to provide patients with information, counseling, prescriptions, and referral on these matters, and to undertake procedures insofar as they can without collaboration of objecting colleagues and the hospital administration. Further, in the same way that principles of equality under the law and of nondiscrimination protect doctors who conscientiously refuse to participate in procedures to which they object, the same principles should protect doctors who are conscientiously committed to delivery of particular care, in hospitals whose administrations disapprove.

Where countries' constitutions and/or laws prohibit discrimination on grounds of conscience or religion, secular hospitals cannot decline to engage service providers on grounds only of their religion. Catholic health care providers seeking positions cannot be rejected simply because they are Catholic. Equally, Catholic hospitals cannot reject applicants because they are not, except for religiously based positions, such as in hospital chaplaincy. Non-Catholic doctors engaged in Catholic hospitals are expected to be respectful of religious directives but should receive reciprocal respect for their conscientious objections and commitments, as do religiously motivated doctors in nonreligious facilities. They should accordingly be free to inform, counsel, refer, prescribe for, and treat their patients according to their conscientious convictions, without subjection to censure, or to discrimination such as is defined, for instance, in Mississippi's Health Care Rights of Conscience Act. That Act is directed, of course, to refusal of care, but a reading according to equal protection principles could apply its key provisions to conscientious delivery of care. Legislation protecting only conscientious objection may deny rights of conscience to those of different conscientious persuasion,[104] in violation of equal protection of the law guaranteed in human rights law and many national constitutions.

On this basis, doctors in Catholic hospitals should be free to exercise their clinical judgment conscientiously to treat pregnant patients suffering premature rupture of membranes according to medical professional standards and guidelines,[105] without subjection to religiously based veto. Similarly, they should be able to treat preeclampsia and eclampsia according to the presenting diagnosis and prognosis, and such conditions as ectopic pregnancy, conscientiously to serve their patients' wishes and best interests, without prohibition because a fetus unavoidably at risk due to treatment indicated for the pregnant woman records a heartbeat. Doctors should not use drugs for pregnant women's treatment, such as for malignant cancer, that risks injury to or loss of their fetuses, without careful review with the patients of available alternatives, out of respect for hospitals' religious directives. If treatment is indicated, such as for cardiovascular emergencies, to preserve the patients' lives but with unavoidable loss of their pregnancies, this may be tolerated by Catholic hospitals' administrations characterizing the treatments not as abortions but as life-saving medical interventions, under the principle of double effect.[106]

More difficult for doctors willing to participate in abortion procedures in hospitals opposed to such procedures may be to react to abortion requests not indicated by any pathology, but of an elective nature, such as to overcome a contraceptive failure or oversight. Even when there is no medical indication for abortion, it is a legitimate health option when the WHO concept of "health" is applied. The state of health means "physical, mental and social well-being and not merely the absence of disease or infirmity."[107] By this measure, unplanned pregnancy may endanger women's health, and its termination may promote women's health.

This provides a legal and ethical framework for the conscientious commitment of health care professionals. Respect for and protection of human rights requires legal protection. In 1991, Pope John Paul II addressed respect for conscience, regarding not abortion but the respect that repressive Communist and other governments should pay to religious conscience. His words were based, of course, on Catholic theology and were intended to be interpreted according to a Catholic understanding of truth, in a somewhat self-serving way to protect rights to Roman Catholic conscience against the hostility of totalitarian, atheistic government, but they also resonate outside that context. The pope observed that "a serious threat to peace is posed by intolerance, which manifests itself in the denial of freedom of conscience to others. The excesses to which intolerance can lead has [sic] been one of history's most painful lessons."[108] Requiring legal protection of conscience, he nevertheless added that "freedom of conscience does not confer a right to indiscriminate recourse to conscientious objection. When an asserted freedom turns into license or becomes an excuse for limiting the rights of others, the State is obliged to protect, also by legal means, the inalienable rights of its citizens against such abuses."[109] This spirit requires of health care institutions and providers, Catholic and secular alike, tolerance both of conscientious objection, and of conscientious commitment, to delivery of abortion-related services.

Chapter 11

Catholic Constitutionalism on Sex, Women, and the Beginning of Life

Julieta Lemaitre

The 1994 U.N. International Conference on Population and Development at Cairo set off a conservative Catholic backlash against feminist ideas on sexuality and reproduction. Catholic lawyers, inspired by Vatican instructions, vigorously argued in constitutional settings across the Americas against the liberalization of abortion laws, same-sex marriage, and embryonic cell research. While some explicitly referenced scripture and religious authorities in their advocacy, many abandoned such references in favor of legal claims based on reason alone. The new strategy marked a profound shift for the conservative Catholic movement against sexual and reproductive rights, and is the object of this chapter.

This move to reason was supported by a robust natural law tradition that claims that even those who do not share the Catholic faith can appreciate and share in its moral order through "our common human reason."[1] Catholic natural law was promoted as a response to sexual and reproductive rights by John Paul II's post-Cairo encyclical *Evangelium Vitae*. It argues for the existence of an objective morality of divine origin, prior to the state, and binding for human law.[2] In other words, since both faith and reason lead to the knowledge of the objective moral order, existing human rights frameworks can be developed through reason to reflect a Catholic morality.[3] It is this necessary link between natural law and human rights—increasingly promoted in legal academia by professors Javier Hervada in Spain and John Finnis, Robert

George, and Christopher McCrudden in the United Kingdom and the United States[4]—that allows advocates to argue in the secular tradition of most contemporary constitutions in support of Catholic conclusions about sexuality and reproduction.[5]

The rebirth of natural law and the recourse to reasoned constitutional argument is a measure of the Catholic Church's cautious relationship with modern democracies, as well as of the hierarchy's response to internal pressure for the church to be more involved in social justice issues. It is important to note that political activism does not come easily to the contemporary Catholic Church. Of course, Catholicism shares with other forms of Christianity the urge to evangelize, including by changing social arrangements to accommodate Christian beliefs. This urge was greatly transformed and limited with the emergence of modern nation-states in the West and their normative call to church-state separation. Renouncing the aspiration to leadership in confessional states—that is, states where Catholicism is the official religion—the church limited its claims to the protection of its own independence, both in the freedom to worship and evangelize, as well as economic and hierarchical independence. In turn, the church conceded to the state issues it considered mainly political or economic. This did not include sexual morality, or more particularly changing sexual mores, which struck at the heart of the church's vision of itself in society, prompting a call to the exercise of Catholic influence led by Pope John Paul II and his successor Benedict XVI.

In the modern democratic states, however, there are limits on how this influence may be exercised. The church has, in a sense, also conceded the liberal position that influence must be exercised in a way accessible to all members of the polity, regardless of faith.[6] While the church may resent the imperative to avoid direct invocation of deeply held beliefs in public debate,[7] it has been willing to argue for those beliefs using only reasoned argument—especially when it finds itself in the uncomfortable position of opposing contemporary democracies, as with the decriminalization of abortion.

The shift to reason in Catholic argument on abortion and other issues of sexuality marks an important transition in the relationship between church and state. Yet secular lawyers, academics, and policy makers have generally failed to engage with Catholic constitutionalism on its own terms—that is, by engaging with the claimed universal moral truths underlying and thereby structuring the logic of legal argument. Since they do not address the Catholic reason underlying these arguments, they fail to respond persuasively to the arguments themselves. Many concentrate only on the damage to gender justice of conservative activism. Others limit themselves to denunciation or avoidance of the theological premises.[8] Rebecca Cook, for example, defines conservative religious activism as an attempt to "secure the supremacy of fundamentalist religions and their hierarchies."[9] Those who do engage conservative arguments refuse to examine the religious dimension of the arguments made "by reason alone." Reva Siegel, for example, who has led the examination of right-wing constitutional arguments in the United States, engages with "the right's reasons" but deals gingerly with the connections between these arguments and their religious premises.[10]

This chapter seeks to address the gap in the study of Catholic constitutionalism, and to do so from the point of view of a nonreligious lawyer who has been part of the pro-choice camp for almost two decades within a deeply Catholic country. Although I do not agree with the implications of Catholic arguments on sexuality and reproduction, I take these arguments seriously, tracing their theological foundations and seeking to engage them on their own merits. In the first part of the chapter, I elaborate core Catholic constitutional arguments about the legal regulation of abortion. While these arguments are without recourse to faith or scripture, I seek to demonstrate how they are in fact deeply rooted in theological reasoning about sexual morality.[11] I cover four core arguments in the abortion debates: that decriminalization violates women's equality rights; that the suffering of women is caused by abortion rather than criminalization; that the right to life begins from conception; and that freedom of conscience extends to all individual and institutional refusals of participation. In the second part of the chapter, I propose modes of engagement with Catholic constitutional arguments by the secular pro-choice community and explore the productive effects of this engagement for both movement on and resistance to sexual and reproductive rights.

Theology in Catholic Constitutional Reasoning

Abortion and Sex Equality

It is untrue that only pro-choice advocates understand the criminalization of abortion as a matter of sex equality. In the 2006 Colombian constitutional case, the National Bishops' Confederation, for example, submitted an amicus brief that did not dispute that state regulation of pregnancy and child-birth affects women's social and economic equality. Rather, they disputed that decriminalization was the necessary means to achieve sex equality, calling instead for "a good orientation of responsible fatherhood . . . as well as work-ing measures to protect motherhood in all its stages, such as the extension of maternity leave, [and] a better subsidy per born child."[12] Similar arguments underpin a Brazilian bill presented by Catholic and Christian legislators to eliminate rape exceptions in the criminal abortion law, and to create grants and subsidies to women to keep and raise their born children.[13]

Catholic constitutional arguments hold that feminist views of equality harm women by forcing them to sacrifice themselves in order to conform to social mandates to be economically productive. In this line of argument women bear disproportionate costs for bearing a child, violating the right to equality. The state is called on to ensure bearing children is not an excessive burden for women, by guaranteeing access to health services, education, nourishment, housing, and so on, as well as adequate standards of living for mothers, nondiscrimination of mothers in workplaces, adequate maternal leave, and the acceptance and support of lifestyles geared toward child rearing.

This gender equality argument is deeply influenced by Catholic concep-tions of human nature, namely naturalized gender roles. The theological sig-nificance of sex difference dates to early Christianity, when the Church upheld the full humanity of women against generalized assumption of radical female inferiority. The Church adopted as its orthodox position St. Augustine's third-century position by which men and women are equal in salvation and in the eyes of God. Lack of equality in this world, and male dominion, was the result of original sin ("thou shalt desire thy husband and he shall rule over you," Genesis 3:16).

In modern times the Vatican engaged little with issues of women's sexuality until the 1978 appointment of Pope John Paul II, who had particular concern for the status of sexuality in Catholic teaching. In his 1988 encyclical on female nature, *Mulieris Dignitatem*, Pope John Paul II elaborated on the significance of this sex difference. He explained that women have a "special dignity" based on "a form of union with God that is specifically female"—that is, the possibility of giving life.[14] This union with God requires a special submission and servitude to God, in likeness of Virgin Mary, who defines herself as the slave to the Lord (Luke 1:38). Salvation for women is thus deeply connected to their fulfillment of the call to motherhood and family life in service and sacrifice.[15]

In *Evangelium Vitae* (1995), issued soon after the 1994 U.N. Cairo Conference on Population and Development, Pope John Paul II further developed these ideas and called for a "new feminism"—a Catholic feminism based on the natural difference between men and women.[16] The *new feminism* opposes male dominion but defends natural gender roles, particularly women's devotion to motherhood and relatedly, opposition to abortion. Abortion is described as sinful not merely because it ends life and opposes God's will, but because it is seen as a form of male dominion over women that forces them to have abortions in societies hostile to motherhood. Christian liberation is therefore to be found in liberation from sin (male dominion), but not from traditional gender roles.

Several Catholic scholars have championed the *new feminism* of the church,[17] which, in the words of Mary Ann Glendon, a Harvard Law professor with ties to the Vatican, remains "practically alone in insisting that there can be no authentic progress for women [in economic, social, and political life] without respect for women's roles in the family."[18] The *new feminism* calls on women to reject the temptation of imitating models of "male domination" and to acknowledge and affirm the *true* genius of women in every aspect of social life.[19] When a feminist pro-choice movement denounces traditional gender roles as exploitative, a new feminist response denounces the movement itself for neglecting the inherent equality and dignity of women's roles as mothers, homemakers, and caregivers.[20]

Catholic constitutional arguments thus support a view of equality that requires the defense, and valuing, of traditional gender roles. In Catholic reasoning, traditional gender roles are inherently virtuous insofar as they reflect God's will for women in motherhood and service. Equality rights thus entail equal protection of the virtue associated with traditional gender roles; conversely, there is no virtue in emancipation from these roles. Equality in Catholic constitutional reasoning, in other words, is constrained by virtue; it is a perfectionist concept. As a right, it is meant to foster desirable behaviors, and cannot be deployed to protect socially repulsive behaviors, such as homosexuality and abortion.[21]

Equality as virtue is evident, for example, in arguments against same-sex marriage. Javier Hervada, a law professor in the Opus Dei Universidad de Navarra in Spain, explains that in marriage men and women have different reproductive roles based on their human nature. Any legal norm that denies this difference, such as one that would permit same-sex marriage, offends human dignity, defined as natural and thus moral behavior. The immorality of the law characterizes its unjustness: the erasure of sex differences or the equalizing of men and women in their naturally different functions.[22]

Arguments of sex equality in the abortion debates are hardly one-sided. Catholic constitutional reasoning deploys sex equality not only against abortion decriminalization, but also in support of greater state involvement to alleviate the economic and social burdens of mothering. Catholic legal reasoning defends traditional roles in reproduction, and it does so inspired by the belief in a universal natural law that prescribes these roles as natural and virtuous. The Catholic argument for sex equality is one of ultimately religious virtue; it is to these ends that abortion must be prohibited, and motherhood valued culturally and supported by the state

Suffering and the Criminalization of Abortion

Feminists frequently argue that the decision to terminate a pregnancy is not merely a matter of economics or lack of social support, but of health and well-being. A woman's right to access abortion is frequently framed as a right to avoid suffering, whether of a physical or emotional kind. The Center for Reproductive Rights, for example, recently filed a case on behalf of "Manuela," a Salvadoran woman convicted of murder and given a thirty-year sentence for having an abortion. The Center claims Manuela did not have an abortion, but suffered from an illness that led to the stillbirth, and eventually to her death.[23] "Manuela" is but an extreme example of the documented suffering caused by the harsh application of criminal abortion laws.

The Catholic constitutional response to the narrative of suffering is often to refuse its cause, suggesting that it is the having of abortions that make women suffer, and thereby demanding greater restrictions on abortion. Reva Siegel gives a compelling account of this "woman-protective argument" and its success in the U.S. Supreme Court case *Gonzales v. Carhart*.[24] The majority of the Court validated abortion restrictions in light of some women having come to regret their decision, and to suffer in consequence. As Siegel points out, however, the only evidence of this was an amicus brief submitted by the Justice Foundation. While the religious affiliation of the organization is unclear (at least one of its founders attended a Catholic university), the woman-protective argument recurs in other documents of the Catholic anti-abortion movement. So too does the argument that all suffering from unwanted pregnancy can be alleviated through state support of women and their pregnancies. In a brief against the decriminalization of abortion in cases of rape,

Catholic lawyers from Argentina argued that the state should provide rape victims with the best possible care for themselves and their children, rather than provide access to abortions.[25]

It seems in general contradictory that a religion so concerned with alleviating suffering through generous charities around the world would be so indifferent to the suffering of women, calling for trial and detention for acts often taken in desperation. Support for criminalization seems in tension with Catholic mandates of charity and forgiveness, but it is a tension in perception alone that weakens with a better appreciation of the role of suffering in the Catholic faith.

In Catholic theology, suffering has a two-fold nature. On the one hand, it is rejected as the wages of original sin—God's words on expelling Adam and Eve from Paradise taken as either punishment or a description of the consequences of their sin. On the other hand, Catholicism has a long history of valuing certain types of suffering as pleasing to God. If the God of the Old Testament appreciated animal sacrifice, the God of the New Testament appreciates human suffering in sacrifice. This sacrifice entails the dedication of one's love to God and the destruction of earthly attachment to pleasure, money, and power. Sometimes suffering is deliberately brought about through the mortification ("the putting to death") of earthly desires: fasting and the desire for food; the wearing of painful garments and the desire for comfort; celibacy and the desire for sexual intimacy.

Suffering is not only pleasing to God, but it is also considered a road to inner knowledge and to knowledge of the comfort of God. For mystical Catholicism, suffering is a gift that brings the mystic closer to God. God incarnate is a man who suffers (Jesus), and his painful death in torture is recreated in the veneration of the stations of the cross, each with its own particular pain and humiliation.

The valuing of deliberate suffering complicates the Catholic commitment to compassion for others. It is true that a basic commandment of faith is to love thy neighbor, and for Catholics this entails a mandate of charity. This love, however, does not shy away from personal suffering, nor from the suffering in the (loved) other if understood to be part of the road to enlightenment and liberation from sin.

In the middle of the twentieth century, Latin American priests and nuns proposed a different understanding of the Catholic commitment to charity: they understood the mandate of love as a mandate to change social structures and alleviate the suffering of the poor. This "liberation theology" resulted in a generation of priests and nuns who took on, at enormous personal costs, lives dedicated to succoring the poor. However, in the mid-1980s, the church signaled the important theological errors of liberation theology, arguing that while the church did consider its works of charity to express a commitment to the poor, it did not confuse this with a Marxist class analysis that ultimately advocated class warfare.[26] The Vatican then expelled and silenced many of the principal exponents of liberation theology, rejecting the possibility that the church should be involved in transforming social structures that distribute wealth.[27] Instead, the church's goal was to usher in salvation, and in light of that goal, suffering in this earth was secondary.

The argument that the criminalization of abortion results in suffering for women is not a compelling argument for a church that still finds redemptive value in suffering. In *Evangelium Vitae*, Pope John Paul II described the abortion decision as "aggravated by a cultural climate which fails to perceive any meaning or value in suffering, but rather considers suffering the epitome of evil, to be eliminated at all costs." He said this was especially the case in "the absence of a religious outlook which could help to provide a positive understanding of the mystery of suffering"[28] and where "suffering while still an evil and a trial in itself can always become a source of good."[29]

Life from Conception

Catholic constitutionalism's strongest claim against abortion decriminalization is that human life begins at conception, or fertilization; abortion is murder of persons who are "unborn" from the moment of fertilization. When challenging the Mexico City law that decriminalized abortion in the first twelve weeks, the human rights commissioner argued that human life is "a process" that requires constitutional protection throughout all its stages, precluding decriminalization at any stage of pregnancy.[30] Defining life as process is critical to denying distinction or line drawing in legal protection.

The definition of life, and the right to life, as beginning in conception has been adopted by states and legislatures across the region and approved by courts.[31] The right-to-life argument was elaborated in a recent case before the Inter-American Court of Human Rights on a ban against in vitro fertilization.[32] Several amicus briefs in support of the ban argued that the production and potential destruction of surplus fertilized eggs breaches the human right to life.[33] The interpretive claim underlying the argument was that a "new genome determines the specific and individual biological identity of the new subject and the eventual natural selection does not change ontological reality."[34] The unique status of the human genome as the marker of the beginning of life was also used in a recent Brazilian case on the constitutionality of pregnancy termination in cases of anencephaly.[35] The claimants argued that since the anencephalic fetus lacked a brain or brain activity, there was no human life requiring legal protection. Father Luiz Antonio Bento, a doctor in bioethics and spokesman for the National Bishops' Confederation, rejected this claim in the public hearing. He argued that "since the fetus has the human genome, all genetic facts needed in the life of this individual are present,"[36] and the fetus was and should be protected as "a living human being" albeit one "with a reduced life expectancy."[37] The Court did not find this argument persuasive, but others have. The Argentinean Supreme Court and Chilean Supreme Court, as well as the Peruvian Constitutional Court, have all adopted injunctions against emergency contraception on the basis that it prevents implantation of a fertilized ovum in the uterine wall, violating the right to life of a person, identified by the presence of unique DNA.[38]

The Catholic argument that defines human life through DNA mirrors medieval claims about the moment the soul enters the human body, and thus the time from which abortion constitutes murder. The debate is known as that of immediate versus delayed hominization—that is, whether ensoulment happens at conception or at a later time. Earlier theories about the soul entering once the fetus took human form were rejected with the advancement of reproductive science.[39] In 1869, the church adopted the position that from the moment of conception there was a human person, which marked a turning point in the Catholic rejection of abortion and resulted in the condemnation of any intervention from conception, but without the elaboration it would have in the twentieth century.[40]

Pope Paul VI was the first to explicitly address the issue of contraception and to link it to abortion. In his 1968 Humanae Vitae, he condemned even therapeutic abortion for its contraceptive properties, claiming that: "every marital act must of necessity retain its intrinsic relationship to the procreation of human life."[41] By 1974—a year after Roe v. Wade—the Congregation for the Doctrine of the Faith, a final arbiter of orthodox interpretation, rearticulated the prohibition as a defense of the "right to life" and thereby for the first time fully expressed the church's contemporary rationale for the prohibition. This articulation was quoted verbatim in the influential 1995 encyclical Evangelium Vitae. Affirmed was the claim that "right from fertilization is begun the adventure of a human life . . . [even] supposing a belated

animation, there is still nothing less than a human life, preparing for and calling for a soul in which the nature received from parents is completed."[42]

Affirmation that human life, and hence a person, is present without any
material attribute other than conception, makes sense within a religious
mode of understanding the world, where material manifestations are contingent and objective. Defining life in terms of a material body with human capabilities and functions that are the foundation of the individual autonomy
and choice is simply alien to a meaning-making system that bases truth on a
transcendental dimension independent of empirical confirmation, and affirms this truth to be objective, universal, and deeply moral.

In pressing for legal recognition of the right to life from conception, lay
Catholic advocates across the Americas are seeking to redefine human life as
essence rather than *existence.* To trace the theological roots of this distinction
is to acknowledge that more than life's beginnings are at stake. To argue that
the product of conception is a person, a legal subject with a right to life, is to
contest the very definition of human life itself. Life, in other words, is defined
not by the existence or material manifestation of any entity, that is, the embryo or the fetus. Instead life as *essence* is defined by an ontological or metaphysical reality, which requires study of the eternal categories of being in the
Platonic tradition that is the breeding ground for Christian ideas of life. Ontological reality, the reality of the thing as an essence, is ultimate, or metaphysical, reality. Since life has such a reality, no material elements are required
to prove that there is "a life," beyond the initiation of a process that signals its
presence as an eternal essence—the nature of life as "being" is present.

In the contemporary era, this initiation and the signaling of life as *essence*
is marked by DNA. Catholic advocates claim that from conception the presence of a human genome, a DNA chain distinct from the mother's, signals a
separate, individual human life. This reasoning can be traced to Jerome
Lejeune, a reputed French genetic scientist and a Catholic pro-life activist,
whose arguments on the definition of life from conception were reproduced
by Pope John Paul II. [43] The reference to a material element, DNA, does not
change the Catholic definition of life from essence to existence, that is, it does
not alter the basic reference to an ontological reality of life. DNA is referenced
and remains relevant only as a marker of life as essence. This can be seen in
an argument ultimately endorsed by the Chilean Supreme Court, that "from
the instant the ovum receives the sperm, the totality of the information necessary and sufficient for life is in that egg, and all is written to form a man that
nine months later we will be able to identify fully."[44] Once the link between

life as essence and the existence of the human genome, or a unique DNA, is established, the argument follows that any intentional interruption of the process by which the product of conception becomes a human child is equivalent to murder. This would include abortion, but also intra-uterine devices and emergency contraception, which purportedly work by interrupting the nesting of the fertilized egg in utero.

The contest over the right to life, and the scope of its application, in the abortion context thus carries implications of a much more serious order: at stake is the very definition of life itself, as a material or metaphysical phenomenon. To argue over by which material properties life should be defined—brain activity or consciousness—is to neglect this more fundamental disagreement. It is a disagreement that threatens to overwhelm our capacity for common resolution—a consequence that may leave the church to demand, as a last resort, a measure of independence to allow its faithful to live according to their understanding of the metaphysical dimension to life and existence.

The Freedom of Conscience and the Right to Refuse

For reason of this fundamental conflict, Catholic advocates have argued often successfully for the freedom of conscience and/or religion to refuse provision of abortion services, or any type of information that may facilitate abortion (including counseling and sex education). Originally claimed for health care professionals—Catholic nurses and doctors—the right to refuse has been increasingly extended to all actors within health care institutions, to the institutions themselves, and more recently, to judges and other public officials. The Colombia Procuraduría, for example, recently argued in a report on abortion services that institutions enjoy a right of conscientious objection[45] and later presented a bill guaranteeing to private institutions and public officials (a judge or public hospital director, for example) a right to refuse implementation of a newly liberalized abortion law.[46] In support of the bill, he argued: "Conscience is in the heart of every decision-making process, and while it does have a subjective character, this does not mean [it is] relative, since it is defined by objective principles of a religious, moral and ethical character that shape decision making in a concrete situation."[47]

Redefined within a natural law tradition, the right of conscience emanates not only from deeply held personal convictions, but also from an objective moral order. Laws that violate that order should not bind the faithful. The bill was thus designed to create, as it were, a legal right to disobey immoral laws. The argument underlying this expansive interpretation of the right to conscience is one of church-state separation. In his book *Institutional Conscientious Objection*, Father Alfonso Llano explains that the state cannot force Catholic health care providers acting in institutional affiliation to follow laws deeply offensive to the religious values that guide them.[48] This reasoning applies not only to temples and parishes, but also to social institutions affiliated with a church such as charities, hospitals, and universities.

Behind arguments for an institutional right of conscientious objection lies a robust understanding of the freedom of religion and the renegotiated status of the Catholic Church in secular states. In confessional states, the relationship between the church and state was one of cohabitation not separation, and until the nineteenth century, the church endorsed this arrangement even when the balance of power was not in its favor. Various popes adopted official positions rejecting liberalism and secularization,[49] opposing church-state separation on the grounds that Catholicism represented the manifestation of God's truth on earth and expressed the knowledge of an objective moral order. To separate this moral knowledge from the stewardship of human destiny was to deny its objective nature and to accept a state indifferent to this truth.

In the twentieth century, with the reform process held during the Second Vatican Council, the church accepted secularism, after a passionate internal fight, but under the condition of a generous right to religious freedom.[50] It reconciled its belief in its own moral superiority by linking the emerging institutions and discourses of international human rights law to Catholic natural law.[51] Pro-secularist leaders within the church argued that since both faith and reason lead to the knowledge of the objective moral order, the incorporation of human rights in state procedures and actions could lead secular states through reason to a morality that did not need to be narrowly Catholic.[52]

This freedom included the right to preach and teach, the right to worship, the right to give itself its own rules and authorities, the right to pass moral judgment on temporal matters, the right to form educational, cultural, and other associations, the right to own property and to use it as it sees fit. The separation of church and the state, in other words, implied the existence of a strong and free church, unharnessed by democratic deliberation that might limit its rights and privileges.

This model of church-state separation, however, had a further particularity: while the church as an institution, with its hierarchies and laws, accepts separation from the state, Catholics themselves need not. On the contrary, the Catholic laity is called to sanctify the state through their actions, presence, and participation, as a means to materialize the objective moral order in the state.[53] Catholics are to participate in political life with a deeper commitment to God than to the state and to resist and disobey laws that may go against their conscience (as in Acts 5:29: "obey God before men").

It is this particularity that explains the robustness of claimed conscientious objection rights in Catholic constitutional argument. These rights are perhaps better articulated as freedoms to resist and disobey law as a materialization of Catholic faith in public life. This reading is supported by the Colombian Procuraduría's expansive proposal for protection of conscience as a religious freedom that consistently trumps other constitutional protections. Values such as equality pale in comparison to religious freedom thus defined, which creates many difficulties for mainstream liberal constitutionalism that fundamentally seeks to balance individual freedoms with other collective and individual goods. It also eschews discussion of the duties borne by a strong church in a secular democracy, emphasizing instead the rights of the church and of the faithful.

Engagement with the state as means to materialize Catholic morality has not, however, been pursued nor encouraged by the church in all matters of social life. While engagement on moral issues is required, Catholic activism on political issues is not. This line between morality and politics has been especially problematic in recent church history. In the twentieth century, some national churches and individual priests took strong positions in favor of the poor and the dispossessed, phrased as the "preferential option for the poor."

It is politically noteworthy that the intensity of Catholic commitment to social justice, thwarted in the 1980s with the silencing of liberation theology, has been redirected and fanned by the church today toward sexual morality. While changes in social structures generally are understood to be the province of politics, social structures of sexual morality call on Catholic activism not only to change laws, *but to actively disobey laws* that allow for abortion and same sex marriage.[54] This rallying cry highlights the tensions between Catholic constitutionalism's definition of religious freedom, conscientious objection, and other values of liberal democracies.

Engaging Catholic Arguments

A better understanding of the appeal and the limitations of Catholic constitutional arguments in abortion debates can contribute to a shift in how the secular pro-choice community not only engages these arguments, but also rethinks and strengthens its own. In this section, I explore the productive effects of engagement with Catholic constitutionalism on three issues: underlying moral orders, depenalization, and the contingent, material, and historical nature of legal truths.

Which Moral Order? Feminism and Social Justice

Catholic constitutional arguments require engagement with natural law and the objective moral order it implies. The most important exponents of Catholic legal thought, and the church itself, claim that human rights are nothing more than natural law recognized and reproduced in legal documents. This claim is not easily rejected because human rights activists themselves make similar appeals to an objective moral order—the human rights order. The existence of such an order and its moral value are the unspoken premises of many claims that demand, for example, less stringent abortion laws.

Strict positivism is the classical counterargument against natural law claims. The philosophical basis for positivism is originally the rebuttal of the possibility of knowing transcendental truths such as the content of God's law. Most Enlightenment philosophers opposed the idea that humans can achieve knowledge of transcendental truths about morality, and thus opposed Aquinas's version of natural law as reflecting God's will. Building on this impossibility, thinkers as diverse as Burke[55] and Bentham[56] considered the French Declaration of the Rights of Man, and its appeal to eternal natural rights, to be a logical error or, in Bentham's words, "nonsense upon stilts." However, strict positivism also runs counter to the natural law implications of many human rights arguments.

A second possibility is to insist the natural law of human rights activists is not the same as Catholic natural law. A liberal definition of natural law insists instead that individual autonomy, as part of human nature, is the cornerstone of human rights. In this version, natural law arguments generally support a women's right to choose whether or not to carry a pregnancy to term insofar as it is an expression of an autonomy that is limited only by other people's dignity and rights, and embryos and fetuses are not people. An unexplored path is to link abortion and civic virtue, upending Catholic arguments that link motherhood and virtue.

Hence, engagement with claims about the moral order underlying legal argumentation may lead to a better articulation of the links between abortion and autonomy, or between abortion and collective aspirations to a liberal definition of civic virtue, or to other moral goods implicit in the objective moral order proposed by human rights discourse as an alternative to Catholicism.[57] Alternatively, it could signal the historical and political moorings of all claims to an objective moral order, and relinquish, at least in part, its own claims to universality and objectivity. This would entail a dialogue with Catholic advocates on the rational foundations of a common moral order.

Such a dialogue would also require reflection for human rights activists on the way that political liberalism includes or excludes women and, more generally, avoids issues of social justice. A moral order based on the defense of individual autonomy must address the historical failings of liberalism in allowing private regimes of discrimination and oppression, such as unjust labor practices, unjust wealth distributions, and undue burdens borne by mothers and caretakers, all of which impinge on female autonomy. While many of the points made by the church's "new feminism" seem to reproduce inequality, others do respond to many women's aspirations to the maintenance and appreciation of some aspects of traditional gender roles. More generally, the issue of the social conditions necessary for reproductive justice is a particularly salient social justice issue sometimes overlooked by human rights activists.

Therefore, engagement with Catholic constitutionalism can lead secular advocates down unexplored paths. It can lead us to examine more closely the moral order implicit in our liberal convictions, and their shortcomings for social justice. It can also build bridges with Catholic concerns for social justice, allowing for agreements on less punitive regimes than the criminalization of abortion, as well as less individualistic responses to the social issues raised by unwanted pregnancies and the care of children more generally.

Casting the First Stone: Suffering and
the Rejection of Criminal Law

Another possibility for engaging Catholics in a reasonable debate is on the issue of incarceration as punishment for abortion. Unlike other Christian denominations, the church has not shown a particular interest in sending women who have abortions to jail. In spite of Catholic acceptance of suffering, the mandates of charity, love, compassion, and forgiveness all support a rejection of deliberately causing suffering. In fact there are numerous Catholic criticisms of jails as institutions and of the inhuman conditions of detention. There is a general disbelief in the importance or effectiveness of human punishment, which is often rejected because of the mandate to forgive or the reluctance to judge others (the refusal to "cast the first stone").

This rejection of imprisonment in mainstream Catholicism sits uncomfortably with an underlying theory of law as the expression of a society's moral order. Criminalization is often supported as a moral sanction for behaviors the church finds deeply disturbing. The church, however, has accepted that other undesirable behaviors not be punished by temporal authorities. On abortion itself, the church has stated, "civil law cannot expect to cover the whole field of morality or to punish all faults."[58] The church may be willing to accept abstention from punishment, if the conduct remains nevertheless illegal.

Engagement with Catholics on their terms could advance agreements on depenalization, while maintaining a symbolic rejection. German law is an important precedent in this regard. While abortion is formally criminalized and remains wrongful in law, women can access abortion services under a counseling regime, in which Catholic organizations participate. In practice, this means abortions, and counseling, are available to women, with expenses often covered by the state in a way that is not antagonistic with Catholic insistence on the holiness of a human life that begins at conception.

Life As an Existence, Not an Essence

The fact that the product of conception has no human attribute except for DNA is not a problem for Catholic advocates, because their premise is that the truth about the world lies not in material existence but in essential reality. Paradoxically, this position is related to the church's acceptance of science in the nineteenth century: while it accepted the general proposition that science produces truth about the world, it also rekindled Thomas Aquinas's philosophical ideas that the myriad manifestations of being do not deny the truth of the oneness of being. In twentieth-century terms, this means that the varied claims made by science, even those that seem to deny religious truths (especially claims about the evolution of the species), merely show variations in forms of life (being) that do not change the essential truth of creation.

Applied to abortion, the claim that life begins at conception does not require scientific confirmation because it is premised in an essential reality rather than a material existence. Engagement with this idea thus requires a debate about the legal status of scientific truths: specifically, whether legal truths refer to transcendental or material truths. In science, there is no transcendental reality, only material phenomena. A strong position would be to reclaim the material nature of legal truths and to problematize the legal recognition of transcendental claims about human beings as claims that, by definition, imply a rejection of secular modes of argument.

Legislation has generally recognized the materiality of human life and limited legal outcomes to tangible evidence, avoiding reference to transcendental truths. For example, the law has given legal effects to personal existence only when there is a material proof of such existence, tied generally to activity in the cerebral cortex that denotes consciousness or the possibility of consciousness. In civil legislation, only separation from the mother and independent breathing signaled existence as a person. Materially, and legally, DNA does not a person make. For example, no one could claim that the many fertilized ova that fail to implant in the uterus are dead children. Arguments with Catholic advocates can easily point out these inconsistencies between legal truths and the basically religious claims that life begins at conception as a stand-in for an essentialist definition of life.

However, once life is defined as an existence, rather than a transcendental essence, it opens the door to debates on the material criteria that limit abortion, which could be present at an early stage of pregnancy. Material criteria for the existence of a person with full human rights, for example the existence of a functioning brain, might be earlier than birth, and even earlier than the possibility of sustaining independent life outside the womb. A serious defense of material criteria for a right to life would then need to face the inconsistencies of insisting in having natural birth and independent breathing be the sole criterion for the definition of human life.

Conclusion

Engaging Catholic constitutional arguments on their own terms can further the possibility of a productive dialogue between radically divergent positions on abortion. The issue of the rights and duties that emanate from sexual difference calls for a more robust discussion of social justice as a frame for both church and state responsibility for the suffering generated by punitive abortion laws. The argument that life, and the right to life, begin at conception, can elicit a dialogue on the legal implications of the difference between life-as-an-essence and life-as-existence. The development of an expansive right to conscientious objection can be engaged through a further discussion of church-state separation and of the duties borne by a strong church in a secular democracy.

Engagement would entail overcoming mutual distrust and repulsion. Sexual and reproductive rights activists are generally concerned with religious activists' disregard of the social suffering generated by punitive abortion laws. They are repulsed by religious claims that regardless of the circumstances, women have a duty to bear unwanted pregnancies to term under threat of imprisonment. They are also surprised by the challenge this activism represents for settled arguments of church-state separation that require obedience to legitimate, democratic regimes.

Religious activists, on the other hand, are generally concerned about the feminist disregard for unborn life and the social and economic pressures that may cause women to give up pregnancies they might otherwise want if circumstances were more welcoming. They are repulsed by claims that there is "no person" there, not even in a well-developed fetus. And they are concerned about their own rights, and duties, as people of faith in a secular democracy, and resent being shamed into silencing deeply held beliefs. Ultimately, however, lay Catholic activists' willingness to engage law "through reason alone" can signal a shift that opens the doors to less divisive arrangements, such as the one achieved in Germany.

While this engagement is possible, another fact remains. Many of these issues are being debated in national and international arenas; the role of courts could be that of mediators, ushering in a middle ground similar to the German example. The growing acceptance of balancing rights as the lingua franca of constitutionalism could allow for some version of this. But it could well be that these same arenas, instead of mediating, choose sides, whether firmly on the side of feminism and reproductive and sexual rights, or firmly on the lay Catholic side. There could be a triumph for the idea that there are no rights to be balanced: either the woman can freely dispose of any fetus that is not viable, or she can be punished for failing to bring to term any pregnancy, regardless of the personal costs. In these arenas, it is important to note that the logical integrity of arguments will probably not be the deciding criterion in courts and legislatures. Instead, it is a deeply political matter, a matter of the political power of secular lawyers and reproductive rights activists ver-sus the power of the organized lay faithful. The years to come will test the strength and numbers of each side, as well as their ability to come to terms with the social and political costs of present stalemate and to find a way forward.

Chapter 12

Bringing Abortion into the Brazilian Public Debate: Legal Strategies for Anencephalic Pregnancy

Luís Roberto Barroso

In October 2003, Gabriela de Oliveira Cordeiro, a poor nineteen-year-old living in the town of Teresópolis, in the outskirts of Rio de Janeiro, was four months into her second pregnancy when she learned that she was carrying an anencephalic fetus. She wanted to terminate the pregnancy. Over the next several months a grim and painful legal battle ensued to obtain a court order to carry out the procedure. Her request was first denied by a judge then granted by a state court, only to be revoked before it could go into effect, and then be granted once again. An organized Catholic anti-abortion group, galvanized to stop the medical procedure from taking place, fought against its authorization all the way to a higher federal court. The case eventually reached the Brazilian Supreme Court. Five days before the Justices were set to hear her case, Gabriela went into labor and delivered a full-term anencephalic child, Maria Vida, who was pronounced dead seven minutes after birth. The Court dismissed the case. This is Gabriela's story.

The case gained attention throughout the entire country and was featured on several media outlets. It gave a face and a name to so many other similar stories of women who, pregnant with anencephalic fetuses, were unsuccessfully knocking on every door of the judicial system to get access to a therapeutic premature delivery. The case also made clear to human rights advocacy groups linked to the Gabriela case that they needed to devise a litigation strategy that could elicit from the Supreme Court a broader decision that could affect the entire country rather than one restricted to a specific case. Less than four months after Maria Vida's birth—and death—a Claim of Noncompliance with a Fundamental Precept (ADPF 54, ADPF being its Portuguese acronym) was filed before the Supreme Court. In Brazil, provided certain conditions are met, some institutional actors can bring a direct constitutional lawsuit before the Supreme Court, to discuss in abstract a certain constitutional matter. The Claim of Noncompliance asserted the right to terminate pregnancies involving anencephalic fetuses; a month later, on July 1, 2004, a request for immediate injunction was granted by the Justice presiding over the case. Suddenly, women carrying anencephalic fetuses all over the country could just go to a public hospital and ask for a lawful termination.

In October 20, 2004, Severina Maria Leôncio Ferreira, resident of the miniscule town of Chã Grande, Pernambuco who was carrying an anencephalic fetus, was admitted to a hospital in the capital, Recife, to terminate her pregnancy. That very same day, the majority of the Brazilian Supreme Court lifted the injunction; Severina was sent home with her bags, the fetus inside her womb, and nowhere else to turn to for relief. Her only option was to pursue the usual and tortuous path of filing a request in her own name for a court order to perform the procedure. That road led her to three months of agony, going from courts to hospitals, and back to courts, until she was finally granted permission to terminate the pregnancy (or rather to induce labor, since she was seven months pregnant by then). The hardship of the very situation she found herself in—carrying a fetus she knew could not and would not live—was compounded by the struggle with judges and health care professionals during the months that followed the dissolution of the injunction. Severina's story is documented in a short movie.[1]

These are two snapshots of the battleground regarding reproductive rights in Brazil, around which the debate over abortion has recently been framed. They depict the comings and goings of a moment of transition from a debate on abortion purely centered on moral or religious beliefs to a legal framework, based on the ideas of women's rights and the legal status of the fetus. The hardiness of the opposition they stirred also offers a glimpse of the deep-rooted taboo against abortion that has ingrained itself not only in Brazil but in most of Latin America as well, especially because of the strong political influence of the Catholic Church within the region.

This chapter outlines the legal strategies set forth in Brazil to assert women's right to terminate pregnancies of anencephalic fetuses as the departure point to break through this taboo and advance the more difficult debate over the decriminalization of abortion. To do so, it focuses on the lessons learned throughout the long and strenuous journey that culminated in the recent conclusion of the ADPF 54. Decided eight years after it was filed, the case was greatly affected by and also highlighted the profound shift in the social perception of women's reproductive rights over the past years. This shift set the foundation for a change in the shared understanding through which the case was decided and made it possible to bring the broader issue of women's abortion rights to the table, along with its impact on public health. The chapter takes advantage of other experiences in Latin American countries, where the opposition to abortion is, in general, just as powerful and in some cases even more so. In hopes of contributing to the replication of these legal strategies elsewhere, the chapter also examines a set of arguments that have proved successful in the Brazilian case and are broadly applicable.

The Brazilian Case: Background

For someone not well versed in the many contradictions that run through Brazilian culture and society, it can be hard to reconcile the very strict abortion laws with the extremely liberal attitude toward sex and sexuality usually associated with the country. But the truth is that as much as the country can be indeed very open toward sexual morality, Brazil is still fairly conservative when it comes to a number of social issues—abortion above all. That helps explain why in a country where nationwide public campaigns for the distribution of free condoms have been carried out for over a decade (with pervasive TV ads and billboards, no less), and where the public health care system offers free HIV screening and medication and routinely performs permanent contraception procedures, abortion is broadly forbidden and carries a three-year incarceration sentence,[2] except when necessary to save the pregnant woman's life or when the pregnancy is the result of rape.[3]

If on paper a vast majority of the country seems to converge to an almost blank condemnation of abortion, in reality the situation is much more nuanced. The general prohibition on abortion yields its intended effects with astounding rates of success when it comes to disadvantaged women, who rely almost exclusively on the public (and free-of-charge) health care system to get the services they need. These women, undoubtedly, do not have access to quality abortion or post-abortion services—and therefore many pay with their own lives when terminating an unwanted pregnancy.[4] On the other hand, middle- and upper-class women, who have the means to seek a private clinic, can count on a wide net of abortion and post-abortion services— clandestine in many cases but also a few that are somewhat more mainstream— usually undisturbed by the legal prohibition or enforcement agencies.

Not surprisingly, the general prohibition on abortion in Brazil disproportionately impacts poor women and their families and creates a public health concern over maternal death related to botched abortions, incorrect use of abortive medication, or lack of post-abortion services (unsafe abortion, in fact, is one of the top five causes of maternal death in Brazil).[5] This disparity is a key element in keeping the widespread public opposition to abortion intact, since a change in the legislation is much less important for the most politically and economically influential segments of society given that they do, to a large extent, get the appropriate abortion services they need. The clandestine and private nature of the access to abortion in Brazil also benefits the already very strong influence of the Catholic Church, as it allows even those who have used such services to keep the matter under wraps and avoid any negative consequences to their social, moral, and religious standing. In this context, devising a legal strategy to advance women's right to terminate a pregnancy was as much about the legal arguments per se as about reframing the discussion in legal, rather than moral or religious terms, as the latter battle seemed unlikely to be won.

Throughout the years, hundreds of pregnant women in Brazil have carried fetuses with a condition called anencephaly,[6] the congenital absence of brain and parts of skull and scalp.[7] Many of them, if not the majority, would have liked to end these pregnancies well before their due date. Because there is no specific rule governing the abortion of nonviable fetuses in Brazil, including anencephalic ones, it was not clear from the outset whether the general prohibition should apply or if this constituted an exception to that rule. The uncertainty over the specific situation of nonviable fetuses led to a somewhat widespread understanding in Brazil that women in this situation would have to first seek a court order authorizing the termination procedure. The outcomes tended to vary widely from judge to judge and court to court.

Though anencephalic fetuses have accounted for about half of the judicial decisions allowing selective abortion in Brazil, this number is still very small,[8] and being in that position meant that a woman going through an entirely nonviable pregnancy would have to peregrinate from court to court until an authorization to get the procedure was obtained. That painful process was often altogether unsuccessful, or took so long that the decision came after the pregnancy had ended naturally (so much so that, because of the unavailability of abortion services in these cases, Brazil has been ranked one of the countries with the highest number of anencephalic newborns).[9] These pregnant women—in the overwhelming majority of the cases, poor women seeking public health care services—were thus completely helpless against the pervasive moral and religious beliefs that penetrated judicial decisions on termination of pregnancy.

Asserting the rights of these pregnant women carrying anencephalic fetuses became an opportunity to remedy one of the gravest and most painful injustices inflicted by the restrictive Brazilian abortion laws, while advancing the general right to abortion, since the nature of anencephalic fetuses offered a chance to bypass the most crucial moral issue against abortion—the fetus' potentiality of life. In these situations, a woman's right to choose to terminate the pregnancy would not have to be balanced against any potential rights of the fetus to live, as anencephaly is a condition that by itself is incompatible with life outside the womb, beyond any trace of doubt.

There was no question that the plight of these women had to be alleviated, and in doing so, our team of lawyers and women's health experts felt that the pursuit of more generous abortion laws would also benefit from the rise in awareness and public debate on the subject, and, most importantly, from the framing of the public debate in legal terms. But even the exceedingly sad situation of women carrying anencephalic fetuses has been the object of tenacious opposition (in this case, mostly of a religious nature), so it was important to tread with caution when putting forth strategies to assert women's right to terminate pregnancies of anencephalic fetuses, even if that meant choosing a more gradual approach to advancing their general right to have an abortion. These strategies were tested in a Claim of Noncompliance with a Fundamental Precept (ADPF 54) before the Supreme Court.

The Making of ADPF 54

The idea to bring a lawsuit before the Brazilian courts to obtain a broader decision recognizing a woman's right to terminate a pregnancy of an anencephalic fetus had been brewing in a small but very articulate section of the medical and women's rights social movement for a few years. Devoted to helping these women in the day-to-day struggle to secure a lawyer (or, more frequently, a public defender) and to seek judicial authorization, these groups were very aware that a unified approach, not tied to a specific case and therefore unrestrained by the urgency that a typical forty-week pregnancy would impose, had to be taken. It was also clear by then that the possibility of advancing an instance of selective termination of pregnancy—even if limited to the very extreme case of pregnancy of anencephalic fetuses—could be beneficial to the general effort to assert women's right to abortion.

This idea made its way from the social movements to our legal team in 2004, amid the frustration and heartbreak over the Gabriela case. The challenge, from a legal perspective, was to marry strong legal arguments with a strategy that would be sensible in regards to the moral and religious opposition that so strongly lingered in the background. Instead of going through the usual channels of the Brazilian judicial system, it was clear to us that we needed to take a fast track to the Supreme Court, using the tools available to obtain a binding decision that would have effects across the entire national territory. We then settled on the ADPF even though it was untested at the time because it was a direct and abstract (not related to any specific case) constitutional action.

The main claim of the action was that any interpretation of the Penal Code that forbade women carrying anencephalic fetuses from seeking an abortion would be unconstitutional, and therefore the Court should settle the interpretation in accordance with the Constitution to declare that such procedures were valid under the law. Given how long it can take for a final decision on ADPFs to be reached by the Supreme Court, it was crucial to pair the main claim with a request for an injunction. Specifically, we requested that the Justice to whom the case was assigned put in place an injunction so that all women were allowed to terminate a pregnancy in these circumstances without having to obtain prior court authorization. According to Brazilian law, however, such a temporary order, granted by monocratic decision, must be submitted to the full Court before it becomes effective unless the order is granted during the Court's recess. And that was the case here. Justice Marco Aurélio, who presided over ADPF 54, granted the injunction on July 1, 2004, during the Court's annual break in the month of July, which made it effective immediately. It was based on this specific decision that Severina planned to terminate her pregnancy.

This much-needed period of respite was, unfortunately, short-lived.

When the Supreme Court gathered again to discuss the case, in October 2004, the full panel revoked the injunction by a 7–4 vote. Though terribly disappointing, the setback was mostly because the Court recognized that the importance, complexity, and magnitude of the case made it unsuitable to the superficial scrutiny involved in temporary orders of injunction. Some of the Justices, in fact, made it clear that they were not anticipating their position on the merits of the case, but simply indicating that they found it improper to deal with this matter without the deep consideration that can be attained only in a final judgment. On the positive side, the Court decided to hear the case, declaring that all the formalities required by law for an ADPF had been met. That was a major victory, since a few Justices took the view that termination of pregnancies of anencephalic fetuses was a matter to be discussed and settled in Congress, and not in a court of law.

In the years that followed, using a prerogative available to him, the Justice presiding over the case did not schedule it to be heard by the full Court. Given the complexity of the case and of its highly controversial nature, the Supreme Court decided to hold a series of public hearings on the matter in 2008. A public hearing is not to be confused with the specific hearing of the case, where the lawyers present their arguments to the Court. A public hearing is a tool that allows the Court to convene a panel of experts from different sectors of society in order to pose some questions that the Court believes to be beyond the realm of law, but which are, nonetheless, considered relevant to the disentanglement of the case. In this specific case, the Court invited representatives of religious groups, medical associations, and advocacy groups in favor of and against the decriminalization of abortion.

The public hearing,[10] broadcast live on the national court television station TV Justiça, was in and of itself a major achievement, since it provided an incredible arena for the discussion of women's rights regarding their pregnancies—which, considering the depth of the abortion taboo in Brazil, was no small matter. On its content, likewise, the hearing proved to be a success, for it demystified many misconceptions that had seeped into the legal aspects of the case. Five findings from the hearing were particularly relevant and reflect facts that may benefit other cases litigating the rights of women to terminate pregnancies of anencephalic fetuses elsewhere as they are not restricted to the Brazilian context.

The first finding established that anencephaly is a condition that is lethal and irreversible in all cases, and that its diagnosis is performed through simple medical exams with a 100 percent degree of certainty. The public health care system in Brazil was found to be entirely capable of performing that diagnosis, as well as the medical procedure to induce early delivery if the mother so desires. The second finding determined that anencephaly was not to be confused with a disability. On the contrary, it found that anencephaly is a condition incompatible with life, and, because of that, there are no children or adults with anencephaly. The third finding was related to maternal health and revealed that a pregnancy involving an anencephalic fetus represented a higher degree of risk for women than typical ones, especially with regard to hypertension, higher levels of amniotic liquid, and preeclampsia. Moreover, it was found that forcing a woman to take the pregnancy of a nonviable fetus to full term can gravely affect her mental health.

The fourth finding dealt with anencephaly and organ donation. The panel indicated that an anencephalic fetus would not be a potential organ donor, because it has multiple associated deformities that increase the rate of organ rejection by the recipient. The fifth and final finding was closely associated with one of the arguments we put forth in the case (and to which we will turn our attention very soon): that the termination of pregnancy of anencephalic fetuses did not constitute abortion because there was no potentiality of life when it came to the fetus. In fact, it must be treated as a therapeutic premature delivery.

After the public hearing, there was a long hiatus during which the Court's composition changed drastically (with five of its eleven Justices being replaced). Our final address to the Court and its final ruling on the case were finally scheduled for April 11, 2012. Eight years after we first brought the claim before the Court, we felt extremely confident that the debate about the therapeutic premature delivery of anencephalic fetuses had matured enough to induce a favorable decision, both because of the change in the composition of the Court and the now stronger social support. The pressure from the Catholic Church and other religious groups, though, had not decreased in the least. Once the Court session was scheduled, an organized opposition movement started to take vigorous action, arranging vigils and communal prayers in front of the courthouse and asking for personal audiences with the Justices.

Interest in the final ruling on ADPF54 also gathered a lot of steam in the news media and on the Internet. The ruling not only dominated the headlines all over the country, but it also boiled over as the main point of contention and discussion among people in general. As all eyes were on the Court, and with the session being broadcast live on TV and streamed in real time on the Internet, we decided to push the envelope and, alongside the three core arguments (which we will detail in the following section), present a fourth one: a general pro-abortion argument.

As the circumstances seemed favorable, we seized the opportunity to highlight the main reasons why we believed abortion should be decriminalized up until the twelfth week. Under the umbrella of Article 1, III of the Federal Constitution, which guarantees "the dignity of the individual," the fourth argument invoked women's reproductive right— stressing the ideas of autonomy and equality—and the public health concern over maternal death caused by unsafe clandestine abortions. Our final address to the Court was a long time coming. It was the first time the decriminalization of abortion was openly argued before the Supreme Court. It is interesting to note that the point was made in an inevitably ambiguous fashion: although it implied a general call for decriminalization, the specific claim was limited to the case of anencephalic fetuses. We were indeed fishing for an obiter dictum recognizing the concept of women's reproductive rights. The strategy succeeded. In the more than fifteen hours, over the two days that the session lasted, every one of the ten Justices decided to write a separate opinion, and to submit it to the panel. An 8–2 majority declared that the prohibition of therapeutic premature delivery of anencephalic fetuses was indeed a violation to the Constitution and conceived a new interpretation to the Penal Code to allow for such exception, as per the opinion by presiding Justice Marco Aurélio. The summary of the decision reads, "Interpreting the interruption of a pregnancy with anencephalic fetus to be typified by articles 124, 126 and 128 I and II of the Penal Code is deemed unconstitutional."[11] Articles 124 and 126 criminalize inducing or allowing an abortion to be performed, and performing an abortion, and article 128 outlines the exemptions from punishment for performing an abortion. The clear message is that terminating a pregnancy with an anencephalic fetus cannot be equated with an abortion. No more Severinas and no more Gabrielas would have to go through their personal tragedies while suffering the hostility and uncertainty of the judicial system.

The Court crafted a predictably minimalist approach to the decision (which, nonetheless, comprises more than 430 pages with all ten decisions), making it very clear that its application was restricted to pregnancies involving anencephalic fetuses. The Justices made the point in several instances. Justice Marco Aurélio's opinion states: "It is thus entirely unsound to say that the Supreme Court will examine, in this case, the decriminalization of abortion, especially because, as we shall see, there is a distinction between abortion and therapeutic premature delivery."[12]

If our more recent and pro-abortion argument, centered on reproductive rights and public health and built on our human dignity framework, was not inscribed into the opinion's holding, it did make its way into the reasoning of individual opinions, thus being acknowledged by the Court for the first time. For example, Justice Rosa Weber's opinion, making express reference to our oral arguments, states, "forcing a woman to continue the pregnancy without minimum biological conditions of development offends . . . her right to reproductive freedom. Protecting women in such situations where the life is unfeasible outside the womb concretely ensures their freedom of choice about the reproductive role they are entitled to and recognizes their fundamental right."[13] As for the public health argument, Justice Luiz Fux's opinion declares: "It is unequivocally revealed, therefore, that the interruption of pregnancies of anencephalic fetuses is a matter of public health, which afflicts mostly the women—as said by Justice Marco Aurélio—that make up the less affluent part of the population. The issue should be treated as an efficient policy of social assistance, which would give to pregnant women all the support needed in such an unfortunate situation, not subject them to criminal prosecution, a prosecution devoid of any reasonable basis."[14]

Although this decision was influenced by the shift in the circumstances and perceptions that surrounded the case, the major achievement and the change in thinking that this decision represented rested on a substantial technical foundation. This foundation was particularly ample in its reach, as it tried to provide a set of arguments that could both appeal to a narrower view on termination of pregnancies involving anencephalic fetuses—one less inclined to a wide recognition of abortion rights—as well as offer a sound legal foundation to advance those rights more broadly. As it turns out, the breadth covered by this set of arguments was precisely what made it possible to push for a more abortion-oriented decision in the final holding, when the circumstances appeared to be ripe, without doing so at the expense of a favorable decision, as the women's reproductive rights and its public health impact argument would not (and were not) sufficient to sway the Court. This wide-ranging approach, however, needs to preserve its bite in order to overcome the hurdles in its way. An overview of the arguments and their reception by the Brazilian Supreme Court are the focus of the next section, while case law from other Latin American countries is also presented when valuable to the discussion.

From Strategy to Practice: The Three Core Arguments

ADPF 54 was conceived with two related but distinct goals. The first, more obvious and visible, was aimed at the recognition of a right of women carrying anencephalic fetuses to have access to induction procedures without having to resort to individual court authorizations. The second and strategic purpose of the lawsuit was to ignite the more sensitive and complex debate on women's right to terminate unwanted pregnancies in general. Due to the impossibility under the current legal and judicial environment to pursue a broader right to abortion, we all had the sense that a victory regarding anencephalic fetuses would not be small by any measure: it would alleviate the incredible suffering of these women while breaking through the abortion taboo. Along these lines, the arguments were crafted attempting to strike a balance between the two goals (which, though related, differed widely in ambition and degree of public sympathy) without being disingenuous or artificial.

The three core arguments on which the ADPF was grounded were thus tailored to advance abortion rights but also to leave the door open for those Justices who, though opposed to the decriminalization of abortion, felt that the specific case of pregnancies of anencephalic fetuses should be interpreted as an exception to the general prohibition of article 124 of the Penal Code which criminalizes "inducing an abortion or allowing another to perform an abortion."[15] This balanced approach was particularly embodied by the first argument, which aimed at differentiating the special legal position of women pregnant with anencephalic fetuses from the general issue regarding abortion rights.

First Argument: Therapeutic Premature Delivery Is Not Abortion

The determination of when life truly begins has been the object of a debate— religious, moral, and also legal—that we felt would not be beneficial to the cause we were pursuing. In fact, we decided to look at the issue from a completely different perspective, afforded by the specific situation of anencephalic fetuses: the beginning of death. In this context, there were legal norms we could count on to establish that there could be no abortion when there was no brain activity as that would be, according to Brazilian law, the precise definition of death. Because there is no crime against life when the victim is already brain dead, it follows that there is no abortion in the absence of brain activity of the fetus.

Indeed, abortion in Brazil is described by specialized doctrine as "interruption of pregnancy with the consequent death of the fetus (the product of the conception)."[16] In other words: death must be the direct result of the abortive means and, therefore, proof of the causal link between action and result, as well as the potentiality of the life of the fetus outside the womb, is absolutely necessary. This does not occur in the case of the therapeutic premature delivery of an anencephalic fetus. In effect, the death of the fetus in these cases is the result of the congenital deformity in and of itself and is certain and inevitable even if the nine months of normal pregnancy were to elapse. The factual basis required for the penal classification of this case, therefore, does not fit the criminal type of abortion.

This line of reasoning is inexorably derived from the legal concept of death adopted in Brazilian law. In fact, the legal system permits the extraction of organs destined for transplant after the donor's "encephalic death is diagnosed."[17] Therefore, a person is considered dead when his/her brain ceases to have any activity. But the anencephalic fetus never even initiates cerebral activity because it lacks cerebral hemispheres and a cortex, possessing merely a residue of the encephalic trunk. Interruption of pregnancy in this case is not the type of act intended to be captured by the law and thus is not punishable. To the contrary, it is a legitimate and even necessary intervention to safeguard the physical and mental health of the pregnant woman, given the higher risks involved in these types of pregnancies.[18] Just as a reference, we did consider the repercussions this argument would hypothetically entail for organ donation. However, as the understanding seemed to prevail within the medical community (settled as one of the findings of the public hearing in the ADPF 54 and later incorporated into the decision by the presiding Justice) that the condition itself, that anencephaly itself, would compromise the state of health and the suitability of the organs for donation, organ donation from a breathing anencephalic baby was not an issue that needed to be addressed—and thus was not. The Brazilian Supreme Court welcomed the argument and rested its decision in ADPF 54 in great part on the fact that the conduct did not amount to an abortion (even though one of the concurring Justices in the majority, Justice Gilmar Mendes, explicitly dismissed it). Writing for the Court, Justice Marco Aurélio stated,

> Because it is absolutely unfeasible, the anencephalic fetus does not expect to be, is not, and will not be entitled to the right to life, which is

why I alluded at the beginning of voting that the conflict between fundamental rights was only apparent. Strictly speaking, at the other side of the scale, as opposed to women's rights, is not the right to life and human dignity of those who are to come, precisely because there is no one to come, there is no viable life. Abortion is a crime against life. The potentiality of life is what it is protected. In the case of anencephalic fetuses, I repeat, there is no life possible.[19]

In a later excerpt of the written opinion, Justice Marco Aurélio confirms: "Mr. Chief Justice, even in the absence of express provision in the Penal Code of 1940, it seems to me that the fetus without potentiality of life cannot be protected by the penal type that protects life."[20]

The different nature of the procedure of premature delivery of anencephalic fetuses when compared to an abortion was also explored in a landmark decision in Argentina, *T., S. v. Gobierno de la Ciudad de Buenos Aires*,[21] in 2001. The Argentine Penal Code prohibits any kind of abortion, unless it is strictly necessary to safeguard the woman's health or if the pregnancy is the result of rape against a mentally incompetent woman.[22] The Supreme Court of Argentina has relaxed the general prohibition over the years, albeit timidly, extending the exception based on rape, more recently, to any woman who has suffered such violence.[23]

The 2001 decision represents the mitigation of the abortion prohibition based on the atypical nature of the conduct. In that case, the Court understood that the specific case of anencephalic fetuses should also be considered an exception to the general prohibition, as the premature delivery of an anencephalic fetus lacked some aspects of the penal type and, therefore, did not constitute the crime of abortion. The framework adopted by the Court, however, is notably peculiar: it was centered on a qualification that the premature delivery occurred only after twenty-eight weeks of gestation, considered the threshold for viability outside the womb. The idea behind the qualification was that, when the delivery was performed after that period (when a viable fetus would be able to survive outside the womb), the death of the fetus was not a result of the procedure, but of its own malformation. That is, the Court understood that the fetus's death was due to anencephaly itself, a condition that is entirely beyond human control, even considering the possible lack of postnatal care received by the anencephalic fetus delivered after the twenty-eighth week.

For this reason, according to the Court, performing the premature delivery could not be considered abortion, for it would lack the *actus reus* of the offense, as the death could not be attributed to human action. The Court understood, also, that the mens rea of abortion was not present in the case of premature delivery of anencephalic fetuses over twenty-eight weeks of gestation, since there was no intent to deprive the fetus of life, even though the fact that its death would, beyond any doubt, follow the delivery was well known and acknowledged.

The troublesome framework established by the Argentine decision derives from its unwillingness to spare women carrying anencephalic fetus from their tragedy before some sort of fictitious viability would have been achieved, even though there is no question from the start that this would never come to be materialized. Basically, the woman has to wait for over four months after diagnosis, under tremendous distress and agony, until her baby would qualify to undergo the premature delivery, even though viability was never a prospect for the anencephalic fetus. That is an unfortunate situation, caused by the need to rely on some sort of specific threshold of fictitious viability to do what could have been done from the beginning, with the same results. It also completely ignores some stark difficulties, such as the impact of the lack of postnatal care available to a fetus delivered at twenty-eight weeks of gestation to the outcome of its death. Though its survival is possible, any fetus delivered at such an early stage of gestation would face immense hardships and most likely would not avoid death unless very high standards of care were available.

Second Argument: Evolving Interpretation of the Penal Code

The first argument was a pragmatic one and rested on a minimalist approach to judicial reasoning, entirely attached to the specific case of anencephalic fetuses, and intended to appeal to Justices who were generally against the decriminalization of abortion but still willing to grant an exception in these cases. The second argument, in contrast, offers more options to advance the right to selective abortion. It seeks to support an evolving interpretation of the general prohibition on abortion and attempts to create exceptions to the general rule other than the one sought for anencephalic fetuses. The argument states that, even if one were to consider the therapeutic premature delivery as abortion in the case of anencephalic fetuses, that would still not be a punishable act, in light of the exceptions put in place by the Penal Code for what is called "necessary" abortion: if there is no other means of saving the life of the woman, or in the case of abortion desired by the woman when the pregnancy was caused by rape. The case of nonviable fetuses, we argued, was not expressly classified as an exception that would prevent punishment merely due to the fact that in 1940, when this segment of the Penal Code was enacted, the technology existing at the time did not permit the precise diagnosis of fetal anomalies incompatible with life.

In fact, the Penal Code's appraisal of factors such as the potentiality of life of the fetus balanced against that of the mother, and the suffering of the mother when she had been the victim of an act of violence, suggests that the lawmaker considered the situation and allowed for the termination of pregnancy. The case of women pregnant with anencephalic fetuses seems actually simpler, and easier to balance, since it involves a less drastic moral and legal choice: the mother's immense suffering and health risk, on the one hand, and the absence of potentiality of life on the other. It thus appears reasonable to argue that, having authorized the more drastic case, the law had merely failed to mention the less drastic one because it was not possible to imagine such situations at the time it was drawn up.

An evolving interpretation of the law requires that, once put into effect, the legal norm becomes free of the subjective will that created it and achieves an objective and autonomous existence.[24] This is what enables the law to adapt to new situations that, though not anticipated by the lawmaker, feature values that inspired its enactment and fall within the possibilities and limits offered by its text. The therapeutic anticipation of delivery when a woman is pregnant with an anencephalic fetus is, indeed, within the logical sphere of situations that the Penal Code considered an exception to the general prohibition of abortion since it is much less drastic than the exception granted in the case of rape.

Embracing this argument, Justice Luiz Fux explains in his individual opinion: "The need for an evolving interpretation, then, is manifestly revealed to the extent that . . . the draft of the new Penal Code includes one more instance of permissible abortion in art. 127, III: when there is justified likelihood, attested by two different doctors, that the unborn fetus present severe and irreversible abnormalities that render it nonviable."[25] Along the same lines, Justice Cármen Lúcia asserts: "Every time has its Law. Justice is not a finished idea, it is something society construes at each time."[26]

A more modern interpretation of criminal abortion laws, though used in our case as an argument anchored in the specific context of the Brazilian law, may, under certain circumstances, be an option in other places where at least some exceptions are made to a general prohibition on abortion, as it advances other exceptions similar to or less drastic than the ones expressly granted by the law.

Third Argument: The Constitutional Principle of Human Dignity

The third argument, entirely based on constitutional interpretation, is the most interesting one. The Brazilian Constitution states that one of the fundamental principles of the Republic is the protection and promotion of human dignity,[27] and therefore all statutory law—including, of course, the Penal Code—shall be read in light of this principle. It thus follows that the prohibition of abortion cannot violate the principle of human dignity, as—we argue—would be the case if the norm were interpreted without granting an exception to women pregnant with anencephalic fetuses. To force a woman to take her pregnancy to full term with an anencephalic fetus, without a viable possibility of life outside the womb, violates two dimensions of human dignity: physical and psychological integrity. From the point of view of physical integrity, the expectant mother will be forced to spend many months going through transformations in her body, preparing for the arrival of a child she will never truly have. With regard to psychological integrity, it is impossible to exaggerate how much suffering will be endured by a person who goes to sleep and wakes up every day for six months with the certainty that her delivery will not bring a baby into life, but rather, into death. In summary: to force a woman to endure prolonged, useless, and unwanted suffering is a violation of her dignity.

A defense of abortion rights based on human dignity can be a powerful tool, as it allows for a number of other arguments to be brought as a subset or as theoretical developments on this central element. This has been the experience in Brazil, where the shift in thinking on reproductive rights throughout the years over which the case was awaiting a ruling by the Supreme Court propelled an expansion of the human dignity argument to encompass two other related ones, more broadly connected to abortion rights in general: women's reproductive rights and the public health concerns involving illegal abortion. Though these two other grounds for abortion rights could easily stand on their own, it was strategically unsound to push them at the time the Brazilian claim was brought. Nonetheless over the course of the eight years that the case eventually lasted, from filing to final decision, the public perception of the matter shifted dramatically. In fact, as time went by and the public debate became broader and more sophisticated, public opinion became increasingly aware of the absurdity of forcing a woman to take a pregnancy to full term in the case of anencephalic fetuses—that is, of course, when that is not what she wants. Suddenly, what appeared to be an implausible claim at the beginning had come to be seen as common sense.

In this new scenario, as the date of the final ruling approached, our assessment was that we would obtain a large majority in the Court. And then ambitions grew bolder. As I personally handed our final brief to the Justices—which is common practice in Brazil—I tried to get a sense of whether the Justices were willing to go as far as asserting women's right to terminate unwanted pregnancies as the basis of their decision, instead of opting for a more timid approach. My "internal" poll, however, indicated that they were not. We thus decided to shift gears once again and limit our pursuit to the inclusion of these arguments into their reasoning, at least as an obiter dictum, which we felt could be achieved. The plunge was taken in a two-page brief explaining and defending women's reproductive rights and public health as a fourth ground for recognizing the right to abortion in the case of anencephalic fetuses, and in my oral closing arguments before the Supreme Court.[28]

First, the public health argument was incorporated into the final stages of the Brazilian claim as a development of the principle of human dignity. Because of the particular (and dire) circumstances surrounding illegal abortion services in many countries such as Brazil, it is fair to say that the denial of the right to terminate unwanted pregnancies puts at risk women's dignity, as it threatens their physical and psychological integrity. This association between human dignity, in its physical and psychological components, and the public health concerns raised by the criminalization of abortion thus opened the door for the latter to be presented later on, as an aspect of the former.

The second argument was related to women's reproductive rights in general and the idea that human dignity supports the right of women to terminate unwanted pregnancies more broadly. The contours of a theoretical human dignity approach to abortion and women's reproductive rights will not be fully discussed in this chapter, as it has been meticulously examined in other academic endeavors.[29] For the moment, it suffices to provide a few comments based on three central elements of human dignity. The first element, centered on Kant's categorical imperative that every individual is an end in himself or herself, encompasses the idea of intrinsic value and asserts that women have the right to terminate unwanted pregnancies, for they cannot be instrumentalized and used as a means to an end, that is, to bring another life into this world.

The second element, private autonomy and self-determination, leads to an understanding of reproductive and child-rearing decisions as within the most intimate and private domain of the individual and thus related to one's right to make free decisions regarding the basic aspects of one's life. The third element is community value. It is no exaggeration to state that abortion continues to be arguably the most divisive moral issue in public life today, both in those countries that allow it and in those that do not. There is, in short, no significant societal consensus on the matter in contemporary society. For that reason, the state should remain neutral and abstain from taking sides, instead of imposing one view over another. In that case, individuals should be free from state regulation to make their autonomous choices; that is, individual autonomy should be placed over mere legal moralism.

Not surprisingly, human dignity emerged as a deeply powerful argument in the Court's decision, embraced by the opinion of the presiding Justice, writing for the Court, and all but one Justice in the majority. Justice Carmén Lúcia proclaimed in her individual opinion:

> The termination of pregnancy of anencephalic fetus is a measure protective of the physical and emotional health of women, avoiding psychological disorders she would suffer were she forced to carry on a pregnancy that she knew would not result in life. Note that termination of pregnancy is a choice, having to respect, of course, also the choice of those who prefer to carry on and live the experience to the end. But respect to this choice is respect for the principle of human dignity.[30]

Then Chief Justice Ayres Britto also noted that the prohibition of abortion in the case of anencephalic fetuses is "a cruel way to ignore feelings which, added up, have the power to collapse any female state of physical, mental and moral health, herein imbedded the loss or significant decrease in self-esteem." And recognition of feelings, he added, "lay on the very starting line of the principle of human dignity."[31]

The human dignity argument has not gone unnoticed by courts

elsewhere. In the *T., S.* case, even though the main argument used to establish women's right to a premature delivery was the atypical nature of the conduct, the Argentine Supreme Court recognized the psychological harms inflicted on women pregnant with anencephalic fetuses and the damage to their families' emotional well-being. The later decision by the Buenos Aires Supreme Court in *C.R. O v. Province of Buenos Aires*[32] also dealt with the importance of taking into account the agony and distress forced on women in achieving their right to terminate the pregnancy when faced with a diagnosis of fatal fetal abnormalities.

A violation to human dignity, on the other hand, was the foundation of another landmark case dealing with premature delivery of anencephalic fetuses: the case of *K.L. v. Peru* before the United Nations Human Rights Committee.[33] The case involved a seventeen-year-old girl who, despite learning early on that she was carrying an anencephalic fetus, had her request for premature delivery denied by state hospital authorities, who subjected her to not only carry her pregnancy to full term, but also to breastfeed the baby once born.

Unlike Brazil and Argentina, which have no specific legislation on the subject, Peru has a particular prohibition of abortion directed against the termination of pregnancies involving fetuses with severe malformations.[34] The sole exception to the general abortion prohibition is if the procedure is the only means to save the mother's life or to avoid a severe and permanent harm to her health. In the *K.L.* case, the U.N. Human Rights Committee recognized that the immense suffering imposed on the mother, as well as the risks that the pregnancy presented to her life, were protected by this exception to the prohibition of abortion, and therefore the conduct of the state personnel in charge of her care had been illegal. The Committee also made it clear that the decision of the State Party could not withhold access to a legal abortion when the requirements had been met, and that causing immense physical and psychological damage to the mother constitutes a violation of the International Covenant on Civil and Political Rights.

The recent rise of human dignity to a position of centrality within several Latin American countries also helps explain the dramatic transformation regarding abortion rights in Colombia. In an unsettling decision in 1997[35] involving a case in which the unwanted pregnancy was the result of rape, the Colombian Constitutional Court concluded that the right to life of the fetus should prevail over the mother's dignity, and therefore, there could be no exception to the general legal prohibition to abortion. Rape, as the decision concluded, could be taken into account only to lessen the sentence for the practice of abortion. This exceedingly harsh decision placed Colombia among the very few countries in Latin America—alongside Chile and El Salvador then (and Nicaragua since 2006)—and in the world to completely forbid abortion, with no exceptions whatsoever.

In 2006, however, human dignity—by then already deemed a foundational principle of the legal system—provided the grounds for the Constitutional Court reversal of its 1997 decision. The Court considered that a complete prohibition to abortion was unconstitutional because it was a violation of a number of fundamental rights demanded by human dignity, especially the physical and psychological health of the mother. The Court went on to establish that, besides any other exception to be determined by the Legislature, abortion must be considered legal in at least three instances: when it imposed a risk to the mother's physical or mental health; when the pregnancy resulted from rape; and when the fetus presented a malformation severe enough to render life outside the womb nonviable.[36] This last exception stresses the close ties between the right to terminate pregnancies involving anencephalic (or other nonviable) fetuses and a protection to human dignity and points to another instance of its successful vindication in court.

Conclusion

After a tenacious eight-year judicial battle, on April 11, 2012, the Brazilian Supreme Court recognized the right of women carrying anencephalic fetuses to terminate their pregnancies without the need to obtain a judicial authorization by an 8–2 vote. It is impossible to overstate what this decision represents for women's rights and the affirmation of a secular State in a country where the Catholic Church has always been a major influence in most social matters. We have learned a few things along this long yet very rewarding process.

The particularities involved in pregnancies of nonviable fetuses, especially anencephalic ones, allow for a more timid, though equally legitimate, legal strategy: the active differentiation of the procedure of therapeutic premature delivery from abortion. This strategy has the advantage of bypassing one of the most crucial moral issues regarding abortion (the fetus's potentiality of life) while testing the waters of the public debate and social perception on the subject. This effort not only evinces a useful strategy in situations where confronting the opposition to abortion is out of question but also stems from a sincere belief that terminating a pregnancy where the fetus has no potentiality for life outside the womb is essentially different from other much more complex situations, where potential opposing rights have to be balanced.

The risks, however, of making an exceptional claim (and thus of reaffirming the general anti-abortion norm) should not be ignored; rather, they should be weighed according to the specific context in which the claim is being brought, taking into account a pragmatic cost-benefit analysis. Given our specific case and its context, we felt the risks were worth it when the lawsuit was brought; eight years later, we were reassured when the final ruling on ADPF 54 showed that the strategy had paid off.

Another lesson we learned was that even legal strategies centered on the specificities of nonviable fetuses can be powerful in advancing abortion rights, just by reframing the issue in legal, rather than moral or religious terms. Our experience in Brazil has shown us that, once these ideas start to float around more freely, the public debate gathers substance, and in consequence there is a palpable rise in awareness of what is really at stake: the discrimination and subordination of women, the disrespect for their dignity, and their continuous subjection to unsafe abortions and maternal death. In fact, testing the waters may sometimes yield the necessary tools to take the plunge and broaden the argumentative foundation. That has been our experience in Brazil, and one that we hope can happen elsewhere.

Though women's reproductive rights and the public health argument were restricted to the Court's reasoning, and not its holding, securing an acknowledgement that women have at least *some* autonomy to choose to terminate unwanted pregnancies—even if only outside the penal definition of abortion—was no easy task and a major victory in a country where abortion had always been an insurmountable taboo and where these concepts had never been presented before the Supreme Court. There is still a long and winding road ahead. But it is not as dark and gloomy as it used to be.

Chapter 13

Toward Transformative Equality in Nepal: The *Lakshmi Dhikta* Decision

Melissa Upreti

In 2009, the Supreme Court of Nepal issued a monumental decision in the case of *Lakshmi Dhikta v. Nepal* recognizing abortion as a constitutionally protected fundamental right.[1] The decision represents a dramatic shift from treating abortion as a matter of crime and punishment to one of reproductive choice and justice grounded in a vision of transformative equality. The *Dhikta* decision underscores that abortion is a matter of personal choice, and that women have rights over their own bodies and to have the final say in decisions concerning their procreation. The Court obligates government to address the multiple barriers women face in accessing safe abortion services, and to ensure that all women, especially those marginalized by socioeconomic and rural status, have access to abortion services. In examining the relationship between women and pregnancy, it repudiates traditional stereotypes of women that reduce them to the role of bearers of children and self-sacrificing mothers, which have been employed for centuries to perpetuate their subordinate status. The Court establishes that pregnancy cannot be imposed on women as an obligation but rather recognizes it as a noble act that must be freely chosen.

The decision concerns Lakshmi Dhikta, an impoverished woman who lives with her husband and six children in far-western rural Nepal. When she became pregnant for the sixth time, she and her husband wanted to terminate the pregnancy because they were simply not in a position to support one more child and Lakshmi's health had deteriorated significantly over the years because of previous pregnancies. Both went to the nearest district hospital to terminate the pregnancy but were required to pay approximately $15 USD for the procedure—an amount that was far beyond their means. Consequently, they were left with no option but to return home without terminating the pregnancy, and Lakshmi was forced to continue the pregnancy to term. She gave birth to a son and continues to live in dire poverty with her family in western Nepal.

Lakshmi's experience embodies the predicament and injustice faced by hundreds of thousands of women living in poverty in Nepal who are denied their legal rights because of financial circumstances. With a population of thirty million, Nepal is one of the poorest countries in the world.[2] Nearly one-quarter of the population lives on less than a dollar a day,[3] and the level of poverty in the rural population is nearly four times higher than in the urban population.[4] Prior to 2002, an estimated 50 percent of maternal deaths were due to unsafe abortion, and women were routinely imprisoned for having abortions. Despite the current legal status of abortion, unsafe abortion remains the third leading cause of maternal mortality in the country.[5] The inability of poor, rural, and marginalized women to realize their legal right to abortion remains a crucial challenge. Numerous reports on the status of women's reproductive health in Nepal reveal that, despite the 2002 amendments that created broad exceptions to the criminal abortion ban[6] and the recognition of reproductive rights as fundamental rights in the 2007 Interim Constitution, women are still unable to access safe and legal abortion services because of economic reasons among others.[7]

While the central issues in the *Dhikta* decision are the accessibility and affordability of abortion, the Court's analysis is also significant for its detailed discussion of how prevailing notions of women's equality, sexuality, and motherhood restrict women's ability to make decisions about pregnancy. The Court takes a particularly strong stance against forced pregnancy and denounces the imposition of pregnancy on women as a violation of their fundamental constitutional rights. Building on its line of court decisions recognizing women's rights to autonomy and nondiscrimination, the Court explains that it is crucial for women both socially and legally to have control over their fertility so that they may live with dignity and be protected against discrimination, coercion, and violence.

The importance of the *Dhikta* decision lies in the Court's assertion that the government must ensure access to safe abortion services for all women.

Despite the government's claims that it has already taken steps to create access to safe abortion services by introducing official guidelines and establishing clinics in all seventy-five districts of the country, the Court concludes that the government has simply not done enough to remove the practical barriers that women face. The *Dhikta* decision recognizes the multiple challenges that women face in trying to access abortion services, which include: lack of information, lack of financial resources, and lack of proximity to quality services. The Court explains that the government has positive obligations to address these barriers as a matter of justice and to protect women's fundamental reproductive rights.

The decision embodies a transformative model of women's equality as envisioned in the Convention on the Elimination of All Forms of Discrimination against Women (CEDAW).[8] This model entails recognition of biological differences between men and women and that gender stratification results in "hierarchical relationships between women and men in the distribution of power and rights favoring men and disadvantaging women."[9] It obligates states to address "the causes and consequences of their de facto or substantive inequality,"[10] and to "ensure the development and advancement of women in order to improve their position and implement their right of de jure and de facto or substantive equality with men."[11] This may even include the adoption of measures providing for the "nonidentical treatment of women and men due to their biological differences."[12] A transformative model of equality also requires recognizing how different forms of discrimination intersect with each other, such as how socioeconomic status and age may intersect with sex and gender, to yield new forms of intersectional discrimination.[13]

In essence, "transformative equality requires rethinking unintended pregnancy from the perspective of the woman affected, recognizing and remedying the disadvantages that women face in making decisions to terminate or continue pregnancy and removing the barriers faced in seeking services."[14] It necessitates "the recognition of abortion as a positive right that states have a duty to provide."[15] While a traditional legal approach to abortion involves criminal restrictions, a transformative equality approach involves recognizing that "women are able to make their own reproductive decisions with dignity and freedom from stereotypes and stigma. It also requires that women have access to safe abortion services at the earliest possible stage of pregnancy, free of judgment about their sexuality and punishment for their failure to conform to the norms of motherhood."[16] It has been observed that "the challenge of transformative equality is to liberate women as moral agents equal to men and let them decide for themselves how to manage their sexuality and family life."[17]

The *Dhikta* decision reflects the prioritization of gender equality and women's empowerment in postconflict Nepal. These priorities are embodied in the Interim Constitution of 2007, which recognizes women's reproductive rights as constitutionally protected fundamental rights and guarantees the right to free health care for the poor. The elevation of reproductive rights to constitutional status is a recent development in Nepalese law. Examining abortion restrictions in an equality framework enables consideration of how they are embedded in historical religious texts resulting in the subjugation of women based on their sex and gender roles.

This chapter explains how the Court's judgment in *Dhikta* reflects the transformative model of equality as envisioned in the CEDAW.[18] The first section discusses the goals of the *Dhikta* litigation strategy and explains their significance in the context of Nepal. The second section analyzes the Court's reasoning and shows that, in line with the goals of transformative equality, the Court understands that "equality for women entails a restructuring [of] society so that it is no longer male defined" and that "full and genuine equality [is] likely to be achieved only when the social structures of hierarchy and dominance based on sex and gender are transformed."[19] The second section concludes by describing the Court's structural remedies. In reflecting the General Recommendation 24 of the Committee on the Elimination of Discrimination against Women, the Court requires the decriminalization of abortion and explains that the state has immediate obligations to eliminate discrimination against women in the field of health and to ensure women have equal access to health care services.[20]

The Goals of the *Dhikta* Litigation Strategy

The *Dhikta* litigation strategy specifically targeted the government's failure to ensure affordable abortion services for poor women and aimed to secure a mandate for a comprehensive legal framework for abortion outside the purview of criminal law. These strategic goals were shaped by the realization that although the Eleventh Amendment to the Country Code had established women's abortion rights on paper, these were not sufficient to ensure access to services, especially for the most vulnerable and socially marginalized who continue to face insurmountable financial, logistical, and systemic barriers and abortion stigma. Public interest litigation was viewed as a strategic route for establishing a broad legal framework for abortion by seeking a directive order from the Court for the enactment of a comprehensive abortion law that could be used to address these barriers.

The Nepalese legal system derives originally from Hindu law and is predominantly patriarchal in character.[21] Modern scholars have criticized the Hindu scriptures for their treatment of women "as non-human objects"[22] and for relegating them to "second class status."[23] For centuries Hindu patriarchal norms, which were "intentionally designed in order to weaken [women's] position in the society so that the men's absolute control over their personality and sexuality is rendered possible," denied equal status to women.[24] The criminal ban on abortion was rooted in Hindu philosophical and moral precepts as expressed in authoritative philosophical texts, specifically the Rigveda and the Atharvaveda.[25] According to these sources, abortion was deemed to be socially, morally, and ethically unacceptable, and women who terminated their pregnancy would face punishment in hell.[26] They instructed society to treat women who had abortions as "social outcasts."[27] The Manusmriti, another such text, went so far as to deny funeral rites to women who had abortions and required a husband whose wife had an abortion without his knowledge to end the marriage.[28] These restrictions have been understood as reflections of the high value that Hindu society places on women's fertility, particularly their ability to bear sons.[29] These norms were codified in the form of a criminal ban for the first time in 1854 when the original Country Code was introduced and survived two subsequent revisions in 1935 and 1963.

Until 2002 Nepal was one of the few countries in the world to criminalize abortion without clear legal exceptions. Although the law appeared to provide an exception for abortions that occurred as an unintended consequence of a benevolent act, there were no guidelines clarifying the scope of legally permissible abortions.[30] Due to lack of clarity about the scope of the exception, abortion stigma, and fear of prosecution among both women and health service providers, this exception was not utilized in practice, leading to a public health crisis due to unsafe abortions. An estimated 50 percent of all maternal deaths were due to unsafe abortion.[31] Common methods of unsafe abortion included oral ingestion of herbs and unregulated drugs and insertion of foreign objects such as sticks coated with cow dung.[32] Over sixty per cent of hospital admissions requiring obstetric care involved cases of abortion complications.[33]

The harshness of Nepal's abortion law was exposed when Min Min Lama, a fourteen-year-old girl was incarcerated in 1999 for allegedly having an illegal abortion after becoming pregnant as a result of having been raped by a relative.[34] By 2000, 20 percent of women incarcerated in Nepal's prisons were charged with abortion or infanticide.[35] Women who had abortions, even spontaneous miscarriages, were frequently prosecuted for infanticide, which carried a much harsher sentence of life imprisonment. Investigations conducted by the police were fraught with procedural lapses,[36] yet the conviction rate was high. An analysis of abortion and infanticide cases reported in the *Nepal Kanoon Patrika*, a periodic official digest of court decisions, between 1979 and 2002 revealed that 70 percent of women who were prosecuted for abortion-related offences were convicted.[37] Legal analysts have noted that the "rate of conviction in abortion-related cases was very high in comparison to other criminal cases" involving women.[38] Further, enforcement of the ban was discriminatory since only poor and illiterate women were ever prosecuted and punished.[39]

The criminal abortion ban was amended in 2002 with the passage of the Eleventh Amendment to the Country Code and the introduction of section number 28 (b), which, while maintaining a general prohibition on abortion, permits termination with the consent of the pregnant woman within the first twelve weeks of the pregnancy; within eighteen weeks where the pregnancy is a result of rape or incest; and if, in the opinion of a legally qualified medical practitioner, failure to terminate the pregnancy may create a threat to the woman's life or her physical or mental health, or if the child born may be impaired.

The broad legalization of abortion was a groundbreaking development that formally ended more than one hundred years of institutionalized discrimination against women based on their reproductive capacity. However, it was limited in the sense that it merely created broad exceptions to an existing prohibition and allowed the aura of criminality to remain by keeping it in the chapter of the Country Code that prescribes criminal punishments for crimes against human life such as homicide. As a result, the goals of the *Dhikta* litigation strategy were to ensure that abortion services are available to all women, irrespective of their socioeconomic status and their geographic location, to reduce abortion stigma resulting from the criminalization of abortion, and to improve the protection of women's rights including their reproductive rights.

Ensuring Women's Equal Access to Health Services

It is widely held[40] that the reforms of 2002 contributed to a 56 percent decline in Nepal's maternal mortality ratio from 1990 to 2008.[41] Currently, abortion services are offered through a national initiative launched in 2004 called the Comprehensive Abortion Care (CAC) program[42] and are reportedly available in all of the country's seventy-five districts.[43] Despite this progress, lack of equal access to health services remains a persistent challenge, particularly in rural and remote parts of Nepal.[44] Abortion (spontaneous and induced) is currently the third leading direct cause of maternal mortality in the country.[45] Although the government has recognized health care as "a basic citizenship right," ensuring equal access to quality services has proven difficult.[46] The difficult geographical terrain creates unique challenges to ensuring the availability of services across the country, and continued lack of awareness of recent changes to the law within the largely rural population has hampered access to safe abortion and drives women to seek clandestine abortions.[47]

Unsafe Abortion, Nepal Country Profile, a detailed field-based study released by the government in 2006, revealed the existence of several practical barriers to safe abortion services faced by women across the country despite law reform, including the prohibitive cost of services in government hospitals,[48] concentration of services in urban areas,[49] and lack of awareness among women of the legal grounds for abortion and where services may be obtained.[50] According to this study, the implementation gap ran so deep that in one survey of 2,293 women, not a single poor woman had received an abortion for free despite hospital guidelines that entitled them to the service.[51] The findings of this report were cited extensively in the *Dhikta* petition.

Improving Protection of Women's Reproductive Health and Rights

Women's formal legal status has undergone a dramatic change in Nepal, especially within the last two decades. Since 1990, when Nepal transitioned from an absolute monarchy to a parliamentary monarchy,[52] there has been a significant expansion of women's rights. The Constitution of the Kingdom of Nepal of 1990 recognized the right to equality as a fundamental right and sex as a prohibited ground of discrimination.[53] It further provided for the introduction of special legal measures "for the protection and advancement of the interests of women."[54] Within a few years of this transition, the government ratified several major international treaties, including the Convention on the Elimination of All Forms of Discrimination against Women, and introduced the Treaty Act of 1990 that gives primacy to international law over national law.[55] The ratification of major international treaties has had a positive impact on the expansion of women's rights in Nepal as a basis both for advocacy and for case law. This expansion of women's rights has been accompanied by a growing recognition of women's reproductive health concerns that have a direct impact on their survival and ability to exercise their other legal rights.

An important legal development in Nepal is the adoption of an Interim Constitution in 2007, following a decade-long violent insurgency. The Interim Constitution is groundbreaking for women as it recognizes women's reproductive rights as constitutionally protected fundamental rights in Article 20(2), which provides that "every woman shall have the right to reproductive health and rights relating to reproduction."[56] Other crucial rights that have been recognized specifically as women's fundamental rights include the right to nondiscrimination guaranteed in Article 20(1), which provides that "a woman must not be discriminated against in any way on the ground that she is a woman"; and the right to freedom from violence in Article 20(3), which says that "no woman shall be subjected to physical, mental or any other form of violence and such as shall be punishable by law."[57] The Interim Constitution is expected to serve as a blueprint for a new Constitution that will be adopted by a Constituent Assembly elected specifically for this purpose in 2013.

The Supreme Court of Nepal has played an important role in advancing women's rights through groundbreaking legal decisions declaring numerous provisions in the Country Code to be discriminatory. Some of these decisions paved the way for sweeping legal reform to the Country Code in 2002, including the legalization of abortion and the introduction of the Gender Equality Act in 2006[58] which brought about further amendments to the Country Code in a second wave of law reform. In *Dhikta*, the Court pushes the boundaries even further and articulates a transformative model of equality to establish the state's obligation to eliminate discrimination and to ensure all women are able to exercise their fundamental reproductive rights. The Court holds that forced pregnancy is a violation of women's of human rights. Further, building on current jurisprudential trends, the Court recognizes the practical barriers to accessing abortion services and instructs the government to take positive steps to ensure women can exercise their legal rights. The

Court explains the necessity of a new legal framework for abortion free of the stigma of criminal law and based on reproductive rights guaranteed in the Interim Constitution of 2007.

The *Dhikta* Decision as a Model of Transformative Equality

Dhikta offers a powerful illustration of the application of a model of transformative equality to the issue of abortion to the extent that it recognizes women as moral agents with full decision-making authority, rejects traditional patriarchal norms based on notions of women's inferiority to men, and holds the government responsible for ensuring the practical realization of women's right to abortion by recognizing and addressing the unequal power dynamics and inequalities that prevent women from enjoying this right. That is, the Court does not simply acknowledge the equality of women. Rather, *Dhikta* recognizes the right to abortion as being crucial for women's health, survival, and empowerment and obliges the state to take appropriate steps to ensure the practical realization of this right, particularly in relation to socioeconomically disadvantaged and marginalized women. It establishes abortion-related decision making as a crucial determinant of women's well-being and dignity by emphasizing that without legal protection of this right, women will be vulnerable to discrimination, stigma, and violence and stripped of moral agency and self-respect, which would not only constitute a violation of their legal rights but also have a dehumanizing impact on their health and lives.

The following section discusses the *Dhikta* decision with the aim of shedding light on its transformative nature. The first part analyzes the Court's holding on the legal issues of women's dignity and equality, the constitutional scope of reproductive rights under the 2007 Interim Constitution of Nepal, and the legal status of the fetus. The second part describes the structural remedies ordered by the Court and describes why decriminalization and positive action by the state, including a comprehensive reform of abortion law, is necessary to ensure women's equality.

The Holdings of the Court

Women's Dignity and Equality

The basic premise of the Court's reasoning is that denial of the right to abortion compromises a woman's dignity, including her physical integrity and autonomy, by forcing her to continue an unwanted pregnancy to term. The opinion is anchored in an understanding of abortion from a woman's perspective that views pregnancy as an honorable act and not an obligation. The Court gives primacy to women's autonomy over patriarchal stereotypes of male dominance that have led to women's inequality within marriage and subordination. In doing so, the Court essentially rejects traditional norms that have historically prevented women from engaging with men as equals in the context of marriage and procreation. By taking this approach the Court essentially calls for a transformation of existing power dynamics in women's relationships with men and within the institution of marriage.

Dhikta reaffirms women's dignity by recognizing a woman as "the master of her own body"[59] and that "whether or not to have sexual relations, whether or not to give birth and how to use one's own body are matters with regards to which a woman has the right to have the final say."[60] This view is consistent with the Court's line of decisions upholding women's sexual autonomy in a series of cases in which it rejected virginity testing,[61] established the crime of marital rape,[62] and rejected a petition to require a woman to obtain her husband's authorization in order to terminate her pregnancy.[63]

In the last example, petitioner Achyut Kharel launched a challenge against the 2002 amended abortion provisions of the Country Code which allows married women to seek abortion during the first twelve weeks of pregnancy without their husbands' authorization.[64] The petitioner claimed that the absence of a spousal authorization requirement discriminated against men contrary to CEDAW, which guarantees the same rights to make decisions about the number and spacing of children "on a basis of equality of men and women."[65] The Court dismissed the claim holding that although the 2002 Amendment does not contain a spousal authorization requirement, it does not prohibit it either.[66] Noting the patriarchal character of Nepalese society and the vulnerability of women within society,[67] the Court explained that the legislature clearly intended to allow married women to unilaterally seek abortion for specific reasons.[68] The Court observed that if men were to be granted the sole right to decide whether and when to have children, as would be the case if their authorization were required, then women would never be able to gain equality.[69]

In *Dhikta,* the Court goes further and recognizes "pregnancy as a woman's right"[70] instead of an obligation that must be fulfilled. The Court reasons that "the fact that women are by nature able to become pregnant does not mean that they must become pregnant."[71] Indeed, the Court holds that the right to reproductive self-determination is central to a broad range of women's human rights. The Court explains: "the right to freedom, including the right to live with dignity, and the right to personal liberty are some of women's most important human rights. The right to health; reproductive health; family planning, to marry freely or found a family; to have or not to have children, and if having children to decide how many and when" are all related issues.[72]

The Court cautions against failing to protect women's dignity in decisions concerning pregnancy, noting that it may lead to women's oppression. The Court explains that if women are forced to continue with unwanted pregnancies, they will be "transformed into mere instruments."[73] Further, denying women any choice in the matter turns pregnancy from "the fulfillment of one's highest duty" into "a form of slavery."[74] The Court emphasizes that the effects of unwanted pregnancies do not end with childbirth. Indeed, "for a woman, the child born from an unwanted pregnancy is a continuous burden," which is good for neither the mother nor the child.[75] Therefore, the Court concludes, "it is of utmost importance to work toward ensuring that pregnancies are wanted and to ensure legal and other protections for such pregnancies."[76]

The Court specifically addresses decision making in the context of marriage because cultural norms and stereotypes typically favor men over women. For example, it is common in Nepalese law to distinguish among women based on chastity, marital status, and the ability to bear children. The legal categorization of women based on their sexual and marital status is pervasive in Hindu law and modern Nepalese legal codes. Common classifications include the designation of women as: *kanya* (virgin); *bihe nagareko* (never married); *lyayeko* (brought as a wife but not formally married); *bahira rakheko* (kept informally outside the home); *santan hune/nahune* (capable of bearing offspring or not); and *bidhawa* (widow).[77] These classifications have been used to determine women's legal rights based on their reproductive status and establish women's "inferiority in competency to contract relations with men."[78] Given these classifications, the Court recognizes that women may be particularly vulnerable in marriage. Accordingly, the Court explains that it is especially important that women "have the final say so that they can be free from such discrimination."[79] The Court observes that "traditionally in a marriage it is not unusual for a woman to make decisions with the consent of her husband or on the basis of mutual understanding, but it is very important for a woman to have the final say about how her body shall be used and whether or not she will have children."[80]

Considering the profound personal impact of pregnancy on a woman's life—her free will and physical integrity and the potential health risks of pregnancy—the Court reasons that a woman's autonomy must be given equal weight to that of a man, who does not face such conditions. The Court explains that a woman who is forced into pregnancy "loses all control over her own body as a result of which she is explicitly and implicitly forced to accept a continuous position of subordination."[81] The Court reasons that a denial of abortion is a form of discrimination and a source of violence against women because of the specific dangers that they may face as a result of forced pregnancies,[82] forced abortions based on the sex of the fetus,[83] and unsafe abortion procedures due to criminalization.[84] Echoing its decision in *Kharel*, the Court notes that the uncertainty created by lack of recognition of women's reproductive rights for their sexual and physical freedom that could result in "the right to become pregnant being transformed into a responsibility" forcing them to suffer such violence in silence.[85] The Court recognizes the broad impact of this type of discrimination as an impediment to women's equality that "could lead to negative outcomes as a result of which women would not be able to live freely with self-respect" and exercise their guaranteed rights.[86]

The Court views the right to abortion as legal protection against forced continuation of a pregnancy. The Court argues, "In a context where reproductive rights and, as part of that, the right to abortion are guaranteed by the constitution and other laws, if a woman is prevented from exercising her right and forced to continue an unwanted pregnancy, it is clear that her rights have been violated."[87] Furthermore, the Court underscores the irreparable harm that results from compelling a woman to continue a pregnancy against her will when it states that "in a situation where a pregnancy has to be continued and a child is born, it is not possible to reinstate a woman's rights."[88] Thus, the Court recognizes the irreparable harm caused by forced continuation of pregnancy and establishes the importance of ensuring access to abortion as a means of protecting women's equality and preserving their ability to exercise their rights.

Underlying the Court's warning against allowing pregnancy to be used to undermine women's dignity and equality is a call to accommodate differences between men and women in terms of their physiology and gender roles since accommodation of sexual differences between men and women is a vital pre-condition for sex and gender equality. By recognizing pregnancy as "an inseparable part of women's reproductive health"[89] and the potential to become pregnant as a unique capability, the Court obligates the government to take positive steps to accommodate this capability by ensuring the delivery of appropriate health services.[90]

The Scope of Reproductive Rights Under the 2007 Interim Constitution

To this end, the *Dhikta* Court defines the scope of reproductive rights under Article 20(2) of the Interim Constitution of 2007, which guarantees the reproductive rights of women, as being anchored broadly in women's health and autonomy. The Court examines the uniqueness of women's reproductive health and takes a life-cycle approach that encompasses specific needs of women at different stages of their reproductive cycle. Importantly, the Court identifies abortion as a key component of women's reproductive health. Since the Court explains that reproduction is an essential aspect of women's health, "reproductive rights are considered to be an inseparable part of women's human rights, and within that the right to abortion is seen to hold an important place."[91] Ultimately, reproductive rights are recognized as a means to ensure the right to self-determination.

Within the umbrella of reproductive rights, the Court identifies several specific rights, including "the right to plan one's family, which includes the right to information about and access to methods of family planning and the right to use such methods to prevent pregnancy; women are also considered to have the right to make decisions relating to reproduction free from interference."[92] The Court further notes that "reproductive health and reproductive rights encompass the decision to have children and not to have children, and within that must be recognized the right of a pregnant woman who does not wish to bear children to discontinue the pregnancy." [93] Thus, the Court clarifies that reproductive rights include the right to abortion with reasonable limits. The Court notes that "the right to abortion is applicable in cases of unwanted pregnancy or in difficult circumstances. It does not include the right to prevent a pregnancy in all circumstances, and it is necessary to consider the right to abortion within appropriate limits."[94] The Court's recognition of limited restrictions is based primarily on concerns about the medical safety of abortions and the increasing complexity of the procedure in more advanced stages of pregnancy.[95]

By clearly defining reproductive rights, the Court aims to protect women from the potential adverse social effects of becoming pregnant. The Court notes that depending on the circumstances, "because of pregnancy women may experience discrimination, be disqualified, ostracized and suffer social stigma."[96] Oftentimes these acts are rooted in violent intent.[97] As such, the *Dhikta* Court emphasizes the importance of recognizing reproductive rights as a means to protect women against violent actions that compromise their physical integrity and reproductive self-determination. Indeed, the Court views forced pregnancy and forced prevention of pregnancy as "acts of violence against women"[98] and holds that "it is necessary to protect women's reproductive health and reproductive rights in order to ensure women's freedom from any form of physical, mental, and other form of violence."[99]

The Legal Status of the Fetus

Having explained that abortion is essential to women's dignity and equality with men and well within the scope of reproductive rights guaranteed by the 2007 Interim Constitution, the *Dhikta* decision clarifies Nepal's position on the legal status of the fetus. The Court takes the view that a pregnant woman cannot be subordinate to the fetus, holding that "issues relating to pregnancy should not be viewed as being limited to the fetus but relate more broadly to women's physical and mental health."[100] The Court notes that "once a pregnancy is established and as the fetus develops, it takes on the form of a life, but not every stage of fetal development can be equated with human life."[101] To consider a fetus a human life, the Court opines, there must be a clear provision in the law that grants legal recognition to the fetus.[102] Given the location of the amended abortion provisions within the Chapter on Homicide in the Country Code, which deals with crimes against human life such as homicide, and the past criminalization of abortion, the Court notes that it may appear that the fetus has been given the status of a human life in Nepalese law.[103] However, the Court explains that since the Chapter does not define human life and in the absence of a constitutional or other legal provision that recognizes a fetal right to life, the fetus is not recognized as a human life, or person, in Nepalese law.[104]

The Court holds that only a born alive child who has reached a certain stage of development is granted the status of human life. The Court notes, "Even in situations where the fetus is capable of life outside the womb, if it suffers demise in the course of being born, it is not considered to be a [human] life."[105] With this explanation, the Court clarifies that a fetus assumes legal rights only upon birth. Taking into account arguments put forward by supporters and opponents of abortion rights, the Court addresses the issue of legal personhood and clarifies that "because a fetus is dependent on the mother and owes its existence to the mother, it cannot be recognized as a separate personality."[106] The Court explains that "these arguments are not practical" since if the full humanity of a fetus were recognized, "even if the mother's existence was in jeopardy, she would be forced to tolerate the risk to her life in order to protect the fetus."[107] In other words, while the fetus is physically dependent on the pregnant woman, this dependency cannot become the basis for elevating its legal status and forcing a woman to continue a pregnancy to term against her will or at risk to her own life.

While the Court acknowledges that fetal interests are worthy of protection, it holds that they cannot be allowed to prevail over women's rights.[108] In its explication of fetal interests, the Court notes that fetal interests and those of a pregnant woman do not necessarily stand in contradiction to each other: "The protection of the fetus has its own special place; the fetus is important to the pregnant mother too. The fetus being such, instead of looking at the fetus's interests and the mother's interests as two separate things, the fetus's interests should be viewed as a crucial part of the mother's interests."[109]

While emphasizing the importance of protecting the rights of pregnant women and not subjugating them to fetal interests, the Court expresses concern about the medical safety of abortions in later stages of pregnancy and once the fetus has reached viability.[110] The Court takes the view that certain restrictions in later stages of pregnancy may be suitable as being in the interest of both the pregnant woman and the fetus.[111] However, such restrictions, the Court notes, must exist "only to a limited extent, to protect pregnancies except when they are unwanted and to create a safe environment for those seeking abortion services."[112]

The Structural Remedies Necessary for Women's Dignity and Equality

Decriminalization

The Court explains that the state has an obligation to decriminalize abortion and to support the creation of a gender-sensitive health system. The Court notes that criminalization has a disproportionate impact on women and is therefore discriminatory. Pointing to the routine prosecution, conviction, and punishment of women, the Court suggests that prior to 2002, "a woman's unique reproductive capacity was used against her in a conspiratorial way."[113] Addressing the situation before the Eleventh Amendment to the Country Code in 2002, the Court explains that the criminal regime forced women, including those who became pregnant as a result of rape, to continue their pregnancies or go to jail.[114] The Court points out that "although these pregnancies were not a consequence of women acting alone, the entire burden of the prosecution for abortion fell on women, and the men did not fall within the purview of the law."[115] The harsh impact of the ban was felt particularly by marginalized women, as "allegations of abortion were mostly made against illiterate and low-income women from rural areas."[116] This regime not only discriminated against women but also drove them to seek unsafe, clandestine abortions as a last resort.

Underlying the Court's approach is concern about abortion stigma resulting from the government's failure to disassociate abortion from criminal law. The Court explains that "abortion is a new serious issue that has evolved through greater public consciousness, and it is important to convey the correct message to the public. As such, it is no longer appropriate to treat it as an issue of criminal law and retain it in the Chapter on Homicide. As long as it remains part of the Chapter on Homicide, abortion will carry the stamp of a crime even though it has been decriminalized in specific circumstances."[117] The Court's concern reveals its awareness of the changing modern day discourse on abortion and the need to change laws in accordance with this new discourse that is less punitive, and based more on human rights than traditional views of women's sexuality and procreation.

The Court explains that maternal mortality "is a serious problem in countries where abortion is criminalized."[118] Noting that Nepal is known worldwide for its high rates of maternal mortality,[119] the Court attributes this trend to the former criminal ban.[120] Based on the harmful impact of criminal abortion bans on women's survival, the Court opposes a criminal approach. The Court frames criminalization of abortion as source of violence against women whereby women are forced to continue unwanted pregnancies to term as a result of "pregnancy being transformed into a responsibility."[121] The Court refers to this phenomenon as the "dehumanization of women's health"[122] and explains that as a result women are unable to exercise a broad range of other crucial rights including their right to live freely with self-respect and equality.[123]

The Court describes the Eleventh Amendment to the Country Code as a "milestone" for women's rights, as it ended years of criminalization in all circumstances as a result of which "women were forced to endure a situation of being deprived of their right to life and their fundamental human rights."[124] Nevertheless, the Court remains critical of the current legal framework, which, in its view, continues to represent a crime-and-punishment approach.[125] The Court expresses concern about the continuing treatment of abortion in the Country Code's Chapter on Homicide, which deals with crimes against people even though abortion has been recognized as a right. The Court notes, "With the recognition of reproductive health and abortion as rights in this changing context, it is necessary to adopt a new way of thinking that is suitable to the establishment of these rights."[126]

The *Dhikta* Court takes the clear position that abortion must be protected as part of women's reproductive rights and must be decriminalized. The Court states that "reproductive health and reproductive rights stand in mutual relationship to each other. It is only when one's reproductive health is in a good state that one can fully enjoy their reproductive rights; similarly, it is only when one has reproductive rights that their reproductive health can be fully protected. This important relationship has been wisely recognized through Article 20 of the Constitution."[127] The Court's rejection of a criminal approach is further illustrated through its support for a new comprehensive abortion law. The Court explains that "it is objectionable and extremely unsuitable to keep the provisions on abortion—this newly recognized right—within a harsh and rigid criminal law framework, and it is necessary to introduce separate legislation to address this important issue."[128]

The Positive Obligation of the State

In addition to requiring decriminalization, the *Dhikta* Court explains that the state is obligated to take positive steps to ensure women's equality in access to health services. The Government of Nepal is required to take positive action to ensure that rights guaranteed on paper are in fact enjoyable in practice and to take concrete steps to make this happen in an equitable manner. The Court holds that rights guarantees are not "merely declaratory and people must be able to benefit from them in practice."[129] This is especially the case with regards to rights recognized as fundamental rights in the Constitution, which include women's reproductive rights as expressed in Article 20(2) of the 2007 Interim Constitution. The Court explains that "the inclusion of these guarantees in the constitution and legislation does not automatically lead to the enjoyment of these rights."[130]

Article 20(2) of the 2007 Interim Constitution was first applied in 2008 by the Court in *Prakash Mani Sharma v. Government of Nepal*,[131] which addressed the widespread occurrence of uterine prolapse, a pregnancy-related morbidity, with high incidence in Nepal, where the uterus sags into the vagina or falls completely out depending on the severity. Women may experience a number of symptoms as a result of uterine prolapse including difficulty urinating or moving their bowels, low back pain and difficulty walking. The petitioners in this case contended that the prevalence of approximately six hundred thousand cases of uterine prolapse and absence of government programs to prevent and effectively deal with these cases violated women's fundamental rights, including their right to reproductive health services, under the 2007 Interim Constitution.[132] They sought orders from the Court for the provision of government health services, including free consultation and treatment for uterine prolapse and the introduction of a comprehensive reproductive health bill in parliament.[133] The Court observed that "the status of reproductive health of women in Nepal is in a serious state, and it is also clear that no plan has been made to address this problem,"[134] and it ordered the government to provide services for the consultation and treatment of uterine prolapse.[135]

Following this precedent, the *Dhikta* Court explicitly recognizes the obligation of the state to ensure that the weaker and poorer segments of society are able to exercise their fundamental rights. The Court criticizes the government for failing to ensure that the health system serves women's sex-specific health needs. The Court notes, "Although half the world's population is comprised of women, the fact remains that governments have not established health systems and health budgets with women's reproductive rights and health in mind as a result of which budget allocations and women-centered health facilities are very limited."[136] Recognizing these health systems limitations, the Court calls for the accommodation of women's distinctive health needs at a systemic level through the creation of a gender-sensitive health system.

The Court holds that equal access to rights and benefits for people of all classes is a matter of justice and a basis for the rule of law.[137] The Court holds that it is the "primary responsibility of the state"[138] to "raise awareness about the law, establish the necessary preconditions to implement laws, create institutions, build the capacity of those working in these institutions, and ensure the distribution of services according to people's needs through proper programs."[139] According to the Court, not only must the state ensure access but also it must ensure equitable enjoyment of fundamental rights. The Court reasons that "a right or benefit guaranteed by law must not be limited to certain people or a particular class. It is mandatory for the state to make such rights and benefits equally accessible."[140] In acknowledging the disproportionate impact of abortion restrictions on poor women, the Court underscores the obligation of the state to pay specific attention to the intersectional discrimination on grounds of gender and poverty in relation to women's reproductive health and rights. The Court's recognition of intersectional discrimination on grounds of gender and poverty is significant because this form of discrimination is an important source of subordination in Nepal.

The Court clearly articulates the steps that need to be taken by the government to ensure that women are able to exercise their legal right to abortion, which includes increasing the number of licensed service providers and medical institutions,[141] ensuring equitable distribution of services across the country,[142] establishing appropriate standards for service fees,[143] and monitoring the quality of services.[144] In order to measure the accessibility of services, the Court notes that it is the duty of the state to ascertain "how many women have been able to obtain abortion services in the districts to determine whether services are fairly distributed."[145] The Court also holds that no woman should be denied an abortion simply because of her inability to pay and requires the state to ensure that abortion services are affordable. The Court contends that "if anyone who needs an abortion is unable to obtain one, merely due to procedural difficulties or unaffordability, and as a consequence is forced to continue an unwanted pregnancy and give birth, then it must be recognized that the benefit created by law has not been attained by its intended beneficiaries."[146]

In examining the scope of the state's responsibility to ensure the affordability of abortion services, the Court holds that free services must be provided where appropriate.[147] The Court reasons that although abortion is a personal matter, given the implications of denial of abortion for a broad range of women's fundamental rights and the duty of the state to protect these rights, the state cannot disregard the reality that abortion services remain beyond the reach of many women. The Court concludes, "abortion and pregnancy-related concerns cannot always be regarded as individual problems and separated from the public duties of the state" because abortion is a health issue and "the right to health has been guaranteed as a fundamental right."[148] The Court also frames this obligation as falling within the ambit of the fundamental right to social justice as expressed in Article 21 of the 2007

Interim Constitution, which recognizes women as a marginalized social group and establishes the government's responsibility to protect women's rights.

The Court also takes the government to task for failing to take steps to clarify the law and explain when abortions shall be provided for free, the process for obtaining abortions, and the locations at which they are available. This lack of clarity, the Court observes, is an impediment to women's access to abortion services. The Court explains that "unless the grounds, process, and locations where services are available for free are established with certainty and such information reaches people, abortion services cannot be considered to be accessible and affordable."[149]

Comprehensive Abortion Law Reform

The shortcomings of the current criminal law framework together with the reproductive rights granted by Article 20 (2) of the Interim Constitution compel the Court to order the government to create an adequate and comprehensive legal framework for abortion to ensure that women are able to exercise their reproductive rights.[150] This holding follows the Court's precedent in its *Prakash Mani Sharma* decision, where it ordered the government to provide services for the treatment of uterine prolapse.[151]

The criminal law, the Court argues, is not suitable for dealing with the range of health issues involved in providing safe abortion services. The government needs to use health regulations and laws to ensure the provision of safe abortion services. Appropriate health laws are needed to address issues such as techniques and procedures for abortion;[152] the competencies and duties of abortion providers;[153] registration and accreditation of abortion facilities;[154] information about abortion and counseling services;[155] confidentiality and privacy of patients;[156] cost schemes;[157] and legal recourse and remedies for legal issues that may arise in the context of abortion.[158] While noting that the Safe Abortion Service Procedure does address some of these issues, the Court criticizes the Procedure for lack of clarity and describes it as something that the government has had to settle for in the absence of a comprehensive legal framework.[159] Stressing that reproductive health and abortion are legal concerns, the Court states that "the right to abortion can be fully realized only through a definite legal framework that defines the related rights, duties, and processes and is implemented through appropriate programs."[160]

Furthermore, in *Dhikta,* the Court specifically questions the appropriateness of retaining the provisions on abortion in penal provisions of the

Country Code and recommends a noncriminal legal approach to abortion. The Court describes the current legal framework established in the Country Code as being too narrow and focused on penalties for abortion.[161] Even with the additional sections created through the Eleventh Amendment, the current framework cannot be considered adequate and discrete enough to address the issues at hand.[162] The Court criticizes the current legal framework as serving more to maintain the overall status of abortion as a crime as opposed to effectively facilitating access to services for women in need.[163] The continued treatment of abortion as a matter of criminal law is inconsistent with its recognition as a new right, and in the more recent context of legal reform it is necessary to introduce separate legislation.[164]

Some of the issues that the Court expects the government to address through a comprehensive law and specific programs include: compensation for denial of abortion services and for harm suffered as a result of the service not being provided in accordance with the proper procedures and standards;[165] safeguards to ensure the privacy of information provided by a woman seeking an abortion;[166] accessibility through the appropriate expansion of services throughout the country;[167] safeguards against the imposition of unreasonable fees;[168] provisions clarifying the availability of free services;[169] protection against adverse consequences of abortion due to lack of correct information about the service and superstitious beliefs prevalent in society;[170] and awareness programs about safe abortion.[171] The Court explicitly requires that a comprehensive law be based on standards of reproductive rights recognized and established in international law.[172]

The Court urges the government to act swiftly and warns against attempts to prevent the enjoyment of these rights by failing to introduce or delaying the adoption of appropriate legislation.[173] As of 2013, comprehensive abortion legislation had not been introduced.

Conclusion

Dhikta is a milestone in Nepal's jurisprudential development as it recognizes the right to abortion as a constitutionally protected right. The recognition of abortion rights is crucial for a country like Nepal that has a history of patriarchal inequality and continues to struggle with high rates of maternal mortality due to unsafe abortion, particularly among poor, rural, and socially marginalized women. By recognizing that it is not enough for the state to grant rights on paper and that these rights must be rendered effective in practice through the introduction of appropriate laws, policies, and programs, the Court puts the onus squarely on the state to introduce measures that take into account the unequal power dynamics and institutional inequalities that prevent women from exercising their right to abortion and ensure that they are able to make autonomous decisions about pregnancy; this includes the state's obligation to ensure that abortions are accessible and affordable, even free if necessary. The Court requires the state to ensure the practical realization of abortion rights, especially for the poor, which is a much-needed step toward ensuring equality and reproductive justice for disadvantaged and marginalized women, in addition to eliminating sex and gender-based discrimination and protecting women from various forms of violence and abortion stigma. Recognition of the denial of abortion rights as an infringement on women's moral agency and a form of discrimination that the state is obligated to remedy is essential for the protection of women's human rights and dignity and must be the premise of Nepal's future laws and policies on abortion, including the future comprehensive abortion law.

PART IV

Narratives and Social Meaning

Chapter 14

Reckoning with Narratives of Innocent Suffering in Transnational Abortion Litigation

Lisa M. Kelly

Over the past decade, reproductive rights advocates have pursued a series of lawful abortion access cases from Latin America before the United Nations and Inter-American human rights systems.[1] Advocates drew in part on the decades-long history of abortion rights litigation in the European human rights system.[2] The Latin American cases have met with resounding legal success. U.N. human rights treaty bodies have recognized state obstructions of lawful abortions as rights violations in each communication brought before them. In 2007, Mexico agreed to a landmark friendly settlement in a case before the Inter-American Commission on Human Rights.[3] Two years later, the Commission granted precautionary measures against Colombia in a case related to the denial of a lawful abortion.[4]

Regional and international reproductive rights advocates celebrate these decisions as important victories for the advancement of abortion rights in international human rights law.[5] As one advocate commented after the U.N. Human Rights Committee's decision in *K.L. v. Peru*, "this ruling establishes that it is not enough to just grant a right on paper. Where abortion is legal it is governments' duty to ensure that women have access to it."[6] These claims aim to ensure access to abortion under enumerated exceptions—such as to preserve the life of the woman or where pregnancy results from rape—in jurisdictions that generally prohibit abortion. Advocates understand these decisions as tools that can be deployed domestically to bridge the gap between abortion exceptions on the books and their realization on the ground.

I offer in this chapter a more ambivalent reading of these cases, specifically of how they narrate abortion and sexuality. All but one of the five Latin American claims has involved rape, and all but one has concerned minors. I identify in these cases a recurring narrative that invokes sexual innocence, violation, and parental beneficence: an adolescent girl, figured often as a child, is raped, becomes pregnant, and with the support of her parents seeks to terminate the pregnancy. When she is denied access to a lawful abortion at a public hospital, the state emerges as the shameful antagonist.

This narrative of innocent suffering is neither new nor limited to international law cases from Latin America. It repeats across time and place, weaving through landmark domestic abortion cases in interwar Britain,[7] late twentieth-century Ireland,[8] and contemporary Argentina,[9] Colombia,[10] and Nicaragua.[11] A recent abortion decision by the European Court of Human Rights similarly concerned a Polish adolescent who was raped, became pregnant, and with the support of her mother sought access to a lawful abortion under the rape exception to Poland's restrictive abortion law.[12] Each of these "innocent suffering" cases arose in jurisdictions with restrictive abortion laws.

Although these other cases figure in my analysis, this chapter focuses on contemporary international abortion rights litigation from Latin America. My reasons for this focus are twofold. First, narratives of innocent suffering are particularly prominent in contemporary abortion discourse in Latin America. A series of highly publicized cases involving the rape of minors has fueled debates in the region over restrictive abortion laws.[13] Second, these are landmark cases in international human rights law. They mark the first time that U.N. human rights treaty bodies have addressed communications concerning abortion and the first time that abortion rights advocates have engaged the Inter-American system. Analyzing how these cases narrate abortion, and to what effect, is crucial for mapping the current state of international abortion jurisprudence, understanding reproductive rights advocates' strategies, and anticipating future legal developments.

The innocent suffering narrative has received only cursory analysis in both the health and human rights literatures.[14] In this chapter, I examine the power and peril of this narrative. The production of narrative is a complex phenomenon, and so I proceed cautiously in naming from where it emerged and by whom it is deployed. Regional and international reproductive rights advocates did not see themselves as seeking out abortion cases from Latin

America involving adolescent rape.[15] Rather, like all cause lawyers, they pursued high-profile international cases that they believed they could win at law and in public opinion.[16] They overwhelmingly advanced sympathetic cases that bracketed the act of abortion from the contested terrains of wanted sex, non-procreative desire, and family discord.

Cases involving adolescent rape and parental beneficence resonate with publics and with legal decision makers. In a region where the word abortion (*aborto*) remains taboo, euphemized often as an interruption (*interrupción; interrupção*), narratives of innocent suffering make abortion utterable. One advocate suggests that "these cases have made it easier to say the word 'abortion,'" as they personalize abortion.[17] Another writes of the *Paulina* case against Mexico, "for the first time, a young girl's experience, instead of abortion in general, was the subject of discussion, and it has had a great influence on abortion law and policy in Mexico."[18]

However, these legal and discursive openings come with costs. Reproductive rights advocates face a dilemma. By narrating sympathetic cases likely to secure greater public support for abortion access, advocates risk reinforcing narrow conceptions of the reasonable or deserved abortion. Narratives of innocent suffering leave out the majority of abortion experiences. Among others, the experiences of women who desire nonprocreative sex, who have no access to claims of extreme suffering, who seek multiple abortions, who terminate for economic reasons, and young women in conflict with their parents are elided by such narratives. This elision has implications for both the kind of legal reforms advocates are likely to secure and the ways that women and abortion are constructed. As one abortion rights advocate in the United States writes of this dilemma, "when I . . . focus on exceptional circumstances, I reinscribe a discourse of 'appropriate abortion' that in turn feeds a cultural climate in which abortion patients feel 'guilty' or 'like bad people.'"[19] This insight applies critical pressure to advocates' representational work. Reproductive rights advocates "represent" women by seeking legal reforms on their behalf and in doing so shape their subjective identities and experiences.

International and regional reproductive rights advocates are sophisticated and experienced agents of progressive struggle. The U.S.-based Center for Reproductive Rights, which litigated three of the five Latin American cases, is a leading international reproductive rights organization working at the domestic, regional and international levels. In regional and international human rights advocacy, advocates face down well-organized opposition from anti-abortion state and civil society groups. I do not claim that advocates are blind to the problematic features of innocent suffering narratives. Rather, I detect in the deployment of these narratives a strategic calculus whereby advocates seek to secure incremental change. In restrictive abortion jurisdictions, advocates may believe that these cases will clear the way for further exceptions and eventual liberalization of law and access. If these narratives work to secure some abortion rights, advocates may argue, some of their troubling features may simply be forgotten afterward, or at least discounted as "'merely' symbolic harms."[20]

I caution against a ready faith in discounting these harms. I do so with an understanding that any advocacy tactic, particularly regarding a highly contested issue such as abortion, will inevitably impose costs and require tradeoffs. Advocates' calculations about the bearable short-and long-term costs of specific moves will differ according to the forum, region, and political moment. Given the remarkable salience of innocent suffering narratives, I urge a more fulsome reckoning with their potential consequences.

Narratives of innocent suffering can sustain lines of argument that are sympathetic to divergent political projects. Anti-abortion advocates have in recent decades proven adept at picking up, flipping, and redeploying narratives of suffering and vulnerability. Reva Siegel's groundbreaking work on the rise of women-protective arguments in the United States illuminates how anti-abortion advocates have repurposed feminist and abortion rights discourses, marrying them with public health and trauma language to claim that abortion hurts women.[21] The uptake of these ideas in American abortion jurisprudence underlines the importance of attending to the intellectual and legal contexts that feminist theorists and advocates help create.[22] Narratives of innocent suffering can cultivate and reinforce discourses of vulnerability and protectionism over which reproductive rights advocates do not enjoy exclusive ownership. In the specific case of young people, social conservatives regularly reference pain, vulnerability, and family harmony to argue against minors' access to health information and services.

Another reason for caution concerns the legal rules that narratives of innocent suffering can produce. Cases that foreground parental support and pregnancy through rape can strengthen parental involvement rights and legitimize rape exceptions. In cases of parent-child harmony, the family may be an effective bulwark against a resistant state. However, by reinvigorating family privacy and parental power, these cases may also redistribute decision-making power away from minors in cases of conflict. Similarly, while rape exceptions may permit safe and legal abortion for some classes of women, they may also reinforce restrictive sexual governance schemes by selectively imposing reproductive burdens on women who choose to have sex.

This chapter proceeds in two parts. First I describe the genesis of these cases from Latin America. I discuss some of the strategic and tactical choices of advocates in bringing these cases, track the case trajectories before international human rights bodies, and consider their contribution to international abortion jurisprudence. In the second part I assess innocent suffering narratives in contemporary abortion litigation by disaggregating the narrative into its constituent parts and reading each for the meaning it gives to the whole. I conclude by considering the costs and benefits of this litigation, in particular for the young people who figure so centrally in it.

A Case Is Born

This part describes how advocates selected the cases they did, traces the legal arguments they developed, and analyzes the cases with a specific emphasis on how the relevant international bodies interpreted abortion denial as a human rights violation.

Local Genesis

The overwhelming majority of abortions induced each year in Latin America contravene formal legal restrictions. While middle- and upper-class women can often access safe abortions at private clinics, poor women and girls must resort to clandestine and less safe terminations.[23] State tolerance of private abortions for wealthier women affirms what Bonnie Shepard calls the "double discourse system" in Latin America. Shepard argues that the *doble discurso* around abortion in many Latin American states sustains formal, public prohibitions in the face of widespread private violation. Politicians and state officials use this duality to "maintai[n] the status quo in repressive or negligent public policies while expanding private sexual and reproductive choices behind the scenes."[24] The worst consequences of this double discourse of public formal prohibition/private informal permission fall on poor women, young people, and those living in rural areas. Unable to access or afford safer private procedures, these women suffer significantly higher rates of abortion-related morbidity and mortality. Studies indicate that poor women and girls are the most likely to come to the attention of law enforcement authorities after attending a public hospital for complications due to unsafe or self-induced termination.[25]

Reproductive rights advocates did not bring cases involving private unlawful abortions. Instead, advocates selected cases that involved public obstruction of lawful abortions. Each of the five challenges from Argentina, Colombia, Mexico, and Peru involved the delay or denial of a lawful abortion at a public hospital. These cases satisfied domestic exceptions for abortions, whether to preserve the life or health of the woman or because the pregnancy resulted from rape.

International advocates learned of these cases through local feminist organization partners, who in turn had either been contacted by families or learned of them through local and national media. This filtering inevitably affected the types of cases international advocates advanced. For example, local feminist organizations learned of the *Paulina* case through media coverage.[26] Paulina's story attracted attention precisely because of its striking elements—a young girl, raped by a stranger during a home robbery, impeded by hospital officials from accessing a lawful abortion that her mother supported. Some advocates also speculate that their bias toward cases involving minors may reflect adult women's distrust of the legal and public health systems.[27] Many adult women opt for clandestine rather than public abortions, even when they believe that they qualify for a lawful exception. Parents may be less willing to subject their minor daughters, pregnant by rape, to less safe abortions. Some families may also initiate petitions, or at least respond to proceedings initiated by hospital officials, because they perceive adolescent rape cases to be less publicly stigmatizing than abortions following consensual sex or even the rape of adult women.[28]

This case selection pattern exemplifies "the procedural turn in abortion law" that Joanna Erdman identifies in this collection.[29] Advocates aim to secure greater procedural fairness for women accessing lawful abortions, rather than to substantively challenge restrictive abortion laws. In procedural rights litigation, advocates press states to enact laws or regulations clarifying the requirements for recognized exceptions. They also make claims on the state to extend to women the right to be heard and to receive a timely decision.[30] Advocates' decision to pursue procedural challenges suggests a strategic calculus about the current probability of success in challenging abortion restrictions themselves.

International Trajectory

International and regional reproductive rights organizations began pursuing this wave of Latin American abortion litigation in the early 1990s. This litigation resulted from sustained cooperation among local, regional, and international reproductive rights groups. Through high-profile litigation, advocates seek to transform public discourse and develop progressive norms at international law that can be cited domestically.[31]

In 2002, the Mexican women's rights organizations Alaíde Foppa and Epikeia, together with the United States–based Center for Reproductive Rights, filed the first case in this wave before the Inter-American Commission on Human Rights.[32] *Paulina del Carmen Ramírez Jacinto v. Mexico* involved a thirteen-year-old who became pregnant as a result of rape. Paulina and her mother requested an abortion at a public hospital in Baja California, pursuant to that state's rape exception. Medical staff dissuaded Paulina's mother from consenting to the abortion by providing "biased and imprecise information" about the dangers of abortion.[33] On April 13, 2000, at the age of fourteen, Paulina gave birth to a son by cesarean section.

The *Paulina* case followed domestic complaints before the Baja California state's attorney for human rights and citizenship protection and the Mexican National Commission for Human Rights.[34] Both institutions recommended compensation for Paulina and her family. They also urged the government to proceed with a preliminary inquiry against the officials who had impeded Paulina's access to abortion and to ensure enforcement of the lawful exception permitting abortion in cases of rape.[35] The Baja California government eventually agreed to award Paulina limited compensation; however, the preliminary inquiry remained stalled by the time Paulina and her mother petitioned the Inter-American Commission.[36]

In their claim before the Commission, the petitioners acknowledged that domestic mechanisms existed by which Paulina's assailants could be criminally convicted and hospital authorities administratively disciplined. They argued, however, that these mechanisms were insufficient because they did not address "the absence of regulations establishing a procedure for exercising the right to terminate a pregnancy caused by an act of rape."[37] By failing to provide Paulina adequate procedures through which she could access lawful abortion, the petitioners claimed, the Mexican state had violated its obligations under human rights treaties and declarations. Her lawyers claimed that Mexico had violated Paulina's rights to humane treatment, privacy, conscience and religion, life, liberty and security of the person, and freedom from sex discrimination in accessing health services.

In 2007, the litigants reached a friendly settlement with Mexico. Mexico agreed to provide Paulina and her son compensation for moral damages, living and ongoing health care expenses, and eventual support for university education. It also pledged to strengthen the federal Health Secretariat's "commitment toward ending violations of the right of women to the legal termination of a pregnancy."[38] The government of Baja California also agreed to submit to and promote before the State Congress regulatory proposals by the petitioners concerning women's access to abortion under the state's rape exception.

Two years after the *Paulina Ramírez* settlement, the international human rights organization Women's Link petitioned the Inter-American Commission for precautionary measures on behalf of XX, a thirteen-year-old Colombian victim of rape who was refused a lawful abortion, and her mother X.[39] The Commission is empowered to request states to take precautionary measures to "prevent irreparable harm" to persons under its jurisdiction.[40] XX and her mother were subject to violent harassment after criminal charges were filed against her assailant and after her baby was put up for adoption. The Commission granted the petitioners' request. It requested Colombia take necessary measures to protect the petitioners' lives and physical integrity and to guarantee to XX medical treatment for the effects of being sexually violated and forced to carry a high-risk pregnancy to term.[41] The *XX and X* case marked the first time that the Inter-American Commission granted precautionary measures in a case related to the denial of a lawful abortion.[42]

In addition to the Inter-American human rights system, reproductive rights advocates have in the last decade pursued three abortion challenges from Latin America before U.N. treaty bodies.

In 2002, the Center for Reproductive Rights and two regional partner organizations—the Latin American and Caribbean Committee for the Defense of Women's Rights and the Counseling Center for the Defense of Women's Rights—filed the *K.L. v. Peru* communication before the U.N. Human Rights Committee.[43] K.L. was seventeen years old when she became pregnant. Some three to four months into her pregnancy, K.L. was informed by her obstetrician-gynecologist that she was carrying an anencephalic fetus and that the pregnancy posed risks to her life. The obstetrician advised terminating the pregnancy by means of uterine curettage.[44] Although Peruvian law permitted abortion in order to preserve the life or health of the woman, hospital officials denied K.L. an abortion. Forced to carry the fetus to term, K.L. described the experience of seeing "her daughter's marked deformities and knowing that her life expectancy was short" as akin to an "extended funeral."[45]

In 2005, the Human Rights Committee found that Peru had violated its obligations under the International Covenant on Civil and Political Rights. The Committee concluded that Peru's denial of abortion caused K.L.'s suffering, and violated her right to be free from cruel, inhuman, and degrading treatment.[46] It emphasized that the prohibition of cruel treatment "relates not only to physical pain but also to mental suffering."[47] The Committee further held that Peru had violated K.L.'s right to privacy by intruding on her medical decision, as well as her right to special protection as a minor.[48]

Two years after the *K.L.* decision, V.D.A., the mother of a developmentally disabled young woman, L.M.R., filed a communication against Argentina before the U.N. Human Rights Committee. V.D.A. was represented by three women's rights organizations: the Gender, Law and Development Institute of Argentina, Catholics for Free Choice–Argentina, and the Latin American and Caribbean Committee for the Defense of Women's Rights.[49] L.M.R. attended a special school and had been diagnosed with the cognitive functioning of an eight- to ten-year-old. She lived with her mother, a domestic worker, in Buenos Aires. At nineteen, L.M.R. was raped, allegedly by her uncle, and became pregnant.[50] She qualified for a legal abortion pursuant to Argentina's exception for victims of rape who have a mental disability.[51] As a result of the obstinacy of hospital officials and interference by religious groups, L.M.R. was denied an abortion at a public hospital and ultimately resorted to a clandestine termination.

In 2011, the Committee held that Argentina had violated L.M.R.'s rights to equality and nondiscrimination, to privacy, and to be free from cruel, inhuman, and degrading treatment. Crucially, the Committee found that Argentina's failure "to guarantee L.M.R.'s right to a termination of pregnancy . . . when her family so requested, caused L.M.R. physical and mental suffering constituting a violation of article 7 of the Covenant."[52] The Committee was persuaded that the state's denial of abortion, as distinct from the rape and pregnancy itself, caused sufficient psychic suffering to constitute cruel, inhuman, and degrading treatment. The Committee deemed the rights violations particularly serious given "the victim's status as a young girl with a disability."[53]

Six months after the Human Rights Committee decided *L.M.R.*, the U.N.

Committee on the Elimination of Discrimination against Women issued its first decision on abortion in *L.C. v. Peru*. L.C. and her mother, T.P.F., the author of the communication, were represented by the Center for Reproductive Rights and the Centre for the Promotion and Protection of Sexual and Reproductive Rights.[54]

L.C. was thirteen years old when "she began to be sexually abused by J.C.R., a man about 34 years old."[55] In 2007, L.C. learned she was pregnant and "in a state of depression, attempted suicide . . . by jumping from a building."[56] She sustained serious spinal cord injuries; on examination at a public hospital, doctors recommended surgery to prevent permanent disability. During the course of a psychological evaluation, L.C. disclosed to medical staff that she had attempted suicide because of ongoing sexual abuse and fear of pregnancy. Hospital officials confirmed her pregnancy and informed L.C. that they were postponing spinal surgery. L.C.'s mother, after consulting with her daughter, requested that hospital officials terminate the pregnancy in accordance with Peru's statutory exception for lawful abortion to preserve the life or health of the woman. Forty-two days after the abortion request, the hospital medical board issued a denial because it considered "the life of the patient was not in danger."[57] L.C.'s mother requested that the medical board reconsider its decision. She included with her request a report by the High-Level Commission on Reproductive Health of the Medical College of Peru, which concluded that L.C. was entitled to a therapeutic abortion because of the "grave risk to the girl's physical and mental health."[58] Nine days later, L.C. spontaneously miscarried. At the time of the complaint before the Committee on the Elimination of Discrimination against Women, she remained "paralyzed from the neck down" and had regained "only partial movement in her hands."[59]

The Committee interpreted abortion in this case through the woman-centered discrimination framework that organizes the Convention on the Elimination of All Forms of Discrimination against Women.[60] In contrast to the Human Rights Committee's focus on the painful *effects* of abortion denied, the Committee on the Elimination of Discrimination against Women emphasized the sex-discriminatory *causes* of abortion denial. The Committee grounded its analysis of abortion denial as a human rights violation in women's biological differences from men and a critique of the state's use of gender stereotypes. It paid far less attention to other axes of disparity in abortion access such as class or age.

The Committee found that "owing to her condition as a pregnant woman,"

L.C. did not have access to adequate procedures to establish her entitlement to necessary medical services, including spinal surgery and therapeutic abortion.[61] Peru's failure to provide these services violated its obligation to "take all appropriate measures to eliminate discrimination against women in the field of health care."[62] The Committee further concluded that the decision to postpone spinal surgery was "influenced by the stereotype that protection of the foetus should prevail over the health of the mother."[63] The state's violations were "even more serious considering that she was a minor and a victim of sexual abuse."[64] In the end, as in the other cases discussed above, L.C.'s youth and sexual violation compounded the state's denial of abortion.

Assessing the Innocent Suffering Narrative

In the following part, I elucidate the key moves that make narratives of innocent suffering both powerful and perilous. I analyze how advocates mobilize ideas of deserved abortions, family privacy, and state shame to advance abortion rights. I caution that in doing so, advocates may (re)produce narrative constructions, lines of argument, and legal rules that undercut their larger emancipatory goals.

Abortion Deservingness

Transposing Innocence from Fetus to Girl

Reproductive rights advocates' mobilization of innocent suffering narratives disrupts anti-abortion advocates' presumed monopoly on innocence claims. Abortion access cases that foreground the abortion claimant as a subject of youthful suffering offer a competing innocence claim to that of the fetus. These cases challenge anti-abortion narratives that see fetal innocence as necessarily trumping abortion rights. By exposing abortion denial as destructive of innocent girls' lives, reproductive rights advocates are able to potentially neutralize conservative emphases on fetal innocence.

Anti-abortion groups advance strong and moderate claims of fetal innocence to oppose abortion access even in cases of rape of minors. In response to a recent Brazilian case involving a nine-year-old girl pregnant by rape, Catholic officials articulated a strong version of fetal innocence to condemn abortion. Explaining the Church's decision to excommunicate the girl's mother and the physicians who terminated the pregnancy, Archbishop José Cardoso Sobrinho stated: "They took the life of an innocent. Abortion is much more serious than killing an adult. An adult may or may not be an innocent, but an unborn child is most definitely innocent."[65] Here, the wrongfulness of terminating life is directly related to innocence, and fetuses enjoy a universal claim to innocence.

A more moderate articulation of fetal innocence suggests that although both girl and fetus are innocent, a wrong against the first does not justify terminating the latter. In *L.M.R.*, the Juvenile Court that initially granted an injunction against the abortion reasoned that the termination should be prohibited because it was not acceptable to right one wrong (the rape of L.M.R.) "with another wrongful assault against *a new innocent victim*, i.e. the unborn child."[66] The Court's framing differs from Archbishop Sobrinho's. It recognized L.M.R. as an "innocent victim," but intervened to protect the fetus from becoming yet another "innocent victim." This moderate articulation establishes a competition between girl and innocence over the terrain of innocence. As one commentator observed of the *Paulina* case: "Paulina put an innocent victim's face on the abortion decision. It was not about the fetus; it was about the girl who had been raped."[67]

The young women at the center of these challenges are often referred to in media and advocacy reports in terms that connote childishness: "the girl"; "*la niña*"; the "child rape victim."[68] This semantic emphasis on childishness evokes ideas of sentimental innocence that the legal or developmental terms "minor" or "adolescent," and the quasi-pejorative term "teenager," may not. In contrast to the promiscuous teenager or Lolita temptress, the "child rape victim" personifies innocent victimization.[69]

Framing Innocence as Pain

Whereas anti-abortion advocates emphasize fetal innocence to demonstrate the wrongfulness of abortion, reproductive rights advocates pursue youthful innocence cases to communicate the exquisite painfulness of abortion denied. At stake in these cases is the painful fracturing of girlhood innocence, first by the rape and then by potentially becoming a "child-mother."[70] By foregrounding this pain, advocates invite a compassionate response to abortion. Referring to the *Paulina* case, a commentator stated: "It is impossible to find a case where the need to perform an abortion is clearer than with this young girl. Unless Paulina or the fetus had been infected with AIDS as a result of the rape, it is difficult to think of a more dramatic scene."[71]

This imbrication of innocence with the pain of sexual violation has analogues in earlier landmark abortion litigation. The seminal English abortion decision of *R. v. Bourne* (1938), which expanded the common law interpretation of exceptions to protect the life of the woman, turned on ideas of innocence.[72] The case involved a fourteen-year-old from a middle-class family who became pregnant after being raped by soldiers in East London. With her parents, she visited a family physician and requested a termination.[73] The physician referred the family to Dr. Aleck Bourne, who later performed the abortion. At the time, England's restrictive abortion law contained an exception only to preserve the life of the woman.[74]

Dr. Bourne had been waiting for an opportunity to challenge England's restrictive abortion law, having previously been subjected to criticism by colleagues for terminating another minor's pregnancy.[75] As he later recounted, "the case of the girl in 1938 seemed to be a God-given opportunity as she had suffered the extremity of cruelty and horror and was, withal, an innocent child."[76] Shortly after performing the termination, Dr. Bourne turned himself in to authorities.

At trial, Judge Macnaghten famously instructed the jury that England's life exception "ought to be construed in a reasonable sense."[77] He said that where a doctor is of the reasonable opinion that "continuance of the pregnancy will . . . make the woman a physical or mental wreck, the jury are quite entitled . . . [to conclude that the doctor] is operating for the purpose of preserving the life of the mother."[78] This jury instruction introduced a liberal interpretation of the life exception to include physical and mental health that would subsequently travel throughout the common law world.[79]

Judge Macnaghten stated that it would only be natural for an innocent girl to suffer immensely if forced to carry a pregnancy by rape to term. Her psychic pain would flow not simply from having to continue an unwanted pregnancy, but more specifically from the pregnancy's reminder of her sexual violation: "No doubt you will think it is only common sense that a girl who for nine months has to carry in her body the reminder of the dreadful scene and then go through the pangs of childbirth must suffer great mental anguish, unless indeed she be feeble-minded or belongs to the class described as 'the prostitute class,' a Dolores 'marked cross from the womb and perverse.'"[80] Although jurors heard extensive medical expert testimony during the trial, Judge Macnaghten suggested the girl's psychic suffering was a point of fact the jury could intuit from "common sense."

Judge Macnaghten juxtaposed the sexually promiscuous and

feeble-minded woman with the girl in order to construct the latter as innocent. The girl's innocence manifested itself as a vulnerability to and capacity
for pain—a sentience that cultural historian Robin Bernstein has argued was
central to American concepts of white "childhood innocence" from the mid-
nineteenth century onward.[81] The prostitute would not experience such psychic pain because she presumably could not suffer the injurious violation of
rape in the first place. That the girl would comprehend her innocence lost
proved the final element of mental suffering, articulated as an opposition to
the feeble-minded woman who lacked such insight. As Judge Macnaghten's
interpretation of the life exception traveled to other jurisdictions, psychic
pain proved crucial to the incremental expansion of lawful abortion.

The expressly moralistic tenor of *Bourne* betrays its interwar dating. Still,
as I discuss in the next section, the emphasis on young women's acute vulnerability to the psychic pain of rape and pregnancy persists in contemporary
international abortion litigation.

Revealing the Pain of Abortion Denied

Contemporary abortion rights litigation renews the emphasis of *Bourne*
on the grievous suffering experienced by young women forced to continue a
pregnancy conceived through rape. In *L.C.*, advocates argued that L.C. would
have experienced "grave and permanent harm to her mental health" if forced
"to bring to term a pregnancy that had resulted from a rape."[82] Peru's statutory
language of "grave and permanent" harm to one's mental health conjures
traumatic suffering that can never be made past. As Ruth Leys explains, "the
experience of trauma, fixed or frozen in time, refuses to be represented *as*
past, but is perpetually re-experienced in a painful, dissociated, traumatic
present."[83] The *L.C.* complaint emphasized that this suffering had already "de-
stabilized [L.C.] to the point of attempting suicide."[84]

The Committee on the Elimination of Discrimination against Women
agreed that L.C. should have qualified for a lawful abortion under Peru's exception for preserving the life or health of the woman. The fact that L.C. had
also been raped provided an opening for the Committee to weigh in on Peru's
lack of a lawful abortion exception for rape. It recommended that Peru "review its legislation with a view to decriminalizing abortion when the pregnancy results from rape or sexual abuse."[85] This nod toward decriminalization
in cases of rape marks the only instance in this body of litigation where an
international body commented on the substance of a state's abortion law.
That it did so in the context of rape is significant. Where enacted and

operationalized domestically, rape exceptions can provide safe abortion access to some women. The Committee's recommendation of a rape exception may presage its future endorsement of additional exceptions. Still, by tying abortion access, even incrementally, to sexual consent, advocates risk reinforcing a particular form of sexual discipline through law.

Rape exceptions condition the legality of abortion on a woman's nonconsent to sex. They "rest on unarticulated assumptions about how women are to comport themselves sexually—a code the state enforces by selectively allowing women access to abortion."[86] Women and girls who do not consent to sex are adjudged at law as deserving of abortion. Drucilla Cornell interprets these prohibition-exception schemes in punitive terms: "Women who suffered incest and rape did not choose to have sex, and therefore should not be punished with an unwanted pregnancy; those who chose to have sex should expect such a punishment."[87] The logic of rape exceptions disciplines women and girls to consent to heterosexual intercourse only when they can bear its potential reproductive consequences. Those who depart from this baseline must either resort to a potentially unsafe, clandestine termination, or face unwanted reproduction.

The *L.M.R.* communication, which concerned access under Argentina's rape exception, struck similar notes to *L.C.* about the painfulness of abortion denied. The petitioners argued that "forcing [L.M.R.] to continue with her pregnancy constituted cruel and degrading treatment and consequently, a violation of her personal well-being."[88] To support this argument, the petitioners filed a psychological evaluation showing that L.M.R. exhibited signs of post-traumatic stress disorder.[89] Given L.M.R.'s mental disability, advocates analogized her situation to "child sexual abuse, with its associated fear and inability to understand the nature of the act and process it emotionally."[90] On this reading, L.M.R. may not necessarily have experienced the sexual violation as traumatic at the time that it occurred because, like a child, she lacked the capacity to understand it as such. Instead, sexual trauma was projected back in time from the pregnancy to the sex, and then forward again onto the pregnancy.

Echoing *Bourne* and *L.C.*, advocates framed abortion in *L.M.R.* as a means to mitigate the suffering of pregnancy as trauma. As the petitioners argued, "although it is difficult to distinguish between the effects of the rape and those attributable to the State's failure to guarantee access to a safe abortion, there are sufficient grounds to maintain that if the termination had been performed in due time and form *its* damaging consequences could have been mitigated."[91] The possessive pronoun "its" here refers back to the rape, suggesting that abortion would mitigate the harmful effects of rape manifested as pregnancy.

Re-Enchanting Family Privacy

The family, particularly mothers, figure prominently in this body of litigation. Mothers are key advocates for their daughters seeking access to lawful abortions, and in subsequently challenging state obstructions to this access. Human rights bodies repeatedly identify abortion as a joint decision. In *L.C.*, the Committee on the Elimination of Discrimination against Women observed the supportive role of the minor's mother: "On 18 April 2007, *the author* [of the communication], *after consulting with her daughter, requested* the hospital officials to carry out a legal termination of the pregnancy."[92] In *L.M.R.*, the Human Rights Committee noted that when hospital officials determined L.M.R. was pregnant, her mother "requested a termination."[93] The agreed statement of facts in the *Paulina* friendly settlement likewise framed the abortion decision as maternal-filial: "Paulina . . . *and her mother decided* that an abortion was the best alternative."[94]

Advocacy materials for these cases likewise emphasize maternal support. A video account of the *L.C.* case, produced by the Center for Reproductive Rights, captures maternal beneficence in the face of filial suffering.[95] The video montage opens not with L.C. herself, but with her mother recounting the moment she first learned that her daughter was pregnant. After jumping from a building in a suicide attempt, L.C. faced potential paralysis. Her mother describes telling the doctor, "'I want my daughter to walk.' 'No,' he says, 'Ma'am, first of all your daughter is pregnant.'" With L.C.'s mother foregrounded in this way, state obstruction appears to violate not only L.C.'s rights, but also those of her mother.

Maternal involvement in these cases is partly a function of the legal incapacity of minors. As advocates working in Latin America note, parental-consent-and-involvement laws and informal hospital practices almost invariably require the involvement of the parents of minors in securing the latter's abortions.[96] For example, even in Mexico City, which has one of the most liberal abortion laws in the region, parental consent is required for minors sixteen years and under seeking abortion services.[97]

Still, the fact that international advocates actively foreground family harmony in these cases marks a significant sea change in abortion advocacy.

During earlier periods of transnational abortion liberalization, reproductive rights advocates worked hard to individualize the abortion decision at law. In a wave of cases from the 1970s onward, women in North America,[98] Western Europe,[99] and Israel[100] successfully defended abortion access against spousal and conjugal veto, notice, or consent provisions. The European Commission and Court of Human Rights likewise rejected notice and consultation claims by spouses and potential fathers.[101] In the case of minors, several influential decisions by courts in the United States and the United Kingdom limited parental vetoes over minors' abortions.[102]

In recent decades, reproductive rights advocates have also argued against parental involvement laws in their international human rights work. Advocates emphasize the specter of family violence as well as public health concerns about young people's ability to access health services. They argue specifically that while many minors will voluntarily involve a parent in their abortion decisions, they should not be mandated to do so by the state. "Young women who avoid parental involvement in that decision," the Center for Reproductive Rights has argued, "usually do so for reasons such as fear of abuse, pressure to carry the pregnancy to term, threats of being thrown out of the house, or other negative repercussions."[103] Young people subjected to mandatory parental disclosure may experience family violence, coercion, or abandonment. Advocates argue that faced with these stakes, some young people will delay or avoid accessing necessary health services and information.[104]

These arguments have found some purchase in the U.N. human rights system. The Committee on the Elimination of Discrimination against Women has encouraged voluntary family consultation, while emphasizing the individuality of the ultimate reproductive decision. In its General Recommendation on Equality in marriage and family life, the Committee stated that "decisions to have children or not, while preferably made in consultation with spouse or partner, must not nevertheless be limited by spouse, *parent,* partner or Government."[105] Similarly, the Committee on the Rights of the Child has emphasized the deleterious public health effects of parental involvement laws. It has expressed concern about the "various factors, including limited availability of contraceptives, poor reproductive health education *and the requirements of parental consent* . . . [that result] in an increasing number of illegal abortions among girls."[106] In other words, background legal rules requiring parental involvement may channel minors into unsafe, clandestine abortions. The U.N. Special Rapporteur on Physical and Mental Health, in his 2011 interim report, likewise cited "*parental* and spousal consent requirements" as examples of "legal restrictions. . . [that] contribute to making legal abortions inaccessible."[107]

Contemporary abortion rights litigation from Latin America instead presents the family as a bulwark against the obstructive state. In contrast to advocacy campaigns against parental involvement laws, which tend to emphasize the potential malignity of parental interference, these cases foreground mother-daughter harmony. Advocates may believe it necessary to harness the cultural and legal capital of the family in regions and countries where abortion is especially contested. The maternal frame inverts representations of abortion as the ultimate rejection of motherhood. Advocates defer for a later day issues concerning young women's sexuality and abortion decision-making. This tactic carries a strong risk of legal boomerang, however. Emphasizing maternal support in the face of state obstruction may reinvigorate parental power and family privacy vis-à-vis the minor's abortion decision. Advocates may set up obstacles that will not be easily undone.

Recent abortion case law from the European Court of Human Rights suggests this is a pressing concern. The facts of *P. and S. v. Poland* (2012) mirror the narrative of innocent suffering. P. was fourteen years old when she was raped by a peer and became pregnant. The Court described P. and her mother as having decided together that she should terminate the pregnancy.[108] Although P. qualified for a legal abortion under the rape exception to Poland's restrictive abortion law, hospital and state officials impeded her access. Eventually, some two months after the rape, officials from the Ministry of Health finally arranged for P. to access a legal abortion at a public hospital five hundred kilometers from her home.[109]

The Center for Reproductive Rights and two Polish lawyers represented P. and her mother S. as coapplicants before the European Court. As a coapplicant, the mother S. claimed that Poland's procedural failings violated her own right to respect for private and family life. The applicants had been "given contradictory and inaccurate information about the legal conditions that had to be met to obtain a lawful abortion . . . ; *they* had thus been hindered in taking a *free decision* on the matter of abortion."[110] The claimants articulated the abortion decision as familial. They argued that the Polish state's obstruction of lawful abortion therefore violated not only the daughter's right to private and family life, but also her mother's.

The Polish state defended against the mother S.'s claim by insisting that abortion is an individual rather than family decision. Poland read the Article 8 "private and family life" clause disjunctively, asserting that "decisions concerning the carrying out of abortions belonged to the sphere of private, not family life."[111] It relied in part on the European Court's earlier decision in *Boso v. Italy*, in which the Court had refused to grant a potential father any procedural rights under Article 8.[112]

At issue in *P. and S.* were two competing visions of the abortion decision— one that emphasized its ultimate residence with the individual woman, and another that admitted a role for the mother (parent) in the case of minors. The Court accepted the latter view. The Court's reasoning on this point warrants a close reading:

> The Court acknowledges that in a situation of unwanted pregnancy *the mother of a minor girl is not affected in the same way*. It is of the view that *legal guardianship* cannot be considered to automatically confer on the *parents of a minor* the right to take decisions concerning the minor's reproductive choices, because proper regard must be had to the minor's personal autonomy in this sphere. . . . However, it cannot be overlooked that the *interests and life prospects of the mother of a pregnant girl* are also involved in the decision whether to carry the pregnancy to term or not. Likewise, it can be reasonably expected that *the emotional family bond makes it natural for the mother to feel deeply concerned by issues arising out of reproductive dilemmas and choices to be made by the daughter*. Hence, the difference in the situation of a pregnant minor and that of *her parents* does not obviate the need for a procedure for the determination of access to a lawful abortion whereby both parties can be heard and their views fully and objectively considered, including, if necessary, the provision of a mechanism for counseling and reconciling conflicting views in favour of the best interest of the minor.[113]

The mother-daughter relationship forms the model by which parents generally, and thus fathers, gain procedural rights concerning their minor daughter's abortion decision. Unlike the adult woman of European human rights jurisprudence who is left alone with her abortion decision, free from masculine notice or consultation obligations, the minor here is nested at law in a parent-child relationship.

The Court took judicial notice of mothers' disparate care obligations as compared to men in observing how pregnancy may specifically affect the "interests and life prospects of the mother of a pregnant girl." The opinion relies on these obligations to sustain a mother's right to be heard concerning her minor daughter's reproduction. What really drives the Court's maternal turn, however, is a vision of the organic emotive bond between mother and daughter. The Court concludes, "it can be reasonably expected that the emotional family bond makes it natural for the mother to feel deeply concerned" about her daughter's "reproductive dilemmas and choices." On this reading, mothers enjoy a unique bond with their daughters, rendering them singularly concerned about their daughters' reproduction and their own potential grandmothering role. This figuration of maternal care marks what Janet Halley calls the "happy face of cultural feminism"—a model of mutual love between mother and child invoked as a guide for other hierarchical relationships.[114]

While the Court embraced this cultural *maternal* care frame, it defined its legal effects in gender-neutral terms. After devoting several sentences to the exceptionality of the mother-daughter relationship, the Court shifts seamlessly to the language of the minor's "*parents.*" Parents of a pregnant minor— mother and father—now enjoy a right to "be heard and [have] their views fully and objectively considered."[115] The Court left open the possibility that where parent and child conflict, the minor's abortion decision may become subject to some form of a balancing inquiry regarding the best interests of the child.

Mothers and daughters unified in a desire to access abortion are the faces of contemporary litigation narratives of innocent suffering. When received into law, cultural feminist visions of mother and child united may redistribute decision-making power away from minors. Rather than opening space for future incremental progress, these cases may produce parental rights that will be hard to challenge. Parental rights to be involved in a minor daughter's abortion decision will apply equally to cases where parent and child are in conflict or where the minor does not want to involve her parents. Cases such as *P. and S.* open the door to parents in other jurisdictions to claim a right to be heard regarding their minor daughter's abortion.

Shaming the State

Advocates' "shaming" of states that deny or delay access to lawful abortion marks the denouement of litigation narratives of innocent suffering. For decades, international human rights advocates have "mobilized shame" to influence state behavior.[116] Reproductive rights advocates share with international lawyers an abiding concern about enforcing international norms in a global order that lacks an overarching sovereign. They argue that the "shaming effect" can be "an effective legal and political strategy for holding states accountable for their actions."[117] International abortion rights cases and the public and media attention they attract advance this project.

"Naming and shaming" is premised on a belief that by exposing wrongdoing, advocates will "shame" states into reforming their conduct.[118] Kenneth Roth, executive director of Human Rights Watch, an organization that has advocated for abortion access in Latin America,[119] describes this tactic as follows: "the core of our methodology is our ability to investigate, expose and shame. We are at our most effective when we can hold governmental (or in some cases, nongovernmental) conduct up to a disapproving public."[120] This revelation-as-progress motif figures crucially in contemporary international abortion litigation. Advocates emphasize the importance of drawing public and global eyes to the wrongfulness of abortion denied, and of putting the state and its courts on notice that they are being watched.[121]

Advocates' faith in the transformative potential of shame presupposes the sociability of states and their agents.[122] Shame is intersubjective and communicative.[123] It requires a social reference point against and through which a subject can be shamed. Commentators articulate state shame in precisely these affective terms. Robert Drinan writes: "this captivating phrase [the 'mobilization of shame'] assumes *that nations, like individuals, experience 'shame'* when its [*sic*] *conduct is perceived to be degrading, unworthy, humiliating, in essence, shameful.*"[124]

Reproductive rights advocates face a stark challenge in mobilizing shame. Unlike acts such as torture, which attract at least rhetorical condemnation as *jus cogens* violations, state obstructions of abortion do not yield a consensus response. Anti-abortion state and civil society groups have developed sophisticated international human rights arguments to advance their agendas.[125] Alice Miller and Mindy Roseman observe that even within the area of sexual and reproductive rights, abortion stands out as especially contested and subject to backsliding in the U.N. system.[126]

To mobilize shame around abortion denial, advocates arguably need cases that include exceptional elements of cruelty and inhumanity. Narratives of innocent suffering satisfy this need. As one advocate observed, "there is a clear objective strategically that the conditions are so extreme and so cruel that it would make evident the need for change and show how shameful the state is for treating girls like this."[127] Advocates are able to persuasively cast the state as cruel, perhaps even barbaric, for denying abortion to an innocent girl suffering grievously.

Shame in this sense can be distinguished from guilt. Advocates aim to find states guilty of human rights violations through international litigation. Their recurring refrain of state "shame" suggests something more. Shame inheres in the state—what sort of government would do this to its own minor citizens?—rather than simply in its acts. To draw from Eve Sedgwick, "shame, as opposed to guilt, is a bad feeling that does not attach to what one does, but what one is."[128] Cases of innocent suffering provoke public interrogations of the *nature* of states that would deny abortion in these circumstances.

Public reaction to a landmark abortion case from the Republic of Ireland exemplifies this shame response. *Attorney General v. X* (1992) involved a fourteen-year-old who became pregnant after being raped by a family friend. With the support of her parents, X attempted to travel to the United Kingdom to terminate the pregnancy. After Irish officials and a High Court injunction initially blocked X from travelling, feminist advocates and the general public castigated the Irish state as cruel and backward.[129] Public discourse suggested that Ireland was regressing into the company of non-European states. An *Irish Times* editorial stated: "What has been done to this Irish Republic, what sort of State has it become that in 1992, its full panoply of authority, its police, its law officers, its courts are mobilised to condemn a fourteen-year-old child to the ordeal of pregnancy and childbirth after rape . . . ? With what are we now to compare ourselves? Ceausescu's Romania? The Ayatollah's Iran? Algeria?"[130] On this view, Ireland's treatment of a child victim of rape spoiled its identity as a civilized Western state. Shame ran in two directions here— externally toward those who had "done" this to the Republic, and inwardly toward the Irish themselves who had chosen representation by an uncivilized, regressive government.

Internalized state shame can produce a crisis of national identity. Feminist ideas can find reception in such moments of crisis and revulsion. With the *X* case "it became possible for Irish feminism to occupy a prominent position, and win a degree of popular support, both in Ireland and abroad, not least due to a wave of intense media interest in what was referred to in the *Irish Independent* as the 'child rape' case."[131] If the Irish state had shown itself to be barbaric (read non-Western), feminist ideas offered a civilized rejoinder.

The civilizational overlay of state shaming should give progressives pause.[132] This overlay risks producing abortion as merely another site of competition between tradition and modernity. When advocates explicitly or implicitly frame abortion law as a choice between local and global, or traditional and modern, they may in the process undermine local sites and modes of political contestation.[133] Human rights advocates may unwittingly "strengthen the hand of self-styled 'traditionalists' who are offered a commonsense and powerful alternative to modernization for whatever politics they may espouse."[134] Groups and individuals who set themselves up as defenders of "tradition" can count abortion restrictions as yet another marker of "national identity." They can flip and embrace the shameful distinction between global and local for their own nationalist or traditionalist projects.

This is not a hypothetical concern in the abortion context. "Euroskepticism" in Ireland has often been forged and articulated in terms of protecting Irish sovereignty over its military neutrality and restrictive abortion laws.[135] Transnational anti-abortion advocates have likewise identified Latin American countries with restrictive abortion laws as "following their historic tradition" of protecting the right to life.[136] Like many other advocacy techniques, shame can be internalized and redeployed for radically different political projects. Shame may hold progressive transformative potential, but advocates should acknowledge and weigh the darker undersides that stem from its powerful mobilization of affect and use of status as a normative condition.

Conclusion

Reproductive rights advocates have achieved landmark legal successes in this recent body of international abortion rights litigation. In each case from Latin America, international human rights bodies found in favor of the petitioners. Perhaps most importantly, these high-profile cases have sparked significant local debates about abortion law and policy.

Narratives of innocent suffering are powerful vehicles for reproductive rights advocates. By narrating the pain of abortion denied for young women who have been raped and their families, abortion rights advocates foreground an innocent subject, for whom publics and lawmakers should be concerned. Images of family harmony further underscore youthful innocence in these cases. Mother-child unity also counters conservative depictions of adolescents seeking abortion as necessarily at odds with their parents. Reproductive rights advocates are able to readily mobilize the power of shame against obstructive states precisely because of these sympathetic narrative elements.

However, these victories may engender troubling closures, erasures, and concessions. Reproductive rights advocates mobilize the cultural and legal power of the family in these cases to advance a progressive agenda. However, re-enchanting family privacy carries a real risk of legal boomerang insofar as parents of all political stripes may gain greater procedural rights concerning their minor daughter's pregnancy. By deploying tropes of youthful suffering and vulnerability, reproductive rights advocates may also reinforce protectionist discourses readily used for more restrictive ends. Anti-abortion groups regularly defend restrictions on minors' access to reproductive health services and information as necessary to protect young women from sexual exploitation and risky behavior. With the global spread of women-protective anti-abortion arguments, progressives should exercise caution in tying abortion rights tightly to discourses of pain and protection.

Reproductive rights advocates face the difficult but necessary challenge of engaging the politics of abortion in its range of exceptional and quotidian forms. Whether advocates believe they can translate everyday abortion stories into viable international litigation cases remains to be seen. At the least, I urge advocates to reckon with how narratives of innocent suffering, while contributing to short-term victories, redistribute power over abortion and sexual decision-making in ways that may produce troubling long-term consequences.

Chapter 15

Narratives of Prenatal Personhood in Abortion Law

Alejandro Madrazo

In August 2008 a majority of the Mexican Supreme Court declared the decriminalization of abortion constitutional.[1] By December, state legislatures throughout the country had adopted constitutional amendments to extend personhood to prenatal life, granting it the constitutional protection of fundamental rights, including the right to life.

The story began in the spring of 2007 when Mexico City's local congress redefined the crime of abortion to exclude pregnancy termination in the first trimester. Accompanying health law regulations required that these services be provided on request and free of charge throughout the city's public hospitals and clinics. The reforms sought to create an institutional framework to protect women from the risks of clandestine abortion, and to support women in the exercise of their constitutional right to choose.

Both the federal government and the National Human Rights Commission challenged the decriminalization as a violation of the constitutional right to life of unborn persons. In 2002, a majority of the Court had established this constitutional right in a nonbinding precedent.[2] By 2008, the Court, in obiter dicta, overturned this precedent. There was no such thing as a prenatal right to life.

While the ruling ultimately turned on the absence of any explicit mandate in the text of the Constitution obligating the state to criminalize abortion,[3] it was widely understood—and reported in the media—that abortion had been deemed constitutional *because* the right to life had been denied to prenatal life. The ruling triggered an intense lobbying campaign by pro-life advocates and Church officials. By the end of 2008, sixteen of thirty-one state constitutions were amended to establish prenatal personhood.[4] These amendments varied in normative structure and drafting, but their central thrust was clear enough: to explicitly establish prenatal protection by recognizing a right to life from conception. Because only persons can be rights holders, these reforms—explicitly[5] or implicitly[6]—attributed personhood to prenatal life.

The legal *status* of something can be as varied as legal imagination allows: prenatal life has been explicitly labeled, among other ways, as a person,[7] a state interest,[8] a constitutionally protected good (*bien*),[9] a value,[10] nonliving tissue.[11] The manifest purpose of these "prenatal-personhood" amendments was to preempt decriminalization of abortion at the state level and to "bulletproof" criminal statutes against future liberalization efforts. This collection of constitutional amendments is thus often explained as a "backlash" to the Court's 2008 decision. While the decision may have *triggered* the wave of local amendments, prior judicial decisions elsewhere, the velocity and scope of this backlash, and similar attempts in other countries to introduce constitutional personhood amendments all point to a phenomenon broader than Mexican judicial politics.

The question of prenatal personhood has long been present in abortion law, but these and other recent legislative initiatives and judicial decisions seem to tell us that it will increasingly become a key battleground in abortion law. In this chapter, I want to address the ramifications of granting the status of a person to prenatal life as explored primarily through recent developments in countries across the Americas. My questions are: What are the consequences when prenatal life, in its different stages, is deemed a "person" for legal purposes? And what are the consequences when it is denied that status? I take a right to imply a titleholder that, in legal terms, can only be a person. Accordingly, throughout the chapter, I treat the question of prenatal personhood and a prenatal right to life as mutually implied.

Prenatal Personhood: Importance and Recurrence in Abortion Law

A historical perspective—even a short one—tells us that the status of prenatal life has been an ongoing topic in contemporary abortion debates. As we shall see, it was central in *Roe v. Wade*, it was the object of heated debate in the drafting of the Pact of San José, and it has proven determinant in foreclosing the Inter-American Human Rights system as a vehicle to reverse the trend of abortion liberalization at the national level.

In 1973, in *Roe v. Wade*, the U.S. Supreme Court addressed the question of whether "the fetus is a 'person' under the Fourteenth Amendment, which prohibits the state from depriving any person of life without due process of law."[12] The question is not minor. Rather the Court reasoned that if "person-hood is established, the appellant's case [in favor of a woman's right to choose], of course, collapses, for the fetus's right to life would then be guaranteed specifically by the Amendment."[13] For the U.S. Court, prenatal personhood is an all-or-nothing question, and determinative of all other questions regarding abortion. Because *Roe* answered the question of prenatal personhood in the negative, abortion became a question of interpreting the constitutional rights of women, against the policy interests of the state. The abortion controversy was played out between these two actors—the woman and the state (and to some degree doctors). Had the Court answered the question differently, the matter would have been cast as a tension between the fundamental rights of women and of prenatal persons, which the Court suggested would not have allowed for any "indulge[nce] in statutory interpretation favorable to abortion in specific circumstances."[14]

The Court, however, did not. It stated unequivocally that "the word 'person', as used in the Fourteenth Amendment, does not include the unborn . . . ; the unborn have never been recognized in the law as persons in the whole sense."[15] If the *Roe* Court presumed to have settled the question of the status of prenatal life, it was wrong. If we look closely, *Gonzales v. Carhart*,[16] decided thirty-four years later, is driven by the same question. The Court held a statute banning some forms of late-term abortion constitutional because it took the statute to protect not what prenatal life is during late term pregnancy (a fetus), but what it *seems* to be (a person). By finding abortion lawfully subject to prohibition not because it *is* abortion but because it *seems* to be infanticide (the murder of an infant), *Gonzales* is a step in the direction of reopening the question of the status of the fetus in U.S. abortion law.

Other events illustrate the importance for the pro-life camp of unsettling *Roe*'s answer. As early as 1977, pro-life groups in the United States sought to reverse *Roe*'s position on prenatal life by turning to the Inter-American Human Rights system in what is known as the *Baby Boy* case.[17] They unsuccessfully petitioned the Inter-American Human Rights Commission to consider legal abortion as a violation of the human right to life of the unborn. The claim was based on the language of the American Convention on Human Rights, which states, "Every person has the right to have his life respected. This right shall be protected by law, in general, from the moment of conception."[18] The Commission rejected the claim, concluding that the States Parties to the convention had consciously rejected language requiring an interpretation of the right to life (and thus personhood) that would outlaw abortion.

More recently, however, the turn toward state legislative and ballot initiatives in the United States has revived the question of the status of prenatal life. Since 2007, at least nineteen states have seen initiatives or attempts to initiate constitutional amendments attributing personhood to prenatal life.[19] In Colorado (2010) and Mississippi (2011) amendment proposals were submitted to voters, and both failed. In Oklahoma, pro-choice advocates challenged a similar initiative before the state Supreme Court and stopped it under *Casey*.[20] In North Dakota a similar initiative found its way to the ballot and will be submitted in 2014. All this suggests that a broad and ambitious strategy to attribute personhood to the fetus via legislative change is at work in a country that allegedly settled the question of prenatal personhood in 1973.

Law and Narrative

Most often, the question of prenatal personhood has been addressed as a narrow question of law: is prenatal life to be considered a "person" under the equal protection clause of the U.S. Constitution?[21] Is a fertilized egg a person and thus entitled to the right to life?[22] Can states enlarge the scope of what a person is for purposes of constitutional rights?[23] But the novel salience of the question of prenatal personhood also suggests that, in order to fully understand it and its implications for broader debates on reproductive rights, we need to rethink our approach to the question. The recent visibility of the question stems from a different and broader function that prenatal personhood plays in debates over abortion law. Prenatal personhood is both important and persistent because of its role in determining the narratives through which debates over abortion are deployed.

Robert Cover most famously articulated the relationship between law and the narrative that locates it and gives it meaning: "law and narrative are inseparably related. Every prescription is insistent in its demand to be located in discourse—to be supplied with history and destiny, beginning and end, explanation and purpose."[24] Cover distinguished the "narrow kind of problem" commonly faced in interpreting laws from the "broader" issues at stake in legal interpretation. The narrow questions address matters such as the proper classification to determine the "correct" normative consequences in a specific case; the "broader" interpretations involve "a complex normative world" that includes a body of law, "but also a language and a mythos" that allow us to both give meaning to the problems at hand and imagine different— alternate—outcomes to the present situation.

The difference between Cover's "narrow" and "broader" problems of interpretation is crucial in understanding the difference between the way prenatal personhood has been most often addressed, and the role it actually plays, in abortion debates. The status of prenatal life is usually employed to determine what technical meaning should be given to some rule. For instance, when a legal text states that life begins from conception, (relatively) narrow technical legal questions arise: does this mean that the fetus has rights and that these extend some protection to the pregnant woman carrying it?[25] If personhood is attributed to a zygote, are forms of contraception that act to stop implantation murder?[26] More prosaically, does this mean that a pregnant woman can use the car-pool lane when driving?[27] The status of prenatal life is relevant and problematic when facing these "narrow" problems, and these narrow problems are not minor. But the strategic importance of prenatal life lies in its role in determining the "broader" interpretative problems that abortion law involves: the construction of a narrative that informs the understanding of the problem at hand and its normative thrust. The status of prenatal life addresses directly *who* is affected and *in what ways* by abortion and abortion law. It speaks to the core of what is at stake and who has a stake. The status of prenatal life plays a role in shaping our fundamental legal understanding of abortion, by informing the narratives through which we understand the debates, and so it is of the utmost importance, strategically. The status of prenatal life determines the protagonist of these narratives and, in doing so, the situation, the conflict, the acceptable resolutions, and, importantly, the antagonist. In short, all of the building blocks of a narrative.

Applying or denying the label of "person" prenatally is politically fraught for both sides. For those supporting liberalization of abortion, it is indelicate to say that prenatal life is not a person.[28] The word "person" is, in common—as opposed to technical legal—language, taken as synonymous with "human being," and common ideas regarding pregnancy involve a happy couple already developing a relationship with their "baby." It is an uncomfortable question for the pro-life camp too, because the technical legal meaning of "person" has many implications, which are not easy to accept or make sense of legally in reference to prenatal life. For instance, if the fetus is a person, what criteria will be employed to determine his/her nationality: where he/she is conceived or where he/she is born?

Reference to prenatal personhood succeeds by blurring the differences between prenatal life and individuals. Prenatal life becomes a subject of law, as opposed to an object of regulation. The Costa Rican Court held that "if we have admitted that the embryo is a subject of law and not a mere object, then it must be protected equally as other human beings."[29] Similarly, in a 2006 Argentinian decision, a Justice commented that "life should be recognized to the child that is about to be born, to the one born, to the young man, the old man, the crazy man, the crippled man and generally to all human beings."[30] The result is that any and all stages of prenatal life is rendered the functional equivalent of a "baby," with all the rhetorical implications of the word.

If the fetus is a person, he relates to the pregnant woman as her baby, defenseless and endearing as are all children, and she comes into the narrative as his mother. Frequently we find the text of the law explicitly referring to the woman whose abortion is procured as a "mother," not a "person" or even a "woman."[31] Such stereotyping has serious implications for issues of representation. Prenatal personhood proponents provide different answers to the question of who can speak for the "baby"—the state, a doctor, the "father"— but they always assume that *whoever* it is, it cannot be the "mother." Why is this so? It is not because abortion cannot conceivably be the worst possible fate: the law—even in jurisdictions that explicitly speak of prenatal personhood—frequently indicates cases when abortion is permissible. Rather, it is because, under the narrative that stems from prenatal personhood, the "mother" in an abortion is defined by the betrayal of her proper role: that of protecting her "child." She is disqualified as a "mother" to make decisions concerning her "child." Abortion can thus only be allowed by a third party: the state, through law, for instance; or the doctor, through expert opinion.

This is not because there is a good reason to think a third party understands the consequences of the decision better, but because it is presumed that *her* decision *should* conform to a specific stereotype. If a woman deems, for instance, that it is in the best interest of the unborn "person" not to be born into a life of extreme poverty or likely abuse, her judgment is a priori discarded; whereas if that same woman should judge that withdrawing her child from having contact with formal schooling or the outside world, her decision is a priori protected. Prenatal personhood casts the woman in a very specific role and thus sets up the range of expectations for her (no longer as pregnant woman, but as mother). If she decides not to fulfill the role, she is deemed unfit to decide.

Both the stereotyping of women and the blurring of distinctions between prenatal life and individuals is best illustrated—to the point of caricature—by the intervention of Justice Pettigiani in the 2006 Argentinian decision referenced above.[32] The Court considered whether a an eighteen-year-old woman with a mental age equivalent to an eight-year-old could lawfully interrupt a pregnancy resulting from rape. The circumstances surrounding the woman could hardly have been more dramatic and could hardly draw more attention to her context and plight. Justice Pettigiani, however, provides us with a lengthy argument in which he claims that the fetus's due process rights were violated in the Court's deliberation for it was not being heard in trial. In his opinion, the pregnant woman having been interviewed, the fetus had a lawful right, in equality, to have been heard by the Court. He argued that an ultrasound should be performed for the benefit of the Court: "The purpose sought with this was that, prior to ruling, the justices . . . could get to know and come into contact with the little body and the person of the nasciturus [unborn] . . . it would have been possible to make effective the right also held by the nasciturus according to Argentinian law: the right that the child be heard whichever way he may manifest himself."[33] As for the pregnant woman, Justice Pettigiani remarked only that despite her incapacity to care for herself, she could still "offer (...) affection to her child and find (...) in maternity a motivation."[34]

In short, prenatal personhood enables and demands an oversimplified narrative in which the differences between the stages of prenatal life, and of prenatal life and individuals, are blurred; and in which women are pushed to the background and stereotyped and reduced to "mothers." Using the concept of person to refer to prenatal life allows the embryo, zygote, or fetus to be fully equated with an individual already born. This is possible because the concept of person is not addressed in its formal legal dimensions, thereby avoiding most of the legal consequences of personhood—such as having legal obligations like carrying a passport for foreign travel, having a specific status such as nationality,[35] having privileges such as being considered for eligibility to use a car-pool lane,[36] or being liable for damages involuntarily imposed on another (for instance, on a woman's health).

For the pro-life use of prenatal personhood to be successful, prenatal personhood must be kept relatively unarticulated so as to maintain its rhetorical and normative thrust. That is why the use of the label of "person" regarding a fetus is typically not followed by a serious engagement of the legal-technical implications of such use outside context of an abortion (or birth control). Proponents shy away from exploring all other situations or issues where equating the fetus with a person would be relevant, because these circumstances require much more concreteness to imagine and engaging them underscores the many aspects in which a zygote, an embryo, or a fetus cannot be treated as a person. In other words, maybe the *only* aspect in which prenatal life and individuals are comparable, is that they are both alive; but that aspect is shared too, with plants, animals, and bacteria. As long as *only* abortion—or situations that only require an alive/not-alive dichotomy—are used as alternative to the fact of a woman going through an unwanted pregnancy, the equation has rhetorical and normative teeth. Asking the concrete questions that highlight the incapacity of prenatal personhood to function elsewhere in law causes the narrative to breaks down.

But what is the importance of choosing one or another broad narrative structure? The narrative—and the underlying position regarding the status of prenatal life—is quite important, but we need to understand *how* it is important. In the following two sections, we will look at what I consider to be two key consequences that derive from the divergent narratives that stem from attributing or denying personhood to prenatal life: first, the functions that prenatal personhood plays in determining the relationships in the narrative; and second, the type of legal reasoning that will be brought to bear on the matter.

Prenatal Personhood

By being proclaimed a person, prenatal life becomes the protagonist of the narrative. This has two central consequences: separation and hierarchy. Prenatal personhood creates a character within the woman's body and thus separates the woman from "the product of conception." While the product remains, in fact, dependent on the woman and, at least for a considerable period, undistinguishable from her in any relevant way, in the imagination, they come to be seen as two different characters in the narrative, with divergent, conflicting interests. Legally, the undistinguishable nature of the zygote or embryo is rendered a circumstantial condition of what are imagined as discrete, discernible, and equivalent entities. The Mexican dissent of 2008 expresses clearly the unimportance of the stages of development: they are merely temporary, accidental conditions, which do not affect the essential equivalence of all life: "an embryo of twelve weeks, one of twenty four or one of thirty six or a baby of a year are different in the same way that a person of twelve years, one of twenty four, one of thirty six and one of seventy. The distinction lies only on the stage of development, in their age, not their nature."[37]

Since prenatal life is imagined as an entity of its own with its own interests, it implies also a separation of the woman from her pregnancy. The pregnancy is no longer a condition in which the woman finds herself, but a process that the fetus is undergoing. The woman's role is, at best, that of "mother"; at worst, it is that of a location—a womb. Whoever has a claim to speak in the name of the zygote/son's interests, has a claim on the woman/mother's body. Pregnancy and body become territories in dispute.

The separation also establishes a hierarchy of value between the prenatal "person" and the "mother," and simultaneously a decision-making hierarchy between the representative of the prenatal "person" and the woman. Proclaiming prenatal personhood and thus establishing prenatal life as protagonist of the narrative necessarily focuses the attention of the debate on the act of abortion itself. This draws attention away from circumstances leading to abortion or the consequences of carrying it out (or not). The key questions become when, and under what circumstances, is an act (murder/abortion) so relevant to the protagonist that it is to be allowed, and why. The complex circumstances leading to or stemming from the decision pale before the enormity of the direct result of the event: death of the protagonist. All other parties—the woman, the state, the doctor, the man—have *something* at stake in the event, but the protagonist—that is, a "baby"—has *everything* at stake in the event.

What is more, from the perspective of both the pregnancy and the abortion, the woman's role is reduced—she just happens to be the location where pregnancy takes place. Her decision regarding abortion is something she decides to inflict on someone else, not a decision regarding her own body and her own life. Thus, her entitlement to decide on the pregnancy is not only questioned but, at best, put on equal footing as that of her male counterpart in conception,[38] or subject to the approval of doctors, or of the state, as in *Gonzales*. In this context, because the third party—usually the state—representing the fetus's interest can impose a decision on the woman, then her decision is trumped, and she is subordinated to another's decision. The extreme version of this is illustrated by reckless endangerment charges brought against pregnant women or mothers. For instance, a decision as personal as choosing vaginal birth over cesarean has been cast as medical neglect, resulting in withdrawal of child custody.[39] Or else, unintentional, non-negligent conduct resulting in abortion is not everywhere accepted as an exception to the criminalization of abortion.[40] In the end, prenatal personhood is a legal stand-in for the interests of whomever is empowered to decide over a woman's reproduction. It is a legal vehicle for hijacking a woman's body, without taking responsibility for the hijacking but rather attributing it to some other "person"; one whose motives and interests will not be questioned because they are simultaneously nonexistent and presupposed.

Because of its impact on narrative, the status of prenatal life also plays a part in determining which area of law—or, more precisely, which modality of legal reasoning—is brought to bear on the question of abortion. If the abortion is a direct threat to the protagonist, then those procuring the abortion, accordingly, are cast as antagonists. When prenatal life is deemed a person, then the meaning of abortion itself is understood as death; and so procured abortion is akin to murder. Women, then, are not only antagonists but also criminals. The Costa Rican Court, which reasons from the premise that a fertilized egg is a person, illustrates the potential for equating abortion to murder by equating prenatal life to persons. In deciding two cases of medical malpractice resulting in fetal death, the Court understood the doctor's fault as a form of manslaughter. Illustratively, the Court found it necessary to explain in detail the differences between homicide and abortion—as two specific crimes—suggesting that the default position is to equate them.[41]

Good examples of both the relative *lack* of importance given to women and their default casting as antagonists come from Mexico. The majority opinion of the Mexican Supreme Court's 2002 decision illustrates this point. A claim had been brought against a legislative reform, known as the *Ley Robles,* liberalizing abortion through an indications model in cases of fetal malformation, artificial insemination without consent, and risk to a woman's health.[42] The plaintiffs argued, among other things, that the reform violated the unborn's right to life. Having spent nearly seventy paragraphs of the opinion's text (almost all of what was not dedicated to procedural questions) in establishing the existence of the right to life in the Constitution—which had no textual grounding back then—and the constitutional protection of the fetus, the Court spends only one paragraph, near the end, considering the woman's plight, and then only in cases of severe fetal malformation. It portrays her as having to choose between two alternatives: "the heroic one of accepting to continue with the pregnancy and that of accepting the interruption of it, with the consequence of it being a crime."[43] What little attention is given to the woman and her circumstances focus on the alternative between being a hero or being a criminal.

In the end, the Mexican Court in 2002 found the reforms constitutional, but it did so for counterintuitive reasons. To the Court, the reforms are constitutional *because* they leave the criminal nature of abortion untouched:

> [The reform liberalizing abortion in certain cases] is not an exception to . . . the crime of abortion, for it does not establish that given the situations there pointed out, it should be understood that the crime of abortion was not committed; it merely states that in such cases no sanction will be applied (. . .) the exceptions, properly understood, do not relieve the active subject [i.e. the woman] from her responsibility in the perpetration of a crime, they only determine they are not subject to punishment.[44]

In other words, starting from the assertion of prenatal personhood, the liberalization of abortion is constitutional *because* abortion remains a crime, and women engaging in abortion retain their casting as criminals; had the language of the reform differed,[45] the ruling would have been adverse. Not everybody can be a hero, and so allowing women who have abortions to escape prison is acceptable, as long as they are still labeled criminals.

When criminal law is presumed to be the proper legal tool for dealing with abortion, the question is framed in terms of what exceptions justify *not* using criminal punishment. Criminal punishment becomes the expected legal tool to address abortion, and that presumption is difficult to defeat. Because people assume that murder, if anything, should be criminally punished, the question of decriminalization of abortion itself seems out of place. In the case of abortion, the woman bears the burden of not only of being the antagonist, but also of being an antagonist in spite of the gender role expected of her: that of the mother.[46] So when the fetus is deemed a person, the motives a woman has for terminating a pregnancy will be judged as those of a *mother* intending to end her *son*'s life. A more noxious villain is hard to cast; and a harder position from which to gain sympathy is difficult to find. So when the question of what *exceptions* are admissible to the rule proscribing abortion comes up, the room for leniency will be narrow. Even though there is no *logical* need to criminalize any conduct unless explicitly stated in a Constitution (especially since criminal law is, in theory, to be used only as a last resort measure),[47] *narratively* it is hard to accept that abortion-turned-murder is not to be criminally punished.

Justice Azuela, in his concurring opinion to the Mexican decision of 2002, illustrates this presumption. In responding to Justice Gudiño's argument holding that decriminalization—that is, incrementing the number of indications in an indications model—is constitutional because there is no constitutional obligation to criminalize abortion, he held:

> The argument seems to me unacceptable, for the Constitution establishes fundamental rights that the constituted bodies of government must preserve, which means that if, in order to do so, it is indispensable to establish criminal rules that define certain conducts as crimes, as well as the need to punish them, then not having such a legislation or including in it rules that would give way to hindering the rights protected by the Constitution, would translate into a violation of the Constitution itself.[48]

The successor case of 2008, when Gudiño's concurring argument of 2002 became the Court's opinion, also illustrates the point. The Court held there is no obligation to criminalize unless it is explicitly mandated in the constitutional text. This ruling did not require denying personhood to prenatal life, yet the Court took care to revert the 2002 precedent affirming fetal personhood. Strictly speaking, the reversal was obiter dicta, but the fact that the majority took pains to make the reversal illustrates the strategic importance of denying prenatal personhood for narratively enabling solutions that do not require criminal law. It illustrates, in this sense, the importance of the narrative—as opposed to the technical legal—dimension of the question of prenatal life. Logically, decriminalization is a legal possibility regardless of the status of what is protected by criminal law, be it a person, a value, or a state interest. Narratively, however, it is much more difficult to hold that the intentional and nonconsensual procurement of death to a person should not be dealt with through the criminal law than it is to hold that a state interest need not be protected specifically through criminal law. As Cover pointed out to us, narrative is at least as important as logic in law.

This does not mean, however, that prenatal personhood precludes any and all exceptions to criminal punishment. Criminal law always admits exceptions to punishment, and so prenatal status seldom translates into an absolute ban on abortion under any and all circumstances. Self-defense is a common exception to criminalization of homicide in general. Others include the doctrine of necessity, need,[49] fulfillment of duty,[50] or impossibility of reasonably expecting a different conduct.[51] Because of the narrative structure that unfolds from affirming prenatal personhood, exceptions are more difficult to accept than in other crimes because, under this framing, abortion is about the very worst type of crime imaginable: murder perpetrated by those primarily charged with the care of a victim as innocent as imaginable. This requires that there be values or goods of considerable weight—of equal or more weight than the life of a (defenseless) "person"—to trump the impulse to turn to criminal punishment; or else it must be deemed that any other conduct, other the termination of the pregnancy, cannot be demanded of the woman, even though there is no equal or more valuable good at stake.

The doctrine of necessity, for example, will tend to allow abortion only when the life of the pregnant woman is at risk. The Irish Court, for instance, states that fetal personhood means that abortion should always be punished "except were there was a real and substantial risk to the life of the mother which could only be avoided by the termination of the pregnancy."[52] The admissibility of abortion in these cases is the result of squarely applying the logic of criminal law: the sacrifice of a value or good protected under criminal law can be admissible only if harming it is the last resort to avoid harming an equal or more valued good.[53] Importantly, even in these exceptional cases, there is still a normative pull toward carrying the pregnancy to term: a woman might not be *forced* to carry a pregnancy to term, but she can be *expected* to do so and *admired* if she does.

Personhood Denied

Now the question needs to be recast in the opposite direction: what narratives are enabled when prenatal personhood is denied? If prenatal life is not a person, then it cannot be a protagonist of the narrative. This doesn't mean that the focus of the narrative shifts automatically to the woman and makes her the protagonist. Even when prenatal life is not deemed a person, it is not infrequent to find that the pregnant woman remains in the background and the spotlight is occupied by some other actor, frequently an authority, be it government or doctors. *Roe* gave a prominent role to doctors; in *Gonzáles v. Carhart*, the state's wishes regarding prenatal life prevails; and Mexico's 2008 decision is focused predominantly on a state actor—Mexico City's local congress and its constitutional powers.

Denial of prenatal personhood does mean, however, that it is easier to engage the woman, her rights and plight, and even allow some room for sympathy. Suppressing prenatal life as protagonist frees women from being cast as the antagonist in the narrative. She can be a protagonist herself—facing a difficult choice, or exercising a right; she can be a marginal player (i.e. not antagonistic) in a policy decision by the state seeking to reduce maternal mortality or enhance fetal protection.[54] Mexico's 2008 decision, for example, follows the health policy track:

> The general justification for the measure resulting from the democratic exercise undertaken by [Mexico City's Legislative Assembly], which resulted in the decriminalization of a conduct, was to end a public health problem derived from the practice of clandestine abortions, assuming that the decriminalization of abortion will allow women to voluntarily interrupt their pregnancy in conditions of hygiene and security.[55]

Thus, the most important consequences of denying prenatal personhood is not that the woman, her rights and plight, *will* now be the focus, but rather that the fetus *no longer needs to be the protagonist* and that *the woman who seeks an abortion is no longer cast as an antagonist*. Denying prenatal personhood also drains dramatic tension away from the act of abortion, for it is no longer a situation in which the very existence of the protagonist of the narrative is at stake. The world no longer hinges on the abortion. This allows room to engage in more complex discussions regarding the context surrounding the act of abortion, and to see beyond abortion itself. It also allows for a more nuanced regulation of abortion, in which different degrees of protection to life fit more comfortably.

Narratively, when prenatal personhood is denied, criminal law is not as easily accepted as the default legal framework. Constitutional law and the kinds arguments that are usually deployed there play a more important role. Balancing rights and interests and considering the complexity of means-to-ends rationality become more attractive options. For instance, the 2008 Mexican Court decision used the language of means-to-ends rationality, arguing that the first trimester time limit on decriminalization was acceptable because it is "the most secure and recommended in medical terms."[56]

But this does not mean that it is *necessary* to deny personhood in order to admit the possibility of moving away from criminal law. Argentinian Justice Kogan, in a debate where prenatal personhood was never questioned, states: "if an act is prohibited by the Constitution, that does not necessarily mean that it must be a crime and . . . abortion can or cannot be defined as a crime."[57] But, I posit, denying prenatal personhood allows more leeway for disengaging from criminal law.

I believe it is not a coincidence that the four decisions in the Americas, which consciously opened broad processes of liberalization of abortion, carefully explained why personhood begins at birth.[58] Just as *Roe* gave detailed reasons for denying prenatal personhood, similar explanations were made by the Canadian Supreme Court, the Colombian Constitutional Tribunal, and Mexican Supreme Court.[59] The Mexican Supreme Court decision of 2008 upheld the constitutionality of legislative decriminalization of abortion on the grounds that there was no constitutional obligation to criminalize abortion. Before doing so, however, it was careful to reverse the 2002 (nonbinding) precedent that affirmed prenatal personhood. The Court explicitly made the point that, even if there was a fundamental right to life in favor of the fetus that did not preclude decriminalization: "the mere existence of a fundamental right does not imply the obligation to criminalize the conduct that offends it."[60] But only after denying prenatal personhood did the Court proceed to inquire whether decriminalization was constitutional, even though to respond to this, the denial of prenatal personhood was not technically necessary. I believe the Court needed the narrative space to disengage from the equation of abortion to murder to make its holding more palatable to the public (and to itself).

Although it is not the most aggressive of the liberalizing decisions in the region, the Colombian Constitutional Court's opinion[61] best illustrates the strategic importance—and use—of denying prenatal personhood to advance women's reproductive rights. The Court carefully tailored its decision so as to not provide the status of person to prenatal life. The Court begins by distinguishing "between life as a constitutionally protected good and the right to life as a subjective right of fundamental character."[62] So the *right* to life is held only by the born, whereas the "protected good" of life covers prenatal life because it is *a potential* being. This allows the Court to start off its discussion of the *constitutional* questions at hand by focusing on the woman. In a section titled "Abortion policy only includes fundamental rights of women as the questions to consider in recent decades," the Court undertakes a historic review of the framing of abortion regulation and concludes, "now, with the arrival of the social and democratic rule of law, the fundamental rights of the true protagonist are taken as the criteria for evaluating [abortion law]: the woman's."[63] For the Colombian Court, denying prenatal personhood does not preclude the use or consideration of criminal law. It can still play an important role, but it now has to be *reintroduced* as a possibility, not presumed to be the default normative framework. We see a similar move in *Roe* when the U.S. Court claims that *even though* the fetus is not a person, but only the potential of life, the state *can* regulate abortion to protect the potential life: "In assessing the State's interest, recognition may be given to the less rigid claim that as long as at least *potential* life is involved, the State may assert interests beyond the protection of the pregnant woman alone."[64] Criminal law is now naturally subject to reasonableness analysis, and so are liberalizing measures.

The logic of constitutional law can play a more important role and this allows for a richer, more contextual consideration of abortion. The dominance of the logic of constitutional law over criminal law is probably best illustrated in the closing passages of the Mexican Court's 2008 decision:

This Tribunal considers that "the measure employed by the Legislature is ideal for safeguarding the rights of women, because the non-criminalization of the interruption of pregnancy translates in the freedom of women to decide over their body, their physical and mental health and, even, their life, for we cannot disregard that today, [as the legislature of Mexico City clearly states . . .], there is maternal mortality. . . .

The criminal reproach, that is, the imposition of punishment in such a case, is not useful in insuring the proper development of the process of gestation, for our social reality is different and, in opposition, it undermines and affirms discrimination against women. Therefore, it cannot be said that the threat of criminal sanction is the first and only solution to the eradication of the practice of clandestine voluntary interruptions of pregnancy, for going beyond the theory we use to justify the imposition of sanctions by the state, the sanction cannot ignore rationality and necessity for, quite the contrary, we would be allowing for the introduction of a criminal justice system that uses vengeance as the foundation for sanction.[65]

In other words, decriminalization is a reasonable policy for enhancing women's rights, while criminalization is not a reasonable measure for protecting prenatal life. Balancing rights and policies, evaluating means-to-ends adequacy of using criminal law as a policy tool: this is first and foremost the logic of constitutional review at play, not the judicial application of criminal law. Moreover, criminal law is here a *tool* subject to evaluation under the parameters of constitutional law; it is no longer the framing normative universe to be deployed.

It is important here to take a moment to distinguish the constitutional exercise of balancing rights and values from the criminal law evaluation of whether an "equal or greater" good was preserved by infringing the general ban on abortion. Both compare two (or more) things; yet the "equal or greater" test is usually geared as an abstract contrast—that is, life versus life; life versus health; life versus life project—whereas balancing under constitutional adjudication orients the discussion to be as concrete as possible, for all fundamental rights are a priori equal, and adjudication must be done case by case. Also, criminal law "protected-value" comparisons to determine "equal or greater" tend to demand a binary response: either A is equal to or greater than B and thus trumps it, or not. In contrast, constitutional balancing exercises seek and carve out multiple possibilities through which to accommodate the two values in tension. It allows a graduated, as opposed to binary, solution. Again, these are not logical necessities, but common rhetorical and argumentative resources that tend to be used in criminal law or constitutional law.

In short, denying prenatal personhood allows for a less rigid narrative. It is not about a "mother" "killing" "her" "baby," but a complex problem in which different values and different actors are pulled in multiple directions. Accordingly, the logic of criminal law in which exceptions are to be carved out from a default impulse to criminalize is displaced by the logic of constitutional law in which criminal law can be assessed as a policy based on both its results and its positive or negative impact on fundamental rights, particularly women's sexual and reproductive rights.

Conclusions

I want to conclude this chapter with three warnings, which I will illustrate with specific cases. First, I want to warn that the status of prenatal life is likely to remain contested turf. Second, I want to insist that the affirmation of prenatal personhood is often not something that is taken seriously by its proponents; rather it is a vehicle for justifying restrictions on women's sexual and reproductive rights and, more specifically, for trumping the right to choose. Last, I want to make the point that leaving such a fundamental question unattended represents important risks, for, when taken seriously and deployed in a principled—as opposed to a strategic—way, the affirmation of prenatal personhood can have catastrophic consequences for women's rights in general, and their sexual and reproductive rights in particular, beyond abortion.

Roe illustrates the persistence of the question of the status of the fetus *in spite* of clear-cut answers in law. *Roe* discarded the argument that the fetus should be deemed a person under constitutional protection based on both textual arguments and historical review. Since, in the United States, judicial debates over abortion have been framed accepting *Roe*'s choice, what is at stake in abortion regulation are, on the one hand, women's constitutional rights, and on the other, a *state* interest in protecting prenatal life. Of course, the issue of abortion has not remained unmoved since *Roe*, but the basic decision regarding the question of the status of prenatal life remains. In spite of all, the legal status of prenatal life has come to be unsettled again in the domestic law of the United States through both legislative and ballot initiatives attempting to explicitly consecrate prenatal personhood in law.

The Irish case exposes the strategic—as opposed to principled—function of the affirmation of prenatal life in pro-life advocacy. An immigrant woman from Nigeria petitioned suspension of her deportation process because being in Nigeria involved higher risks during pregnancy, during childbirth, and after and thus affected her unborn child's right to life.[66] The Court's response illustrates how prenatal personhood is often strategic rather than principled: "The passage from Article 40.3.3° on which counsel relied, as explained by the judgments of the majority in this Court in *Attorney General v. X* [1992] 1 IR 1, was intended to prevent the legalization of abortion either by legislation or judicial decision within the State."[67]

The Court denied the petition to trump deportation on the grounds of a fetus's right of life by explicitly stating that the law establishing prenatal personhood was specifically tailored to ensure against the liberalization of abortion, not to actually protect prenatal life from risks other than abortion. The case illustrates how prenatal personhood functions as a vehicle for restricting reproductive liberty, not really as grounds for actually protecting prenatal life. Of course, the hypocrisy so cynically flaunted by the Irish Court is not necessarily shared by others proposing fetal personhood.

If anything, the Costa Rican Court has been sadly consistent: prenatal personhood trumps abortion, but it also trumps in vitro fertilization and turns medical negligence into manslaughter. The Costa Rican case regarding in vitro fertilization warns us about the concrete and catastrophic consequences that can follow from affirming prenatal personhood in the abstract, and—unlike the Irish Court—following through in a principled manner. In 2000, it ruled on a case in which the bylaws governing in vitro fertilization were challenged on the grounds that, as established, the procedure violated the right to life of human fertilized eggs.[68] The plaintiff argued that, in allowing up to six fertilized eggs to be implanted in the womb, the bylaws violated the right to life of the eggs that would not come to be implanted on the uterus. The Costa Rican Court, invoking article 4 of the San José Pact,[69] which speaks of the right to life from conception, agreed and consequently struck down the bylaws. The case was the direct precedent of the two manslaughter cases that we have touched on in this chapter and provide the grounds for criminalizing doctors when they are deemed to be negligent in cases of stillbirths.[70] Criminalizing assisted reproduction and the medical profession will hardly advance women's rights or reproductive health.

In fact, the aftermath of the Costa Rican in vitro fertilization case, though not engaging abortion on its face, brings home many of the points I make in this chapter. It its 2012 ruling on the matter, the Inter-American Human Rights Court deemed Costa Rica's in vitro fertilization policy resulting from it's Court's 2002 ruling a violation of several human rights of its citizens, notably reproductive autonomy. It does so after subjecting the policy to a test of proportionality.[71] In order to deploy its proportionality exercise, however, the Court held, among other things, that "it is not admissible to grant the status of person to the embryo."[72]

With astounding clarity, Judge Eduardo Vio Grossi's dissenting opinion, the only one, noted that this ruling meant that prenatal life "does not have, *per se*, the right" and that, therefore, its protection was to be "respected in relation to the pregnant woman" and thus accessory to her wishes.[73] That is, denying prenatal personhood gives the woman a more central role. Second, that this had profound implications beyond in vitro fertilization, for it is "evidently . . . related to issues such as the legal regime on abortion."[74] This, of course, illustrates that the question of prenatal personhood affects all reproductive rights, from in vitro fertilization to abortion, including birth control and contraception. Finally, Judge Grossi notes that having reproductive autonomy take the day is the result of the fact that the Court "does not compare two rights, but rather some rights with a technique." That is, that the logic used was that of constitutional balancing and not of justifying criminal exceptions. Judge Grossi is correct in his assessment of the implications of the ruling. Let us hope that its impact will reflect its implications in the future.

The affirmation of prenatal personhood inhibits women's rights, whether in law or in fact. Much hinges on the mere affirmation of prenatal personhood, even if it does not translate into a more punitive abortion regime. Justice Sanchez, from Mexico's Supreme Court, clearly identified the overarching threat that prenatal personhood represents to women, their control over their bodies, and the exercise of their rights. While debating a challenge to the state constitutional reform establishing fetal personhood from conception in the state of Baja California, she argued that deeming a fertilized egg a person would problematize the use of contraception methods that *may* have anti-implantatory effects such as certain types of emergency contraception or IUDs. If a fetus is a person, then a woman using such methods would not know whether she was exercising the fundamental right of reproductive liberty or incurring in the crime of murder. This, she argued, produced a "chilling effect" (*efecto inhibidor*) in the exercise of such rights. She argues:

> Under these conditions and under such circumstances when the sensible attitude any woman will take will be to withdraw from the possibility of being arbitrarily sanctioned by authorities as a murderer and thus avoid fully exercising her right to reproductive freedom through the use of an IUD, the incertitude is derived from the existence of the norm itself, not its application, and thus, it inhibits the exercise of a right without there being a need for the authority to apply it. That is what I mean, with this chilling effect of an undetermined norm, when the uncertain norm inhibits the exercise of a right, it makes its enjoyment null and thus cancels it.[75]

Prenatal personhood has major repercussions for women, in narrative, in law, and in practice. To say that it chills women's exercise of their sexual and reproductive rights is to put it mildly: in truth, it trumps women's power over their bodies, transferring it to some other person, who claims the woman's body for his own interests, in the name of the (unborn) son.

And with their bodies, their lives.

Chapter 16

Stigmatized Meanings of Criminal Abortion Law

Rebecca J. Cook

The meaning of induced abortion is constructed and contested, in part, through how abortion laws are framed, enforced, and interpreted. The social meaning of abortion—and by implication the meaning ascribed to women who seek abortion and those persons who provide it—is historically and culturally contingent. Social meaning provides "a way to speak of the frameworks of understanding within which individuals live; a way to describe what they take or understand various actions, or inactions, or statuses to be; and a way to understand how the understandings change."[1] It is derived from the socially perceived situation or context. The "social" in social meaning is meant "to emphasize its contingency on a particular society or group or community within which social meanings occur."[2]

When a state criminalizes induced abortion (hereinafter abortion), it is constructing its social meaning as inherently wrong and harmful to society. Through criminal prohibition, a state is signaling conditions in which abortion is criminally wrong, reflecting the historical origin of crime in sin that can and should be punished.[3] In contrast, the legal framing of abortion as a health issue constructs meanings of preservation and promotion of health. A state is signaling that abortion is a public health concern, and should be addressed as a harm reduction initiative.[4] However a state regulates abortion, it is increasingly required to ensure that its chosen approach is compliant with its obligations under constitutional[5] and human rights law.[6] Where contests emerge about constitutional and human rights compliance, they generate new meanings relating to rights to private life, to be free from inhuman and degrading treatment, and to sexual nondiscrimination.

Over time and across cultures, governments have employed the criminal law to attribute different social meanings and different degrees of wrongfulness to individual conduct, in part through determining who is punishable and the nature of the punishment. For example, in England before 1803, abortion was treated in Common law (customary law) as a misdemeanor, that is, a lesser offense. Moreover, it was a misdemeanor only for someone to cause an abortion; the woman who underwent the procedure faced no criminal sanction. After 1803, procuring a woman's abortion was legislated a felony, that is, a more serious offense. By enactments of 1837 and 1861, however, the criminal law allowed a woman who terminated her own pregnancy or who permitted another to procure her "miscarriage" to be prosecuted under a felony charge.[7]

Currently, states vary in whether and how they punish those performing abortion, women undergoing abortion, and other criminal accessories such as those supplying the means of abortion. Criminal law primarily penalizes providers of abortion. The penalties for providers range from life imprisonment to imprisonment of varying years.[8] Some criminal laws, but not all, punish women who undergo abortions, sometimes with lesser penalties if certain conditions are met, such as if they do not have "bad reputations".[9] Where pregnant women's conduct is not specifically criminalized, they might still be charged as parties to, or with conspiracy to commit, their unlawful abortion, unless legislation expressly excludes them. Some countries criminalize those who provide or sell methods for procuring abortion, including for women's self-induction.[10]

These sketches from the historical evolution of criminal abortion law and from how different jurisdictions criminalize it illustrate how law constructs *abortion* as a crime and the different meanings ascribed to it. Criminal abortion, like crime generally, is a legal and social construct.[11] It has been explained that "socially descriptive legal rules establish essences: Nature did not create felons or tortfeasors, but law nonetheless imposes on them irreducible and constitutive characteristics."[12] Criminal law gives abortion an "essence"— that it is a wrong against the individual or society. The criminal essence of abortion then implicates the social construction of those who actually and potentially seek abortion and those who provide and assist in its provision. By framing abortion as a crime, societies ascribe deviance to those seeking and providing it. They label them as an underclass of potential or actual criminals and so perpetuate prejudices against them. By criminalizing induced abortion, societies, in the words of Erving Goffman, are "spoil[ing the] social identity" of those seeking and providing abortion, which "has the "effect of cutting [them] off from society and from [themselves] so that [they stand as] discredited person[s] facing an unaccepting world."[13] The criminal prohibition of abortion contributes to exceptionalizing women seeking abortion as deviant,[14] medical providers as "abortionists,"[15] and supportive parents as "negligent" or "unfit."[16] It also places lawful abortion under a negative shadow of criminality.

The impact of criminalized abortion can be measured quantitatively by maternal mortality (death of a woman while pregnant or within 42 days of pregnancy)[17] and morbidity due to unsafe abortion,[18] but also qualitatively, such as through examining the stigmatizing harms that aborting women suffer. In order adequately to capture the injury caused by criminal abortion laws, it is important to expand beyond the bare statistics of maternal mortality and morbidity due to unsafe abortion to articulate the harms of criminalized abortion to women's worth. It is necessary to advance beyond thinking about the consequences of criminal law solely in quantitative terms in order to better understand the qualitative consequences of how criminal law constructs women as individuals and their worth in society. In short, the chapter urges moving beyond the focus on the woman as a statistic, the "statistical" woman, to understand the woman as constructed by criminal law, the "criminally constructed" woman.

The construction of abortion is iterative: societies criminalize abortion in part because of preconceptions about women, their sexuality, and prenatal life—for example, fetal personhood; and criminalization then reinforces those preconceptions. Criminal abortion laws construct an image of a socially unsuitable or socially endangering pregnant or potentially pregnant woman, thus constraining the world in which such women live. Such laws frequently attribute immorality to women seeking abortion, thus marking them as threats to their societies' values, exacerbating prejudices against them. In criminalizing abortion, the state stigmatizes women, undermining their capacities, and questions their sexuality and their social roles. The state thereby further subordinates and taints women, provokes hostility toward them, and contributes to gender-based animus.[19]

It has been explained that law affects the operation of stigma in society in three broad ways: "Law can be a means of preventing or remedying the enactment of stigma as violence, discrimination or other harm; it can be a medium through which stigma is created, enforced or disputed; and it can play a role in structuring individual resistance to stigma."[20] This chapter focuses on the first two ways in order to understand how abortion law is used to create stigma and to explore how legal reasoning can more fully acknowledge the stigmatizing effects of criminal abortion law. It poses the question: given its stigmatizing effects, how, if at all, can societies justify the criminalization of abortion?

In exploring answers to this question, the chapter begins with a sketch of the normative justifications that societies employ for criminalizing abortion. It then explores how societies use these justifications to criminalize abortion to create social meanings about women, which in turn reinforce justifications for criminalization. The chapter applies social psychology scholarship to better articulate the stigmatizing harms attributable to criminalization of abortion and the processes by which the stigma is produced, and to identify the locations in which it exists. The chapter continues by examining how the formal criminal abortion law, the informal law, and background rules stigmatize women. It then analyzes how the European Court of Human Rights in *R.R. v. Poland* might have more effectively acknowledged the stigmatizing harms resulting from the application of Poland's criminal abortion law in finding violations of R.R.'s rights to be free from inhuman and degrading treatment and to private life, and how it could have found a violation of R.R.'s entitlement to secure these rights without discrimination on grounds of sex. The chapter concludes by answering the question about whether societies can justify criminalizing abortion, given its stigmatized meanings.

Normative Justifications for Criminalizing Abortion

Theories of criminalization that explain normative justifications for criminalizing abortion vary over time and across jurisdictions. The concept of criminalization is a "hugely encompassing" social and political phenomenon,[21] and well beyond the scope of this chapter. For purposes of understanding the justifications societies use to criminalize abortion, it might be useful to think about criminalization as an outcome or prescription, since it addresses "what has been or should be criminalised." Criminalization could also be considered a social practice, since it addresses "who criminalises, or should criminalise, on what assumptions and according to what processes and principles."[22]

In considering criminalization as a prescription or as a social practice, this section sketches the justifications for criminalizing abortion, recognizing that a fuller explanation is necessary. It has been explained that there are two general theories of modern thinking of why societies criminalize certain conduct: "those that begin from questions of harm and harm reduction or prevention, and those theories, often called legal moralism, which are centered around questions of wrongdoing and retribution. The first derives from, and is animated by John Stuart Mill's famous 'harm' principle: that 'the only purpose for which power can be rightfully exercised against any member of a civilised community, against his will, is to prevent harm to others.'"[23] The justification based on harm to others originated in harm risked through injury to women themselves,[24] which developed to address harm to society itself, including by women who seek abortions.

The dominant justifications for criminalizing abortion are morally based. They are centered on religious convictions embedded in retributive punishment. The convictions are that individuals should pay tribute to God by observing His ordinances, but when they withhold tribute through commission of a sin, society must reinstate the denied tribute by punishment of the sin through the legal process of "re-tribution." Society imposes, and the sinning individual suffers, retributive punishment through the criminal law and procedure identifying and condemning the sin as criminal.

Societies have further developed the morally based justifications for criminalizing abortion through rationales relating to women, sex, and fetuses. The criminal law has shown ambivalence about women, seeing them as requiring protection against unskilled or forced abortion, but also as perpetrators of wrongs against women's proper roles as caregiving mothers in their societies. The sex-focused rationale justifying abortion punishment condemns unmarried women seeking to disguise illicit sex causing pregnancy, and married women denying their husbands their children. A related sex-focused rationale is that punishment is justifiable when individuals engage in non-procreative sex, because it is alleged such engagement is hedonistic. Fetal-focused rationales emerge from concepts of ensoulment and personification of fetuses, wrongly denied birth, baptism, and eternal life in heaven through abortion. An associated fetal-focused rationale is that the prohibition of abortion is necessary to protect the state's interest in prenatal life.[25]

Empirical evidence on the actual implementation of abortion laws contradicts many of these justifications. The prosecution rates are low relative to the high rates of termination, and the conviction rates are lower still, granting that these rates are hard to substantiate.[26] Abortion is an ancient practice and remains prevalent in many if not all societies. For example, it is reported that in one country, three in ten women will have an abortion during their reproductive lifetime.[27] Restrictive laws affect the safety but not the overall incidence of abortion.[28] Lawful abortions by qualified providers are safe, and many unlawful abortions by unskilled providers have been unsafe, but the increasing use of medication abortion has further blurred this distinction.[29] The justification of protecting women who seek abortion offends Mill's harm principle, and, in directing women toward unlawful, frequently unskilled abortion, the law itself becomes a source of harm.

The alleged harm to society is similarly contradicted where women's lives and health are endangered by pregnancies that come too early, too late, too often or too closely spaced in their reproductive lives. These conditions of pregnancy endanger not only women's lives and health, but also the survival and well-being of their young dependent children and the well-being of their families. Here again, restrictive laws are themselves the source of harm to women, children, families, and societies, contradicting the claim that abortion must be prohibited as a harm. The fetal-focused rationale is dysfunctional in overlooking the ways the state can actually protect prenatal life consistently with women's rights by, for example, ensuring availability of emergency obstetric care and reducing recurrent miscarriage and violence against pregnant women.[30]

Constructing Social Meanings Through Abortion Stigma

In criminally prohibiting abortion, societies create a category called "abortion" distinct from other medical services and treats those accessing and performing such services in categorically different ways. In exceptionalizing abortion, criminal law perpetuates stigma, and that stigma has social meaning.[31] Social meaning of abortion exists in different forms, such as in law and in the discourses that are used to describe procedures and experiences of abortion, women seeking abortion, and those providing it. Social meaning is attached to the narratives of women considering abortion, such as rape victims in need of protection,[32] or women considering abortion as vectors of the social contagion of immorality.[33] The language used to describe abortion, such as lost pregnancy,[34] to explain the means of abortion, such as menstrual regulation[35] or the "moral property of women,"[36] and to describe abortion providers, such as human rights' defenders,[37] or as murderers,[38] contributes to the construction of various social meanings of abortion. Meaning is generated in how communities consider women seeking services,[39] such as through networks that facilitate women's access to the abortion pill through the internet,[40] or that limit or deny women's access,[41] and in how health institutions treat women seeking abortion services.[42] Health systems can be inclusive, by covering abortion like a routine health service, or exclusive, by refusing to provide abortion services or to train doctors and nurses in service provision.[43]

Social meaning about abortion, those pregnant women seeking it, and those providing it is generated in part through the use of stigma. While different types of stigma are subject of extensive research,[44] it can generally be said that stigma refers to an attribute or characteristic that is designated as defective or tainted in a particular context. "Stigma . . . is the situation of the individual who is disqualified from full social acceptance."[45] Stigmatized individuals are thus "reduced in our minds from a whole and usual person to a tainted, discounted one."[46] The social identity of the bearers of that attribute or characteristic is "spoiled," and their full humanity is called into question. They may become social pariahs or outcasts. Stigmatized individuals are valued less than individuals without spoiled social identities, that is, so-called "normal" persons. Stigma requires reflection on how the recognition of certain behaviors and conditions as deviant transforms persons tending to such behaviors or conditions into deviants.[47] It also requires focusing on those constructing deviancy, to better understand their motives to dehumanize others. Stigma relates to such judgmental characteristics as "abominations of the body" (e.g., physical deformities), "blemishes of individual character" (e.g., mental ill-health, addictions), or for example, "tribal identities" (e.g., race, religion).[48]

While abortion stigma is applied to both those who seek and supply abortion,[49] one of its definitions focuses on those negative attributes that are "ascribed to women who seek to terminate a pregnancy that marks them, internally or externally, as inferior to ideals of womanhood. While ideals of womanhood vary depending on local culture and histories, a woman who seeks an abortion is inadvertently challenging widely-held assumptions about the 'essential nature' of women."[50] Some ideals of womanhood that are transgressed through abortion have been identified as: (1) female sexuality as solely for the purpose of procreation, (2) the inevitability of motherhood, and (3) women's instinctual nurturance of the vulnerable.[51] Other ideals of womanhood might be found upon examining gender prejudices about women manifested in stereotypes. For example, the prescriptive stereotypes that women should be passive and subordinate to men, and not autonomous or assertive, might be transgressed through women voluntarily deciding to terminate their pregnancies.

Thinking about abortion stigma as a way societies counteract the transgressions of the ideals of womanhood is one approach. Another approach by Bruce Link and Jo Phelan focuses on how stigma functions by considering the components of its production.[52] Stigma production has five components, all of which have to be present in order for stigma to exist. These components of stigma production might be applied to criminalized abortion in the following ways: Criminalization *marks* those seeking and providing abortion as different, the first component of stigma production. Criminalization *links* those differences to undesirable characteristics through stereotyping, the second component. Linking the labeled persons to criminal deviance *separates* labeled persons from the dominant culture, the third component. The separation *justifies* a loss of status in, or even discrimination against, the labeled persons, the fourth component. Through each of these components of stigma production, the criminal law allows the labeling agents to *exert power* over the labeled persons, the fifth component.[53]

How labeled people are marked will vary.[54] For example, how women are targeted by stigma might depend on where women are situated along the abortion pathway or their circumstances: women with unwanted pregnancies, women who are considering or seeking abortions, or women who induced their own abortions. Certain subgroups of women are differently constructed;[55] for example adolescents and unmarried women are linked to promiscuity, and married women are tainted as selfish. Which women are labeled by society through criminal laws and their justifications relate to their reasons for seeking abortions. Acceptable and unacceptable abortions stem from good (acceptable) and bad (unacceptable) reasons for having them.[56] Reasons are expressed in the particular exceptions to the criminal prohibition that laws make justifiable or at least excusable.[57] However abortion stigma is targeted, aborting women are labeled by society without regard to their individual needs and circumstances. Moreover, stigma makes it easier to envisage such women as falling into the criminal category.

The location of abortion stigma is the subject of exploration and can be understood to range from structural to individual domains.[58] At the individual level, stigma is located in at least three separate domains: perceived, experienced and internalized stigma.[59] Applied to abortion, *perceived stigma* "refers to an individual's perception of how other people feel about abortion or how others might react to knowing that she has had an abortion or is intending to have one. This domain also includes what women think might happen to them if others knew about their abortion, such as spousal or family rejection."[60] Perceived stigma might cause women to delay[61] or avoid seeking therapeutic abortion services,[62] or, for example, delay or avoid seeking necessary post-abortion care.[63] Perceived stigma might heighten the need for women to conceal their abortion, resulting in reduced opportunities for them to find social and emotional support.[64]

Experienced stigma is the actual experience of being discriminated against or treated negatively by others and having that discrimination or negative treatment be directly related to the stigmatized condition.[65] In the abortion context, experienced stigma includes women being denied information necessary for them to make an abortion decision in a timely manner,[66] being harassed, humiliated or condemned in accessing abortion services,[67] being denied services entirely,[68] including through health professionals objecting on grounds of conscience,[69] or being imprisoned.[70] Experienced stigma also extends to those providing abortion services through their experience of harassment, intimidation, and violence,[71] and to others such as abortion researchers being silenced or dismissed.[72]

Internalized stigma is defined as the extent to which the stigmatized individual incorporates negative perceptions, beliefs, and/or experiences into his or her own self.[73] Women who have safe abortions in private with no breaches of their confidentiality or dignity might still internalize a tainted identity associated with the experience.[74] When women do so, stigma "can manifest itself as feelings of guilt or shame or other negative feelings about oneself."[75] Severe manifestations of internalized abortion stigma have resulted in, for example, subsequent anti-abortion activism for expiation of guilt, or suicide attempts.[76] While experienced stigma might have the most direct legal consequences, it is important to consider how perceived and internalized stigma might at least indirectly affect women's exercise of their rights.

It is a matter of debate how enduring abortion stigma is or need be. It has been explained that "if an abortion is performed safely and early, there [are] no enduring stigmata to indicate that a woman has had an abortion."[77] Where this is the case, abortion stigma primarily concerns the internalization of blemished attributes.[78] Other forms of internalized stigma, such as self-silencing, closeting, or covering, might have enduring psychological effects, such as lowered self-esteem. Covering requires people to hide disfavored, stigmatized attributes in order to fit into the mainstream.[79] Examples of resistance to abortion silencing include dresses produced by a nongovernmental organization, Women on Web, that say "I had an abortion"[80] and the early "speak-outs."[81] These examples of resistance remain somewhat exceptional, however, suggesting that abortion stigma, particularly in its internalized and perceived forms, might be endemic. Given the statistics on the prevalence of unsafe abortion,[82] the silencing, closeting, or covering of abortion are major obstacles to dismantling ongoing prejudicial treatment of women and to the provision and uptake of safe abortion services.

There is an important debate about whether the creation of stigma is inherently wrong or whether its wrongness depends on the severity or intensity of the stigma.[83] Abortion stigma operates through criminalization to rationalize animosity against pregnant women and their use of animosity against themselves by internalizing stigma. In arguing that the creation of stigma is inherently wrong, one legal scholar explains how it is an arbitrary and cruel form of social control: "It is arbitrary in that it is decentralized and unlinked to any explicit form of institutional authorization or accountability. No one need take responsibility for imposing the sanction. It simply happens. There is no form of appeal or clarification."[84] Stigma's cruelty works by enrolling stigmatized women into enforcing their discredited status: "to cut a person off from the esteem and support of others is bad enough, but then to turn the individual into [her] own jailor, [her] own chorus of denunciation, takes inhumanity to an ultimate pitch."[85] For the state to participate in this inhumanity through its formal criminal law, its misapplication through informal law, and the failure to apply background norms on patients' rights and doctors' professional duties is contrary to its obligations to promote the human rights of pregnant women.

Stigmatized Meanings of Formal and Informal Law and Background Rules

Formal criminal law provides a framework that makes the act of abortion inherently wrong, and makes those deliberately performing or facilitating abortion criminal. Stigmatized meaning about abortion is located beyond the formal law in its commonplace operation through, for example, informal law and background rules.[86] Informal (mis)interpretation and (mis)application of law by people and institutions in health care settings generate negative social meanings about those seeking and providing services. Background rules affect the delivery of medical services more generally, such as laws and regulations that dictate patients' rights to information. Informal law and background rules often do the stigmatizing work. They evolve under the shadow of the criminal law and stigmatize those seeking and providing abortion, but they are not directly enforceable by criminal procedures.

The way in which the formal criminal law prohibits abortion and punishes those associated with it, and the way in which it specifies any exemptions from criminal prohibition, convey social meaning. For example, a state conveys a particular prejudice against pregnant women when the criminal law specifically provides for their punishment. Many criminal laws indicate circumstances in which abortion is permitted, or at least exempt from punishment, such as during a period early in pregnancy, known as the periodic model of legislation. Other laws, following what is known as the indications model, permit abortion for certain indications, such as to save life, to preserve health, in cases of rape or incest, or for eugenic or socioeconomic reasons. Sometimes the models are mixed, with abortion permitted in early pregnancy on a periodic model and then on specified indications thereafter. In the periodic, indications, or mixed models, abortion is justified or excusable, and therefore not punishable.

In exempting abortion from criminal punishment on specified indications,[87] a state conveys social meanings about which abortions are tolerable and which are not, about women who seek them, about sexuality, and about fetal protection.[88] A state prejudices women where its law allows exceptions from criminal prohibition of abortion to preserve only a woman's life. The prejudice embedded in this narrow exception is that women's physical existence is alone worthy of protection, and that preservation of their health and well-being do not matter.[89] The fueling of such prejudices is discriminatory against pregnant women because the state does not embed such prejudices about the value of men's health and well-being in its criminal law. A woman who terminates a pregnancy she would survive, but with long-term harmful health consequences, is punishable. Where prohibition of abortion is justified by the construction of non-procreative sexual relations as morally and criminally wrong, the rape exemption suggests that women should not be punished when they did not intend to have such relations.

In contrast to states that justify lawful abortion for specified indications, some frame their criminal laws to excuse abortion from punishment only in certain circumstances. When states excuse abortion from punishment, it is still criminally wrong.[90] Exempting providers from criminal punishment, while retaining overall criminality, leaves open the possibility that providers could be required to experience stigma through threats of professional disciplinary sanctions for committing or advising a criminally wrongful act. It is not a defense to a charge of ethical misconduct that it was legally excusable. While the distinction between what act is justified and what is unjustified, but excusable, might be a refinement in criminal law terms, what matters for purposes of stigma is that the state is applying its criminal law power to spoil women and their health providers, and so jeopardize women's health and well-being. By retaining criminal prohibition for abortion, albeit with some exceptions, the state is signaling that criminalization is necessary to exert overall control over pregnant women's bodies and reproductive choices, contributing to their internalization of stigma by undermining their self-worth.

In criminal law enforcement, the legal burden is on the prosecution to prove beyond reasonable doubt that the commission of the prohibited abortion was outside any permitted time period or indications. However, because society presupposes that performance of the act constitutes the full crime, and therefore is punishable, there is a social burden on the accused woman to show that the performance was justifiable or excusable. If the prosecution fails to prove performance outside permitted grounds such as to preserve health, the public will suppose acquittal to mean that "she got away with it" rather than that she did not commit a crime. Even if the prosecution fails to meet its legal burden of proof of the crime, the woman has a social burden to show that she is a "worthy" victim.[91] The burden to escape social stigma is on the woman to show that she is a legitimate victim, such as of rape, or of life- or health-endangering pregnancy.

When criminal abortion laws allow for exceptions to criminal prohibition, they often contain administrative requirements regarding the availability of and access to services that can have stigmatizing consequences. Administrative requirements, such as of third party authorizations, rape certifications, or reflection delays, categorically separate women seeking abortion from other patients and so construct them as deviant, exacerbating stigma. In order for women to access lawful abortion services, they often need first to obtain the authorization of their spouses or parents, heightening women's experience and internalization of stigma. Such authorization requirements label women as inherently incapable of making autonomous decisions, or as inherently subordinate. They perpetuate pejorative labels that discriminate against women.[92] In effect, women who are subject to legally or informally required spousal or parental authorization may have to bear the children, irreparably harm themselves, or die trying to continue and complete hazardous pregnancies. The choice is not the woman's own to make.

Regulations that require third parties, such as doctors, police officers, or courts, to certify that women have been raped in order for them to access abortions signal that heightened scrutiny is necessary to guard against women's deceptive resort to exceptions.[93] The state disproportionately degrades women as liable not to be telling the truth about suffering a serious violation, or not being worthy of respect for the decisions they make in good faith about their health and well-being. The state does not degrade men through its laws and policies by, for example, requiring independent scrutiny and approval of their health-preserving decisions following injury by assault. Reflection delay requirements, ranging from twenty-four hours[94] to three days,[95] stereotype women with unwanted pregnancies as impetuous, emotional, and unreflective about the implications of the choices they make for their health and family well-being. As a result, laws mandating additional time for reflection to make "correct" decisions are claimed to be justified. Such justifications, which are rarely made explicit, contribute to women's internalization of infantilizing sexist stereotypes as their not being fully capable of making difficult moral decisions.

Where acts of pregnant women's reproductive preference do not fall within explicit exceptions to criminal prohibition, abortion remains criminal, and the threat of criminal sanctions always exists. The degree to which providers and women are actually prosecuted for criminal abortion varies by jurisdiction and socioeconomic factors.[96] Even where the criminal law is rarely enforced, the threat of criminal sanctions perpetuates all forms of stigma. The threat of criminal sanctions or the uncertainty about the scope of the law heightens perceived stigma, causing abortion providers to delay or deny services.[97] Stigma might deter women seeking safe abortion because they perceive that they might be exposed and socially ostracized. The threat of criminal sanctions closets those associated with abortion, furthering the internalization of stigma in ways similar to how social stigma attached to gay men through unenforced laws criminalizing sodomy closets gay men.[98]

Beyond the formal criminal law, informal rules and background rules are often misapplied with impunity to stigmatize those who seek and provide abortion services. Examples of informal law are the social practices that emerge to restrict offer of services, and determine who does not qualify for health exceptions[99] or, for instance, eugenic exceptions,[100] to the criminal prohibition of abortion. The informal law that emerges to determine which women are "undeserving" of such abortions stigmatizes those subgroups of women.

Background rules relate to clinical services, or to health systems. Take the example of a rule regulating patient confidentiality: sometimes such rules require doctors to notify law-enforcement authorities of patients who show evidence of possible criminal activity, including abortion or miscarriage.[101] Such rules offend professional ethical duties of confidentiality, stigmatize women, and disproportionately impact poorer women because reporting requirements are more likely to be applied in public health facilities, which low-income women generally use.

Background rules may target providers by imposing medically unnecessary requirements,[102] deliberately causing them to experience stigma. An example of background rules that operate at the health system level includes rules requiring specified training and certification to provide abortion services in ways that are more onerous than for comparable health services. They exceptionalize abortion providers and differentiate them from other medical providers. In so doing, they construct the meaning of abortion providers as hazardous and bad. The hyper-regulation of abortion providers through background rules might be so stigmatizing that service provision might be considerably more difficult than under unenforced formal criminal abortion law.

Addressing Stigmatized Meanings— Rethinking *R.R. v. Poland*

Over time and across jurisdictions, women have faced obstacles in accessing legal reproductive health services or have been denied them entirely, with the result that their physical or mental well-being and their socioeconomic status have been further compromised. National courts, regional human rights courts, and international treaty-monitoring bodies have determined how these obstacles have variously violated pregnant women's human rights, including their rights to freedom from inhuman and degrading treatment,[103] to privacy,[104] to security of the person,[105] and to nondiscrimination.[106]

To illustrate how judicial reasoning in decisions on obstructed access could better articulate the harms of abortion stigma, this section focuses on the decision of the European Court of Human Rights in *R.R. v. Poland*[107] and refers to other human rights decisions as appropriate. Poland's Family

Planning Act allows for three exceptions to the overall prohibition of abortion in Poland's Criminal Code, when doctors alone may terminate pregnancies within varying gestational limits: (1) when there is danger to the life or health of the woman, abortion is permitted at any stage of the pregnancy; (2) when there is a high probability of severe and irreversible fetal malformation, abortion is permitted until fetal viability; and (3) when the pregnancy is a result of a crime, such as rape, abortion is permitted during the first twelve weeks of pregnancy.[108] A doctor who terminates a pregnancy outside these exceptions, but not the pregnant woman, is guilty of a criminal offense that is punishable by up to three years' imprisonment.[109]

R.R.'s ultrasound examination raised suspicion of a serious fetal malformation, but she was repeatedly denied the necessary referrals for genetic testing that could have confirmed or refuted the suspicion. These denials prevented R.R. from obtaining timely information on the health of the fetus and ultimately barred her from accessing a legal abortion, in which she had shown an interest, in that by the time the tests were completed, the local hospital refused to perform the abortion on the ground that the fetus was then viable. Unable to access diagnostic services, and a subsequent lawful abortion, R.R. gave birth to a baby who had Turner syndrome. Additionally, after the birth, R.R.'s doctor stigmatized her by disclosing her confidential health information to the press and making derogatory comments about her character.

The European Court found Poland responsible for violating R.R.'s right to freedom from inhuman and degrading treatment and her right to respect for private life. While the holding of this decision is significant, the Court failed to analyze how the state's treatment of R.R. spoiled her identity, causing social inferiority. This failure is unfortunate because it prevented the Court from examining how the stigmatization of R.R. aggravated violations of these rights, and from finding a violation of the right to exercise these rights, and the right to freedom of conscience, without discrimination.

The Right to be Free from Inhuman and Degrading Treatment

In considering the claim of a violation of the right to be free from inhuman and degrading treatment, the Court addressed several aspects of R.R.'s ill treatment and consequent suffering. Importantly, the Court explored how R.R. was "in a situation of great vulnerability" as a pregnant woman "deeply distressed by the information that the foetus could be affected with some malformation."[110] The Court described R.R.'s mental suffering in terms of her "acute anguish" caused by "having to think about how she and her family would be able to ensure the child's welfare, happiness and appropriate long-term medical care."[111] The Court stressed the mental suffering she experienced as result of the doctors' deliberate procrastination, and emphasized that this suffering was "aggravated by the fact that the diagnostic services which she had requested early on were at all times available and that she was entitled as a matter of domestic law to avail herself of them."[112]

The Court noted that the purpose of an individual's mistreatment is a factor that must be taken into account, "in particular whether it was intended to humiliate or debase the victim."[113] The Court recognized that the doctors' treatment of R.R. was humiliating. It explained that in previous cases the Court had found violations of individuals' rights to freedom from inhuman and degrading treatment when there has been "callous disregard for their vulnerability and distress,"[114] and that such findings had been made in the field of health care.[115] The majority of the Court found that R.R.'s suffering reached the minimum threshold of severity required to justify finding a violation of her right to be free from inhuman and degrading treatment.[116] However, the then president of the Court, Nicolas Bratza, dissented from this holding. Without elaborating reasons, he simply said that the treatment, in his view, did not meet that minimum threshold.[117] To overcome reservations such as Judge Bratza's, the majority might have analyzed the calculated nature of stigma production in order to better articulate how the health professionals, with one exception, degraded and exploited R.R. As social psychologists have explained, perpetrators of stigma use it to elicit "negative emotions, interactional discomfort, social rejection and other forms of discrimination, status loss and other harmful effects on life chances of targets."[118]

The first component of stigma production is the *marking* of human difference. That is, "there is a social selection process determining which differences are deemed relevant and consequential [to difference], and which are not."[119] The doctors marked R.R. as different from other women because she was actively seeking information necessary for possibly obtaining a legal abortion. The purpose of the doctors' denial of diagnostic services was to mark R.R. as unworthy of medical information to make a decision about her pregnancy, ignoring with impunity their professional obligations as outlined in the background rules of the Medical Professions Act.[120]

Having been marked as different in the first stage, R.R. was then "*linked* to undesirable characteristics" through stereotyping.[121] In this stage, it is important to name the stereotypes at work because they are often implicit or buried in the unconscious realm. In naming the operative stereotypes, the Court could have contributed to their modification because the ability to modify wrongful gender stereotypes is contingent on the stereotypes first being named and their harms exposed. To borrow from a medical metaphor, a pathology first needs to be diagnosed and named in order for it to be effectively treated.[122]

There are several stereotypes that the European Court could have identified, exposed, and contested, such as the stereotype of R.R. as an object, an incubator, a disrupter of the moral order, and incapable of "correct" moral decision making. The Court might have named these stereotypes of R.R., and explained that the male health professionals treated R.R. as an object of their control, not as a self-determining subject lawfully deciding the outcome of her own pregnancy. The imposition of this stereotype is evidenced in that all but one of the doctors failed to treat R.R. in accordance with her own medical needs as a patient. Moreover, the Court could have discussed how the doctors linked her to undesirable characteristics of disruptors of the moral order, because she did not comply with the doctors' gender ideology of women as self-sacrificing mothers passively carrying their pregnancies to term. In denying her access to the medical information necessary to determine the outcome of her pregnancy, the doctors stereotyped her as incapable of making the "correct" moral choice.

In the third stage of the production of abortion stigma, the doctors treated R.R. according to their degrading stereotypes, and so *separated* R.R. from the compassionate care accorded to other patients seeking diagnostic services. They assigned her a spoiled identity on the basis of her marked difference and its attached derogatory stereotypes.[123]

In the fourth component of stigmatization, the doctors *denied* R.R. legitimate diagnostic services, because they treated her as unworthy according to their hostile stereotypes, not according to her medical needs and legitimate requests as their patient whom they were obligated to serve under the background rules on patients' rights, detailed in the Medical Institutions Act.[124] The criminal nature of abortion enabled the doctors to mark her as deviant, and to apply their informal law, which in effect limited the scope of the eugenic indication. It is during this phase of stigma production that most human rights violations occur, which in this case was the degrading denial of legitimate information necessary to choose lawful health services.

Through all of these phases of stigma production, R.R. was *disempowered* by the attending doctors (with only one exception) who controlled her by denying her medically necessary referrals.[125] General criminal prohibition allows the labeling agents, in this case the doctors, to mark pregnant women considering abortion as a suspect group, intensifying their internalization of stigma by exacerbating their shame, fueling prejudices against them, and enabling violations of their rights.

Had the Court analyzed the sequence of components of stigma production through doctors' *marking* R.R. as different from other women, *linking* her to undesirable characteristics, *separating* her from other patients, and so *denying* her medical information and services to which she was legally entitled, it would have provided insights into the degrading nature of her choice-denying treatment. The doctors targeted her in order to promote their ideology, callously disregarding her own needs and circumstances. The various obstacles that the doctors erected functioned to exploit R.R.'s vulnerability and dependency on the information only they could provide. The obstacles were created with the purpose of dehumanizing R.R. Through all the phases of stigma production, the doctors *disempowered* her by denying her appropriate referrals and by violating her right to private and family life.

The Court might have explained that the stigmatizing way in which R.R. was denied access to lawful and available care was a distinct harm that contributed to the severity of the human rights violations. When women are treated in ways that require them to experience stigma, such experiences contribute to the severity of the inhuman and degrading treatment. Had the Court majority systematically analyzed the components of stigma production, it might have equipped them to convince the dissenting judge that R.R.'s treatment amounted to a level of severity that constituted inhuman and degrading treatment.

The Right to Private Life

The Court in *R.R.* held the state responsible for a violation of the complainant's right to private life because it failed to institute "effective procedural mechanisms capable of determining whether the conditions existed for obtaining a lawful abortion on the grounds of danger to the mother's health which the pregnancy might present, or of addressing the mother's legitimate fears."[126] In holding that Poland contravened its positive obligations to respect R.R.'s private life,[127] the Court yet again called on the state to institute transparent legal procedures to enable women, like R.R., to have timely access to diagnostic information about fetal health to be able to make informed decisions on whether to carry their pregnancies to term.[128] To be effective, such procedures would need to "guarantee to the pregnant woman at least a possibility to be heard in person and to have her view considered," and to have written grounds for its decision from the relevant body or person.[129]

The Court recognized that the possibility of doctors incurring liability to prosecution and conviction under the Criminal Code as "abortionists" can have a "chilling effect" when they have to read the Code to determine whether its requirements for a legal abortion have been met in a particular case.[130] The Court noted that any procedural framework would have to be formulated so as to alleviate this chilling effect of criminalization on the provision of services. As a result, the burden is on the state to establish a procedural framework that will eliminate the risk of that threat.

The Court might have elaborated the discussion of the chilling effect that the risk of stigmatization can have on the delivery of abortion services. This stigmatizing effect can interfere with patients' right to private life, as it was found to have done regarding two accused but acquitted persons,[131] and the equal exercise of this right regarding a mature gay adolescent.[132] Doctors face the risk of criminal prosecution and its stigmatizing effects. Fear of stigmatizing prosecutions disposes doctors to favor their own interests in not being prosecuted over their patients' interests in receiving health protection. The Court could have explained that when doctors have to read the criminal law to determine what types of medically indicated health services they can provide to their patients, this requirement places them in a conflict of interest, because patients are liable to be denied access to legal abortion services that would serve their right to private life.

The Court might have usefully expanded on its point that the "essential object of Article 8 is to protect the individual against arbitrary interference by public authorities"[133] to address the arbitrary way in which stigma works. Stigma is produced through ongoing, but indeterminate, threats of criminal prosecution and conviction. It is a decentralized mode of social control, unlinked to any form of accountability for the harm that it causes to patients and doctors.[134]

As of this writing, Poland has not formulated any procedural framework, so it remains to be seen whether and how such a framework might alleviate both the chilling and stigmatizing effects that taint those seeking and providing lawful abortion services.

The Right to Nondiscrimination

Had the Court found a violation of R.R.'s ability to secure her rights to private and family life, freedom of conscience, and freedom from inhuman and degrading treatment without discrimination, it could have elaborated how stigma fuels discrimination. The state discriminated against R.R. because it allowed its doctors to stigmatize her as a moral deviant, denying her the ability to determine her treatment equally with all patients seeking lawful diagnostic services. The Court could have explained how the doctors' prejudices about pregnant women considering lawful abortion contributed to the discriminatory denial of lawful diagnostic procedures.

The state through its doctors allowed R.R. to be stigmatized for defying the prescriptive sex role stereotype that all pregnant women should be mothers and should not be allowed to exercise their moral agency. In doing so, the doctors treated her as though she had no conscience and ignored her right to exercise her conscience equally with other patients.[135] Their stigmatization based on hostile stereotypes functioned to blind the doctors to their obligation to ensure that R.R. had the relevant information on her fetus's health, in a timely manner, necessary for exercising her conscience within the law. In allowing doctors to deny R.R. her right to the equal exercise of her conscience, the state permitted doctors "to treat [her] as means to an end, to deprive [her] . . . of [her] 'essential humanity'"[136] to accommodate the doctors' own self-assessed superior consciences.

In focusing on how R.R.'s stress and anxiety were fueled by the doctors' denials of necessary diagnostic services,[137] the Court overlooked that her individual suffering was systematically caused by the overall criminalization of abortion. The Court avoided addressing how the criminalization contributed to R.R.'s experience of stigma by causing the failure to provide her with diagnostic services equally with other patients. The Court failed to see how the doctors' application of their own informal rules regarding which women should be referred for genetic testing and which not were based on their discriminatory prejudices, resulting in the unequal application of the background rules on patients' rights and doctors' duties. That is, the Court did not examine how the state's framing of abortion as a criminal matter contributed to the doctors' unequal application of the background rules regarding patients' rights to information about their conditions[138] and the professional duties to provide comprehensive health information.[139]

In contrast, the Court in *Kiyutin v. Russia* found a violation of the right to nondiscrimination in the exercise of private life because of the state's re-fusal to issue a residence permit to a foreign national solely on the basis of HIV-positive status.[140] The Court explained that it is particularly sensitive to prejudice against "vulnerable groups" who have "historically been subject to prejudice with lasting consequences," because such prejudice can result in stereotyping and stigmatization which prohibits "the individualized evalua-tion of their capacities and needs."[141] The Court identified a "false nexus" between HIV infection and personal irresponsibility, which reinforced "other forms of stigma and discrimination, such as racism, homophobia or misogyny."[142] In *R.R.*, the Court might have similarly identified how the false nexus between R.R. and her incapacity to make "correct" moral decisions reinforced discrimination against her. R.R. was "subject to prejudice with lasting consequences," since she was denied testing necessary to provide the medical information to make an informed decision on whether she would mother a child.

International human rights treaty-monitoring bodies have found dis-crimination when states failed to implement legal exceptions to criminal pro-hibition, due in part to judges' and doctors' application of their own informal rules. For example, in *L.M.R. v. Argentina*, a case concerning the rape of a nineteen-year-old disabled woman with the mental capacity of an eight- to ten-year-old, the Human Rights Committee found Argentina responsible for failure to ensure women's equal exercise of their rights protected by the Inter-national Covenant on Civil and Political Rights. However, the Committee did not explain how the operation of prejudices and stigma contributed to the discrimination, despite the applicant's submissions that "since abortion is an issue that affects women only and is shrouded in all kinds of prejudices in the collective imagination, the attitude of the judicial officer and the medical staff . . . , and the authorities' failure to enforce the law, were discriminatory, depriving L.M.R. of her right to a safe, lawful abortion."[143]

The Committee's holding would have been more robust had it identified the prejudices at work, and exposed how they functioned to permit state of-ficials and doctors to stigmatize L.M.R. in order to exploit her for their ideo-logical purposes, thus denying her right to equal exercise of the law. [144] The prejudices were evidenced by a juvenile court judge refusing to certify the abortion that was lawful under the Criminal Code of Argentina,[145] and by the medical staff refusing to treat her according to her actual circumstances, as a young girl with mental disabilities pregnant by rape.[146] The criminalization of abortion fueled the stigma and prejudices, enabling the development of informal rules that arbitrarily denied L.M.R. the equal exercise of her rights to be free from inhuman and degrading treatment and to private life.

In contrast to the *L.M.R.* decision, the Committee on the Elimination of Discrimination against Women in its decision in *L.C. v. Peru* found that Peru failed to eliminate discrimination against L.C., a thirteen-year-old sexually abused pregnant girl denied access to lawful abortion services. She was denied the right to be treated free of "prejudices . . . which are based on the idea of [her] inferiority," and free of the stereotyped role of a reproductive instrument.[147] The Committee explained that Peru did not take appropriate steps "to modify the social and cultural patterns of conduct" that privilege prenatal life over women's health and well-being.[148] When the state allows stigma and prejudices, which are based on the inferiority of women and on the degrading gender stereotype of women as reproductive instruments, to prevent the distribution of health services that only women need, it violates women's rights to nondiscriminatory access health care services.[149]

In focusing in *R.R.* on individual suffering and procedural lapses, the European Court failed to see the structural dimensions of discrimination, as envisaged in *L.M.R.* and *L.C.* The European Court did not address how criminalization has "stigmatising, socially exclusionary and divisive outcomes" that damage women's equal citizenship.[150] The Court could not see that the denial of diagnostic services to R.R. was based on abortion stigma and discriminatory prejudices against women who seek genetic information about their pregnancies. In denying R.R. access to prenatal genetic diagnosis, the doctors applied the degrading stereotype that condemns pregnant women who decline to be self-sacrificing and nurturing mothers carrying their pregnancies to term, irrespective of the health of the fetus. The doctors discriminated against R.R. by applying their own informal rules, not the actual law. They treated her according to the degrading stereotype, not according to the professional standards by which they should care for all patients irrespective of their gender and pregnant status. In so doing, the doctors stigmatized R.R. as a criminally constructed woman in order to confine her within a discriminatory gender ideology.

Conclusion

Stigma and criminalization of abortion reproduce and reinforce each other. Understanding why societies stigmatize abortion will provide insights into why they criminalize abortion, and vice versa. Abortion is constructed and constituted as a crime, a serious offense against society for which people are liable to prosecution and imprisonment. Criminal abortion law then facilitates stigmatization of people who have had or performed abortions, silencing and closeting them. The enforced silence allows for the perpetuation of hostility against those associated with abortion, which in turn justifies its criminalization. Closeted women are reluctant to speak about their abortions, thus enabling further stigmatization of women associated with abortion, further justifying the criminalization of abortion.

The chapter started by questioning how, if at all, given the stigmatizing effects of criminal abortion law, societies can justify criminalizing abortion. The chapter begins answering this question by showing how the purported justifications for criminalization do not withstand scrutiny. The answer requires acknowledging that stigmatization is a dehumanizing process by which power is exerted to mark individuals, link them to undesirable characteristics by hostile stereotyping, and separate them in order to justify their degrading treatment. The way in which criminal abortion laws are framed, implemented, and interpreted can have degrading and discriminatory effects on pregnant women seeking abortion and those persons providing it. As a decentralized mode of social control, the effects of stigmatization are unending and arbitrary with no form of accountability. The stigmatizing effects extend well beyond the formal criminal law to facilitate the development of informal rules that misapply the formal law and ignore the background rules on patients' rights and professional duties with impunity. As a result of its stigmatizing effects of criminally constructing women, criminal abortion law cannot be justified.

The hope is that the chapter will help to stimulate much needed thinking beyond quantitative statistics of unsafe abortion mortality and morbidity to better articulate the stigmatizing harms of criminalizing abortion. It invites the conclusion that the harms criminal laws cause to individual pregnant women in particular and to all women in general, as well as to conscientious health care providers committed to their patients' best interests, show such laws to be unjustified.

Table of Cases

Domestic Jurisprudence

Argentina

Austria

Verfassungsgerichtshof [Constitutional Court] October 11, 1974, Erklaerungen des Verfassungsgerichtshofs 221, 20n40, 37n2

Brazil

Supremo Tribunal Federal [Supreme Court] 2008, Ação Direta de Inconstitucionalidade No. 3510, 246n33

Supremo Tribunal Federal [Supreme Court] April 12, 2012, ADPF 54/DF, 247nn35–37, 262–77

Canada

McInerney v. MacDonald, [1992] 2 S.C.R. 138, 93 D.L.R. (4th) 415 (Supreme Court of Canada), 229n69

R. v. Morgentaler, [1988] 1 S.C.R. 30, 44 D.L.R. (4th) 385 (Supreme Court of Canada), 165, 221nn33–34, 360n105, 366n136

Tremblay v. Daigle, [1989] 2 S.C.R. 530 (Supreme Court of Canada), 319n98, 341nn58–59

Chile

Corte Suprema de Justicia [Supreme Court] August 30, 2001, Sentencia Rol 2.186-2001, 248n44

Tribunal Constitucional [Constitutional Court] April 18, 2008, Sentencia Rol 740-07-CDS, 90, 91n46, 219n27

Colombia

Corte Constitucional [Constitutional Court] 1997, Sentencia C-013/97, 276n35

Corte Constitucional [Constitutional Court] 2002, Sentencia C-370/02, 87n34

Corte Constitucional [Constitutional Court] May 10, 2006, Sentencia C-355/06, 31nn103–8, 87, 90n44, 91n49, 93nn57–60, 94n62, 95, 100, 105nn45–46, 241–42, 249n45, 276–77, 328n10, 341nn58–59, 341nn61–62, 342n63

Corte Constitucional [Constitutional Court] 2008, Sentencia T-209/08, 214–15, 225, 304n10, 328n10

Corte Constitucional [Constitutional Court] 2011, Sentencia T-841/2011, 109n73

Corte Constitucional [Constitutional Court] August 10, 2012, Sentencia T-627, 249n45

Costa Rica

Corte Suprema de Justicia de Costa Rica, Sala Constitucional [Supreme Court of Justice of Costa Rica, Constitutional Chamber] 2000, Sentencia No. 2000-02306, 79n3, 328n7, 330n22, 332n29, 345

Corte Suprema de Justicia de Costa Rica, Sala Constitucional [Supreme Court of Justice of Costa Rica, Constitutional Chamber] 2004, Sentencia 442/2004, 328n7, 336, 345n70
Corte Suprema de Justicia de Costa Rica, Sala Constitucional [Supreme Court of Justice of Costa Rica, Constitutional Chamber] 2005, Sentencia 1267/2005, 328n7, 336, 345n70

Ecuador

Corte Constitucional [Constitutional Court] June 14, 2006, *José Fernando Roser Rohde c. Instituto Nacional de Higiene y Medicina Tropical "Leopoldo Izquiéta Pérez y el Ministro de Salud S/Acción de Amparo,* 219

France

Conseil Constitutionnel [Constitutional Court] January 15, 1975, D.S. Jur. 529 [1975] A.J.D.A. 134, 20n40, 37n1
Conseil Constitutionnel [Constitutional Court] June 27, 2001, Decision No. 2001-446 DC, 231
Conseil d'État [Council of State] 1982, D.S. Jur. 19, 732, 319n99

Germany

Bundesverfassungsgericht [Federal Constitutional Court] February 25, 1975, 39 BVerfGE 1, 15n7, 20n40, 23–24, 26n81, 37n3, 39, 40–41, 52n93, 78, 79–81, 85, 87, 92n52, 93, 98, 99–100, 351n25
Bundesverfassungsgericht [Federal Constitutional Court] May 28, 1993, 88 BVerfGE 203, 26–27, 48–49, 52, 56n2, 63, 65n52, 72n87, 73, 85–86, 94n61, 96, 99–104

Hungary

Alkotmánybíróság [Constitutional Court] 1998, 48/1998 (XI. 23), Magyar Közlöny [MK] 1998/105, 33, 37n4, 56n2, 63, 65, 67–68

Ireland

Attorney General v. X, [1992] I.E.S.C. 1 (Supreme Court of Ireland), 31, 125, 304n8, 324, 344
Baby Oladapo v. Minister for Justice, [2002] I.E.S.C. 44 (Supreme Court of Ireland), 331n25, 333n35, 339n52, 344n66, n67
McGee v. Attorney General, [1974] I.R. 284 (Supreme Court of Ireland), 31n100

Israel

A. v. B., 35 (iii) P.D. 57 (1981) (Supreme Court of Israel), 319n100

Italy

Corte Costituzionale [Constitutional Court] February 18, 1975, no. 27, 98 Foro It. I, 515, 20n40, 39n19

Mexico

Suprema Corte de Justicia de la Nación [Supreme Court] 2002, Acción de Inconstitucionalidad 10/2000, 327n2, 328n9, 337–38

Suprema Corte de Justicia de la Nación [Supreme Court] 2008, Acción de inconstitucionalidad 146/2007 y su acumulada 147/2007, 30n96, 87–88, 91n49, 246n30, 327–28, 335, 340–42

Suprema Corte de Justicia de la Nación [Supreme Court] 2010, Controversia constitucional 54/2009, 345n70

Suprema Corte de Justicia de la Nación [Supreme Court] 2011, Acción de inconstitucionalidad 11/2009, 328n9, 330n23

Suprema Corte de Justicia de la Nación [Supreme Court] 2011, Acción de inconstitucionalidad 62/2009, 328n9, 330n23

Nepal

Achyut Kharel v. Government of Nepal, Writ No. 3352, 2061 (2008) (Supreme Court of Nepal), 288

Annapurna Rana v. Kathmandu District Court, Writ No. 2187, 2053 (1998) (Supreme Court of Nepal), 288n61

Lakshmi Dhikta v. Government of Nepal, Writ No. 0757, 2067, Nepal Kanoon Patrika, para. 25 (2009) (Supreme Court of Nepal), 279, 282–83, 287–99

Meera Dhungana v. Government of Nepal, Writ No. 55, 2058 (2002) (Supreme Court of Nepal), 288n62

Prakash Mani Sharma v. Government of Nepal, Writ No. 064 (2008) (Supreme Court of Nepal), 296, 298

New Zealand

Right to Life New Zealand Inc. v. Abortion Supervisory Committee, [2008] 2 N.Z.L.R. 825 (High Court of New Zealand), 128

Right to Life New Zealand Inc. v. Abortion Supervisory Committee, [2012] N.Z.S.C. 68 (Supreme Court of New Zealand), 127–28

Peru

Tribunal Constitucional [Constitutional Court], November 13, 2006, Sentencia Exp. No. 7435-2006-PC/TC, 248n44

Tribunal Constitucional [Constitutional Court] 2009, *ONG Acción de Lucha Anticorrupción Sin Componenda c. MINSA*, 219n24

Tribunal Constitucional [Constitutional Court] October 16, 2009, Sentencia Exp. No. 02005-2009-PA/TC, 219n28

Poland

Trybunal Konstitucyjny [Constitutional Tribunal] May 28, 1997, K 26/96, Orzecznictwo Trybunału Konstytucyjnego, Rok 1997, 37n5, 56n2, 63–64, 67

Portugal

Tribunal Constitucional [Constitutional Court]1984, Acórdão No. 25/84, Acórdãos do Tribunal Constitucional II, 37, 40

Tribunal Constitucional [Constitutional Court]1985, Acórdão No. 85/85, Acórdãos do Tribunal Constitucional V, 37, 40–41

Tribunal Constitucional [Constitutional Court] 1998, Acórdão No. 288/98, Diário da República 91/98 Suplemento I-A Série, 37, 42–45

Tribunal Constitucional [Constitutional Court] 2006, Acórdão No. 617/2006, Diário da República I Série, 37, 45–47

Tribunal Constitucional [Constitutional Court] 2010, Acórdão No. 75/2010, Diario da Republica vol. 60, 3, 33nn117–18, 37–38, 47–54, 84n20, 86, 88, 90n45, 91n50, 96, 100, 102, 104, 105nn48–49, 110nn79–81, 359n95

Slovakia

Ústavný Súd [Constitutional Court] 4 December 2007, PL. ÚS 12/01, Collection of Laws of the Slovak Republic, No. 14/2008, vol. 8, 3, 52n94, 57, 62, 65–76, 90, 96

South Africa

Christian Lawyers Association of South Africa & Others v. Minister of Health & Others 1998 (4) SA 113 (T) (Transvaal Provincial Division of the High Court of South Africa), 116–17

Christian Lawyers Association v. Minister of Health and Others, [2004] 4 All SA 31 (South African Supreme Court of Appeal), 29, 99

Spain

Tribunal Constitucional [Constitutional Court] April 11, 1985, S.T.C. 53/1985, 1985-49 BJC 515, 31, 91n49

United Kingdom

Barr v. Matthews, (1999) 52 B.M.L.R. 217 (High Court of England and Wales, Queen's Bench Division), 229n68

British Pregnancy Advisory Serv. v. Sec'y of State for Health, [2011] E.W.H.C. 235 (Admin) (High Court of England and Wales), 201n55, 201n57, 202n59, 202n63, 207

Family Planning Association of Northern Ireland v. Minister for Health, Social Services and Public Safety, [2005] Northern Ireland Law Reports 188 (Court of Appeal, Northern Ireland), 122n6, 359n97

Gillick v. West Norfolk and Wisbech Area Health Authority, 3 All E.R. 402 (1985) (House of Lords), 319n102

Paton v. Trustees of British Pregnancy Advisory Service and Another [1978] QB 276 (High Court of Justice, Queen's Bench Division), 319n99

Petition of Mary Teresa Doogan and Concepta Wood, [2012] C.S.O.H. 32 (Outer House, Court of Session, Scotland), 231n74, 232nn80–81

Petition of Mary Teresa Doogan and Concepta Wood, [2013] C.S.I.H. 36, P876/11 (Extra Division, Inner House, Court of Session, Scotland), 231n74, 232n83

R. (on the application of Purdy) v. Dir. of Pub. Prosecutions, [2009] U.K.H.L. 45 (House of Lords), 190n4

R. (on the application of Smeaton) v. Secretary of State for Health, [2002] E.W.H.C. 610 (Admin) (High Court of England and Wales), 218n22

R. (S.B.) v. Governors of Denbigh High School, [2006] U.K.H.L. 15, [2007] 1 A.C. 100 (House of Lords), 232n82

R. v. Bourne, [1938] 3 All E.R. 615 (Crown Court of England and Wales), 170, 195–96, 304n7, 315–16

R v Sarah Louise Catt [2013] EWCA Crim 1187 (Crown Court of England and Wales), 205–6

R. v. Smith [1974] 1 All E.R. 376, 381 (Court of Appeal of England and Wales), 196n31

Royal College of Nurses v. Department of Health and Social Security, [1981] 1 All E.R. 545 (House of Lords), 198n46

United States

Bellotti v. Baird, 443 U.S. 622 (1979) (U.S. Supreme Court), 319n102

Brownfield v. Daniel Freeman Marina Hospital, 208 Cal. App. 3d 405, 256 Cal. Rptr. 240 (1989) (California Second District, Court of Appeal), 218n20–21

Gonzales v. Carhart, 550 U.S. 124 (2007) (U.S. Supreme Court), 244, 328n8, 329, 335–36, 340

In RE Initiative Petition No. 349, State Question No. 642, 1992 OK 122 (1992) (Supreme Court of Oklahoma), 330n20

N.J. Div. of Youth & Family Serv. v. V.M., 974 A.2d 448 (2009) (Superior Court of New Jersey, Appellate Division), 336n39

Planned Parenthood v. Danforth, 428 U.S. (1976) (U.S. Supreme Court), 319n98, 319n102

Planned Parenthood of Kansas City v. Ashcroft, 462 U.S. 476 (1983) (U.S. Supreme Court), 319n102

Planned Parenthood of Minn., N.D. & S.D. v. Rounds, 530 F.3d 724 (2011) (Eighth Circuit Court of Appeals), 103n34

Planned Parenthood of Southeastern Pa. v. Casey, 505 U.S. 833 (1992) (U.S. Supreme Court), 24–26, 39n18, 68, 73n91, 93, 99, 103n33, 104, 319n98, 328n8, 330, 359n94

Rodriguez v. City of Chicago, 156 F. 3rd 771 (1998) (Seventh Circuit Court of Appeals), 233n85

Roe v. Wade, 410 U.S. 113 (1973) (U.S. Supreme Court), 15n6, 20n40, 22–23, 24n70, 39, 43, 68, 73n91, 90, 98–99, 100, 103, 225, 247, 328n8, 329, 330n21, 340, 341, 342n64, 344

Stenberg v. Carhart, 530 U.S. 914 (2000) (U.S. Supreme Court), 349n15

Regional Jurisprudence

African Regional Courts

Mehar Singh Bansel v. R., (1959) E.A.L.R. 813 (East African Court of Appeal), 170n23

R. v. Edgal, Idike and Ojugwu, (1938) W.A.C.A. 133 (West African Court of Appeal), 170n22, 173

European Commission of Human Rights

Ahmad v. United Kingdom (1981) 4 E.H.R.R. 126, 232n79

Brüggemann and Scheuten v. Federal Republic of Germany, App. No. 6959/75 (1981) 3 E.H.R.R. 244, Eur. Comm'n H.R., 137

Church of Scientology v. Sweden, App. No. 7805/77, 16 Eur. Comm'n. H.R. Dec. and Rep. 68 (1979), 214n11

Hercz (R.H.) v. Norway, App. No. 17004/90, Eur. Comm'n H.R. (1992), 128n41

Paton (X.) v. United Kingdom, App. No. 8416/78, Eur. Comm'n H.R. (1980), 71n84, 128n41, 319n101

X v. Austria, App. No. 7045/75, Eur. Comm'n H.R. (1976), 132n66

X v. Norway, App. No. 867/60, Eur. Comm'n H.R. (1961), 132n66

European Court of Human Rights

A, B, and C v. Ireland, [2010] E.C.H.R. 2032, 95n63, 125, 129n43, 130–31, 132n69, 133, 135, 137–38, 168n11, 176, 353n42, 355n63

Airey v. Ireland, [1979] 2 E.H.R.R. 305, 132n73

Belgian Linguistic Case (No. 2) (1968) 1 E.H.R.R. 252, 130n56

Boso v. Italy, App. No. 50490/99, Eur. Ct. H.R. (2002), 128nn41–42, 321

D. v. Ireland, App. No. 26499/02, Eur. Ct. H.R. (2006), 133

Kiyutin v. Russia, App. No. 2700/10, Eur. Ct. H.R. (2011), 366–67

Marckx v. Belgium, (1979) 2 E.H.R.R. 330, 136n95

Open Door Counselling and Dublin Well Woman v. Ireland, App. Nos. 14234/88 and 14235/88, Eur. Ct. H.R. (1992), 129

P. and S. v. Poland, App. No. 57375/08, Eur. Ct. H.R. (2012), 126–27, 132n73, 136, 137, 140nn119–20, 168n11, 176, 223–24n42–44, 304n12, 320–21, 322, 349n16, 355n67, 360nn103–4

Pichon and Sajous v. France, Case No. 49853/99, Eur. Ct. H.R. (2001), 231

Pretty v. United Kingdom, 35 Eur. Ct. H.R. Rep. 1 (2002), 190n4

R.R. v. Poland, App. No. 27617/04, Eur. Ct. H.R. (2011), 126, 128, 131n64, 132n69, 132n73, 133n77, 135n88, 136nn93–94, 136n96, 137–38, 140nn119–20, 168n11, 176, 180n54, 213n7, 349n14, 350, 355n66, 355n68, 359n100, 360–68

S. and Marper v. United Kingdom, App. Nos. 30562/44 and 30566, Eur. Ct. H.R. (2008), 365n131

S.L. v. Austria, App. No. 45330/99, Eur. Ct. H.R. (2003), 359n98, 365n132, 366n140

Tysiąc v. Poland, 45 E.H.R.R. 42 (2007), 124–25, 129–30, 132n69, 132n73, 135n88, 136–37, 140, 168n11, 176, 353n42, 355n68, 359n99, 360n104

Table of Legislation, Treaties, and Other Relevant Instruments

Domestic Legislation, Guidelines, and Instruments

Argentina

Constitution of the Republic of Argentina, August 22, 1994, 146, 150

Criminal Code of Argentina, 1984, 143, 145–48, 156, 175–76, 270, 311n51, 367

Law No. 25.673, National Sexual Health and Responsible Parenthood Program, May 26, 2003, 147n15

Law XV No. 14, Act of the Province of Chubut to Develop Public Heath Facilities for the Treatment of Nonpunishable Abortions, May 31, 2010, 154

Brazil

Constitution of the Federative Republic of Brazil, 1988, 266, 273–77

Law No. 9.347/1997, 269n17

Penal Code, Decree No. 2.848 of December 7, 1940, 260nn2–3, 266, 268, 271–73

Norma Técnica: Atenção Humanizada ao Abortamento (Brasilia: Ministerio da Saúde, 2005), 275n30

Cape Verde

Law of December 31, 1986, 170–71n24

Colombia

Agreement 350/2006 (Bogotá: Ministerio de la Protección Social, 2006), 108n68, 109

Decree 4444/2006 (Bogotá: Ministerio de la Protección Social, 2006), 108n68, 109

Norma Técnica para la Atención de la Interrupción Voluntaria del Embarazo (IVE) Resolution 4905/2006 (Bogotá: Ministerio de la Protección Social, 2006), 108n68, 109, 275n31

Ethiopia

Criminal Code of the Federal Democratic Republic of Ethiopia, 2005, 171n28

Technical and Procedural Guidelines for Safe Abortion Services in Ethiopia (Family Health Department, 2006), 183n64

France

Law 75-17 of 17 January 1975 on the Voluntary Interruption of Pregnancy, 222n35

Law 79-1204 of 31 December 1979 on the Voluntary Interruption of Pregnancy, 222n35

Germany

Basic Law of the Federal Republic of Germany, 1990, 23–24, 32–33nn109–11, 34, 80

Fifth Penal Reform Act, June 18, 1974, 23

Penal Code (StGB), 1977, 27n90

Ghana

Criminal Code 1960 (as consolidated), 182n60

Criminal Code (Amendment) Law, Act 102, 1985, 182n60

Prevention and Management of Unsafe Abortion: Comprehensive Abortion Care Services, Standards and Protocols (Accra: Ghana Health Service, 2006), 182–83nn61–63

Ireland

Constitution of Ireland, 1937, 21n43, 89–90n41

Eighth Amendment of the Constitution Act, 1983, 21n43, 30–31, 125

Offences Against the Person Act (1861), reprinted in 7 *The Statutes* 266 (3d ed. 1950), 125

Protection of Life During Pregnancy Act 2013 (Act No. 35 of 2013), 134–36, 139–40

Kenya

Constitution of Kenya, Rights and Fundamental Freedoms, Part 2 (2010), 107–8

Standards and Guidelines for Reducing Morbidity and Mortality from Unsafe Abortion in Kenya (Nairobi: Ministry of Medical Services, 2012), 183n66

Mexico

Constitution of Mexico, 1917, 29–30n94, 336–38

Constitution of the State of Baja California, 1953, 328n6, 346

Constitution of the State of Chiapas, 1921, 328n6

Nepal

New Zealand

Peru

Penal Code, Legislative Decree No. 635, 1991, 276n34
General Law on Health, Law No. 26842, 1997, 360n101

Poland

Act Amending the Act on Family Planning, Protection of the Human Fetus and Conditions for
    Termination of Pregnancy and Amending Certain Other Acts, August 30, 1996, 64n48
Family Planning, the Protection of the Human Fetus and the Conditions for the Admissibility of
    Abortion Act, January 7, 1993, 61n34, 124, 361n108
Medical Institutions Act 1992, 363, 366n138
Medical Professions Act 1996, 362, 366n139

Portugal

Constitution of the Portuguese Republic, 1976, 38–39, 42n36
Law No. 6/84 of May 11, 1984 amending the Penal Code, 40n21
Law No. 16/2007 of April 17, 2007 amending the Penal Code, 37n7, 47n66, 49, 359n95
Ministry of Health Normative Circular No. 11/SR on the Organization of Services for the Imple-
    mentation of Law No. 16/2007 of 17 April 2007, 105n50

Slovakia

Act No. 73/1986 Coll. on Artificial Interruption of Pregnancy, as amended, 1986, 59n19, 61n36,
    62n37, 74n95, 75n98
Regulation of the Ministry of Health No. 74/1986 Coll. Implementing Act No. 73/1986 Coll. on
    Artificial Interruption of Pregnancy, as amended, 59nn20–21, 59n24, 61n36
Act No. 345/2009 Coll. of Laws on Amending and Supplementing Act No. 576/2004 Coll. of Laws
    on Healthcare, Healthcare-Related Services, and on Amendments and Supplements to Certain
    Acts as Amended, 2009, 74n96, 75nn98–99
Constitutional Act No. 23/1991 Coll., Introducing the Charter of Fundamental Rights and Free-
    doms as a Constitutional Act of the Federal Assembly of the Czech and Slovak Federal Repub-
    lic, 1991, 60
Constitution of the Slovak Republic, 460/1992 Coll., as amended, 1992, 60–62, 64, 65–71

South Africa

Choice on Termination of Pregnancy Act No. 92 of 1996, 29, 99, 110, 171n25
Choice on Termination of Pregnancy Amendment Act No. 1 of 2008, 99, 114, 169, 171n25
Constitution of the Republic of South Africa, 1996, 99n10

Spain

Organic Law 2/2010 of March 3, 2010, on Sexual and Reproductive Health and Voluntary Interruption of Pregnancy, 34n119, 34, 54, 55n97

Tunisia

Law No. 65-25 of 1 July 1965, 169, 171n26

United Kingdom

Abortion Act, 1967, c. 87 (Gr. Brit.), 194–98, 201–2, 204, 208–9, 211, 224–25, 232
Abortion Regulations, 1991, S.I. 1999/499 (Eng. and Wales), 204n70
Act 43 Geo. III, c. 58 (1803) (U.K.), 348, 351n24
Health and Social Care Act, 2012, c. 7 (U.K.), 203n64
Human Fertilisation and Embryology Act, 1990, c. 37 (U.K.), 197, 199–200
Human Fertilisation and Embryology Act, 2008, c. 22 (U.K.), 199–200
Human Rights Act, 1998, c. 42 (U.K.), 190
Infanticide Act, 1938, 1 & 2 Geo. VI, c. 36 (U.K.), 236n100
Offences Against the Persons Act, 1861, 24 and 25 Vict., c. 100 (U.K.), 195, 205, 315n74
Scientific Developments Relating to the Abortion Act 1967, Report of the Science and Technology Committee (2007), 199–200, 208

United States

California Health and Safety Code, §§ 123420–123450, 225
Michigan, *Compiled Laws*, Ch. 333, 17015 (2013), 234
Mississippi Code Annotated, §§ 41-107-1–41-107-13 (2012) (Health Care Rights of Conscience), 225–26, 229, 237
Texas, Health and Safety Code Annotated,§ 171.012 (West 2012), 222
Wisconsin Statutes and Annotations, § 253 (2013), 103n35

Zambia

Standards and Guidelines for Reducing Unsafe Abortion Morbidity and Mortality in Zambia (Lusaka: Ministry of Health, 2009), 183n65
Termination of Pregnancy Act, 1972, 171n27

Zimbabwe

Termination of Pregnancy Act, 1977, 171-172

Regional Treaties, Guidelines, and Instruments

Africa

African Charter on Human and Peoples' Rights, June 27, 1981, 1520 U.N.T.S. 217, O.A.U. Doc. CAB/LEG/67/3 Rev.5 (entered into force October 21, 1986), 166–67, 173

Constitutive Act of the African Union of 2009, 182

Maputo Plan of Action for the Operationalisation of the Continental Policy Framework for Sexual and Reproductive Health and Rights 2007–2010, Special Sess. of the African Union Conference of Ministers of Health, September 18–22, 2006, O.A.U. Doc. Sp/MIN/CAMH/5(I), 168, 183

Protocol to the African Charter on Human and Peoples' Rights on the Rights of Women in Africa, July 11, 2003, 2nd Ordinary Sess. of the Assembly of the African Union, AHG/Res. 240 (XXXI) (entered into force November 25, 2005), 167, 172–73

Protocol to the African Charter on the Establishment of an African Court on Human and Peoples' Rights, June 10, 1998, O.A.U. Doc. OAU/LEG/MIN/AFCH/PROT(I) Rev. 2 (entered into force on June 25, 2004), 173

Americas

American Convention on Human Rights, November 21, 1969, 1144 U.N.T.S. 143, O.A.S.T.S. 36 (entered into force July 18, 1978), 146, 150, 329–30, 345n69

Inter-American Convention on the Prevention, Punishment and Eradication of Violence against Women (Convention Belém do Pará) (entered into force March 5, 1995), 147

Rules of Procedure of the Inter-American Commission on Human Rights, approved by the Commission at its 137th regular period of sessions, held from October 28 to November 13, 2009, and modified on September 2, 2011, 310n40

Europe

European Convention for the Protection of Human Rights and Fundamental Freedoms, November 4, 1950, 213 U.N.T.S. 222, E.T.S. 5 (entered into force September 3, 1953), 66, 122, 136–37, 214, 231–32

International Treaties, Guidelines, and Instruments

International

Notes

Introduction

1. Rebecca J. Cook and Bernard M. Dickens, "Human Rights Dynamics of Abortion Law Reform," *Human Rights Quarterly* 25 (2003): 1–59, 7.

2. James G. March, "Parochialism in the Evolution of a Research Community: The Case of Organizational Studies," *Management and Organization Review* 1 (2004): 5–22, 16.

3. March, "Parochialism," note 2, at 19.

Chapter 1. The Constitutionalization of Abortion

This chapter originally appeared as chapter 52 of *The Oxford Handbook of Comparative Constitutional Law*, ed. Michel Rosenfeld and András Sajó (Oxford: Oxford University Press, 2012). It is reprinted here with the kind permission of Oxford University Press. For comments on the manuscript, I am grateful to Rebecca Cook, Tom Ginsburg, Vicki Jackson, Julieta Lemaitre, Miguel Maduro, Susanna Mancini, Robert Post, Judith Resnik, Ruth Rubio-Marín, and Hunter Smith. I was fortunate to explore the cases in this chapter with the research assistance of Joanna Erdman and in conversation with her. I look forward to continuing to learn together. Thanks also to Alyssa King, Jena McGill, and Danieli Evans.

1. See, e.g., Mary Ann Glendon, *Abortion and Divorce in Western Law* (1987); Donald P. Kommers, "Autonomy, Dignity and Abortion," in Tom Ginsburg and Rosalind Dixon (eds.), *Comparative Constitutional Law* (2011), 441–58 (discussing Ireland, Germany, and the United States). See also Norman Dorsen, Michel Rosenfeld, András Sajó, and Susanne Baer, *Comparative Constitutionalism: Cases and Materials* (2nd ed., 2010), 539–64 (discussing the United States, Canada, Germany, Poland, and Mexico); Vicki C. Jackson and Mark V. Tushnet, *Comparative Constitutional Law* (2nd ed., 2006), 2–139, 196–210 (discussing Canada, Germany, Ireland, and the United States). Comparative studies of abortion legislation are more comprehensive. See, e.g., Albin Eser and Hans-Georg Koch, *Abortion and the Law: From International Comparison to Legal Policy* (2005); Reed Boland and Laura Katzive, "Developments in Laws on Induced Abortion: 1998–2007" (2008) 34 *International Family Planning Perspectives* 110; see also Anika Rahman, Laura Katzive, and Stanley K. Henshaw, "A Global Review of Laws on Induced Abortion, 1985–1997" (1998) 24 *International Family Planning Perspectives* 56.

2. See, e.g., Richard E. Levy and Alexander Somek, "Paradoxical Parallels in the American and

German Abortion Decisions" (2001) 9 *Tulane Journal of International and Comparative Law* 109; Udo Werner, "The Convergence of Abortion Regulation in Germany and the United States: A Critique of Glendon's Rights Talk Thesis" (1996) 18 *Loyola of Los Angeles International and Comparative Law Review* 571. For dynamic accounts attentive to transnational influence, see Federico Fabbrini, "The European Court of Human Rights, the EU Charter of Fundamental Rights and the Right to Abortion: *Roe v. Wade* on the Other Side of the Atlantic?" (2011) 18 *Columbia Journal of European Law* 1; Sjef Gevers, "Abortion Legislation and the Future of the "Counseling Model" (2006) 13 *European Journal of Health Law* 27.

3. One comparative study that begins by investigating the political origins of the first constitutional decisions on abortion is Machteld Nijsten, *Abortion and Constitutional Law: A Comparative European-American Study* (1990).

4. On the relationship of law and politics in the abortion cases, see Reva B. Siegel, "Dignity and Sexuality: Claims on Dignity in Transnational Debates over Abortion and Same Sex Marriage" (2012) 10.2 9 *International Journal of Constitutional Law* (forthcoming):355. See also Linda Greenhouse and Reva B. Siegel, "Before (and After) *Roe v. Wade*: New Questions About Backlash" (2011) 120 *Yale Law Journal* 2028; Robert Post and Reva B. Siegel, "Roe Rage: Democratic Constitutionalism and Backlash" (2007) 42 *Harvard Civil Rights–Civil Liberties Law Review* 373; and Reva B. Siegel, "Dignity and the Politics of Protection: Abortion Restrictions Under Casey/Carhart" (2008) 117 *Yale Law Journal* 1694.

5. For comparative literature on abortion legislation, see note 1.

6. *Roe v. Wade* 410 U.S. 113 (1973).

7. BVerfGE 1 (1975), translated in Robert E. Jonas and John D. Gorby, "West German Abortion Decision: A Contrast to *Roe v. Wade*" (1976) 9 *John Marshall Journal of Practice and Procedure* 605–684 (the *Abortion I* case).

8. Ruth Roemer, "Abortion Law: The Approaches of Different Nations" (1967) 57 *American Journal of Public Health* 1906, 1908–18.

9. Rebecca J. Cook and Bernard M. Dickens, "A Decade of International Change in Abortion Law: 1967–1977" (1978) 68 *American Journal of Public Health* 637, 643–44. See also Ruth Roemer, "Abortion Law Reform and Repeal: Legislative and Judicial Developments" (1971) 61 *American Journal of Public Health* 500, 504–5.

10. Nijsten (note 3).

11. See Glendon (note 1), 45; Kim Lane Scheppele, "Constitutionalizing Abortion" in Marianne Githens and Dorothy McBride Stetson (eds.), *Abortion Politics: Public Policy in Cross-Cultural Perspective* (1996), 29–54.

12. This theme recurs but it is not clearly developed in the literature, see Glendon (note 1), 45; Scheppele (note 11), 29–30; Donald P. Kommers, "The Constitutional Law of Abortion in Germany: Should Americans Pay Attention?" (1994) 10 *Contemporary Journal of Health Law and Policy* 1, 31 (limiting claim to U.S. judicialization).

13. Nijsten (note 3), 1, 228, 232.

14. On the relationship of constitutional politics and constitutional law, see note 4.

15. See Dagmar Herzog, *Sexuality in Europe: A Twentieth-Century History* (2011), 156, 159; Greenhouse and Siegel (note 4), 2036.

16. See Herzog (note 15), 156; Greenhouse and Siegel (note 4), 2037; Christopher Tietze, "Abortion in Europe" (1967) 57 *American Journal of Public Health* 1923, 1926.

17. Nijsten (note 3), 29–33.

18. Greenhouse and Siegel (note 4), 2038–39; Nijsten (note 3), 33.

19. Greenhouse and Siegel (note 4), 3029–46; Herzog (note 15), 156–60; Nijsten (note 3), 30; Reva B. Siegel, "*Roe's* Roots: The Women's Rights Claims that Engendered *Roe*" (2010) 90 *Boston University Law Review* 1875. See also Myra Marx Ferree, William Anthony Gamson, Jurgen Gerhards, and Dieter Rucht, *Shaping Abortion Discourse: Democracy and the Public Sphere in Germany and the United States* (2002), 131–53; Dorothy McBride Stetson (ed.), *Abortion Politics, Women's Movements, and the Democratic State: A Comparative Study of State Feminism* (2003); Joni Lovenduski and Joyce Outshoorn (eds.), *The New Politics of Abortion* (1986).

20. "La liste des 343 françaises qui ont le courage de signer le manifest 'je me suis fait avorter'" [The list of 343 French women who have the courage to sign the manifesto "I have had an abortion"] *Le Nouvel Observateur*, April 5, 1971, at 5 (author's translation).

21. See Herzog (note 15), 156.

22. "Wir haben abgetrieben!" [We Aborted] *Stern* (Hamburg), June 6, 1971, at 16 (author's translation). See also Alice Schwarzer (ed.), *Frauen gegen den §218: 18 Protokolle, aufgezeichnet von Alice Schwarzer* [*Women Against §218: Eighteen Interviews, Recorded by Alice Schwarzer*] (1971), 146 (author's translation).

23. "Anche in Italia 'autodenunce' per l'aborto," *Liberazione Notizie*, August 4, 1971, reprinted at *Even in Italy "autoenunce" for abortion*, available at http://old.radicali.it/search_view.php?id=44852&lang=&cms=. See Herzog (note 15), 159 n. 24; Marina Calloni, "Debates and Controversies on Abortion in Italy" in Stetson (note 19), 181.

24. Barbaralee D. Diamonstein, "We Have Had Abortions," *Ms. Magazine*, Spring 1972, 34; cf. Siegel, "*Roe's* Roots" (note 19), 1880, 1885. For the language of some of the manifestos, see Siegel, "Dignity and Sexuality" (note 4), ms. at 7 (on file with author).

25. Betty Friedan, President, National Organization for Women, Address at the First National Conference on Abortion Laws: Abortion: A Woman's Civil Right (February 1969), reprinted in Linda Greenhouse and Reva B. Siegel (eds.), *Before* Roe v. Wade: *Voices That Shaped the Abortion Debate Before the Supreme Court's Ruling* (2010), 38.

26. Greenhouse and Siegel (note 25), 39.

27. Ibid., 39–40.

28. Jean C. Robinson, "Gendering the Abortion Debate: The French Case" in Stetson (note 19), 86, 88.

29. Maria Mesner, "Political Culture and the Abortion Conflict: A Comparison of Austria and the United States," in David F. Good and Ruth Wodak (eds.), *From World War to Waldheim: Culture and Politics in Austria and the United States* (1999), 187–209, 196 (citing Maria Mesner, *Frauensache? Zur Auseinandersetzung um den Schwangerschaftsabbruch in Österreich nach 1945* [1994], 207).

30. Greenhouse and Siegel (note 4), 2048–52 (United States); Anne Egger and Bill Rolston (eds.), *Abortion in the New Europe: A Comparative Handbook* (1994), 33, 40 (Britain and Austria).

31. Greenhouse and Siegel (note 4), 2046–51, 2077–79.

32. Ibid., 2049. See generally Greenhouse and Siegel (note 25), 69–115 (surveying religious and secular arguments against abortion reform in the United States in the decade before *Roe*).

33. Dagmar Herzog, *Sex After Fascism: Memory and Morality in Twentieth Century Germany* (2005), 225; Lewis Joachim Edinger, *West German Politics* (1986), 281.

34. Manfried Spieker, *Kirche und Abtreibung in Deutschland: Ursachen und Verlauf eines Konflikts* (2nd ed., 2008), 22 (author's translation).

35. Siegel, "Dignity and Sexuality" (note 4), ms at 9, 16, 19–20; Spieker (note 34), 23.

36. Spieker (note 34), 22–23.

37. Edinger (note 33), 282.

38. Robert Spaemann, *Kein Recht auf Leben? Argumente zur Grundsatzdiskussion um die Reform des §218* (1974), 10 (author's translation). For a history of Catholic Church opposition to reform in the years leading up to the Court's ruling, see Hermann Tallen, *Die Auseinandersetzung über §218 StGB* (1977).

39. Nijsten (note 3), 232.

40. In the United States, movements seeking repeal of abortion legislation began litigation in a number of states in a quest to move federal courts to address the constitutionality of restrictions on abortion, ultimately prevailing in January of 1973 in the Supreme Court. *Roe* (note 6). See Siegel (note 19), 1884–94. Over two years (1974–75), four courts in Western Europe issued judgments on the constitutionality of the legal regulation of abortion: *Abortion I* (note 7), Judgment of October 11, 1974, Verfassungsgerichtshof [1974] Erklärungen des Verfassungsgerichtshof 221, translated and reprinted in Mauro Cappelletti and William Cohen, *Comparative Constitutional Law: Cases and Materials* (1979), 615 (Austria); Judgment of January 15, 1975, Conseil constitutionnel, 1975 DS Jur 529, translated and reprinted in Cappelletti and Cohen, ibid. 577 (France); Judgment of February 18, 1975, Corte costituzionale [Rac uff corte cost] 201, 98 Foro It I 515, translated and reprinted in Cappelletti and Cohen, ibid. 612 (Italy). See Nijsten (note 3), 232. See also Donald P. Kommers, "Liberty and Community in Constitutional Law: The Abortion Cases in Comparative Perspective" (1985) 3 *Brigham Young University Law Review* 371, 371–72.

41. Nijsten (note 3), 232. See also note 34 and accompanying text.

42. See note 1. For an early example, Donald P. Kommers, "Abortion and the Constitution: United States and West Germany" (1977) 25 *American Journal of Comparative Law* 255, 276–85.

43. Commentators do not generally look to constitutional text to explain the divergent approaches of the U.S. and German courts; constitutions do not begin expressly to address abortion until after the decisions of the 1970s. See, e.g., Republic of Ireland, Eighth Amendment of the Constitution Act, 1983, 1983 Acts of the Oireachtas, October 7, 1983 (amending Irish Constitution, Art 40.3.3): "The State acknowledges the right to life of the unborn and, with due regard to the equal right to life of the mother, guarantees in its laws to respect, and, as far as practicable, by its laws to defend and vindicate that right."

44. See Gerald L. Neuman, "Casey in the Mirror: Abortion, Abuse, and the Right to Protection in the United States and Germany" (1995) 43 *American Journal of Comparative Law* 273, 274.

45. Kommers (note 1), 452–53 (describing the United States as a liberal democracy and Germany as a social democracy).

46. Simone Mantei, *Nein und Ja zur Abtreibung: Die Evangelische Kirche in der Reformdebatte um §218 StGB (1970–1976)* (2004), 448 (author's translation); Edinger (note 33), 283; Siegel, "Dignity and Sexuality" (note 4), [TAN 56–58].

47. See, e.g., Levy and Somek (note 2); Nijsten (note 3); Siegel, "Dignity and Sexuality" (note 4); see also Ferree, Gamson, Gerhards, and Rucht (note 19).

48. See sources in note 19 (feminist advocates of liberalization); nn. 30–38 (opponents of liberalization).

49. Greenhouse and Siegel (note 25), 256–58.

50. Ibid., 155.

51. Ibid., 164–65.

52. See *Roe* (note 6), 153.

53. See the first section; Siegel (note 19), 1885–94.

54. Brief for Appellants, *Roe v. Wade* 410 U.S. 113 (1973), (No. 70–18) 1971 WL 128054, reprinted in Greenhouse and Siegel (note 25), 230, 234.

55. *Roe* (note 6), 153. Siegel (note 19), 1897.

56. *Roe* (note 6), 153.

57. See Siegel (note 19), 1899.

58. Reva B. Siegel, "Reasoning From the Body: An Historical Perspective on Abortion Regulation and Questions of Equal Protection" (1992) 44 *Stanford Law Review* 261, 275–77.

59. *Abortion I* (note 7), 605.

60. Ibid., 641 (citing Arts. 2[2] [1] and 1[1] [2]).

61. Ibid., 661. See also ibid., 662.

62. Ibid., 643 (citing German Federal Parliament, Seventh Election Period, 96th Sess., Stenographic Reports, 6492).

63. Ibid., 644.

64. Ibid., 644.

65. Ibid., 647.

66. Ibid.

67. Ibid., 653.

68. Ibid., 624, 647–48. The Court gave the legislature discretion whether to allow abortion on eugenic, rape, and social emergency indications. Ibid.

69. Ibid., 649.

70. East Germany allowed abortion during the first twelve weeks of pregnancy as West Germany did not, and so, in the 1990s, the abortion issue became entangled in negotiations over reunification, leading to the enactment of more liberal abortion legislation. See Peter H. Merkl, *German Unification in the European Context* (1993), 176–80.

In the United States, abortion became entangled in the competition of the national political parties for voters. Even before *Roe*, leaders of the Republican Party changed position on abortion to attract Catholics who had historically voted with the Democratic Party, as well as Americans opposed to feminist understandings of the family. By the late 1980s, a majority of Republican voters opposed abortion, and the party had reshaped the composition of the Supreme Court in ways that threatened *Roe*. Greenhouse and Siegel (note 4); Post and Siegel (note 4).

For an account of the changing political context of the 1990s and renewed feminist and Catholic mobilization in Germany and the United States, see Ferree, Gamson, Gerhards, and Rucht (note 19), 39–43.

71. 505 U.S. 833 (1992).

72. Ibid., 844.

73. Ibid., 871.

74. Ibid., 877.

75. Ibid., 877.

76. See Siegel, "Dignity and the Politics of Protection" (note 4), 1735–66, 1773–80. For an account tracing these arguments from the 1970s to the U.S. Supreme Court's most recent abortion decision, see Siegel (note 19). See also Siegel, "Dignity and Sexuality" (note 4) (analyzing competing claims about dignity and abortion historically and transnationally). Since *Casey*, scholars in the United States have increasingly discussed the abortion right as grounded in equality as well as

liberty. See Reva B. Siegel, "Sex Equality Arguments for Reproductive Rights: Their Critical Basis and Evolving Constitutional Expression" (2007) 56 *Emory Law Journal* 815.

77. Ibid., 851 (O'Connor, Kennedy, Souter JJ, Joint Opinion).

78. Ibid., 852 (O'Connor, Kennedy, Souter JJ, Joint Opinion); ibid., 856 (O'Connor, Kennedy, Souter JJ, Joint Opinion): "for two decades of economic and social developments, people have organized intimate relationships and made choices that define their views of themselves and their places in society, in reliance on the availability of abortion in the event that contraception should fail. The ability of women to participate equally in the economic and social life of the Nation has been facilitated by their ability to control their reproductive lives."

The opinion ties constitutional protection for women's abortion decision to the understanding, forged in the Court's sex discrimination cases, that government cannot use law to enforce traditional sex roles on women.

79. *Casey* (note 71), 893–98.

80. Ibid., 896–98 (citation omitted).

81. *Abortion I* (note 7) at 653; see nn. 63–68.

82. See note 70.

83. See 88 BVerfGE 203 (1993), [36]–[37] available at http://www.bverfg.de/entscheidungen/fs19930528_2bvf000290en.html (the *Abortion II* case) (official court translation).

84. Ibid., [149].

85. Ibid., [173]–[174]; see also ibid., [170]–[172].

86. Ibid., [178].

87. Ibid., [183].

88. Ibid., [185].

89. Ibid., [214].

90. See German Penal Code (StGB), para. 218a; in English available at http://www.gesetze-im-internet.de/englisch_stgb/englisch_stgb.html#StGB_000P218.

91. Mary Anne Case, "Perfectionism and Fundamentalism in the Application of the German Abortion Laws" in Susan H. Williams (ed.), *Constituting Equality: Gender Equality and Comparative Constitutional Law* (2009) 93, 96; Nanette Funk, "Abortion Counselling and the 1995 German Abortion Law" (1996–97) 12 *Connecticut Journal of International Law* 33.

92. South Africa, *The Choice on Termination of Pregnancy Act, 1996* (Act No. 92 of 1996).

93. *Christian Lawyers Association v. Minister of Health* [2004] 4 All SA 31 (T), 39. See also ibid. 39: "The South African Constitution recognises and protects the right to termination of pregnancy or abortion in two ways, firstly under section 12(2)(a), that is, the right to bodily and psychological integrity which includes the right to make decisions concerning reproduction, and secondly, under section 12(2)(b), that is, the right to control over one's body."

In an earlier judgment, the law was upheld as constitutional against claims of violation of the right to life on the view that legal personhood commences only at live birth. *Christian Lawyers Association of South Africa & Others v. Minister of Health & Others* 1998 (4) SA 113 (T).

94. Constitucion Politica de los Estados Unidos Mexicanos, as amended, Art. 4, Diario Oficial de la Federacion, February 5, 1917 (Mexico) (Right to Choose Clause) (author's translation).

95. Mexico, Federal District, Decree Reforming the Federal District Penal Code and Amending the Federal District Health Law, Official Gazette of the Federal District No. 70, April 26, 2007 (author's translation) (emphasis added).

96. Accion de inconstitucionalidad 146/2007 y su acumulada 147/2007, Pleno de la Suprema

Corte de Justicia de la Nacion, Novena Epoca, August 28, 2008, available at http://www.informa
.scjn.gob.mx/sentencia.html.

97. On gender, see Catharine A. MacKinnon, "Gender in Constitutions," chapter 19 of *The Oxford Handbook of Comparative Constitutional Law*, ed. Michel Rosenfeld, András Sajó (Oxford: Oxford University Press, 2012), 397–416.

98. Republic of Ireland, Eighth Amendment of the Constitution Act, 1983 (note 43) (emphasis added).

99. *Attorney General v. X and others* [1992] 1 IR 1, para. [44].

100. Ibid., para. 32 (citing *McGee v. Attorney General* [1974] IR 284, 318–19).

101. Tribunal Constitucional, STC 53/1985, Pt. 11(b), April 11, 1985, 1985–49 Boletin de Jurisprudencia Constitucional 515 (Spain), available at http://www.boe.es/aeboe/consultas/bases_datos /doc.php?coleccion=tc&id=SENTENCIA-1985–0053. Official court translation available at http:// www.tribunalconstitucional.es/es/jurisprudencia/restrad/Paginas/JCC531985en.aspx.

102. See, e.g., ibid., Pt. 9: "We are required to consider whether legislation [*sic*] is *constitutionally permitted* to use a different technique [to protect unborn life], by means of which punishability is specifically excluded for certain offences." A dissenting judgment objects that the majority employs rights rhetoric without conferring rights: "despite the rhetorical claims to the contrary, it totally ignores the fundamental rights of physical and moral integrity and that of privacy enshrined in the Constitution, and to which pregnant women are indeed entitled." Ibid., dissenting opinion of Senior Judge Francisco Rubio Llorente (no paragraph numbering in the judgment).

103. Corte Constitucional (Constitutional Court), May 10, 2006, Sentencia C-355/2006, 25, Gaceta de la Corte Constitucional (Colombia) (partial translation is available in *Women's Link Worldwide, C-355/2006: Excerpts of the Constitutional Court's Ruling that Liberalized Abortion in Colombia* (2007).

104. Ibid., 36.

105. Ibid., 50 (emphasis added).

106. Ibid., 51 (emphasis added).

107. Ibid., 53.

108. Ibid., 54–57.

109. For discussion of counseling and its normative bases as a "third model" in abortion regulation (supplemental to periodic/indication models), see Eser and Koch (note 1); for analysis of the counseling framework attentive to its gendered premises, see Ruth Rubio-Marín, "Constitutional Framing: Abortion and Symbolism in Constitutional Law" (2009 draft, and Ruth Rubio-Marín, "Abortion in Portugal: New Trends in European Constitutionalism," in this volume. For discussion of counseling in the United States see Siegel, "Dignity and the Politics of Protection" (note 4).

110. See text accompanying note 69.

111. See text accompanying notes 83, 89.

112. Alkotmanybirosag (Constitutional Court), Decision 48/1998 (XI.23), Official Gazette (MagyarKozlony) MK 1998/105 (Hungary), Section III, Pt. (3)(d) (p. 26), official court translation available at http://www.mkab.hu/admin/data/file/710_48_1998.pdf.

113. Ibid., Section III, Pt. (3)(c) (p. 24).

114. Ibid., Section IV, Pt. (2)(a) (p. 34).

115. Ibid., Section IV, Pt 2(a) (p 35) (emphasis added).

116. For rich discussion, see Rubio-Marín (note 109).

117. Tribunal Constitucional, Acordao no 75/2010, Processos nos 733/07 and 1186/07, March

26, 2010, Diario da Republica vol 60, at 15566 (Portugal), available at http://w3.tribunalconstitucional
.pt/acordaos/acordaos10/1–100/7510.htm (author's translation).

The Court observed at 11.4.15: "Our legislature has made clear the goal of the counseling by
stating that such counseling is aimed at providing the pregnant woman access to all relevant information necessary to make a free, genuine ('*consciente*'), and responsible decision."

The Court further observed that the legislation directed that the pregnant woman would receive information concerning government assistance should she carry the pregnancy to term, and
stated at 11.4.15 that: "the body of information to be provided to the pregnant woman in a mandatory counseling process . . . has the objective effect of promoting in her the consciousness of the
value of the life that she carries in her (or, at least, it will clearly be perceived by her as an attempt
to do so). . . . The fact that the counseling process is not, expressly and ostensively, orientational
does not impose, ipso facto, its qualification as merely informative and deprived of any intention to
favor a decision to carry on with the pregnancy."

118. See ibid., 11.4.16: "By abstaining, even at a communicational level, from any indication
that might be felt by the woman as an external judgment imposing a particular decision, the legislator acted in line with the underlying reasoning supporting the decision not to punish abortion. This
is based on the belief that only the free adhesion of the woman to carry on with the pregnancy
guarantees, at this stage, the protection of the unborn life. . . .

"It is objectively founded for a legislator that has decided, also for reasons of efficiency, to trust
in the sense of responsibility of the pregnant woman by calling her to cooperate in the duty of
protection that belongs to the State, not to create a context of decision that may run counter that
purpose.

"The trust in the sense of responsibility of the woman and in her predisposition to be open to
the reasons contrary to abortion would not be compatible with a tutelage and paternalistic approach. The protection of the woman's dignity is also affirmed by the way in which the counseling
process imposed on her takes place."

119. Ley Organica 2/2010, de 3 de marzo, de salud sexual y reproductiva y de la interrupcion
voluntaria del embarazo (Spain) (author's translation).

120. See Eser and Koch (note 1); Gevers (note 2).

121. See Rubio-Marín (note 109).

122. See Siegel, "Dignity and the Politics of Protection" (note 4).

123. See, e.g., Myra Max Ferree, "Resonance and Radicalism: Feminist Framing in the Abortion Debates of the United States and Germany" (2003) 109 *American Journal of Sociology* 304;
Siegel, "Dignity and the Politics of Protection" (note 4). For similar reasons, appeals to dignity now
play a significant role on both sides of the abortion debate, transnationally. See Siegel, "Dignity and
Sexuality" (note 4).

Chapter 2. Abortion in Portugal

This chapter reflects legal changes up to June 30, 2013.

1, Conseil Constitutionnel [Constitutional Court] January 15, 1975, D.S.Jur. 529 [1975]
A.J.D.A. 134 (Fr.).

2. Verfassungsgerichtshof [Constitutional Court] October 11, 1974, Erklaerungen des Verfassungsgerichtshofs 221 (Austria).

3. Bundesverfassungsgericht [Federal Constitutional Court] February 25, 1975, 39 BVerfGE 1 (Ger.) [hereinafter 39 BVerfGE 1], translated in Robert E. Jonas and John D. Gorby, "West German Abortion Decision: A Contrast to *Roe v. Wade*", *John Marshall Journal of Practice and Procedure* 9 (1976): 605–684.

4. Alkotmánybíróság [Constitutional Court] 1998, 48/1998 (XI. 23), Magyar Közlöny [MK] 1998/105 (Hung.).

5. Trybunal Konstitucyjny [Constitutional Tribunal] May 28, 1997, K 26/96, Orzecznictwo Trybunału Konstytucyjnego, Rok 1997 [Case Law of the Constitutional Tribunal, 1997] (Pol.).

6. Tribunal Constitucional [Constitutional Court] February 23, 2010, Acórdão No. 75/2010 [hereinafter Acórdão No. 75/2010].

7. Código Penal [Criminal Code], art. 142, as amended by Law No. 16/2007 (Port.) [hereinafter Law No. 16/2007].

8. Tribunal Constitucional [Constitutional Court] 1984, Acórdão No. 25/84, Acórdãos do Tribunal Constitucional II, 7 [hereinafter Acórdão No. 25/84].

9. Tribunal Constitucional [Constitutional Court] 1985, Acórdão No. 85/85, Acórdãos do Tribunal Constitucional V, 245 [hereinafter Acórdão No. 85/85].

10. Tribunal Constitucional [Constitutional Court] 1998, Acórdão No. 288/98, .nst 117. 833 (1992) (US Supreme Court). tion of pregnancy, f recognizing prenatal personhood. Diário da República 91/98 Suplemento I-A Série [hereinafter Acórdão No. 288/98].

11. See Tribunal Constitucional [Constitutional Court] 2006, Acórdão No. 617/2006, Diário da República I Série [hereinafter Acórdão No. 617/2006].

12. Acórdão No. 75/2010, note 6.

13. See Ruth Rubio-Marín and Wen-Chen Chang, "Sites of Constitutional Struggle for Women's Equality," in *Routledge Handbook of Constitutional Law*, ed. Mark Tushnet, Thomas Fleiner, and Cheryl Saunders (New York: Routledge, 2013), 301–12.

14. Reva Siegel, "The Constitutionalization of Abortion," in this volume.

15. Siegel, "Constitutionalization," note 14.

16. *Roe v. Wade*, 410 U.S. 113 (1973) (U.S. Supreme Court).

17. *Roe v. Wade*, note 16, at 164–65.

18. See *Planned Parenthood of Southeastern Pa. v. Casey*, 505 U.S. 833 (1992) (U.S. Supreme Court).

19. See Corte Costituzionale [Constitutional Court] February 18, 1975, No. 27, 98 Foro It. I, 515 (It.).

20. 39 BVerfGE 1, note 3.

21. Código Penal [Criminal Code of Portugal] as amended by Law No. 6/84, of May 11.

22. Acórdão No. 85/85, note 9.

23. Acórdão No. 25/84, note 8, cfr. VII, §1.

24. 39 BVerfGE 1, note 3, at C.I.1. (b); Jonas Trans. at 638, author's italics.

25. 39 BVerfGE 1, note 3, at C.I.2; Jonas trans. at 641.

26. 39 BVerfGE 1, note 3, at, CII.2; Jonas trans. at 642.

27. 39 BVerfGE 1, note 3, at CIII.1; Jonas trans. at 644.

28. 39 BVerfGE 1, note 3, at C.III.3; Jonas trans. at 648.

29. Acórdão No. 85/85, note 9, cfr. 2, §2.

30. Acórdão No. 85/85, note 9, cfr. 2, §2.

31. 39 BVerfGE 1, note 3, at D.III; Jonas trans. at 660.

32. 39 BVerfGE 1, note 3, at D.II.2; Jonas trans. at 653–57.

33. 39 BVerfGE 1, note 3, at D.II.2; Jonas trans. at 653.

34. 39 BVerfGE 1, note 3.

35. Acórdão No. 288/98, note 10.

36. Constitution of the Portuguese Republic, April 25, 1976, art. 115(11).

37. See J. Bacelar Gouveia and H. Mota, eds., *Vida e direito: Reflexões sobre um referendo* (Cascais: Principia, 1998) (collecting articles against abortion from twenty-nine right-wing law professors).

38. André Freire and Michael A. Baum, "1998 Portuguese Referendums: Explaining the Results and Speculating on the Future of Direct Democracy in Portugal," *Portuguese Journal of Social Science* 2.1 (2003): 5–19, at 18.

39. Freire and Baum, "Portuguese Referendums," note 38, at 23, 29.

40. Freire and Baum, "Portuguese Referendums," note 38, at 19, 22, 23.

41. Acórdão No. 288/98, note 10, cfr. §§45, 47.

42. Acórdão No. 288/98, note 10, cfr. §46.

43. Acórdão No. 288/98, note 10, cfr. §48.

44. Acórdão No. 288/98, note 10, cfr. §48.

45. Acórdão No. 288/98, note 10, cfr. §49.

46. Acórdão No. 288/98, note 10, cfr. §§28–42.

47. Acórdão No. 288/98, note 10, cfr. §§28–42.

48. Acórdão No. 288/98, note 10, cfr. §32.

49. Acórdão No. 288/98, note 10, cfr. §42.

50. Acórdão No. 288/98, note 10, cfr. §52.

51. Acórdão No. 288/98, note 10.

52. Acórdão No. 288/98, note 10, see the dissenting votes by A. Tavares da Costa, P. Mota Pinto, V. Nunes de Almeida, M. P. Pizarro Beleza, and Chief Justice J. M. Cardoso da Costa.

53. Acórdão No. 288/98, note 10, see in particular the dissenting vote by Messias Bento but also those of V. Nunes de Almeida and Chief Justice J. M. Cardoso da Costa.

54. See Madalena Duarte, Carlos Barradas, Ana Cristina Santos, and Madga Alves, "Representações em torno da lei do aborto em Portugal: Cenários passados e futuros," *Revista do Ministério Público* 30.120 (2009): 191–217.

55. See Acórdão No. 617/2006, note 11.

56. Duarte et al., "Representações," note 54, at 208.

57. See Acórdão No. 617/2006, note 11, cfr. §§15, 30–31.

58. Acórdão No. 617/2006, note 11, cfr. §32.

59. Acórdão No. 617/2006, note 11, cfr. §32.

60. Acórdão No. 617/2006, note 11, cfr. §33.

61. Acórdão No. 617/2006, note 11, cfr. §34.

62. Acórdão No. 617/2006, note 11, see the dissenting votes by Chief Justice R. M. Moura Ramos, M. P. Pizarro Beleza, and P. Mota Pinto.

63. Acórdão No. 617/2006, note 11, see the dissenting votes by B. Rodrigues and M. Torres.

64. Exclusion of wrongdoing in cases of interruption of pregnancy, Law No. 16/2007, of April 17 (Port.).

65. Law No. 16/2007, note 7.

66. Código Penal, note 63, at art. 6.

67. Acórdão No. 75/2010, note 12, cfr. §46.

68. Acórdão No. 75/2010, note 12, cfr. §46.

69. Acórdão No. 75/2010, note 12, cfr. §46.

70. Acórdão No. 75/2010, note 12, cfr. §14.4.2.

71. Acórdão No. 75/2010, note 12, cfr. §11.4.4.

72. Acórdão No. 75/2010, note 12, cfr. §§11.4.5, 11.4.6.

73. Acórdão No. 75/2010, note 12, cfr. §11.4.3.

74. Acórdão No. 75/2010, note 12, cfr. §11.4.3.

75. Acórdão No. 75/2010, note 12, cfr. §11.4.4.

76. See Bundesverfassungsgericht [Federal Constitutional Court] May 28, 1993, 88 BVerfGE 203 [hereinafter 88 BVerfGE 203].

77. Acórdão No. 75/2010, note 12, cfr. §11.4.4.

78. See 88 BVerfGE 203, note 76.

79. 88 BVerfGE 203, note 76.

80. 88 BVerfGE 203, note 76, at D.II.

81. Acórdão No. 75/2010, note 12, cfr. §11.4.13.

82. Acórdão No. 75/2010, note 12, cfr. §§11.4.13 and 11.4.17.

83. Acórdão No. 75/2010, note 12, see dissent by Chief Justice Rui Manuel Moura Ramos (§§2–3).

84. Acórdão No. 75/2010, note 12, cfr. §11.4.15.

85. Acórdão No. 75/2010, note 12, cfr. §11.9.2.

86. Acórdão No. 75/2010, note 12, cfr. §11.4.10.

87. Acórdão No. 75/2010, note 12, cfr. §11.4.10.

88. Acórdão No. 75/2010, note 12, cfr. §11.4.16.

89. Acórdão No. 75/2010, note 12, cfr. §11.4.16.

90. Acórdão No. 75/2010, note 12, cfr. §11.4.16.

91. Acórdão No. 75/2010, note 12, cfr. §11.4.18.

92. Acórdão No. 75/2010, note 12, cfr. §11.4.18.

93. Acórdão No. 75/2010, note 12, cfr. §11.6.

94. Acórdão No. 75/2010, note 12, cfr. §11.6.

95. Acórdão No. 75/2010, note 12, cfr. §11.6.

96. Acórdão No. 75/2010, note 12, cfr. §11.6.

97. Statute on *Sexual and Reproductive Health and the Voluntary Interruption of Pregnancy* (Ley Orgánica 2/2010, of March 3) (Spain).

Chapter 3. Abortion, Women, and the Slovak Constitutional Court

I am grateful to Janka Debrecéniová, Johanna B. Fine, Martin Fotta, Lisa Kelly, Ľubica Kobová, Jarmila Lajčáková, Michaela Potančoková, Agata Szypulska, Johanna Westeson, and Christina Zampas for comments on earlier versions of this chapter. I would also like to thank the editors of this book for their comments and the participants of the Shifting Paradigms in Abortion Law workshop held at Faculty of Law, University of Toronto in May 2012, for their stimulating discussion. All translations are by the author. This chapter reflects legal changes up to June 30, 2013.

1. Ústavný Súd [Constitutional Court] December 4, 2007, PL. ÚS 12/01, Collection of Laws of

the Slovak Republic, No. 14/2008, vol. 8 (Slovakia), unofficial translation [hereinafter PL. ÚS 12/01].

2. Bundesverfassungsgericht [Federal Constitutional Court] May 28, 1993, 2 BvF 2/90, paras. 1–434, (Germany), [hereinafter BVerfG 1993]; Alkotmánybíróság [Constitutional Court] 1998, Decision 48/1998 (XI.23), Magyar Közlöny [MK] 1998/105 (Hungary), http://www.mkab.hu/letoltesek/en_0048_1998.pdf [hereinafter Decision 48/1998]; Trybunal Konstytucyjny [Constitutional Tribunal] May 28, 1997, K 26/96, Orzecznictwo Trybunału Konstytucyjnego, Rok 1997 [Case Law of the Constitutional Tribunal, 1997] (Poland), http://www.trybunal.gov.pl/eng/Judical _Decisions/1986_1999/K_%2026_96a.pdf [hereinafter Decision K 26/96].

3. Katarína Zavacká, "Prerušenie tehotenstva v práve na území Slovenska," in *Možnosť voľby. Aspekty práv a zodpovednosti,* ed. Jana Cviková and Jana Juráňová (Bratislava: ASPEKT, 2001), 23–26. See also Gabriela Nikšová, *Nedovolené prerušenie tehotenstva v československom trestnom práve* (Martin: Slovenská akadémia vied, 1971).

4. Nikšová, *Nedovolené,* note 3; Bill No. 3851, 1922, National Assembly of the Czechoslovak Republic, http://www.psp.cz/eknih/1920ns/ps/tisky/T3851_00.htm (accessed January 21, 2013).

5. See, e.g., Bill No. 3851, note 4; Bill No. 694, 1920, National Assembly of the Czechoslovak Republic, http://www.psp.cz/eknih/1920ns/ps/tisky/t0694_00.htm; Chamber of Deputies of the National Assembly of Czechoslovak Republic, 370th sess., 1925, http://www.psp.cz/eknih/1920ns/ps/stenprot/370schuz/s370001.htm; Chamber of Deputies of the National Assembly of Czechoslovak Republic, 74th sess., 1927, http://www.psp.cz/eknih/1925ns/ps/stenprot/074schuz/s074001.htm (accessed January 21, 2013).

6. See Radka Dudová, *Interrupce v České republice: Zápas o ženská těla* (Praha: Sociologický ústav AV ČR, 2012), 50; Radka Dudová, "The Framing of Abortion in the Czech Republic: How the Continuity of Discourse Prevents Institutional Change," *Sociologický časopis/Czech Sociological Review* 46 (2010): 945–75, at 955.

7. Trestní zákon [Criminal Code] č. 86/1950 Sb., s. 218.

8. See Dudová, "The Framing," note 6, at 950–51.

9. Zákon č. 68/1957 Sb. o umělém přerušení těhotenství [Act No. 68/1957 Coll. on Artificial Interruption of Pregnancy] [hereinafter Act 68/1957].

10. Act 68/1957, note 9, ss. 3, 7, 8. See also Vyhl. MZ č. 104/1961 Sb., kterou se provádí zákon o umělém přerušení těhotenství [Regulation of the Ministry of Health No. 104/1961 Coll. Implementing the Act on Artificial Interruption of Pregnancy], September 13, 1961 [hereinafter Regulation 104/1961]; Vládní nař. č. 126/1962 Sb., kterým se zřizují interrupční komise a provádí zákon o umělém přerušení těhotenství [Government Decree No. 126/1962 Coll. Establishing Abortion Commissions and Implementing the Act on Artificial Interruption of Pregnancy], December 21, 1962 [hereinafter Decree 126/1962]; Vládní nař. č. 95/1964 Sb., jímž se mění vládní nařízení č. 126/1962 Sb. [Government Decree No. 95/1964 Coll. Amending Government Decree No. 126/1962 Coll.], May 27, 1964; Nařízení vlády SSR č. 70/1973 Sb. o zrušení vládního nařízení č. 126/1962 Sb. [Decree of the Government of the SSR No. 70/1973 Coll. Repealing Government Decree No. 126/1962 Coll.], May 16, 1973; Vyhl. MZ SSR č. 72/1973 Sb., kterou se provádí zákon č. 68/1957 Sb. [Regulation of the Ministry of Health of the SSR No. 72/1973 Coll. Implementing the Act No. 68/1957 Coll.], May 16, 1973 [hereinafter Regulation 72/1973]; Vyhl. MZ SSR č. 141/1982 Sb. o zmene a doplnení vyhl. č. 72/1973 Zb. [Regulation of the Ministry of Health of the SRR No. 141/1982 Coll. Amending and Supplementing Regulation No. 72/1973 Coll.], October 15, 1982.

11. Regulation 104/1961, note 10, s. 2; Decree 126/1962, note 10, at s. 6.

12. See Dudová, *Interrupce,* note 6, at 47–57.

13. Act 68/1957, note 9, at s. 1.

14. Dudová, *Interrupce,* note 6, 73–74. See also Act 68/1957, note 9, at ss. 3, 7; Decree 126/1962, note 10, at s. 3.

15. Dudová, "The Framing," note 6, at 955, 957.

16. Dudová, "The Framing," note 6, at 963.

17. Dudová, *Interrupce,* note 6, at 67 (emphasis added).

18. Regulation 72/1973, note 10, at ss. 1, 2(3). See also Dudová, *Interrupce,* note 6, at 67.

19. Explanatory Report of the Bill on Artificial Interruption of Pregnancy, adopted as Act No. 73/1986 Coll., at 117 [hereinafter Explanatory Report of Act No. 73/1986].

20. Zákon č. 73/1986 Zb. o umelom prerušení tehotenstva [Act No. 73/1986 Coll. on Artificial Interruption of Pregnancy] October 23, 1986 [hereinafter Act 73/1986], s. 4.

21. Explanatory Report of Act No. 73/1986, note 19, at 118–119; Dudová, *Interrupce,* note 6, at 69–70.

22. Dudová, *Interrupce,* note 6, at 69–71, 171.

23. Dudová, "The Framing," note 6, at 964.

24. Explanatory Report of Act No. 73/1986, note 19, at 121.

25. Slovak National Council, 3rd sess., Bratislava, 1986, http://www.nrsr.sk/dk/Download .aspx?MasterID=75214 (accessed January 21, 2013).

26. See, e.g., Susan Gal, "Gender in the Post-Socialist Transition: The Abortion Debate in Hungary," *East European Politics and Societies* 8 (1994): 256–86; Janine P. Holc, "The Purest Democrat: Fetal Citizenship and Subjectivity in the Construction of Democracy in Poland," *Signs: Journal of Women in Culture and Society* 29 (2004): 755–82.

27. Federal Assembly of the Czech and Slovak Federal Republic, 11th sess., 1991, http://www .psp.cz/eknih/1990fs/slsn/stenprot/011schuz/s011001.htm (accessed January 21, 2013) [hereinafter Transcript Federal Assembly, 1991].

28. Transcript Federal Assembly, 1991, note 27, Magyar.

29. Transcript Federal Assembly, 1991, note 27, Krejcar. See, e.g., Gail Kligman, "The Politics of Reproduction in Ceauşescu's Romania: A Case Study in Political Culture," *East European Politics and Societies* 6. 3 (1992): 364–418.

30. Úst. zákon č. 23/1991 Zb., ktorým sa uvádza Listina základných práv a slobôd ako ústavný zákon Federálneho zhromaždenia Českej a Slovenskej Federatívnej Republiky [Constitutional Act No. 23/1991 Coll., which Introduces the Charter of Fundamental Rights and Freedoms as a Constitutional Act of the Federal Assembly of the Czech and Slovak Federal Republic], art. 6(1).

31. Constitution of the Slovak Republic, 460/1992 Coll., art. 15(1) [hereinafter Constitution].

32. National Council of the Slovak Republic, 45th sess., 2001, http://www.psp.cz/eknih/1998nr/ stenprot/045schuz/s045040.htm (accessed January 21, 2013) [hereinafter Transcript, National Council, 2001].

33. Transcript, National Council, 2001, note 32.

34. Family Planning, the Protection of the Human Fetus and the Conditions for the Admissibility of Abortion Act, January 7, 1993, (Pol.).

35. Transcript, National Council, 2001, note 32.

36. Act 73/1986, note 20, ss. 4, 5; Vyhl. č. 74/1986 Zb., ktorou sa vykonáva zákon Slovenskej národnej rady č. 73/1986 Zb. o umelom prerušení tehotenstva [Regulation of the Ministry of Health of the SSR No. 74/1986 Coll. Implementing Act No. 73/1986 Coll. on Artificial Interruption of Pregnancy], s. 2.

37. Návrh podľa čl. 125 písm. a), písm. b) Ústavy Slovenskej republiky, Rvp 278/01, May 3, 2001 [hereinafter Rvp 278/01].

38. Constitution, note 31, at arts. 125(1)(a), 130(1).

39. Rvp 278/01, note 37, at II-B, II-C.

40. PL. ÚS 12/01, note 1.

41. Zora Bútorová and Jarmila Filadelfiová, "Women, Men and the Increasing Diversity of Life," in *She and He in Slovakia: Gender and Age in the Period of Transition*, ed. Zora Bútorová et al. (Bratislava: Institute for Public Affairs, 2008), 43–72, at 62–64.

42. BVerfG 1993, note 2, at para. 158.

43. BVerfG 1993, note 2, at paras. 3, 157.

44. Decision 48/1998, note 2, addressing Act LXXIX/1992 on the Protection of Foetal Life.

45. Decision 48/1998, note 2, at Section III Pt. (1)(b).

46. Decision 48/1998, note 2, at Section III Pts. (5), (2)(a), (3)(c).

47. Decision 48/1998, note 2, at Section III Pts. (1)(a), (3)(c), (5).

48. Decision K 26/96, note 2, addressing Act Amending the Act on Family Planning, the Protection of the Human Fetus and the Conditions for the Admissibility of Abortion and Amending Certain Other Acts, August 30, 1996.

49. See also Decision K 26/96, note 2, (Garlicki L., dissenting).

50. Decision K 26/96, note 2, at para. 4.3.

51. Constitution, note 31, art. 1(1); PL. ÚS 12/01, note 1, at II.A.

52. BVerfG 1993, note 2, at paras. 147, 158.

53. Decision 48/1998, note 2, at 45 (Holló A., concurring).

54. PL. ÚS 12/01, note 1, at II.A Pt. (1.2). See also Constitution, note 31, art. 14.

55. PL. ÚS 12/01, note 1, at II.A Pt. (4).

56. PL. ÚS 12/01, note 1, at II.A Pt. (3.1); International Covenant on Civil and Political Rights, December 16, 1966, 999 U.N.T.S. 171 (entered into force March 23, 1976) (acceded to by Slovakia May 28, 1993); Convention for the Protection of Human Rights and Fundamental Freedoms, E.T.S. 5 (entered into force September 3, 1953) (acceded to by Slovakia, January 1, 1993).

57. PL. ÚS 12/01, note 1, at II.A Pt. (1.2).

58. PL. ÚS 12/01, note 1, at II.A Pt. (1.2).

59. PL. ÚS 12/01, note 1, at II.A Pt. (1.3).

60. PL. ÚS 12/01, note 1, at II.A Pt. (1.3).

61. PL. ÚS 12/01, note 1, at II.A Pt. (1.4).

62. Decision K 26/96, note 2, at para. 4.3.

63. Decision 48/1998, note 2, at Section III Pt. (3)(c).

64. *Roe v. Wade*, 410 U.S. 113 (1973) (U.S. Supreme Court); *Planned Parenthood of Southeastern Pa. v. Casey*, 505 U.S. 833 (1992) (U.S. Supreme Court).

65. PL. ÚS 12/01, note 1, at II.A Pt. (2.1).

66. PL. ÚS 12/01, note 1, at II.A Pt. (2.1).

67. PL. ÚS 12/01, note 1, at II.A Pt. (2.1).

68. Constitution, note 31, at art. 2(3).

69. PL. ÚS 12/01, note 1, at II.A Pt. (2.1).

70. PL. ÚS 12/01, note 1, at II.A Pt. (2.2).

71. PL. ÚS 12/01, note 1, at II.A Pt. (3.4); Convention on the Elimination of All Forms of

Discrimination against Women, December 18, 1979 (entered into force September 3, 1981), 1249 U.N.T.S. 13, reprinted in 19 *I.L.M.* 33 (1980) (acceded to by Slovakia May 28, 1993).

72. PL. ÚS 12/01, note 1, at II.A Pt. (2.2).

73. PL. ÚS 12/01, note 1, at II.A Pt. (2.3).

74. PL. ÚS 12/01, note 1, at II.A Pt. (2.3).

75. Donald P. Kommers, "Germany: Balancing Rights and Duties," in *Interpreting Constitutions: A Comparative Study,* ed. Jeffrey Goldsworthy (Oxford: Oxford University Press, 2006), 161–214, at 203.

76. PL. ÚS 12/01, note 1, at II.A Pt. (2.4).

77. PL. ÚS 12/01, note 1, at II.A Pt. (2.4).

78. PL. ÚS 12/01, note 1, at II.A Pt. (2.4).

79. Constitution, note 31, at art. 13(4).

80. PL. ÚS 12/01, note 1, at II.A Pt. (2.4).

81. PL. ÚS 12/01, note 1, at II.A Pt. (2.4).

82. PL. ÚS 12/01, note 1, at II.A Pt. (2.4).

83. PL. ÚS 12/01, note 1, at II.B Pt. (1–2).

84. *Paton v. United Kingdom,* App. No. 8416/78, 3 Eur. H.R. Rep. 408 (1980), (also cited as *X. v. U.K.*), para. 19.

85. PL. ÚS 12/01, note 1, at II.B Pt. (2).

86. PL. ÚS 12/01, note 1, at II.B Pt. (3).

87. BVerfG 1993, note 2, at D.II–IV.

88. PL. ÚS 12/01, note 1, at II.B Pt. (3).

89. PL. ÚS 12/01, note 1, at II.B Pt. (3).

90. Rvp 278/01, note 37, at II-B.

91. PL. ÚS 12/01, note 1, at II.B Pt. (4), addressing *Vo v. France,* App. No. 53924/00, Eur. Ct. H.R. (July 8, 2004); *Roe,* note 64; *Planned Parenthood,* note 64.

92. PL. ÚS 12/01, note 1, at II.B Pt. (4) (emphasis added).

93. BVerfG 1993, note 2, at paras. 373–417 (Mahrenholz and Sommer JJ., dissenting).

94. PL. ÚS 12/01, note 1, at II.B Pt. (4).

95. Návrh na vydanie zákona, ktorým sa mení a dopĺňa zákon Slovenskej národnej rady č. 73/1986 Zb. o umelom prerušení tehotenstva v znení zákona č. 419/1991 Zb. [Bill Amending and Supplementing Act No. 73/1986 Coll. on Artificial Interruption of Pregnancy as Amended by Act No. 419/1991 Coll.], print 539, 2008 [hereinafter Print 539].

96. Návrh na vydanie zákona, ktorým sa mení a dopĺňa zákon č. 576/2004 Z. z. o zdravotnej starostlivosti, službách súvisiacich s poskytovaním zdravotnej starostlivosti a o zmene a doplnení niektorých zákonov v znení neskorších predpisov [Bill Amending and Supplementing Act No. 576/2004 Coll. of Laws on Healthcare, Healthcare-Related Services, and on Amendments and Supplements to Certain Acts as Amended], print 1030, 2009, adopted as Act No. 345/2009 Coll. of Laws [hereinafter Print 1030].

97. PL. ÚS 12/01, note 1, at II.A Pt. (2.1).

98. Explanatory Report of Print 539, note 95; Explanatory Report of Print 1030, note 96.

99. Explanatory Report of Print 1030, note 96.

100. PL. ÚS 12/01, note 1, at II.B Pt. (3).

101. National Council of the Slovak Republic, 35th sess., 2009, http://www.nrsr.sk/dl /Browser/ Default?legId=13&termNr=4 (accessed January 21, 2013).

102. See, e.g., Reva B. Siegel, "The Right's Reasons: Constitutional Conflict and the Spread of Woman-Protective Antiabortion Argument," *Duke Law Journal* 57 (2008): 1641–92.

Chapter 4. Proportionality in the Constitutional Review of Abortion Law

1. Verónica Undurraga, *Aborto y Protección del que Está por Nacer en la Constitución Chilena,*(Santiago: Legal Publishing Chile [Thomson Reuters], forthcoming 2014).

2. Robert Alexy, *A Theory of Constitutional Rights*, trans. Julian Rivers (Oxford: Oxford University Press, 2002), 49.

3. Corte Suprema de Justicia de Costa Rica, Sala Constitucional [Constitutional Chamber of the Supreme Court] 2000, Sentencia No. 2000-02306.

4. Alexy, *Theory*, note 2, at 47.

5. Alexy, *Theory,* note 2, at 47–48.

6. Alexy, *Theory,* note 2, at 50–54.

7. Bundesverfassungsgericht [Federal Constitutional Court] February 25, 1975, 39 BVerfGE 1, para. 151 [hereinafter 39 BVerfGE 1] translated in Robert E. Jonas and John D. Gorby, "West German Abortion Decision: A Contrast to *Roe v. Wade*," *John Marshall Journal of Practice and Procedure* 9 (1976): 605–684.

8. 39 BVerfGE 1 note 7, at para. 152; Jonas trans. at 644.

9. 39 BVerfGE 1 note 7, at para. 151; Jonas trans. at 643.

10. 39 BVerfGE 1 note 7, at para. 151; Jonas trans. at 643.

11. 39 BVerfGE 1, note 7, at para. 151; Jonas trans. at 643.

12. 39 BVerfGE 1, note 7, at para. 151; Jonas trans. at 643.

13. 39 BVerfGE 1, note 7, at paras. 160 and 162; Jonas trans. at 647, 648.

14. 39 BVerfGE 1, note 7, at para. 162; Jonas trans. at 648.

15. 39 BVerfGE 1, note 7, at para. 162; Jonas trans. at 648.

16. 39 BVerfGE 1, note 7, at para. 162.; Jonas trans. at 648

17. See a recent Brazilian case in Luís Roberto Barroso, "Bringing Abortion into the Brazilian Public Debate: Legal Strategies for Anencephalic Pregnancy," in this volume.

18. Antonio Bascuñán, "La Licitud del Aborto Consentido en el Derecho Chileno," *Revista Derecho y Humanidades* 10 (2004): 143–81, at 156.

19. Reva Siegel, "The Right's Reasons: Constitutional Conflict and the Spread of Woman-Protective Antiabortion Argument," *Duke Law Journal* 57, No. 6 (2008): 1641–92.

20. Tribunal Constitucional [Constitutional Court] 2010, Acórdão No. 75/2010, at para. 11.4.8 (Port.) [hereinafter Acórdão No. 75/2010].

21. Vanessa MacDonnell and Jula Hughes, "The German Abortion Decisions and the Protective Function in German and Canadian Constitutional Law," *Osgoode Hall Law Journal* 50.4 (2013) 999-1050.

22. Gilda Sedgh et al., "Induced Abortion: Incidence and Trends Worldwide from 1995 to 2008," *Lancet* 379, No. 9816 (2012): 625–32, at 626, doi: 10.1016/S0140-6736(11)61786-8 (accessed June 30, 2013); David A. Grimes et al., "Unsafe Abortion: The Preventable Pandemic," *Lancet* 368, No. 9550 (2006):1908–19, doi:10.1016/S0140-6736(06)69481-6 (accessed January 31, 2013); Alan Guttmacher Institute, "Sharing Responsibility: Women, Society and Abortion Worldwide," *Abortion, Reports* (1999), http://www.guttmacher.org/pubs/sharing.pdf; Alan Guttmacher Institute, "Facts on Induced Abortion Worldwide," *Abortion, Fact Sheets* (October, 2009), http://www.

guttmacher.org/pubs/fb_IAW.html; Cicely Marston and John Cleland, "Relationships Between Contraception and Abortion: A Review of the Evidence," *International Family Planning Perspectives* 29, No.1 (2013): 6–13; Gilda Sedgh et al., "Induced Abortion: Estimated Rates and Trends Worldwide," *Lancet* 370, No. 9595 (2007):1338–45; Marge Berer, "National Laws and Unsafe Abortion: The Parameters of Change," *Reproductive Health Matters* 12 (2004): 1–8.

23. Ronald D. Bachman, ed., "Romania: A Country Study," Washington, D.C., GPO for the U.S. Library of Congress, 1989, http://countrystudies.us/romania/37.htm (accessed January 31, 2013).

24. 39 BVerfGE 1, note 7, at para. 181; Jonas trans. at 655.

25. Bundesverfassungsgericht May 28, 1993, 88 BVerfGE 203, at para. 189 [hereinafter 88 BVerfGE 203].

26. 88 BVerfGE 203, note 25, at para. 189.

27. Acórdão No. 75/2010, note 20, at para. 11.4.18.

28. Acórdão No. 75/2010, note 20, at para. 11.4.8.

29. Acórdão No. 75/2010, note 20, at para. 11.4.8.

30. 39 BVerfGE 1, note 7, at para. 158.

31. Suprema Corte de Justicia de la Nación [Supreme Court] 2008, Acción de inconstitucionalidad 146/2007 y su acumulada 147/2007. Minority Vote of Justices Aguirre, Azuela y Ortiz, 131–32 [hereinafter Acción de inconstitucionalidad 146/2007 y su acumulada 147/2007].

32. 39 BVerfGE 1, note 7, at paras. 209–10; Jonas trans. at 662–663.

33. Corte Constitucional May 10, 2006, Sentencia C-355/06, para. VI.5 [hereinafter Sentencia C-355/06].

34. Corte Constitucional [Constitutional Court] 2002, Sentencia C-370/02, para. VI.22 .

35. Sentencia C-355/06, note 33.

36. Acción de inconstitucionalidad 146/2007 y su acumulada 147/2007, note 31, at 189.

37. Acción de inconstitucionalidad 146/2007 y su acumulada 147/2007, note 31, at 189.

38. Acórdão No. 75/2010, note 20, at para. 11.4.8.

39. John Cleland et al., "Family Planning: The Unfinished Agenda," *Lancet* 368, No. 9549 (2006):1810–27.

40. Alexy, *Theory*, note 2, at Postscript.

41. Bunreacht Na hÉireann [Constitution of Ireland] 1937, at art. 40.3.3.

42. *Roe v. Wade*, 410 U.S. 113 (1973) (U.S. Supreme Court).

43. Sentencia C-355/06, note 33, at para. VI.5; Acórdão No. 75/2010, note 20, at para. 11.4.2; Ústavný Súd [Constitutional Court] December 4, 2007, PL. ÚS 12/01 (Slovak Republic) [hereinafter PL. ÚS 12/01].

44. Sentencia C-355/06, note 33, at para. VI.5.

45. Acórdão No. 75/2010, note 20, at para. 11.4.11.

46. Tribunal Constitucional [Constitutional Court] April 18, 2008, Sentencia Rol 740-07-CDS, at para. 64.

47. Katharine T. Bartlett, "Feminist Legal Method," *Harvard Law Review* 103, No. 4 (1990): 829–88.

48. Reva Siegel, "Dignity and the Abortion Debate," paper presented at SELA (Seminario en Latinoamérica de Teoría Constitucional y Política—Seminar in Latin America on Constitutional and Political Theory), June 2009 (Asunción, Paraguay).

49. Tribunal Constitucional [Constitutional Court] April 11, 1985, S.T.C. 53/1985, 1985-49 BJC 515, para. 11 b (Spain); Sentencia C-355 (Colombia), note 33, para. 8.1; Acción de

Inconstitucionalidad 146/2007 y su acumulada 147/2007 (Mexico), note 31, concurring vote of Justice Valls Hernández, p. 11, and concurring vote of Justice Sánchez Cordero de García Villegas, p. 15.189.

50. Acórdão No. 75/2010, note 20, at para. 11.4.11.

51. Sedgh et al., "Induced," note 22, at 625–26.

52. 39 BVerfGE 1, note 7, at para. 162; Jonas trans. at 648.

53. *L.M.R. v. Argentina*, Communication No. 1608/2007, CCPR/C/101/D/168/2007 (Human Rights Committee) (2011); *K.L. v. Peru*, Communication No. 1153/2003, U.N. Doc. CCPR/C/85/D/1153/2003 (Human Rights Committee) (2005).

54. 39 BVerfGE 1, note 7, at para. 154; Jonas trans. at 644.

55. 39 BVerfGE 1, note 7, at para. 161; Jonas trans. at 647.

56. *Planned Parenthood of Southeastern Pa. v. Casey*, 505 U.S. 833 (1992), at 852 (U.S. Supreme Court).

57. Sentencia C-355/06, note 33, at para. VI.10.1.

58. Sentencia C-355/06, note 33, at para. VI.10.1.

59. Sentencia C-355/06, note 33, at para. VI.8.1.

60. Sentencia C-355/06, note 33, at para. VI.10.1.

61. 88 BVerfG 203, note 25, at para. 201.

62. Sentencia C-355/06, note 33, at para. VI.11.

63. *A, B, and C v. Ireland*, Eur. Ct. H.R., [2010] E.C.H.R. 2032, at para. 254.

64. 88 BVerfG 203, note 25, at para. 159.

65. PL. ÚS 12/01, note 43, at para. II.A.2.4.

66. Acórdão No. 75/2010, note 20, at paras. 11.4.11, 11.4.18.

67. Acórdão No.75/2010, note 20, at para. 11.4.18.

Chapter 5. A Functionalist Approach to Comparative Abortion Law

1. *Roe v. Wade*, 410 U.S. 113 (1973) (U.S. Supreme Court).

2. Bundesverfassungsgericht [Federal Constitutional Court] February 25, 1975, 39 BVerfGE 1 (Ger.) [hereinafter 39 BVerfGE 1] translated in Robert E. Jonas and John D. Gorby, "West German Abortion Decision: A Contrast to *Roe v. Wade*," *John Marshall Journal of Practice and Procedure* 9 (1976): 605–684.

3. Rachel Rebouché, "Comparative Pragmatism," *Maryland Law Review* 72, No. 1 (2012): 85–155 (citing Mary Ann Glendon, *Abortion and Divorce in Western Law* (Cambridge, Mass.: Harvard University Press, 1987), 22–23, 33–38). See also Vicki C. Jackson and Mark Tushnet, *Comparative Constitutional Law* (New York: Foundation Press, 2006), 1–142.

4. *Roe*, note 1, at 164.

5. *Roe*, note 1, at 164–65.

6. See Center for Reproductive Rights, "*Roe v. Wade* and the Right to Privacy" (3rd ed., New York, 2003) 54–58, http://reproductiverights.org/sites/crr.civicactions.net/files/documents/roepri vacy_0.pdf. See also Naomi Cahn and Anne T. Goldstein, "*Roe* and Its Global Impact: The Constitution, Reproductive Rights, and Feminism," *University of Pennsylvania Journal of Constitutional Law* 6 (2004): 695–722.

7. *Planned Parenthood of Southeastern Pa. v. Casey*, 505 U.S. 833 (1992) (U.S. Supreme Court).

8. Julia L. Ernst, Laura Katzive, and Erica Smock, "The Global Pattern of U.S. Initiatives Curtailing Women's Reproductive Rights: A Perspective of the Increasingly Anti-Choice Mosaic," *University of Pennsylvania Journal of Constitutional Law* 6 (2004): 752–95, at 753.

9. Choice on Termination of Pregnancy Act 92 of 1996 (S. Afr.), amended by Choice on Termination of Pregnancy Amendment Act 1 of 2008.

10. *Christian Lawyers Association v. Minister of Health,* 2004 (4) All S.A. 31, 42 (South African Supreme Court of Appeal). See also South African Constitution, 1996, ch. 2, § 39.

11. *Christian Lawyers,* note 10, at 43.

12. *Christian Lawyers,* note 10, at 46.

13. 39 BverfGE 1, note 2, A.II.2.; Jonas trans. at 624.

14. 39 BVerfGE 1, note 2, at 39.; Jonas trans. at 643.

15. 39 BVerfGE 1, note 2, at 39.

16. 39 BVerfGE 1, note 2, at 49–50; Jonas trans. at 648.

17. Bundesverfassungsgericht May 28, 1993, 88 BverfGE 203 (Ger.).

18. Tribunal Constitucional [Constitutional Court] February 23, 2010, Acórdão No. 75/2010 (Port.), § 11.4.11 [hereinafter Acórdão No. 75/2010].

19. Acórdão No. 75/2010, note 18, at 11.4.6.

20. Acórdão No. 75/2010, note 18, at 11.4.5–6.

21. Acórdão No. 75/2010, note 18, at 11.4.3.

22. Corte Constitucional [Constitutional Court] May 10, 2006, Sentencia C-355/2006 (p. 280) (Colom.) [hereinafter Sentencia C-355/06]; See also Women's Link Worldwide, *C-355/2006: Excerpts of the Constitutional Court's Ruling that Liberalized Abortion in Colombia,* (2007), http://www.womenslinkworldwide.org/pdf_pubs/pub_c3552006.pdf, [hereinafter C-355/2006 Excerpts].

23. Sentencia C- 355/06, note 22.

24. Sentencia C- 355/06, note 22, at pt. 9, 272.

25. Sentencia C- 355/06, note 22, at pt. 9, para. 6.

26. Sentencia C- 355/06, note 22.

27. Günter Frankenberg, "Critical Comparisons: Re-Thinking Comparative Law," *Harvard International Law Journal* 26 (1985): 411–55, at 455.

28. Guttmacher Institute, *State Policies in Brief: Counseling and Waiting Periods for Abortion* (New York: Guttmacher Institute: 2012), 1, http://www.guttmacher.org/statecenter/spibs/spib_MWPA.pdf.

29. Rebouché, "Comparative," note 3, at 90.

30. European Women's Health Network, *State of Affairs: Concepts Approaches, Organizations in the Health Movement, Country Report: Germany* (Hanover: Landesvereinigung für Gesundheit Niedersachsen e.V, 2000), 123.

31. European Women's Health Network, *State of Affairs,* note 30.

32. European Women's Health Network, *State of Affairs,* note 30, at 124.

33. European Women's Health Network, *State of Affairs,* note 30; see also *Casey,* note 7, at 882–83.

34. European Women's Health Network, *State of Affairs,* note 30, but see *Planned Parenthood of Minn., N.D. & S.D. v. Rounds,* 530 F.3d 724, 733–37 (2011) (Eighth Circuit Court of Appeals).

35. See, e.g., Wis. Stat. §253.10(3)(c)(1)(f) (2013).

36. See, e.g., West Virginia Department of Health and Human Resources, *Information on Fetal Development, Abortion & Adoption* (2003), 15, http://www.wvdhhr.org/wrtk/wrtkbooklet.pdf.

37. Guttmacher, *State Policies,* note 28, at 1.

38. Rachel K. Jones et al., *Characteristics of U.S. Abortion Patients, 2008* (New York: Guttmacher Institute, 2010), 1, http://www.guttmacher.org/pubs/US-Abortion-Patients.pdf.

39. Adam Sonfield et al., "Public Funding for Family Planning, Sterilization and Abortion Services, FY 1980–2006," Occasional Report No. 38 (New York: Guttmacher Institute, 2008), 6, tbl. A, http://www.guttmacher.org/pubs/2008/01/28/or38.pdf; Elke Thoss and Joachim von Baross, "Mifegyne in Germany: Were All the Efforts in Vain?" *Choices* 28, No. 2 (2000): 26–28, at 28.

40. See National Abortion Federation, *Public Funding for Abortion: Medicaid and the Hyde Amendment* (2006), 1, http://www.prochoice.org/pubs_research/publications/downloads/about_abortion/publ ic_funding.pdf (noting that in 1979 Congress removed the physical health exception, and in 1981, the rape and incest exceptions, which were reintroduced in 1993).

41. Mary Anne Case, "Perfectionism and Fundamentalism in the Application of German Abortion Laws," in *Constituting Equality: Gender Equality and Comparative Constitutional Law*, ed. Susan H. Williams (Cambridge: Cambridge University Press, 2009), 93–106, at 100.

42. See, e.g., Laura Reichenbach, "The Global Reproductive Health and Rights Agenda: Opportunities and Challenges for the Future," in *Reproductive Health and Human Rights: The Way Forward*, ed. Laura Reichenbach and Mindy Jane Roseman (Philadelphia: University of Pennsylvania Press, 2009), 21–39, at 24–25 (citing the International Conference on Population and Development); Center for Reproductive Rights, *Abortion Worldwide: Twelve Years of Reform* (2007), 1.

43. Reva B. Siegel, "The Constitutionalization of Abortion," in this volume; see also Vicki Jackson, "Gender and Transnational Legal Discourse," *Yale Journal of Law and Feminism* 14 (2002): 377–91, at 378.

44. Siegel, "Constitutionalization," note 43.

45. Sentencia C-355/06, note 22, at § 7, 242.

46. Sentencia C-355/06, note 22, at § 7, 242.

47. See, e.g., Reva Siegel, "Dignity and Sexuality: Claims on Dignity in Transnational Debates over Abortion and Same-Sex Marriage," *International Journal of Constitutional Law* 10 (2012): 355–79.

48. Acórdão No. 75/2010, note 18, at 49–50 (listing the United Kingdom, Belgium, Switzerland, Bosnia/Herzegovina, Macedonia, Turkey, Estonia, Netherlands, Romania, Sweden, Greece, Denmark, France, and Austria).

49. Acórdão No. 75/2010, note 18, at § 11.4.13.

50. Direcção-Geral da Saúde, Circular Normativa No. 11/SR, Organização dos Serviços para implementação de Lei 16/2007 de 17 de Abril [Portugal Ministry of Health Normative Circular No. 11/SR on the Organization of Services for the Implementation of Law 16/2007 of April 17].

51. Fernanda Nicola, "Family Law Exceptionalism in Comparative Law," *American Journal of Comparative Law* 58 (2010): 777–810, at 785.

52. Center for Reproductive Rights, *The World's Abortion Laws 2007*, http://reproductive rights.org/sites/crr.civicactions.net/files/documents/Abortion%20Map_FA.pdf.

53. Annelise Riles, "Wigmore's Treasure Box: Comparative Law in the Era of Information," *Harvard International Law Journal* 40 (1999): 221–83, at 228.

54. David Kennedy, "New Approaches to Comparative Law: Comparativism and International Governance," *Utah Law Review* 2 (1997): 545–637, at 548; but see Mathias Reimann, "The Progress and Failure of Comparative Law in the Second Half of the Twentieth Century," *American Journal of Comparative Law* 50 (2002): 671–700, at 699.

55. Rudolf Schlesinger, "The Past and Future of Comparative Law," *American Journal of Comparative Law* 43 (1995): 477–81.

56. Theresa Glennon, "An American Perspective on the Debate over the Harmonization or Unification of Family Law in Europe," *Family Law Quarterly* 38 (2004): 185–211.

57. Darren Rosenblum, "Internalizing Gender: Why International Law Theory Should Adopt Comparative Methods," *Columbia Journal of Transnational Law* 45 (2007): 760–828, at 768.

58. Riles, "Wigmore's," note 53, at 226.

59. See, e.g., Aníbal Faúndes and Ellen Hardy, "Illegal Abortion: Consequences for Women's Health and the Health Care System," *International Journal of Gynecology and Obstetrics* 58 (1997): 79–80.

60. Karen Knop, "Here and There: International Law in Domestic Courts," *New York University Journal of International Law and Policy* 32 (2000): 501–35, at 529.

61. World Health Organization, *Safe Abortion: Technical and Policy Guidance for Health Systems* (Geneva: World Health Organization, 2012), 63–65.

62. The Constitution of Kenya, Rights and Fundamental Freedoms, Part 2 (2010), § 26(4).

63. Rubina Hussain, "Abortion and Unintended Pregnancy in Kenya," Guttmacher Institute, *In Brief* 2 (2012): 1.

64. Ministry of Medical Services, *Standards and Guidelines for Morbidity and Mortality from Unsafe Abortion in Kenya*, 2012.

65. James Gordley, "The Functional Method," in *Methods of Comparative Law,* ed. Pier Giuseppe Monateri (Cheltenham: Edward Elgar Publishing, 2012), 107–19, at 109.

66. Ralf Michaels, "The Functional Method of Comparative Law," in *The Oxford Handbook of Comparative Law*, ed. Konrad Zimmerman and Mathias Reimann (Oxford: Oxford University Press, 2006), 339–82, at 347–49.

67. See, e.g., Martha Davis, "Abortion Access in the Global Marketplace," *North Carolina Law Review* 88 (2010): 1657–85, at 1675–76.

68. Eduardo Amado et al., "Obstacles and Challenges Following the Partial Decriminalisation of Abortion in Colombia," *Reproductive Health Matters* 18 (2010): 118–26, at 123–4 (citing the Decree 4444/2006, Resolution 4905/2006, and Agreement 350/2006 of the Colombian Ministry of Social Protection).

69. Mónica Roa, *Ensuring Reproductive Rights in Colombia: From Constitutional Court Success to Reality* (2008), http://www.isiswomen.org/downloads/wia/wia-2008–1/1wia08_05TalkPoints_Monica.pdf.

70. Cyra Akila Choudhury, "Exporting Subjects: Globalizing Family Law Progress through International Human Rights," *Journal of International Law* 32 (2011): 259–324 at 297; see also Sharad D. Iyengar, "Introducing Medical Abortion Within the Primary Health System: Comparison with Other Interventions and Commodities," *Reproductive Health Matters* 13 (2005): 13–19.

71. Public Administration of Mexico City, "Mayor's Office Decrees the Reform of the Mexico City Penal Code and Additions to the Mexico City Health Law," 70 *Official Mexico City Gazette*, Penal Code art. 144, Health Code art. 16, § 6 (April 26, 2007).

72. Raffaela Schiavon et al., "Characteristics of Private Abovtion Services in Mexico City After Legalisationn," *Reproductive Health Matters* 18 (2010):127–135, 133.

73. Corte Constitucional [Constitutional Court] 2012, Sentencia T-841/2011 (Colom.), http://www.promsex.org/docs/varios/Sentencia_T-841_de_2011.pdf.

74. Choudhury, "Exporting," note 70, at 122.

75. Choudhury, "Exporting," note 70, at 294.

76. See Joanna N. Erdman, "Access to Information on Safe Abortion: A Harm Reduction and Human Rights Approach," *Harvard Journal of Law and Gender* 34 (2011): 413–462 at 413–14; Riles,

"Wigmore's," note 53, 252; but see Lance Gable, "Reproductive Health as a Human Right," *Case Western Reserve Law Review* 60 (2010): 957–96, at 965–66.

77. Choudhury, "Exporting," note 70, at 294.

78. Choudhury, "Exporting," note 70, at 294.

79. Acórdão No. 75/2010, note 18, at 44; see Diana Curado, *Portugal, 3 Years of Legal, Safe and Free Abortion*, IWL-FI, December 13, 2010, http://www.litci.org/en/index.php?option=com_content&view=article&id=1748 (describing the "pro-choice" movement that "campaigned on the streets and on television").

80. Acórdão No. 75/2010, note 18, at 44.

81. Banwari Meel and Ram P. Kaswa, "The Impact on the Choice on Termination of Pregnancy Act of 1996," *African Journal of Primary Health Care and Family Medicine* 79–81, 79; Amado et al., "obstacles," note 66, at 120.

82. Meel and Kaswa, "Impact," note 81, at 1.

83. Amado et al., "Obstacles," note 68, 118. See also Jennifer Lee and Cara Buckley, "For Privacy's Sake, Taking Risks to End Pregnancy," *New York Times*, January 4, 2009, http://www.nytimes.com/2009/01/05/nyregion/05abortion.html?hp=&adxnnl=1&adxnnlx=1328529736-oyNlVbXyBr1yhn5lljvVGw (accessed July 23, 2013).

84. Choudhury, "Exporting," note 70, 294; see also Jacqueline Sherris et al., "Misoprostol Use in Developing Countries: Results from a Multicountry Study," *International Journal of Gynecology and Obstetrics* 88 (2005): 76–81, at 80; María Mercedes Lafaurie et al., "Women's Perspectives on Medical Abortion in Mexico, Colombia, Ecuador, and Peru: A Qualitative Study," *Reproductive Health Matters* 13 (2005): 75–83, 78.

85. See, e.g., Sherris et al., "Misoprostol," note 84, at 80; Lafaurie et al., "Women's Perspectives," note 84, at 78.

86. Sherris et al., "Misoprostol," note 84, at 79.

87. Lafaurie et al., "Women's Perspectives," note 84, at 79–80.

88. See Iyengar, "Introducing," note 70, at 14.

89. See Iyengar, "Introducing," note 70, at 14.

90. See Iyengar, "Introducing," note 70, at 14.

91. See Iyengar, "Introducing," note 70, at 14.

92. Karen Knop, Ralf Michaels, and Annelise Riles, "From Multiculturalism to Technique: Feminism, Culture, and the Conflict of Laws Style," *Stanford Law Review* 64 (2012): 589–656, 640. See also Janet Halley, *Split Decisions: How and Why to Take a Break from Feminism* (Princeton Princeton University Press, 2007), 304.

93. Scott Burris, "From Health Care to the Social Determinants of Health: A Public Health Law Research Perspective," *University of Pennsylvania Law Review* 159 (2011): 1649–1667, 1663.

94. Burris, "From Health," note 93, at 1665.

95. Rachel Rebouché, "The Limits of Reproductive Rights in Improving Women's Health," *Alabama Law Review* 63 (2011): 1–46, at 36.

96. International Conference on Population and Development, Cairo, Egypt, September 5–13, 1994, *Report*, ch. 8, U.N. Doc. A/CONF.171/13 (October 18, 1994).

97. Peer Zumbansen, "Transnational Comparisons: Theory and Practice of Comparative Law as a Critique of Global Governance," in *Theory and Practice in Comparative Law*, ed. Jacco Bomhoff and Maurice Adams (Cambridge: Cambridge University Press, 2012), 186–211.

98. Scott Burris et al., "Making the Case for Laws that Improve Health: A Framework for Public Health Law Research," *Milbank Quarterly* 88, No. 2 (2010): 169–210, 170.

99. Burris, "From Health Care," note 93, at 1652.

100. Burris, "From Health Care," note 93, at 1655.

101. Scott Burris and Alexander Wagenaar, "Integrating Diverse Theories for Public Health Research," *Public Health Law Research Methods Monograph Series* (2012), http://ssrn.com/abstract2118690.

102. Burris and Wagenaar, "Integrating," note 101, at 12–15.

103. Burris and Wagenaar, "Integrating," note 101, at 18.

104. Burris, "Making," note 98, at 174–75.

105. Burris, "Making," note 98, at 183.

106. See Rebouché, "The Limits of Reproductive Rights," note 95, at 26–36. See also Jake Naughton, Jina Moore, and Estelle Ellis, "South Africa's Barriers to Abortion," *Nation*, January 3, 2013, http://www.thenation.com/slideshow/171989/south-africas-barriers-abortion# (accessed July 23, 2013).

107. Rachel K. Jewkes et al., "Why Are Women Still Aborting Outside Designated Facilities in Metropolitan South Africa?" *British Journal of Obstetrics and Gynaecology* 112 (2005): 1236–42, at 1237.

108. Jewkes et al., "Why," note 107, at 1237–38.

109. Jewkes et al., "Why," note 107, at 1241. See also Rebouché, "The Limits of Reproductive Rights," 26–27.

110. Jewkes et al., "Why," note 107.

111. WHO, "Safe," note 61, at 81.

112. WHO, "Safe," note 61, at 82.

113. Special Programme of Research, Development and Research Training in Human Reproduction, "What Health-Care Providers Say on Providing Abortion Care in Cape Town, South Africa: Findings from a Qualitative Study," *Social Science Research Policy Brief*, WHO Reference No. WHO/RHR/HRP/10.18 [hereinafter "Health-Care Providers"].

114. "Health-Care Providers," note 113, at 2, see Rebecca J. Cook, "Stigmatized Meanings of Criminal Abortion Law," in this volume.

115. "Health-Care Providers," note 113, at 5.

116. Scott Burris, Glen P. Mays, F. Douglas Scutchfield, and Jennifer K. Ibrahim, "Moving from Intersection to Integration: Public Health Law Research and Public Health Systems and Services Research," *Milbank Quarterly* 90 (2013): 375–408.

117. See Heads of Argument on Behalf of the Reproductive Rights Alliance, *Christian Lawyers* (on file with author).

118. Heads of Argument, *Christian Lawyers*, note 117, at 18.

119. Konrad Zweigert and Hein Kotz, *An Introduction to Comparative Law* (Oxford: Clarendon Press, 1992), 10–11.

120. Meel and Kaswa, "Impact" note 81, at 80.

121. Meel and Kaswa, "Impact," note 81, at 80.

Chapter 6. The Procedural Turn

Written with much appreciation to Reva Siegel for my year at Yale Law School and in New Haven, Connecticut.

1. Guttmacher Institute, *Making Abortion Services Accessible in the Wake of Legal Reforms: A Framework and Six Case Studies* (New York: Guttmacher Institute, 2012), http://www.guttmacher .org/pubs/abortion-services-laws.pdf.

2. Kenneth Culp Davis, *Discretionary Justice: A Preliminary Inquiry* (Baton Rouge: Louisiana State University Press, 1969). See also: William J. Stuntz, "The Uneasy Relationship Between Criminal Procedure and Criminal Justice," *Yale Law Journal* 107 (1997): 1–76; William J. Stuntz, "The Pathological Politics of Criminal Law," *Michigan Law Review* 100 (2001): 505–600.

3. Joanna N. Erdman, "Procedural Turn in Transnational Abortion Law," *American Society of International Law Proceedings* 104 (2011): 377–80; Rebecca J. Cook, Joanna N. Erdman, and Bernard M. Dickens, "Achieving Transparency in Implementing Abortion Laws," *International Journal of Gynecology and Obstetrics* 99 (2007): 157–61.

4. See Lisa Kelly, "Reckoning with Narratives of Innocent Suffering in Transnational Abortion Litigation" in this volume for a discussion of the following procedural rights cases in the U.N. system: *K.L. v. Peru*, Communication No. 1153/2003, U.N. Doc. CCPR/C/85/D/1153/2003 (Human Rights Committee) (2005); *L.C. v. Peru*, Communication No. 22/2009, U.N. Doc. CEDAW/ C/50/D/22/2009 (Committee on the Elimination of Discrimination against Women) (2011); *L.M.R. v. Argentina*, Communication No. 1608/2007, U.N. Doc. CCPR/C/101/D/1608/2007 (Human Rights Committee) (2011); *X and XX v. Colombia*, MC-270/09, Inter-Am. C.H.R. (2011); *Paulina Ramirez v. Mexico*, Case 161–02, Report No. 21/07, Inter-Am. C.H.R., Friendly Settlement (2007).

5. See Paola Bergallo, "The Struggle Against Informal Rules on Abortion in Argentina" in this volume for a rich discussion of the procedural turn in abortion law in Argentina.

6. *Family Planning Association of Northern Ireland v. Minister for Health, Social Services and Public Safety*, [2005] Northern Ireland Law Reports 188 (Court of Appeal, Northern Ireland). See: Eileen V. Fegan and Rachel Rebouché, "Northern Ireland's Abortion Law: The Morality of Silence and the Censure of Agency," *Feminist Legal Studies* 11 (2003): 221–54; Ruth Fletcher, "Abortion Needs or Abortion Rights? Claiming State Accountability for Women's Reproductive Welfare," *Feminist Legal Studies* 13 (2005): 123–34; Marie Fox, "The Case for Decriminalising Abortion in Northern Ireland," in *Bioethics, Medicine and the Criminal Law*, ed. Amel Alghrani, Rebecca Bennett, and Suzanne Ost (Cambridge: Cambridge University Press, 2013), 203–19.

7. Convention for the Protection of Human Rights and Fundamental Freedoms (European Convention), 213 U.N.T.S. 222 (November 4, 1950).

8. *Tysiąc v. Poland*, 45 E.H.R.R. 42, Eur. Ct. H.R. (2007).

9. Law on Family Planning (Protection of The Human Fetus and Conditions Permitting Pregnancy Termination) 1993 (Poland) Statute Book 93.17.78.

10. *Tysiąc v. Poland*, note 8, at para. 104.

11. *Tysiąc v. Poland*, note 8, at para. 76.

12. *Tysiąc v. Poland*, note 8, at para. 107.

13. *Tysiąc v. Poland*, note 8, at para. 116.

14. *Tysiąc v. Poland*, note 8, at para. 116.

15. *Tysiąc v. Poland*, note 8, at para. 124.

16. *Tysiąc v. Poland*, note 8, at para. 116.

17. *Tysiąc v. Poland*, note 8, at para. 116.

18. *A, B, and C v. Ireland*, [2010] E.C.H.R. 2032.

19. *Offences Against the Person Act*, ss. 58–59 (1861), reprinted in 7 *The Statutes* 266 (3rd ed. 1950).

20. Eighth Amendment to the Constitution Act, 1983 (Amendment No. 8/1983), Art. 40.3.3 (Constitution of Ireland).

21. *Attorney General v. X* [1992] 1 I.R. 1 (Supreme Court of Ireland). See also Jennifer Schweppe, ed., *The Unborn Child, Article 40.3.3° and Abortion in Ireland: Twenty-Five Years of Protection?* (Dublin: Liffey Press, 2008).

22. *A, B, and C v. Ireland*, note 18, at paras. 22–25.

23. *A, B, and C v. Ireland*, note 18, at para. 178.

24. *A, B, and C v. Ireland*, note 18, at paras. 253–63.

25. *A, B, and C v. Ireland*, note 18, at para. 253.

26. *R.R. v. Poland*, Application No. 27617/04, Eur. Ct. H.R. (2011).

27. *R.R. v. Poland*, note 26, at para. 198.

28. *R.R. v. Poland*, note 26, at paras. 201, 203–4.

29. *R.R. v. Poland*, note 26, at para. 200.

30. *P. and S. v. Poland*, Application No. 57375/08, Eur. Ct. H.R. (2012).

31. *P. and S. v. Poland*, note 30, at para. 83.

32. *P. and S. v. Poland*, note 30, at para. 108.

33. Jakob Cornides, "Human Rights Pitted Against Man," *International Journal of Human Rights* 12 (2008): 107–34, at 126.

34. For the relationship between over- and underinclusion in criminal law and procedure, see Carol S. Steiker and Jordan M. Steiker, "Sober Second Thoughts: Reflections on Two Decades of Constitutional Regulation of Capital Punishment," *Harvard Law Review* 109 (1995): 355–438, at 366.

35. *Right to Life New Zealand Inc. v. Abortion Supervisory Committee*, [2012] NZSC 68 (Supreme Court of New Zealand).

36. *Right to Life New Zealand Inc. v. Abortion Supervisory Committee*, [2008] 2 NZLR 825, paras. 5, 135 (High Court of New Zealand).

37. Right to Life New Zealand [2012], note 35, at para. 39.

38. Right to Life New Zealand [2012], note 35, at paras. 45–46.

39. *R.R. v. Poland*, note 26, at para. 66, citing Law on Family Planning, note 9, at §1(1).

40. *R.R. v. Poland*, note 26, at para. 163.

41. *Paton (X.) v. United Kingdom*, Application No. 8416/78, Eur. Comm'n H.R. (1980) (admissibility); *Hercz (R.H.) v. Norway*, Application No. 17004/90, Eur. Comm'n H.R. (1992) (admissibility); *Boso v. Italy*, Application No. 50490/99, Eur. Ct. H.R. (2002).

42. *Boso v. Italy*, note 41.

43. *Open Door Counselling and Dublin Well Woman v. Ireland*, Application Nos. 14234/88 and 14235/88, Eur. Ct. H.R. (1992), at para. 63. See also *A, B, and C v. Ireland*, note 18, at paras. 222, 227.

44. *Vo v. France*, Application No. 53924/00, 40 E.H.R.R. 12, Eur. Ct. H.R. (2004).

45. *Vo v. France*, note 44, at para. 86.

46. Nicolette Priaulx, "Testing the Margin of Appreciation: Therapeutic Abortion, Reproductive 'Rights' and the Intriguing Case of *Tysiąc v. Poland*," *European Journal of Health Law* 15 (2008): 361–79, 378. See also: Daniel Fenwick, "The Modern Abortion Jurisprudence Under Article 8 of the European Convention on Human Rights," *Medical Law International* 12 (2013): 249–76; Daniel

Fenwick, "'Abortion Jurisprudence' at Strasbourg: Deferential, Avoidance and Normatively Neutral?" *Legal Studies* (forthcoming).

47. Barbara Hewson, "Dancing on the Head of a Pin? Foetal Life and the European Convention," *Feminist Legal Studies* 13 (2005): 363–75, at 375.

48. See Heinz Klug, "Transnational Human Rights: Exploring the Persistence and Globalization of Human Rights," *Annual Review of Law and Social Science* 1 (2005): 85–103.

49. *Tysiąc v. Poland*, note 8, at para. 3 (Borrego Borrego, J., *dissenting*).

50. *Tysiąc v. Poland*, note 8, at para. 13 (Borrego Borrego, J., *dissenting*).

51. See Andrzej Kulczycki, "Abortion Policy in Postcommunist Europe: The Conflict in Poland," *Population and Development Review* 21 (1995): 471–505; Anne-Marie Kramer, "The Polish Parliament and the Making of Politics Through Abortion: Nation, Gender and Democracy in the 1996 Liberalization Amendment Debate," *International Feminist Journal of Politics* 11 (2009): 81–101; Joanna Diane Caytas, "Women's Reproductive Rights as a Political Price of Post-Communist Transformation in Poland," *Amsterdam Law Forum* 5 (2013): 64–89.

52. Caytas, "Women's Reproductive Rights," note 51, at 67.

53. See: Ruth Fletcher, "Post-Colonial Fragments: Representations of Abortion in Irish Law and Politics," *Journal of Law and Society* 28 (2011): 569–89; Siobhán Mullally, "Debating Reproductive Rights in Ireland," *Human Rights Quarterly* 27 (2005): 78–104; Lisa Smyth, *Abortion and Nation: The Politics of Reproduction in Contemporary Ireland* (Aldershot, U.K.: Ashgate, 2005).

54. Mullally, "Debating," note 53, at 104.

55. See Paolo G. Carozza, "Subsidiarity as a Structural Principle of International Human Rights Law," *American Journal of International Law* 97 (2003): 38–79.

56. The *Belgian Linguistic Case (No. 2)* (1968) 1 E.H.R.R. 252, at para. 10.

57. See Howard C. Yourow, *The Margin of Appreciation Doctrine in the Dynamics of European Human Rights Jurisprudence* (Dordrecht, Netherlands: Martinus Nijhoff Publishers, 1996).

58. *A, B, and C v. Ireland*, note 18, at paras. 239; see also paras. 225–26, 28–76.

59. *A, B, and C v. Ireland*, note 18, at paras. 223, 232–33.

60. See, e.g., Sheelagh McGuiness, "A, B and C Leads to D for Delegation!" *Medical Law Review* 19 (2011): 476–91; Elizabeth Wicks, "*A, B, C v. Ireland*: Abortion Law Under the European Convention on Human Rights," *Human Rights Law Review* 11 (2011): 556–66.

61. Steven Greer, *The European Convention on Human Rights: Achievements, Problems and Prospects* (Cambridge: Cambridge University Press, 2006), 223.

62. *Vo v. France*, note 44, at para. 86.

63. Hewson, "Dancing," note 47, at 372.

64. *A, B, and C v. Ireland*, note 18, at para. 266. See also *R.R. v. Poland*, note 26, at para. 213.

65. See Fenwick, "The Modern Abortion Jurisprudence Under Article 8," note 46; Fenwick, "Abortion Jurisprudence at Strasbourg," note 46.

66. *X v. Norway*, Application No. 867/60, Eur. Comm'n H.R. (1961) (admissibility), *X v. Austria*, Application No. 7045/75, Eur. Comm'n H.R. (1976) (admissibility).

67. *Z. v. Poland*, Application No. 46132/08, Eur. Ct. H.R. (2012), at para. 111.

68. Dimitros Xenos, *The Positive Obligations of the State Under the European Convention of Human Rights* (London: Routledge, 2012), 100.

69. *Tysiąc v. Poland*, note 8, at paras. 123; *A, B, and C v. Ireland*, note 18, at para. 266; *R.R. v. Poland*, note 26, at paras. 213.

70. Alec Stone Sweet, "A Cosmopolitan Legal Order: Constitutional Pluralism and Rights

Adjudication in Europe," *Global Constitutionalism* 1 (2012): 53–90, at 77. See also Wojciech Sadurski, "Partnering with Strasbourg: Constitutionalisation of the European Court of Human Rights, the Accession of Central and East European States to the Council of Europe, and the Idea of Pilot Judgments," *Human Rights Law Review* 9 (2009): 397–453; Luzius Wildhaber, "A Constitutional Future for the European Court of Human Rights," *Human Rights Law Journal* 23 (2002): 161–65.

71. See Sweet, "Cosmopolitan Legal Order," note 70; Steven Greer and Luzius Wildhaber, "Revisiting the Debate About 'Constitutionalising' the European Court of Human Rights," *Human Rights Law Review* 12 (2012): 655–87.

72. Alastair Mowbray, "The Creativity of the European Court of Human Rights," *Human Rights Law Review* 5 (2005): 57–79, at 72–78.

73. *Tysiąc v. Poland*, note 8, at para. 113; *R.R. v. Poland*, note 26, at para. 191; *P. and S. v. Poland*, note 30, at para. 99, citing to *Airey v. Ireland*, [1979] 2 E.H.R.R. 305, at para. 24.

74. Laurence R. Helfer, "Redesigning the European Court of Human Rights: Embeddedness as a Deep Structural Principle of the European Human Rights Regime," *European Journal of International Law* 19 (2008): 125–59.

75. Sadurski, "Partnering," note 70, at 421.

76. *A, B, and C v. Ireland*, note 18, at para. 258.

77. *A, B, and C v. Ireland*, note 18, at para. 265. See also *R.R. v. Poland*, note 26, at para. 203.

78. *D. v. Ireland*, App. No. 26499/02, Eur. Ct. H.R. (2006).

79. *D. v. Ireland,* note 78, at para. 85.

80. Health Service Executive, *Final Report: Investigation of Incident 50278 from Time of Patient's Self Referral to Hospital on the 21st of October 2012 to the Patient's Death on the 28th of October, 2012* (2013) http://www.hse.ie/eng/services/news/nimtreport50278.pdf, 73.

81. Health Service Executive, *Final Report*, note 80, at 73.

82. Department of Health, *Report of the Expert Group on the Judgment in A, B, and C v. Ireland*, November 2012, www.dohc.ie/publications/Judgement_ABC.html.

83. Irish Human Rights Commission, *Right to Life Review Under the Human Rights Commission Act 2000*, January 2013, http://www.ihrc.ie/download/pdf/right_to_life_review.pdf.

84. Houses of the Oierachtas (National Parliament of Ireland), *Protection of Life During Pregnancy Bill 2013* (Bill Number 66 of 2013), as initiated (June 14, 2013), http://www.oireachtas.ie/documents/bills28/bills/2013/6613/b6613d.pdf. The Bill was enacted into force after the writing of this chapter, see *Protection of Life During Pregnancy Act 2013* (Act No. 35 of 2013)

85. See, e.g., Abortion Rights Campaign, *Legislation We Can't Live With*, June 27, 2013, http://www.abortionrightscampaign.ie/2013/06/27/legislation-we-cant-live-with-2/; Abortion Rights Campaign, *21 Years, and 14 Hours of Debate—How Long Must Women in Ireland Wait?* July 11, 2013, http://www.abortionrightscampaign.ie/2013/07/11/21-years-and-14-hours-of-debate-how-long-must-women-in-ireland-wait/.

86. See, e.g., access concerns raised on an earlier draft of the bill, Irish Family Planning Association, *Submission on General Scheme of the Protection of Life During Pregnancy Bill 2013*, May 2013, http://ifpa.ie/sites/default/files/ifpa_submission_protection_of_life_in_pregnancy_heads_of_bill.pdf. See also Rachel Rebouché, "A Functionalist Approach to Comparative Abortion Law" in this volume for a discussion of procedural access barriers.

87. *A, B, and C v. Ireland*, note 18, at para. 189.

88. *Tysiąc v. Poland*, note 8, at para. 112; *A, B, and C v. Ireland*, note 18, at para. 248; *R.R. v. Poland*, note 26, at paras. 190.

89. *See* Stéphanie Henette-Vauchez, "Constitutional v. International? When Unified Reformatory Rationales Mismatch the Plural Paths of Legitimacy of ECHR Law," in *The European Court of Human Rights Between Law and Politics*, ed. Jonas Christoffersen and Mikael Rask Madsen (Oxford: Oxford University Press, 2011), 144–63.

90. Department of Health, *Government Decision to Approve the Publication of the Protection of Life During Pregnancy Bill*, June 12, 2013, http://www.dohc.ie/press/releases/2013/20130612a.html.

91. Albin Eser and Hans-Georg Koch, *Abortion and the Law: From International Comparison to Legal Policy*, trans. Emily Silverman (The Hague: TMC Asser, 2005), 241.

92. *Tysiąc v. Poland*, note 8, at para. 1 (Bonello, J., *separate*).

93. *P. and S. v. Poland*, note 30, at para. 1 (De Gaetano, J., partly *dissenting*). See also *R.R. v. Poland*, note 26, at paras. 2, 4–5 (De Gaetano, J., partly *dissenting*).

94. *P. and S. v. Poland*, note 30, at para. 1 (De Gaetano, J., partly *dissenting*). See also *R.R. v. Poland*, note 26, at paras. 4–5 (De Gaetano, J., partly *dissenting*).

95. *Marckx v. Belgium*, (1979) 2 *E.H.R.R.* 330, 31 Eur. Ct. H.R. See also Xenos, *Positive Obligations of State*, note 68, at 13; Eva Brems and Laurens Lavrysen, "Procedural Justice in Human Rights Adjudication: The European Court of Human Rights," *Human Rights Quarterly* 35 (2013): 176–200.

96. *Tysiąc v. Poland*, note 8, at para. 113; *R.R. v. Poland*, note 26, at paras. 191; *P. and S. v. Poland*, note 30, at para. 99.

97. See also Priaulx, "Testing the Margin," note 46, at 363 on this point.

98. *Tysiąc v. Poland*, note 8, at para. 107; *A, B, and C v. Ireland*, note 18, at para. 212; *R.R. v. Poland*, note 26, at paras. 180; *P. and S. v. Poland*, note 30, at para. 96.

99. *Brüggemann and Scheuten v. Federal Republic of Germany*, Application No. 6959/75 (1981) 3 E.H.R.R. 244, Eur. Comm'n H.R.

100. *Tysiąc v. Poland*, note 8, at paras. 107, 127.

101. *A, B, and C v. Ireland*, note 18, at paras. 157–58, 250.

102. *P. and S. v. Poland*, note 30, at para. 96, 111.

103. *Tysiąc v. Poland*, note 8, at para. 109; *A, B, and C v. Ireland*, note 18, at para. 244; *R.R. v. Poland*, note 26, at paras. 183; *P. and S. v. Poland*, note 30, at para. 94.

104. *Tysiąc v. Poland*, note 8, at paras. 112, 117; *R.R. v. Poland*, note 26, at paras. 190; *P. and S. v. Poland*, note 30, at para. 94. See: Brian Z. Tamanaha, "Formal Theories" in *On the Rule of Law: History, Politics and Theory* (Cambridge: Cambridge University Press, 2004), 91–101.

105. *A, B, and C v. Ireland*, note 18, at para. 248; *R.R. v. Poland*, note 26, at para. 210; *P. and S. v. Poland*, note 30, at para. 111.

106. Michael Rosenfeld, "The Rule of Law and the Legitimacy of Constitutional Democracy," *Southern California Law Review* 74 (2001): 1307–51, at 1309.

107. *R.R. v. Poland*, note 26, at para. 2 (De Gaetano, J., partly *dissenting*).

108. Stuntz, "Uneasy Relationship," note 2, at 53.

109. Louise Finer and Johanna B. Fine, "Abortion Law Around the World: Progress and Pushback," *American Journal of Public Health* 103 (2013): 585–89, at 586, citing: "Sejm odrzucił obywatelski projekt zakazuja □cy aborcji," Gazeta Wyborcza, August 31, 2011, http://wiadomosci.gazeta.pl/wiadomosci/1,114873,10209867, Sejm_odrzucil_obywatelski_projekt_ zakazujacy_aborcji.html.

110. Caytas, "Women's Reproductive Rights," note 51, at 73–75.

111. See Colin S. Diver, "The Optimal Precision of Administrative Rules," *Yale Law Journal* 93 (1984): 65–109.

112. See Eser and Koch, *Abortion and the Law,* note 91, at 277–85.

113. *A, B, and C v. Ireland*, note 18, at para. 178.

114. *R.R. v. Poland*, note 26, at para. 165.

115. See e.g. Prolife Campaign, *Briefing: Abortion Bill Is Dangerous, Unjust and Irretrievably Flawed*, June 2013, http://prolifecampaign.ie/plc/wp-content/uploads/PLC%20Briefing%20Document%20 June%202013%20web.pdf. See also Fiona de Londras and Laura Graham, "Impossible Floodgates and Unworkable Analogies in the Irish Abortion Debate," *Irish Journal of Legal Studies* 3.3 (2013): 54–75.

116. "Cardinal Seán Brady Raises Legal and Constitutional Concerns About the Protection of Life During Pregnancy Bill 2013," *Irish Catholic Bishops Conference*, July 1, 2013, http://www .catholicbishops.ie/2013/07/01/cardinal-sean-brady-raises-legal-constitutional-concerns-protection -life-pregnancy-bill-2013/.

117. John Finnis, "Abortion and Legal Rationality," *Adelaide Law Review* 3 (1970): 431–67, at 444–48.

118. See Eser and Koch, *Abortion and the Law*, note 91, at 277–85.

119. *Tysiąc v. Poland*, note 8, at para. 113; *R.R. v. Poland*, note 26, at para. 191; *P. and S. v. Poland*, note 30, at para. 99.

120. *Tysiąc v. Poland*, note 8, at para. 117; *R.R. v. Poland*, note 26, at para. 191; *P. and S. v. Poland*, note 30, at para. 99.

121. *Tysiąc v. Poland*, note 8, at paras. 12–14 (Borrego Borrego, J., *dissenting*).

122. See Charles Ngwena, "Reforming African Abortion Laws and Practice: The Place of Transparency" in this volume for a discussion of procedural abortion rights and the pure proceduralism of John Rawls, *Theory of Justice* (Oxford: Oxford University Press, 1971).

123. See Robert J. MacCoun, "Voice, Control and Belonging: The Double-Edged Sword of Procedural Fairness," *Annual Review of Law and Social Science* 1 (2005): 171–201, at 188–93.

124. See Reva B. Siegel, "The Constitutionalization of Abortion," in *The Oxford Handbook of Comparative Constitutional Law*, ed. Michel Rosenfeld and András Sajó (Oxford: Oxford University Press, 2012), 1057–78, reprinted in this volume. See also Ruth Rubio-Marín, "Abortion in Portugal: New Trends in European Constitutionalism" and Adriana Lamačková, "Women's Rights in the Abortion Decision of the Slovak Constitutional Court" in this volume.

125. Siegel, "Constitutionalization of Abortion," note 124, at 1059.

Chapter 7. The Struggle Against Informal Rules on Abortion in Argentina

I am grateful for the observations of participants in the workshop "Shifting Paradigms in Abortion Law," convened by the International Reproductive and Sexual Health Law Program, Faculty of Law, University of Toronto. All translations in this chapter are by the author. This chapter reflects legal changes up to June 30, 2013.

1. Código Penal de la Nación Argentina [National Criminal Code], art. 86 (Boletin Oficial, Buenos Aires, 1985). The word "idiot" actually appears in the Criminal Code that dates from 1921.

2. Silvina Ramos, Paola Bergallo, Mariana Romero, and Jimena Arias Feijóo, "El aborto no punible: Una cuestión de derechos humanos," *Informe Anual 2008*, (Buenos Aires: Centro de Estudios Legales y Sociales y Siglo XXI Editores, 2009).

3. Gretchen Helmke and Steven Levitsky, *Informal Institutions and Democracy: Lessons from Latin America* (Baltimore: Johns Hopkins University Press, 2006).

4. Guillermo O'Donnell, "Polyarchies and the (Un)Rule of Law in Latin America: A Partial

Conclusion," in *The (Un)Rule of Law and the Underprivileged in Latin America*, ed. Juan E. Mendez, Paul Sergio Pinheiro, and Guillermo O'Donnell (Notre Dame: University of Notre Dame Press, 1999), 303–38.

5. Corte Suprema de Justicia de la Nación [Supreme Court] 2012, *F., A.L.*, Expediente Letra "F," No. 259, Libro XLVI, (Arg.)

6. Mónica Gogna, et al., "Abortion in a Restrictive Legal Context: The Views of Obstetrician-Gynaecologists in Buenos Aires, Argentina," *Reproductive Health Matters* 10, No. 19 (2002): 128–37.

7. Helmke and Levitsky, *Informal,* note 3.

8. Constitución Nacional de la República Argentina, August 22, 1994, art. 33; American Convention on Human Rights, art. 4, November 21, 1969, 114 U.N.T.S. 143.

9. Merike Blofield, *The Politics of Moral Sin: Abortion and Divorce in Spain, Chile and Argentina* (New York: Routledge, 2006).

10. Gene Burns, *The Moral Veto: Framing Contraception, Abortion, and Cultural Pluralism in the United States* (Cambridge: Cambridge University Press, 2005).

11. Alicia Gutierrez, "Mujeres Autoconvocadas para decidir en Libertad (MADEL)," in *La Sociedad Civil Frente a las Nuevas Formas de Institucionalidad Democrática*, ed. Martín Abregú and Silvina E. Ramos (Buenos Aires: CEDES, CELS, 2000), 83–106.

12. Rebecca Cook, Joanna Erdman, Martin Hevia, and Bernard Dickens, "Prenatal Management of Anencephaly," *International Journal of Gynecology and Obstetrics* 102 (2008): 304–8.

13. Martin Hevia, "The Legal Status of Emergency Contraception in Latin America," *International Journal of Gynecology and Obstetrics* 116 (2012): 87–90.

14. Mónica Petracci and Mario Pecheny, *Argentina, derechos humanos y sexualidad* (Buenos Aires: CEDES, 2007).

15. Ley No. 25.673, Nov. 22, 2002, Programa Nacional de Salud Sexual y Procreación Responsable [National Sexual Health and Responsible Parenthood Program].

16. Consejo Federal de Salud, "Compromiso para la reducción de la mortalidad materna en la Argentina" (Commitment for the reduction of maternal mortality in Argentina), 2004, http://www.msal.gov.ar/promin/archivos/pdf/comp-red-mort-mat.pdf.

17. "Ginéz García despenalizaría el aborto," *La Nación*, February 15, 2005, http://www.lanacion.com.ar/679770-gines-garcia-legalizaria-el-aborto.

18. Helmke and Levitsky, *Informal,* note 3.

19. Edurne Cárdenas and Leah Tandeter, *Derechos sexuales y reproductivos en Argentina* (Buenos Aires, CONDERS, 2008).

20. Suprema Corte de la Provincia de Buenos Aires [Supreme Court of the Province of Buenos Aires] 2005, *C.P. d. P., A.K. s/autorización*, LLBA, July 2005, 629.

21. Mercedes Cavallo, "La falta de *enforcement* del aborto no punible en Argentina," *Revista Jurisprudencia Argentina*, Suplemento Especial, June 2011.

22. Suprema Corte de la Provincia de Buenos Aires [Supreme Court of the Province of Buenos Aires] 2006, "R., L.M., 'NN Persona por nacer. Protección. Denuncia.'" Causa Ac. 98.830, also known as the *L.M.R.* case.

23. Mariana Carbajal, *El aborto en debate: Aportes para una discusión pendiente* (Buenos Aires: Paidós, 2009).

24. Marianne Mollmann, *Illusions of Care: Lack of Accountability for Reproductive Rights in Argentina* (New York: Human Rights Watch, 2010), 45.

25. Mollmann, *Illusions*, note 24, at 47.

26. U.N. General Assembly, *Convention on the Rights of the Child*, November 20, 1989, United Nations, Treaty Series, vol. 1577, p. 3, Argentina's Declarations, http://treaties.un.org/untc/Pages/ViewDetails.aspx?src=TREATY&mtdsg_no=IV-11&chapter=4&lang=en#EndDec.

27. Instituto Nacional contra la Discriminación y la Xenofobia, *Recomendación No. 2*, http://www.inadi.gob.ar/uploads/recomendaciones/rec_gral_abortoslegales.pdf.

28. Ramos et al., "El aborto," note 2.

29. World Health Organization, *Safe abortion: Technical and Policy Guidance for Health Systems* (Geneva: World Health Organization, 2003).

30. *Norma Técnica: Atenção Humanizada ao Abortamento* (Brasilia: Ministerio da Saúde, 2005).

31. *Norma Técnica para la Atención de la Interrupción Voluntaria del Embarazo (IVE)* (Bogotá: Ministerio de la Protección Social, 2006).

32. Paola Bergallo and Mariana Romero, *Guide for the Comprehensive Care of Nonpunishable Abortions* (Buenos Aires: NPRHRP, 2007) (drafted but never implemented) [hereinafter 2007 Guide].

33. Programa de Salud Reproductiva de la Provincia de Neuquén, "Percepciones, prácticas y actitudes de los profesionales médicos en la atención del aborto" (Provincia de Neuquén: Ministerio de Salud, 2011), http://www.hypermedios.com/aborto/aborto%20final.pdf.

34. Tribunal de Familia de Bahía Blanca [Family Court of the City of Bahía Blanca] October 1, 2008, *S.G.N s/situación*, Causa 30.790 [hereinafter *S.G.N.*, Causa 30.790].

35. Suprema Corte de la Provincia de Buenos Aires [Supreme Court of the Province of Buenos Aires] 2006, "R., L.M., 'NN Persona por nacer. Protección. Denuncia.'" Causa Ac. 98.830, also known as the *L.M.R.* case, note 22.

36. 2007 Guide, note 32.

37. Guide for the Comprehensive Care of Nonpunishable Abortions (Buenos Aires: Ministry of Health, 2010) (drafted but never implemented) [hereinafter 2010 Guide].

38. Virginia Menéndez, "Iniciativas regulatorias para el acceso al aborto no punible," in *Aborto y justicia reproductiva,* ed. Paola Bergallo (Buenos Aires: Editores del Puerto, 2011), 201–45.

39. "Legislatura porteña: Aprobaron en comisión un proyecto sobre aborto no punible," *TN*, August 24, 2010, http://tn.com.ar/politica/00041055/legislatura-portena-aprobaron-en-comision-un-proyecto-sobre-aborto-no-punible.

40. The 2009 provincial resolution was the Administrative Resolution 886 of the Ministry of Health of the Province of Santa Fe, adopted on April 20, 2009.

41. 2007 Guide, note 32.

42. Sala "B" de la Cámara en lo Criminal de la Provincia de Río Negro [Criminal Court of Appeal of the Province of Río Negro] 2009, *F.N.M.*; Superior Tribunal de la Provincia de Chubut [Supreme Court of the Province of Chubut] 2010, *F., A.L. s/ medida autosatisfactiva*, Expte. 21.912-f-2010 [hereinafter *F., A.L.*,]; Sala "A" de la Cámara de Apelaciones de la Provincia de Chubut [Court of Appeal of the Province of Chubut] *M.*, Expte. 93/10 [hereinafter *M.*, Expte. 93/10].

43. *F., A.L.*, note 5.

44. *M.*, Expte. 93/10, note 42.

45. Ley XV No. 14, Chubut, May 31, 2010, Ley provincial de procedimientos a desarrollar en los establecimientos de salud pública, respecto de la atención de los casos de abortos no punibles [Act to Develop Public Health Facilities for the Treatment of Non-Punishable Abortions].

46. Peña Fago, Angélica and Edurne Cárdenas, "Barreras judiciales al acceso al aborto legal: La intervención ilegitima de la justicia en casos de Aborto No Punible en Argentina" (Buenos Aires:

Instituto de Investigaciones Gino Germani, 2011), http://webiigg.sociales.uba.ar/saludypoblacion/ixjornadas/principal.php?resumenid=78 (accessed July 23, 2013).

47. U.N. Committee on the Elimination of Discrimination against Women, *Concluding Observations of the CEDAW Committee on the Report of Argentina*, August 16, 2010, U.N. Doc. CEDAW/C/ARG/CO/6; U.N. Human Rights Committee, *Concluding Observations of the Human Rights Committee: Argentina*, March 31, 2010, U.N. Doc. CCPR/C/ARG/CO/4; and the U.N. Committee on the Rights of Children, *Final Recommendations of the Committee on the Rights of Children*, June 21, 2010, U.N. Doc. CRC/C/ARG/CO/34.

48. *L.M.R.* note 22.

49. *L.M.R. v. Argentina*, Communication No. 1608/2007, CCPR/C/101/D/168/2007 (Human Rights Committee) (2011).

50. *S.G.N.*, Causa 30.790; "Bahía Blanca, disputa por el freno al aborto de una joven violada," *La Nación*, October 1, 2008, http://www.lanacion.com.ar/1055239–bahia-blanca-disputa-por-el-freno-al-aborto-de-una-joven-violada.

51. 2007 Guide, note 32, and 2010 Guide, note 37.

52. Mariana Carbajal, "Puerta abierta al golpe bajo en un hospital," *Página 12*, September 6, 2008, http://www.pagina12.com.ar/diario/sociedad/3–111093–2008–09–06.html.

53. Vladimir Hernández, "Embarazo en niña de 11 años reaviva el debate sobre aborto en Argentina," *BBC Mundo, Argentina*, January 20, 2012, http://www.bbc.co.uk/mundo/noticias/2012/01/120118_argentina_casos_joven_embarazada_aborto_vh.shtml.

54. Juzgado en lo Contencioso Administrativo y Tributario Poder Judicial de la Ciudad de Buenos Aires [Administrative and Fiscal Court of the City of Buenos Aires] 2008, *Profamilia Asoc. Civil. c. Gobierno de la Ciudad de Buenos Aires y otros s/impugnación de actos administrativos*, Expte: EXP 31117/0.

55. 2007 Guide, note 32.

56. Daniel Gallo, "Confusión por la guía sobre el aborto que sigue vigente," *La Nación*, July 22, 2010, http://www.lanacion.com.ar/1287135–confusion-por-la-guia-sobre-el-aborto-que-sigue-vigente.

57. *F., A.L,* note 5.

58. *F., A.L.,* note 5.

59. *F., A.L.,* note 5, at Considerando 24.

60. *F., A.L.,* note 5, at Considerando 25.

61. "Suspensión del primer aborto no punible: 'Macri se tiene que hacer cargo,' aseguró Manzur Telam," *Télam*, October 9, 2012, http://www.telam.com.ar/nota/40334.

62. Mercedes Cavallo and Roberto Amette, "El aborto no punible a cuatro meses de *F., A.L. s/ medida autosatisfactiva* ¿Qué Obtuvimos y qué nos queda por obtener?" *Cuestión de Derechos, Revista Electronica* 2 (August 2012): 60–81, http://www.cuestiondederechos.org.ar/pdf/numero2/09-Aborto-no-punible.pdf; Mercedes Cavallo and Roberto Amette, "El aborto no punible a nueve meses de *F.A.L. s/ medida autosatisfactiva* ¿Qué Obtuvimos y qué nos queda por obtener?" 1–27 (Buenos Aires: Asociación por los Derechos Civiles, 2012), http://www.adc.org.ar/sw_contenido.php?id=968.

63. Cavallo and Amette, "El aborto no punible a nueve meses de *F.A.L.*," note 62.

64. "Macri vetará la ley de aborto no punible en la Ciudad de Buenos Aires," *Infobae*, October 6, 2012, http://www.infobae.com/notas/674376-Macri-vetara-la-ley-de-aborto-no-punible-en-la-Ciudad-de-Buenos-Aires.html.

65. "La Corte autorizó el aborto tras revocar el amparo," *La Nación*, October 12, 2012, http://www.lanacion.com.ar/1516568-la-corte-autorizo-el-aborto-tras-revocar-el-amparo.

66. *R. v. Morgentaler*, [1988] 1 S.C.R. 30, 44 D.L.R. (4th) 385 (Supreme Court of Canada).

Chapter 8. Reforming African Abortion Laws and Practice

This chapter reflects legal changes up to June 30, 2013.

1. Reed Boland and Laura Katzive, "Development of Laws on Induced Abortion: 1998–2007," *International Family Law Planning Perspectives* 34 (2008): 110–20, at 115–16.

2. Anand Grover, "Interim Report of the Special Rapporteur on the Right of Everyone to the Enjoyment of the Highest Attainable Standard of Physical and Mental Health" (Part IV concerns criminalization of sexual and reproductive health), U.N. Doc. A/66/254 (August 2011).

3. Eunice Brookman-Amissah and Josephine B. Moyo, "Abortion Law Reform in Sub-Saharan Africa: No Turning Back," *Reproductive Health Matters* 12 (2004): 227–34.

4. African Charter on Human and Peoples' Rights, adopted June 27, 1981, O.A.U. Doc. CAB/LEG/67/3 Rev. 5, 1520 U.N.T.S. 217, entered into force October 21, 1986 [hereinafter African Charter].

5. Protocol to the African Charter on Human and Peoples' Rights on the Rights of Women in Africa, adopted July 11, 2003, 2nd Ordinary Session of the Assembly of the African Union, AHG/Res. 240 (XXXI), entered into force November 25, 2005 [hereinafter Women's Protocol].

6. African Union, "List of Countries Which Have Signed, Ratified/Acceded to the Protocol to the African Charter on Human and Peoples' Rights on the Rights of Women in Africa," http://www.au.int/en/sites/default/files/Rightsof%20of%20Women_0.pdf.

7. Charles G. Ngwena, "Inscribing Abortion as a Human Right: Significance of the Protocol on the Rights of Women in Africa," *Human Rights Quarterly* 32 (2010): 783–864, at 852–56.

8. *K.L. v. Peru*, Communication no. 1153/2003, CCPR/C/85/D/1153/2003 (2005) (Human Rights Committee) (2005); *L.C. v. Peru*, Communication no. 22/2009, CEDAW/C/50/D/22/2009 (Committee on the Elimination of Discrimination against Women) (2011); *L.M.R. v. Argentina*, Communication no. 1608/2007, CCPR/C/101/D/168/2007 (Human Rights Committee) (2011).

9. Frans Viljoen, *International Human Rights Law in Africa* (Oxford: Oxford University Press, 2007), 101–2, 127–29.

10. Rebecca J. Cook, Joanna N. Erdman, and Bernard M. Dickens, "Achieving Transparency in Implementing Abortion Laws," *International Journal of Gynecology and Obstetrics* 99 (2007): 157–61; Ngwena, "Inscribing," note 7, at 805–8.

11. *Tysiąc v. Poland*, 45 E.H.R.R., 42, Eur. Ct. H.R. (2007); *A, B, and C v. Ireland*, [2010] E.C.H.R. 2032, Eur. Ct. H.R.; *R.R. v. Poland*, Application no. 27617/04, Eur. Ct. H.R. (2011); *P. and S. v. Poland*, Application No. 57375/08, Eur. Ct. H.R. (2012).

12. World Health Organization, *Safe Abortion: Technical and Policy Guidance for Health Systems*, 2nd edition (Geneva: WHO, 2012), 87–103.

13. African Union, Maputo Plan of Action for the Operationalization of the Continental Policy Framework for Sexual and Reproductive Health and Rights 2007–2010, Special Sess. of the African Union Conference of Ministers of Health, September 18–22, 2006, O.A.U. Doc. Sp/MIN/CAMH/5(I).

14. World Health Organization, *Unsafe Abortion: Global and Regional Estimates of the Incidence of Unsafe Abortion and Associated Mortality in 2008*, 6th ed. (Geneva: WHO, 2011).

15. General Assembly, United Nations Millennium Declaration, adopted September 18, 2000, G.A. Res. 55/2, U.N. GAOR 55th Session (2000).

16. Oren Asman, "Abortion in Islamic countries," *Medicine and Law* 23 (2004): 73–89.

17. Janie Benson, Kathryn Andersen, and Ghazaleh Samandari, "Reduction in Abortion-Related Mortality Following Policy Reform: Evidence from Romania, South Africa and Bangladesh," *Reproductive Health* 8 (2011): 39, http://www.ncbi.nlm.nih.gov/pmc/articles/PMC3287245/.

18. Guttmacher Institute, "Unsafe Abortion in Zambia," *In Brief* 3 (2009): 1–4, at 1; Emily Jackson et al., "A Strategic Assessment of Unsafe Abortion in Malawi," *Reproductive Health Matters* 19 (2011): 133–43, at 136; Brooke R. Johnson et al., "Reducing Unplanned Pregnancy in Zimbabwe Through Postabortion Contraception," *Studies in Family Planning* 13 (2002): 195–202, at 195; Center for Reproductive Rights, *In Harm's Way: The Impact of Kenya's Restrictive Abortion Law* (New York: Centre for Reproductive Rights, 2007), 31–35.

19. Charles G. Ngwena, "Access to Legal Abortion: Developments in Africa from a Reproductive and Sexual Health Rights Perspective," *South Africa Public Law* 19 (2004): 328–48, at 336.

20. Rebecca J. Cook and Bernard M. Dickens, "Abortion Laws in African Commonwealth Countries," *Journal of African Law* 25 (1981): 60–79.

21. *R. v. Bourne*, [1938] 3 All E.R. 615 (Crown Court of England and Wales).

22. *R. v. Edgal, Idike and Ojugwu*, (1938) W.A.C.A. 133 (West African Court of Appeal).

23. *Mehar Singh Bansel v. R.*, (1959) E.A.L.R. 813 (East African Court of Appeal).

24. Law of December 31, 1986, of Cape Verde.

25. Choice on Termination of Pregnancy Act No. 92 of 1996 as amended by the Choice on Termination of Pregnancy Act No. 1 of 2008 of South Africa.

26. Law No. 65–25 of 1 July 1965 as amended of Tunisia.

27. Termination of Pregnancy Act of 1972 of Zambia.

28. Criminal Code of Ethiopia of 2005, Article 551.

29. Center for Reproductive Rights, *World's Abortion Laws Map 2013*, http://worldabortionlaws.com/map/.

30. Charles G. Ngwena, "An Appraisal of Abortion Laws in Southern Africa from a Reproductive Health Rights Perspective," *Journal of Law, Medicine and Ethics* 32 (2004): 708–17, at 713.

31. Brook R. Johnson et al., "Unplanned Pregnancy and Abortion in Zimbabwe Through Postabortion Contraception," *Studies in Family Planning* 33 (2002): 195–202, at 195.

32. Zimbabwe, Ministry of Health and Child Welfare, *National Health Profile* (Harare: Ministry of Health and Child Welfare, 2009).

33. Ngwena, "Inscribing," note 7, at 810–18.

34. On the genesis of the Women's Protocol, see Fareda Banda, *Women, Law and Human Rights: An African Perspective* (Portland, Ore.: Hart, 2005), 66–82; Frans Viljoen, "An Introduction to the Protocol to the African Charter on Human and Peoples' Rights on the Rights of Women in Africa," *Washington and Lee Journal of Civil Rights and Social Justice* 16 (2009): 11–46.

35. Women's Global Network for Reproductive Rights, "Rwanda: MPs to Harmonise Legislation on Abortion," http://www.wgnrr.org/news/rwanda-mps-harmonise-legislation-abortion (accessed February 14, 2013).

36. African Charter, note 4, at arts. 30, 45, 47, and 45.

37. Protocol to the African Charter on the Establishment of an African Court on Human and

Peoples' Rights, adopted June 10, 1998 (entered into force June 25, 2004), O.A.U. Doc. OAU/LEG/MIN/ AFCH/PROT(I) Rev.2 (Protocol to the African Charter on the Establishment of an African Court).

38. African Commission, Concluding Observations, Fourth Periodic Report of Nigeria at the 50th Ordinary Session of Nigeria, October 24 to November 5, 2011 (2011) [hereinafter African Commission].

39. African Commission, note 38, at para. 67.

40. African Commission, note 38, at para. 93.

41. *R. v. Edgal, Idike and Ojugwu*, note 22; Olaide Gbadamosi, *Reproductive Health and Rights* (Benin City: Ethiope Publishing Corporation, 2007), 71–72.

42. *K.L. v. Peru*, at note 8.

43. *L.C. v. Peru*, at note 8.

44. *L.M.R. v. Argentina*, note 8.

45. *L.C. v. Peru*, note 8, at para. 8.16.

46. *L.C. v. Peru*, note 8, at para. 8.11.

47. *L.C. v. Peru*, note 8, at para. 12(b)(ii).

48. *L.M.R. v. Argentina*, note 8, at para. 9.4.

49. *Tysiąc v. Poland*, note 11; *A, B, and C v. Ireland*, note 11; *R.R. v. Poland*, note 11; *P. and S. v. Poland*, note 11.

50. John Rawls, *Political Liberalism* (New York: Columbia University Press, 2005), 133–72.

51. Rawls, *Political*, note 50, at 133.

52. John Rawls, *Theory of Justice* (Oxford: Oxford University Press, 1971).

53. Martha Minow, "Interpreting Rights: An Essay for Robert Cover," *Yale Law Journal* 96 (1987): 1860–915, at 1867; Peter Gabel, "The Phenomenology of Rights-Consciousness and the Pact of Withdrawn Selves," *Texas Law Review* 62 (1984): 1563–99, at 1590.

54. *R.R. v. Poland*, note 11, para. 206; see Bernard M. Dickens "The Right to Conscience" in this volume for a discussion of conscientious objection and its reciprocal rights and duties.

55. Rebecca J. Cook and Susannah Howard, "Accommodating Women's Differences under the Women's Anti-Discrimination Convention," *Emory Law Journal* 56 (2007): 1039–91, at 1040–41.

56. Nancy Fraser, "Rethinking Recognition," *New Left Review* 3 (2000): 107–20, at 113–16.

57. Martha C. Nussbaum, *Women and Human Development: The Capabilities Approach* (Cambridge: Cambridge University Press, 2000).

58. Rachel Murray, *Human Rights in Africa* (Cambridge: Cambridge University Press, 2004), 73–115; Viljoen, *International Human Rights Law in Africa*, note 9, at 169.

59. Constitutive Act of the African Union of 2009, arts. 3(g) and 3(h).

60. Criminal Code (Amendment) Law, PNDC Law 102 of 1985 of Ghana as incorporated into section 58 of the consolidated Criminal Code of 1960.

61. Ghana Health Service, *Prevention and Management of Unsafe Abortion: Comprehensive Abortion Care Services* (2006), 1.

62. Ghana Health Service, *Prevention*, note 61.

63. Ghana Health Service, *Prevention*, note 61, at 1.

64. Family Health Department, *Technical and Procedural Guidelines for Safe Abortion Services in Ethiopia* (2006), http://phe-ethiopia.org/resadmin/uploads/attachment-161-safe_abortion _guideline_English_printed_version.pdf.

65. Zambia, Ministry of Health, *Standards and Guidelines for Reducing Unsafe Abortion, Morbidity and Mortality in Zambia* (2009).

66. Kenya, Ministry of Medical Services, *Standards and Guidelines for Reducing Morbidity and Mortality from Unsafe Abortion in Kenya* (2012).

67. African Union, *Maputo*, note 13.

68. Guttmacher Institute, "Abortion in Ghana," *In Brief No 2* (2010).

69. Clement Ahiadeke, "Incidence of Induced Abortion in Southern Ghana," *International Family Planning Perspectives* 27 (2001): 96–108.

70. U.N. Committee on Economic, Social and Cultural Rights, *General Comment No 14: The Right to the Highest Attainable Standard of Health*, U.N. Doc. E/C12/2000/4 (2000), para. 12.

71. Kim Dickson-Tetteh and Deborah L. Billings, "Abortion Care Services Provided by Registered Midwives in South Africa," *International Family Planning Perspectives* 28 (2002): 144–50.

72. Anne McClintock, "Family Feuds: Gender, Nationalism and the Family," *Feminist Review* 44 (1993): 61–80 at 77.

Chapter 9. The Medical Framework and Early Medical Abortion in the U.K.

This chapter reflects legal changes up to June 30, 2013.

1. E.g., Sally Sheldon, *Beyond Control: Medical Power and Abortion Law* (London: Pluto, 1997).

2. Society for the Protection of Unborn Children, *A Dose of Lies: False Claims About RU486, the Abortion Drug* (London: SPUC, 1993).

3. David Feldman, *Civil Liberties and Human Rights in England and Wales*, 2nd ed. (Oxford: Oxford University Press, 2002), 70.

4. *R. (on the application of Purdy) v. Dir. of Pub. Prosecutions*, [2009] U.K.H.L. 45 (House of Lords); *Pretty v. U.K.*, 35 Eur. Ct. H. R. Rep. 1 (2002).

5. "Health," sense 1.a., *Oxford English Dictionary* (Oxford).

6. "Health," *English-Word Information*, http://wordinfo.info/unit/2924 (accessed November 22, 2012).

7. World Health Organization, "Reproductive Health" webpage, http://www.who.int/topics/reproductive_health/en/ (accessed November 22, 2012).

8. World Health Organization, "Reproductive," note 7.

9. See, e.g., Rebecca J. Cook, Bernard M. Dickens, and Mahmoud F. Fathalla, *Reproductive Health and Human Rights: Integrating Medicine, Ethics and Law* (Oxford: Oxford University Press, 2003).

10. World Health Organization, *Safe Abortion: Technical and Policy Guidance for Health Systems*, 2nd ed. (Geneva: World Health Organization, 2012).

11. Regina Kulier et al., "Medical Methods for First Trimester Abortion," *Cochrane Database of Systematic Reviews* 2011, Issue 11, No.: CD002855.

12. Alan Templeton and David A. Grimes, "A Request for Abortion," *New England Journal of Medicine* 365 (2011): 2198–204.

13. Ellen Goodman, as cited in Renate Klein, Janice G. Raymond, and Lynette J. Dumble, *RU 486: Misconceptions, Myths and Morals* (Melbourne: Spinifex, 1991), 25, 29.

14. Sheldon, *Beyond*, note 1, at 141–43.

15. Étienne-Émile Baulieu, *The Abortion Pill* (London: Century, 1991), 18.

16. Suzanna S. Banwell and John M. Paxman, "The Search for Meaning: RU486/PG, Pregnancy and the Law of Abortion," *Reproductive Health Matters* 1, No. 2 (1993): 68–76.

17. See, e.g., 195 Parl. Deb. U.K., H.C., (6th ser.) (July 22, 1991) 898 (Campbell-Savours).

18. Sheldon, *Beyond*, note 1, 141.

19. Catherine Francoise, as cited in Anne-Marie Sapsted "Abortion: The New Pill," *Sunday Times Magazine* (January 6, 1991), 41.

20. Joanna Erdman, "Access to Information on Safe Abortion: A Harm Reduction and Human Rights Approach," *Harvard Journal of Law and Gender* 34 (2011): 413–62, at 414, citing Iqbal Shah and Elisabeth Ahman, "Unsafe Abortion in 2008: Global and Regional Levels and Trends," *Reproductive Health Matters* 18 (2010): 90–101, at 91.

21. Generally, see Frances Kissling, "Abortion: The Link Between Legality and Safety," *Reproductive Health Matters* 1, No. 2 (1993): 65–67.

22. Erdman, "Access," note 20.

23. Marge Berer, "Medical Abortion in Britain and Ireland: Let's Join the 21st Century," *RH Reality Check* blog, http://rhrealitycheck.org/article/2011/02/16/medical-abortion-britain-ireland-let-join-21st-century/. February 16, 2011.

24. Sheldon, *Beyond*, note 1.

25. U.K., Abortion Act 1967, *U.K. Statutes* 1967, Ch. 87, s.1(1)(a).

26. Abortion Act 1967, note 25, at s.1(1)(b)–(d).

27. Sheldon, *Beyond*, chapter 3.

28. 750 Parl. Deb. U.K., H.C., (5th ser.) (July 13, 1967) 570 (David Steel).

29. Abortion Act 1967, note 25, at s.1(2).

30. *R. v. Bourne*, [1938] 3 All E.R. [1938] 615, 619 (Crown Court of England and Wales).

31. Scarman L.J., *R. v. Smith* [1974] 1 All E.R. 376, 381 (Court of Appeal of England and Wales).

32. Abortion Act 1967, note 25, at s.1(1) and s.1(3), respectively.

33. *Abortion Statistics, England and Wales 2010* (London: Department of Health, 2011).

34. Sheldon, *Beyond*, note 1, chapter 6.

35. Abortion Act 1967, note 25, at s.1(3A).

36. 174 Parl. Deb. U.K., H.C., (6th ser.) (June 21, 1991) 1193.

37. Sheldon, *Beyond*, note 1, chapter 7.

38. E.g., Baulieu, *Abortion Pill,* note 15, chapters 2 (on the French case), 7 (on the United States), and 6 (on licensing elsewhere).

39. Denise Chicoine, "RU486 in the United States and Great Britain: A Case Study in Gender Bias," *Boston College International and Comparative Law Review* 16 (1993): 81–113, at 111–12.

40. Sheldon, *Beyond*, note 1, chapter 7.

41. 195 Parl. Deb. U.K., H.C., (6th ser.) (July 22, 1991) 890 (Bernard Braine).

42. 195 Parl. Deb. U.K., H.C., (6th ser.) (July 22, 1991) 884–87 (Kenneth Hind); 888–92 (Bernard Braine); 895–96 (Ann Winterton).

43. 195 Parl. Deb. U.K., H.C., (6th ser.) (July 22, 1991) 884 (Kenneth Hind).

44. 195 Parl. Deb. U.K., H.C., (6th ser.) (July 22, 1991) 892, 893, 894 (Jo Richardson); 897 (Peter Thurnham); 899 (Stephen Dorrell).

45. Abortion Act 1967, note 25, at s.1(1).

46. *Royal College of Nurses v. Department of Health and Social Security*, [1981] 1 All E.R. 545 (House of Lords).

47. Jonathan Montgomery, "Doctors' Handmaidens: The Legal Contribution," in *Law, Health and Medical Regulation*, ed. Sally Wheeler and Shaun McVeigh (Aldershot: Dartmouth, 1992), 145.

48. Abortion Act 1967, note 25, at s.1(3).

49. House of Commons, Science and Technology Committee (2007), *Scientific Developments Relating to the Abortion Act 1967*, 12th Report of Session 2006–7, Vol. 1 (HC 1045–I) and 2 (HC 1045–II).

50. Science and Technology Committee, note 49, Conclusion and Recommendations, at 53–57.

51. Science and Technology Committee, note 49, at 71–83.

52. Ben Goldacre, respectively, "Oooooh I'm in the Minority Report!" *Guardian,* October 31, 2007, and "Minority Retort," *Guardian*, November 3, 2007.

53. Science and Technology Committee, note 49, at para. 46.

54. Sally Sheldon, "A Missed Opportunity to Reform an Outdated Piece of Legislation," *Clinical Ethics* 4 (2009): 3.

55. *British Pregnancy Advisory Serv. v. Sec'y of State for Health*, [2011] E.W.H.C. 235 (Admin), at para. 12 [hereinafter BPAS decision].

56. Jennie Bristow, "Misoprostol and the Transformation of the 'Abortion Pill,'" *Abortion Review*, January 26, 2011.

57. *BPAS decision*, note 55, at paras. 32, 30, respectively.

58. Ann Furedi, "Our 10-Year Struggle to Improve Abortion Care," *Abortion Review*, February 17, 2011.

59. Secretary of State for Health, Skeleton Argument, in *BPAS decision*, note 55, at para. 22, on file with the author.

60. Kate Greasley, "Medical Abortion and the 'Golden Rule' of Statutory Interpretation," *Medical Law Review* 19, No. 2 (2011): 314–25.

61. Secretary, Skeleton Argument, note 59, at paras. 9, 10, 38, and 39 respectively.

62. Secretary, Skeleton Argument, note 59, at para. 41.

63. *BPAS decision*, note 55 at para. 2.

64. Health and Social Care Act, 2012, c. 7 (U.K.).

65. Nadine Dorries, "Abortion Guidelines Need to Be Drawn Up by an Independent Body Which Is Accountable to Parliament," *Conservative Home* blog, http://conservativehome.blogs.com/platform/2011/03/nadine-dorries-.html (accessed November 27, 2012).

66. Holly Watt, Claire Newell, and Robert Winnett, "Abortion Investigation: Doctor Caught Falsifying Sex Selection Paperwork," *Telegraph*, February 24, 2012.

67. Cited in Robert Winnett, Claire Newell, and Holly Watt, "One in Five Abortion Clinics Breaks Law," *Telegraph*, March 22, 2012.

68. Winnett, Newell and Watt, "One in Five," note 67.

69. Care Quality Commission, "Findings of Termination of Pregnancy Inspections Published," press release, July 12, 2012.

70. Abortion Act 1967, note 25, at s.1(1); Abortion Regulations 1991 (S.I. No. 1991/499), at S.3(2).

71. Barbara Hewson, "The Public Is Being Misled About Pre-Signed Abortion Certificates," *Solicitors Journal*, April 16, 2012, http://www.solicitorsjournal.com/node/9428.

72. BBC News, "Abortion Clinic Checks Cost £1m," April 5, 2012.

73. Andy Burham, Shadow Health Secretary, cited in BBC News, "Abortion" note 7272.

74. Randeep Ramesh, "NHS Watchdog Attacks Blitz on Abortion Clinics," *Guardian*, April 4, 2012.

75. Sam Coates, Rachel Sylvester, and Alice Thomson, "Jeremy Hunt Backs 12-Week Limit for Abortions," *Times*, October 6, 2012.

76. Coates, Sylvester, and Thomson, "Jeremy," note 75.

77. BBC News, "Abortion Law: David Cameron Has 'No Plans' for New Rules," October 6, 2012.

78. Nick Collins, "Maria Miller: I Would Vote to Lower Abortion Limit from 24 to 20 Weeks," *Telegraph*, October 3, 2012.

79. *R. v. Sarah Louise Catt,* Sentencing Remarks, September 17, 2012 (Crown Court of England and Wales).

80. *Catt,* note 79, at paras. 4, 7, 11, and 17.

81. See, however, Barbara Hewson, "Sarah Catt Should Never Have Been Convicted," *Spiked,* September 25, 2012.

82. John Cooper, "Sarah Catt: An Anti-Abortion Judgment?" *Criminal Law and Justice Weekly,* September 22, 2012.

83. Lawyers' Christian Fellowship website, http://www.lawcf.org/index.asp?page=About+Us (accessed November 27, 2012).

84. *Catt,* note 79, at paras. 15 and 16.

85. Cooper, "Sarah Catt," note 82.

86. *R. v. Sarah Louise Catt* [2013] EWCA Crim. 1187.

87. Ingeborg Retzlaff, "Anti-Progestins—A Feminist Medical View," in *Medical Abortion Services: European Perspectives on Anti-Progestins,* ed. Ann Furedi (London: International Planned Parenthood Federation, 1993), 24.

Chapter 10. The Right to Conscience

This chapter reflects legal changes up to June 30, 2013.

1. John D. Swales, "The Leicester Anti-Vaccination Movement," *Lancet* 340 (1992): 1019–21.

2. Glanville Williams, *The Sanctity of Life and the Criminal Law* (London: Faber and Faber, 1958).

3. Sophia J. Kleegman and Sherwin A. Kaufman, *Infertility in Women* (Philadelphia: F. A. Davis, 1966), 178.

4. Abortion Act, 1967, *U.K. Statutes 1967,* Ch. 87.

5. Mark R. Wicclair, *Conscientious Objection in Health Care: An Ethical Analysis* (New York: Cambridge University Press, 2011).

6. Elizabeth Sepper, "Taking Conscience Seriously," *Virginia Law Review* 98 (2012):1501–75; Bernard M. Dickens and Rebecca J. Cook, "Conscientious Commitment to Women's Health," *International Journal of Gynecology and Obstetrics* 113 (2011): 163–66; Steph Sterling and Jessica L. Waters, "Beyond Religious Refusals: The Case for Protecting Health Care Workers' Provision of Abortion Care," *Harvard Journal of Law and Gender* 34 (2011): 463–502.

7. *R.R. v. Poland,* Application No. 27617/04, Eur. Ct. H.R. (2011), at para. 206.

8. Julieta Lemaitre, "Catholic Constitutionalism on Sex, Women, and the Beginning of Life," in this volume.

9. World Health Organization, Preamble to the Constitution of the World Health Organization as adopted by the International Health Conference, New York, June 19–22, 1946; signed on July 22, 1946, by the representatives of sixty-one states (Official Records of the World Health Organization, No. 2, p. 100) and entered into force on April 7, 1948, at para. 1.

10. Frans Viljoen, "International Human Rights Law: A Short History," *U.N. Chronicle Online* (2009), http://unchronicle.un.org/article/international-human-rights-law-short-history/.

11. *Church of Scientology v. Sweden*, Application No. 7805/77, 16 Eur. Comm'n. H.R. Dec. & Rep. 68 (1979), Decision on admissibility.

12. Corte Constitucional [Constitutional Court] 2008, Sentencia T-209/08, (Colom.) [hereinafter Sentencia T-209/08]; See Rebecca J. Cook, Monica Arango Olaya, and Bernard M. Dickens, "Healthcare Responsibilities and Conscientious Objection," *International Journal of Gynecology and Obstetrics* 104 (2009): 249–52.

13. Reva B. Siegel, "The New Politics of Abortion: An Equality Analysis of Women-Protective Abortion Restrictions," *University of Illinois Law Review* (2007): 991–1053.

14. David A. Grimes and Gretchen Stuart, "Abortion Jabberwocky: The Need for Better Terminology," *Contraception* 81 (2010): 93–96.

15. Paul F. A. Van Look, "Emergency Contraception: A Brighter Future?" in *New Insights in Gynecology and Obstetrics Research and Practice*, ed. B. Ottesen and A. Tabor (New York: Parthenon, 1998), 179.

16. FIGO Committee for the Study of Ethical Aspects of Human Reproduction and Women's Health, *Ethical Issues in Obstetrics and Gynecology* (London: FIGO, 2012), 90.

17. 42 Parl. Deb. U.K., H.C., (6th ser.) (May 10, 1983) 235–36 (Attorney General Sir Michael Havers, Written Answer).

18. M. Kemal Irmak, "Beginning of Individual Human Life at 13th Week of Development," *Journal of Experimental and Integrative Medicine* 1 (2011): 235–39.

19. The term "embryo" is used here to describe the pre-fetal product of conception or fertilization, without drawing biological distinctions between zygotes, blastocysts, conceptuses, or otherwise classified products of fertilization.

20. *Brownfield v. Daniel Freeman Marina Hospital*, 208 Cal. App. 3d 405; 256 Cal. Rptr. 240 (1989) (California Second District, Court of Appeal).

21. *Brownfield*, note 20, at 412; 245.

22. *R. (on the application of Smeaton) v. Secretary of State for Health*, [2002] E.W.H.C. 610 (Admin) (High Court of England and Wales), at para. 50.

23. Martin Hevia, "The Legal Status of Emergency Contraception in Latin America," *International Journal of Gynecology and Obstetrics* 116 (2012): 87–90.

24. Tribunal Constitucional [Constitutional Court] 2009, *ONG Acción de Lucha Anticorrupción Sin Componenda c. MINSA* (Peru).

25. Corte Suprema de Justicia de la Nación [Supreme Court] March 5, 2002, *Portal de Belén—Associación Civil sin Fines de Lucro c. Ministerio de Salud y Acción Social de La Nación s/* amparo, No. P.709.XXXVI (Argentina).

26. Corte Constitucional [Constitutional Court] June 14, 2006, *José Fernando Roser Rohde c. Instituto Nacional de Higiene y Medicina Tropical "Leopoldo Izquiéta Pérez y el Ministro de Salud S/ Acción de Amparo* (Ecuador).

27. Tribunal Constitucional [Constitutional Court] April 18, 2008, Sentencia Rol 740–07–CDS (Chile).

28. Tribunal Constitucional [Constitutional Court] October 16, 2009, Sentencia Exp. No. 02005–2009-PA/TC (Peru).

29. *Artavia Murillo et al. v. Costa Rica*, Inter-Am. Ct. H.R. (ser. C) No. 257 (November 28, 2012), at paras. 264, 315.

30. WHO, Preamble to the Constitution, note 9, at para. 1.

31. Rebecca J. Cook and Simone Cusack, *Gender Stereotyping: Transnational Legal Perspectives* (Philadelphia: University of Pennsylvania Press, 2010).

32. Paul Alvaro, "Controversial Conceptions: The Unborn and the American Convention on Human Rights," *Loyola University Chicago International Law Review* 9 (2012): 209–47.

33. *R. v. Morgentaler*, [1988] 1 S.C.R. 30, 44 D.L.R. (4th) 385 (Supreme Court of Canada), Chief Justice Dickson at 402.

34. *Morgentaler*, note 33, at 410–3.

35. Law 75–17 of January 17, 1975, reenacted in Law 79–1204 of December 31, 1979 (Fr.).

36. Mary Anne Case, "Perfectionism and Fundamentalism in the Application of the German Abortion Laws," in *Constituting Equality: Gender Equality and Comparative Constitutional Law,* ed. Susan H. Williams (Cambridge: Cambridge University Press, 2009), 93–106.

37. Texas, Health and Safety Code Ann. § 171.012(a)(4) (West 2012).

38. Susan Frelich Appleton, "Reproduction and Regret," *Yale Journal of Law and Feminism* 23 (2011): 255–333.

39. *L.M.R. v. Argentina*, Communication No. 1608/2007, U.N. Doc. CCPR/C/101/D/168/2007 (Human Rights Committee) (2011).

40. Salvatore Rino Fisichella, "On the Side of the Brazilian Girl," *L'Osservatore Romano*, March 15, 2009.

41. Dickens and Cook, "Conscientious," note 6.

42. *P. and S. v. Poland*, Application No. 57375/08, Eur. Ct. H.R., (2012).

43. *P. and S.*, note 42, at para. 20.

44. *P. and S.*, note 42, at para. 107.

45. Abortion Act, 1967, note 4, at s. 4(3).

46. Manfred Nowak, *U.N. Covenant on Civil and Political Rights: CCPR Commentary*, 2nd rev. ed. (Kehl, Strasbourg: N. P. Engel, 2005), 426.

47. U.K., Abortion Act, 1967, note 4, at s. 4(2).

48. Sentencia T-209, note 12.

49. Catholics for a Free Choice, *In Good Conscience: Respecting the Beliefs of Health-Care Providers and the Needs of Patients* (Washington, D.C.: Catholics for a Free Choice, 2007).

50. R. Alta Charo, "The Celestial Fire of Conscience—Refusing to Deliver Medical Care," *New England Journal of Medicine* 352 (2005): 2471–73.

51. California Health and Safety Code, § 123420(a) (West 2011).

52. *Roe v. Wade*, 410 U.S. 113 (1973) (U.S. Supreme Court).

53. Mississippi Code Ann., §§ 41–107–1 to 41–107–13 (2012) (Health Care Rights of Conscience).

54. Mississippi Code, note 53, § 41–107–3(a).

55. Mississippi Code, note 53, § 41–107–3(b).

56. Mississippi Code, note 53, § 41–107–3(c).

57. Mississippi Code, note 53, § 41–107–3(f).

58. Mississippi Code, note 53, § 41–107–3(h).

59. Mississippi Code, note 53, § 41–107–5(1)).

60. Mississippi Code, note 53, § 41–107–5(1).

61. Mississippi Code, note 53, § 41–107–5(3).

62. Mississippi Code, note 53, § 41–107–11(1).

63. National Health Law Program (NHeLP), *Health Care Refusals: Undermining Quality Care for Women* (Los Angeles: NHeLP, 2010).

64. National Health Law Program (NHeLP), note 63, at 47.

65. American College of Obstetricians and Gynecologists Committee on Ethics, "The Limits of Conscientious Refusal in Reproductive Medicine, ACOG Committee Opinion No. 385," *Obstetrics and Gynecology* 110 (2007): 1203–8.

66. See, e.g., United States Conference of Catholic Bishops, *Ethical and Religious Directives for Catholic Health Care Services* (Washington, D.C.: USCCB, 2001).

67. Mississippi Code, note 53, §§ 41–107–1 to 41–107–13.

68. *Barr v. Matthews*, (1999) 52 B.M.L.R. 217, at 227 (High Court of England and Wales, Queen's Bench Division).

69. *McInerney v. MacDonald*, [1992] 2 S.C.R. 138, 93 D.L.R. (4th) 415 (Supreme Court of Canada).

70. Health Practitioners Competence Assurance Act 2003, *New Zealand Statutes*, No. 48, s. 174(2).

71. Holly Fernandez Lynch, *Conflicts of Conscience in Health Care: An Institutional Compromise* (Boston: Massachusetts Institute of Technology Press, 2008).

72. Nowak, *U.N. Covenant*, note 46, at 406–36.

73. Jim Murdoch, *Protecting the Right to Freedom of Thought, Conscience and Religion under the European Convention on Human Rights* (Strasbourg Cedex: Council of Europe, 2012).

74. *Petition of Mary Teresa Doogan and Concepta Wood*, [2012] C.S.O.H. 32 (Outer House, Court of Session, Scotland), Lady Smith at para. 48, judgment reversed on other grounds, see *Petition of Mary Teresa Doogan and Concepta Wood*, [2013] C.S.I.H. 36, P876/11 (Extra Division, Inner House, Court of Session, Scotland).

75. Conseil Constitutionnel [Constitutional Court] June 27, 2001, Decision No. 2001–446 DC (Fr.).

76. *Pichon and Sajous v. France*, Case No. 49853/99, 381 Eur. Ct. H.R. 381 (2001).

77. Mark Campbell, "Conscientious Objection, Health Care and Article 9 of the European Convention on Human Rights," *Medical Law International* 11 (2011): 284–304.

78. Adriana Lamačková, "Conscientious Objection in Reproductive Health Care: Analysis of *Pichon and Sajous v. France*," *European Journal of Health Law* 15 (2008): 7–43.

79. *Ahmad v. United Kingdom* (1981), 4 Eur. H.R. Rep. 126, at para. 11.

80. *Petition of Mary Teresa*, note 74, Outer House.

81. *Petition of Mary Teresa*, Outer House, note 74, at para. 49.

82. *R. (S.B.) v. Governors of Denbigh High School*, [2006] U.K.H.L. 15, [2007] 1 A.C. 100 (House of Lords), Lord Hoffman, at para. 50.

83. *Petition of Mary Teresa*, note 74, Inner House, Lady Dorrian, at para. 38.

84. Carole Joffe, *Doctors of Conscience: The Struggle to Provide Abortion Before and After Roe v. Wade* (Boston: Beacon Press, 1995); Dickens and Cook, "Conscientious Commitment," note 6.

85. *Rodriguez v. City of Chicago*, 156 F. 3rd 771 (1998) (Seventh Circuit Court of Appeals).

86. Ian Vandewalker, "Abortion and Informed Consent: How Biased Counseling Laws Mandate Violations of Medical Ethics," *Michigan Journal of Gender and Law* 19 (2012): 1–70.

87. Center for Reproductive Rights, "CRR Files Lawsuit Challenging Texas Abortion

Sonogram Law," press release of June 13, 2011, http://reproductiverights.org/en/press-room/crr-files-lawsuit-challenging-texas-abortion-sonogram-law.

88. Texas Department of Health, *A Woman's Right to Know* (Austin: Department of Health, 2003), 17.

89. Rachel Benson Gold and Elizabeth Nash, "State Abortion Counseling Policies and the Fundamental Principles of Informed Consent," *Guttmacher Policy Review* 10, No. 4 (2007): 6–13, at 11.

90. Michigan, *Compiled Laws*, Ch. 333, 17015 (11) (b) (iii) (2013).

91. West Virginia Department of Health and Human Resources, *Information on Fetal Development, Abortion and Adoption*, [rev. 2010], http://www.wvdhhr.org/wrtk/wrtkbooklet.pdf, 15.

92. Robert Post, "Informed Consent and Abortion: A First Amendment Analysis of Compelled Physician Speech," *University of Illinois Law Review* (2007): 939–90.

93. Reva B. Siegel, "New Politics," note 13, at 1011 n. 92.

94. Brenda Major et al., "Abortion and Mental Health: Evaluating the Evidence," *American Psychologist* 64 (2009): 863–85.

95. Trine Munk-Olsen et al., "Induced First-Trimester Abortion and Risk of Mental Disorder," *New England Journal of Medicine* 364 (2011): 332–39.

96. Dieter Giesen, *International Medical Malpractice Law: A Comparative Law Study of Civil Liability Arising from Medical Care* (Tubingen: Mohr [Paul Siebeck] and Dordrecht: Martinus Nijhoff, 1988), 376–92.

97. Ian Vandewalker, "Abortion," note 86, at 28–31.

98. Elizabeth G. Raymond and David A. Grimes, "The Comparative Safety of Legal Induced Abortion and Childbirth in the United States," *Obstetrics and Gynecology* 119 (2012): 215–9 (Part 1).

99. Uriel Halbreich and Sandhya Karkun, "Cross-Cultural and Social Diversity of Prevalence of Postpartum Depression and Depressive Symptoms," *Journal of Affective Disorders* 91 (2006): 97–111.

100. U.K. Infanticide Act, 1938, 1&2 Geo. VI, Ch. 36, section 1(1), replacing the original Act of 1922.

101. Sterling and Waters, "Beyond Religious Refusals," note 6, at 465.

102. Reed Abelson, "Catholic Hospitals Expand, Religious Strings Attached," *New York Times*, February 21, 2012, A 1, B 5; Barbra Mann Wall, *American Catholic Hospitals: A Century of Changing Markets and Missions* (New Brunswick, N.J.: Rutgers University Press, 2011).

103. Abelson, "Catholic," note 102, A1.

104. Sepper, "Taking Conscience Seriously," note 6.

105. American College of Obstetricians and Gynecologists Committee on Ethics, "Limits," note 65.

106. Joseph M. Boyle, "Toward Understanding the Principle of Double Effect," *Ethics* 90 (1980): 527–38.

107. WHO, Preamble to the Constitution, note 9, at para. 1.

108. Pope John Paul II, "If You Want Peace, Respect the Conscience of Every Person," Message of His Holiness Pope John Paul II for the XXIV World Day of Peace, Vatican City, January 1, 1991, at para.11.

109. Pope John Paul II, "Respect the Conscience," note 108, at para. 24.

Chapter 11. Catholic Constitutionalism on Sex, Women, and the Beginning of Life

All translations are by the author.

1. Robert P. George, Sherif Girgis, and Ryan T. Anderson, "What Is Marriage?" *Harvard Journal of Law and Public Policy* 34 (2010): 245–87, at 247; For an analysis of this trend, see also Julieta Lemaitre, "By Reason Alone: Catholicism, Constitutions, and Sex in the Americas," *International Journal of Constitutional Law* 10, No. 2 (2012): 493–511.

2. See the Manhattan Declaration (2009) promoted by a variety of Christian leaders and drafted by Robert P. George, et al., http://www.manhattandeclaration.org/the-declaration/read .aspx (accessed August 29, 2012).

3. See Pope John XXII, *Pacem in Terris*, April 11, 1963, http://www.vatican.va/holy_father/ john_xxiii/encyclicals/documents/hf_j-xxiii_enc_11041963_pacem_en.html; see also encyclical of Pope Paul VI, *Dignitatis Humanae*, December 7, 1965, http://www.vatican.va/archive/hist _councils/ii_vatican_council/documents/vat-ii_decl_19651207_dignitatis-humanae_en.html.

4. Christopher McCrudden, "Catholicism, Human Rights and the Public Sphere," *International Journal of Public Theology* 5 (2011): 331–51; Christopher McCrudden "Legal and Roman Catholic Conceptions of Human Rights: Convergence, Divergence and Dialogue?" *Oxford Journal of Law and Religion* (2012): 1–17; John Finnis, *Natural Law and Natural Rights*, 2nd ed. (Oxford: Oxford University Press, 2011).

5. See Samuel Moyne, *The Last Utopia: Human Rights in History* (Cambridge, Mass.: Harvard University Press, 2010).

6. As developed in John Rawls, *Political Liberalism*, 2nd ed. (New York: Columbia University Press, 2005).

7. See Jurgen Habermas and Joseph Ratzinger, *The Dialectics of Secularization* (San Francisco: Ignatius Press, 2007).

8. For the United States, see: Nicholas Bamforth and David A. J. Richards, *Patriarchal Religion, Sexuality and Gender: A Critique of New Natural Law* (Cambridge: Cambridge University Press, 2007); for Catholic participation in the U.S. Christian right in the international arena, see Doris Buss and Didi Herman, *Globalizing Family Values: The Christian Right in International Politics* (Minneapolis: University of Minnesota Press, 2003); for its spread to Latin America, see Jaris Mujica, *Economía Política del Cuerpo: La Reestructuración de los Grupos Conservadores y el Biopoder* (Lima: Promsex, 2007); Roberto Blancarte, "El porqué de un estado laico," in *Fomentando el Conocimiento de las Libertades Laicas*, ed. George Lliendo, Violeta Barrientos, and Marco Huaco (Lima: Universidad de San Marcos; Mexico City: El Colegio Mexiquense, 2008); Juan Marco Vaggione, "Sexualidad, Religión y Política en América Latina," 2009, http://www.sxpolitics.org/pt/wpcontent/ uploads/2009/10/sexualidad-religion-y-politica-en-america-latina-juan-vaggione.pdf.

9. Rebecca Cook, "Modern Day Inquisitions," *Miami University Law Review* 65 (2011): 767–96, at 767.

10. Reva Siegel, "The Right's Reasons: Constitutional Conflict and the Spread of the Women-Protective Argument," *Duke Law Journal* 67 (2008): 1641–92.

11. Paul VI, *Humanae Vitae*, July 25, 1968, http://www.vatican.va/holy_father/paul_vi/encyclicals/documents/hf_p-vi_enc_25071968_humanae-vitae_en.html; Congregation for the Doctrine of the Faith, *Doctrinal Note on Some Considerations Regarding the Participation of Catholics in Public Life*, November 24, 2002, http://www.vatican.va/roman_curia/congregations/cfaith/documents/ rc_con_cfaith_doc_20021124_politica_en.html; *See also Congregation for the Doctrine of the Faith,*

Considerations Regarding Proposals to Give Legal Recognition to Unions Between Homosexual Persons, June 3, 2003, http://www.vatican.va/roman_curia/congregations/cfaith/documents/rc_con_cfaith_doc_20030731_homosexual-unions_en.html *(accessed August 29, 2012)*; Pope John Paul II, *Evangelium Vitae*, March 25, 1995, http://www.vatican.va/holy_father/john_paul_ii/encyclicals/documents/hf_jp-ii_enc_25031995_evangelium-vitae_en.html; Pope John Paul II, *Mulieris Dignitatem*, August 15, 1998, at http://www.vatican.va/holy_father/john_paul_ii/apost_letters/documents/hf_jp-ii_apl_15081988_mulieris-dignitatem_en.html; Pope Benedict XVI, *Deus Caritas Est*, December 25, 2005 at http://www.vatican.va/holy_father/benedict_xvi/encyclicals/documents/hf_ben-xvi_enc_20051225_deus-caritas-est_en.html; Congregation for the Doctrine of the Faith, *On the Collaboration Between Men and Women in the Church and in the World*, July 31, 2004, http://www.vatican.va/roman_curia/congregations/cfaith/documents/rc_con_cfaith_doc_20040731_collaboration_en.html; Pontifical Council for the Family, *The Family and Human Rights*, November 21, 2000, http://www.vatican.va/roman_curia/pontifical_councils/family/documents/rc_pc_family_doc_20001115_family-human-rights_en.html; Congregation for the Doctrine of the Faith, *Letter on the Pastoral Care of Homosexual Persons*, October 1, 1986, http://www.vatican.va/roman_curia/congregations/cfaith/documents/rc_con_cfaith_doc_19861001_homosexual-persons_en.html.

12. Corte Constitucional [Constitutional Court] May 10, 2006, Sentencia 355/06, (Colom.), at 83–84.

13. Proyecto Legislativo PL 489 of 2007 (Braz.).

14. Pope John Paul II, *Mulieris Dignitatem*, note 11, 4; See also Pope Benedict XVI, *Deus Caritas Est*, note 11.

15. Congregation for the Doctrine of the Faith, *Collaboration*, note 11.

16. In the same line, although less developed, see John Paul II's "Apostolic Letter to Women prior to the 1995 Beijing Women's Conference," June 29, 1995, http://www.vatican.va/holy_father/john_paul_ii/letters/documents/hf_jp-ii_let_29061995_women_en.html.

17. Tina Beattie, *New Catholic Feminism* (London: Routledge, 2006).

18. Mary Ann Glendon, "The Pope's New Feminism," *Crisis* 15, No. 3 (March 1997): 28–31, reproduced in: http://www.catholiceducation.org/articles/feminism/fe0004.html.

19. Pope John Paul II, *Evangelium Vitae*, note 11.

20. Reva Siegel, "*Dignity and the Politics of Protection: Abortion Restrictions Under Casey/Carhart,*" *Yale Law Journal* 117 (2008): 1694–800; Siegel, "Right's Reasons," note 10; Reva Siegel and Robert Post, "Roe Rage: Democratic Constitutionalism and Backlash," *Harvard Civil Rights–Civil Liberties Law Review* 42 (2007).

21. Robert George, *Making Men Moral: Civic Liberties and Public Morality* (London: Oxford University Press, 1995).

22. Javier Hervada, *Escritos de Derecho Natural* (Pamplona: Universidad de Navarra, 1993), 648.

23. Center for Reproductive Rights, "Center for Reproductive Rights Files Case Revealing the Horrifying Reality of El Salvador's Ban on Abortion," press release, March 21, 2012, http://reproductiverights.org/en/press-room/center-for-reproductive-rights-files-case-revealing-the-horrifying-reality-of-el-salvador.

24. Siegel, "Right's Reasons," note 10.

25. El Espejo de la Argentina, "Abogados y médicos denuncian ante la CIDH a la Corte Suprema por su fallo sobre el aborto," http://elespejodelaargentina.com/2012/abogados-y-medicos

-denuncian-ante-la-cidh-a-la-corte-suprema-por-su-fallo-sobre-el-aborto/ (accessed August 29, 2012).

26. For the Vatican's repeal of Liberation Theology, see Congregation for the Doctrine of the Faith, *Instruction on Christian Freedom and Liberation*, March 22, 1986, http://www.vatican.va/roman_curia/congregations/cfaith/documents/rc_con_cfaith_doc_19860322_freedom-liberation_en.html.

27. See e.g., "Theologian in Brazil Says He Is Silenced by Order of Vatican," *New York Times*, May 9, 1985, http://www.nytimes.com; Marlise Simons, "Vatican Reported to Have Sought Rebukes for 2 Other Latin Clerics," *New York Times*, September 11, 1984, http://www.nytimes.com; *For the Vatican's rejection of the class struggle as a source of liberation see Congregation for the Doctrine of the Faith, Instruction on Certain Aspects of the "Theology of Liberation," August 6, 1984, http://www.vatican.va/roman_curia/congregations/cfaith/documents/rc_con_cfaith_doc_19840806_theology-liberation_en.html.*

28. Pope John Paul II, *Evangelium Vitae*, note 11, at 15.

29. Pope John Paul II, *Evangelium Vitae*, note 11, at 67.

30. See Suprema Corte de Justicia de la Nación [Supreme Court] 2008, Acción De Inconstitucionalidad 146/2007 y su acumulada 147/2007. Promoventes: Comisión Nacional de los Derechos Humanos y Procuraduría General De La República. Ponente: Ministro Sergio Salvador Aguirre Anguiano. Encargado Del Engrose: Ministro José Ramón Cossío Díaz, México, Distrito Federal. On file with author. I thank Alejandro Madrazo Lajous for providing me with copies of the aforementioned actions and the cumulative document (*engrose*).

31. For examples of law textbooks that develop these definitions, see Hervada, *Escritos*, note 22, 723, and Ilva Miriam Hoyos, *La persona y sus derechos* (Bogotá: Editorial Temis, 2000).

32. *Artavia Murillo et al. v. Costa Rica*, Inter-Am. Ct. H.R. (ser. C) No. 257 (November 28, 2012),

33. The Briefs of the Association Crece Familia (CreceFam) of Peru, the Bioethics Defense Fund, the Bioethics Institute of the Sacred Heart Catholic University, Human Life International, and Italian Movement for Life; for these arguments see also Ligia de Jesús, "Revisiting *Baby Boy v. United States*," *Florida Journal of International Law* 23 (2011): 222–74 and Alvaro Paúl "Controversial Conceptions: The Unborn and the American Convention on Human Rights," *Loyola University Chicago International Law Review* 9, No. 2 (2012): 209–47.

34. *Artavia Murillo*, note 32.

35. Supremo Tribunal Federal [Supreme Court], Audiência Pública [Public Hearing], August 26, 2008, Arguicao de descumprimento de preceito fundamental 54–8, http://www.stf.jus.br/portal/cms/verTexto.asp?servico=processoAudienciaPublicaAdpf54 [hereinafter ADPF 54, Public Hearing]; See for a discussion of this case Luís Roberto Barroso, "Bringing Abortion into the Brazilian Public Debate: Legal Strategies for Anencephalic Pregnancy" in this volume.

36. ADPF 54, Public Hearing, note 35, at 10.

37. ADPF 54, Public Hearing, note 35, at 6.

38. Martin Hevia, "The Legal Status of Emergency Contraception in Latin America," *International Journal of Gynecology and Obstetrics* 116 (2012): 87–90.

39. John T. Noonan, ed., *The Morality of Abortion: Legal and Historical Perspectives* (Cambridge, Mass.: Harvard University Press, 1970); Joseph F. Donceel, S.J., "Immediate Animation and

Delayed Hominization," *Theological Studies*, vols. 1 and 2 (New York: Columbia University Press, 1970), 86–88.

40. Pope Pius XI, *Casti conubii: On Christian Marriage*, 1930, at http://www.vatican.va/holy _father/pius_xi/encyclicals/documents/hf_p-xi_enc_31121930_casti-connubii_en.html; See also Pope Paul VI, *Gaudium et Spes: Pastoral Constitution on the Church in the Modern World*, 1965, http://www.vatican.va/archive/hist_councils/ii_vatican_council/documents/vat-ii_cons_19651207 _gaudium-et-spes_en.html.

41. Pope Paul VI, *Humanae Vitae*, note 11, at 11.

42. Congregation for the Doctrine of the Faith, "Declaration on Procured Abortion" (1974), http://www.vatican.va/roman_curia/congregations/cfaith/documents/rc_con_cfaith _doc_19741118_declaration-abortion_en.html, para. 13 (accessed August 29, 2012); See also Pope John Paul II, *Evangelium Vitae*, note 11.

43. For his biography see Clara Lejeune, *Life Is a Blessing: The Biography of Jerome Lejeune Geneticist, Doctor, Father* (Philadelphia: National Catholic Bioethics Center, 2011).

44. Corte Suprema de Justicia [Supreme Court] August 30, 2001, Sentencia Rol 2.186–2001 (Chile), in "Anticoncepción de Emergencia: Antecedentes del Debate" *Estudios Públicos*, 95 (2004): 402–8, at 405, http://www.cepchile.cl/1_3400/doc/anticoncepcion_de_emergencia_antecedentes _del_debate.html#.UegQLo3wrT4; In the same direction see Tribunal Constitucional [Constitutional Court], November 13, 2006, Sentencia Exp. No. 7435–2006–PC/TC (Peru), as well as Corte Suprema Justicia de la Nación [Supreme Court] March 5, 2002, en Portal de Belén contra Ministerio de Salud y Acción Social de la Nación s/amparo en anticoncepción de emergencia, No. P.709.XXXVI (Arg.).

45. Procuraduría General de la Nación [Attorney General's Office], Informe de Seguimiento Sentencia C-355 de 2006 [Report on Judgment C-355 of 2006], August 15, 2010, http://www.procuraduria .gov.co/portal/media/file/INFORME%20A%20LA%20SENTENCIA%20C-355%20%28ebook%29 .pdf; see also, Corte Constitucional [Constitutional Court] August 10, 2012, Sentencia T-627, (Colom.), where the Court orders the Procuraduría to recant publicly on this and other issues.

46. House of Representatives (Colombia), Proyecto de Ley Estatutaria 022, 2011 [Statutory Bill N. 022, 2011], "Por medio de la cual se reglamenta el artículo 18 de la Constitución Política" [Regulating article 18 of the Political Constitution] (Statutory Bill filed by the Office of the Attorney General of Colombia to regulate conscientious objection) at http://www.procuraduria.gov.co/portal /media/file/Proyecto%20Ley%20Objecion%20de%20Conciencia%20con%20 Exposici%C3%B3n%20de%20Motivos.pdf, [hereinafter Bill Regulating art. 18].

47. Bill Regulating art. 18, note 46, at 7.

48. Alfonso Llano, *Objeción de Conciencia Institucional* (Bogotá: Pontificia Universidad Javeriana, 2010).

49. E.g., from Popes Gregory XVI and Pius IX, the letters *Mirari Vos* (1832) and *Singulari Nos* (1834); and *Quanta Cura* and *Syllabus* (1864).

50. For the church's perspective on this issue, see Vicente Prieto, *Relaciones Iglesia-Estado: La perspectiva del Derecho Canónico* (Salamanca: Pontificia Universidad de Salamanca, 2005).

51. Moyne, *Last Utopia*, note 5.

52. John XXII, *Pacem in Terris*, note 3; see also Pope Paul VI, *Dignitatis Humanae*, note 3.

53. Encyclical of Pope Paul VI, *Apostolicam Actuositatem*, November 18, 1965, http://www .vatican.va/archive/hist_councils/ii_vatican_council/documents/vat-ii_decree_19651118 _apostolicam actuositatem_en.html.

54. Congregation for the Doctrine of the Faith, *Catholics in Public Life*, note 11, and *Congregation for the Doctrine of the Faith, Unions Between Homosexual Persons*, note 11.

55. Edmund Burke, *Reflections on the Revolution in France* (1790).

56. Jeremy Bentham, *Anarchical Fallacies* (1843).

57. On this point, see Rebecca Cook, "Stigmatized Meanings of Criminal Abortion Law" in this volume.

58. See, for example, Congregation for the Doctrine of the Faith, *Procured Abortion*, note 42, at paras. 20–21.

Chapter 12. Bringing Abortion into the Brazilian Public Debate

I wrote this chapter while I was a professor at the School of Law, State University of Rio de Janeiro. I am greatly indebted to the superb assistance provided by Renata Campante for the elaboration of this article. All translations are by the author. This chapter reflects legal changes up to June 30, 2013.

1. Debora Diniz and Eliane Brum, *Severina's Story*, film, 23 min., 2005, http://hub.witness .org/en/node/8605 (accessed December 5, 2012).

2. Decreto No. 2.848, December 7, 1940, Código Penal [Penal Code], arts. 124–27 (Braz.) (hereinafter Penal Code).

3. Penal Code, note 2, art. 128.

4. Andrzej Kulczycki, "Abortion in Latin America: Changes in Practice, Growing Conflict, and Recent Policy Developments," *Studies in Family Planning* 42, No. 3 (2011): 199–220, at 204–5.

5. Beatriz Galli, "Negative Impacts of Abortion Criminalization in Brazil: Systematic Denial of Women's Reproductive Autonomy and Human Rights," *University of Miami Law Review* 65 (2011): 969–80, at 970–71; Ministério da Saúde, Secretaria de Ciência, Tecnologia e Insumos Estratégicos. Departamento de Ciência e Tecnologia, *Aborto e Saúde Pública no Brasil: 20 Anos* (Brasília: Ministério da Saúde, 2009), http://bvsms.saude.gov.br/bvs/publicacoes/livro_aborto.pdf, 17.

6. Debora Diniz, "Selective Abortion in Brazil," *Developing World Bioethics* 7, No. 2 (2007): 64–67, at 66.

7. Rebecca J. Cook, Joanna N. Erdman, Martin Hevia, and Bernard M. Dickens, "Prenatal Management of Anencephaly," *International Journal of Gynecology and Obstetrics* 102 (2008): 304–8, at 304.

8. Galli, "Negative," note 5, at 973.

9. International Centre for Birth Defects of the International Clearinghouse for Birth Defects Monitoring Systems, *World Atlas for Birth Defects* (Geneva: World Health Organization, 2003).

10. Audiência Pública [Public Hearing], ADPF 54, August 26–September 19, 2008, http:// www.stf.jus.br/portal/cms/verTexto.asp?servico=processoAudienciaPublicaAdpf54.

11. Supremo Tribunal Federal [Supreme Court] April 12, 2012, ADPF 54/DF, (Braz.), http:// redir.stf.jus.br/paginadorpub/paginador.jsp?docTP=TP&docID=3707334 [hereinafter ADPF 54].

12. ADPF 54, note 11, at 33.

13. ADPF 54, note 11, at 45–46.

14. ADPF 54, note 11, at 17.

15. Penal Code, note 2, at art. 124,

16. Damásio E. de Jesus, *Código Penal Anotado* (São Paulo: Saraiva, 2002), 424.

17. Brazilian Law No. 9.347/1997, art. 3.

18. Cook et al., "Prenatal," note 7, at 306.

19. ADPF 54, note 11, at 147.

20. ADPF 54, note 11, at 56.

21. Corte Suprema de Justicia de la Nación [Supreme Court] 2001, *T., S. c. Gobierno de La Ciudad de Buenos Aires*, No. T.421.XXXVI, (Arg.).

22. Código Penal [Penal Code], arts. 85–86 (Arg.).

23. Corte Suprema de Justicia de la Nación [Supreme Court] 2012, *A.F. s/medida autosatisfactiva*, No. F. 259. XLVI, (Arg.).

24. David A. Strauss, "Common Law Constitutional Interpretation," *University of Chicago Law Review* 63 (1996): 877–935, at 877, 879; Cass Sunstein, *One Case at a Time: Judicial Minimalism on the Supreme Court* (Cambridge, Mass.: Harvard University Press, 1999), 70; Luís Roberto Barroso, *Interpretação e Aplicação da Constituição* [*Interpretation and Application of the Constitution*] (São Paulo, Brazil: Editora Saraiva, 2009), 151–54.

25. ADPF 54, note 11, at 166.

26. ADPF 54, note 11, at 216.

27. Constitution of the Federative Republic of Brazil, October 5, 1988, Article 1, III.

28. Luís Roberto Barroso, Closing Arguments, April 11, 2012, in *National Confederation of Health Workers (CNTS) v. Courts of Justice of the States, ADPF 54* (before the Supreme Court of Brazil), http://www.youtube.com/watch?v=1sx34zhzw7g.

29. Luís Roberto Barroso, "'Here, There and Everywhere': Human Dignity in Contemporary Law and in the Transnational Discourse," *Boston College International and Comparative Law Review* 35, No. 2 (2012): 331–93.

30. ADPF 54, note 11, at 235.

31. ADPF 54, note 11, at 264.

32. Suprema Corte de Justica [Supreme Court of the Province of Buenos Aires] 2002, *C.R.O v. Province of Buenos Aires*, Case C 85566 (Arg.).

33. *K.L. v. Peru*, Communication No. 1153/2003, U.N. Doc. CCPR/C/85/D/1153/2003 (2005) (Human Rights Committee).

34. Peruvian Penal Code, art. 120.

35. Corte Constitucional [Constitutional Court] 1997, Sentencia C-013/97 (Colom.).

36. Corte Constitucional [Constitutional Court] May 10, 2006, Sentencia C-355/06 (Colom.).

Chapter 13. Toward Transformative Equality in Nepal

All translations are by the author unless otherwise noted. This chapter reflects legal changes up to June 30, 2013.

1. *Lakshmi Dhikta v. Government of Nepal*, Writ No. 0757, 2067, Nepal Kanoon Patrika, para. 25 (2009) (Supreme Court of Nepal).

2. World Bank, Nepal Overview, http://www.worldbank.org/en/country/nepal/overview (accessed February 11, 2013).

3. Government of Nepal, National Planning Commission and United Nations Country Team Nepal, *Nepal Millennium Development Goals Progress Report 2010* (2010), 13, http://www.undp.org.np/pdf/MDG-Layout-Final.pdf, [hereinafter Nepal MDG Report 2010].

4. Nepal MDG Report 2010, note 3, at 13.

5. Ministry of Health (Nepal), *Nepal Maternal Mortality and Morbidity Study 2008/2009*, (Kathmandu: Ministry of Health, 2010), 9 [hereinafter Nepal MMMS].

6. Muluki Ain 2020 [Country Code 1963], Eleventh Amendment, Chapter on Homicide, art. 28 (2002).

7. Center for Research on Environment, Health and Population Activities, *Policy Brief Number 16* (CREHPA, 2000), http://www.crehpa.org.np/download/policy_brief_16.pdf.

8. United Nations, Convention on the Elimination of All Forms of Discrimination against Women (CEDAW), adopted December 18, 1979, G.A. Res. 34/180, U.N. GAOR, 34th Sess., Supp. No. 46, at 193, U.N. Doc. A/34/46 (1979) (entered into force September 3, 1981).

9. United Nations, Committee on the Elimination of Discrimination against Women, General Recommendation No. 28 on the core obligations of States Parties under article 2 of the Convention on the Elimination of All Forms of Discrimination against Women, 47th sess., December 16, 2010, CEDAW/C/GC/28, at para. 5.

10. CEDAW General Recommendation No. 25, on article 4, para. 1, of the Convention on the Elimination of All Forms of Discrimination against Women, on temporary special measures, 30th sess., 2004, at para. 14.

11. CEDAW General Recommendation 28, note 9, at para. 16 .

12. CEDAW General Recommendation 25, note 10, at para. 16.

13. CEDAW General Recommendation 28, note 9, at para. 18.

14. R. J. Cook and S. Howard, "Accommodating Women's Differences Under the Women's Anti-Discrimination Convention," *Emory Law Journal* 56 (2007): 1045.

15. Cook and Howard, "Accommodating," note 14, at 1054.

16. Cook and Howard, "Accommodating," note 14, at 1045.

17. Cook and Howard, "Accommodating," note 14, at 1047.

18. CEDAW General Recommendation No. 28, note 9, at paras. 8, 18, 19, 22; Andrew Byrnes, "Article 1," *The U.N. Convention on the Elimination of All Forms of Discrimination against Women: A Commentary*, ed. Marsha A. Freeman, Christine Chinkin, and Beate Rudolf (Oxford: Oxford University Press, 2012), 51–70; CEDAW General Recommendation No. 24: Women and Health, 55th sess., 1999, contained in U.N. Doc. A/54/38 Rev. 1 (1999); Rebecca J. Cook and Verónica Undurraga, "Article 12," *The U.N. Convention on the Elimination of All Forms of Discrimination against Women: A Commentary*, ed. Marsha A. Freeman, Christine Chinkin, and Beate Rudolf (Oxford: Oxford University Press, 2012), 311–33.

19. Byrnes, "Article 1," note 18, at 55.

20. CEDAW General Recommendation No. 24, note 18, at paras. 2, 7, and 14.

21. Geeta Sangroula, "Law and Existing Problem of Nepalese Women," in *Gender and Democracy in Nepal*, ed. Laxmi Keshari Manandhar and Krishna B. Bhattachan (Tribhuvan University, Nepal: Central Department of Home Science–Women's Studies Program and Friedrich-Ebert-Stiftung, 2001), 59–61.

22. Krishna B. Bhattachan, "Sociological Perspectives on Gender Issues in Changing Nepalese Society," in *Gender and Democracy in Nepal*, note 21, at 82.

23. Bhattachan, "Sociological," note 22, at 83.

24. Yubaraj Sangroula, "Women's Personality: Defined in Terms of Their Sex and Marital Status," in *Gender and Democracy in Nepal*, note 21, at 106

25. Forum for Women, Law and Development and Planned Parenthood Partners, *Struggles to Legalize Abortion in Nepal and Challenges Ahead* (Forum for Women, Law and Development, 2003), 2.

26. Forum for Women, *Struggles*, note 25, at 2.

27. Forum for Women, *Struggles*, note 25, at 2.

28. Forum for Women, *Struggles*, note 25, at 2.

29. Forum for Women, *Struggles*, note 25, at 2.

30. Country Code 1963, note 6, Chapter on Partition, section number 28.

31. Center for Reproductive Law and Policy and Forum for Women Law and Development, *Abortion in Nepal: Women Imprisoned* (Center for Reproductive Law and Policy, 2002), 11 [hereinafter *Abortion in Nepal*].

32. *Abortion in Nepal*, note 31, at 13.

33. Nepal MMMS, note 5, at 22.

34. Sue Lloyd Roberts, "South Asia's Abortion Scandal," BBC News, November 8, 1999, http://news.bbc.co.uk/2/hi/south_asia/501929.stm.

35. See Center for Research on Environment, Health and Population Activities, *Women in Prison in Nepal for Abortion: A Study on Implications of Restrictive Abortion Law on Women's Social Status and Health*, (CREHPA, 2000), preface.

36. *Abortion in Nepal*, note 31, at 74.

37. Forum for Women, *Struggles*, note 25, at 16.

38. Forum for Women, *Struggles*, note 25, at 16.

39. *Abortion in Nepal*, note 31, at 63.

40. Nepal MMMS, note 5, at 22.

41. World Health Organization (WHO), *Trends in Maternal Mortality: 1990 to 2008: Estimates Developed by WHO, UNICEF, UNFPA, & the World Bank* (Geneva: WHO, 2010), 30, http://whqlibdoc.who.int/publications/2010/9789241500265_eng.pdf.

42. Government of Nepal, Ministry of Health and Population et al., *Unsafe Abortion: Nepal Country Profile* (Teku, New Delhi: Government of Nepal, WHO, CREHPA, July 2006), vi, http://www.crehpa.org.np/download/unsafe_abortion_nepal_country_profile_2006.pdf.

43. Nepal MMMS, note 5, at 22.

44. Asian Development Bank (ADB), *Overview of Gender Equality and Social Inclusion in Nepal* (Manilla: Asian Development Bank, 2010), at 19.

45. Nepal MMMS, note 5, at 104.

46. Asian Development Bank (ADB), *Overview*, note 44, at 21.

47. Nepal MMMS, note 5, at 149.

48. Government of Nepal, *Unsafe Abortion*, note 42, at 39–40.

49. Government of Nepal, *Unsafe Abortion*, note 42, at 39.

50. Government of Nepal, *Unsafe Abortion*, note 42, at 36–39.

51. Government of Nepal, *Unsafe Abortion*, note 42, at 40.

52. Constitution of the Kingdom of Nepal 1990, art. 4(1) Part 1, http://www.nepaldemocracy.org/documents/national_laws/constitution1990.htm.

53. Constitution, note 52, art. 11 (1) (2) and (3) Part 3.

54. Constitution, note 52, article 11 (3).

55. Nepal Treaty Act, 2047 (1990), section 9. (2047 denotes the Nepalese calendar year.)

56. Interim Constitution of Nepal, 2063 (2007) art. 20(2) Part 3 Fundamental Rights [hereinafter Interim Constitution].

57. Interim Constitution, note 56, art. 20(2) Part 3 Fundamental Rights.

58. Amending Some Nepal Acts to Maintain Gender Equality Act 2063 (2006), http://www

.lawcommission.gov.np/en/activities/func-startdown/459/%20%20–%20gender%20equality%20
law (accessed February 11, 2013).

59. *Dhikta*, note 1, at para. 25.

60. *Dhikta*, note 1, at para. 25.

61. *Annapurna Rana v. Kathmandu District Court*, Writ No. 2187, 2053 (1998) (Supreme Court of Nepal).

62. *Meera Dhungana v. Government of Nepal*, Writ No. 55, 2058 (2002) (Supreme Court of Nepal).

63. *Achyut Kharel v. Government of Nepal*, Writ No. 3352, 2061 (2008) (Supreme Court of Nepal) [hereinafter *Kharel*].

64. *Kharel*, note 63.

65. CEDAW, note 8, Article 16(1) (e).

66. *Kharel*, note 63, at 8.

67. *Kharel*, note 63, at 11.

68. *Kharel*, note 63, at 10.

69. *Kharel*, note 63, at 11.

70. *Dhikta*, note 1, at para. 32.

71. *Dhikta*, note 1, at para. 32.

72. *Dhikta*, note 1, at para. 24.

73. *Dhikta*, note 1, at para. 33.

74. *Dhikta*, note 1, at para. 33.

75. *Dhikta*, note 1, at para. 34.

76. *Dhikta*, note 1, at para. 34.

77. Sangroula, "Women's Personality," note 21, at 116.

78. Sangroula, "Women's Personality," note 21, at 116.

79. *Dhikta*, note 1, at para. 38.

80. *Dhikta*, note 1, at para. 25.

81. *Dhikta*, note 1, at para. 26.

82. *Dhikta*, note 1, at para. 27.

83. *Dhikta*, note 1, at para. 27.

84. *Dhikta*, note 1, at para. 28.

85. *Dhikta*, note 1, at para. 36.

86. *Dhikta*, note 1, at para. 36.

87. *Dhikta*, note 1, at para. 92.

88. *Dhikta*, note 1, at para. 92.

89. *Dhikta*, note 1, at para. 32.

90. *Dhikta*, note 1, at para. 32.

91. *Dhikta*, note 1, at para. 23.

92. *Dhikta*, note 1, at para. 25.

93. *Dhikta*, note 1, at para. 40.

94. *Dhikta*, note 1, at para. 41.

95. *Dhikta*, note 1, at para. 17.

96. *Dhikta*, note 1, at para. 42.

97. *Dhikta*, note 1, at para. 42.

98. *Dhikta*, note 1, at para. 42.

99. *Dhikta*, note 1, at para. 42.

100. *Dhikta*, note 1, at para. 42.

101. *Dhikta*, note 1, at para. 9.

102. *Dhikta*, note 1, at para. 9.

103. *Dhikta*, note 1, at para. 87.

104. *Dhikta*, note 1, at paras. 87–88.

105. *Dhikta*, note 1, at para. 12.

106. *Dhikta*, note 1, at para. 14.

107. *Dhikta*, note 1, at para. 13.

108. *Dhikta*, note 1, at para. 15.

109. *Dhikta*, note 1, at para. 15.

110. *Dhikta*, note 1, at para. 17.

111. *Dhikta*, note 1, at para. 17.

112. *Dhikta*, note 1, at para. 19.

113. *Dhikta*, note 1, at para. 86.

114. *Dhikta*, note 1, at para. 18.

115. *Dhikta*, note 1, at para. 18.

116. *Dhikta*, note 1, at para. 18.

117. *Dhikta*, note 1, at para. 89.

118. *Dhikta*, note 1, at para. 19.

119. *Dhikta*, note 1, at para. 19.

120. *Dhikta*, note 1, at para. 19.

121. *Dhikta*, note 1, at para. 36.

122. *Dhikta*, note 1, at para. 36.

123. *Dhikta*, note 1, at para. 36.

124. *Dhikta*, note 1, at para. 20.

125. *Dhikta*, note 1, at para. 90.

126. *Dhikta*, note 1, at para. 88.

127. *Dhikta*, note 1, at para. 39.

128. *Dhikta*, note 1, at para. 90.

129. *Dhikta*, note 1, at para. 55.

130. *Dhikta*, note 1, at para. 55.

131. *Prakash Mani Sharma v. Government of Nepal*, Writ No. 064 (2008) (Supreme Court of Nepal), unofficial English translation in National Judicial Academy, *The Landmark Decisions of the Supreme Court, Nepal on Gender Justice,* ed. Dr. Ananda Mohan Bhattarai (Lalitpur: National Judiciary Acaemy, 2010).

132. *Sharma*, note 131, at para. 148.

133. *Sharma*, note 131, at para. 148.

134. *Sharma*, note 131, at para. 48.

135. *Sharma*, note 131.

136. *Dhikta*, note 1, at para. 69.

137. *Dhikta*, note 1, at para. 55.

138. *Dhikta*, note 1, at para. 55.

139. *Dhikta*, note 1, at para. 55.

140. *Dhikta*, note 1, at para. 54.

141. *Dhikta*, note 1, at para. 60.
142. *Dhikta*, note 1, at para. 60.
143. *Dhikta*, note 1, at para. 68.
144. *Dhikta*, note 1, at para. 68.
145. *Dhikta*, note 1, at para. 72.
146. *Dhikta*, note 1, at para. 65.
147. *Dhikta*, note 1, at para. 75.
148. *Dhikta*, note 1, at para. 75.
149. *Dhikta*, note 1, at para. 67.
150. *Dhikta*, note 1, at para. 101.
151. *Sharma,* note 131.
152. *Dhikta*, note 1, at para. 90.
153. *Dhikta*, note 1, at para. 90.
154. *Dhikta*, note 1, at para. 90.
155. *Dhikta*, note 1, at para. 90.
156. *Dhikta*, note 1, at para. 90.
157. *Dhikta*, note 1, at para. 90.
158. *Dhikta*, note 1, at para. 90.
159. *Dhikta*, note 1, at para. 90.
160. *Dhikta*, note 1, at para. 90.
161. *Dhikta*, note 1, at para. 90.
162. *Dhikta*, note 1, at para. 90.
163. *Dhikta*, note 1, at para. 99.
164. *Dhikta*, note 1, at para. 90.
165. *Dhikta*, note 1, at para. 98.
166. *Dhikta*, note 1, at para. 99.
167. *Dhikta*, note 1, at para. 99.
168. *Dhikta*, note 1, at para. 99.
169. *Dhikta*, note 1, at para. 100.
170. *Dhikta*, note 1, at para. 99.
171. *Dhikta*, note 1, at para. 100.
172. *Dhikta*, note 1, at para. 101.
173. *Dhikta*, note 1, at para. 90.

Chapter 14. Narrating Innocent Suffering in Abortion Law

I thank the editors of this collection, as well as Aziza Ahmed, Deval Desai, Karen Engle, Janet Halley, Nkatha Kabira, Julieta Lemaitre, Heidi Matthews, Zinaida Miller and Anna Su for comments on earlier drafts. I am especially grateful to the lawyers and advocates who spoke with me about their work. All errors remain my own. This chapter reflects legal changes up to June 30, 2013.

1. *K.L. v. Peru,* Communication No. 1153/2003, U.N. Doc. CCPR/C/85/D/1153/2003 (Human Rights Committee) (2005); *L.C. v. Peru,* Communication No. 22/2009, U.N. Doc. CEDAW/C/50 /D/22/2009 (Committee on the Elimination of Discrimination Against Women) (2011); *L.M.R. v. Argentina,* Communication No. 1608/2007, U.N. Doc. CCPR/C/101/D/1608/2007 (Human Rights

Committee) (2011); *X and XX v. Colombia*, MC-270/09, Inter-Am. C.H.R. (2011); *Paulina Ramirez v. Mexico*, Case 161–02, Report No. 21/07, Inter-Am. C.H.R., Friendly Settlement (2007).

2. Personal interview, lawyer, Center for Reproductive Rights, New York (October 25, 2012).

3. *Paulina Ramirez*, note 1.

4. *X and XX v. Colombia*, note 1, at para. 17.

5. See, e.g., Eszter Kismödi et al., "Human Rights Accountability for Maternal Death and Failure to Provide Safe, Legal Abortion: The Significance of Two Ground-Breaking CEDAW Decisions," *Reproductive Health Matters* 20 (2012): 31–39.

6. Luisa Cabal, "UN Human Rights Committee Makes Landmark Decision Establishing Women's Right to Access to Legal Abortion," November 17, 2005, http://reproductiverights.org/en/press-room/un-human-rights-committee-makes-landmark-decision-establishing-womens-right-to-access-to.

7. *R. v. Bourne* [1938] 3 All E.R. 615 (Crown Court of England and Wales).

8. *Attorney General v. X*, [1992] I.E.S.C. 1 (Supreme Court of Ireland).

9. Corte Suprema de Justicia de la Nación [Supreme Court] 2012, *F., A.L.*, Expediente Letra "F," No. 259, Libro XLVI, (Arg.).

10. Corte Constitucional [Constitutional Court] 2008, Sentencia T-209/08 (Colom.).

11. Heather Luz McNaughton Reyes, Charlotte E. Hord, Ellen M. H. Mitchell, and Marta Maria Blandon, "Invoking Health and Human Rights to Ensure Access to Legal Abortion: The Case of a Nine-Year-Old Girl from Nicaragua," *Health and Human Rights* 9 (2006): 63–86.

12. *P. and S. v. Poland*, Application No. 57375/08, Eur. Ct. H.R., (2012).

13. See Andrew Downie, "Nine-Year-Old's Abortion Outrages Brazil's Catholic Church," *Time Magazine*, March 6, 2005; International Planned Parenthood Federation, "México: El embarazo de una niña de 10 anos encien del debate mexicano sobre el aborto" (April 20, 2010), http://www.ippfwhr.org/es/noticias/m%C3%A9xico-el-embarazo-de-una-ni%C3%B1-de-10-a%C3%B1os-enciende-el-debate-mexicano-sobre-el-aborto; CNN World, "10-Year-Old's Pregnancy Fuels Mexican Abortion Debate" (April 19, 2010), http://www.cnn.com/2010/WORLD/americas/04/19/mexico.abortion/index.html; Elwyn Lopez, "Raped 11-Year-Old Stirs an Abortion Debate in Chile," CNN (July 11, 2013), http://www.cnn.com/2013/07/11/world/americas/chile-abortion-debate; Vladimir Hernández, "Embarazo en niña de 11 años reaviva debate de aborto en Argentina," BBC Mundo (January 20, 2012), http://www.bbc.co.uk/mundo/noticias/2012/01/120118_argentina_casos_joven_embarazada_aborto_vh.shtml.

14. But see Ruth Fletcher, "Post-Colonial Fragments: Representations of Abortion in Irish Law and Politics," *Journal of Law and Society* 28 (2001): 568–89; Lisa Smyth, "Narratives of Irishness and the Problem of Abortion: The X Case 1992," *Feminist Review* 60 (1998): 61–83.

15. Phone interview, lawyer, Center for Reproductive Rights (August 21, 2012); e-mail correspondence with reproductive justice lawyer, Buenos Aires, Argentina (August 8, 2012); Personal interview, lawyer, Center for Reproductive Rights, New York (October 25, 2012).

16. Phone interview, lawyer, Center for Reproductive Rights (August 21, 2012).

17. Phone interview, lawyer, Center for Reproductive Rights (August 21, 2012).

18. Rosario Taracena, "Social Actors and Discourse on Abortion in the Mexican Press: The Paulina Case," *Reproductive Health Matters* 10 (2002): 103–10, at 104.

19. Jeannie Ludlow, "The Things We Cannot Say: Witnessing the Traumatization of Abortion in the United States," *WSQ: Women's Studies Quarterly* 36 (2008) 28–41, at 37.

20. See Janet Halley, "'Like-Race' Arguments," in *What's Left of Theory? New Work on the*

Politics of Literary Theory, ed. Judith Butler, John Guillory, and Thomas Kendall (New York: Routledge, 2000), 40–74, at 52.

21. Reva B. Siegel, "The Right's Reasons: Constitutional Conflict and the Spread of Woman Protective Antiabortion Argument," *Duke Law Journal* 57 (2008): 1641–92.

22. Jeannie Suk, "The Trajectory of Trauma: Bodies and Minds of Abortion Discourse," *Columbia Law Review* 110 (2010): 1193–252.

23. Guttmacher Institute, *An Overview of Clandestine Abortion in Latin America* (New York: Alan Guttmacher Institute, 1996), 2.

24. Bonnie Shepard, "The 'Double Discourse' on Sexual and Reproductive Rights in Latin America: The Chasm Between Public Policy and Private Actions," *Health and Human Rights* 4 (2000): 110–43, at 111.

25. S. Singh et al., *Abortion Worldwide: A Decade of Uneven Progress* (New York: Guttmacher Institute, 2009), 23–29; Bonnie L. Shepard and Lidia Casas Becerra, "Abortion Policies and Practices in Chile: Ambiguities and Dilemmas," *Reproductive Health Matters* 15 (2007): 202–10, at 202.

26. Taracena, "Social Actors," note 18, at 104.

27. Phone interview, lawyer, Center for Reproductive Rights (August 21, 2012); e-mail correspondence with reproductive justice lawyer, Buenos Aires, Argentina (August 8, 2012).

28. Phone interview, lawyer, CLADEM and INSEGNAR, Rosario, Argentina (October 5, 2012).

29. Joanna N. Erdman, "The Procedural Turn: Abortion at the European Court of Human Rights," in this volume.

30. *L.C. v. Peru*, note 1, at paras. 7.11–7.13.

31. Luisa Cabal, Mónica Roa, and Lilian Sepúlveda-Oliva, "What Role Can International Litigation Play in the Promotion and Advancement of Reproductive Rights in Latin America?" *Health and Human Rights* 7 (2003): 50–88, at 56–57; Personal interview, lawyer, Center for Reproductive Rights, New York (October 25, 2012).

32. *Paulina Ramirez*, note 1, filed March 8, 2002.

33. *Paulina Ramirez*, note 1, at para. 13.

34. See Adriana Ortiz-Ortega, "The Politics of Abortion in Mexico: The Paradox of Doble Discurso," in *Where Human Rights Begin: Health, Sexuality, and Women in the New Millennium*, ed. Wendy Chavkin and Ellen Chesler (New Brunswick, N.J.: Rutgers University Press, 2005), 154, 155–56.

35. See Grupo de Información sobre Reproducción Elegida (GIRE), *Paulina: Five Years Later* (Mexico: GIRE, 2005), 7.

36. GIRE, *Paulina*, note 34, at 8.

37. *Paulina Ramirez*, note 1, at para. 15.

38. *Paulina Ramirez*, note 1, at para. 16.

39. *X and XX v. Colombia*, note 1; see Women's Link Worldwide, "Lines of Work: X and XX v. Colombia, precautionary measures," (August 17, 2011), http://www.womenslinkworldwide.org /wlw/new.php?modo=detalle_proyectos&dc=12&lang=en.

40. *Rules of Procedure of the Inter-American Commission on Human Rights*, approved by the commission at its 137th regular period of sessions, held from October 28 to November 13, 2009, and modified on September 2, 2011, art. 25.

41. *Rules of Procedure*, note 39.

42. *Rules of Procedure*, note 39.

43. *K.L. v. Peru*, note 1; see Center for Reproductive Rights, "*K.L. v. Peru* (Human Rights Com-

mittee)," (December 10, 2008), http://reproductiverights.org/en/case/kl-v-peru-united-nations-human -rights-committee.

44. *K.L. v. Peru*, note 1, at para. 2.2.

45. *K.L. v. Peru*, note 1, at para. 3.4.

46. *K.L. v. Peru*, note 1, at para. 6.3.

47. *K.L. v. Peru*, note 1, at para. 6.3.

48. *K.L. v. Peru*, note 1, at para. 6.4–6.5.

49. CLADEM, "Resumen: Caso LMR, Argentina (aborto)," http://www.cladem.org/index .php?option=com_content&view=article&id=409:caso-lmr-argentina-aborto&catid=47&Itemid =132 (accessed January 20, 2013); *L.M.R. v. Argentina*, note 1, at para. 2.2.

50. CLADEM, *Caso LMR v. Argentinam Comité de Derechos Humanos*, Boletín No. 2 (2011), http://www.cladem.org/index.php?option=com_content&view=article&id=411&Itemid=548 (accessed December 14, 2012), 3.

51. Código Penal de la Nación Argentina [Criminal Code of Argentina], Ley 11.179 (T.O. 1984) actualizado, art. 86(2).

52. *L.M.R. v. Argentina*, note 1, at para. 9.2.

53. *L.M.R. v. Argentina*, note 1, at para. 9.2.

54. Center for Reproductive Rights, press release, "Teen Rape Victim Files Case Against Peru in U.N. Committee: Government Continues to Refuse Women Access to Legal Abortion," (June 18, 2009), http://reproductiverights.org/en/press-room/teen-rape-victim-files-case-against-peru-in-un -committee.

55. *L.C. v. Peru*, note 1, at para. 2.1.

56. *L.C. v. Peru*, note 1, at para. 2.1.

57. *L.C. v. Peru*, note 1, at para. 2.6.

58. *L.C. v. Peru*, note 1, at para. 2.7.

59. *L.C. v. Peru*, note 1, at para. 2.10.

60. See U.N. General Assembly, *Convention on the Elimination of All Forms of Discrimination Against Women*, December 18, 1979, United Nations, Treaty Series, vol. 1249, p. 13.

61. *L.C. v. Peru*, note 1, at para. 2.10.

62. *L.C. v. Peru*, note 1, at para. 8.5.

63. *L.C. v. Peru*, note 1, at para. 8.15.

64. *L.C. v. Peru*, note 1, at para. 8.15.

65. Downie, "Nine-Year-Old's," note 13.

66. *L.M.R. v. Argentina*, note 1, at para. 2.4 (emphasis added).

67. Phone interview, lawyer, Supreme Court of Justice of Mexico, Mexico City, Mexico (December 27, 2012).

68. Center for Reproductive rights, press release, "Mexico Admits Responsibility for Denying Child Rape Victim's Rights: Landmark Settlement Reached in Case of 13-Year-Old Mexican Rape Victim Denied Abortion," (March 8, 2006), http://reproductiverights.org/en/press-room/mexico -admits-responsibility-for-denying-child-rape-victims-rights.

69. See Sharon Luker, *Dubious Conceptions: The Politics of Teenage Pregnancy* (Cambridge, Mass.: Harvard University Press, 1997), 35–37.

70. GIRE, *Paulina*, note 34, at 52.

71. Arnoldo Kraus, "Paulina: Does Morality Exist?" *La Jornada* (April 19, 2000), as translated and cited in *Paulina: In the Name of the Law* (Mexico: Grupo Información en Reproucción, 2000), 51.

72. *Bourne*, note 7.

73. "Charge Against Surgeon," *Times* (London), July 19, 1938, 4; see Stephen Brooke, "A New World for Women? Abortion Law Reform in Britain During the 1930s," *American Historical Review* 106 (2001): 431–59, 444–51.

74. Offenses Against the Person Act 1861, 24 and 25 Vict., c. 100, s. 58; Infant Life (Preservation) Act 1929, 19 and 20 Geo. 5, c. 34.

75. Aleck Bourne, *A Doctor's Creed: The Memoirs of a Gynaecologist* (London: Victor Gollancz, 1962), 99.

76. Bourne, *Doctor's*, note 75, at 99.

77. *Bourne*, note 7, at 687.

78. *Bourne*, note 7, at 687.

79. See Rebecca J. Cook and Bernard M. Dickens, *Abortion Laws in Commonwealth Countries* (Geneva: World Health Organization, 1979), 13.

80. *Bourne*, note 7, at 694.

81. Robin Bernstein, *Racial Innocence: Reforming American Childhood from Slavery to Civil Rights* (New York: New York University Press, 2011).

82. *L.C. v. Peru*, note 1, at para. 7.6.

83. Ruth Ley, *Trauma: A Genealogy* (Chicago: University of Chicago Press, 2000), 2.

84. *L.M.R. v. Argentina*, note 1, at para. 7.6.

85. *L.C. v. Peru*, note 1, at para. 9 (iii).

86. Reva Siegel, "Concurring," in *What* Roe v. Wade *Should Have Said: The Nation's Top Legal Experts Rewrite America's Most Controversial Decision*, ed. Jack M. Balkin (New York: New York University Press, 2005), 63–85, at 77.

87. Drucilla Cornell, *The Imaginary Domain: Abortion, Pornography, and Sexual Harassment* (New York: Routledge, 1995), 81.

88. *L.M.R. v. Argentina*, note 1, at para. 7.6.

89. CLADEM, *Caso LMR vs Argentina*, at 5.

90. CLADEM, *Caso LMR vs Argentina*, at 5.

91. *L.M.R. v. Argentina*, note 1, at para. 3.1 (emphasis added).

92. *L.C. v. Peru*, note 1, at para. 2.5 (emphasis added).

93. *L.M.R. v. Argentina*, note 1, at para. 2.2 (emphasis added).

94. *Paulina Ramirez*, note 1, at para. 11 (emphasis added).

95. Center for Reproductive Rights, "LC: I Have to Tell What Happened to Me," video clip, http://reproductiverights.org/en/feature/center-for-reproductive-rights-video-archive#lcenglish (accessed October 21, 2012).

96. Phone interview, lawyer, CLADEM and INSEGNAR, Rosario, Argentina (October 5, 2012).

97. Phone interview, lawyer, Supreme Court of Justice of Mexico, Mexico City, Mexico (December 27, 2012).

98. *Planned Parenthood v. Danforth*, 428 U.S. (1976) (U.S. Supreme Court); *Planned Parenthood of Southeastern Pa. v. Casey*, 505 U.S. 833 (1992) (U.S. Supreme Court); *Tremblay v. Daigle*, [1989] 2 S.C.R. 530 (Supreme Court of Canada).

99. *Paton v. Trustees of British Pregnancy Advisory Service and Another* [1978] QB 276 (High Court, Queen's Bench Division); Conseil d'État [Council of State] 1982, D.S. Jur. 19, 732.

100. *A. v. B.*, 35 (iii) P.D. 57 (1981) (Supreme Court of Israel); see Carmel Shalev, "A Man's Right to be Equal: The Abortion Issue," *Israel Law Review* 18 (1983): 381–430.

101. *Paton v. United Kingdom*, Application No. 8416/78, 3 Eur. H.R. Rep. 408 (1980); *Boso v. Italy*, Application No. 50490/99 Eur. Ct. H.R., (2002).

102. *Danforth*; *Planned Parenthood of Kansas City v. Ashcroft*, 462 U.S. 476 (1983) (U.S. Supreme Court); *Bellotti v. Baird*, 443 U.S. 622 (1979) (U.S. Supreme Court); *Gillick v. West Norfolk and Wisbech Area Health Authority*, 3 All E.R. 402 (1985) (House of Lords).

103. Center for Reproductive Rights, *Adolescents Need Safe and Legal Abortion: Briefing Paper* (New York: Center for Reproductive Rights, 2005), 4.

104. World Health Organization, *Safe Abortion: Technical and Policy Guidance for Health Systems*, 2nd ed. (Geneva: WHO, 2012), 68.

105. United Nations, Committee on the Elimination of Discrimination Against Women, General recommendation No. 21 on Equality in Marriage and Family Relations, 13th sess., April 12, 1994, U.N. Doc. A/49/38, para. 22 (emphasis added).

106. United Nations Committee on the Rights of the Child, *Concluding Observations: Krygystan*, 24th Sess., para. 45, U.N. Doc. CRC/C/15/Add. 127 (2000) (emphasis added).

107. U.N. General Assembly, Interim report of the Special Rapporteur on the right of everyone to the enjoyment of the highest attainable standard of physical and mental health, U.N. Doc. A/66/254 (August 2011), para. 24.

108. *P. and S. v. Poland*, note 12, at para. 2.

109. *P. and S. v. Poland*, note 12, at para. 93.

110. *P. and S. v. Poland*, note 12, at para. 93 (emphasis added).

111. *P. and S. v. Poland*. note 12, at para. 90.

112. *Boso v. Italy*, note 101.

113. *P. and S. V. Poland*,, note 12, at para. 109 (emphasis added).

114. Janet Halley, *Split Decisions: How and Why to Take a Break from Feminism* (Princeton N.J.: Princeton University Press, 2006), 71.

115. *P. and S. v. Poland*, note 12, at para. 109.

116. See Robert F. Drinan, *The Mobilization of Shame: A World View of Human Rights* (New Haven: Yale University Press, 2001).

117. Cabal et al., "UN Human Rights," note 6.

118. See Thomas Keenan, "Mobilizing Shame," *Atlantic Quarterly* 103 (2004): 435–49.

119. Human Rights Watch, "Illusions of Care: Lack of Accountability for Reproductive Rights in Argentina" (2010); Human Rights Watch, "My Rights, and My Right to Know: Lack of Access to Therapeutic Abortion in Peru" (2008).

120. Kenneth Roth, "Defending Economic, Social and Cultural Rights: Practical Issues Faced by an International Human Rights Organization," *Human Rights Quarterly* 26 (2004): 63–73, 67.

121. Phone interview, lawyer, DESC de la Asociación por los Derechos Civiles (ADC), Buenos Aires, Argentina (October 1, 2012).

122. See Ryan Goodman and Derek Jinks, "How to Influence States: Socialization and International Human Rights Law," *Duke Law Journal* 54 (2004): 621–703.

123. Eve Kosofsky Sedgwick, "Henry James's The Art of the Novel," *GLQ: A Journal of Lesbian and Gay Studies* 1 (1993): 1–16, at 4.

124. Drinan, *Mobilization*, note 117, at 32 (emphasis added).

125. See, e.g., *San Jose Articles* (San José, Costa Rica: March 25, 2011) http://www.sanjosearticles .com/?page_id=2; Nicholas Windsor, "The World Doesn't Have a Right to Abortion," *Telegraph*, October 10, 2011.

126. Alice M. Miller and Mindy J. Roseman, "Sexual and Reproductive Rights at the United Nations: Frustration or Fulfilment?" *Reproductive Health Matters* 19 (2011): 102–18.

127. Personal interview, lawyer, Center for Reproductive Rights, New York (October 25, 2012).

128. Sedgwick, "Henry," note 123, at 4.

129. Fletcher, "Post-Colonial," note 14, at 580.

130. *Irish Times*, February 18, 1992 as cited in Fletcher, "Post-Colonial Fragments."

131. Smyth, "Narratives of Irishness," note 14, at 62.

132. See Makau W. Mutua, "Savages, Victims, and Saviors: The Metaphor of Human Rights," *Harvard International Law Journal* 42 (2001): 201–45.

133. Rachel Rebouché, "A Functionalist Approach to Comparative Abortion Law," in this volume.

134. David Kennedy, *The Dark Sides of Virtue: Reassessing International Humanitarianism* (Princeton, N.J.: Princeton University Press, 2004), 21.

135. Sibylle Christina Aebi, "Ireland: An Emerging Eurosceptic or an Exemplary EU Member State? An Examination of Irish Attitudes Toward the EU and European Integration," (master's thesis, Copenhagen Business School, 2009), 151, http://studenttheses.cbs.dk/bitstream/handle/10417/449 /sibylle_christina_aebi.pdf?sequence=1.

136. M. Laura Farfán Bertrán, "Overview–Latin America Reaffirms Its Commitment to Life," in *Defending the Human Right to Life in Latin America* (Washington, D.C.: Americans United for Life, 2012) 15–19, at 19.

Chapter 15. Narratives of Prenatal Personhood in Abortion Law

I am grateful to Joanna Erdman for her insightful comments on early drafts of this chapter. All translations are by the author. This chapter reflects legal changes up to June 30, 2013.

1. Suprema Corte de Justicia de la Nación [Supreme Court] 2008, Acción de Inconstitucionalidad 146/2007 y su acumulada 147/2007 [hereinafter Acción de Inconstitucionalidad 146/2007].

2. Suprema Corte de Justicia de la Nación [Supreme Court] 2002, Acción de Inconstitucionalidad 10/2000 (Mex.) [hereinafter Acción de Inconstitucionalidad 10/2000]. See also Alejandro Madrazo Lajous, "The Evolution of Mexico City's Abortion Laws: From Public Morality to Women's Autonomy," *International Journal of Gynecology and Obstetrics* 106 (2009): 266–69.

3. Acción de Inconstitucionalidad 146/2007, note 1.

4. See Estefanía Vela, "Current Abortion Regulation in Mexico," Documento de Trabajo, CIDE, México, 2010, Núm. 50, http://www.cide.edu/publicaciones/status/dts/DTEJ%2050.pdf.

5. Constitución Política para el Estado de Guanajuato [Constitution for the State of Guanajuato], para. 2, art. 1, T. I.

6. Constitución Política para el Estado de Colima [Constitution for the State of Colima], fr. I, § I, T. I; Constitución Política para el Estado de Morelos [Constitution for the State of Morelos], art. 2, T. I; Constitución Política para el Estado de Puebla [Constitution for the State of Puebla], fr. IV, art. 26, § V, T. I; Constitución Política para el Estado de Baja California [Constitution for the State of Baja California], art. 7, § IV, T. I; Constitución Política para el Estado de Chiapas [Constitution for the State of Chiapas], para. 4, art. 4, § I, T. II; Constitución Política para el Estado de Durango [Constitution for the State of Durango], art. I, § I, T. I; Constitución Política para el Estado de Jalisco [Constitution for the State of Jalisco], art. 4, § III, T. I; Constitución Política para el Estado de Nayarit [Constitution for the State of Nayarit], fr. XIII, art. 7, § IV, T. I; Constitución Política para

el Estado de Oaxaca [Constitution for the State of Oaxaca], art. 12, T. I; Constitución Política para el Estado de Querétaro [Constitution for the State of Querétaro], para. 4, art. 2, T. I; Constitución Política para el Estado de Quintana Roo [Constitution for the State of Quintana Roo].

7. Sala Constitucional [Constitutional Chamber] 2000, Sentencia 2000–02306 (Costa Rica) [hereinafter Sentencia 2000–02306]; Sala Constitucional [Constitutional Chamber] 2004, Sentencia 442/2004 (Costa Rica) [hereinafter Sentencia 442/2004]; Sala Constitucional [Constitutional Chamber] 2005, Sentencia 1267/2005 (Costa Rica) [hereinafter Sentencia 1267/2005].

8. *Gonzales v. Carhart*, 550 U.S. 124 (2007) (U.S. Supreme Court); *Planned Parenthood of Southeastern Pa. v. Casey*, 505 U.S. 833 (1992) (U.S. Supreme Court); *Roe v. Wade*, 410 U.S. 113 (1973) (U.S. Supreme Court).

9. Acción de Inconstitucionalidad 10/2000, note 2; Acción de Inconstitucionalidad 146/2007, note 1; Suprema Corte de Justicia de la Nación [Supreme Court] 2011, Acción de inconstitucionalidad 11/2009 (Mex.) [hereinafter Acción de inconstitucionalidad 11/2009]; Suprema Corte de Justicia de la Nación [Supreme Court] 2011, Acción de inconstitucionalidad 62/2009, (Mex.), [hereinafter Acción de inconstitucionalidad 62/2009].

10. Corte Constitucional [Constitutional Court] May 10, 2006, Sentencia C-355/06 (Colom.) [hereinafter Sentencia C-355/06]; Corte Constitucional [Constitutional Court] February 28, 2008, Sentencia T-209/08 (Colom.).

11. Ley General de Salud en materia de control sanitario de la disposición de órganos, tejidos y cadáveres de seres humanos [General Health Law] fr. III, art. 389 § III, T. 16, Diario Oficial de la Federación [DO], February 7, 1984 (Mex.).; Reglamento de la Ley General de Salud en materia de control sanitario de la disposición de órganos, tejidos y cadáveres de seres humanos [Regulations of the General Health Law] fr. XIV, art. 6, § I, Diario Oficial de la Federación [DO], February 18, 1985 (Mex.).

12. *Roe*, note 8, at 157 n.54.

13. *Roe*, note 8, at 156–57.

14. *Roe*, note 8, at 159.

15. *Roe*, note 8, at 158.

16. *Gonzales*, note 8.

17. *White and Potter v. United States (Baby Boy)*, Case 2141, Report No. 3/81, OAS/Ser.L/V/ II.54, doc. 9 rev. para. 1, Inter-Am. C.H.R. (1981).

18. American Convention on Human Rights, November 21, 1969, 114 U.N.T.S. 143, art. 1.

19. H.B. 409, Reg. Sess. (Ala. 2011); Ballot Initiative "The Right to Life" (Ark. 2012); Initiative 090043 art. I § 7 (Calif. 2009); Colorado Ballot Proposal 25 art. II, § 32 (Colo. 2010); Colorado Ballot Proposal #62 art. II, § 32 (Colo. 2010); Constitutional Amendment Petition art. I, § 28 (Fla. 2011); H.R. 5, Reg. Sess. art. I, § 1, pp. XXIX (Ga. 2009); H.R. 536, Reg. Sess. art. I, § 1, pp. XXIX, XXX (Ga. 2007); H.J.R. 2003 art. 2, 3 § 1 (Iowa 2010); H.C.R 5029 § 1 (Kan. 2012); H.B. 1040 art. 24 (Md. 2011); H.J.R. II art. 1, § 28 (Mich. 2009); Initiative 26 art. III, § 33 (Miss. 2011); Initiative Petition 2010–068 art. I, § 35 (Mo. 2010); Constitutional Initiative No. 102 (CI-102) art. II, §17 (Mont. 2010); Initiative Petition 2010–068 art. I, § 35 (Nev. 2010); Ballot Initiative for Personhood Amendment (Ohio 2012); Initiative Petition 395 State question 761 art. 2, § 38 (Okla. 2012); Initiative 83 (Or. 2007); Initiative 117 art. 1, 2, 3 § 46 (Or. 2007); SB 0278 (Utah 2012); JR 77 art. I, § 1 (Wis. 2011).

20. *Planned Parenthood*; *In RE Initiative Petition No. 349, State Question No. 642*, 1992 OK 122 (1992) (Supreme Court of Oklahoma).

21. *Roe,* note 8.

22. Sentencia 2000–02306, note 7.

23. Acción de inconstitucionalidad 11/2009, note 9; Acción de inconstitucionalidad 62/2009, note 9.

24. Robert Cover, "The Supreme Court 1982 Term. Foreword: Nomos and Narrative," *Harvard Law Review* 97, No. 4 (1983): 4–68, at 5.

25. *Baby Oladapo v. Minister for Justice,* [2002] I.E.S.C. 44 (Supreme Court of Ireland).

26. Contenido de la versión taquigráfica de la sesión pública ordinaria del Pleno de la Suprema Corte de Justicia de la Nación, celebrada el martes 27 de septiembre de 2011, Mexico (2011), "Versiones taquigráficas" [Transcript of Ordinary Public Session of the Mexico's Supreme Court *en banc* of Tuesday, September 27, 2011], http://www.scjn.gob.mx/PLENO/ver_taquigraficas/pl20110927v3 .pdf [hereinafter Public Session of September 27]; Contenido de la versión taquigráfica de la sesión pública ordinaria del Pleno de la Suprema Corte de Justicia de la Nación, celebrada el Jueves 29 de septiembre de 2011, Mexico (2011), "Versiones taquigráficas" [Transcript of Ordinary Public Session of the Mexico's Supreme Court *en banc* of Tuesday, September 29, 2011], http://www.scjn.gob .mx/PLENO/ver_taquigraficas/pl20110929v2.pdf [hereinafter Public Session of September 29].

27. See Steve Contorno, "Virginia Senate Buries Personhood Bill for Rest of 2012," *Examiner,* February 23, 2012, http://washingtonexaminer.com/article/304616#.UclBtJgflEQ.

28. Public Session of September 27, note 26, Justice Cossío's intervention arguing such language "diminishes respect for this subject, this protected good."

29. Sentencia 2000–02306, note 7, Considerando VII.

30. Suprema Corte de la Provincia de Buenos Aires [Supreme Court of the Province of Buenos Aires] 2006, Causa Ac. 98.830, "R., L.M., 'NN Persona por nacer. Protección. Denuncia,'" at 83 [hereinafter Causa Ac. 98.830].

31. See for instance the case of Mexican local legislation: Código Penal para el Estado de San Luis Potosí [Penal Code of the State of San Luis Potosí], art. 128; Código Penal para el Estado de Campeche [Penal Code of the State of Campeche] art. 297; Código Penal para el Estado de Guerrero [Penal Code of the State of Guerrero], art. 119; Código Penal para el Estado de Jalisco [Penal Code of the State of Jalisco], art. 228; Código Penal para el Estado de Morelos [Penal Code of the State of Morelos], art. 117; Código Penal para el Estado de Nayarit [Penal Code of the State of Nayarit], art. 336; Código Penal para el Estado de Nuevo León [Penal Code of the State of Nuevo León], art. 328; Código Penal para el Estado de Oaxaca [Penal Code of the State of Oaxaca], art. 315; Código Penal para el Estado de Puebla [Criminal Code of the State of Puebla], art. 342; Código Penal para el Estado de Querétaro [Penal Code of the State of Querétaro] art. 139; Código Penal para el Estado de Quintana Roo [Penal Code of the State of Quintana Roo], art. 139; Código Penal para el Estado de Tlaxcala [Penal Code of the State of Tlaxcala] art. 278; Código Penal para el Estado de Yucatán [Penal Code of the State of Yucatán], art. 342; and Código Penal para el Estado de Zacatecas [Penal Code of the State of Zacatecas] art. 311.

32. Causa Ac. 98.830, note 30.

33. Causa Ac. 98.830 note 30, at 32.

34. Causa Ac. 98.830, note 30, at 32.

35. *Baby Oladapo,* note 25.

36. See Contorno, "Virginia," note 27.

37. Acción de Inconstitucionalidad 146/2007, note 1, at 171.

38. See Acción de Inconstitucionalidad 146/2007, note 1, at 174–75.

39. *N.J. Div. of Youth & Family Serv. v. V.M.*, 974 A.2d 448 (2009) (Superior Court of New Jersey, Appellate Division) (*per curiam*) (Carchman, P.J., concurring); for some cases and the phenomenon in general, see Emma S. Ketteringham, Allison Korn, and Lynn M. Paltrow, "Proposition 26: The Cost to All Women," *Mississippi Law Journal* 81 (2011).

40. See Vela, "Current," note 4.

41. Sentencia 442/2004 and Sentencia 1267/2005, note 7.

42. Madrazo, "Evolution," note 2.

43. Acción de Inconstitucionalidad 10/2000, note 2, at 111.

44. Acción de Inconstitucionalidad 10/2000, note 2, at 71.

45. See Madrazo, "Evolution," note 2.

46. See Rebecca J. Cook and Simone Cusack, *Gender Stereotyping: Transnational Legal Perspectives* (Philadelphia: University of Pennsylvania Press, 2010).

47. Juan J. Bustos Ramírez and Hernán Hormazábal Malarée, *Lecciones de derecho penal: Parte general* (Madrid: Editorial Trotta, 2006), 94–99.

48. Acción de Inconstitucionalidad 10/2000, note 2, at 194.

49. See Código Penal para el Distrito Federal [Criminal Code of the Federal District] (2002), § 1-2-V-29–V [hereinafter CPDF].

50. When the criminal conduct is understood as necessary to fulfilling an obligation, see CPDF, note 49, § 1-2–V-29–VI.

51. CPDF, note 49, § 1-2-V-29–IX (2002).

52. *Baby Oladapo*, note 25, at 19.

53. See Bustos Ramírez and Hormazábal Malarée, *Lecciones*, note 47, at 274–87.

54. For the woman as an instrument of a fetal-protection policy, see the German cases as explained by Ruth Rubio-Marín, "Abortion in Portugal: New Trends in European Constitutionalism" in this volume.

55. Acción de Inconstitucionalidad 146/2007, note 1, at 181–82.

56. See Acción de Inconstitucionalidad 146/2007, note 1, 12–13 for Justice Sánchez opinion; for the Court's opinion, see Acción de Inconstitucionalidad 146/2007, note 1, at 182.

57. Causa Ac. 98.830, note 30, at 47.

58. *Tremblay. v. Daigle* [1990] 62 D.L.R. (4th) 634 (Supreme Court of Canada); Sentencia C-355/06 (Colomian Constitutional Tribunal), note 10; Acción de Inconstitucionalidad 146/2007 (Mexican Supreme Court), note 1; *Roe*, note 8 (United States Supreme Court).

59. *Roe*, note 8; *Tremblay. v. Daigle* note 58; Sentencia C-355/06, note 10; Acción de Inconstitucionalidad 146/2007, note 1.

60. Acción de Inconstitucionalidad 146/2007, note 1, at 176.

61. Sentencia C-355/06, note 10.

62. Sentencia C-355/06, note 10, at 162.

63. Sentencia C-355/06, note 10, at 135 at para.8.3.

64. *Roe*, note 8, at 150.

65. Acción de Inconstitucionalidad 146/2007, note 1, at 183–84.

66. *Baby Oladapo*, note 25.

67. *Baby Oladapo*, note 25, at 19.

68. Sentencia 2000–02306, note 7.

69. American Convention on Human Rights, note 18, art. 4.

70. Sentencia No. 442/2004, note 7; Sentencia 1267/2005, note 7; see also Mexico, Suprema Corte de Justicia de la Nación [Supreme Court] 2010, Controversia constitucional 54/2009.

71. *Artavia Murillo et al. v. Costa Rica*, Inter-Am. Ct. H.R. (ser. C) No. 257 (November 28, 2012).

72. *Artavia*, note 71, at para. 223

73. *Artavia*, note 71, Dissenting Opinion of Eduardo Vio Grossi, at 18.

74. *Artavia*, note 71, Dissenting Opinion of Eduardo Vio Grossi, at 18.

75. Public Session of September 27, note 26, 26–27. She made a similar case two days later in Public Session September 29, 2011, note 26.

Chapter 16. Stigmatized Meanings of Criminal Abortion Law

I am immensely grateful to Andy Sprung and Ken Vimalesan for their research assistance, and to Simone Cusack, Joanna Erdman, Lindsay Farmer, Lisa Kelly, and Alejandra Timmer for their insightful comments on early drafts of this chapter.

1. Lawrence Lessig, "The Regulation of Social Meaning," *University of Chicago Law Review* 62, No. 3 (1995): 943–1045, at 952 (footnote omitted).

2. Lessig, "Regulation," note 1, at 952.

3. Harold J. Berman, *Law and Revolution: The Formation of the Western Legal Tradition* (Cambridge, Mass.: Harvard University Press, 1983), 181–85.

4. Joanna Erdman, "Access to Information on Safe Abortion: A Harm Reduction and Human Rights Approach," *Harvard Journal of Gender and the Law* 34 (2011): 413–62, at 417–24.

5. See, for example, Luís Roberto Barroso, "Bringing Abortion into the Brazilian Public Debate: Legal Strategies for Anencephalic Pregnancy"; Paola Bergallo, "The Struggle Against Informal Rules on Abortion in Argentina"; Adriana Lamačková, "Women's Rights in the Abortion Decision of the Slovak Constitutional Court"; Ruth Rubio-Marín, "Abortion in Portugal: New Trends in European Constitutionalism"; Reva B. Siegel, "The Constitutionalization of Abortion"; Verónica Undurraga, "Proportionality in the Constitutional Review of Abortion Law"; and Melissa Upreti, "Toward Transformative Equality in Nepal: The *Lakshmi Dhikta* Decision," all in this volume.

6. Rebecca J. Cook and Bernard M. Dickens, "Human Rights Dynamics of Abortion Law Reform," *Human Rights Quarterly* 25 (2003): 1–59; Charles G. Ngwena, "Inscribing Abortion as a Human Right: Significance of the Protocol on the Rights of Women in Africa," *Human Rights Quarterly* 32 (2010): 783–864; Johanna Westeson, "Reproductive Health Information and Abortion Services: Standards Developed by the European Court of Human Rights," *International Journal of Gynecology and Obstetrics* 122, No. 2 (2013): 173–76; Christina Zampas and Jaime M. Gher, "Abortion as a Human Right—International and Regional Standards," *Human Rights Law Review* 8, No. 2 (2008), 249–94.

7. Bernard M. Dickens, *Abortion and the Law* (London: MacGibbon and Kee, 1966), 23–28; Lindsay Farmer, "Criminal Wrongs in Historical Perspective," in *The Boundaries of Criminal Law*, ed. R. A. Duff, L. Farmer, S. Marshall, M. Renzo, and V. Tadros (Oxford: Oxford University Press, 2010), 214–37.

8. Albin Eser and Hans-Georg Koch, *Abortion and the Law: From International Comparison to Legal Policy* (The Hague: T.M.C. Asser Press, 2005), 139–43, 152.

9. Alejandro Madrazo, "The Evolution of Mexico City's Abortion Laws: From Public Morality

to Women's Autonomy," *International Journal of Gynecology and Obstetrics* 106 (2009): 266–269, 267.

10. Eser and Koch, "Abortion," note 8, at 164–65.

11. Lindsay Farmer, "Criminal Law as an Institution: Rethinking Theoretical Approaches to Criminalization," in *Criminalization: The Political Morality of the Criminal Law* ed. R. A. Duff, L. Farmer, S. Marshall, M. Renzo, and V. Tadros (Oxford: Oxford University Press, forthcoming).

12. Janet E. Halley, "Sexual Orientation and the Politics of Biology: A Critique of the Argument from Immutability," *Stanford Law Review* 46 (1993–1994): 503–68, at 548.

13. Erving Goffman, *Stigma: Notes on the Management of Spoiled Identity* (Englewood, N.J.: Prentice Hall, 1963), 19.

14. *R.R. v. Poland*, Application No. 27617/04, Eur. Ct. H.R. (2011).

15. *Stenberg v. Carhart*, 530 U.S. 914 (2000) (U.S. Supreme Court) (Scalia, J., dissenting), at 953–54, (Kennedy, J., dissenting) at 957–60, 964–65, 968, 974–76; Paula Abrams, "The Scarlet Letter: The Supreme Court and the Language of Abortion Stigma," *Michigan Journal of Gender and Law* 19 (2012) 293–337, at 299–301.

16. *P. and S. v. Poland*, Application No. 57375/08, Eur. Ct. H.R. (2012), paras. 29–38.

17. World Health Organization et al, *Trends in Maternal Mortality: 1990 to 2010: WHO, UNICEF, UNFPA and The World Bank* estimates (Geneva: WHO, 2012), at 4.

18. World Health Organization, *Unsafe Abortion: Global and Regional Estimates of the Incidence of Unsafe Abortion and Associated Mortality in 2008*, 6th ed. (Geneva: WHO, 2011).

19. Susannah W. Pollvogt, "Unconstitutional Animus," *Fordham Law Review* 81 (2012): 887–937, at 924–30.

20. Scott Burris, "Stigma and the Law," *Lancet* 367, No. 9509 (2006): 529–31 at 529; Scott Burris, "Disease Stigma in U.S. Public Health Law," *Journal of Law, Medicine and Ethics* 30, No. 2 (2002): 179–90, at 188.

21. Nicola Lacey, "Historicising Criminalisation: Conceptual and Empirical Issues," *Modern Law Review* 72, No. 6 (2009): 936–60 at 942; R. A. Duff et al., "Introduction: The Boundaries of the Criminal Law," *The Boundaries of Criminal Law* (Oxford: Oxford University Press, 2010), 1–26, at 14–23.

22. Lacey, "Historicising," note 21, at 943–58.

23. Farmer, "Criminal," note 11, quoting John Stuart Mill, *On Liberty and Other Essays* (1859), ed. John Gray (Oxford: Oxford World Classics, 1991), at 14.

24. Preamble, Act 43 Geo. III, c. 58 (1803) (U.K.), cited in Dickens, *Abortion*, note 7, at 23, and discussed at 23–25.

25. Bundesverfassungsgericht [Federal Constitutional Court] February 25, 1975, 39 BVerfGE 1 Translated in Robert E. Jonas and John D. Gorby, "West German Abortion Decision: A Contrast to *Roe v. Wade*," *John Marshall Journal of Practice and Procedure* 9 (1976): 605–684. [hereinafter 39 BVerfGE 1].

26. Eser and Koch, "Abortion," note 8, at 185–89, 199–201, 232–33.

27. Guttmacher Institute, "Facts on Induced Abortion in the United States," *In Brief: Fact Sheet* (New York: Guttmacher Institute, 2011), http://www.guttmacher.org/pubs/fb_induced_abortion.html.

28. Gilda Sedgh et al., "Induced Abortion: Incidence and Trends Worldwide from 1995 to 2008," *Lancet* 379, No. 9816 (2012): 625–32; World Health Organization, *Safe Abortion: Technical and Policy Guidance for Health Systems*, 2nd ed. (Geneva: World Health Organization, 2012), at 23.

29. Joanna Erdman, "Harm Reduction, Human Rights, and Access to Information on Safer Abortion," *International Journal of Gynecology and Obstetrics* 118 (2012): 83–86 at 83.

30. Rebecca J. Cook, "Modern Day Inquisitions," *University of Miami Law Review* 65, No. 3 (2011): 767–97, 788–89.

31. Lessig, "Regulation," note 1, at 951.

32. See Lisa M. Kelly, "Reckoning with Narratives of Innocent Suffering in Transnational Abortion Litigation" in this volume.

33. E.g., Anuradha Kumar, Leila Hessini, and Ellen M. H. Mitchell, "Conceptualising Abortion Stigma," *Culture, Health and Sexuality* 11, No. 6 (2009): 625–39, at 627.

34. Kumar et al., "Conceptualising," note 33, at 631.

35. Kumar et al., "Conceptualising," note 33, at 631.

36. Sally Sheldon, *Beyond Control: Medical Power and Abortion Law* (London: Pluto Press, 1997), at 127, citing Jean-Ives Nau and Franck Nouchi, "La pilule abortive au nom de la loi," *Le Monde,* 30–31 October 1988, at 9.

37. Center for Reproductive Rights, *Defending Human Rights: Abortion Providers Facing Threats, Restrictions, and Harassment,* (New York: Center for Reproductive Rights, 2009), at 52–53, 78.

38. Kumar et al., "Conceptualising," note 33, at 631.

39. Kumar et al., "Conceptualising," note 33, at 632.

40. Women on Web, https://www.womenonweb.org (accessed July 20, 2013).

41. Kumar et al., "Conceptualising," note 33, at 632.

42. *K.L. v. Peru,* Communication No. 1153/2003, U.N. Doc. CCPR/C/85/D/1153/2003 (2005) (Human Rights Committee) (2005); *L.M.R. v. Argentina,* Communication No. 1608/2007, U.N. Doc. CCPR/C/101/D/168/2007 (Human Rights Committee) (2011); *L.C. v. Peru,* Communication No. 22/2009, U.N. Doc CEDAW/C/50/D/22/2009 (Committee on the Elimination of Discrimination against Women) (2011); *Tysiąc v. Poland,* 45 E.H.R.R. 42 Eur. Ct. H.R. (2007); *A, B, and C v. Ireland,* [2010] E.C.H.R. 2032 [hereinafter *A, B, and C v. Ireland*].

43. Kumar et al., "Conceptualising," note 33, at 632.

44. See Arjan E. R. Bos, John B. Pryor, Glenn D. Reeder and Sarah E. Stutterheim, "Stigma: Advances in Theory and Research," *Basic and Applied Social Psychology* 35, No. 1 (2013): 1–9.

45. Goffman, *Stigma,* note 13, at preface.

46. Goffman, *Stigma,* note 13, at 3.

47. Goffman, *Stigma,* note 13, at 140–47

48. Goffman, *Stigma,* note 13, at 4–5.

49. See Lisa H. Harris, Lisa Martin, Michelle Debbink, and Jane Hassinger, "Physicians, Abortion Provision and the Legitimacy Paradox," *Contraception* 87 (2013): 11–16, at 12–13.

50. Kumar et al., "Conceptualizing Abortion," note 33, at 628.

51. Kumar et al., "Conceptualizing Abortion," note 33, at 628.

52. Bruce G. Link and Jo C. Phelan, "Stigma and Its Public Health Implications" *Lancet* 367 (2006): 528–29 at 528; Bruce G. Link and Jo C. Phelan, "Conceptualizing Stigma," *Annual Review of Sociology* 27 (2001): 363–85, at 367–76.

53. Link and Phelan, "Stigma," note 52, at 528; Link and Phelan, "Conceptualizing," note 52, at 375–76.

54. See Robin A. Lenhardt, "Understanding the Mark: Race, Stigma, and Equality in Context," *New York University Law Review* 79 (2004): 803–931, at 816–36.

55. Sheldon, *Beyond,* note 36, at 35–41.

56. Alison Norris et al., "Abortion Stigma: A Reconceptualization of Constituents, Causes, and Consequences," *Women's Health Issues* 21(3rd Suppl.) (2011): 549–54, at 550; Reva Siegel,

"Reasoning from the Body: A Historical Perspective on Abortion Regulation and Questions of Equal Protection," *Stanford Law Review* 44 (1992): 261–381, at 365.

57. Sheldon, *Beyond*, note 36, at 41–48.

58. Kumar et al., "Conceptualising," note 33, at 630–33.

59. Kristen M. Shellenberg et al., "Social Stigma and Disclosure About Induced Abortion: Results from an Exploratory Study," *Global Public Health: An International Journal for Research, Policy and Practice* 6 (supplement) (2011): S111–S125, at S113; Bruce G. Link et al., "On Stigma and Its Consequences: Evidence from a Longitudinal Study of Men with Dual Diagnoses of Mental Illness and Substance Abuse," *Journal of Health and Social Behavior* 38 (1997): 177–90.

60. Shellenberg et al., "Social," note 59, at S113.

61. Jane Harries, Phyllis Orner, Mosotho Gabriel, and Ellen Mitchell, "Delays in Seeking an Abortion Until the Second Trimester: A Qualitative Study in South Africa," *Reproductive Health* 4, No. 7 (2007), http://www.reproductive-health-journal.com/content/4/1/7.

62. Shellenberg et al., "Social," note 59, at S113.

63. *A, B, and C v. Ireland*, note 42 at paras. 16, 21.

64. David J. Schneider, *The Psychology of Stereotyping* (New York: Guilford Press, 2004), at 481;

65. Link et al., "On Stigma," note 59, at 179.

66. *R.R. v. Poland*, note 14, at paras. 43, 48, 62.

67. Kristen M. Shellenberg and Amy O. Tsui, "Correlates of Perceived and Internalized Stigma Among Abortion Patients in the USA: An Exploration by Race and Hispanic Ethnicity," *International Journal of Gynecology and Obstetrics* 118 (supp. 2) (2012): S152–S159, at S157; Cynthia Steele and Susanna Chiarotti, "With Everything Exposed: Cruelty in Post-Abortion Care in Rosario, Argentina," *Reproductive Health Matters* 12, No. 24 (2004): 39–46; *L.M.R. v. Argentina*, note 42; *P. and S. v. Poland*, note 16.

68. *Tysiąc v. Poland*, note 42; *R.R. v. Poland*, note 14; *K.L. v. Peru*, note 42; *L.C. v. Peru*, note 42; for Brazilian cases where women were denied abortions, see Luís Roberto Barroso, note 5.

69. National Health Law Program (NHeLP), *Health Care Refusals: Undermining Quality Care for Women* (Los Angeles: NHeLP, 2010); see Bernard M. Dickens, "The Right to Conscience," in this volume.

70. See, e.g., Center for Reproductive Law and Policy and Forum for Women, Law, and Development, *Abortion in Nepal: Women Imprisoned* (Nepal: Forum for Women, Law, and Development, 2002). See also Upreti, note 5.

71. Center for Reproductive Rights, *Defending Human Rights*, note 37, at 25, 34, 40; Center for Reproductive Rights, Human Rights Watch, and Latin American and Caribbean Committee for the Defense of Women's Rights, "Defenders of Sexual Rights and Reproductive Rights: A Briefing Paper to the Special Rapporteur on Human Rights Defenders," http://reproductiverights.org/sites/crr.civicactions.net/files/documents/CRR_HRW_CLADEM_BriefingPaper_SRHRD.pdf, at 13–14.

72. Cook, "Modern," note 30, at 802.

73. Betsy L. Fife and Eric R. Wright, "The Dimensionality of Stigma: A Comparison of its Impact on the Self of Persons with HIV/AIDS and Cancer," *Journal of Health and Social Behavior* 41, No. 1 (2000): 50–67, at 55.

74. Kumar et al., "Conceptualising," note 33, at 630.

75. Shellenberg et al., "Social," note 59, at S114.

76. *L.C. v. Peru*, note 42.

77. Kumar et al., "Conceptualising," note 33, at 630.

78. Norris et al., "Abortion," note 56, at 550.

79. See Kenji Yoshino, *Covering: The Hidden Assault on Our Civil Rights* (New York: Random House, 2006), 74–164.

80. Women on Web, https://www.womenonweb.org/en/page/864/in-collection/521/about-the -i-had-an-abortion-project (accessed July 20, 2013).

81. See Siegel, note 5.

82. World Health Organization, *Unsafe Abortion*, note 18; Sedgh et al., "Induced," note 28, at 625–32.

83. Ronald Bayer, "Stigma and the Ethics of Public Health: Not Can We but Should We," *Social Science and Medicine* 67 (2008): 463–72, at 466; Scott Burris, "Stigma, Ethics and Policy: A Commentary on Bayer's 'Stigma and the Ethics of Public Health: Not Can We but Should We,'" *Social Science and Medicine* 67 (2008): 473–75; Ronald Bayer, "What Means This Thing Called Stigma? A Response to Burris," *Social Science and Medicine* 67 (2008): 476–77.

84. Burris, "Stigma," note 83, at 475.

85. Burris, "Stigma," note 83, at 475.

86. See Patricia Ewick and Susan S. Silbey, *The Common Place of Law* (Chicago: University of Chicago Press, 1998), 33–53; see also Rachel Rebouché, "A Functionalist Approach to Comparative Abortion Law" in this volume.

87. Reed Boland and Laura Katzive, "Developments in Laws on Induced Abortion: 1998–2007," *International Family Planning Perspectives* 34, No. 3 (2008): 110–20; Rebecca J. Cook, Bernard M. Dickens, and Laura E. Bliss, "International Developments in Abortion Law from 1988 to 1998," *American Journal of Public Health* 89, No. 4 (1999): 579–86; Eser and Koch, "Abortion," note 8, at 72–89, 223–28.

88. Norris et al., "Abortion," note 56, at 550; Siegel, "Reasoning," note 56, at 362–63.

89. Siegel, "Reasoning," note 56, at 365.

90. Madrazo, note 9 at 266; 39 BVerfGE 1, note 25.

91. Sally Engle Merry, *Human Rights and Gender Violence: Translating International Law into Local Justice* (Chicago: University of Chicago Press, 2005), 193; Keri Bennett, "Limitations of Advocacy and Exceptions to the Criminal Law in Brazil: The Struggle for Reproductive and Sexual Rights," *Canadian Woman Studies* 27, No. 1 (2009): 112–20, at 116–17; Alice M. Miller, "Sexuality, Violence Against Women, and Human Rights: Women Make Demands and Ladies Get Protection," *Health and Human Rights* 7, No. 2 (2004): 16–47 at 28.

92. United Nations, Committee on the Elimination of Discrimination against Women, General Recommendation No. 24: Women and Health, 55th sess., 1999, contained in U.N. Doc. A/54/38 Rev. 1 (1999), at paras. 14 and 21.

93. See, for example, Report of Bolivia to the Committee on the Elimination of Discrimination against Women, CEDAW/C/Bol/1 (1995), para. 239.

94. See, e.g., *Planned Parenthood of Southeastern Pa. v. Casey*, 505 U.S. 833 (1992) (U.S. Supreme Court) where the court upheld a twenty-four-hour waiting period as constitutionally valid.

95. See, e.g., Código Penal [Criminal Code], art. 142(3)(a), as amended by Law No. 16/2007 (Port.), which imposes a three-day mandatory reflection period and Tribunal Constitucional [Constitutional Court] February 23, 2010, Acórdão No. 75/2010, upholding the law; see also Rubio-Marín, note 5.

96. See Upreti, note 5, explaining how it was usually poorer Nepalese women who were imprisoned; see also Alice Jenkins, *Law for the Rich* (London: Gollancz, 1960).

97. *Family Planning Association of Northern Ireland v. Minister for Health, Social Services and Public Safety*, [2005] Northern Ireland Law Reports 188, at paras. 6, 9 (Court of Appeal, Northern Ireland).

98. *S.L. v. Austria*, Application No. 45330/99, Eur. Ct. H.R. (2003), paras. 10, 30, 44.

99. *Tysiąc v. Poland*, note 42; *L.C. v. Peru*, note 42; see Bergallo, note 5.

100. See *R.R. v. Poland*, note 14.

101. Ley General de Salud [General Law on Health], Ley No. 26842, 1997, art. 30 (Peru); see also *Women's Rights in Peru: A Shadow Report* (New York: Center for Reproductive Law and Policy, 2000), 8, http://reproductiverights.org/sites/default/files/documents/sr_peru_1000_eng.pdf; Eser and Koch, "Abortion," note 8, at 138, 171–74.

102. See Center for Reproductive Rights, *Targeted Regulation of Abortion Providers* (New York: Center for Reproductive Rights, 2009), http://reproductiverights.org/en/project/targeted-regulation -of-abortion-providers-trap..

103. *K.L. v. Peru*, note 42; *R.R. v. Poland*, note 14; *P. and S. v. Poland*, note 16; *L.M.R. v. Argentina*, note 42.

104. *Tysiąc v. Poland*, note 42; *R.R. v. Poland*, note 14; *P. and S. v. Poland*, note 16; *L.M.R. v. Argentina*, note 42.

105. *R. v. Morgentaler* [1988] 1 S.C.R. 30 (Supreme Court of Canada).

106. *L.M.R. v. Argentina*, note 42; *L.C. v. Peru*, note 42.

107. *R.R. v. Poland*, note 14.

108. Law on Family Planning (protection of the human foetus and conditions permitting pregnancy termination) 1993 (Poland) Statute Book 93.17.78, art. 4a.1(1–3), (Family Planning Act 1993).

109. *R.R. v. Poland*, note 14, at paras. 70, 192.

110. *R.R. v. Poland*, note 14, at para. 159.

111. *R.R. v. Poland*, note 14, at para. 159.

112. *R.R. v. Poland*, note 14, at para. 160.

113. *R.R. v. Poland*, note 14, at para. 151.

114. *R.R. v. Poland*, note 14, at para. 151.

115. *R.R. v. Poland*, note 14, at para. 152.

116. *R.R. v. Poland*, note 14, at paras. 161–62.

117. *R.R. v. Poland*, note 14, N. Bratza dissenting, at para. 5.

118. Jo C. Phelan, Bruce G. Link, and John F. Dovidio, "Stigma and Prejudice: One Animal or Two?" *Social Science and Medicine* 67, No. 3 (2008): 358–67, at 364.

119. Link and Phelan, "Stigma," note 52, at 528.

120. *R.R. v. Poland*, note 14, at para. 157.

121. Link and Phelan, "Stigma," note 52, at 528.

122. Rebecca J. Cook and Simone Cusack, *Gender Stereotyping: Transnational Legal Perspectives* (Philadelphia: University of Pennsylvania Press, 2010), at 3, 39–70.

123. Link and Phelan, "Stigma," note 52, at 528; Gregory Herek, "Sexual Prejudice," in *Handbook of Prejudice, Stereotyping, and Discrimination*, ed. Todd D. Nelson (New York: Psychology Press, 2009) 441–67, at 445.

124. *R.R. v. Poland*, note 14, at para. 52, 72.

125. Link and Phelan, "Stigma," note 52, at 528.

126. *R.R. v. Poland*, note 14, at para. 195.

127. *R.R. v. Poland*, note 14, at paras. 163–214.

128. *R.R. v. Poland*, note 14, at paras. 195, 200, 203, 209, 213, 214.

129. *R.R. v. Poland*, note 14, at para. 191.

130. *R.R. v. Poland*, note 14, at para. 193.

131. *S. and Marper v. the United Kingdom*, Application Nos. 30562/44 and 30566, Eur. Ct. H.R. (2008), at paras. 122, 124, 125.

132. *S.L. v. Austria*, note 98, at paras. 10, 30, 44, 46.

133. *R.R. v. Poland*, note 14, at para. 183.

134. Burris, "Stigma," note 83, at 475.

135. *R.R. v. Poland*, note 14, at para. 206; see Dickens, note 69.

136. *R. v. Morgentaler*, note 105, at para. 253, per Justice Bertha Wilson.

137. *R.R. v. Poland*, note 14, at paras. 159–60.

138. Medical Institutions Act 1992 discussed in *R.R. v. Poland*, note 14, at paras. 52, 72.

139. Medical Professions Act 1996 discussed in *R.R. v. Poland*, note 14, at paras. 61, 73, 74.

140. *Kiyutin v. Russia*, Application No. 2700/10, Eur. Ct. H.R. (2011); see also *S.L. v. Austria*, note 98.

141. *Kiyutin v. Russia*, note 140, at para. 63; see Alexandra Timmer, "Toward an Anti-Stereotyping Approach for the European Court of Human Rights," *Human Rights Law Review* 11, No. 4 (2011): 707–38, at 716.

142. *Kiyutin v. Russia*, note 140, at para. 64.

143. *L.M.R. v. Argentina*, note 42, at para. 3.6.

144. Phelan, Link, and Dovidio, "Stigma," note 118, at 362–65.

145. *L.M.R. v. Argentina*, note 42, at paras. 2.4, 2.5, 5.4.

146. *L.M.R. v. Argentina*, note 42, at paras. 2.7, 3.5, 3.10, 5.3, 5.5, 7.2.

147. United Nations, Convention on the Elimination of All Forms of Discrimination against Women (CEDAW), adopted December 18, 1979, G.A. Res. 34/180, U.N. GAOR, 34th Sess., Supp. No. 46, at 193, U.N. Doc. A/34/46 (1979) (entered into force September 3, 1981), article 5(a); *L.C. v. Peru*, note 42, at para. 8.15.

148. CEDAW, note 147, article 5(a); *L.C. v. Peru*, note 42, at para. 8.15.

149. CEDAW, note 147, article 12(1); *L.C. v. Peru*, note 42, at para. 8.15.

150. Lacey, "Historicising," note 21, at 945.

Contributors

Luís Roberto Barroso, formerly on Faculty of Law, State University of Rio de Janeiro; now Justice, Supreme Federal Court of Brazil
Paola Bergallo, Faculty of Law, University of Palermo, Buenos Aires, Argentina
Rebecca J. Cook, Faculty of Law, University of Toronto, Canada
Bernard M. Dickens, Faculty of Law, University of Toronto, Canada
Joanna N. Erdman, Schulich School of Law, Dalhousie University, Halifax, Canada
Lisa M. Kelly, doctoral candidate (S.J.D.) and Trudeau Scholar, Harvard Law School, Cambridge, Massachusetts
Adriana Lamačková, Legal Adviser for Europe, Center for Reproductive Rights
Julieta Lemaitre, Faculty of Law, University of los Andes, Bogotá, Colombia
Alejandro Madrazo, CIDE Law School, Aguascalientes, Mexico
Charles G. Ngwena, Center for Human Rights, University of Pretoria, South Africa
Rachel Rebouché, Beasley School of Law, Temple University, Philadelphia, Pennsylvania
Ruth Rubio-Marín, European University Institute, Florence, Italy
Sally Sheldon, Kent Law School, Canterbury, U.K.
Reva B. Siegel, Yale Law School, New Haven, Connecticut
Verónica Undurraga, Faculty of Law, Adolfo Ibáñez University, Santiago, Chile
Melissa Upreti, Regional Director for Asia, Center for Reproductive Rights

Index

For page references to individual cases, legislation and treaties see the Tables of Cases and Legislation, Treaties, and Other Relevant Instruments, beginning on page 379

abortion access: and conscientious objection, 227–28; and discriminating stigmatization, 367–68; for the poor, 280–81, 282–85, 307–8; relationship to laws, 4–5, 101–2, 105; threatened in procedural turn, 138

abortion counseling. *See* counseling regulations

abortion funding: and abortion practice, 112; publicly funded health care, 47, 196, 254, 285; United States and Germany compared, 103. *See also* public health and public health care

abortion methods: early medical abortion/self-use (mifepristone/misoprostol), 110–11, 114, 192–99, 200–208; vacuum aspiration (mini-abortion), 59, 185, 219

abortion practice: background rules and, 112, 357; common reasons for abortion versus "innocent suffering," 305; counseling regulations in practice, 102–3; delaying tactics, 180; discretion in, 121–22, 124, 132; illegal/informal methods, 110–11 (*see also* maternal mortality and abortion); inspection of clinic (U.K.), 204; obstruction of lawful abortion, 126–27, 164, 173–77, 362–64; of poor and rich in Brazil, 261; and public health law research, 113–16; risks of childbirth versus abortion, 235–36; self-referral from public to private clinics, 215; as shaping formal rules, 110; and stigma, 359–60; study in Ghana, 184; underground by

gynecologists, 138. *See also* maternal mortality and abortion; procedural turn in abortion rights; public health and public health care

abortion rates, 84–85, 352

administrative procedures/law: accessibility of, 176–82, 184–86, 228; fight for, 151–56; as guidelines for practice, 107, 109, 168; lack of, 171, 174, 176, 309; refusal to follow, 234–35; and stigma, 358. *See also* procedural turn in abortion rights

adolescent girls and abortion: and abortion rights narratives, 8, 174–75, 304–5, 308–17, 320–22; agency and autonomy of, 31, 222–23, 318–22; autonomy (parental consent), 104, 222–23, 318–19; with mental disabilities, 149, 156, 175–76, 311–12, 367–68; and prejudice and stigma, 354, 367–68; and regulating informal obstructive practices, 126–27, 154, 160–61

Africa: abortion rates in, 84; colonial penal codes (list of countries with), 170; historical development of abortion laws, 170–73, 186; maternal mortality rates, 169; procedural abortion rights, 5; reforming abortion laws and practice, 166–86; transparency requirements in abortion laws, 181–85. *See also* South Africa

African Commission on Human and Peoples' Rights, 173, 182

African Court on Human and Peoples' Rights, 173, 182

African Union, 168, 171

Aktion 218 (Germany), 17

Alaíde Foppa (Mexico), 309

Alexy, Robert, 79, 89

Acknowledgments

The editors are tremendously grateful to those who have supported us in the journey that ended in the publication of this book. The planning and execution of the book, including an authors' workshop at the Faculty of Law, University of Toronto, in May, 2012, would not have been possible without a grant from the Ford Foundation. In particular, we want to thank Lourdes Rivera, our program officer at the Foundation, who challenged and supported us to expand our vision throughout this project, for which we will always be grateful.

Our thinking about the design of the book benefitted greatly from discussions with various colleagues, including Luisa Cabal, Markus Dubber, Tatjana Hoernle, Isabel Jaramillo, Lisa Kelly, Karen Knop, Fernanda Nicola, Reva Siegel and Catherine Valcke, whose insights from various perspectives proved invaluable. We are grateful to Reva Siegel and Ruth Rubio-Marín for the inspirations we derived from a workshop on comparative and transnational perspectives on reproductive rights they organized in 2010. We thank Sonia Lawrence and participants of the Osgoode Institute for Feminist Legal Studies Series for an afternoon of stirring conversation about the book concept. We thank Oxford University Press for their permission to reprint Reva Siegel's chapter, "The Constitutionalization of Abortion," in this book. We are grateful to Peter Agree, Editor in Chief of the University of Pennsylvania Press, and Bert Lockwood, editor of its Pennsylvania Studies in Human Rights series, for their guidance throughout this project.

We are indebted to Linda Hutjens, Coordinator of the International Reproductive and Sexual Health Law Program, University of Toronto, for the constancy of her support throughout this project, from the very drafting of the grant proposal to the submission of the final manuscript. We simply could not have completed this project without her thoughtful and meticulous ways.

We are grateful to Susan Barker, of the Bora Laskin Law Library of the Faculty of Law, University of Toronto, for providing bibliographic assistance. We sincerely thank our research assistants, Y. Y. Brandon Chen, Sandra Dughman, Jenny Leon, Andy Sprung, and Ken Vimalesan, who helped in countless ways, including researching, checking sources, editing drafts, or formatting citations.

Finally, we owe a tremendous debt of gratitude to our respective home institutions: the Faculty of Law, University of Toronto, and the Schulich School of Law, Dalhousie University, for facilitating this project.